Lecture Notes in Artificial Intelligence 6317

Edited by R. Goebel, J. Siekmann, and W. Wahlster

Subseries of Lecture Notes in Computer Science

Philipp Cimiano H. Sofia Pinto (Eds.)

Knowledge Engineering and Management by the Masses

17th International Conference, EKAW 2010
Lisbon, Portugal, October 11-15, 2010
Proceedings

Springer

Volume Editors

Philipp Cimiano
Universität Bielefeld
Cognitive Interaction Technology
Excellence Center (CITEC)
Universitätsstraße 21-23
33615 Bielefeld, Germany
E-mail: cimiano@cit-ec.uni-bielefeld.de

H. Sofia Pinto
IESC-ID, IST/DEI
Rua Alves Redol 9
1000-029 Lisboa, Portugal
E-mail: sofia@ontol.inesc-id.pt

Library of Congress Control Number: 2010936194

CR Subject Classification (1998): I.2, H.4, H.3, J.1, C.2, H.5, D.2

LNCS Sublibrary: SL 7 – Artificial Intelligence

ISSN 0302-9743
ISBN-10 3-642-16437-4 Springer Berlin Heidelberg New York
ISBN-13 978-3-642-16437-8 Springer Berlin Heidelberg New York

springer.com

Printed in Germany

Typesetting: Camera-ready by author, data conversion by Scientific Publishing Services, Chennai, India
Printed on acid-free paper 06/3180

Preface

Knowledge Management and Knowledge Engineering is a fascinating field of research these days. In the beginning of EKAW[1], the modeling and acquisition of knowledge was the privilege of – or rather a burden for – a few knowledge engineers familiar with knowledge engineering paradigms and knowledge representation formalisms. While the aim has always been to model knowledge declaratively and allow for reusability, the knowledge models produced in these early days were typically used in single and very specific applications and rarely exchanged. Moreover, these models were typically rather complex, and they could be understood only by a few expert knowledge engineers.

This situation has changed radically in the last few years as clearly indicated by the following trends:

- The creation of (even formal) knowledge is now becoming more and more collaborative. Collaborative ontology engineering tools and social software platforms show the potential to leverage the wisdom of the crowds (or at least of "the many") to lead to broader consensus and thus produce shared models which qualify better for reuse.
- A trend can also be observed towards developing and publishing small but high-impact vocabularies (e.g., FOAF[2], Dublin Core[3], GoodRelations[4]) rather than complex and large knowledge models.
- Everybody can become a knowledge engineer nowadays since data models and tools with lower entry barriers are available for the masses. RDF as a datamodel is simple to understand and use, and has penetrated many applications and fields. There are further user-friendly ontology engineering tools which hide technical details and allow people to model at a more intuitive level.
- The division between knowledge consumers and knowledge producers is fading, especially in a Web 2.0 context.
- Domains of public interest, such as open government, tourism, cultural heritage, etc. are attracting more and more attention in the community.
- Games with a purpose have been successfully applied to knowledge acquisition and have been shown to have the potential to leverage the knowledge of the masses for knowledge engineering purposes.

Overall, the time is more than ripe for developing methods and techniques allowing us to leverage the wisdom of the crowds for knowledge engineering and

[1] The first EKAW workshop took place in London in 1987.
[2] http://www.foaf-project.org/
[3] http://dublincore.org/
[4] http://www.heppnetz.de/projects/goodrelations/

management purposes. Thus, we decided to consider *"Knowledge Management and Knowledge Engineering by the Masses"* as a special focus for EKAW 2010. Our claim that the time is indeed ripe for collaborative approaches involving the masses is corroborated by the fact that we indeed received a number of contributions addressing our topic of focus. Tudorache et al. for example discuss how to use collaborative protégé to develop widely used ontologies such as ICDE. The paper by Martin Hepp discusses how to use Twitter for collaborative ontology engineering and Tramp et al. show how to use RDFa for collaborative ontology engineering. The call for papers covered the following topics in particular.

Call for Papers

We specifically called for submissions on the following topics:

- Knowledge Management
  - Methodologies and tools for KM
  - Aspects of collaboration, distribution, and evolution of knowledge in KM
  - Advanced knowledge modeling languages and tools
  - Best practices / experiences in KM
  - Foundations of KM
  - Entity-oriented approaches to KM
  - Layered intelligence in KM
  - Provenance, reliability, and trust in KM
  - KM for collaboration and decision support
  - Methods for accelerating take-up of KM technologies
  - Corporate memories for KM
  - Case-based reasoning for KM
  - Large-scale distributed reasoning
- Knowledge Engineering and Acquisition
  - Methodologies for knowledge engineering
  - Knowledge acquisition, ontology learning
  - Knowledge sharing
  - Knowledge evolution
  - Collaborative knowledge engineering
  - Design patterns
  - Techniques for knowledge acquisition based on machine learning, NLP, etc.
  - Uncertainty and vagueness in knowledge modeling
  - Knowledge engineering and software engineering
  - Ontology localization
  - Ontology alignment
  - Evolution of knowledge (including ontology evolution)
  - Knowledge acquisition from non-ontological resources (thesauri, folksonomies, lexica, etc.)
  - Knowledge acquisition and knowledge integration from heterogeneous sources (multimedia and 3D data, databases, sensor data streams, social interaction data)

  - Knowledge authoring and knowledge markup languages
  - Ontology evaluation
  - Dynamic, distributed, and process knowledge (including web services, grid services, P2P systems, rules and business processes, problem solving methods, procedural knowledge)
  - Agent-based approaches to knowledge management
  - Knowledge mashups
- Knowledge in Use
  - Retrieval and proactive delivery of pertinent knowledge
  - Multimedia applications
  - Life and e-sciences
  - E-government and public administration
  - Health and medicine
  - Automotive and manufacturing industry
  - Semantic desktop applications
  - The legal domain
  - Cultural heritage applications
  - Digital broadcasting and film, game, and 3D media content production and sharing
  - Digital libraries
  - Virtual worlds
  - Storytelling
  - Management in critical applications
  - Organizing user-contributed content
  - Transition across organizations
- Social and Cognitive Aspects of Knowledge Engineering
  - Sustainability and cost analysis of knowledge engineering
  - Human-knowledge interaction
  - Cognitive systems and knowledge engineering
  - Knowledge ecosystems
  - Knowledge and social network analysis and modeling
  - Knowledge in trust networks
  - Personal sphere in knowledge engineering and management
  - Collaborative and social approaches to knowledge management and acquisition
- Special Focus Knowledge Management and Engineering by the Masses
  - Human-machine synergy in knowledge acquisition
  - Incentives for knowledge creation and semantic annotation
  - Enhancing human productivity (e.g., knowledge workers)
  - Social and human factors in knowledge management
  - Collective and collaborative intelligence in knowledge management
  - Social tagging and folksonomies, social networks
  - Web2.0 approaches to KM (including semantic wikis, folksonomies, etc.)
  - Games with a purpose and KM
  - Linked open data / web of data

Paper Types

As an important difference with respect to earlier editions of EKAW, we decided to call for different types of papers in order to acknowledge the fact that there are very different (and all legitimate) methodologies of enquiry and types of scientific contributions. We feel that the type of contributions typically represented at computer science conferences is rather limited, in most cases showing that a "novel" approach outperforms a baseline on one or several datasets. This is clearly not the only possible contribution or way of addressing a research problem. In fact, it is a very limited approach, which in many cases does not even advance our understanding of the characteristics of the problem. Thus, we decided to encourage researchers to consider other research methodologies and ways of approaching a scientific problem. At submission time, each paper had to be clearly identified as belonging to one of the following categories:

- **Standard research papers:** presenting a novel method, technique, or analysis with appropriate empirical or other types of evaluation as proof-of-concept. The main evaluation criteria here were originality, technical soundness, and validation.
- **In-use papers:** describing applications of knowledge management and engineering in real environments. Contributions of this type were expected to address a sufficiently interesting and challenging problem on real and large datasets, involving many users, etc. The focus was less on the originality of the approach and more on presenting real, large-scale, and complex systems solving significant problems. Technical details to understand how the problems were solved were required. Evaluations were expected to involve real users of a system rather than representing a pure academic exercise. The papers were evaluated according to the significance and practical relevance of the research described as well as with respect to the technical soundness of the solution described and the accompanying evaluation.
- **Problem analysis papers:** were not expected to present a novel technique or approach to solving a problem, but help to understand the problem itself. Understanding the characteristics of a problem itself is an important task in research and can benefit many people working on the same or at least similar problems. In-depth discussion and analysis of a certain phenomenon or problem was expected, with clear definitions as well as qualitative and quantitative analysis of the main characteristics of the problem. We also expected a reasonable review of the state of the art stating to what extent current solutions fall short. Papers were mainly evaluated with respect to how general and technically sound their problem analysis was and how useful the analysis would be for other researchers working on the same or similar problems. We expect that such papers will guide future research by highlighting critical assumptions, motivating the difficulty of a subproblem, or explaining why current techniques are not sufficient, all corroborated by quantitative and qualitative arguments. Evaluation criteria included appropriate categorization of the problem area and description of existing solutions as well as an appropriate description of the limitations of the present approaches.

- **Validation papers:** In some disciplines, reproduction of results by others is a basic research activity. This is typically not the case in computer science. However, reproduction of previous results and solutions is clearly an important activity as it helps to validate results independently. Further, it helps to better understand the assumptions and conditions under which a certain solution works as well as the reason why it shows the observed behavior. In addition, it creates baselines that one can control better, allowing an accurate comparison with previous work and a deeper understanding of the reason why an approach works better. Therefore, we encouraged researchers to reproduce and validate methods, results, and experiments, etc. proposed previously by others in a new context or application, on new datasets, under new assumptions, etc. The goal was clearly to reach interesting and significant new conclusions about the method/approach in question that would warrant a stand-alone publication. We expected the reproduction of results to lead to new knowledge about the method in question or to reveal inherent problems in the assumptions of the original research or limitations of previous solutions. Papers were evaluated with respect to the soundness of the rationale for reproducing a certain approach as well as with respect to the new knowledge that was generated by reproducing the approach in question. A clear comparison between the results obtained through the reproduction and the original results was regarded as mandatory.

Submission and Acceptance Statistics

We received a total number of 166 papers: 128 standard research papers, 23 in-use papers, 14 problem analysis papers, and 1 validation paper. This corresponds to a significant increase with respect to earlier editions. EKAW 2002 had 110 submissions, EKAW 2004 had 75, EKAW 2006 had 119, EKAW 2008 had 102. As expected, research papers constituted the vast majority followed by in-use and problem analysis papers. Validation was the category with the lowest number of submissions. We anticipate that this might hopefully change in the future as validation and reproduction become increasingly recognized as important research activities. Regarding the geographic distribution, we received papers from 34 different countries. Central and Western Europe was the most active area, but all inhabited continents were represented, indicating the international nature of the event, the considerable interest this conference attracts, and the perceived high quality of the conference. The 10 countries with the most submissions were (in this order, the number of papers is indicated in brackets): Germany (30), France (21), UK (18), Spain (14), Italy (13), The Netherlands (11), Ireland (10), Austria (9), USA (5) and Canada (5).

All papers were reviewed by at least three different reviewers. Intensive discussions were held whenever reviewers had contradictory views on the same paper. In some cases, further reviewers were called in. In the end, we accepted 22 as full and 25 as short papers, which gives an acceptance rate a little above 28%. Of the full papers accepted, 16 were standard research papers, 5 in-use papers, and 1 problem analysis paper. Of the short papers, 21 were standard research papers and 4 in-use papers.

Invited Speakers

Our goal was to find three invited speakers who would cover our topic of focus - Knowledge Management and Engineering by the Masses - from very different perspectives. After intense discussion with our program committee members, we decided to invite one invited speaker from the EKAW community, one speaker from some other related area in computer science, as well as one speaker from industry working on real applications of knowledge management and engineering. As a well-known member of our community, Enrico Motta kindly agreed to accept our invitation as keynote speaker. What better way is there to reach the masses than embedding KM techniques into those devices that we use everyday, even in our leisure time? Enrico Motta talked about embedding knowledge technologies into everyday devices. Our second invited speaker, Bernardo Huberman, is very renowned for his contributions on analyzing the behavior of the masses on the World Wide Web as well as in Web 2.0 applications such as Wikipedia, Twitter, tagging systems such as delicious, etc. Bernardo Huberman talked about how content is produced, shared, and classified on the Web, focusing in particular on issues related to attention. Finally, Tom Scott will show how the BBC has adopted Linked Data Techniques to turn their web presence into an open API that can be used by application developers to repurpose content and develop applications on top of BBC data. Further, by linking content across autonomously maintained sites using Linked Data techniques, the BBC has managed to create an information ecosystem which allows the masses of consumers to access broadcasting-related information in a uniform fashion. Detailed information about our speakers and the topics of their keynotes can be found below:

- Enrico Motta
  Professor of Knowledge Technologies, Knowledge Media Institute
  The Open University, Milton Keynes
  UK
  http://people.kmi.open.ac.uk/motta/

  New Frontiers for Knowledge Engineering and Management: Embedding Knowledge Technologies in Everyday Devices

  The notion of "Smart Product" has recently emerged, which refers to "an autonomous object designed for self-organized embedding into different environments in the course of its lifecycle, supporting natural and purposeful product-to-human interaction". For instance, a smart product may be a car, which at different times of its lifecycle may be interacting with workers on the assembly line, dealers, garage mechanics, and a number of owners, and is able to exploit its awareness of its own history and the current context, to improve the level of interaction and proactive support provided to the user in any particular context. In order to realise this vision, several challenges need to be addressed: in particular, in the context of smart products knowledge acquisition is no longer a structured process under the control of a knowledge engineer but it is a highly dynamic process where contextual knowledge is continuously acquired from a variety of sources, including sensors, databases, the internet, and different types of users, at different stages of the lifecycle. Effective knowledge acquisition is in turn crucial to support proactive behaviour, where the smart product is able to initiate communication and action on the basis of its understanding of the current situation and goals. Again, this scenario provides a major departure from classic decision-making support scenarios, which are relatively static with respect to problem solving contexts and types of users. Finally, the dynamic nature of the decision-making support provided by smart products, for different contexts and different classes of users, also introduces new challenges with respect to human-computer interaction: depending on the user and the current context, different interaction modalities may be needed, thus introducing the need for smart, adaptive, multi-modal interaction methods. In my talk I will discuss these new scenarios for knowledge technologies in the context of the SmartProducts project, in particular illustrating these ideas in two everyday application scenarios: smart products in the car and in the kitchen.

– Bernardo Huberman
Senior Fellow and Director, Social Computing Lab
HP Labs
Palo Alto, CA 94304, USA
http://www.hpl.hp.com/research/scl/people/huberman

Social Media and Attention

The past decade has witnessed a momentous transformation in the way people interact and exchange information with each other. Content is now co-produced, shared and classified, and rated on the Web by millions of people, while attention has become the ephemeral and valuable resource that everyone seeks to acquire. This talk will describe how social attention determines the production and consumption of content within social media, and the role it plays in the prediction of future events and trends.

– Tom Scott
Executive Product Manager
BBC
UK
http://derivadow.com/

Using Linked Data to describe the natural world

Linked Data is a deceptively simple yet powerful idea, an idea that provides the foundations for much of the Semantic Web project. It has the potential to offer organisations and users new ways of using the Web by publishing and linking data using standard web technologies and paradigms. Tim Berners-Lee originally proposed a web of things in contrast to a mere "web of documents", i.e. a web that establishes semantic links between documents, people and "things" existing in the real world. By publishing HTTP URIs for people and things as well as documents and describing the relationship between those things with semantic links, Linked Data allows publishers to provide descriptions of things and make assertions about relationships between those things on the Web. The BBC has adopted the principles of Linked Data in publishing significant sections of its Web site, including: programme information (www.bbc.co.uk/programmes) and natural history content (www.bbc.co.uk/wildlifefinder). This presentation provides an introduction to Linked Data and describes how the BBC has used the approach in the development of Wildlife Finder and BBC Programmes; including how Wildlife Finder reuses data from across the Web (e.g. IUCN, WWF, Zoological Society of London, Animal Diversity Web and Wikipedia) and from across the BBC to build the site.

Acknowledgments

Our further thanks go to the following people:

- Ursula Cimiano for designing and producing the flyers, advertisements in the Nodalities Magazine, as well as the program.
- Anja Vigouroux for support in compiling the proceedings and help with the conference organization.
- Ana Jesus for support in the local organization of the conference.
- Andre Grandoch and Ícaro Medeiros for setting up and maintaining the website.

July 2010

Philipp Cimiano
H. Sofia Pinto

Organization

Conference Organization

General and PC Chairs	Helena Sofia Pinto (INESC-ID, Lisbon) Philipp Cimiano (CITEC, Universität Bielefeld)
Workshop Chair	Siegfried Handschuh (DERI, NUI Galway)
Tutorial Chair	Victoria Uren (University of Sheffield)
Demo and poster Chairs	Oscar Corcho (UPM, Madrid) Johanna Völker (University of Mannheim)

Program Committee

We thank the following program committee members for their invaluable support in helping to compile a high-quality program for EKAW 2010 and for their heroic effort of reviewing between 7 and 8 papers in three weeks! As the number of papers submitted to future editions is likely not to decrease, we will need to recruit more people to serve as program committee members in the future.

Andreas Abecker (FZI, Karlsruhe)
Stuart Aitken (University of Edinburgh)
Lora Aroyo (Vrije Universiteit Amsterdam)
Harith Alani (Knowledge Media Institute, The Open University)
Jon Atle Gulla (Norwegian University of Science and Technology)
Nathalie Aussenac-Gilles (IRIT-CNRS, Toulouse)
Richard Benjamins (Telefónica I+D, Madrid)
Eva Blomqvist (ISTC-CNR, Semantic Technology Lab)
Johan Bos (Sapienza University of Rome)
Paulo Bouquet (University of Trento)
Joost Breuker (Universiteit van Amsterdam)
Christopher Brewster (Aston University)
Paul Buitelaar (DERI, NUI Galway)
Pablo Castells (Universidad Autónoma de Madrid)
Jean Charlet (INSERM Paris)
Vinay K. Chaudri (SRI International)
Paolo Ciancarini (University of Bologna)
Paul Compton (UNSW, Sydney)
Olivier Corby (INRIA Sophia Antipolis - Mediterranée)
Claudia d'Amato (University of Bari)
Mathieu D'Aquin (Knowledge Media Institute, The Open University)
Stefan Decker (DERI, NUI Galway)

Nenad Stojanovic (FZI, Karlsruhe)
Heiner Stuckenschmidt (University of Mannheim)
Gerd Stumme (University of Kassel)
Vojtech Svatek (University of Economics, Prague)
Valentina Tamma (University of Liverpool)
Christoph Tempich (Detecon International GmbH)
Annette Ten Teije (Vrije Universiteit Amsterdam)
Francky Trichet (University of Nantes)
Fabio Vitali (University of Bologna)
Hannes Werthner (Vienna University of Technology)
Michael Witbrock (Cycorp Europe, Ljubljana)
Susumu Yamasaki (Okayama University, Japan)

Additional Program Committee Members

Tutorial PC	Trevor Collins (Knowledge Media Institute, The Open University)
	Vitaveska Lanfranchi (OAK Group, University of Sheffield)
	Kinga Schumacher (DFKI, Kaiserslautern)
Workshop PC	Michael Sintek (DFKI, Kaiserslautern)
	Heiner Stuckenschmidt (University of Mannheim)
Demo/Poster PC	Sofia Angeletou (Knowledge Media Institute, The Open University)
	Eva Blomqvist (STLab, ISTC-CNR)
	Klaas Dellschaft (WeST, Universität Koblenz-Landau)
	Frank Dengler (Institute AIFB, KIT)
	Paul Doran (University of Liverpool)
	Kai Eckert (University of Mannheim)
	Guillaume Ereteo (INRIA)
	Tudor Groza (DERI, NUIG, Galway)
	Michiel Hildebrand (CWI, Amsterdam)
	Laura Hollink (Delft University of Technology)
	Simon Jupp (University of Manchester)
	Zoi Kaoudi (University of Athens)
	Malte Kiesel (DFKI, Kaiserslautern)
	Ralf Krestel (L3S, Hanover)
	Holger Lewen (Institute AIFB, KIT)
	Véronique Malaisé (Vrije Universiteit Amsterdam)
	Christian Meilicke (University of Mannheim)
	Elena Montiel-Ponsoda (Universidad Politécnica de Madrid)
	Andriy Nikolov (Knowledge Media Institute, The Open University)
	Vit Novacek (DERI Galway)

Raul Palma (Poznań Supercomputing and Networking Center)
Hector Pérez Urbina (Oxford University)
Simon Schenk (WeST, Universität Koblenz-Landau)
Katharina Siorpaes (STI Innsbruck and playence)
Ondrej Svab-Zamazal (University of Economics, Prague)
Christopher Thomas (Wright State University)
Tania Tudorache (BMIR, Stanford University)
Mark van Assem (Vrije Universiteit Amsterdam)
Fouad Zablith (Knowledge Media Institute, The Open University)

Additional Reviewers (Main Conference)

Alessandro Adamou (ISTC-CNR, Semantic Technology Lab)
Sofia Angeletou (Knowledge Media Institute, The Open University)
Max Arends (Vienna University of Technology)
Nacéra Bennacer (Supelec, Gif/Yvette)
Georgeta Bordea (DERI, NUIG, Galway)
Davide Cerri (STI Innsbruck)
Pasquale De Meo (DIMET, Università Mediterranea di Reggio Calabria)
Frank Dengler (Institute AIFB, KIT)
Birgit Dippelreiter (Vienna University of Technology)
Marco de Gemmis (University of Bari)
Anna Fensel (STI Innsbruck)
Miriam Fernandez (Knowledge Media Institute, The Open University)
Thomas Franz (WeST, Universität Koblenz-Landau)
Andrea Giovanni Nuzzolese (ISTC-CNR, Semantic Technology Lab)
Paul Groth (Vrije Universiteit Amsterdam)
Thomas Gottron (WeST, Universität Koblenz-Landau)
Christoph Grün (Vienna University of Technology)
Heiko Haller (FZI, Karlsruhe)
Karl Hammar (School of Engineering, Jönköping University)
Sung-Kook Han (STI Innsbruck)
Daniel Herzig (Institute AIFB, KIT)
Geert-Jan Houben (TU Delft)
Zhisheng Huang (Vrije Universiteit Amsterdam)
Michael Kassoff (Stanford)
Beate Krause (University of Würzburg)
Markus Krötzsch (Oxford University)
Reto Krummenacher (STI Innsbruck)
Barbara Kump (Know-Center Granz)
Günter Ladwig (Institute AIFB, KIT)
Agnieszka Lawrinowicz (Poznan University of Technology)
Florian Lemmerich (University of Würzburg)
Holger Lewen (Institute AIFB, KIT)

Vanessa Lopez (Knowledge Media Institute, The Open University)
Markus Luczak-Rösch (Freie Universität Berlin)
Laura Moss (The University of Aberdeen)
Nadejda Nikitina (Institute AIFB, KIT)
Andriy Nikolov (Knowledge Media Institute, The Open University)
Santiago Ontañón (IIIA-CSIC)
Nathalie Pernelle (Université Paris-Sud CNRS and INRIA)
Michael Pöttler (Vienna University of Technology)
Behrang Qasemizadeh (DERI, NUIG, Galway)
Brigitte Safar (Université Paris-Sud CNRS and INRIA)
François Scharffe (INRIA and LIG, Grenoble)
Thomas Scharrenbach (Swiss Federal Institute for Forest, Snow and Landscape Research WSL)
Rainer Schuster (Vienna University of Technology)
Katharina Siorpaes (STI Innsbruck)
Olga Streibel (Freie Universität Berlin)
Stuart Taylor (The University of Aberdeen)
Ed Thomas (The University of Aberdeen)
Ioan Toma (STI Innsbruck)
Cássia Trojahn dos Santos (INRIA and LIG, Grenoble)
Chris van Aart (Vrije Universiteit Amsterdam)
Marieke van Erp (Vrije Universiteit Amsterdam)
Pierre-Yves Vandenbussche (INSERM, Paris)
Paola Velardi (La Sapienza University of Rome)
Denny Vrandecic (Institute AIFB, KIT)
Shenghui Wang (Vrije Universiteit Amsterdam)
Tobias Wunner (DERI, NUIG, Galway)
Fouad Zablith (Knowledge Media Institute, The Open University)
Valentin Zacharias (FZI Karlsruhe)
Ondrej Svab-Zamazal (University of Economics, Prague)
Marco Zapletal (Vienna University of Technology)
Amal Zoaq (Athabasca University)

Sponsors

We thank all our sponsors for kindly agreeing to support the conference. We thank in particular:

- ISOCO[5] for sponsoring the invited talk of Tom Scott (Platin Sponsor)
- The Monnet project[6] (Platin Sponsor)
- The Cognitive Interaction Technology Excellence Cluster[7] (CITEC) in Bielefeld (Platin Sponsor)
- Calouste Gulbenkian Foundation[8] for providing the rooms at reduced price (Platin Sponsor)
- IOS Press[9] for sponsoring the best research paper award (Gold Sponsor)
- The LARKC project[10] for sponsoring the best in-use paper (Gold Sponsor)
- The Insemtives project[11] for sponsoring the best problem analysis paper (Gold Sponsor)
- The ACTIVE project[12] for sponsoring the best poster award (Gold Sponsor)
- BeInformed[13] for sponsoring the best demonstration award (Gold Sponsor)
- The SEALS project[14] for sponsoring the best student paper award (Gold Sponsor)
- Talis[15] for including conference advertisements in the Nodalities Magazine[16] (Gold Sponsor)

Platin Sponsors

iSOCO enabling the networked economy

monnet

CITEC

FUNDAÇÃO CALOUSTE GULBENKIAN

5 http://www.isoco.com/
6 http://www.monnet-project.eu/
7 http://www.cit-ec.de/
8 http://www.gulbenkian.pt/
9 http://www.iospress.nl/
10 http://www.larkc.eu/
11 http://www.insemtives.org/
12 http://www.active-project.eu/
13 http://www.beinformed.nl/
14 http://www.seals-project.eu/
15 http://www.talis.com/
16 http://www.talis.com/nodalities/

Gold Sponsors

Silver Sponsors

Table of Contents

Knowledge Engineering: Alignment and Identity

Knowledge Acquisition

Collaboration in Knowledge Engineering

Knowledge Engineering: Patterns

Social Aspects and Tagging

Semantic Web, Web of Data and Linked Data

Ontology Evolution / Refinement

Knowledge Access

Annotation, Retrieval and Natural Language Processing

Short Papers

Pattern-Based Mapping Refinement

Fayçal Hamdi, Chantal Reynaud, and Brigitte Safar

CNRS - University of Paris-Sud 11 (LRI) & INRIA Saclay Ile-de-France (LEO)
Parc Orsay Université 4 rue Jacques Monod 91893 Orsay France
{Faycal.Hamdi,Chantal.Reynaud,Brigitte.Safar}@lri.fr

Abstract. Semantic alignment between ontologies is a crucial task for information integration. There are many ongoing efforts to develop matching systems implementing various alignment techniques but it is impossible to predict what strategy is most successful for an application domain or a given pair of ontologies. Very often the quality of the results could be improved by considering the specificities of the ontologies to be aligned. In this paper, we propose a pattern-based approach implemented in the TaxoMap Framework helping an engineer to refine mappings to take into account specific conventions used in ontologies. Experiments in the topographic field within the *ANR* (The French National Research Agency) project *GéOnto* show the usefulness of such an environment both for a domain expert and an engineer, especially when the number of mappings is very large.

Keywords: Ontology alignment, Mapping refinement.

1 Introduction

The explosion of the number of data sources available on the web increases the need for techniques which allow their integration. The ontologies which provide definitions of domain concepts are essential elements in integration systems and the task of ontology alignment is particularly important for making different heterogeneous resources interoperable. The current alignment tools [4] do not have the same efficiency in all application domains or for all pairs of ontologies. They may be very good in some cases, worse in others. The quality of their results is not always guaranteed and could often be improved if the alignment process took more into account the specificities of the aligned ontologies.

Taking into account these specific aspects can be done in different ways: (1) during the alignment process itself or (2) by refining the results generated by the alignment, considered as preliminaries. In the first case, the adaptation of the handled ontologies is made possible by the modification of the alignment process parameters or by the definition of a particular combination of the alignment systems. No differentiation is thus made in the way the different elements of the ontologies are treated. Inversely, the refinement of mappings (the alignment results) extends the alignment process, applied in the same way to all the elements of the ontologies, and completes it. This second solution allows a finer adaptation of the alignment to the specificities of the handled ontologies. It also

P. Cimiano and H.S. Pinto (Eds.): EKAW 2010, LNAI 6317, pp. 1–15, 2010.

allows performing differentiated refinements according to the generated results. Our work follows this research direction.

Currently, there is no tool which helps to specify mapping refinement treatments to take into account specific conventions used in the ontologies. The TaxoMap Framework allows such specifications.

The paper is organized as follows. In the next section, we present the context of this work, in particular the ontology alignment tool TaxoMap and the goals of the conception of the TaxoMap Framework. In Section 3 we present our main contributions: a pattern-based approach to help refining mappings, the mapping refinement work-flow implemented in the framework and MRPL (Mapping Refinement Pattern Language), the language used in this environment to define patterns. In Section 4 we present some mapping refinement patterns built in the setting of the ANR project *GéOnto* [5]. Experiments in the topographic field which show the usefulness of this environment both for the domain expert and the engineer are described in Section 5. In Section 6 we present some related works. Finally we conclude and give some perspectives in Section 7.

2 Context

We describe the alignment tool TaxoMap [14][6] in Section 2.1 and the objectives of the approach in Section 2.2.

2.1 TaxoMap

TaxoMap has been designed to align owl ontologies $O = (C, H)$. C is a set of concepts characterized by a set of labels and H is a subsumption hierarchy which contains a set of *isA* relationships between nodes corresponding to concepts. The alignment process is an oriented process which tries to connect the concepts of a source ontology O_S to the concepts of a target ontology O_T. The correspondences found are equivalence relations (*isEq*), subsumption relations (*isA*) and their inverse (*isMoreGnl*) or proximity relations (*isClose*).

To identify these correspondences, TaxoMap implements techniques which exploit the labels of the concepts and the subsumption links that connect the concepts in the hierarchy [6]. The morpho-syntactic analysis tool, *TreeTagger* [18], is used to classify the words of the labels of the concepts and to divide them into two classes, *full words* and *complementary words*, according to their category and their position in the labels. At first the repartition between *full* and *complementary words* is used by a similarity measure that compares the trigrams of the labels of the concepts [12] and gives more weight to the common *full words*. Then it is used by the alignment techniques. For example, one technique named t_2 generates an *isA* mapping between X and Y if (1) the concept Y is the concept of O_T having the highest similarity value with the concept X of O_S, (2) one of the labels of Y is included in one of the labels of X, (3) all the words of the included label of Y are classified as *full words* by *TreeTagger*.

Mappings identified by TaxoMap are generated in the Alignment format [3] used as a standard in the OAEI campaign [9]. We added to this format the information about the names of the techniques that generated mappings. The aim is to facilitate the specification of treatments exploiting the mappings generated by those techniques. All these pieces of information are stored in a relational mappings database which can then be queried using *SQL* queries. This allows, in particular, to present the generated mappings to the expert in the validation phase, technique by technique.

2.2 Objectives

Many ontology alignment tools have been developed in these last years but as shown in the results of the OAEI campaigns [9] organized every year since 2004 [1], no tool reaches 100% of precision and recall, even though the results obtained by some of these tools are very good. This also applies to TaxoMap results, either in the OAEI competition in the two last years [7][6] or in the setting of the ANR project *GéOnto* [5]. The aim of this project is the construction of a topographic ontology and its enrichment with elements coming from other geographic ontologies using alignment techniques. In this setting, tests performed on taxonomies provided by the *COGIT-IGN* (project partner) have shown that TaxoMap gives good results (precision 92%) but these results could still be improved.

A closer study showed that the improvements desired by the domain experts are rather specific to the aligned ontologies because they depend on the specific conventions used in the pair of ontologies. Our aim was not to turn TaxoMap into a tool dedicated to the alignment of such topographical taxonomies (the quality of the results would not be guaranteed when TaxoMap would be used to align ontologies coming from other domains). Therefore, we proposed to the experts of the *GéOnto* project an environment allowing to specify and perform refinement treatments applied on the prior obtained mappings. At first, this environment will be used to improve the quality of an alignment provided by TaxoMap. Subsequently, it will be used for other treatments based on mappings as enriching, restructuring or merging ontologies.

Such a mapping refinement environment must satisfy two main objectives. First, it must provide the domain experts with a tool helping them to detect and propose corrections for invalid mappings. The validation task is sometimes very difficult because the number of generated mappings can be enormous when the ontologies are very large. The expert may have difficulties to browse all the mappings and to have the global view he requires in order to propose the right modifications. In consequence, he may ask to modify some mappings without realizing that the requested modifications have an undesirable impact on other mappings. The observations of the consequences of the requested updates can be a means for the expert to clarify the right refinement treatments to be performed. Second, thanks to the iterative validation/correction process, such an environment must help the engineer to specify correct treatments. The validation phase performed by the expert allows to check whether the specification of a treatment intended to be applied to a given set of mappings is correct or not (i.e. if it does not also generate undesirable mappings).

3 The Approach

The approach implemented in the TaxoMap Framework has been designed to meet the objectives described in Section 2.2. We describe the approach and a diagram representing the mapping refinement work-flow respectively in Section 3.1 and 3.2. This work-flow allows the specification of treatments according to a pattern-based approach. The language MRPL used to define mapping refinement pattern is presented in Section 3.3.

3.1 Presentation of the Approach

An important feature of the approach is to allow a declarative specification of treatments based on particular alignment results, concerning particular ontologies and using a predefined vocabulary. Treatments which can be specified depend on the characteristics of the concerned ontologies and on the task to be performed (at first mapping refinement and subsequently ontology merging, restructuring, enriching). These treatments are thus associated to independent specification modules, one for each task, each having their own vocabulary. The approach is extensible and a priori applicable to any treatment based on alignment results.

In the setting of mapping refinement, the approach should help to specify, for example, that the subsumption mapping *isA* generated between “Road and coast trail” and “Trail”, as shown in Fig. 1 must be replaced by a mapping of the same type but between “Road and coast trail” and “Road”. Indeed, “Trail” is defined in O_T as a kind of “Road” and the term “Road” itself appears in the label “Road and coast trail”. The expert would thus prefer to establish a mapping directly between “Road and coast trail” and “Road”.

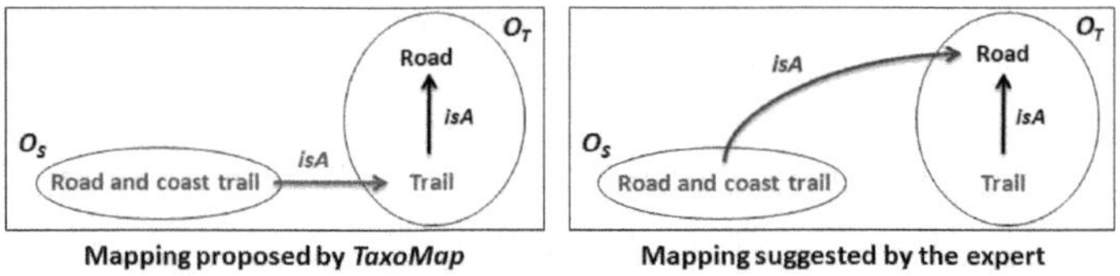

Fig. 1. Example of update asked by the expert

The specification of treatments must be as generic as possible. Thus, the specification of the treatment illustrated in Fig. 1 should not refer directly to the concepts denoted by “Road”, “Trail” and “Road and coast trail”. Instead, we provide the engineer with a vocabulary allowing to specify mapping refinement patterns. These patterns are generic specifications of mapping refinements which can then be instantiated and thus applied many times.

By analyzing the examples of mapping refinement delivered by the domain expert, the engineer will be able to identify groups requiring the same refinement treatment and to specify the appropriate pattern to apply to each of them. The specification will be declared in such a generic way, then instantiated on the alignment results and the concerned ontologies in order to perform the expected treatments. The patterns are stored and can be reused from one mapping refinement task to another.

3.2 The Mapping Refinement Work-Flow

Fig. 2 presents the mapping refinement work-flow implemented in the TaxoMap Framework. First, TaxoMap is performed on two ontologies, a source one and a target one (cf. 1). The alignment results, i.e. the mappings, are stored in a database (cf. 2) and have to be validated by a domain expert or an engineer (cf. 3). When the expert/engineer examines closely the built alignment, he may notice the existence of incorrect mappings or of mappings which are different from what he would have liked. These mappings are grouped by the engineer when they correspond to a similar case. The examples related to a similar case are generalized (cf. 4) and the corresponding pattern is described (cf. 5). The patterns are then applied to the whole mappings database, i.e. to the mappings cited by the expert as examples of mappings having to be refined but also to other ones that the expert has not seen but which are also instances of the patterns (cf. 6). Results of the mapping transformation process have then to be validated (cf. 3). The validation phase helps to check whether a treatment generates undesirable mappings. In case mappings are updated where they should not be, these mappings are a means to clarify the right treatments to be performed (the right patterns to be applied). Thus, the mapping refinement process must be viewed as an iterative validation/correction process needed by the great number of mappings to be examined. The validation, the generalization and the specification of patterns are manual treatments. The mapping transformation based on the use of patterns is automatic.

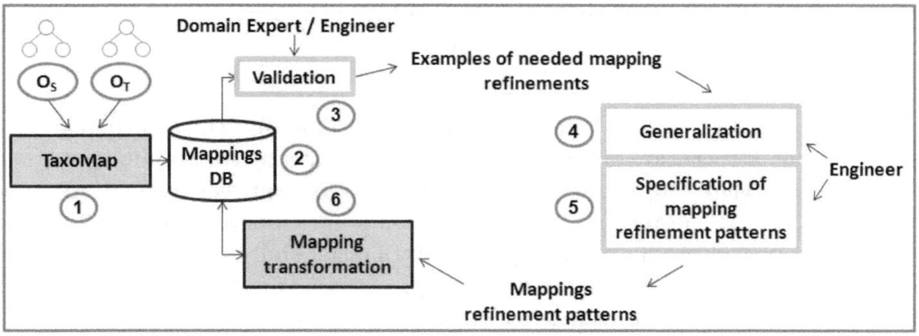

Fig. 2. The mapping refinement work-flow

3.3 MRPL, the Mapping Refinement Pattern Language

The language MRPL is used to specify mapping refinement pattern. This language differs from the one defined in [16] especially because it includes patterns which test the existence of mappings generated by alignment techniques. MRPL is defined as follows:

Definition 1 (Vocabulary)
The vocabulary of MRPL contains:

- a set of predicate constants. We distinguish three categories of predicate constants: the predicate constants relating to the type of techniques applied in the identification of a mapping by TaxoMap, the predicate constants expressing structural relations between concepts of a same ontology, the predicate constants expressing terminological relations between labels of concepts.
- a set of individual constants: $\{a, b, c, ...\}$
- a set of variables: $\{x, y, z, ..., \_\}$ where $\_$ is an unnamed variable used to represent parameters which do not need to be precised.
- a set of built-in predicates: $\{Add\_Mapping,\ Delete\_Mapping\}$
- a set of logical symbols: $\{\exists,\ \wedge,\ \neg\}$

MRPL allows the definition of a **context part** which must be satisfied to make the execution of a pattern possible, and of a **solution part** which expresses the process to achieve when the **context part** is satisfied. The **context part** is a logical formula defined as follows.

Definition 2 (Terms)
Variables and constants are terms.

Definition 3 (Syntax)
If α and β are terms and P is a predicate symbol with two places then $P(\alpha, \beta)$ is a formula.

If α, β and γ are terms and P is a predicate symbol with three places then $P(\alpha, \beta, \gamma)$ is a formula.

If ϕ and ψ are formulae then $[\phi \wedge \psi]$ is a formula.

If ϕ is a formula then $[\neg\ \phi]$ is a formula.

If ϕ is a formula and v is a variable then $\exists v\phi$ is a formula.

The **context part** tests (1) the technique used to identify the considered mapping, (2) the structural constraints on mapped elements, for example, the fact that they are related by a subsumption relation to concepts verifying or not some properties, or (3) the terminological constraints, for example, the fact that the labels of a concept are included in the labels of other concepts. These conditions are represented using formulae built from predicate symbols. So, we distinguish three kinds of formula according to the kind of predicate symbols used.

The formulae related to the type of techniques applied in the identification of a mapping by TaxoMap. By testing the existence in the mappings database of a particular relation generated by a given technique, we build formulae that implicitly test the conditions for the application of this technique. For example the formula $isAStrictInclusion(x, y)$ tests the existence of a mapping isA generated between two concepts x and y using the technique t_2. It validates implicitly at the same time all the conditions for the application of t_2, i.e. (1)

the concept y is the concept of O_T having the highest similarity value with the concept x of O_S, (2) one of the labels of y is included in one of the labels of x, and (3) all the words of the labels of y are classified as *full words* by *TreeTagger*. TaxoMap includes several alignment techniques. Thus, several predicate symbols leading to formulae of that kind are needed. More formally, let:

$R_M = \{isEq, isA, isMoreGnl, isClose\}$, the set of correspondence relations used by TaxoMap,

$T = \{t_1, t_2, t_3, t_4, t_5, t_6, t_7, t_8, t_9\}$, the set of techniques.

T_M, the table storing generated mappings in the form of *4-tuple* (x, y, r, t) where $x \in C_S, y \in C_T, r \in R_M, t \in T$. The pairs of variables (x, y) which can instantiate these formulae will take their values in the set $(x, y) \mid (x, y, r, t) \in T_M$. The predicate symbols necessary for the task of refinement presented in this paper are $isEquivalent$, $isAStrictInclusion$ and $isCloseCommonDescendant$ the semantics of which are the following:

- $isEquivalent(x, y)$ is true iff $\exists(x, y, isEq, t_1) \in T_M$
- $isAStrictInclusion(x, y)$ is true iff $\exists(x, y, isA, t_2) \in T_M$
- $isCloseCommonDescendant(x, y)$ is true iff $\exists(x, y, isClose, t_9) \in T_M$

The formulae expressing structural relations between concepts x and y of the same ontology $O = (C, H)$. Since the aim of TaxoMap is the alignment of taxonomies, the structural relations considered here are subsumption relations. If the approach was used with another alignment tool, other relations could be considered. Note that the instances of variables in these formulae will be constrained, either directly because they instantiate the previous formulae, related to the type of the applied techniques, or indirectly by having to be in relation with other instances.

- $isSubClassOf(x, y, O)$ is true $\Leftrightarrow isA(x, y) \in H$
- $isParentOf(x, y, O)$ is true $\Leftrightarrow isA(y, x) \in H$

The formulae expressing terminological relations between the labels of the concepts:

- $strictInclusionLabel(x, y)$ is defined as follows:

Algorithm 1. strictInclusionLabel(x,y)

Require: $\{x, y\} \in C_S \cup C_T$
1: **for** each label L_1 of x and each label L_2 of y **do**
2:    **if** $L_1 \subseteq FullWords(L_2, L_1)$ **then**
3:       **return** *true*
4:    **end if**
5: **end for**

where $FullWords(L_2, L_1)$ is a function which calculates the common terms to L_1 and L_2 considered as *full words*.

- $appearInLabel(c, y)$ is true $\Leftrightarrow \exists$ a label L_1 of y such as $c \subset L_1$, where c is a string and $y \in C_S \cup C_T$.

Algorithm 2. extractFromLabel(x,c,y,r)

Require: $\{x, y\} \in C_S \cup C_T$ and $c \in \{$"*and*", "*or*"$\}$
for each label L_1 of x **do**
  $SplitLabelPart(L_1, c, Part_1, Part_2)$
  if one label of $y = Part1$ **then**
    $r = Part_2$, **return** *true*
  else if one label of $y = Part_2$ **then**
    $r = Part_1$, **return** *true*
  else
    return *false*
  end if
end for

- $extractFromLabel(x, c, y, r)$ is defined as follows: where $SplitLabelPart(L_1, c, Part_1, Part_2)$ is a function which extracts from the label L_1 two new labels $Part_1$ and $Part_2$, where $Part_1$ and $Part_2$ consist of words that appear respectively before and after c.
- $inclusionInLabel(x, c, y)$ is true $\Leftrightarrow$ $extractFromLabel(x, c, y, \_)$ is true.
- $conceptsDifferent(x, y)$ is true $\Leftrightarrow$ $ID(x) \neq ID(y)$ with $ID(x)$ is the identifier of the concept x.

A **context part** is associated to a **solution part** which is a set of actions to be performed. This set of actions is modeled by a conjunction of built-in predicates executed in a database. The built-in predicates are defined as follows:

- $Add\_Mapping(x, y, r)$ has the effect of adding a tuple to the table T_M which becomes $T_M \cup \{(x, y, r, t)\}$ where r and t are fixed in the treatment condition by instantiating the predicate corresponding to the type of technique associated with the considered mapping.
- $Delete\_Mapping(x, y, \_)$ has the effect of removing a tuple from the table T_M which becomes $T_M - \{(x, y, \_, \_)\}$.

4 Mapping Refinement Patterns

In this section, we present some mapping refinement patterns designed in the setting of the ANR project, *GéOnto* [5]. At first, TaxoMap performed an alignment between *Topo-Cogit* and *Carto-Cogit*, two taxonomies provided by the *COGIT-IGN* and containing respectively 600 and 495 concepts. 340 mappings have been generated and stored in the mappings database. 27 mappings (precision 92%) have been deemed as invalid by the domain expert. For other mappings, the expert proposed alternative mappings. We used the TaxoMap Framework to specify the changes to be done through mapping refinement patterns.

Pattern-1: This first pattern is illustrated in Fig. 3. It concerns mappings detected by the technique t_2, connecting by a subsumption relation *isA* a concept

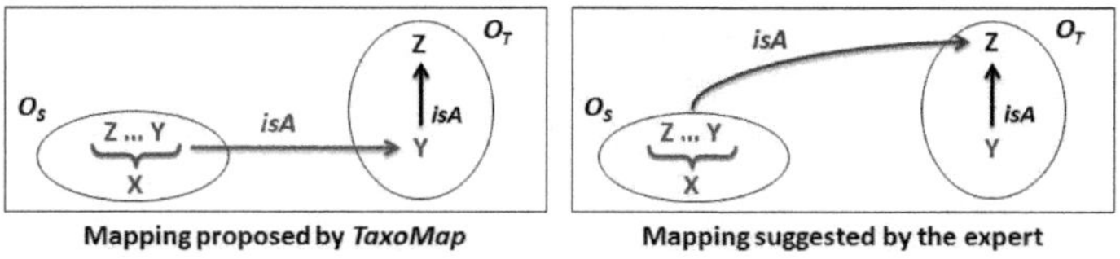

Fig. 3. Illustration of Pattern-1

x of the source ontology O_S to a concept y of the target ontology O_T, such as one of the labels of y is included in one of the labels of x. If one of the labels of the concept z that subsumes y in O_T is also included in the label of x, the expert prefers to link x to z, the most general concept of O_T.

Context part of Pattern-1:

$\exists x \exists y\ (isAStrictInclusion(x, y)$
$\wedge\ \exists z\ (isSubClassOf(y, z, O_T) \wedge strictInclusionLabel(z, x)))$

Solution part of Pattern-1:

$Delete\_Mapping(x, y, \_) \wedge Add\_Mapping(x, z, isA)$

The application of this pattern on the example presented in Fig. 1 allows first to select the mapping (id_1, id_2, isA, t_2) where one of the labels of id_1 is "Road and coast trail", one of the labels of id_2 is "Trail" and such as the formula $isAStrictInclusion\ (id_1, id_2)$ is satisfied in the mappings database. The variables x and y are instantiated by id_1 and id_2 respectively. The use of the formula $isSubClassOf(id_2, z, O_T)$ based on a structural predicate symbol leads to the instantiation of the variable z by id_3, where one of the labels of id_3 is "Road", and to the verification of the formula $strictInclusionLabel(id_3, id_1)$. The mapping (id_1, id_2, isA, t_2) is then removed from the mappings database and replaced by the mapping (id_1, id_3, isA, t_2).

Pattern-2: This second pattern concerns also the mappings generated by the technique t_2. If none of the labels of the concept z that subsumes y in O_T is included in the labels of x (see the two last conditions of the pattern) but if instead it contains one of the connectors "and" or "or", the expert considers that x is not a specialization of y but rather a generalization of it, that we represent by the relation "isMoreGnl" (see Fig. 4). An example of the application of the Pattern-2 is given in the Fig. 5.

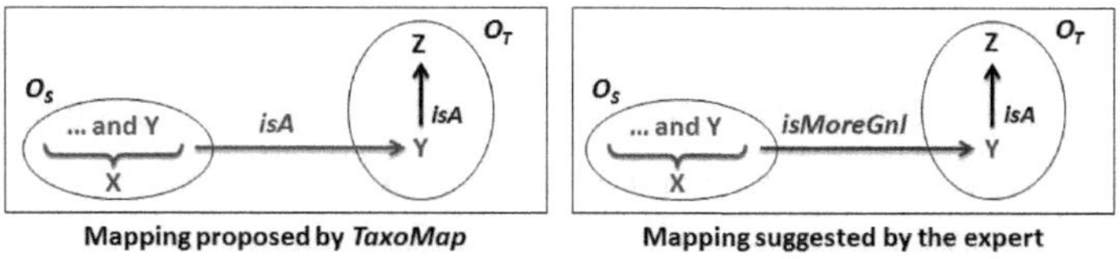

Fig. 4. Illustration of Pattern-2

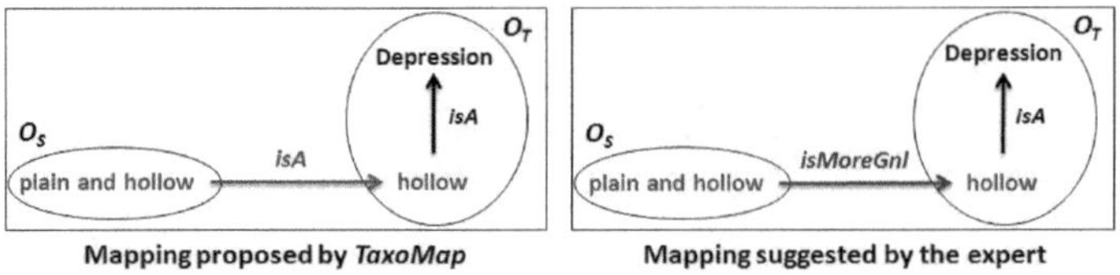

Fig. 5. Example of the application of the Pattern-2

Context part of Pattern-2:
$\exists x \exists y\ (isAStrictInclusion(x, y) \wedge inclusionInLabel(x, \text{“}and\text{”}, y)$
$\wedge\ \exists z\ (isSubClassOf(y, z, O_T) \wedge \neg strictInclusionLabel(z, x)))$

Solution part of Pattern-2:
$Delete\_Mapping(x, y, \_) \wedge Add\_Mapping(x, y, isMoreGnl)$

Pattern-3: Let the set $SD(c, O)$ be composed of c and of all its sub-concepts in O. The measure $M_{SD}(c_1, O_1, c_2, O_2)$ is defined as the ratio between the number of equivalence relations verified in the mapping table between concepts in $SD(c_1, O_1)$ and in $SD(c_2, O_2)$ and the total number of concepts belonging to the union of these two sets. The technique t_9 connects by a relation of proximity *isClose*, a concept x of O_S to a concept y of O_T, if y is the concept in O_T which has at least two descendants in common with x and which maximizes the M_{SD} for x.

If there is a concept $d \in O_S$ such that $isEquivalent(d, y)$ and $d \in SD(x, O_S)$, the expert prefers to connect x to the father P of y in O_T by a subsumption relation. An illustration is given in Fig. 6.

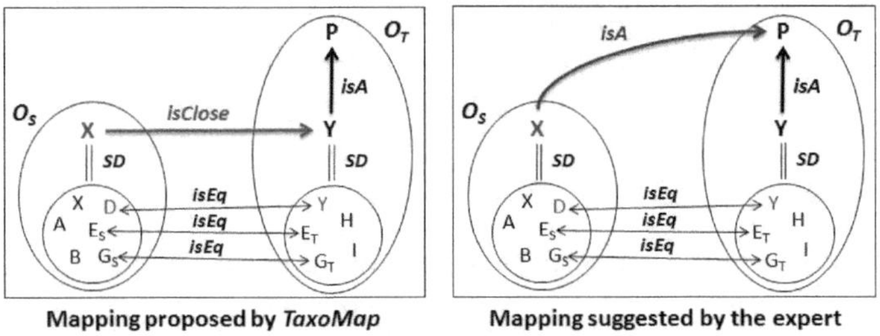

Fig. 6. Illustration of Pattern-3

Context part of Pattern-3:
$\exists x \exists y\ (isCloseCommonDescendant(x, y) \wedge \exists d\ isEquivalent(d, y)$
$\wedge\ isSubClassOf(d, x, O_S) \wedge \exists p\ isParentOf(p, y, O_T))$

Solution part of Pattern-3:
$Delete\_Mapping(x, y, \_) \wedge Add\_Mapping(x, p, isA)$

5 Experiments in the Context of the *GéOnto* Project

This section illustrates the mapping refinement work-flow presented in Section 3.2, the interactions between the expert, the engineer and our tool leading to the design of refinement patterns. The experimentation described here is that guiding the expert and the engineer to refine the numerous mappings generated by the technique t_2. t_2, represented by the predicate *isAStrictInclusion*, constructs an *isA* mapping between x and y if (1) y is the concept of O_T having the highest similarity value with the concept x of O_S, (2) one of the labels of y is included in one of the labels of x, (3) all the words of the included label are full words. The 3 iterations described below are needed to specify the right pattern operating the right modifications. Note that mappings produced by TaxoMap are presented technique by technique. This allows to easily validate mappings generated by a given technique.

Iteration 1

The evaluation of the mappings produced by the technique t_2 leads the expert to identify 3 mappings as examples of what needs to be modified: "plain and hollow *isA* hollow" should become "plain and hollow *isMoreGnl* hollow", "wood and forest *isA* forest" should become "wood and forest *isMoreGnl* forest", "road or street *isA* street" should become "road or street *isMoreGnl* street".

These 3 examples are generalized by the engineer as follows: in the context of this alignment technique, when the label of the concept x in O_S contains a connector "and/or", x is not a specialization of y but rather a more general concept. This change is implemented in a pattern as follows:

Context part:

$\exists x \exists y\ (isAStrictInclusion(x, y) \wedge appearInLabel(\text{“and”}, x)$
$\wedge\ \exists z\ (isSubClassOf(y, z, OT) \wedge \neg strictInclusionLabel(z, x)))$

Solution part:

$Delete\_Mapping(x, y, \_) \wedge Add\_Mapping(x, y, isMoreGnl)$

The application of this pattern to the whole mappings database leads to the modification of 20 mappings. 3 of them are the examples proposed by the expert but 17 additional mappings have also been updated. For example, "rocks and sand *isMoreGnl* rock", "local or private museum *isMoreGnl* museum", "campanile and not adjacent belfry *isMoreGnl* belfry". Their evaluation is necessary. That leads to a new cycle of mapping refinement.

Iteration 2

For 5 additional mappings, the modifications are consistent with what the expert asks (for example "rocks and sand *isMoreGnl* rock"). But it reveals also undesirable modifications, especially when the part of x containing the label of y denotes a more specific concept than x (for example, in "local or private museum", the part of x "private museum" is more specific than the label of y "museum"). In this case, x must not be considered as more general than y. Consequently, the only presence of a connector "and/or" is not enough to guarantee that x is more general than y. It is necessary to check that the connector separates effectively the exact label of y and something else (which we will called the remaining part), in the form "P_1 and/or P_2" where the label of y is exactly P_1 or P_2.

This leads the engineer to modify the previous pattern by using instead of $appearInLabel(\text{"}and\text{"}, x)$, the formula $inclusionInLabel(x, c, y)$, which allows to check if one of the two parts connected by the connector c is exactly the label of y: *InclusionInLabel("water treatment and pumping station", and, "pumping station")* is true, while *InclusionInLabel("local or private museum", or, "museum")* and *InclusionInLabel("campanile and not adjacent belfry", and, "belfry")* are false. The pattern becomes:

Context part:
$\exists x \exists y\ (isAStrictInclusion(x, y) \wedge inclusionInLabel(x, \text{"}and\text{"}, y)$
$\wedge\ \exists z\ (isSubClassOf(y, z) \wedge \neg strictInclusionLabel(z, x)))$
Solution part:
$Delete\_Mapping(x, y, \_) \wedge Add\_Mapping(x, y, isMoreGnl)$

The application of this new pattern to the original whole mappings database leads to the modification of 8 mappings. 3 of them are the examples proposed by the expert. Only 5 additional mappings (among 17 modified by the pattern in iteration 1) have been updated. This leads to a new iteration where the expert has to evaluate these 5 additional mappings and 12 mappings modified in iteration 1 but not in iteration 2, which are considered as counterexamples.

Iteration 3
In this phase, the expert validates the modifications of the 5 additional mappings, as well as the preservation of 10 of the 12 mappings presented as counterexamples. Two mappings were not updated by the pattern in its final version but the expert would have wanted them to be modified: "campanile and not adjacent belfry *isA* belfry" "Highway or lane road with divided ways *isA* road with divided ways".

The analysis of these two counterexamples shows that in both cases, the label of x is in the form "P_1 and/or P_2" with the label of y included in P_2 without being exactly equivalent. However the string P_1 is the label of a domain concept ("campanile" in the first case, "highway" in the second). The concept identification would be simple to perform automatically in the second case because "highway" is a label of a concept in O_T. It is more difficult in the first case, since "campanile" is not a label of any concept, either in O_T or in O_S. So only one of the two new desired changes can be performed automatically by introducing an additional pattern. The pattern previously defined must not be modified. The expert has validated its results. The new pattern addresses a new case identified by the expert during iteration 3. Note that the results are unchanged regardless of the order of applying these 2 patterns (the pattern previously defined and the new one).

The whole experiment in the topographic field led to specify 6 refinement patterns related to 4 alignment techniques of TaxoMap. 25 mappings have been modified. 23 satisfy the wishes of the expert. Two refinements are incorrect.

Table 1. The number of initially found, false and refined mappings per technique

Technique	T_1	T_2	T_3	T_4	T_5	T_6	T_7	T_8	T_9	Total
# mappings	197	86	13	13	5	4	0	8	14	340
# false mappings	1	13	5	0	0	0	0	6	2	27
# refined mappings	0	16	3	0	0	0	0	4	2	25
# false mappings after refinement	1	6	2	0	0	0	0	3	0	10

6 Related Works

Many alignment tools existing today generate good results in certain cases and not so good results in other cases. This observation should direct research to treat several problems [19] such as: the choice of the most adapted tool, the combination of the alignment techniques and the problem of the regulation of the parameters (thresholds, coefficient of formulas, etc.) used in the alignment tools. Our works are issued from the same observation but have been developed in a different direction, the alignment refinement, and subsequently the assistance to the specification of treatments based on mappings.

The closest work we know is the COMA++ system [2]. It aims to build powerful alignment tools by the combination of existing matchers then to refine the obtained alignment results considered as preliminary. The refinement process is here totally automatic. The COMA++ alignment process is re-applied on groups of elements whose proximity has been established by a first treatment applied to ontologies. The refinement of the alignment can also be seen as an adaptation of the alignment solutions to the context of an application. Thus, the system eTunes [11] adapts an alignment by looking automatically to the most adapted values for the parameters of the alignment system. Other works deal with alignment refinement or alignment transformation which are close but not similar activities. In [17] and [15], correspondences patterns are used to assist the design of precise and complex ontology alignments when parts of both ontologies represent the same conceptualizations but modeled in two different ways. This approach can be seen as a way to refine one-to-one correspondences which can then be used to transform an ontology into another as in [17]. Other works propose services to transform alignments. The Alignment API [3] generates transformations which are implementations for rendering the alignments, but the alignments are not modified.

Regarding our environment, another related work is PROMPT-Suite integrating the ontology merging tool IPROMPT [13], the alignment tool Anchor-PROMPT, versioning, comparison, translation functionalities. All these tools are interactive and semi-automatic. For example, in the fusion process the system makes suggestions. The expert can hold one of them or specify an operation to perform. The system then executes the operation, calculates the resulting changes, makes other suggestions and detects any inconsistencies.

All systems combining several alignment systems are very modular. The possibility of defining the strategy of combination makes them adaptable to a new field of application. This modularity and adaptability are strong points which also characterize our approach. The treatments which can be specified in the TaxoMap Framework are indeed modular and conceived to integrate the very particular characteristics of the treated ontologies. It goes beyond the possibilities of the tools previously mentioned. However, the TaxoMap Framework differs from existing tools such COMA++, eTunes or PROMPT-Suite by considering that the performance of an alignment tool implementing general alignment algorithms is necessarily limited (even if the values of parameters are optimal). Some improvements can be obtained only after taking into account the particularities of the aligned ontology which involves various improvements depending on the ontologies. Specifying such improvements needs to be familiar with the aligned ontologies. So this process cannot be automatic. Only an expert of the domain is able to suggest them. As in PROMPT-Suite, we offer an interactive environment to help an expert assisted by an engineer to carry out this task, but we do it differently. We allow the definition of particular generic treatments able to take into account specific conventions used in the ontologies. In PROMPT-Suite, this is not possible. The treatments are all pre-defined.

7 Conclusion and Future Work

In this paper, we have presented an environment for the specification of treatments based on alignment results generated by TaxoMap. We presented the context of this work, the approach, the mapping refinement work-flow and the Mapping Refinement Pattern Language MRPL. We described the use of our mapping refinement approach applied in the topographic field. This approach has been implemented in the TaxoMap Framework. We illustrated its use and the usefulness of the approach through experiments made in the setting of the ANR project *GéOnto*.

The engineer can select all the elements of the vocabulary of MRPL through an appropriate GUI accessible at the following Web address [20]. Note that the approach is based on the use of TaxoMap as an alignment tool, but it could be based on another tool. If the predicate symbols associated with this other tool have been defined, the specification of refinement treatments is simplified. If these predicates have not been defined, it will be necessary to further specify the conditions that must be satisfied in the context part of the pattern. Anyway, the method is usable for any alignment tool.

The TaxoMap Framework has also been designed to allow the specification of other treatments such as merging, restructuring and enriching ontologies based on alignment results. Future work will be devoted to the design and the implementation of the modules corresponding to these additional functionalities. It will be devoted also to the extension of the approach for refining the mappings between ontologies that have a more richer axiomatisation.

Acknowledgement

This research was supported by the French National Research Agency (ANR), through the *GéOnto* project ANR-O7-MDCO-005 on Creation, Comparison and Exploitation of Heterogeneous Geographic Ontologies [5].

References

1. Euzenat, J., Ferrara, A., Hollink, L., Isaac, A., Joslyn, C., Malaisé, V., Meilicke, C., Nikolov, A., Pane, J., Sabou, M., Scharffe, F., Shvaiko, P., Spiliopoulos, V., Stuckenschmidt, H., Sváb-Zamazal, O., Svátek, V., Trojahn dos Santos, C., Vouros, G., Wang, S.: Results of the Ontology Alignment Evaluation Initiative 2009. In: Proc. 4th ISWC Workshop on Ontology Matching (OM), Chantilly (VA US), pp. 73–126 (2009)
2. Do, H.-H., Rahm, E.: Matching large schemas: Approaches and Evaluation. Information Systems 32, 857–885 (2007)
3. Euzenat, J.: An API for ontology alignment. In: McIlraith, S.A., Plexousakis, D., van Harmelen, F. (eds.) ISWC 2004. LNCS, vol. 3298, pp. 698–712. Springer, Heidelberg (2004)
4. Euzenat, J., Shvaiko, P.: Ontology Matching. Springer, Heidelberg (2007)
5. GéOnto Project, `http://geonto.lri.fr`
6. Hamdi, F., Safar, B., Niraula, N., Reynaud, C.: TaxoMap in the OAEI 2009 alignment contest. In: ISWC Workshop on Ontology Matching, Chantilly (VA US), pp. 230–237 (2009)
7. Hamdi, F., Zargayouna, H., Safar, B., Reynaud, C.: TaxoMap in the OAEI 2008 alignment contest. In: The 3rd ISWC Workshop on Ontology Matching, Karlsruhe (DE), pp. 206–213 (2008)
8. Kamel, M., Aussenac-Gilles, N.: Ontology Learning by Analysing XML Document Structure and Content. In: Knowledge Engineering and Ontology Development (KEOD), Madère, Portugal, pp. 159–165 (2009)
9. Ontology Alignment Evaluation Initiative, `http://oaei.ontologymatching.org/`
10. Kergosien, E., Kamel, M., Sallaberry, C., Bessagnet, M.-N., Aussenac, N., Gaio, M.: Construction automatique d'ontologie et enrichissement à partir de ressources externes. In: JFO proceedings, Poitiers, pp. 1–10 (2009)
11. Lee, Y., Sayyadian, M., Doan, A., Rosenthal, A.S.: eTuner: tuning schema matching software using synthetic scenarios. The VLDB Journal 16, 97–122 (2007)
12. Lin, D.: An Information-Theoretic definition of Similarity. In: Proc. of ICML 1998, Madison, pp. 296–304 (1998)
13. Noy, N.F., Musen, M.A.: The PROMPT Suite: Interactive Tools For Ontology Merging And Mapping. IJHCS 59(6), 983–1024 (2003)
14. Reynaud, C., Safar, B.: Techniques structurelles d'alignement pour portails Web. In: du Web, F. (ed.) Revue RNTI W-3, Cépaduès, pp. 57–76 (2007)
15. Ritze, D., Meilicke, C., Svab-Zamazal, O., Stuckenschmidt, H.: A pattern-based Ontology Matching Approach for detecting Complex Correspondences. In: ISWC Workshop on Ontology Matching, Chantilly (VA US), pp. 25–36 (2009)
16. Scharffe, F.: Correspondence Patterns Representations. PhD thesis, University of Innsbruck (2009)
17. Scharffe, F., Euzenat, J., Fensel, D.: Towards Design patterns for Ontology Alignment. In: SAC, pp. 2321–2325 (2008)
18. Schmid, H.: Probabilistic Part-of-Speech Tagging Using Decision Trees. In: Int. Conf. on New Methods in Language Processing (1994)
19. Shvaiko, P., Euzenat, J.: Ten Challenges for Ontology Matching. In: Proc. of the 7th International Conference on Ontologies, DataBases, and Applications of Semantics (ODBASE), Monterey (MX), pp. 1163–1181 (2008)
20. TaxoMap FrameWork, `http://www.lri.fr/~hamdi/TaxoMap/TaxoMap.html`

Practical Considerations on Identity for Instance Management in Ontological Investigation

Kouji Kozaki, Satoshi Endo, and Riichiro Mizoguchi

The Institute of Scientific and Industrial Research, Osaka University
8-1 Mihogaoka, Ibaraki, Osaka, 567-0047 Japan
{kozaki,miz}@ei.sanken.osaka-u.ac.jp

Abstract. For knowledge representation based on ontology and its use, it is desirable to understand phenomena in the target world as precisely and deeply as possible. The ontology should reflect the understanding of them and provide a fundamental framework to manage the behavior of instances adequately. The management of instance model requires identity of things. Contrary to the common understanding, there are several kinds of identity according to the purpose of its use. This paper discusses how many kinds of identity exist and what kind of identity suits to what purpose. Based on the consideration result we suggest four kinds of identity and discuss what situation to be applied.

Keywords: Identity, Instance management, Roles, Ontology.

1 Introduction

Ontology has been used as the basis of knowledge systems in various domains, and its utility is recognized more widely day by day. An ontology provides "an explicit specification of a conceptualization" [1] underlying any knowledge representation (an instance model), and it is one of the important roles to keep the consistency and reusability of knowledge by describing them based on the ontology. Many researchers study ontological theories intended to contribute to building a well-founded ontology. Especially, theory of roles is one of the critical topics. Roles have various characteristics such as anti-rigidity [2], dynamics [3], context dependency, and so on. We have been investigating these characteristics of roles and how to deal with them on computer systems as accurately as possible. As a result, we have developed an ontology development/use tool, named Hozo, based on fundamental consideration of roles [4].

In spite of the intensive work on theory of roles, however, there still remains some room for investigation of instance management problems such as the counting problem [5], appearance/disappearance of instances of roles, dynamic change of roles which players play, and so on. It is important to establish an ontological theory for instance management of roles so that we can capture their behavior and manage them in a sound manner.

Especially, identity of an instance of role concept and role holder has various characteristics [4], and we can observe several kinds of identity according to target tasks. This motivated us to investigate the issue of identity of roles and normal

P. Cimiano and H.S. Pinto (Eds.): EKAW 2010, LNAI 6317, pp. 16–30, 2010.

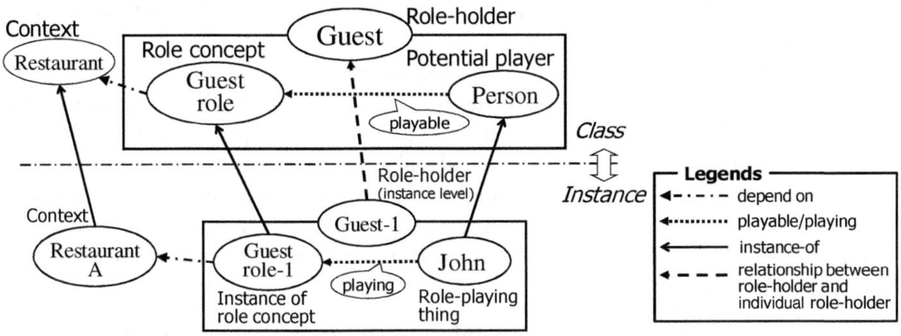

Fig. 1. Fundamental scheme of role concept and a role holder

types as well from practical point of view. We discuss what kinds of identity we need and try to enumerate its kinds so that we can study instance management. In addition, in developing a system based on ontology and Semantic Web technologies, the importance of identity problem, e.g. identity of resource on the Web, the same name problem, identity through links and so on, are discussed [6, 7].

This paper discusses a property of identity to talk about instances, and introduces four kinds of identity that seem useful from practical point of view. The next section summarizes problems of identity in instance management and presents some motivating examples. Section 3 discusses classification of identity recognized generally. Section 4 discusses a nature of identity which is our subject in this paper, and introduces four kinds of identity. Section 5 discusses identity of role concept based on the four kinds of identity. Section 6 gives some discussion about applying those identities to instances of role concept and normal types. Related work is discussed in Section 7, followed by concluding remarks.

2 Motivating Examples

Let us show our model of roles in Fig.1. We divided the conventional notion of "Role" into two kinds: role concept and role holder in our model. The fundamental scheme of our role model is the following:

> "In a context, there are potential players who can play role concepts and thereby become role holders" [4, 8].

For example, "In restaurants, there are persons who play guest roles and thereby become guests." (Fig.1). The link from Guest-1 to Guest is not completely same as instance-of relation because the individual role holder to be instantiated inherently requires first an instance of a potential player (e.g., person) class and of a role concept class (e.g., guest role). Identity of the role holder is composed by that of the role concept and that of the player. For example, identity of the guest role holder is determined according to the identity of guest role and that of person. Note here that our model assumes the existence of role concepts that are not played, we call them "unplayed roles" in this paper and they are understood as possessing identities.

Before presenting some motivating examples, we mention the identity discussed in philosophy.

Any P, P(X) = P(Y) ⇔ X and Y are identical

It is called numerical identity. Although it is philosophically very important and interesting to investigate what it means, it is not very practical for talking about identities of individuals, since it is useful only for saying that any thing is identical to itself and since every individual changes as time goes. In practice, it is often the case to talk about diachronic identity rather than synchronic identity. This suggests we would need other kinds of identity in everyday practice of ontological investigation. Consider the following examples:

(1) Imagine you are renewing your bike by changing its parts. How many parts or what parts can you change before you say "It is not my bike anymore!"?
(2) Assume you are replacing a part of a bike one by one to fix it, or you are removing skin of an orange to eat it. What do you answer when you are asked what bike you are fixing, or what skin you are removing? You will answer "I'm fixing ***this*** bike[1]" at any time or "I'm removing skin of ***this*** orange" at any time and "***this bike***" and "***this orange***" must denote "the same thing", respectively, independently of when you are asked. What identity do you use in such a case?
(3) When you have three four-sided figures, one figure is pressed to change its form from a square to a diamond. The thing is not square anymore, but you still have three four-sided figures. What identities do you use to say "this square has lost its identity" and "I have three four-sided figures independently of the change." Ontologically, counting needs no time, but it needs time in practice. Then what happens if one figure changes and looses its identity while you are counting the number of figures you have? The resulting number is influenced by the change or not? Is the change of the number influenced by what identity you use for counting?
(4) We consider a problem of counting the number of guests a restaurant served in a month. In the problem, there is no need to identify who are the guests. Rather, it is sufficient to count the number of guests role holders in the month independently of who came when. When we interpret the calculated number from the identity of guest role, the number coincides with the number of instances of guest roles played by persons within a month. What identity of guest roles do we use in such a case? When you, as an owner of the restaurant, want to serve more nicely to frequent guests than others, you need to count number of guests in the month paying attention who played guest role to count how many time particular person came to your restaurant. What identity do you use in such a case?
(5) How about the number of parliament members? The number of Japanese lower house is 480. When a member resigned, then a vacancy appears. It is interpreted that an *unplayed* parliament member role appears. What identity does the unplayed role individual has? Is it the 138th position of the member role, or the 41st roles? Of course, not. There is no difference between all the 480 unplayed roles. But, we should be able to count how many unplayed role individuals exist in the lower house.
(6) In a school, a Math teacher resigns, and then an unplayed teacher role appears in the school. What happens if the same person comes back to the school and starts to

[1] By "this", we do not mean the referent but mean the one the person is manipulating.

play a Math teacher role after a year. Does the person play the same teacher role individual or another teacher role individual?
(7) We assume John, an associate professor of Osaka University gets promoted to full professor. If we model this promotion process as that John directly plays the associate professor role and he changes the role to play, he has to stop being a member of Osaka University at the instance of he stops to be an associate professor. To avoid such a difficulty, a new mechanism is necessary for guaranteeing the continuity of his being a member of Osaka University while he changes roles to play.
(8) When the Prime Minister of Japan changes from Aso to Hatoyama, we can regard that they play the same role as the head of the Japanese Government. However, we also can recognize they play different roles (e.g. 92th and 93th Prime Ministers). What kind of role instances do we need to explain this?

It is apparent that the numerical identity is useful for neither of the above examples. At first glance, numerical identity would seem to be useful for the role of parliament members. This is because unless the constitution changes the role of parliament members, all parliament roles seem to be numerically identical. However, those 480 unplayed roles cannot be identical, if so, there would be only one member in the lower house. What is salient in the above examples is that there seem to be multiple kinds of notion of *identity*. When we count who came how many times to a restaurant, we need to identify who is the person. But that identity should be weaker than numerical identity since the same person might gain weight at the next visit. On the other hand, the identity must be stronger than that used for just counting the number of things because counting needs no identification of what the counted objects are. The identity in the example (1) is similar to the one in (2), but is different in that your bike cannot change by replacing all the parts with new ones until becoming a totally different bike from your original one. So, we can investigate how far we can change its parts before it becomes not your bike. A very weak identity is found in (2) in which whatever change is made, "*this bike/orange*" keeps its identity until the very maximum change, since you must be able to fix the bike you are given first and to eat the orange you are given first.

Example (3) has a very special notion of identity. Some researchers say "a thing loses its identity when it changes the class it belongs to due to its change" It is correct in most of the cases where we are interested in each thing in usual tasks. Such a notion of identity is not at the instance level but at the class level. That is, such an identity could be called "class-level identity" since it loses its essential property for belonging to the original class, while it is not certain if it also loses another (instance-level) identity or not. On the other hand, if we are only counting four-sided figures, the change of a figure from a square to a diamond has no influence. This strongly suggests that we need a special identity for counting which is weaker than class-level identity. On the basis of the observation thus far, we investigate the kind of identity and characteristics of them.

3 Classification of Identity

In this section, we summarize kinds of identity which are discussed in general. There are two kinds of identity of an instance; identity which discusses the sameness of the class (*Class identity which we called class-level identity in the above*) it belongs to and identity which discusses the sameness of instances (*Instance identity*).

Instance identity is further divided into the following two kinds:

- ***Synchronic identity***
- ***Diachronic identity***

The main target we consider in this paper includes synchronic identity and diachronic identity of individuals(instances) which are discussed in the following sections.

3.1 Class Identity vs. Instance Identity

Class identity and instance identity are discussed based on essential properties of concepts as follows:

Essential property: A property which determines the identity of its instances. In other words, it loses its identity[2] when the property changes.

For example, we can consider that essential property of bikes, which is an artifact, is "aggregates of the parts such as two wheels, and functions such as to carry a person by human power", and so on. From an engineering viewpoint, we permit arbitrariness to capture an essential property of a concept unlike the philosophy. Class identity and instance identities are defined using *Essential property* as follows:

Class identity of a thing: Identity for discussing the sameness of the class the thing belongs to. It is also defined as belongingness of things to the class which is determined by essential property.

For example, we assume the necessary condition (essential property) of being a bike as having two wheels. When a wheel is removed, the bike loses its class identity and thereby it stops to be an instance of bike. This identity can apply to the example of four-sided figures discussed in section 2.

Instance identity: Identity for discussing the sameness of instances. The conventional numerical identity is a kind of instance identity.

For example, when a saddle and a wheel of Taro's bike (i.e. an instance of bike) have been replaced with new ones, it is discussed using the instance identity whether the bike after the replacement is the same or not for Taro, that is, if Taro is happy to accept it is his bike or not. Although difference between these two types of identity has not attracted much attention to date, it is practically important. In fact, while replacing the engine of a Porsche with one of a Beatle cannot change class identity, it changes its instance identity.

3.2 Synchronic and Diachronic Identities

There is another set of identities such as synchronic identity and diachronic identity.

Synchronic identity: Identity which represents the fact that two individuals are the same thing at a given time.

For example, let us assume a question that "Are they the same one hour from 10:00 to 11:00 and one hour from 11:00 to 12:00?" The answer is "Although they are different

---

[2] This should usually read "class identity".

as a time interval, they are ***the same*** as a quantity of time." The *synchronic identity* means ***the same*** in the answer. The identity corresponds to the sameness in another example such as "the evening star and the morning star are ***the same*** star, that is, Venus, though they have different names".

Diachronic identity: Identity which discusses the sameness of instances at two time points.
For example, the diachronic identity is used to discuss the sameness of individuals in the cases such as "Whether Taro, an instance of person, at present is the same person with the person five minutes ago or not", "Whether an instance of bike and the bike some of whose parts are replaced are the same or not" and so on.

4 Consideration on Instance Identity

In this section, we discuss the sameness of instances and kinds of identity of normal types to prepare for investigation on that of roles in next section. The target of our consideration is instance identity, that is, we focus on the sameness of instances in the scope of the same class identity. We consider kinds of identity according to their strength by which, we mean how strictly the sameness of instances is judged. For example, we assume a case where a bolt of an instance of bike is replaced with another one. In this case, there could be two positions:

1. Strictly speaking, the bike whose bolt is replaced becomes a different bike from the bike before the replacement.
2. The bike has been the same bike before and after the replacement of a bolt because the change is negligible.

While the identity of the former is stronger than one of the latter, it is needed some more discussions about the latter case to judge whether the change is negligible or not when you are renewing your bike. We can also find a weaker identity. In the example of counting the number of guests at a restaurant, identity used for just counting the number of them is weaker than that used for counting who came how many times. The above example suggests that there would be several kinds of identity according to their strength. In this paper, we introduce four kinds of identity according to its strength and features of each identity in the following sections. Three of them are diachronic identity and the last one is synchronic identity. The four kinds of identity can be applicable to all instances.

4.1 Identity for Exactness

- **Identity for exactness** (denoted as ***Iex*** in the following) that corresponds to numerical identity: Identity which means the exact sameness.

For example, we consider an instance of bike. When a bolt of the bike is replaced, ***Iex*** tells us the bike changes because the bike has a different bolt after the replacement. Therefore, the bike whose bolt is replaced is different from the previous bike before the replacement in the meaning of ***Iex*** (Fig.2).

Fig. 2. ***Iex*** applied for bike

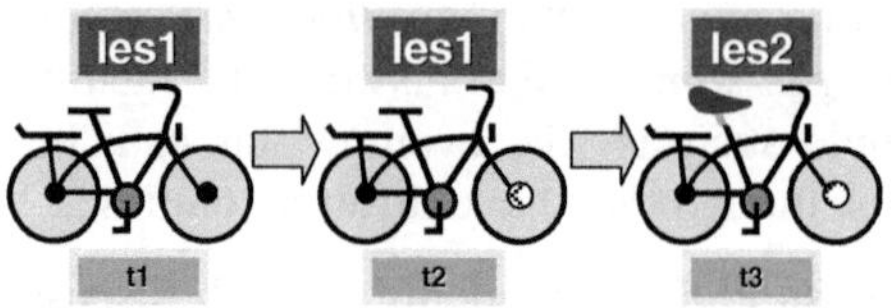

Fig. 3. ***Ies*** applied for bike

The meaning of the exact sameness in the definition of ***Iex*** implies the change of instance as time goes by. For example, because an instance of bike rusts as time goes it changes without replacements of parts in terms of *Iex*. In the actual world, because all individuals can be regarded they undergo change at least in molecular level as time goes. In practice, however, we often recognize that an instance of bike is the same even if a bolt of it is replaced. We can find similar recognition when we suppose instances of person. For example, John at present can be recognized as the same person with him five minutes ago while he is different in terms of ***Iex*** at the two time points. It is necessary to define identity which is weaker than Identity for exactness to deal with such sameness adequately.

4.2 Identity for Essentiality

Identity for essentiality (denoted as ***Ies*** in the following): Identity which is defined by essential property

For example, we assume essential property of John's bike as a comfortable saddle which he has used for ten years. We consider ***Ies1*** which the bike has (Fig.3, t1). When a part of the bike is replaced with a new part, the bike has kept ***Ies1*** unless the essential property (essential to John), it is the saddle in this example, is replaced. Therefore, the bike is treated as the same bike to John even if a bolt is exchanged because the essential property does not change (t2). However, when the saddle is replaced with other one, ***Ies1*** changes to ***Ies2*** because the essential property of the bike to John is changed (t3).

4.3 Identity for Counting

In a task of counting numbers of instances, we do not consider the details of each instance discussed in terms of ***Iex*** and ***Ies*** if following two conditions are satisfied: (1) we can recognize whether instances are the target to count or not, (2) we can distinguish each from others, and (3) we can avoid duplicate counting. Because the existence and the number of target entity are theoretically already fixed when a counting task is started, identity which is used for the counting task is synchronic identity independent of time.

Identity for counting (denoted as ***Ico*** in the followings):

Identity which argues about the number of instances (Synchronic identity) satisfying the above three conditions.

For example, when we count the number of bikes in Fig.4, we can recognize that there are five bikes in terms of $\boldsymbol{Ico_{bike}}$ ***1~5*** which is associated with each bike. If we want to count the number of mountain bike in those five, we should count only the number of ***Ico*** of instance which is belong to mountain bike class. We can also use ***Ico*** for comparing only the number of instances at two different time points because ***Ico*** is identity representing the number of instances. However, ***Ico*** cannot discuss the sameness of instances at two time points because it is synchronic identity.

Fig. 4. ***Ico*** applied for counting bikes

4.4 Identity for Replacement

Now, we assume a case where a counting as a real-world task which needs non-zero time to accomplish. If some parts of the target instance of counting are replaced during the counting task, we would fail to count them correctly. For example, we assume there are three bikes (A~C) and the situation that the two wheels of bike A was replaced during counting them. We also assume the essential property of these bikes as two wheels. Because ***Ico*** cannot discuss whether the bike changes its identity after replacement of parts or not, we try to use ***Ies*** for the counting task here (Fig.5). At first bike A~C have ***Ies1~3,*** respectively. If the two wheels of bike A are removed after we have counted bike A and B, ***Ies1*** disappears because the essential property of bike A disappears during (t1, t2). And when new two wheels are installed to bike A, bike A has new ***Ies*** (e.g. ***Ies4***) because new essential property of bike A is generated at t3. Then, we will count bike which have ***Ies3*** and ***Ies4***, bike C and bike A whose wheels are replaced, because we have not counted instances which have these identities yet. As a result, the number of bikes is four while actually there are only three bikes. This example shows that parts replacement of the instance can cause that we might fail to count the number of instances correctly in practice.

When we assume the parts replacement in the above example, we can consider bike A at t2 as "a bike during parts replacement". This consideration suggest we need another identity which does not change during parts replacement. We now introduce the fourth identity for replacement to solve such a problem.

Identity for replacement (denoted as ***Ire*** in the following):

Identity which an instance of the whole continues to be itself without becoming another thing *while* whose parts are being replaced independently of their kinds and number of the replaced parts.

For example, we consider the same situation as the example discussed in Fig.5. Here, we suppose bike A~C has ***Ire1 - 3*** before the counting task (Fig.6). Even if the two wheels of bike A are removed after we have counted bike A and B, bike A has kept the sameness in terms of ***Ire***. Then, we count only instance having ***Ire3*** after counting A and B, and as a result we can count the number of three bikes successfully. In this way, we can achieve a correct counting using ***Ire*** in the instance model in which the parts replacement can cause inappropriate counting using ***Ies*** .***Ire*** also can handle that bike A continues to be the same instance during the parts replacement.

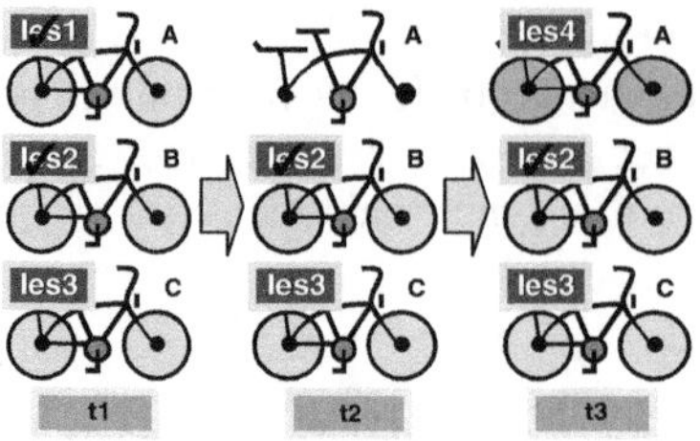

Fig. 5. *Ies* applied for counting bikes

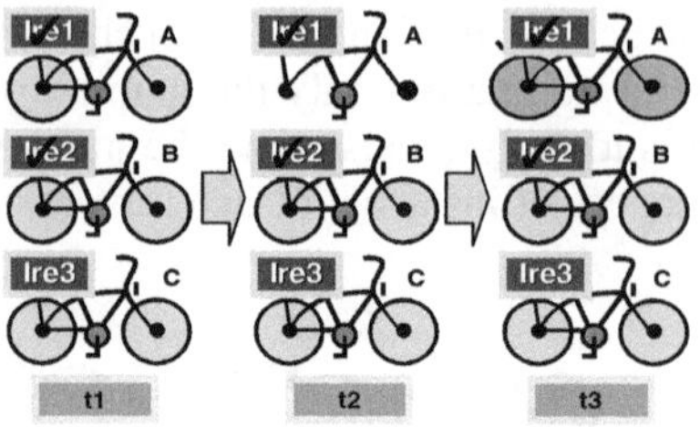

Fig. 6. *Ire* applied for bike (count for bikes)

5 Identity of Role Concept

5.1 Identities of Constituent Role and Post Role

In order to cope with the continuity of membership while changing roles to play as shown in example (7) discussed in section 2, we introduce two new concepts such as ***constituent role*** and ***post role*** by dividing role concept into two parts: one is the player's participation in the context and the other is what kinds of post the player is required to fulfill. We call the former *constituent role* and the latter *post role*. In addition, the post role is played not by the player directly but by constituent role-holder. See details [9]

In the case of promotion, not John but John as a Osaka university constituent role holder is playing the associate professor post role, so when he gets promoted, he can stop to play the associate professor post role while keeping the continuity of his participation in the Osaka University. In the case where he resigned, on the other hand, the constituent role individual disappears. If he returns to Osaka University in a few years later, he will play another Osaka university constituent role different from the one he played a few years before. This is consistent with the reality in handling personnel ID in companies where no personnel ID is reused and for each employment a new ID is assigned to the employee independently of he/she had been an employee of this company or not.

Fig.7 shows a revised model of roles shown in Fig.1 after introduction of ***constituent role*** and ***post role.*** The modeling methodology is the same as that used for modeling Japanese prime minister role must be played by Japanese citizen, that is, the methodology used for modeling compound roles [4]. While we are designing formal representation of this model using OWL based on our previous work [10], it is beyond the scope of this article. Note, however, that the methodology is not the issue. What we claim here is that constituent role must exist in any role model, and any role (post role) must be played by constituent role holder.

5.2 Instances of Constituent Role and Post Role

Post role should correspond to a kind of specification of properties and functions of what a player is expected to play and is almost equivalent to what is claimed by Guarino and Massolo in [2, 3], that is, there is only one post role for each role concept in a context. Therefore, we do not need to discuss ***Ico*** for it, while, similarly to the

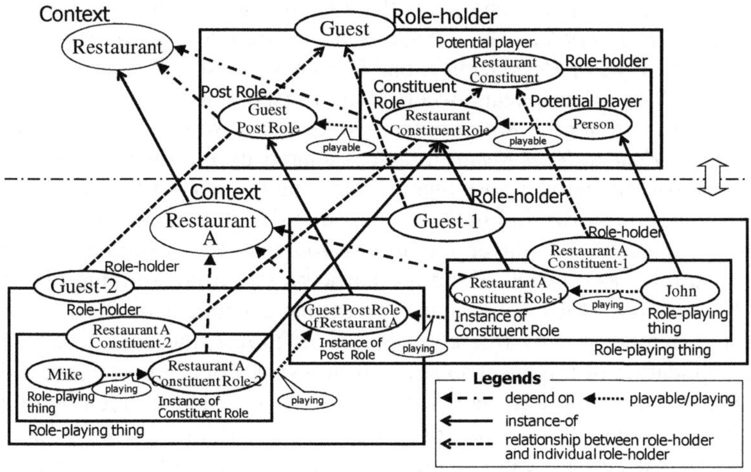

Fig. 7. Revised model of roles

basic type, ***Iex***, ***Ies*** and ***Ire*** should be investigated for post roles to see how it changes diachronically.

Contrary to the fact that basic types necessarily change in any second because of natural degradation of its material, however, post role does not change in such a sense because it is immaterial. Note here that it is true unless the context changes its definition. For example, a school can change the role of teacher when its policy changes, which would suggest that post role does not have ***Iex***.

The creation of constituent role is done synchronized with the event of player's participation in the context. So, when the participation is finished, then it disappears. While the player is participating in the context, it keeps playing the constituent role. Therefore, we can consider the essential property of each constituent role is determined by the event of any player's participation in the context. That is, we can discuss its identity using ***Ies*** based on that essential property. Multiple constituent roles for a context have different identities in terms of ***Ies***.

We can distinguish between instances of constituent role by the time when it is created (in what order it is created) in terms of ***Ies***, while we can use ***Ico*** if there is no need to discuss in what order they are created like in the case of parliament constituent roles. In the case where fixed number of roles are predetermined, like teachers of a school and parliament members, instances of constituent roles are created in advance by that number and exist in unplayed states. When vacancies appear by resignation of members, then same numbers of constituent roles should be created. On the other hand, in the case of no predetermined quota, like guests of a restaurant, they are created at the same time of new players' participation.

Let us see the example shown in Fig.7 in which there exists one *Guest Post Role of Restaurant A* as an instance of *Guest Post Role*. When John participates in the restaurant, an instance of *Restaurant A Constituent Role* as an instance of *Restaurant*

Constituent Role is created[3]. John plays the constituent role and becomes *Restaurant A Constituent-1 Role-holder*. Then, John as *Restaurant A Constituent-1 Role-holder* plays *Guest Post Role of Restaurant A* and becomes *Guest-1 Role-holder. Restaurant A Constituent Role-1* disappears when John finished his dinner, and hence both *Restaurant A Constituent-1 Role-holder* and *Guest-1 Role-holder disappear.* Note here that *Guest Post Role of Restaurant A* is shared by multiple constituent roles to form different role holders because there is only one *Guest Post Role of Restaurant A*.

From the diagram shown in Fig. 7, it seems that five individuals such as *Restaurant A Constituent roles-1*, its player (John), *Restaurant A Constituent-1 Role-holder*, *Guest Post Role of Restaurant A* and are participating in determining the identity of *Guest-1 Role-holder.* However, things are not that complicated. Because identity of role-holder is synthesized by role concept and its player, the goal is realized by the recursive application of this mechanism as follows: identity of constituent role-holder is determined by those of constituent role and its player, and then identity of post role-holder is determined by those of the post role and the constituent role-holder. In terms of identity introduced here can explain the examples shown in (4) through (8) as is discussed in section 5.

6 Discussion

This section discusses some examples to demonstrate what kind of problems we can deal with using these four kinds of identity which we introduced in the previous section. We discuss counting problem in next section, then we explain the examples of identities of roles discussed in section 2.

6.1 Counting Problem

The first is counting problems for the guest management in a restaurant discussed in section 2 and counting the number of river flows, the second is a more complicated problem of the parts replacement of bikes.

When we count only the total number of guests of a restaurant in a month, we can use weak identity, *identity for counting (**Ico**)*, which can discuss only the number of guests. On the other hand, it is necessary to identify the individual guest using stronger identity, *Identity for essentiality* (***Ies***) of person, when we want to know how many times each guest comes. We explain this example in detail using identities of roles later. In the case of river flows for example, we cannot use ***Ies*** for counting the number of the flow of the water in the river because it cannot identify particular water of the river itself. We can count the number of river flow only if we use ***Ico***. These examples show, a kind of identity to apply is different according to whether we want to deal with particular property of the instance or only the number of instances.

Next, we consider a complicated problem of parts replacement of bikes. We here assume the essential property of the bikes as a two wheels, and apply ***Ies(Ies1)*** and ***Ire(Ire1)*** to the instance of bike A at t1 (Fig.8). When we replaced all parts of the bike

[3] When we discuss another role such as chef role at the same context, constituent role is divided to into multiple roles such as restaurant guest constituent role and restaurant staff constituent role.

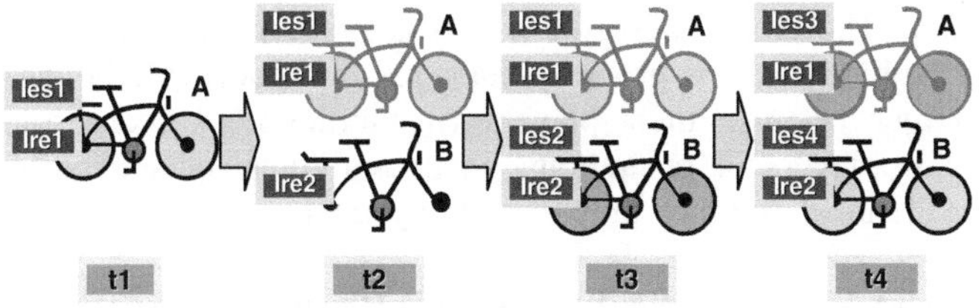

Fig. 8. ***Ies*** and ***Ire*** applied for bike

A except the two wheels of it (t2), ***Ies1*** and ***Ire1*** of this bike are maintained. At the same time (t2), another ***Ire (Ire2)*** is generated when we are going to make another bike B using the parts which we removed from bike A. And another ***Ies (Ies2)*** is generated when new two wheels are installed to bike B (t3). Then, when we exchanged the two wheels of bike A and the ones of bike B each other, ***Ies1*** and ***Ies2*** are changed to ***Ies3*** and ***Ies4*** respectively (t4). In this example, the bikes at t3 and them at t4 are regarded as different bikes because of difference of ***Ies***, while bike A and B have kept same Ire, ***Ire1*** and ***Ire2*** respectively, because ***Ire1*** and ***Ire2*** are maintained regardless of parts replacement. In this way, we can deal with such complicated change of instances in each time points appropriately by applying ***Ies*** and ***Ire*** to the parts replacement.

6.2 Instance Identities of Roles

6.2.1 Guests at a Restaurant (e.g. Example (4) Discussed in Section 2)

When we count the number of guests of a restaurant in a month, we can count the number of instances of restaurant constituent role-holders which play guest post role of the restaurant while it is not necessary to identify particular players (persons) who play the constituent roles. If we need to know in what order each guest comes because an owner of the restaurant wants to give a special souvenir to the 1000th guest, we should use ***Ies*** of the restaurant constituent roles, which can discuss in what order they are created and their role-holders play the guest post role. If we want to count only total number of guests, we can use weak identity, ***Ico***, which can discuss only the number of the restaurant constituent roles.

Next, we consider services for guests. Only one instance of guest post role can exist at a restaurant and all players of guest role holders (restaurant constituent role holders) at the restaurant play the same post role. It implies that all guests are served the same service at the restaurant.

On the other hand, when you want to serve special menu to frequent guests who comes to the restaurant more than 3 times a month, you need to define sub classes of guest post role such as "guest post role for person who comes not more than 3 times a month" and "guest post role for person who comes more than 3 times a month". In such a case, we need to know how many times each person comes and plays the guest post role, using ***Ies*** of person.

Note, when the same person comes to the restaurant twice, the same guest post role is played by him/her while different restaurant constituent roles are created and played each time. Therefore, guest role-holder at first time and that at second time are not identical. In this way, it is properly managed that guest role-holders are different from one another because their players (restaurant constituent role-holders) are different even if players of restaurant constituent roles, persons who come to the restaurant, are identical and they play the same guest post role.

6.2.2 Parliament Members (e.g. Example (5) Discussed in Section 2)

At Japanese lower house, only one instance of parliament member post role exists and it is played by all parliament constituent role-holders. Parliament constituent roles are created by the quota number, that is 480, and exist in unplayed state before particular persons play them. Because there is no need to discuss in what order they are created or what number of parliament constituent role, such as the 138th constituent role, or the 41st constituent role, we can use ***Ico*** for them. When the house has dissolved, all of parliament constituent roles disappear and 480 new parliament constituent roles for next period are created. Then, period of the parliament, which is a non essential attribute of parliament member post role, is renewed, e.g. from 79th to 80th, without losing the identity of parliament member post role in term of ***Ies***. This enables us to properly represent the facts that the current parliament members of Japanese lower house is the 80th and that the member A who has recently elected by the election to fill a vacancy is the XYZ^{th} member in its whole history using ***Ies*** of parliament constituent role.

6.2.3 Math Teacher (e.g. Example (6) Discussed in Section 2)

When a Math teacher resigns in a school, the teachers' Math teacher post role remains same unless the policy of the school changes education to modify the role of teachers, while his/her school constituent role disappears. If the same person returns to the school and starts to play the Math teacher role again in a few years later, he/she plays the same Math teacher post role while he/she plays a school constituent role different from the one he/she played a few years before. Therefore, his/her Math teacher role-holder and the one a few years before are different in terms of *Ies*.

6.2.4 Japanese Prime Minister (e.g. Example (8) Discussed in Section 2)

When Japanese Prime Minister changes, Japanese Prime Minister post role keeps same identity as the head of the Japanese Government while identity of Japanese Prime Minister role-holder changes because its constituent role changes. Even if the same person becomes Japanese Prime Minister continuously two periods, its constituent role also changes because he/she resigns at once and then is reappointed. The period of Japanese Prime Minister is represented as non essential attribute of Japanese Prime Minister post role like parliament members, and its value is renewed synchronized with the change of its player. Unlike parliament members, however, the value of the period corresponds to in what order the instance of Japanese Prime Minister constituent role is created because of its predetermined quota is only one.

7 Related Work

In philosophy, two interpretations of "sameness" are discussed. The one is "qualitatively same" which means attributes of entities are same. The other is "numerically same". The former corresponds to *identity for essentiality*, and the latter corresponds to *exact sameness*. Graeme S. Cumming et.al discusses metamodel to define changing nature of complex systems. They refer to philosophical problem of parts replacement, called Theseus' ship, and discuss a metamodel based on this problem with engineering handling it [11]. The replacement metamodel does not support continuous identity. The identity corresponds to *identity for essentiality*. However, it seems their metamodel does not support *identity for replacement*.

Secondly, we summarize studies of identity in the point of view of engineering. Guarino applied identity to class recognition and proposed ontology construction methodology based on "identity criterion". He established a principle "a class can have only one identity criterion" [2]. Although all classes do not have identity criterions, it is useful for class recognition because we may think that "object" has identity criterion. Identity which used in the methodology is class identity described in 3.1. However, it is difficult to solve the parts replacement problem discussed in Section 4 by "identity criterion". Compared with them, we have classified instance identity in this paper and can handle the problem adequately according to kinds of identity.

In object-oriented modeling some researchers discuss identity which role concept has. [12]. Kristensen defines identity in object-oriented modeling as "An object and its role have the same identity". Furthermore, Alan Colman expanded this definition to "Roles have an organizational identity that is independent from their players even though the role and player constitute a unity within the organization" [13]. We can agree to the definition of Colman, because role concept is defined depending on context and independent of the identity of its player. However, they do not discuss enough about handling of diachronic identity of instances of role concepts such as generation/continuation/extinction of identity of the instance of the role concept depending on the existence of its player.

As discussed in the above, identity has been discussed in the field of philosophy, ontology engineering, and object-oriented modeling. Nevertheless, we do not know someone count up and discuss kinds of identity which is necessary for discussion of identity. That is, they cannot treat properly all of motivated examples discussed in section 2 because they do not support the four kinds of identity we proposed.

In semantic web technology some researchers discuss how identify resources on web. Presutti pointed out five distinct issues concerning identification of resources on the Web and has proposed IRE (identity of resources and entities on the Web) model to solve them. IRE is an ontology built on top of DOLCE+ and its extensions [6]. Halpin discusses identifying non-Web accessible entity and has proposed identity which is defined through relationships given on the Web as links [7]. These approaches are lower-level aspect of identity to represent identity practically on computer systems. They are very informative when we design implementation of our theory of identity.

8 Conclusion and Future Work

In this paper, we have discussed the sameness of instances at two time points and the property of identity on counting instances. As a result, we have identified four kinds of identity and suggested what task to be applied to them through some examples. These considerations provide fundamental theory to discuss identity and contribute theoretically to instance management on computer system based on ontology. For example, we could use the theory as a reference model when we design how a system should treat identify of instances, i.e. to identify whether some instances which have same id in different time point are same thing or not. As future work, we plan to in-depth develop a theoretical framework for management of identity based on the consideration. Furthermore, we plan to implement the framework in Hozo, an ontology building tool developed by us [8, 14].

Acknowledgment

We gratefully acknowledge the helpful discussions with Professor Nicola Guarino.

References

1. Gruber, T.: A translation approach to portable ontologyspecifications. In: Proc. of JKAW 1992, pp. 89–108 (1992)
2. Guarino, N.: Some Ontological Principles for Designing Upper Level Lexical Resources. In: Proceedings of the First International Conference on Language Resources and Evaluation, Granada, Spain, pp. 527–534 (1998)
3. Masolo, C., et al.: Social Roles and their Descriptions. In: Proceedings of the 9th International Conference on the Principles of Knowledge Representation and Reasoning (KR 2004), pp. 267–277 (2004)
4. Mizoguchi, R., et al.: A Model of Roles within an Ontology Development Tool: Hozo. J. of Applied Ontology 2(2), 159–179 (2007)
5. Guizzardi, G.: Agent Roles, Qua Individuals and The Counting Problem. In: Invited Chapter in Software Engineering of Multi-Agent Systems, vol. IV, pp. 143–160 (2006)
6. Presutti, V., Gangemi, A.: Identity of Resources and Entities on the Web. Int'l Journal on Semantic Web & Information Systems 4(2), 49–72 (2008)
7. Halpin, H.: The Principle of Self-Description: Identity Through Linking. In: Proc. of the 1st International Workshop on Identity and Reference on the Semantic Web (IRSW 2008), Tenerife, Spain, June 2 (2008)
8. Kozaki, K., et al.: Hozo: An Environment for Building/Using Ontologies Based on a Fundamental Consideration of "Role" and "Relationship". In: Gómez-Pérez, A., Benjamins, V.R. (eds.) EKAW 2002. LNCS (LNAI), vol. 2473, pp. 213–218. Springer, Heidelberg (2002)
9. Kozaki, K., Endo, S., Mizoguchi, R.: Instance Management Problems in the Role Model of Hozo. In: Ho, T.-B., Zhou, Z.-H. (eds.) PRICAI 2008. LNCS (LNAI), vol. 5351, pp. 614–625. Springer, Heidelberg (2008)
10. Kozaki, K., et al.: Role Representation Model Using OWL and SWRL. In: Proc. of 2nd Workshop on Roles and Relationships in Object Oriented Programming, Multiagent Systems, and Ontologies, Berlin, July 30-31 (2007)
11. Cumming, G.S., Collier, J.: Change and identity in complex systems. Ecology and Society 10(1), 29 (2005), http://www.ecolotyandsociety.org/vol10/iss1/art29/
12. Kristensen, B.B., et al.: Roles: conceptual abstraction theory and practical and practical language issues. Theory and Practice of Object Systems 2(3), 143–160 (1996)
13. Colman, A., Han, J.: Roles, players and adaptable organizations. Applied Ontology 2(2), 105–126 (2007)
14. Hozo:Ontology Editor, http://www.hozo.jp

Involving Business Users in Formal Modeling Using Natural Language Pattern Sentences

Jeroen van Grondelle, Ronald Heller, Emiel van Haandel, and Tim Verburg

Be Informed, De Linie 620, 7325 DZ Apeldoorn, The Netherlands
{j.vangrondelle,r.heller,e.vanhaandel,t.verburg}@beinformed.nl
http://www.beinformed.nl/

Abstract. With knowledge representation based technologies reaching the enterprise, involving business users in modeling is more important than ever. When primary processes and business decisions are driven by models, business knowledge needs to be captured and only business users can establish whether the models created are correct.

A natural language based representation of models can help business users get involved in the modeling process. We have used a representation based on natural language pattern sentences to improve business user participation in our business modeling projects. Based on the lessons learned, user interfaces have been developed that use this representation for both communicating and editing formal models.

Keywords: Natural language, knowledge authoring, knowledge acquisition, knowledge representation, user interfaces.

1 Introduction

The adoption of model driven technologies such as Enterprise Decision Management and Business Process Management is growing. As a result, involving business users in modeling is more important than ever. Their ability to capture business knowledge in models correctly is a key factor in the adoption of these technologies. They enable businesses to run processes based on models alone, eliminating the need for expensive and time consuming systems development to implement changes. The feasibility and success of implementations using these technologies, depend heavily on the level of control that business users have in the modeling process.

In practice, we see business users involved in different roles. The ultimate goal is often to enable business users to create and maintain the models themselves. This is of course the most efficient way to keep regularly changing knowledge models up to date, and it reduces the number of transfers of information and intentions before formally capturing knowledge.

Traditionally however, business users have transferred their knowledge or requirements informally to information professionals, such as information analysts and systems designers. Beyond that point, the role of business users is often

P. Cimiano and H.S. Pinto (Eds.): EKAW 2010, LNAI 6317, pp. 31–43, 2010.

limited to reviewing the models and specifications that these information professionals produce. In environments based on modeling, this means that business users are required to review more formal representations than before. Although the involvement level might seem limited, it can prove challenging in practice. In this paper we describe how to equip business users to better participate in this process.

Modeling policy candidates and reviewing the resulting models can improve the policy making process considerably, by integrating formal modeling techniques as early as the decision stages. Allowing for consistency checking and 'what if' analyses, the model driven environment leads to better policies.

The main challenge in involving business users in knowledge modeling is the fact that most business users are not trained in formal knowledge representation techniques. A formal, concise, visual representation can be quite intimidating to the uninitiated. As a result, these users experience problems relating these representations to their working knowledge of the domain concerned. When presented with a model representation of knowledge they provided themselves, they often do not understand how their knowledge is represented in the model. This means they will not be able to verify the accuracy of the model directly.

Be Informed develops a software suite that is used by complex, knowledge intensive organizations to capture their business knowledge and run model driven services based on these knowledge models. This paper shows how a model visualization based on natural language has helped Be Informed users to actively participate in modeling business knowledge. User interfaces were developed that can help business users to review models created by others and develop these models themselves. Furthermore, the natural language based visualization is used to communicate the formal models further, to users that are not participating in modeling, but whose work is influenced by the resulting models.

2 Related Work

Using natural language to represent formal models is an active field of research. The representation presented in this paper is in many respects part of the field of Controlled Natural Languages. Using controlled languages to represent ontologies has been done before in Attempto Controlled Language by Kaljurand and Fuchs [1] and in CLOnE by Funk et al. [2]. The textual syntax definition proposed in this paper is quite similar to the definition used in CLOnE.

Furthermore, work has been done to enable business users to actively express their knowledge based on these controlled natural languages. As controlled languages are designed to avoid ambiguity and complexity, NLP has been used to parse sentences into modeling constructs or even roundtrip between textual representation and formal ontology specification, for instance by Davis et al. [3]. Our approach towards editing a model, based on a natural language visualization is different: The formal model remains the single source at all times. The textual representation is just used as a view on the formal model and editing operations by the user in the view are translated into updates to that underlying formal model. Of course, the view needs (partial) updating as a consequence, following the Model-View-Controller paradigm.

The fact that no NLP or parsing needs to be performed on the textual representation provides a lot of freedom in choosing the pattern sentences. This enables us to benefit from areas such as requirement engineering and business rules. Methods such as RuleSpeak [4] and the OMG standard SBVR [5] have rationalized the use of natural language by business users by introducing syntactic guidelines and best practices. These guidelines have proven to be useful in choosing our pattern sentences.

3 Representing Formal Models Using Pattern Sentences

3.1 Separating Syntax from Semantics

Knowledge representation in Be Informed is based on concept graphs, containing concepts, relations between concepts and properties of both concepts and relations. To add semantics, the concepts, relations and properties are typed, using types from a meta model associated with the graph.

For the purpose of presenting and editing these models, they are visualized to users using a syntax that matches the semantic information in the meta model. These syntaxes can be both graphical and textual. For instance, the default visualization in Be Informed is a graphical visualization, based on a visual syntax that maps iconography, line styles and colors to meta model types.

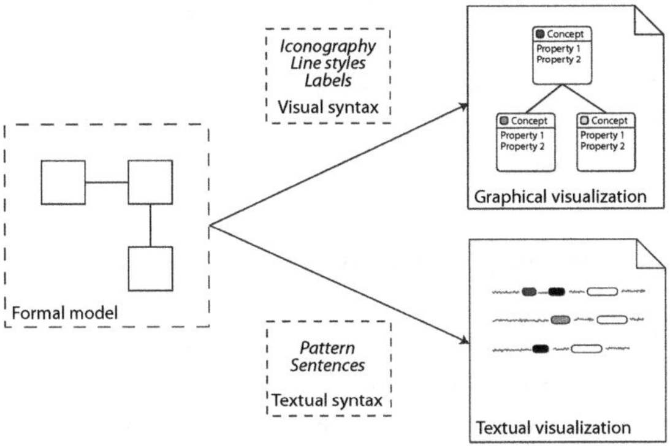

Fig. 1. Visualizing models using both visual and textual syntaxes

The visualization proposed in this paper represents the graph using pattern sentences based on natural language. Visualization is defined by a grammar of pattern sentences, which consists of natural language text with placeholders that map to the graphs concepts and properties by their types and relations. These sentences are hand crafted to communicate the semantics of the graph constructs they represent.

3.2 Visualizing Graphs Using Pattern Sentences

On visualizing a graph, the structural mapping constraints that follow from the pattern sentences are applied to the graphs concepts and relations. Then, instances of the pattern sentences are shown for each matching combination of concepts and relations.

Pattern sentences consist of different kinds of parts. They have their own properties that are used as constraints when mapping the pattern sentences to a graph.

1. Static text fragments contain the wording of the sentences;
2. Subject placeholders map to concepts that act as the subject of a sentence and include its label in the text;
   (a) The subject placeholder maps to subjects of specified type;
3. Object placeholders map to the objects of the sentences' subjects relations and include their label in the text;
   (a) The object placeholder maps to objects of specified type;
   (b) The object placeholder maps to objects of relations with the subject of specified type;
   (c) The object placeholder concats the objects labels according to the number of objects and with configurable infixes;
4. Property placeholders map to the subjects properties and include their value in the text;
   (a) The property placeholder maps to properties of specified type.

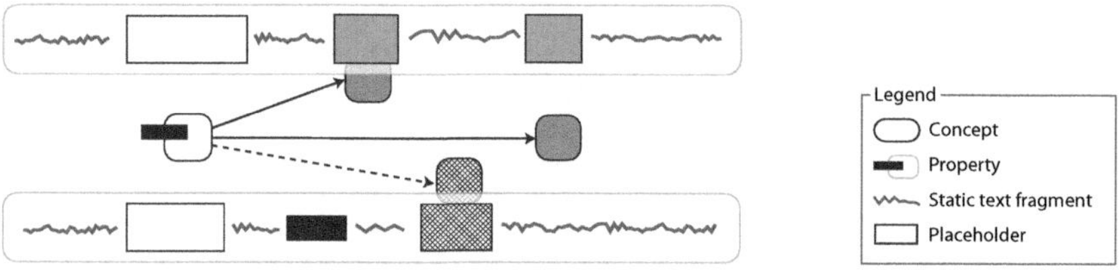

Fig. 2. Mapping pattern sentences to a concept graph

Fragments and placeholders are grouped into sentence parts, in order to make certain parts of the sentence optional. If the graph construct they map to does not exist, the other parts of the sentence might still apply and form a valid textual representation.

Pattern sentences have to deal with cardinality in the (meta)model. In a trivial case, where sentences encode for one relation instance only, having more than one relation is represented in language by introducing a sentence for each relation. Pattern sentences can also represent multiplicity within a sentence, so that one sentence encodes a number of relations and concepts. A grammar can contain one sentence to encode for more multiple relations of the same type. For any subject, all these relations are then represented in a single sentence with the objects of the relations enumerated inside. A sentence can also encode for relations of more than one type. In that case, sentence parts encode for the different relation types, and they are concatenated into a single sentence.

3.3 Influencing the Sentence Generation

Although the mechanism presented in the last section does not require additional information to generate sentences based on a model, the resulting sentences can be influenced at a number of levels.

A grammar may contain alternative sentences that map to the same graph fragments. These may be equivalent sentences, mapping to exactly the same graph constructs. Alternatively, a grammar contains both sentences that map to more general and more specific constructs. The sentences have a precedence within the grammar, indicating which sentence to use first if possible. Alternatively, a user could be given a choice if more than one sentence applies.

The same holds for the order of the sentences in the document. This order depends on the order of both sentences in the grammar and concepts in the graph. Typically, a user could be allowed to choose a more appropriate order.

Variants can also be chosen at the grammar level. As grammar and meta model are strictly decoupled, alternative grammars can be developed for a single meta model. As a result, a single model can be represented into different textual representations, as displayed in Figure 3. This can be used to target different user groups for instance. A grammar containing more formal, precise language could be used for legally trained employees, where a more informal grammar is suitable for wider audiences.

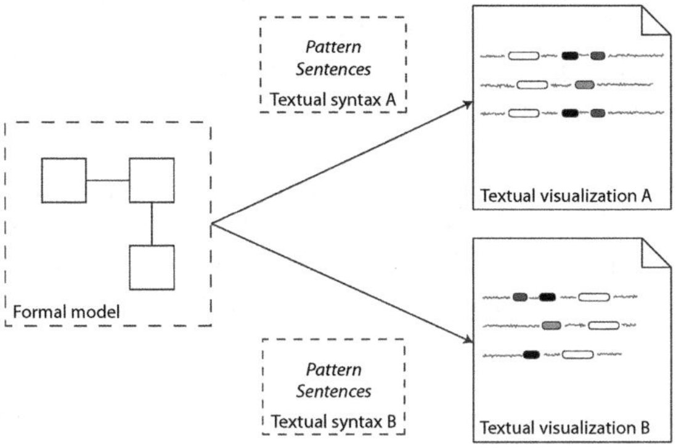

Fig. 3. Mapping a model to two different textual representations

The same mechanism could be used to represent a single model into different languages. Apart from translating the pattern sentences in the grammar, the model will have to be available in multiple languages. This requires manually specifying multi-lingual labels or using automated translation, such as is being developed in the EU's Monnet project[1].

[1] http://www.monnet-project.eu/

3.4 An Example: A Telecom Product Model

In this section we present an example based on the product model of a telecom provider.

The meta model in Figure 4 is based on typical taxonomical structures for modeling products and associated discounts. The requirement relations connect the discounts with the products, or combinations of products, they apply to. This basic meta model enables the modeling of both the provider's product portfolio structure and the requirements its client must meet to apply for specific target group discounts.

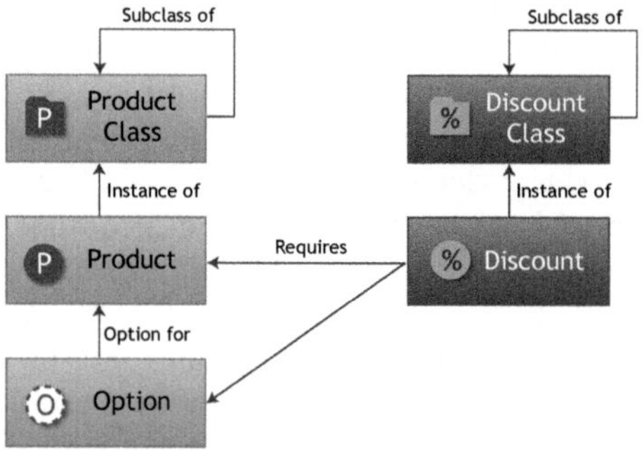

Fig. 4. Meta model for the Telecom example

An example of a product and discount model in the traditional graphical notation is given in Figure 5. It describes the telephone, television and internet products the provider has and how customers apply for specific discounts. For example, a consumer ordering all three products (Internet, Telephone and TV) applies for a triple play discount.

To visualize the product model in natural language, we need to specify a grammar first; such a grammar should mirror the information in the meta model shown in Figure 4. The example grammar introduces product classes and individual products in short, structural sentences. The following two patterns are possible parts of this grammar:

1. "THERE IS A CLASS OF PRODUCTS NAMED *PC*." $\leftrightarrow \{ProductClass\}$.
2. "THE PRODUCT *P* IS A *PC* PRODUCT."
   $\leftrightarrow \{Product, instanceof, ProductClass\}$.

The first sentence pattern can be used to declare a class of products, while the second is meant to declare a specific product and to which class it belongs. The following two sentences are examples of such a specific declaration:

I THERE IS A CLASS OF PRODUCTS NAMED **Internet**.

II THE PRODUCT **Fast ADSL** IS AN **Internet** PRODUCT.

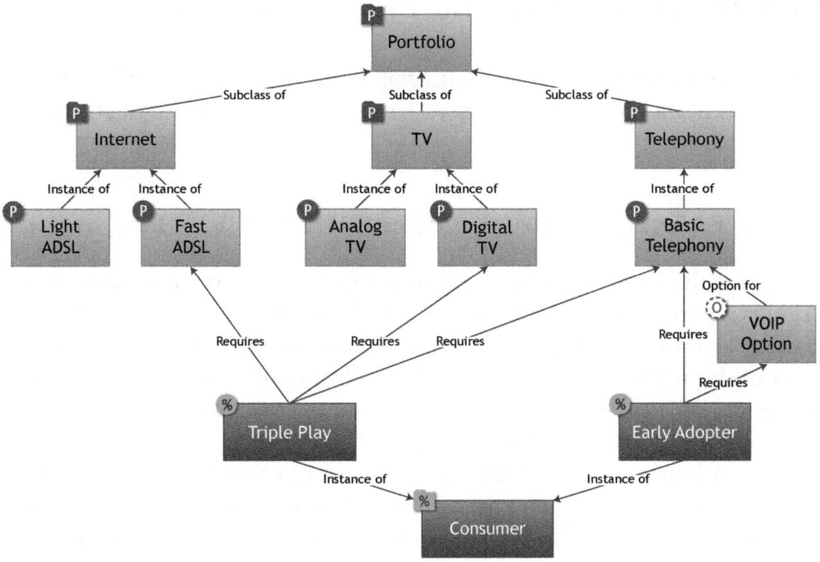

Fig. 5. Product model for the Telecom example

Introducing discounts requires a more complex structure of several sentence parts that can be linked together.

3. a) "THE DISCOUNT D IS A DC DISCOUNT," $\leftrightarrow \{Discount, instanceof, DiscountClass\}$
   b) "AND CUSTOMERS APPLY FOR IT BY ORDERING THE PRODUCT P," $\leftrightarrow \{Discount, requires, Product\}$
   c) "WITH OPTIONS O." $\leftrightarrow \{Discount, requires, Option\}$

The first part introduces a discount and encodes for its type relation, as it is mandatory. The second part encodes for the products required to apply for the discount. The third part encodes for the options that are required to apply for the discount, if any.

Based on the product model from Figure 5, the following textual representation of the two types of discounts can be constructed:

III THE DISCOUNT **Triple Play** IS A **Consumer** DISCOUNT, AND CUSTOMERS APPLY FOR IT BY ORDERING ALL OF THE PRODUCTS **Fast ADSL**, **Digital TV** AND **Basic Telephony**.

IV THE DISCOUNT **Early Adopter** IS A **Consumer** DISCOUNT, AND CUSTOMERS APPLY FOR IT BY ORDERING THE PRODUCT **Basic Telephony**, WITH OPTION **VOIP**.

4 User Interfaces Based on Pattern Sentences

Based on the experiences with the representation described, user interfaces were developed to enable Be Informed users to use the natural language representations in their work.

4.1 Using Language Representation in Knowledge Base Access

Often, the results of knowledge representation efforts are published online to assist reviewing and querying of the models. Typically, such an interface is based on directory-style navigation and search. A concept, or topic, is represented by a page, containing all its properties and resources and navigation links to other related topics. The types of both concepts and relations are visualized through by instance icons or by grouping items in categories.

The natural language representation presented in Section 3 can be integrated into such an interface. On each page, a textual representation of its concept and all its relations is shown. The textual representation can offer hyperlinks for the concepts in the sentences, linking to their respective knowledge base pages.

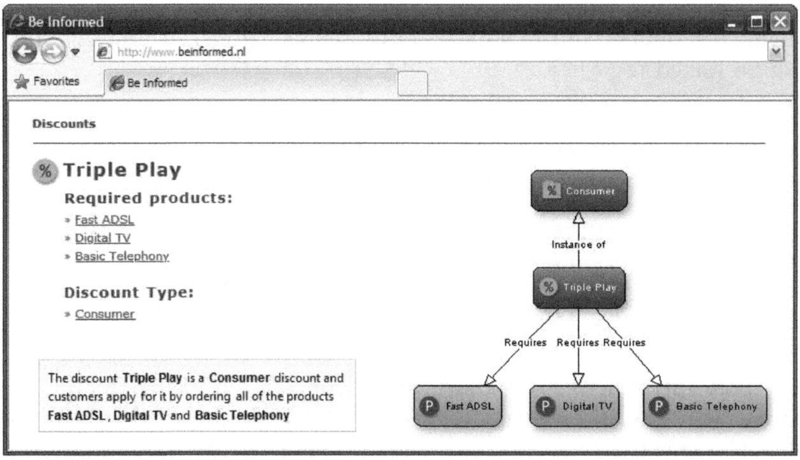

Fig. 6. Multi syntax knowledge base: Navigation, natural language and visual

The pattern sentence representation does not need to be a replacement of conventional knowledge base interface elements. As shown in Section 3.1, multiple representations can be presented in parallel. Even the visual graph representation can be integrated into a knowledge base, which can be useful if the knowledge base is used for analysts as well as end users. Typically, the appropriate representation is selected based on user profile or roles. However, adding representations in parallel allows user to focus on the representation of their personal choice, while possibly getting familiar with the other representations.

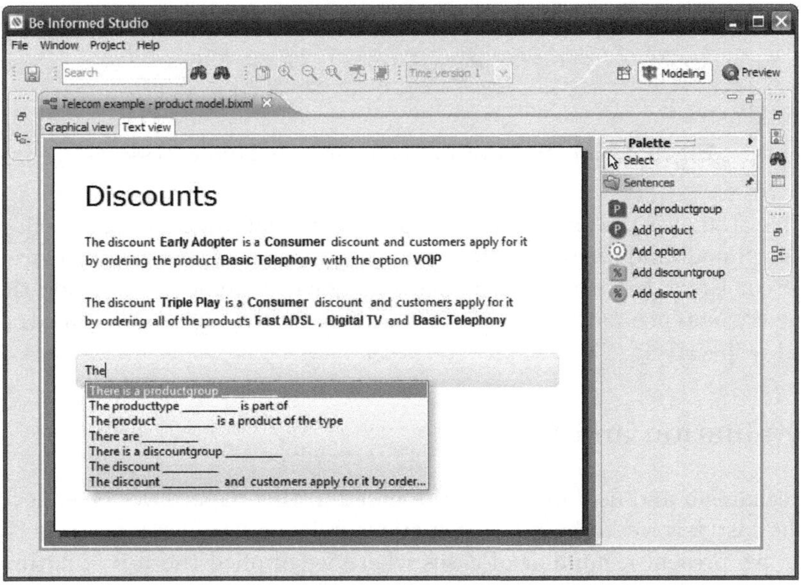

Fig. 7. Task centric and word processor style editing

4.2 Editing Models by Manipulating Sentences

We have also developed an editor for knowledge models based on the pattern sentences representation. It uses the interaction metaphor of a text document with sentences, however without the cursor as the main means of manipulating the document. Instead, the user can edit the model by adding and removing pattern sentences and filling in the placeholders of these pattern sentences.

The biggest interaction challenge in such an interface is supporting users in selecting the pattern sentences that match the knowledge they want to express. At modeling time, users have little freedom in creating their own sentences, so only a carefully designed grammar that is offered to the user in a very contextual way leads to a good user experience.

In the current editor, available pattern sentences are offered to the user in two ways. The pattern sentences are offered in a task centric way in a Tool Palette. Users can drag available pattern sentences from the palette onto the document, where they appear with variable parts that need to be completed. The Tool Palette presents the pattern sentences by a task-oriented name, that summarizes the effect or goal of the particular sentence.

They are also offered in a more word processor style: By typing at the end of the document, pattern sentences matching the typed text are presented in a popup menu. Selecting a pattern sentence from the menu inserts it into the document. Creating references to other concepts is also performed by combo boxes that show a relevant subset of the available concepts based on typed text and placeholder constraints.

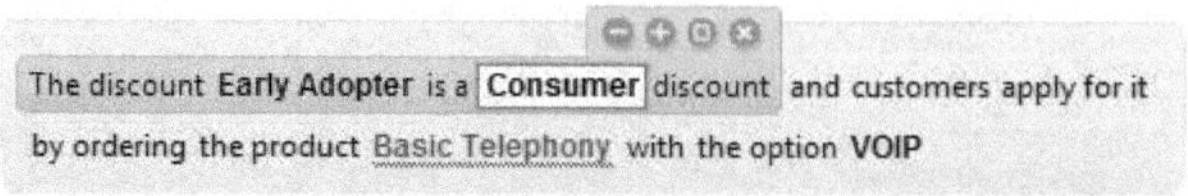

Fig. 8. Contextual controls and embedded error messages

To offer the user the experience of a text document, all controls are embedded in the document and are only visible when a specific sentence part or placeholder is selected. Error feedback is provided by showing annotations inside the text document. Sentence parts containing warnings or errors are underlined, orange and red respectively.

5 Evaluation and Cases

The mechanism and user interfaces presented in this paper have been developed over the last few years based on experiences in actual client projects. In this section, we present a number of cases where we applied the use of natural language in formal modeling. We describe observations and lessons learned from these projects. They have either guided the development of this mechanism or are the basis for future work.

5.1 Reviews Based on Language Representation

Centraal Beheer Achmea, a large Dutch insurer, has developed a self service portal for transport insurance, that enables logistic firms to insure their shipments. Applications are automatically accepted or rejected and context specific advice about possible risks and relevant regulatory requirements is presented, both based on knowledge models.

One of the early iterations of this mechanism has been used to help the underwriters to review and validate the models that were created by analysts based on their input.

The models in this project included context taxonomies to classify a shipments type of goods, conveyance and information about destinations etc. A central Risk taxonomy was associated to these context taxonomies to express how shipments individuals belonged to specific risk classes.

- We find that business users often have trouble evaluating formal models using visual diagrams. Our clients underwriters, who were owners of the knowledge being captured, actively participated in the workshops where we elicited the knowledge, but they had trouble reviewing the result. We got the impression that, although a lack of experience with formal methods contributed to this problem, there was a cultural dimension to it: graphical diagrams were regarded as just too technical.
- We found that graphical visualization of tree structured graphs can be improved by using a hierarchical layout using indenting. The associative parts

of models with many to many relations are the hardest part for business users.
- We experienced that natural language representation improves greatly the business users understanding of the models. A first version of the algorithm described above was developed at that time and applied to the risk models. Although the sentences produced were rough and still very triple oriented, the business users immediately spotted language constructs that appeared odd to them. It turned out that the recall rate of modeling errors improved drastically and investigating sentences they marked was a very good reviewing strategy.

5.2 Improving the Quality of Legislation through Early Modeling

The Dutch Immigration Office has recently implemented their primary process based on a knowledge driven architecture, as described in [6]. Based on their experiences in retro actively converting existing policy into formal, executable models, they are now assessing whether formal modeling as early as in the policy making process can help to keep the policy consistent and executable.

This project of the Dutch Immigration Office is called the Modern Migration Policy, meaning a complete redesign of migration legislation where the validation of implementation possibility and separation of law, policy and application is done up front.

The mechanism proposed in this paper is being used to validate candidate policy decisions for consistency even before they are finalized into active policy. In workshops with business representatives, legal advisors and knowledge analysts, the policy is defined according to a strict set of textual rules, which is a mixture of company vocabulary and business rules oriented syntax.

These sentence rules are also implemented in our software and using the described mechanism we are able to capture the sentences in the same form as the business users define them. This way, we can validate and demonstrate in realtime whether or not the defined policy rule is indeed executable using a knowledge based decision system.

Although it is too early to conclude anything from these workshops, as it is work in progress, there are some observations that are interesting enough to share.

- We find that representing knowledge in structured language helps the business users recognize and understand the knowledge they are responsible for. The graphical representation proved to be unsuitable for most policy makers, who seem to be very text oriented.
- We observe that business users have a hard time recognizing the captured knowledge in textual representation if it is not represented in the exact same manner as they have originally stated the rule. For example, a set of criteria represented as a comma separated list was not recognizable to users who originally stated the rule as a bullet list.
- Another lesson learned is the enthousiasm about the possibility to execute the newly defined policy against test cases almost realtime. As soon as the

knowledge is captured in the knowledge system, one is able to execute services like classification and decision services. This provides direct feedback and verification of the defined rules. Business users can see that their own rules are being used. They see the effects they have in real life cases. All this, and as early as in the policy creation phase, should make for better law and legislation, a conviction shared by all project members involved.

5.3 Dissemination of Finished Models

A risk when implementing a knowledge modeling based application, is that it is regarded as a black box afterwards. In that case, the knowledge is hidden for the rest of the organization and is only used for the decision making process. The application described in Section 5.2 heavily depends on the models it is based on and the Dutch Immigration Office is aware that sharing the models is important.

A company wide knowledge infrastructure requires that the knowledge models are available to the whole organization, or at least a large part. It would seem logical to use this knowledge as a basis for multiple company processes. We believe that the textual representation of this knowledge helps in the company wide adoption, especially if this knowledge proves to be the fundamental part in the primary process.

In the previous sections we used the textual representation as a means to review and validate captured knowledge by business users. Other examples of processes where the knowledge is applied and where the mechanism described in this paper can deliver support, are:

- The call center employee needs to understand the rules applied. The textual representation can act as another instrument for quick overview and understanding. The mechanism presented in this paper has support for multiple configurations, meaning that the sentence patterns can be custom designed for identified user groups.
- In the operational process, a decision maker is supported in this activity with knowledge models that specify which rules apply and how to apply them. The decision maker needs to be able to understand the rules when questions arise. The textual representation is an instrument that will aid the decision maker in this.
- External parties, like auditors, reviewers or other experts in the field, meaning the knowledge domain, will be able to view the knowledge without the need for a thorough understanding of for example formal models and ontologies. The textual representation will enable them to participate at any moment in the knowledge lifecycle.

6 Discussion and Future Work

In this paper we have presented a mechanism for representing formal concept graphs as natural language, using natural language pattern sentences.

This mechanism is not using natural language processing for interpreting the sentences to update the models as many related technologies do. Natural language generation is used to create sentences from a graph, but updates to these sentences are performed directly on the underlying graph. This gives a large degree of freedom in choosing pattern sentences. Sentences that might seem too informal or complex from a parsing perspective, are feasible in our approach and may be very understandable to business users.

Another important choice is the fact that the textual syntax, like the meta model and visual syntax, is chosen before the actual modeling. In other words: a language has to be chosen before one can start to speak. This relieves the modeler of choosing the appropriate words in every sentence, as he would not choose iconography for individual diagrams in visual notation. As the number of things that can be said are limited by the meta model, the number of ways to say it is now limited by the available pattern sentences.

We have demonstrated a number of user interfaces based on this representation that can be used for creating, maintaining en reviewing formal models. Its use in practical cases shows that the use of pattern sentences has helped business users to actively participate in various phases of knowledge representation based projects.

However, a thorough quantitative analysis of business users performance based on this representation as opposed to the more common, graphical notation is needed. Especially, the ability of business users to actually create models using this representation and the editor itself have to be evaluated in more detail.

References

1. Kaljurand, K., Fuchs, N.E.: Verbalizing OWL in Attempto Controlled English. In: Proceedings of Third International Workshop on OWL: Experiences and Directions, Innsbruck, Austria, June 6-7 (2007)
2. Funk, V., Tablan, K., Bontcheva, H., Cunningham, B., Davis, S.: CLOnE: Controlled Language for Ontology Editing. In: Aberer, K., Choi, K.-S., Noy, N., Allemang, D., Lee, K.-I., Nixon, L.J.B., Golbeck, J., Mika, P., Maynard, D., Mizoguchi, R., Schreiber, G., Cudré-Mauroux, P. (eds.) ASWC 2007 and ISWC 2007. LNCS, vol. 4825, pp. 142–155. Springer, Heidelberg (2007)
3. Davis, B., Iqbal, A.A., Funk, A., Tablan, V., Bontcheva, K., Cunningham, H., Handschuh, S.: RoundTrip Ontology Authoring. In: Sheth, A.P., Staab, S., Dean, M., Paolucci, M., Maynard, D., Finin, T., Thirunarayan, K. (eds.) ISWC 2008. LNCS, vol. 5318, pp. 50–65. Springer, Heidelberg (2008)
4. Ross, R.G.: RuleSpeak Sentence Forms: Specifying Natural-Language Business Rules in English. Business Rules Journal 10(4) (April 2009)
5. Semantics of Business Vocabulary and Business Rules (SBVR), Version 1.0, `http://www.omg.org/spec/SBVR/1.0/PDF/`
6. Heller, R., van Teeseling, F., Gülpers, M.: A Knowledge Infrastructure for the Dutch Immigration office. In: 7th Extended Semantic Web Conference, ESWC 2010 Heraklion, Greece, May 30-June 3 (2010)

Knowledge Acquisition from Sources of Law in Public Administration

Alexander Boer and Tom van Engers

Leibniz Center for Law, University of Amsterdam, The Netherlands
{A.W.F.Boer,T.M.vanEngers}@uva.nl

Abstract. Knowledge acquisition from text, and sources of law in particular, is a well established technique. Text is even – certainly in the context of the Semantic Web – increasingly conceived of as a raw knowledge resource that can be mined for knowledge routinely and automatically.

As experience by large public administrations shows, the maintenance of traceability to the original sources of law from context-dependent knowledge representation resources of various kinds is hardly a solved problem, though. The use of IT in general has increased the organization's capacity for change in many dimensions, but because of the increasing use of IT the organization has to manage an increasing number of executable pseudo-specifications that contain knowledge of the law but fail to present a coherent picture of it.

In this paper we present some of the guiding principles and ontological distinctions we use in the *Agile project* to accurately document the use of the law as a knowledge resource in administrative organizations.

1 Introduction

Knowledge acquisition from text, and from sources of law in particular, is a well established knowledge engineering technique. In the field of AI & Law the meaning of units of discourse in sources of law (e.g. sentences) from a knowledge representation point of view is a constant subject of study. It is well understood that *isomorphism* between units of discourse in the sources of law and knowledge representation units is important for both the ability to maintain the knowledge representation in the face of changes to the sources of law, and the ability to provide credible justifications of legal decisions [1,2].

In the field of law there is also great awareness of the ways in which the meaning of units of discourse of a source of law depends on the social and informational context of its production. Legislative drafters consider context dependence undesirable and try to minimize it, resulting in the Byzantine language often associated with law.

For administrative organizations the challenge is to associate sources of law, whose meaning depends on the context of their production, to concrete activities. In this process, the organizations experience that knowledge representation for specific decision support systems introduces new forms of dependence on the context of use. It is therefore not possible to use one executable specification of the sources of law as a general purpose account of how the organization implements the law.

P. Cimiano and H.S. Pinto (Eds.): EKAW 2010, LNAI 6317, pp. 44–58, 2010.

In the knowledge acquisition community this fact has been known for some time [3]. The same unit of discourse in the sources of law can play different roles in different tasks at the same time, and ends up with subtly different operational meanings in each. The meaning of the sources of law is interpreted in the context of a problem definition, of an informational, social, epistemic, and circumstantial context, and usually forced into a logic of limited expressiveness dictated by commitments to IT infrastructure.

While the task has succesfully functioned as a conceptual coatrack for the contextual aspect of knowledge in knowledge engineering (cf e.g. [4]), the problem setting adddressed in this paper involves task definitions that themselves may change considerably as the sources of law change.

For organizations that mainly execute official public functions, it is not very helpful to say that knowledge of the sources of law is task-dependent. In public administration the task itself often does not exist independent from the law: without the legal effects of its performance, there is no reason for its performance. Bringing about legal effects is essential to the problem definition. If the problem definition lacks the required inertia, it fails as a knowledge management device.

At the same time, organizations obviously never implement the law in a green field situation. They have to take into account the efficient reuse of resources and data, the knowledge and skills of their workforce, and the expectations and needs of their clients and network partners. Increasingly, this includes reuse and maintenance of decision support systems and knowledge bases.

A typical recurrent challenge is for instance to establish a new legal interpretation for existing data about clients in databases when the activities that produced and used them, and the concepts that described them, are redefined in the relevant sources of law. Another recurrent challenge is the problem of dealing with long term commitments: a tax administration or immigration authority deal with open cases that are handled with deprecated rules and procedures for many years after the sources of law changed.

An increasingly complicating factor in this is the increasing dependence of public service provision on negotiated network arrangements between – otherwise uncoordinated – organizations, and the increasing formalization of communication through ICT [5].

The adoption of public administration-wide shared ontologies and open standards is, at least now, for instance more often perceived as an extra burden than as a solution. The potential for reuse of existing knowledge structures in for instance communication protocols is critically evaluated, since reuse outside of the original context, even if superficially possible, may lead to legal trouble.

The Agile project [6], presented in section 2, aims to provide practical concepts for the legal provenance issue involved in evaluating and legally justifying the structures and knowledge resources of the organization. In this section we position the proposed knowledge representation as a knowledge resource produced and used in a layered problem solving cycle connecting case handling processes on the work floor to the legislative process.

Our approach to knowledge representation, explained in section 3, is based in a distinction between three different universes of discourse – an application of ontological stratification that is also found in positivist legal theory – that often leads to confusion. On each of the layers we find agents, knowledge, capabilites, tasks, and actions.

The concepts of institution and constitutiveness, representation, and applicability (sections 3.1 and 3.2) play a central role in structuring the domain. Applicability is based on provenance information about the sources of law from the MetaLex standard, introduced in section 4 about sources of law. Because the nature of sources of law is in our view most interesting to this community, the small example of section 5.1 is about the production of sources of law.

In the concluding section (section 5) we also address the role of tasks and agent roles, and their relationship to the important issue of defeasibility in law. We expect that our approach to knowledge representation leads to improved traceability from law to implementation and more accurate documentation of the impact of changes to the law and the theory construction process that takes place over time in an organization. The *Agile* project, and the pilot implementation projects that are part of it, test this hypothesis.

2 Problem Context

The work reported in this paper was performed in the context of the Agile project (acronym for Advanced Governance of Information services through Legal Engineering). Agile aims to develop concepts helping administrative organizations to reduce the time from a request for changes based on a change in the relevant law to implementation in the organization.

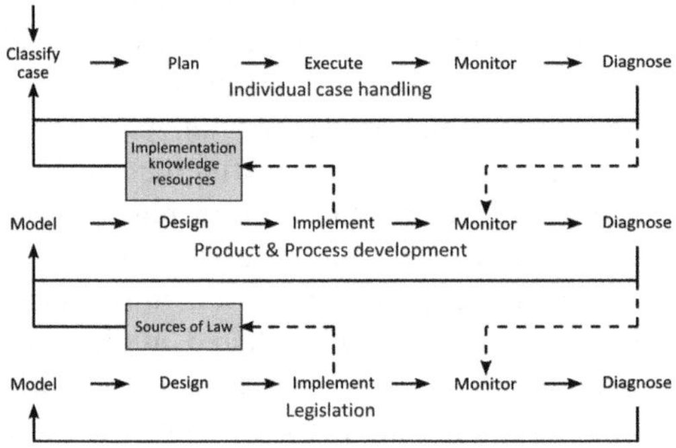

Fig. 1. The implementation and legislation problem solving cycles

Implementation of changes in the law is in public administration not an occasional isolated interruption of peaceful stasis, but a core activity of the organization. Moreover, the organizations in this category usually have a close working relationship with the legislator, at least some direct influence on the formation of positive law, and their interpretation of codified law is of direct relevance to many others. There is a direct feedback cycle between legislator, these organizations that implement the law, and the courts that judge those implementations, which drives theory construction in many areas of law. Fig. 1 shows an interpretation of this feedback cycle within the generic task framework of [4].

Involved in the Agile project are the Dutch Immigration and Naturalisation Service (IND) and the Dutch Tax and Customs Administration (DTCA). In both organizations, timely and efficient adaptation to changing legislation, case law, and patterns of behaviour accommodating or evading law in the relevant environment, is seen as an important organizational objective, and one whose realization is a constant cause of problems. Immigrants and taxpayers are notoriously capricious customers to have. The IND and DTCA have to reinvent themselves continually, and sometimes move to have the law changed, in response to problems and opportunities arising from their environment.

Both organizations also use decision support systems with executable rules. The DTCA heavily depends on electronic exchange of data with taxpayers, and has fully automated important decision-making processes.

2.1 The Role of Network Arrangements

The IND and DTCA are representative of modern, large public administrations. Modern public administrations increasingly depend on so-called network arrangements for the realization of their institutional responsibilities. Typical for such network arrangements are voluntary co-operation between agents (and agencies) and a dynamic serialization of services provided by different actors. No larger organizational framework creates and enforces the network arrangements. An administrative organization like the IND may for instance use an electronic service of the DTCA to perform an income check on behalf a client, yielding a simple yes/no answer, instead of asking the client to claim an income and provide evidence. This saves work, increases the reliability of data, and – if used properly – protects the client's privacy. It however also creates dependencies, in our example on the tax administration, and thus a need to understand the requirements and constraints – including but not restricted to the legal ones – that motivate and constrain service delivery, and a need to monitor for changes to these requirements and constraints.

Network arrangements create opportunities for increasing efficiency and quality, but they also increase exposure to risk. The organization that depends on service delivery of others becomes increasingly responsible for (intelligently monitoring and reacting to) what happens outside its organization.

The management of effective and legally compliant network arrangements is complex and puts high demands on the organizations involved. Implementation depends on service contracts, resource sharing, automated and standardized data exchange, etc, between independent agents that only enter into such arrangements if and as long as these are beneficial to the participants. Such loose network arrangements make it harder to organize durable compliance to the law: meeting obligations does not necessarily translate to straightforward control objectives, to allocation of responsibilities to roles in fixed business processes and specific groups of employees in departments.

The automation approach to compliance, for instance found in [7], presumes a degree of multi-agent task coordination and a capacity for change that is non-existent in practice within the participating organizations. The translation of obligations into task definitions is an important aspect of legal compliance, but not one in which we aim for scientific advance over the state-of-the-art approaches found in [7].

The Agile project definition reflects this changed view on implementation of the law by focusing its attention on the maintenance of diverse *implementation knowledge resources* – including shared resources, agreed standards for data exchange, service contracts, etc – rather than on the implementation of legal rules into effective and compliant decision making processes (generally for instance [8,7]).

2.2 Objectives of the Agile Project

In the Agile project we aim at developing a knowledge representation and design methodology, distributed service architecture simulation environment, and supporting tools for legal requirements and knowledge representation. A central aim to take the resilience of existing systems and dependencies on the environment explicitly into account [9,10]. We intend to demonstrate the effectiveness of the use of methodological guidelines in pilot projects in the participating organizations in a later stage of the project.

The Agile project started in the second half of 2008 and will last for four years. The project uses knowledge representation technology developed within the semantic web community: OWL2, and the extension to description graphs described in [11]. It also uses ontologies and technologies (partially) developed within our institute, like the Legal Knowledge Interchange Format [12] (LKIF), MetaLex [13,12], and the LKIF Core ontology and its predecessor [14], as a starting point.

A central objective is to properly distinguish knowledge about the presentation of legal rules in written form, the context of production of legal rules, and the contexts of use of legal rules.

The purpose of modeling implementation of legislation in OWL2 is to account for that implementation, to validate it, to do impact analysis if something changes, to simulate candidate new service arrangements, and to provide feedback to the legislator. Real world deployment of OWL2-based web services is not an object: actual technical implementation has to take into account the existing technical infrastructure of an organization, and the modernization of infrastructure or selection of delivery platforms is not the focus of the project.

3 Knowledge Representation Design Principles

Conceptually, Agile knowledge representation is based on a distinction between three universes of discourse [6]:

1. the production of law, which creates
2. legal institutional reality, and
3. its implementation(s) in brute reality.

The first domain, described in section 4, addresses the relevant provenance and efficacy information about the sources of law. This is in essence the metadata of the sources of law that is relevant in positioning them and deciding on their *applicability* in a decision making process.

In the next domain we find abstract legal institutions, whose presence is produced by the sources of law (cf. e.g. [15,16] and our work in [5].

Finally, in the third domain, there is the implementation of the legal institutions in brute reality. The institutional reality as represented in the sources of law only comes to life through the brute reality that constitutes (or "counts as") it. The raising of a hand for instance counts as a bid in an auction. The issuing of a document invented by some administrative agency tasked with issuing residence permits similarly counts as an official residence permit.

3.1 Constitutiveness and Representation

Between these three domains we find simple and uniform interfaces, existing of a *representation*[1] relation, which relates legal documents and data structures to entities in legal institutional reality represented by them, and a constitutiveness or *counts as* relation, which relates occurrences in legal institutional reality to their constituting implementation in brute reality.

Constitutiveness is the central issue when talking about implementation, because implementation is to a large extent a matter of designing ways to perform legal acts. The centrality of constitutiveness is itself only a relatively recent realization in academic legal knowledge engineering and requirements engineering [17], which certainly hasn't been fully absorbed by the business community yet.

The *legal rules* presented by the sources of law as part of legal institutional reality, constrain 1) the structure of institutional reality (institutional rules) and 2) the superposition of institutional reality on brute reality (constitutive rules) [5].

We assume that the organization aims for a transparent and unambiguous interpretation of the ontological structure of the individual three domains at any point in time, and that the legislator, at least in the administrative law domain, has the intention of resolving ambiguities in institutional reality wherever they arise. *Institutional rules* map out a logical space of possible models of the institution: they form the institution's ontology, and can be interpreted as terminological axioms [15,5]. They are not considered defeasible as a matter of policy.

Institutional occurrences are constituted by occurrences in brute reality. The main function of the *constitutive rule* is to present necessary and indicative conditions on changes to the state of the institution. Indicative conditions are defeasible [5].

We model constitutiveness with the *constitutes* (inverse *constitutedBy*) property in OWL2 [5]. This property applies to *legal occurrences*, and not legal propositions: we do not follow the custom of talking about *legal facts* arising from brute facts in representation. Legal occurrences *must* be constituted by another occurrence, which means in essence that one of the constitutive rules that indicates the legal fact *must* be applicable [5], and none of the necessary conditions violated.

In [18,5] we found useful reconstructions of normative concepts like obligation and violation in terms of constitutiveness.

In implementation in administrative processes, representation, modeled with the *represents* (inverse *representedBy*) property, also plays a central role. It is a marriage certificate that represents a relevant marriage, a receipt that represents a financial transaction, a written administrative decision that represents a change of legal position, and an

[1] Or presentation if one prefers to take that ontological stance.

update in some database that represents official recognition of some legally relevant new fact in some administrative procedure.

The uses of representation in law for the production of a paper trail as evidence is a source of confusion in knowledge representation.

For immigration, the proposition that someone is married may for instance be legally relevant; In implementation it for instance becomes the proposition that someone has supplied a marriage certificate. But even if the marriage certificate must be renewed every year, a certificate may in fact be still valid at the moment of decision making while the marriage is not at that point in time in existence. Moreover, some issuers of certificates in foreign countries may be notoriously unreliable, etc. Behind a single proposition in the law are often complete procedures, and many subtle differences in meaning in all those places where the same proposition is inferred. The formal act of marriage is an unambiguous event, but it is not the only relevant context of use for the applicable rules.

3.2 Applicability

Applicability plays a central role for knowledge engineers as soon as the reified legal rule and the interpretation of its logical meaning are distinguished. The logical rule must assert explicitly that the legal rule is being applied. The law also frequently identifies rules: a special class of legal rules, *applicability rules* (e.g. [19,20,5], constrains the applicability of other rules, or make the application of one legal rule conditional on the application of another legal rule.

Applicability is modeled through the *applicable* (inverse *appliesTo*) property [5]. This property applies to the *legal* thing the rule is about, regardless of its left hand or right hand side position in the axiom. Together *constitutedBy* and *applicable* explain how a legal occurrence happened.

Applicability is wherever possible attached to legal actions as a methodological choice, for practical and legal theoretical reasons [5]. Since we do not determine confluence of applicability rules from subsumption between propositions, or sets of them, we have to be sure that rules about the same subject apply to the same thing. Actions are the focal objects.

We do not attempt to account directly for metalegal principles like lex specialis (more specific rules defeat general rules), and lex posterior (newer rules defeat older rules). Based on our work in [5] we are of the opinion that lex specialis and lex posterior are based on generic principles of practical communication and cognitive function that give rise to temporal and logical defeasibility, and do not as such have to be specifically accounted for in legal knowledge representation. The metalegal conflict resolution principles are interpreted as generators of applicability rules.

One of the great challenges in understanding application of legal rules is the distinction between the dispositional and categorical meanings of applicability. The dispositional use in essence tries to capture *it is consistent to assume that the rule is applicable*, which refers to reasoning strategy rather than to the meaning of the legal rules per se. In its epistemological applications (of which [20] is an excellent and paradigmatic example) in defeasible reasoning, and in implementation resources, it is generally taken to be dispositional. Why make explicit the application of a rule at all, unless it is defeasible?

The effect of switching "switching OWL2 axioms on and off" for specific cases or in specific task contexts may be realized by an extra condition to an OWL2 axiom styled as a form of dispositional applicability statement about the legal rule, but this is an epistemological commitment not explicitly warranted by the law itself. For our task-neutral interpretation we prefer a categorical interpretation, and keep track only of whether a rule has matter-of-factly been applied, as the example in 5.1 will show.

4 Sources of Law

Some of the innovations we introduce in the project relate to the management of sources of law. Generally, we try to build on analogies between the legislative domain and the implementation domain, choosing the same representation solutions for both. The source of law is in our view:

1. a writing that may be used to back an argument concerning the presence of a legal rule, or another legal entity, in a certain legal institution [13],
2. the result of a legislative act performed with the intent of creating that legal rule, and
3. evidence of the occurrence of that legislative act.

The legislative act belongs to a broader category of *formal* legal acts that are characterized by 1) the requirement that one intends to bring about a certain institutional change, and 2) that this intent is represented in writing [5]. Knowledge engineers tend to focus on the representation issue when talking about the sources of law simply because this, and not the context of the legislator's abstract legal act, is the access point to the law.

The sources of law in a sense function as a log book of relevant legislative changes to a legal institution. A well-picked body of sources of law may also be considered a blueprint or a snapshot of the rules and structures of a specific legal institution of interest in time, but this notion should not be taken for granted (cf. our work in [5]).

4.1 MetaLex and Bibliographic Identity

To implement traceability from knowledge representation to sources of law, the Agile project builds on the results of our work on MetaLex XML (cf. for instance [12,13,5]), an XML metastandard for legal and legislative resources. MetaLex is a common document format, processing model, metadata set, and ontology for software development, standardized by a CEN/ISSS[2] committee specification in 2006 and 2010.

MetaLex is especially useful for our purposes because it standardizes legal bibliographic identity. The determination of bibliographic identity of sources of law is essential for deciding on the applicability in time of legal rules presented in those sources of law. MetaLex requires adherence to a URI[3] based, open, persistent, globally unique, memorizable, meaningful, and "guessable" naming convention for legislative resources based on provenance information. This provenance information can be extracted in RDF form and used in OWL2 [21].

[2] `http://www.cen.eu`
[3] Uniform resource identifier.

MetaLex and the MetaLex naming convention strictly distinguish the source of law as a published work from its set of expressions over time, and the expression from its various manifestations, and the various locatable items that exemplify these manifestations, as recommended by the Functional Requirements for Bibliographic Records (FRBR; cf. [22]).

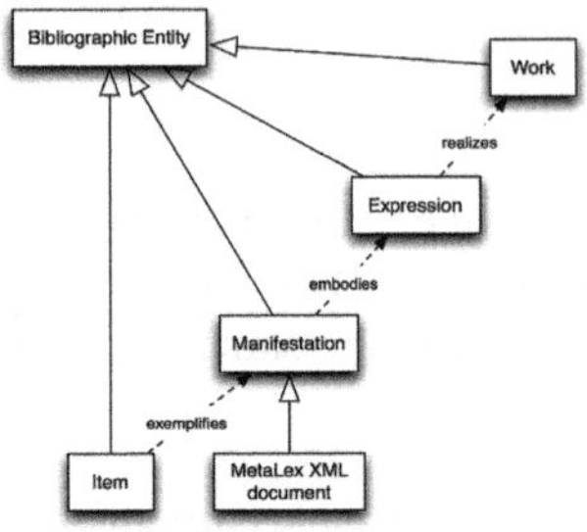

Fig. 2. Taxonomy of bibliographic entities in MetaLex, and their relata, based on FRBR

MetaLex extends the FRBR with a detailed but jurisdiction-independent model of the lifecycle of sources of law, that models the source of law as a succession of consolidated versions, and optionally *ex tunc* consolidations to capture the possibility of retroactive correction (errata corrige) or annulment after the fact of modifications to a legislative text by a constitutional court. In these cases the version timeline is changed retroactively: the conceptual time travel involved is an excellent example of the weird applications of constitutiveness. See for instance [23] for an explanation of the practical ramifications of annulment, and more generally an overview of the complexities involved in change of the law. Note that while MetaLex permits the identification of versions in different timelines, the involved reasoning requires defeasibility.

The use of MetaLex identification and referencing solves one aspect of the traceability problem. In current organizational practice links are more often than not made to locatable items, often without formal agreements about the permanence of the used item identifiers *even* between different departments of the same organization. Correct traceability to the right bibliographic abstraction (generally work or expression depending on the purpose of the reference) is – particularly at the levels below *formal* law – a notable weak point in organizational practice, and *ex tunc* change scenarios are not explicitly modeled, or even recognized. MetaLex makes this aspect of the traceability problem at least explicit, and provides some tools to address it.

In the MetaLex metadata set, specified in an OWL ontology, the *realizes* property between expressions and works represents the connection between the two ontological levels at which documents exist that are of relevance to their real world use (see Fig. 2). The source of law on the expression level for instance *cites* other rules on the work level, while the legal rules we represent knowledge about are necessarily identified by their representation in a discrete number of expressions [5].

A citation *(text fragment)* w *applies to (concept)* C should for instance be read as *each legal rule that is represented by an expression-level text fragment that realizes work fragment* w *applies to* C. This representation technique plays an important role in the Agile project, and is observed to significantly cut down on rather pointless maintenance operations redirecting reference pointers.

The idea of the MetaLex standard is of course that provenance metadata will be supplied by the publisher of the used XML manifestation, and is extracted from it in RDF form by organizations that use it.

4.2 Actions Performed on Documents

An important design feature of MetaLex from our perspective, is that provenance information is organized around actions performed on documents. Because actions play a central role in all relevant domains, we have chosen for a uniform representation of action inspired by MetaLex.

An action generally plays the mediating role between relevant entities and the resource the metadata description is about. The natural coherence between for instance *author*, *publication date*, and *publication channel* information (e.g. state gazette bibliographic information) is apparent to all: all are participants in the publication (promulgation) event. There is also a natural coherence between an old consolidation, the new consolidation, the modifying legislation, the modifying authority, and the modification date: the modification event links them together.

Provenance metadata often consists of simple predicate-object statements about electronic documents. This permits representation of different perspectives on the same action, because its identity was not made explicit, and may yield incompatible metadata descriptions. This results in unnecessary duplication of metadata, and separate occasions in which to make mistakes. It therefore creates unnecessary maintenance, and, lastly, the loss of relevant references between documents [24].

4.3 Identity of Legal Concepts and Rules over Time

In [5] (chapter 5) we discussed the subject of aligning version expressions of the knowledge representation with expressions of the sources of law, and the identity of legal concepts over time. The MetaLex source of law at the expression level *refers* to a set of *terms*, and it *represents* a set of *legal rules* and other *legal assertions*. A knowledge representation of a source of law represents its meaning in a specific point in time, from a specific vantage point in time.

One might think of the set of terms and legal rules occurring in *all* known expressions of a work as the shared set of terms and rules at the work level. The shared work level set however only exists from a specific vantage point in time, or only once the source of law has become immutable after its repeal, and the shared work level set – which can no longer change – has become largely irrelevant. This commonly used abstraction is unsafe, since it may lead to (ex tunc) versioning problems.

5 Conclusions and Discussion

A prominent place in this paper sofar was taken by the distinction between the institution and its implementation. For every institutional event, there must be something that counts as it. This distinction helps us determine whether, and how, existing capabilities and data can be given a second life with a new legal meaning. The decision to apply this distinction to all legal rules [17], and to ontologically stratify brute (or implementation) and institutional domains instead of classifying *propositions* as *legal facts* or *brute facts*, is a departure from standard practice in AI & Law.

In addition, we introduced the FRBR distinction between the source of law as an expression and as a work, and pointed out its significance for the interpretation of intra-textual references in knowledge representation. We also propose that legal documents, and the sources of law specifically, should be considered as evidence and as a descriptive medium for *changes to* legal institutional reality, rather than as a self-contained specification of it. Generally the representation and constitutiveness senses of documents are separate; The sources of law may represent a rule without being constitutive of it, and marriage certificates may attest of a marriage that doesn't exist anymore.

Moreover, we believe that the presented categorical method of representing applicability results in better and more durable isomorphism [1] between sources of law and implementation resources over time.

5.1 Representation Example

Let us turn to an integrated example of task-neutral interpretation, using a contrived source of law that consists of two sentences presenting two simple rules:

t_1 The publication of a text presenting a rule counts as the creation of that rule.
t_2 Rule t_1 applies to text published by a rule maker.

This legislative example is *qua* use of design patterns representative of formal legal acts in bureaucratic environments, like the issuing of a permit, claim, or income tax declaration, and many in the private sphere, like the issuing of a receipt for a purchase.

It is important at this point to stress that legal rules are *objects* in legal institutional reality, residing in the abox, and not terminological axioms. OWL2 axioms about rules are built according to the following pattern: if certain conditions on an occurrence are met – in the brute or legal institutional domains – then the legal rule is applicable and a certain legal occurrence is produced in the legal institutional domain.

We distinguish the text, which is a MetaLex expression object, from the legal rules: t_1 represents legal rule r_1, and t_2 represents legal rule r_2. We moreover also distinguish the legal rules from the (logical) OWL2 rules describing their meaning. Rule r_1 (written in a compact Manchester syntax-like notation for purposes of readability) demonstrates an interesting pattern relating the *constitutes* and *represents* relations:

```
if :Publication that
 (:resultsIn some (:Text that
  (agile:represents some :Rule)))
 then
  (agile:constitutes some (:Creation that
   (:resultsIn some :Rule) and
   (agile:applicable value :r1)))
```

This pattern is typical of implementation of legal acts as *formal* acts, and occurs often in public administration.

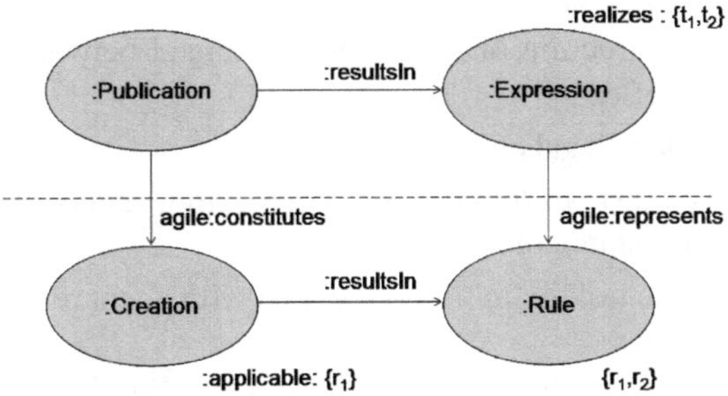

Fig. 3. The structure of interest in rule 1 of section 5.1

The second rule r_2 limits the applicability of r_1, but also of any other rules derived from any *future or alternative* version of t_1, as follows, showcasing the subtle bibliographic identity distinctions made by MetaLex:

```
if (agile:representedBy some
 (metalex:realizes value :t1))
 then
  (agile:appliesTo all ((:actor some :RuleMaker) and
   (agile:applicable value :r2)))
```

Because of the distinction allowed by MetaLex, we can *refer* to the work, and *represent* the expression in Agile rules.

Note that, although these two rules are consistent, the applicability assertions may turn out to be in logical conflict with respect to common and anticipated types of cases. We intentionally do not resolve this defeasibility between the rules, because there are alternative, equally reasonable ways to resolve it depending on the knowledge representation language semantics used, and on the disposition one has towards these rules, as pointed out in section 3.2.

5.2 Tasks and Agent Roles

While the legislator may occasionally want to reconceptualize the tasks and services of public administration, the organization itself is best helped with reusability in administrative task designs. There are clearly design patterns to be found that survive even the most radical reorganizations.

Generally, we try to find a practical middle road between interpreting the law strictly within the context of an implementation project, and the alternative of a shared, necessarily defeasible, decontextualized, monolithic interpretation of what the law means. We have pointed to the importance of network arrangements and the lack of global coordination as important factors creating inertia in implementation of the law in public administration, and a reason to be skeptical about decontextualization and reductive approaches to compliance like [7].

The institutional interpretation of law tells us little about the functions of law for its users. To explain the functions of various legal acts, we use *agent simulation* [10]. The agent metaphor positions knowledge resources as:

1. sets of beliefs linked to an agent role,
2. descriptions of the structure of messages exchanged between agents in order to achieve some legal effect,
3. capabilities to produce legal effects,
4. sets of beliefs that must be *shared* by communicating agents (in for instance information leaflets for clients), or
5. as components of the task definition associated with agent roles.

Generally, for simulation we always need to fill in gaps. Problem definitions don't follow directly from the law.

The analysis of obligations is for instance usually based on the expectation that people generally avoid the circumstances in which they are liable to be punished. Obligations therefore usually set us concrete tasks to change some situation in some direction or to leave it unchanged. There is however no reason in principle why an agent couldn't use them as soft requirements, or decide to violate obligations based on reasoning about whether it will be caught.

Our views on the roles of law in *normal* agent behaviour is based loosely on Hohfeld's theoretical work in [25] on *jural relationships* between parties. Hohfeld asserts that there are eight such entities: right, privilege, power, and immunity along with their respective correlates of duty, no-right, liability, and disability.

Hohfeld's relationships in essence distinguish between the capability (or power) and incapability to play a certain legal agent role (buyer, minister, tax inspector), between the task of bringing a certain change about or its absence, and between the one who acts and the one who predicts, monitors, and interprets the actions of another. The most obvious reason that we are actively monitoring and predicting someone else's actions that change our situation is because we are committed to a task that involves that other person as an actor.

The organization's conceptualization of its tasks represent its intention to use (legal) capabilities in a predictable manner. Services publicly advertise this intention, so that it creates capabilities of prospective clients. These clients use this ability by requesting a service.

To explain the normalizing effect of legal rules one must ascribe tasks to agents based on their agent role: People intentionally use their capabilities to try to bring about or avoid certain positions in legal institutional reality. In an organization like the DTCA we for instance want to predict the effect of changes to the law to for instance the behaviour of tax evaders, who intentionally misrepresent what they try to do (for instance by misrepresenting gifts as sales below or above market prices). The guiding principle for recognition of such misrepresentations, is that the agents – directly or indirectly – involved in the transaction are not really independent, uncoordinated agents in that transaction (parent and child, company and executive or shareholder). Evasion patterns are specific to the law being evaded, but the evading agent role is reusable.

Of central importance is the adoption of agent roles: the client becomes a client by requesting a service and – thereby – adopting a well-defined role, while the employee of the administrative organization adopts or is allocated an agent role in an associated business process. Agent simulation as a tool for impact analysis and exploration of design options assumes the development of prototypical agents representing both the organization itself and its relevant environment.

It is only when the allocation of OWL2 rules to agent roles and tasks takes place, that their potential to conflict with eachother becomes an issue. There are various approaches to dealing with the resultant defeasible reasoning requirement. We can add extra conditions to remove contradictions, use task-specific assumptions, and use a belief base revision approach [26,5]. Decisive are in the end the specific limitations of the logic used for knowledge representation in each intended delivery platform.

Acknowledgements

Agile is a Jacquard project funded by the Netherlands Organisation for Scientific Research (NWO), that involves, besides the Leibniz Center for Law, the Technical University of Delft, and commercial and public administration partners.

References

1. Bench-Capon, T., Coenen, F.: Exploiting isomorphism: development of a KBS to support British coal insurance claims. In: Sergot, M. (ed.) Proceedings of the Third International Conference on AI and Law, pp. 62–69. ACM, New York (1991)
2. Bench-Capon, T., Gordon, T.F.: Isomorphism and argumentation. In: ICAIL 2009: Proceedings of the 12th International Conference on Artificial Intelligence and Law, pp. 11–20. ACM, New York (2009)
3. Chandrasekaran, B., Johnson, T.R.: Generic tasks and task structures: History, critique and new directions. In: David, J.M., Krivine, J.P., Simmons, R. (eds.) Second Generation Expert Systems. Springer, Heidelberg (1993)
4. Breuker, J.: A suite of problem types. In: Breuker, J., de Velde, W.V. (eds.) CommonKADS Library for Expertise Modelling, pp. 57–88. IOS-Press/Ohmsha, Amsterdam/Tokyo (1994)
5. Boer, A.: Legal Theory, Sources of Law, & the Semantic Web. In: Frontiers in Artificial Intelligence and Applications, vol. 195. IOS Press, Amsterdam (2009)
6. Boer, A., van Engers, T., Winkels, R.: Traceability and change in legal requirements engineering. In: Casanovas, P., Pagallo, U., Ajani, G., Sartor, G. (eds.) AI Approaches to the Complexity of Legal Systems. LNCS. Springer, Heidelberg (2010)
7. Governatori, G., Sadiq, S.: The journey to business process compliance. In: Handbook of Research on BPM, pp. 426–454. IGI Global (2009)
8. Siena, A., Mylopoulos, J., Perini, A., Susi, A.: From laws to requirements. Requirements Engineering and Law, 6–10 (2008)
9. Janssen, M.: Adaptability and accountability of information architectures in interorganizational networks. In: ICEGOV 2007: Proceedings of the 1st International Conference on Theory and Practice of Electronic Governance, pp. 57–64. ACM, New York (2007)
10. Gong, Y., Janssen, M., Overbeek, S., Zuurmond, A.: Enabling flexible processes by eca orchestration architecture. In: ICEGOV 2009: Proceedings of the 3rd International Conference on Theory and Practice of Electronic Governance, pp. 19–26. ACM, New York (2009)
11. Glimm, B., Horridge, M., Parsia, B., Patel-Schneider, P.F.: A syntax for rules in owl 2. In: OWL Experiences and Directions (OWLED 2009), Washington D.C., USA (2009)
12. Boer, A., Winkels, R., Vitali, F.: Metalex XML and the Legal Knowledge Interchange Format. In: Casanovas, P., Sartor, G., Casellas, N., Rubino, R. (eds.) Computable Models of the Law. LNCS (LNAI), vol. 4884, pp. 21–41. Springer, Heidelberg (2008)

13. Boer, A., Vitali, F., de Maat, E.: CEN Workshop Agreement on MetaLex XML, an open XML Interchange Format for Legal and Legislative Resources (CWA 15710). Technical report, European Committee for Standardization, CEN (2006)
14. Breuker, J., Hoekstra, R.: Core concepts of law: taking common-sense seriously. In: Proceedings of Formal Ontologies in Information Systems FOIS 2004, pp. 210–221. IOS Press, Amsterdam (2004)
15. MacCormick, N.: Norms, institutions, and institutional facts. Law and Philosophy 17(3), 301–345 (1998)
16. Hindriks, F.A.: Rules & Institutions; essays in meaning, speech and social ontology. PhD thesis, Erasmus University Rotterdam (2005)
17. Mazzarese, T.: Towards the semantics of "constitutive" in judicial reasoning. Ratio Luris 12, 252–262 (1999)
18. Boella, G., van der Torre, L.W.N.: Obligations as social constructs. In: AI*IA, pp. 27–38 (2003)
19. Prakken, H., Sartor, G.: On the relation between legal language and legal argument: assumptions, applicability and dynamic priorities. In: ICAIL 1995: Proceedings of the 5th International Conference on Artificial Intelligence and Law, pp. 1–10. ACM, New York (1995)
20. Kowalski, R.A., Toni, F.: Abstract argumentation. Artificial Intelligence and Law 4, 275–296 (1996)
21. Boer, A.: Metalex naming conventions and the semantic web. In: Governatori, G. (ed.) Legal Knowledge and Information Systems, pp. 31–36. IOS Press, Amsterdam (2009)
22. Saur, K.G.: Functional requirements for bibliographic records. UBCIM Publications - IFLA Section on Cataloguing 19 (1998)
23. Governatori, G., Rotolo, A.: Changing legal systems: legal abrogations and annulments in Defeasible Logic. Logic Jnl IGPL, jzp075 (2009)
24. Boer, A.: Using event descriptions for metadata about legal documents. In: Winkels, R., Francesconi, E. (eds.) Electronic Proceedings of the Workshop on Standards for Legislative XML, in conjunction with Jurix 2007 (2007)
25. Hohfeld, W.: Fundamental Legal Conceptions as Applied in Legal Reasoning. Yale University Press (1919); Cook, W.W.(ed.): fourth printing (1966)
26. Halaschek-Wiener, C., Katz, Y., Parsia, B.: Belief base revision for expressive description logics. In: Online Proceedings of the Second OWL: Experiences and Directions Workshop (OWLED), Athens, Georgia, USA (2006), `http://owl-workshop.man.ac.uk/accepted06.shtml`

Enriching the Gene Ontology via the Dissection of Labels Using the Ontology Pre-processor Language

Jesualdo Tomas Fernandez-Breis, Luigi Iannone, Ignazio Palmisano, Alan L. Rector, and Robert Stevens

Departamento de Informatica y Sistemas
Facultad de Informatica
Universidad de Murcia
CP 30100, Murcia, Spain
jfernand@um.es
School of Computer Science
University of Manchester
Oxford Road
Manchester
United Kingdom
M13 9PL
lastname@cs.manchester.ac.uk

Abstract. In this paper we describe the process of taking an axiomatically lean ontology and enriching it through the automatic application of axioms using ontology design patterns (ODP). Our exemplar is the Gene Ontology's Molecular Function Ontology; this describes an important part of biology and is widely used to describe data. Yet much of the knowledge within the GO's MF is captured within the term's that label the concepts and within the natural language definitions for those concepts. Whilst both of these are absolutely necessary for an ontology, it is also useful to have the knowledge within the textual part of the ontology exposed for computational use. In this work we use an extension to the Ontology PreProcessor Language (OPPL) to dissect terms within the ontology and add axiomatisation, through OPPL's application of ODP, that make the knowledge explicit for computational use. We show the axiomatic enriching of the GO MF; that this can be accomplished both rapidly and consistently; that there is an audit trail for the transformation; and that the queries supported by the ontology are greatly increased in number and complexity.

1 Introduction

In this paper we describe the automatic transformation of an axiomaticaly lean ontology to one that is axiomatically richer through the application of ontology design patterns (ODP). We do this by exploiting the semantics within the labels on classes and the relatively systematic and explicit nature of naming within

P. Cimiano and H.S. Pinto (Eds.): EKAW 2010, LNAI 6317, pp. 59–73, 2010.

the ontology in question [1] and related ontologies. As the authoring of large, axiomatically rich ontologies by hand, whether *de novo* or by enhancing an existing ontology, involves considerable effort, the ability to automatically enrich ontologies by 'dissecting' their labels and generating the axioms they imply is attractive. Also, ontologies, like software, will need re-factoring during development as testing reveals problems and conceptualisations of the domain change. Applying changes consistently across an ontology by hand is difficult, prone to errors of commission and omission—particularly inconsistency between two changes of the same 'type'.

Many ontologies have much information within the labels on concepts that are not apparent axiomatically for computational inference. One such ontology is the molecular function (MF) aspect of the Gene Ontology (GO) [2]. GO MF describes the activities that occur at the molecular level for gene products such as proteins. There is a great deal of knowledge about the entities described within the labels and text definitions held on classes; these are useful for human users of GO, but not much good for machine processing. For example, as biochemists we can see that the label "vitamin binding" means the binding of a vitamin (and that a vitamin is a chemical) and that 'isoprenoid binding' means the binding of the chemical isoprenoid. However, the ontology does not contain an axiomatic description of what either binding or vitamin means. Similarly, 'oxidoreductase activity, acting on peroxide as acceptor' captures a considerable amount of knowledge in the function's label, but not axiomatically. Consequently, the reasoner cannot take advantage of such knowledge.

If we analyse the structure of the labels of the families of functions in GO, we could identify some regularities. Most binding functions have a label with the structure 'X binding', where X is a biochemical substance. Most types of structural molecule activity have a label with the structure "structural constituent of Y", where Y is a macromolecular complex. Given such regularity, we should be able to systematically pull out patterns of axioms that can make the semantics explicit. We explore a technique for using these naming conventions within labels as a way of mapping to patterns of axioms that make the information in the label computationally explicit.

Ontology Design Patterns (ODPs) are templates that define best practices in Ontology Engineering [3]. An ODP can then be viewed as a template that can be systematically applied for the representation of a given situation.

The Ontology Preprocessor Language (OPPL) is a scripting language for OWL that can be used to apply ODP across an ontology [4,5]; it is a way of programmatically manipulating an ontology at a higher level of abstraction than, for instance, the Java OWL API (`http://owlapi.sourceforge.net/`). It has the typical advantages of consistent, rapid application of the patterns. If the patterns to be applied change, those changes can also be rapidly applied. Thus, the OPPL scripts act as a documentation of the changes applied to the ontology.

We have extended OPPL2 to include regular expressions that will capture patterns within labels on concepts. This means we can *dissect* a label and use the elements within the label to populate a pattern that has been conceptualised to match a particular pattern of elements within a label. This technique has been used before [6,7] by using bespoke programmes to do the dissection and application of axioms. Here we present a generic tool for this technique and describe its application to a large ontology.

2 Materials and Methods

The method applied in the transformation is:

1. Inspect current GO molecular function labels and text definitions to find out what needs to be revealed as axioms;
2. Develop patterns of axioms that capture the knowledge about the concepts, relating the need for axioms to elements within the term label for the concept.
3. Identify supporting ontologies or modules that capture entities within the developed patterns;
4. Apply patterns across source ontology using OPPL2 to both apply ODP and to recognise lexical patterns in labels;
5. Run a reasoner and inspect the resulting ontology.

Analysing the GO Molecular Function Ontology: In this work we have used the version 1.550 of this ontology, which was downloaded on 19th April 2009 from `http://www.geneontology.org` This ontology had 8 548 classes, 5 object properties, 5 data properties and 9954 subclass axioms. We transformed only some parts of the GO MF ontology: binding; structural molecule activities; chaperone activities; proteasome regulator activities; electron carrier activities; enzyme regulator activities and translation regulator activities. The labels of the classes within each of these areas were inspected and the patterns from the naming conventions extracted. In addition, the text definitions of the class were inspected to help elucidate the patterns.

Producing the ODP: The analysis of the names and text definitions identifies what needs to be made explicit; this stage prescribes how those semantics will be made explicit as a set of axioms. The underlying technique is that of *normalisation* [8]:

- A tree is formed along the primary axis of classification; in this case the functions.
- Other axis of classification, such as chemical type, are separated into *supporting ontologies.*
- A restriction can be formed from the tree of functions of the supporting ontology to capture the aspects separated out into the supporting ontologies. For example, *vitamin binding* might have the restriction *binds some vitamin.*

As described in Section 1, the knowledge held within the labels, the text definitions of each class and the background knowledge of the ODP creator are combined to develop the ODP. The relationships used were taken from OBO's relationship ontology (RO) [9] to retain consistency with OBO.

The auxiliary ontologies: The creation of the ODP suggests the need for a range of supporting ontologies. The application of the ODP strongly depends on the availability of these ontologies. Wherever possible, we used ontologies already developed—especially those from the OBO Foundry `http://www.obofoundry.org/`, the original creators of the GO. Otherwise, or if the chosen ontologies were incomplete, sufficient ontology was created to fulfil the needs of this work.

Application of ODP using OPPL: The Ontology Pre-Processing Language's main motivation was to provide a declarative language for: (a) Specifying how an ontology should be modified; (b) Optionally specifying the conditions under which such modifications should be enacted [4,5]. A generic OPPL 2 statement looks like:

```
<PREAMBLE> SELECT Axiom,...,Axiom BEGIN ADD
| REMOVE Axiom ... ADD | REMOVE Axiom END
```

An OPPL 2 statement is decomposable into the following sections:

1. Variables (before `SELECT`): here all the variables to be used in the following sections must be declared.
2. Selection (between `SELECT` and `BEGIN`): here a set of axioms are specified using the variables declared in the previous section. The resulting matches will consist of all those axioms[1] that hold in the knowledge base under consideration, for every possible variable substitution.
3. Actions (between `BEGIN` and `END`): here a set of axioms to be added or removed are specified. Such axioms could also depend on variables, but only on those bound by one or more select clauses.

The OPPL grammar is available at `http://oppl2.sourceforge.net/grammar.html`. The syntax for encoding axioms in OPPL 2 is based on the Manchester OWL Syntax described in [10], expanded in order to accommodate variables in its constructs. Currently there are only two kinds of actions that can be performed in an OPPL 2 Script: additions and removals. A full description of OPPL2's features may be found in [4,5].

The extension to OPPL2 that makes the current work possible is the inclusion of regular expressions for variable declaration and constraint specification; a variable can now be built on the basis of a regular expression match, i.e.,: $?x\ :\ CLASS\ =\ Match("(\backslash w+)\backslash s\backslash w+")$ represents the set of classes whose label is composed of two alphanumeric sequences divided by a spacing character. The same construct can be used to model a constraint, e.g.,: $SELECT\ ?x\ WHERE\ ?x\ Match("(\backslash w+)\backslash s\backslash w+")$ will restrict the possible matches for $?x$ to those whose label matches the regular expression.

Java regular expressions are used to evaluate the input expression; therefore the syntax constraints and expressive power are those of Java regular expressions. Matching groups can be used, for example to build other generated variables:

[1] Asserted or inferred.

$?y = create(?x.GROUPS(1))$ will use the string captured by the first group in the expression used to define $?x$.

We have already observed that a large portion of the 'binding' sub-hierarchy of GO MF conforms to the label pattern X *binding*, where X is a chemical. We can therefore create a regular expression $(\backslash w+)\backslash sbinding$ that will match said labels; the captured group will be the label of the chemical X. This value can then be used to allow for the dissection of GO MF's labels to expose the implicit semantics of the class explicitly as axioms.

3 Results

We show detailed results for only the binding part of GO MF. The full set of patterns and OPPL2 scripts; together with the ontologies may be found at `http://miuras.inf.um.es/~mfoppl/`

3.1 Analysing Labels and Text Definitions for Binding Functions

Binding activities are defined in GO as "The selective, non-covalent, often stoichiometric, interaction of a molecule with one or more specific sites on another molecule". The bindings are then produced with substances or cellular components. In some cases, the binding is produced with a particular part of the substance or the component. There are different forms of binding according to the labels: binding, pairing and self-binding. The subtypes of binding activities are mainly due to the different types of substances and components that are bound.

This version of the molecular function ontology contains 1567 descendant classes of binding. 36 binding subclasses define their own subtaxonomy, and 18 do not. The *binding* subclasses have the following pattern for the label: "X *binding*", where X is the substance. In some cases the lexical pattern is "X Y *binding*", where X is the substance and Y is the type of substance; for instance for *receptor bindings* and *protein domain specific bindings*, which follow the pattern "*X domain binding*" and "*X receptor binding*", respectively, and this affects 354 (out of 398) classes in the case of receptors and 35 subclasses in the case of protein domain specific labels.

The *molecular adaptor activity* class does not follow the basic pattern above. This function is defined in GO as "the binding activity of a molecule that brings together two or more molecules, permitting those molecules to function in a coordinated way". This class has 72 descendants that follow the pattern "*X Y adaptor activity*", where X and Y are the substances that are brought together.

Another type of binding is *base pairing* that is defined in GO as "interacting selectively and non-covalently with nucleic acid via hydrogen bonds between the bases of a gene product molecule and the bases of a target nucleic acid molecule". The labels of these classes follow the pattern "base pairing with X", where X is a nucleic acid. This pattern is followed by 7 out of 9 classes in the first two taxonomic levels. At this point, the pattern changes: "X modification guide activity", where X is a nucleic acid. The other is "X codon-amino acid adaptor activity", where X is an mRNA triplet. These classes follow the previously described molecular adaptor activity pattern.

3.2 The Auxiliary Ontologies

The analysis above reveals the types of biological entities implied within the labels and text definitions of GO MF. In general these are chemicals, both large and small, to which the functions apply. The following ontologies were used to provide these entities ontologically:

- Chemical Entities of Biological Interest (CHEBI)[11]: CHEBI is a freely available dictionary of molecular entities. It is an ontological classification, whereby the relationships between molecular entities or classes of entities and their parents and/or children are specified. in this work, we have used the OWL version of its release 59.
- Relation Ontology (RO)[9]: The ontology of biomedical relations provides a common set of biomedical relationships being used in the development of OBO ontologies to facilitate knowledge sharing and interoperability.
- Biochemical ontologies (`http://dumontierlab.com/`): These are a set of ontologies developed by Dumontier's lab whose goal is the representation of biological and scientific concepts and relations.
- Amino acid ontology(`http://www.co-ode.org/ontologies/amino-acid/`): This is a small ontology focused on providing the specific, explicit semantics of amino acids and their properties.
- Protein ontology: Some ontologies about proteins have been developed, although they did not provide the kind of knowledge we needed for this work. Some examples are PRO (`http://pir.georgetown.edu/pro/`), and the ProteinOntology (`http://proteinontology.org.au/`). Therefore, we developed a small protein ontology following the classification of proteins suggested in `http://proteincrystallography.org/protein/`
- Enzyme ontology (`http://ontology.dumontierlab.com/ec-primitive`): This ontology implements the Enzyme Commission (EC) classification, which is a numerical classification scheme for enzymes, based on the chemical reactions they catalyze.
- FMA (`http://www.berkeleybop.org/ontologies/owl/FMA`): The Foundational Model of Anatomy ontology represents the classes and relationships necessary for the symbolic structural representation of the human body.
- Other GO ontologies: The ontologies developed by the Gene Ontology Consortium for representing cellular components and biological processes [2].

In addition to this, we also added to the ontology biochemical substances and types of substances that did not appear in any of these ontologies. In some cases, the same biochemical entity was found in more than one ontology, so different concepts had to be merged.

3.3 Binding Function Ontology Design Patterns

Binding The general axiomatisation for the binding function is:

```
binding = molecular_function and enables some
(binds some chemical_substance or binds some cellular_component)
```

The actual OPPL2 scripts for applying this axiomatisation are:

```
?x:CLASS, ?y:CLASS
BEGIN
ADD ?y subClassOf molecular_function,
ADD
?y subClassOf enables some (binds some ?x)
END;
?y is a molecular function that binds the chemical substance
or cellular component ?x
```

There, we can see how the label is processed and the linguistic expression contained in the label and that is different from "binding" is assigned to the variable ?y. This corresponds to the particular substance or cellular component that participates in the function.

```
?y:CLASS=Match("((\w+))_binding"), ?x:CLASS=create(?y.GROUPS(1))
SELECT ?y subClassOf Thing WHERE ?y Match("((\w+))_binding")
BEGIN
ADD ?y subClassOf molecular_function,
ADD ?y subClassOf enables some (binds some ?x)
END;
```

The patterns for domain and receptor bindings only change in the regular expression that is used for processing the labels to "(((\w+))_domain_binding)" and "(((\w+))_receptor_binding)" respectively.

Molecular adaptor activity. The general axiomatisation for the molecular adaptor binding function is:

```
molecular_adaptor_activity= molecular_function
and enables some (adapts some molecule and
                              adapts min 2 molecule)
```

The ODP for applying this pattern of axioms is:

```
?x:CLASS, ?y:CLASS
BEGIN
ADD ?y subClassOf molecular_function,
ADD ?y subClassOf enables some (adapts some ?x and
                                  adapts min 2 molecule)
END;
?y is a molecular function that adapts ?x
```

The actual OPPL2 script that does the matching and application of axioms is:

```
?y:CLASS=Match("((\w+))_adaptor_activity"),
?x:CLASS=create(?y.GROUPS(1))
SELECT ?y subClassOf Thing WHERE ?y Match("((\w+))_adaptor_activity")
BEGIN
ADD ?y subClassOf molecular_function,
ADD ?y subClassOf enables some
                        (adapts some ?x and adapts min 2 molecule)
END;
```

Triplet codon amino acid adaptor activity. This pattern allows a more precise definition that the first one. These functions are types of molecular adaptor activities. The general axiomatisation is:

```
triplet_codon_amino_acid_adaptor_activity=
molecular_function and enables some (adapts some triplet and adapts
some amino_acid )
```

The OPPL2 pattern is:

```
?x:CLASS, ?y:CLASS
BEGIN
ADD ?y subClassOf molecular_function,
ADD ?y subClassOf enables some
              (adapts some (amino_acid and recognizes some ?x))
END;
```

?y is a molecular function that adapts `?x` and a triplet codon-amino acid and recognizes the codon ?x. Finally, the script that executes the pattern is:

```
?y:CLASS=Match("((\w+))_codon_amino_acid_adaptor_activity"),
?x:CLASS=create(?y.GROUPS(1))
SELECT ?y subClassOf Thing
WHERE ?y Match("((\w+))_codon_amino_acid_adaptor_activity")
BEGIN
ADD ?y subClassOf molecular_function,
ADD ?y subClassOf enables some
          (adapts some (amino_acid and recognizes some ?x))
END;
```

Base pairing. This biological function has been explicitly defined using the OWL axioms:

```
 base_pairing = molecular_function and
enables some (pairs some nucleic_acid and through some hydrogen_bond)
```

This general axiomatisation corresponds to the OPPL2 pattern:

```
?x:CLASS, ?y:CLASS
BEGIN
ADD ?y subClassOf molecular_function,
ADD ?y subClassOf enables some
          (pairs some ?x and through some hydrogen_bond)
END;
?y is a molecular function that pairs ?x molecules through hydrogen
bonds.
```

This pattern has been extracted from the textual definition of the function and encoded in the pattern. The pattern is executed through the script:

```
?y:CLASS=Match("base\_pairing\_with\_((\w+))"),
?x:CLASS=create(?y.GROUPS(1)) SELECT ?y subClassOf Thing WHERE ?y
Match("base_pairing\_with_((\w+))") BEGIN ADD ?y subClassOf
molecular_function, ADD ?y subClassOf enables some
                          (pairs some x and through some hydrogen_bond)
END;
```

Modification guide activity. The general axiomatisation is:

```
modification_guide_activity
= molecular_function and enables some (pairs some nucleic_acid and
through some hydrogen_bond and guides some nucleic_acid)
```

The same axiomatisation realised as an OPPL2 pattern is:

```
?x:CLASS, ?y:CLASS, ?z:OBJECTPROPERTY
BEGIN
ADD ?y subClassOf molecular_function,
ADD ?y subClassOf enables some
(pairs some ?x and through some hydrogen_bond and ?z some ?x)
END;
?y is a molecular function that pairs ?x molecules through hydrogen
bonds and guides the ?x ?z operation.
```

The full OPPL2 script is:

```
?y:CLASS=Match("((\w+))_((\w+))_guide\_activity"),
?x:CLASS=create(?y.GROUPS(1)),
?z:OBJECTPROPERTY=create(?y.GROUPS(3))
SELECT ?y subClassOf Thing
WHERE ?y Match("((\w+))_((\w+))_guide_activity")
BEGIN
ADD ?y subClassOf molecular_function,
ADD ?y subClassOf enables some (pairs some ?x
         and through some hydrogen_bond and ?z some ?x)
END;
```

3.4 Execution of the OPPL Patterns against Binding Functions

The version of GO used in this work has 1 567 descendant classes of the class *binding*, among which 54 are direct subclasses. The results of applying the basic pattern are shown in Table 1, where the results are grouped by binding subclass. The global result shows that 1 228 (around 78%) of the classes are matched by the pattern. This result includes the domain and receptor binding patterns. Most of the labels of the non-matched classes are also encoding other biological functions than binding, such as molecular adaptor; this is due to the multiple inheritance in GO MF. In addition, around 200 non-matched classes are types of receptor activities that have multiple parents (more than one function), so the binding pattern needs to be combined with another to accommodate this other function.

Base pairing: There are 84 subclasses of *base pairing* although the pattern only matches 6, because the rest are also kinds of *molecular adaptor activity* and *guide activity.*

Molecular adaptor activity: There are 72 descendant classes and the pattern matches correctly 71. The non-matching is due to inconsistency of naming in the labels, because its label is "*X adaptor protein activity*".

Triplet codon amino acid: There are 64 descendant classes and the pattern correctly matches all of them.

Modification guide activities: There are 12 descendant classes that are correctly matched by the pattern.

In summary, these patterns match 1 336 binding activities, that is, around 85%, and up to 94% if the 157 receptor activities are not included.

3.5 Findings

The original molecular function ontology had 8 548 classes, 5 object properties, 5 data properties and 9954 subclass axioms, having ALER(+D) DL expressivity. The object properties are *part_of*, *regulates*, *negatively_regulates*, *positively_regulates* and *ObsoleteProperties* (which is used for archiving purposes). However, part_of is used in only 8 axioms of the ontology. This ontology is classified in less than 1 second (average time over 5 runs under the same conditions: 842,8 ms).

The transformed ontology has 58 624 classes, 254 object properties, 16 data properties, 107 631 subclass axioms, 264 equivalent class axioms and 488 disjoint class axioms, with SRIQ(D) DL expressivity. This ontology is classified in around 120 seconds (average time over 5 runs under the same conditions: 123 283 seconds). All the classification times have been measured using Protege 4.0.2 and the Fact++ reasoner (version 1.3.0, may 2009), and Protege has been launched with 2GB of memory.

Table 1. Results of the application of the binding pattern by subclass

subclass	number of subclasses	number of correct matches
alcohol	4	4
amide	2	2
amine	29	19
antigen	5	5
bacterial	6	6
base pairing	84	0
carbohydrate	31	28
carbon monoxide	2	1
carboxylix acid	8	8
cell surface	5	5
chromatin	6	6
cofactor	19	17
DNA	78	69
drug	10	10
extracellular matrix	6	6
hormone	23	18
host cell surface	1	1
ion binding	33	30
isoprenoid	9	9
lipid	50	48
metal cluster	5	5
molecular adaptor	72	0
neurotransmitter	39	3
nucleobase	8	8
nucleoside	9	9
nucleotide	38	38
odorant	2	2
oxygen	2	1
pattern	20	14
peptide	87	28
phthalat	3	3
pigment	2	2
protein	920	766
ribonucleoprotein	5	5
RNA	135	52
tetrapyrrole	5	5
translation factor	8	2
vitamin	19	19
TOTAL	1790	1254

This means that the knowledge that can be now exploited has increased by 50 076 classes, 249 object properties, 11 data properties, 97 677 subclass axioms, 264 equivalent class axioms, and 488 disjoint class axioms. Much of this knowledge is provided by the auxiliary ontologies. If we consider just the knowledge added by the execution of the patterns, the numbers are then 584 classes, 13 object properties and 3 608 subclass axioms. The object properties added correspond to the biological functions defined in the patterns such as *binds* or *formation_of*. The subclass axioms correspond to the ones added by the patterns.

Non-matched classes that have been extracted as groups in the regular expressions (mostly chemicals) are created automatically by OPPL2. These are made children of *NotInAuxiliary*. The non-matched substances include D1 Dopamine, eye lens, vasopressin, type X Y, where X is a number and Y is a substance, etc. These classes may refer to substances that exist in the auxiliary ontology but whose labels are different. This can be due to use of abbreviations (e.g., IgX vs 'immunoglobulin X', where X indicated the type of immunoglobulin, mitogen activated protein kinases vs MAPKs, etc. Otherwise meaning is embedded in the taxonomic relation. For instance there are 55 classes (grouped in *NotInAuxiliaryComplex*) whose label in the transformed ontology is 'X' and their label in the auxiliary ontologies is 'X complex'. For 14 of them, the application of a complex binding pattern would work, in the sense that we could add the suffix complex to the label. However, this would not work for 41, and it is not clear in some cases whether they refer to complexes or substances in the labels and the textual definitions.

One of the most important benefits of the transformed ontology is that we can now make more queries. The original ontology could not be asked queries such as:

1. Query 1:"Molecular functions that participate in the formation of a cellular component".
2. Query 2: "Molecular functions that bind substances that can play a chemical role"
3. Query 3:"Molecular functions that bind nitrogenous bases"

These queries can now be asked as follows:

1. Query1: molecular_function and enables some (formation_of some cellular _component). This query returns 20 direct subclasses and 30 descendants. This query benefits from using the cellular component ontology and the axiomatization provided by the patterns.
2. Query 2: molecular_function and enables some (binds some ('chemical substance' and 'has role' some 'chemical role')). This query returns 27 direct subclasses and 74 descendants. This query benefits from the axiomatization provided by the patterns and the auxiliary ontologies.
3. Query 3: molecular_function and enables some (binds some 'nitrogenous base'). This query returns 10 direct subclasses and 45 descendants. As in the previous case, this query benefits from the axiomatization provided by the patterns and the auxiliary ontologies.

3.6 Transformation Times

A graphical representation of the time needed for executing the OPPL patterns is shown in Figure 1in the following order: base pairing (6), modification guide

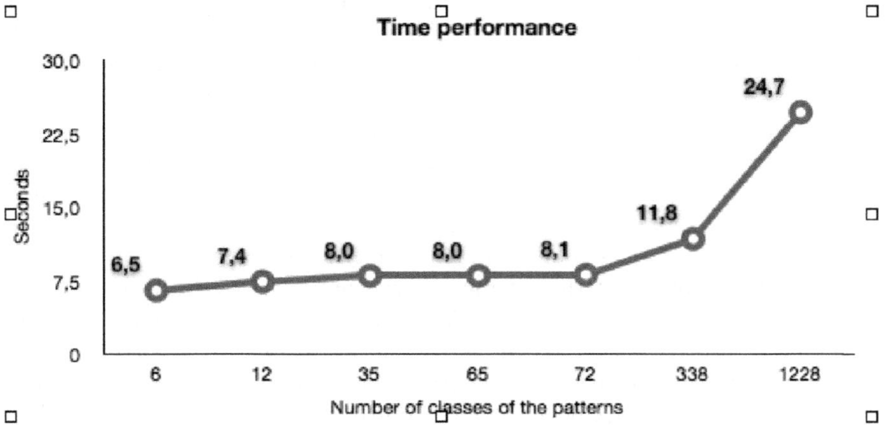

Fig. 1. Graphical representation of time performance

activities (12), domain binding (35), triplet codon amino acid adaptor activity(65), molecular adaptor activity (72), receptor binding (338), and binding (1228).

The increase of the time required to apply the pattern is rather stable for less than 100 classes, whereas it increases for more than 100 classes. In this particular experiment, the slope between 72 and 338 (0,139) is similar to the one between 338 and 1228 (0,144), This means that, although the figure does not allow to appreciate clearly this issue, the time increases linearly with the number of classes affected by the pattern.

4 Conclusions

In this paper, the automatic transformation of a part of the molecular function ontology has been addressed by applying Ontology Design Patterns implemented using OPPL. An important goal of this work was to extract the knowledge that is embedded in the labels of the classes and this was also a limitation that we imposed ourselves in this work, since we did not attempt to capture the complete semantics of the classes, but the one that might be extracted from the analysis of the labels.

Our OPPL scripts have been designed and executed to improve the semantic definition of the targeted molecular functions, but this does not mean that the semantics of such functions is complete. For instance, binding-related patterns provide axioms only from the binding perspective, whereas some functions may encode other biological functions. For instance, some binding functions are also related to structural molecule such as protein scaffold activities. Given the structure of the labels, only the scaffold pattern has been applied to them. This is a limitation of the label processing approach. However, since we have modelled the binding pattern, we can just apply it directly to those classes, so improving the number of binding functions modelled. This is also one of the benefits of applying OPPL patterns, since it allows for executing to all the classes that hold some criteria or to individually selected ones.There are other cases in which binding functions are also transport functions. The same process could be followed but we have not included the modelling of transport functions in this study.

This work has exploited the relatively systematic naming within life science ontologies and the naming conventions of the OBO ontologies in particular. Without these aspects this technique is much less applicable. Some of the non-matches do, however, highlight defects in some entity's labels and this is a useful side-effect. That such consistent naming and naming conventions can be thus exploited can also act as a spur to adopt such best practices.

It should be pointed out that the auxiliary ontologies are far from being perfect, hence they can be improved in different ways. On the one hand, its content can be improved by including, for instance, more substances. Nevertheless, those will be eventually added with the evolution of the source ontologies. On the other hand, the quality of myauxiliarontology can be enhanced. First, its semantics can be optimized by increasing the axiomatization concerning types of substances. In this ontology, we can find that some types of substances have been defined as equivalent classes but some have not. The consequences of this is that the results of the queries are potentially suboptimal. Second, this ontology has been obtained by the partial, manual integration of a set of ontologies. This result could be improved if ontology mapping and alignment techniques were used for supporting this integration process.

This work has shown OPPL to be useful for applying patterns to ontologies, since it provides a flexible way of adding axioms to ontologies in a systematic way. It has been capable of adding axioms to more than 1 600 classes by applying the patterns in a reasonable time. This time is mainly due to the need for matching the label patterns, which have to be compared for every class. The time performance also suggests an acceptable behaviour for larger numbers of classes matched by patterns. Nevertheless, this is one of the first applications of OPPL for executing label-based patterns and the management of regular expressions in OPPL can still improve.

In addition to this, we can see that regular expressions for dissecting labels or identifiers on classes to expose implicit axioms through the application of ODPs can be highly effective and relatively low cost. Therefore, we plan to continue the definition of the patterns for the rest of families of functions contained in GO MF.

Acknowledgements. JTFB has been supported by the Spanish Ministry of Science and Innovation through the grants JC2008-00120 and TSI2007-66575-C02-02.

References

1. Ogren, P., Cohen, K., Acquaah-Mensah, G., Eberlein, J., Hunter, L.: The Compositional Structure of Gene Ontology Terms. In: Pacific Symposium on Biocomputing, vol. 9, pp. 214–225 (2004)
2. GOConsortium: Gene ontology: tool for the unification of biology. Nature Genetics 25(1), 25–29 (2000)

3. Presutti, V., Gangemi, A.: Content ontology design patterns as practical building blocks for web ontologies. In: Li, Q., Spaccapietra, S., Yu, E., Olivé, A. (eds.) ER 2008. LNCS, vol. 5231, pp. 128–141. Springer, Heidelberg (2008)
4. Iannone, L., Rector, A.L., Stevens, R.: Embedding knowledge patterns into owl. In: Aroyo, L., Traverso, P., Ciravegna, F., Cimiano, P., Heath, T., Hyvönen, E., Mizoguchi, R., Oren, E., Sabou, M., Simperl, E. (eds.) ESWC 2009. LNCS, vol. 5554, pp. 218–232. Springer, Heidelberg (2009)
5. Egaña, M., Rector, A.L., Stevens, R., Antezana, E.: Applying ontology design patterns in bio-ontologies. In: Gangemi, A., Euzenat, J. (eds.) EKAW 2008. LNCS (LNAI), vol. 5268, pp. 7–16. Springer, Heidelberg (2008)
6. Solomon, W.D., Roberts, A., Rogers, J.E., Wroe, C.J., Rector, A.L.: Having our cake and eating it too: How the GALEN Intermediate Representation reconciles internal complexity with users' requirements for appropriateness and simplicity. In: Overhage, J.M. (ed.) Proceedings of the 2000 American Medical Informatics Association Annual Symposium (AMIA 2000), Los Angeles, American Medical Informatics Association, pp. 819–823. Hanley and Belfus Inc. (2000)
7. Wroe, C., Stevens, R., Goble, C., Ashburner, M.: A Methodology to Migrate the Gene Ontology to a Description Logic Environment Using DAML+OIL. In: 8th Pacific Symposium on biocomputing (PSB), pp. 624–636 (2003)
8. Rector, A.L.: Modularisation of domain ontologies implemented in description logics and related formalisms including owl. In: Proceedings of the 2nd International Conference on Knowledge Capture, Sanibel Island, USA (October 2003)
9. Smith, B., Ceusters, W., Klagges, B., Köhler, J., Kumar, A., Lomax, J., Mungall, C., Neuhaus, F., Rector, A.L., Rosse, C.: Relations in biomedical ontologies. Genome Biology 6, R46 (2005)
10. Horridge, M., Drummond, N., Godwin, J., Rector, A., Stevens, R., Wang, H.: The Manchester OWL Syntax. In: Proceedigns of OWLED 2006 OWL: Experiences and Directions, Athens GA, USA (2006)
11. de Matos, P., Alcántara, R., Dekker, A., Ennis, M., Hastings, J., Haug, K., Spiteri, I., Turner, S., Steinbeck, C.: Chemical entities of biological interest: an update. Nucleic Acids Research 38(Suppl. 1:D249) (2010)

Ontology Development for the Masses: Creating ICD-11 in WebProtégé

Tania Tudorache[1], Sean Falconer[1], Natalya F. Noy[1], Csongor Nyulas[1], Tevfik Bedirhan Üstün[2], Margaret-Anne Storey[3], and Mark A. Musen[1]

[1] Stanford Center for Biomedical Informatics Research, Stanford University, US
[2] World Health Organization, Geneva, Switzerland
[3] University of Victoria, Canada
{tudorache,sfalc,noy,nyulas}@stanford.edu, ustun@who.int, mstorey@uvic.ca, musen@stanford.edu

Abstract. The World Health Organization is currently developing the 11th revision of the International Classification of Diseases (ICD-11). ICD is the standard diagnostic classification used in health care all over the world. In contrast to previous ICD revisions that did not have a formal representation and were mainly available as printed books, ICD-11 uses OWL for the formal representation of its content. In this paper, we report on our work to support the collaborative development of ICD-11 in WebProtégé—a web-based ontology browser and editor. WebProtégé integrates collaboration features directly into the editing process. We report on the results of the evaluation that we performed during a two-week meeting with the ICD editors in Geneva. We performed the evaluation in the context of the editors learning to use WebProtégé to start the ICD-11 development. Participants in the evaluation were optimistic that collaborative development will work in this context, but have raised a number of critical issues.

1 Creating a Formal Representation of ICD-11

Ontologies and terminologies are a critical component of many knowledge-intensive systems. In recent years, we have seen a considerable growth both in the tools that support the development of ontologies collaboratively and the projects that include contribution by a community of experts as a critical part of their workflow.

The development of large biomedical terminologies and ontologies is possible only in a collaborative setting. The Gene Ontology (GO) is one of the more prominent examples of an ontology that is a product of a collaborative process [3]. GO provides terminology for consistent description of gene products in different model-organism databases. Members of the GO community constantly suggest new terms for this ontology and several full-time curators review the suggestions and incorporate them into GO. The National Cancer Institute's Thesaurus (NCI Thesaurus) is another example of a large biomedical ontology that is being developed collaboratively [4]. The Biomed Grid Terminology (BiomedGT) restructures the NCI Thesaurus to facilitate terminology federation and open content development. NCI is using a wiki environment to solicit the feedback about the terminology from the community at large. The Ontology for Biomedical Investigations (OBI), a product of the OBI Consortium, is a federated ontology, which has more than 40 active curators, each responsible for a particular scientific

P. Cimiano and H.S. Pinto (Eds.): EKAW 2010, LNAI 6317, pp. 74–89, 2010.

community (e.g., cellular assay, clinical investigations, immunology, etc.). Developers of these ontologies use a variety of tools and a broad range of editorial workflows to achieve consensus and to ensure quality [11].

The International Classification of Diseases (ICD) is the standard diagnostic classification developed by the World Health Organization (WHO) to encode information relevant for epidemiology, health management, and clinical use. Health officials use ICD in all United Nations member countries to compile basic health statistics, to monitor health-related spending, and to inform policy makers. In the United States, use of the ICD is also a requirement for all medical billing. Thus, ICD is an essential resource for health care all over the world. The ICD traces its formal origins to the 19th Century, and the classification has undergone revisions at regular intervals since then. The current revision of ICD, ICD-10, contains more than 20,000 terms. In 2007, WHO initiated the work on the 11th revision of ICD (ICD-11) with the mission "to produce an international disease classification that is ready for electronic health records that will serve as a standard for scientific comparability and communication."[1]

ICD-11 will introduce major changes to ICD, which the WHO characterizes as (1) evolving from a focus on mortality and morbidity to a *multi-purpose and coherent classification* that can capture other uses, such as primary care and public health; (2) creating a *multilingual international reference standard* for scientific comparability and communication purposes; (3) ensuring that ICD-11 can function in electronic health records (EHRs) by *linking ICD to other terminologies and ontologies* used in EHRs, such as SNOMED CT; (4) introducing *logical structure and definitions* in the description of entities and representing ICD-11 in OWL and SKOS. In addition to these changes in structure and content, the WHO is also radically changing the revision process itself. Whereas the previous revisions were performed by relatively small groups of experts in face-to-face meetings and published only in English and in large tomes, development of ICD-11 will require a Web-based process with thousands of experts contributing to, evaluating, and reviewing the evolving content online.

We have developed a custom tailored version of WebProtégé, called iCAT, for authoring the alpha draft of ICD-11 (Section 2).[2] WebProtégé is a Protégé client that supports collaboration and enables distributed users to edit an ontology simultaneously, and to use their Web browsers for editing. The application presents users with simple forms that reflect the fields in the ICD-11 content model. The tool also incorporates many collaborative features, such as the ability to comment on ontology entities.

In September 2009, WHO gathered its ICD-11 managing editors for iCamp—a two week meeting with the goal of introducing the editors to the new development process and to the customized WebProtégé tool, developing requirements for further tool support, and evaluating the open development process. In this paper, we report results from an evaluation performed during iCamp, where we focused on the feasibility of an open process for ontology development and the requirements for such a process.

To the best of our knowledge, the development of ICD-11 is the largest open collaborative ontology-development experiment of its kind. Thus, we believe that the insights

---

[1] `http://sites.google.com/site/icd11revision/home`

[2] A demo version is available at `http://icatdemo.stanford.edu`

that we gained from our evaluation will be informative to the organizers and developers of similar projects. Specifically, this paper makes the following contributions:

- We describe the customized WebProtégé system that is being used in the collaborative development of ICD-11.
- We use WebProtégé as the context for an evaluation of feasibility and requirements of a collaborative ontology-development process.

2 WebProtégé and the ICD-11 Customization

Our goal in developing a customized version of WebProtégé is to support the collaborative development of the ICD-11 content. In this section, we give an overview of the main artifact that we are building—the ICD Ontology (Section 2.1) and describe the WebProtégé architecture (Section 2.2). We highlight the key elements of the user interface in iCAT, the custom-tailored version of WebProtégé, in Section 2.3.

We joined the ICD revision project in its infancy, when many fundamental issues (content model, representation, workflow) and requirements for the tooling were undefined. Thus, we had to build tools that we can adapt on the fly when changes are made to the underlying model, user-interface requirements and the workflow. In Section 2.4, we describe our design of WebProtégé as a pluggable and extensible platform to enable each project to customize it according to its own requirements. iCAT is in fact a particular configuration of WebProtégé.

Finally, we present the support for collaboration among a large number of distributed users as an integral requirement of the ICD revision process. We discuss the collaboration features of WebProtégé in Section 2.5.

2.1 The ICD Ontology

The previous revisions of ICD stored only limited information about a disease, such as the code, title, synonyms, example terms, and simple conditions. The goal of the 11th revision process is to extend the description of diseases to include other attributes: a textual definition of the disease, clinical descriptions (body system, signs and symptoms, severity), causal mechanisms and risk factors, and the functional impact of a disease. To support the richer representation of diseases, the WHO has defined a formal representation of the model in OWL, the *ICD Content Model*. The content model describes both the attributes of a disease (e.g., Definition, Body System, Severity, Functional Impact, and so on) and the links to external terminologies, mainly to SNOMED CT [14].

The ICD Ontology[3] is the formal representation of the ICD content model in OWL (Figure 1). The class *ICDCategory* is the top level class of the ICD disease hierarchy. The ontology uses a meta-model layer to describe the attributes that a disease class may or should have. For example, the class representing *Acute Myocardial Infarction* disease has as a type (among others) the *ClinicalDescriptionSection* metaclass that prescribes that the range for the property *bodySystem* should be the class *BodySystemValueSet*. In this example, the class *Acute Myocardial Infarction* has the *CirculatorySystem* as a value for the property *bodySystem*.

[3] Accessible at `http://icatdemo.stanford.edu/icd_cm/`

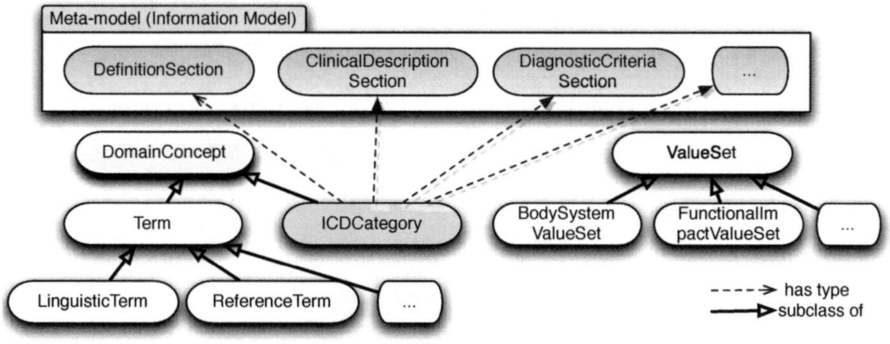

Fig. 1. A snippet of the ICD Ontology. The *ICDCategory* is the top-level class in the ICD disease hierarchy and has as types the metaclasses from the meta-model (gray background). The property values of a disease class are instances of the class *Term*. The *ValueSet* has as subclasses the different value set hierarchies used in the ontology.

All property values describing diseases are reified—they are instances of the class *Term*. For each value, we use this reification to record the source of the value (e.g., for a definition of a disease we need to record the supporting evidence in the form of citations or references) and other salient information. We use *LinguisticTerms* to represent property values that have different labels in different languages. ICD aims to become a multi-language classification, providing support for multi-linguality is paramount.

Property values that are instances of the class *ReferenceTerm* represent links to other terms in external terminologies, such as SNOMED CT. For example, a disease has an associated body part. Rather than defining its own anatomy hierarchy to serve as values for the *bodyPart* property of a disease, ICD-11 references classes in SNOMED CT that represent anatomical parts. Since it is not practical to import the entire SNOMED CT into ICD-11, the *ReferenceTerm* class models all the information needed to identify uniquely an entity in an external terminology: the fully qualified name of the external entity, the name of the ontology, the label of the term, and other auxiliary information. This construct allows us to import references to terms in external terminologies and ontologies in a uniform and practical way.

2.2 Architecture of WebProtégé

Figure 2 shows a high level WebProtégé architecture diagram and the interaction of the software components. The core functionality of the application is supported by the *Protégé server*, which provides access to the ontology content, such as retrieving and changing classes, properties and individuals in the ontology. The ontologies that the server accesses are stored in a database on the server side. To facilitate the management and reuse of the ICD ontology, we modularized it into several smaller ontologies that import each other. Both the Web-based Protégé client (WebProtégé) and the "traditional" Protégé desktop client access the Protégé server to present the ontologies to the users. Any number of clients of either type can access and edit the same ontology on the server simultaneously. All changes that a user makes in one of the clients are

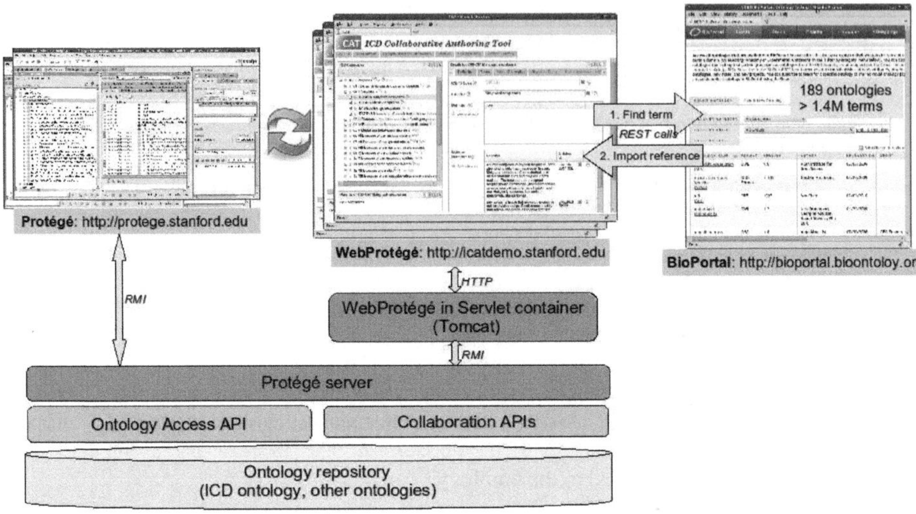

Fig. 2. An architecture diagram of the customized WebProtégé for ICD. The ICD ontology content is accessible through both a Protégé desktop client and in a Web browser. WebProtégé accesses BioPortal for searching terms to import as external references. Both WebProtégé and the Protégé desktop clients connect to a Protégé server to read and write the ontology content and information that supports the collaboration features.

immediately visible in all other clients. The ICD editors use the WebProtégé client to browse and edit ICD-11. The technical-support team often uses the desktop client to make corrections or perform operations that are not supported in the Web interface.

In order to search external biomedical terminologies and to import terms from these terminologies, WebProtégé accesses *BioPortal*, a repository of about 200 biomedical ontologies and terminologies [9]. BioPortal provides REST service access that enables search across different ontologies and access to information about specific terms.

Support for collaboration among users is one of the key features of WebProtégé. We have developed a general-purpose collaboration framework in Protégé [15] and we use the same framework in WebProtégé. This framework provides Java APIs for tracking changes in an ontology, and for storing notes and discussion threads attached to ontology entities. We also reuse the generic access policy mechanism of the Protégé server that allows us to define customized access policies for an ontology (e.g., a user who has only read access will not be able to edit the ontology).

2.3 Features of the WebProtégé User Interface

WebProtégé is a web portal, inspired by other portals, such as myYahoo or iGoogle. Our vision is to enable users to build a custom user interface by combining existing components in a form that is appropriate for their project. The user interface is composed of *tabs*—either predefined ones or user-defined. A new tab is an empty container in which users can add and arrange by drag-n-dropping *portlets*. A portlet is a user interface component that provides some functionality. For example, the *Class tree portlet*

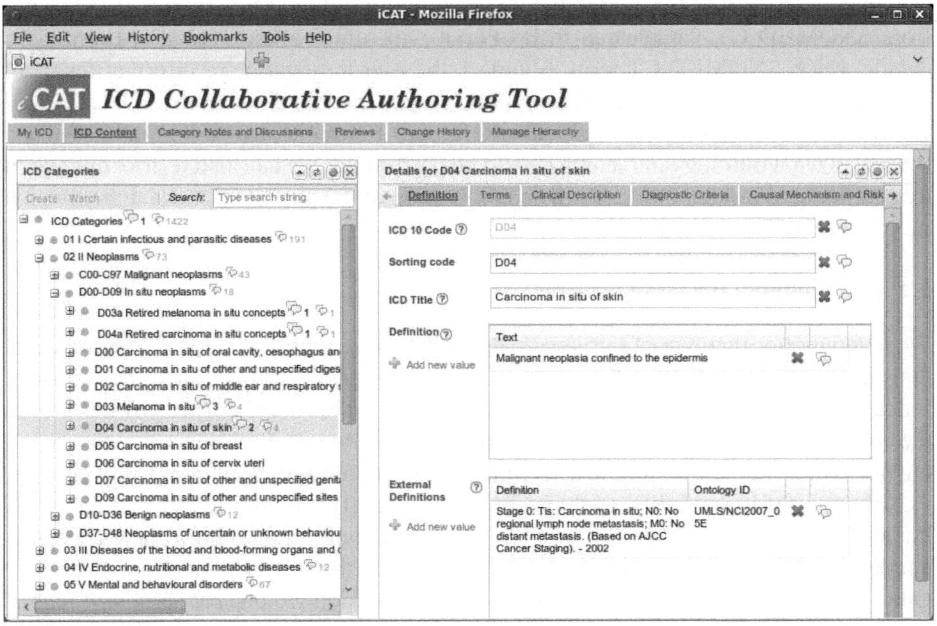

Fig. 3. The WebProtégé user interface customized for ICD. The interface is composed of tabs. Each tab contains one or more panels, called *portlets* that can be arranged by drag-n-drop. The left hand-side portlet shows the disease class hierarchy of the ICD ontology. The right portlet shows the fields of the selected disease in the tree, in this case *D04 Carcinoma in situ of skin*.

displays the class hierarchy in an ontology and has support for class level operations (create and delete class, move class in hierarchy, etc.).

Figure 3 shows one of the tabs in the customized WebProtégé interface for ICD, known to the domain experts as iCAT. The *ICD Content* tab contains two portlets: the class tree portlet—showing only a branch of the ICD ontology, and a details portlet—showing the property values of the class selected in the class tree in a simple form-based interface. The domain experts are familiar with this type of interface from many other applications. For each property, we use a specific *widget* to acquire the property values. For example, we use a text-field widget to record the values of the *ICD title* property (Figure 3). As we have mentioned in Section 2.1, all values of properties describing a disease are reified as instances of the *Term* class. We use an *instance-table widget* to hide this extra reification layer from the user and to present all the details about the reified instance directly in the form for the disease. The widget presents a pre-configured set of property values for the term instance as columns in the table. You can see an example of this widget for the *External Definition* property in Figure 3.

Most attributes for diseases have values that are references to terms in external terminologies and ontologies. For example, the property *bodyPart* takes as values references to the Anatomy branch of SNOMED CT (see Section 1). We have developed a generic *Reference Portlet* that supports the simple import of an external reference with a single mouse click. The portlet uses RESTful Web services to search terms in BioPortal. For example, the *bodyPart* for *Acute Myocardial Infarction* should be a reference to "heart" from SNOMED CT. The search in BioPortal will return a list of matched terms. To decide which SNOMED CT term to import, the user may get more information about each search result either in textual form or as a graph visualization that are also retrieved via Web Service calls to BioPortal. The Reference Portlet is also configurable. We can specify in what ontology the search should be performed. We can also restrict the search to a particular ontology branch in the configuration of the portlet (e.g., Anatomy branch in SNOMED CT).

2.4 Configuring the User Interface

We noted earlier that one of our key goals in designing WebProtégé was to have a tool that can be configured easily for many different settings, workflows, and types of users. Indeed, users can configure almost everything in the WebProtégé portlets, by describing the configuration in an XML file with a a predefined schema[4]. Building a new tool based on WebProtégé can be as simple as defining a layout configuration for existing portlets.

To support this flexibility, each portlet has a property list attached to it in the XML layout file, which we can use to provide additional configuration information. For example, the class tree portlet in Figure 3 displays only the disease hierarchy of the ICD Ontology, with the *ICDCategory* class as the root. We defined one property *topClass* of the portlet that points to the *ICDCategory* class in the configuration file. Thus, we can reuse the class tree portlet to display different class-tree views by simply changing a property of the portlet.

The declarative user interface also allows us to define custom views for different users. In WebProtégé, layout configurations can be defined per user and per project. Therefore, different users can see the same ontology rendered in different ways. One can imagine a scenario in which a user works only on a branch of an ontology, or one in which users should see only a selection of portlets. We can support these scenarios by defining different configuration files for users.

We mentioned earlier that portlets provide independent pieces of functionality. Therefore, we tried to avoid creating hard-coded dependencies between portlets in order to be able to reuse them in different configurations. For example, selecting a class in the class tree portlet should trigger the display of property values in a different portlet. Rather than hard coding this dependency, we defined a generic selection-model mechanism. Each tab has a *controlling portlet*—the portlet that provides the selection for the other portlets in the tab. Each time the selection in the controlling portlet (e.g., the class tree portlet) changes, the other portlets are informed via a listener mechanism about the change and can update their content accordingly. XML layout configuration file specifies the controlling portlet for a tab that can be changed at runtime.

2.5 Support for Collaboration

We implemented the collaboration framework on the server side (Section 2.2) and we expose it in the user interface. Distributed users can edit the same ontology simultaneously and see immediately the results of one another's changes.

[4] XML layout configuration examples available at: `http://tinyurl.com/y35qazg`

Users can add notes to classes, properties, and individuals in the ontology. They can also reply to notes that were posted by others. At the time of this writing, there are more than 1,300 notes in the production version of WebProtégé for ICD. Notes may have different types, such as *Comment* or *Explanation*. When a user browses the class hierarchy, he can see the number of notes that are attached to each class, and the number of notes in the subclasses of that class. In Figure 3, the icon next to the class name indicates, for example, that the class *D04 Carcinoma in situ of skin* has two notes attached to it. The shaded icon next to it indicates that there are also two notes in the subtree rooted at this class. Knowing the number of notes in a subtree, enables users to identify quickly the branches of ontologies that have most activity and discussions, and also to find the notes that are attached somewhere deeper in the class hierarchy. Users can also attach notes to specific triples. For example, a user may want to comment on a particular definition of a disease. The user may do so by clicking on the comment icon next to a particular property value (see Figure 3). The *Notes and Discussions Tab* is a dedicated interface for browsing and creating notes and discussions.

WHO plans to use peer review to ensure the quality of the ICD content. In the current implementation, WebProtégé supports a prototypical implementation of a reviewing mechanism in the *Reviews Tab*. A user with the appropriate priviledges can request a review for a particular disease class. The user may choose from a list of predefined reviewers who are specialized on the particular domain of the disease. Once the review is complete, the reviewer may log into the system and add a review to a class. Internally, we represent Reviews as a specific type of notes in WebProtégé.

The WHO is still working to define the workflow of the ICD-11 revision process. We envision that WebProtégé will support this workflow in a generic and flexible way. Currently, we support only parts of the workflow. WebProtégé already has a generic access-policy mechanism, which we use to define the different user roles (TAG member, managing editor, etc.) and their access rights. The user interface enforces the access rights and we can configure it for different user roles. However, much remains to be done. The main workflow defining how the operations should flow for different user roles is still under development. We currently plan to expose the WebProtégé platform to a larger audience, which will likely have a lower level of expertise than the current users. Members of this broader community should be able to make proposals for changes. We are currently working out the details on how such a proposal mechanism should work. Once we have a well-defined workflow, we will investigate how to develop the tool to support a flexible and generic workflow mechanism.

3 Evaluation

We evaluated the customized WebProtégé tool during *iCamp*—a two-week meeting of the members of the ICD-11 revision project. The meeting took place in September 2009 in Geneva. It brought together editors who will manage the revision process and classification experts. The goal of the iCamp was to discuss the plans for the ICD-11 revision and to gain experience using the WebProtégé software. The objective of the evaluation that we performed during that meeting was two-fold: (1) perform formative evaluation of the WebProtégé software and determine requirements for further development of the tool; and (2) to use WebProtégé and the users' experience with it during the iCamp as the context to evaluate the feasibility of and requirements for collaborative ontology-development process in general. In this paper, we report on the results of the second part of this evaluation—analysis of collaborative ontology development.

3.1 Research Questions for the Evaluation

Our objective for this evaluation was to determine how a collaborative authoring tool can support a diverse community of domain experts in developing a large terminology. Specifically, we wished to address the following research questions:

Q1: Do domain experts find a collaborative development process promising?
Q2: What are the features that users find useful? Which features are required?
Q3: What is the workflow for collaborative ontology-development that a tool must support?
Q4: What coordination and communication mechanisms do the users need?

By answering these questions, we hope to elicit further requirements for tool support for large scale collaborative ontology-development and to understand better the process of collaborative development itself.

3.2 Participants

The participants involved in the tool evaluation consisted of eleven medical professionals that will be working as managing editors for ICD-11 and nine classification experts working to ensure the integrity of the terminology. The domain experts (i.e. managing editors) had varied areas of expertise: rare diseases, dermatology, external causes and injury, and so on. Each managing editor is responsible for the development of the part of ICD-11 in his area of expertise. The revision of ICD-11 is a large international project, thus, English is not the native language for many of the participants.

3.3 Materials and Procedures

Developers of the WebProtégé software introduced the iCamp participants to the customized WebProtégé tool through a series of tool demonstrations and presentations. Then participants worked in pairs over several semi-structured ICD-11 editing sessions. Each of these sessions lasted for two to three hours, and took place over four of the iCamp days. The organizers instructed the pairs to explore the areas of the current ontology that they will be responsible for as managing editors and to begin filling out the different attributes of the content model. However, where users could make changes and the type of changes they could make was not controlled. The organizers encouraged iCamp participants to use social media, such as Twitter and Facebook as well as the collaborative features of WebProtégé. There was also a team shooting daily videos—a few minutes each—that described the activities in the iCamp for that day and included interviews with participants, software developers, and iCamp organizers.[5]

[5] `http://www.youtube.com/user/whoicd11`

Table 1. iCamp survey: Impressions about the collaborative development process

#	Question
1	Do you think the WebProtégé tool is developing into the right tool for authoring ICD-11?
2	Do you have faith that the open process of developing ICD-11 will succeed?
3	What are the two or three most important features you feel need to be incorporated into WebProtégé?
4	Did you find the use of social networking and media tools during iCamp like YouTube, Facebook, Twitter, and Blogger to be useful to the process?
5	Do you have any suggestions about how to evaluate the process of developing ICD-11?

Table 2. Questions to guide the iCamp focus group

#	Question
1	Will the current WebProtégé approach/process work for you in terms of how you want or need to work as a managing editor?
2	Will the current annotation/commenting support fulfill your collaboration needs?
3	Based on what you have been able to produce so far during iCamp, do you feel that you will be able to develop an ICD-11 that is going to address your use cases or is the project moving in the wrong direction?
4	In terms of the review process, how do you see the process working?

Our evaluation consisted of two parts: a **survey** of the participants and a **focus group**. At the last day of the iCamp meeting, participants filled out a Web-based survey. Table 1 shows the survey questions. We also conducted a focus group with the managing editors on the last day of the first week of the iCamp. The focus group was moderated by a researcher and the four questions shown in Table 2 guided the discussion.

3.4 Results

Once the ICD-11 editing sessions were complete, a total of 3,977 changes were made and 392 notes were created. Out of these changes, 244 ICD-11 category terms were involved and 19 of these involved multiple authors. This implies that a substantial amount of activity took place over a relatively short period of time. In the following two subsections, we discuss the specific results from the survey and the focus-group. We use these results to derive findings that help address our research questions (Section 4).

Survey Results

The goal of the survey (Table 1) was to evaluate the participants' impressions of the proposed open process for developing ICD. Eleven participants responded to the survey.

We first asked participants whether the approach taken by WebProtégé was the right one for the development of ICD-11. The responses were primarily positive. Five of the eleven responses were a clear "yes," others were optimistic but had some concerns, e.g., one respondent indicated that the "tool is focused on expert editing, not casual users."

The second question asked whether the participants felt that the open process of developing ICD-11 would succeed. Four out of eleven respondents answered "yes" to this question, while others had some level of concern. In particular, one participant was concerned that an open process will engage users with limited knowledge. Monitoring the contributions of these users will require extra time on behalf of the managing editors. Others were concerned that the editors will be overwhelmed with the feedback that they get or that a lack of ontological expertise among the participants will result in a poor terminology. However, one respondent felt that the "wisdom of the crowd is good."

Following this question, participants were allowed to describe their top three feature requests. Seven participants responded to this question with at least one feature request. The following features were listed by more than one participant: six respondents requested better hierarchy management support, two wanted to view the list of proposals in progress, two requested communication support, and two requested status reports.

We also asked participants about the use of social networking and media tools during iCamp. There was mixed feedback, only a few of the responses were positive. Many participants felt that face-to-face meetings are far more effective, and that the information needs to be centralized rather than spread across multiple social networks. One respondent suggested that the information should be integrated into the WebProtégé tool and one felt that the use of so many media was "media overkill."

Next, we asked for suggestions on how to evaluate the development process of ICD-11. Respondents were keen on eliciting feedback about the development through future face-to-face meetings as well as periodic web-based surveys. One respondent also suggested monitoring participation by editors and the general public.

Focus Group

The focus group consisted of a two-hour semi-structured moderated discussion. The participants felt that WebProtégé was a good initial step, but a lot of work needed to be done in terms of supporting an open collaborative process where anyone can propose a terminology change. Participants indicated that it was unclear to them at that moment what this process should entail in terms of peer review and conflict resolution.

Participants indicated that the current WebProtégé support for commenting was very granular, enabling users to comment on anything in the system. Participants proposed that another, higher-level type of discussion also needed to be supported. Such discussions would not be attached to any specific element in the terminology.

Awareness and tracking of changes to the model was also a key discussion issue. Participants felt that appropriate users need to be notified when certain changes take place. Moreover, participants felt that the WebProtégé model, where changes are immediately committed and visible to everyone, was "too permanent": There was no obvious way to experiment with changes to the terminology without having the changes immediately impact everyone else who was editing or navigating the terminology.

Finally, participants felt that the process of managing proposed changes needed to be defined better and eventually supported by WebProtégé. Participants raised the concerns about privacy for the reviewers of a change. Some participants felt that if a review was not anonymous, then reviewers would be reluctant to be completely honest about a proposal or that it would create more pressure for the reviewers.

4 Findings and Discussion

In this section we return to the research questions that we introduced in Section 3.1. Based on the results from our two evaluation procedures, we attempt to answer these questions in order to address our research objective.

4.1 Q1: Do Domain Experts Find a Collaborative Development Process Promising?

Our survey results indicated that participants had mixed impressions about the collaborative development process. Their central concern about the open process was not only the resources that are required in order to develop the process and software for handling such an ambitious goal, but also the time it would take to manage change proposals by unqualified users of ICD-11. Such a "crowdsourcing" approach has the advantage that potentially many participants will help with the development process and with maintaining the integrity of the terminology, yet it also opens the development to anyone who is interested, regardless of their expertise level.

We can compare the collaborative-development process of a terminology, such as ICD-11, to other "crowdsourcing" projects. We can draw parallels, for example, with open-source software development: the potential number of contributors is probably on a similar scale to the number of contributors to specialized terminologies, since making contributions requires expertise in a specific domain of knowledge (software development in one case, medicine in the other).

In open source software development, the openness of the source code can actually help increase the overall quality of the code. Because everything that a developer produces is freely available to the public, there is both social pressure to make the source code as readable, maintainable, and stable as possible and there are more people available to evaluate the code quality: "given enough eyeballs, all bugs are shallow" [10]. Mockus and colleagues [7] found that both the open source projects Mozilla and Apache had very low defect density levels after release in comparison to commercial software, in part due to the larger community of users contributing to bug reports.

Few code contributions to large open-source projects come from unqualified developers. Instead, highly qualified developers often make up the core set of contributors, as their only incentive is to improve the software for their own use or for the intellectual challenge [6,16]. Finally, since open-source developers often pick and choose what to contribute to, they choose the components that most interest them. This flexibility ensures that the developers are typically engaged in their work, versus a commercial project where they are generally assigned work, regardless of interest [7].

Researchers have observed similar results with the articles contributed to Wikipedia. The online encyclopedia provides a means for those with specialized knowledge to share that information with the rest of the world [1].

However, there is also a significant difference between contributing to open-source software projects or contributing to Wikipedia and contributing to ICD-11. Contributing to source code requires certain level of technical expertise with the tools, if only to compile your contribution. Tools such as WebProtégé are designed to require little or no technical expertise to contribute. Thus, we must develop other mechanisms to control who can contribute content. For instance, we may require that contributors to ICD-11 have accounts that are validated by WHO or its subsidiaries in the respective countries.

At the same time, Wikipedia benefits from an extremely large user community, which helps ensure its quality. Naturally, the number of users who can understand and evaluate the ICD-11 content is far smaller than the number of Wikipedia users. Hence, WHO needs to develop a more structured revision and quality-assurance process.

4.2 Q2: What Are the Features That Users Find Useful? Which Features Are Required?

Among the features that participants felt were critical for a tool to support collaborative terminology development, multi-lingual support was mentioned by several participants both in the survey and during the focus group discussion. In a large, international development effort, this feature is critical. Participants also requested better hierarchical editing support. Although the users found the terminology navigation easy to use, they struggled with making modifications to the actual hierarchy. This is particularly interesting, as WebProtégé uses the same hierarchy navigation and editing paradigm as many other ontology-development tools. The participants struggled with understanding how to rename category entries or moving parts of the hierarchy using the drag-n-drop feature. They also struggled with tracking and revising changes that they made.

In collaborative terminology development, awareness of terminology changes is extremely important. Editors need to be aware of change proposals as well as have support for working together with other editors to incorporate or review proposals. Users need to be able to see an overview of an entire change proposal. Also, users need to know when major changes take place, changes that may influence their use of the terminology.

The software will need to support an audit trail for tracking how a category and its associated attributes change over time. There will need to be visibility about who made certain changes and how a proposal was reviewed. As mentioned, in the WebProtégé version that we used for the evaluation, it was difficult to track your own changes and navigation history, both of which will need to be present to help support the continued development of the terminology.

4.3 Q3: What Is the Workflow for Collaborative Ontology-Development That a Tool Must Support?

The workflow for incorporating change proposals to the terminology was a major concern of the participants in our evaluation. Currently, WebProtégé allows any authorized user to make direct changes to the terminology. However, once the wider community starts contributing to the content, they will be able to do so by creating change proposals. General users will make the proposals for changes, and there will be a series of steps that will be required to review and accept the proposal. For example, managing editors will receive the change-proposal and determine whether it should be reviewed. If review is necessary, the change-proposal will pass through a peer review stage and if approved, the change-proposal will then be reviewed by the Topic Advisory Group.

Any large scale collaborative development process will need tool support for incorporating, tracking, and reviewing changes. The exact process for performing this tracking and how it can be best supported is not yet clear, but it will most likely blend ideas from journal review processes, open source software development, and existing work on conflict resolution in ontology versions [5]. However, our analysis of workflows in several large-scale collaborative ontology-development projects [12,8,13] shows that the workflow for each project is different and involves different steps required by a changed approval. Indeed, there are several efforts to develop a declarative representation of customizable collaborative workflows [2,11].

4.4 Q4:What Coordination and Communication Mechanisms do the Users Need?

Our participants indicated that they needed at least two levels of communication support: low-level commenting on ontology elements and changes (already supported by WebProtégé) and higher-level discussion that could encompass multiple parts of the terminology (supported by the collaboration framework on the Protégé server, but not yet exposed in the user interface). Separate, perhaps private, communication support mechanisms will be necessary for editors working together to review proposals. These comments will possibly involve cross-cutting concerns that include categories within separate branches of the hierarchy or may be of a general nature, for example, comments relating to the review and editing process. The results or verdict of these reviews will also need to be communicated to the public.

Our analysis did not produce a clear picture of what role, if any, common social-networking sites, such as Twitter and Facebook, can play in the social process of terminology development. The participants did not enthusiastically embrace the use of this media in the context of iCamp. However, this may have been in part due to the participants all being co-located, thus, face-to-face communication was most effective. This may also be biased if most of the participants were not already Facebook and/or Twitter users. Unfortunately we do not have statistics about this information.

Again, drawing parallels to open source software (OSS) development, successful projects like Apache and Mozilla rely heavily on somewhat archaic technologies like mailing lists and bugzilla as their main coordination and feedback tools [7]. However, these are older OSS projects. Newer companies like EclipseSource[6], make heavy use of tools like Twitter, blogs, YouTube, and Skype. There is great potential to re-use such tools in collaborative ontology development, but there needs to be buy in from the users as well as integration into the development process. As the ICD-11 project progresses, contributors will be working distributively. At that point, existing social-networking sites may play a larger role.

5 Conclusions

We have presented WebProtégé, a Web-based tool for distributed collaborative development of ontologies. WebProtégé is currently being used by the World Health Organization as the primary development environment for ICD-11, a key international medical

[6] `http://eclipsesource.com/`

terminology. Developers of other terminologies within the WHO Family of International Classifications (WHO-FIC) are beginning to use WebProtégé as well.

The open development of ICD-11 promises to be an exciting experiment in how far collaborative terminology development can go. At the same time, WHO members depend critically on the high quality and timely availability of the 11th revision of the ICD. Hence, the cost of failure is extremely high. However, the ICD experts believe that opening ICD development to a wider international audience is the only way to assure its comprehensive coverage, availability in multiple languages, and correspondence to the latest understanding of clinical practice.

Participants in our evaluation—none of whom are ontology experts or have previously participated in such an open development process—were optimistic that collaborative development will indeed work in this context. They have raised a number of critical issues, including the trade-off of having more experts contribute to the content and requiring more resources to assess the quality of these contributions. They also highlighted critical requirements for tool support such as change tracking, awareness of the state of the change proposals, discussions and notifications mechanisms.

We are currently working on the next version of WebProtégé that will address many of the requirements for the initial state of the development. Simultaneously with the tool development, ICD-11 contributors are already developing and extending content using the current version of the tool. Indeed, in the past month, 12 users have made over 4000 changes and more than 1400 comments.

Acknowledgments

We are very grateful to Jennifer Vendetti, Timothy Redmond and Martin O'Connor for their help with the design and implementation of WebProtégé, and to Robert Jacob, Can Celik, and Sara Cottler for their work in developing the requirements for the project and in organizing and running the iCamp. Samson Tu has been instrumental in designing the ICD Content Model and his help during iCamp was invaluable. The work presented in this paper is supported by the NIGMS Grant 1R01GM086587-01. Protégé is a national resource supported by grant LM007885 from the U.S. National Library of Medicine.

References

1. Baker, N.: The charms of wikipedia. The New York Review of Books 55(4) (2008), http://www.nybooks.com/articles/21131 (retrieved)
2. Gangemi, A., Lehmann, J., Presutti, V., Nissim, M., Catenacci, C.: C-ODO: an owl meta-model for collaborative ontology design. In: Workshop on Social and Collaborative Construction of Structured Knowledge at 16th International World Wide Web Conference (WWW 2007), Banff, Canada (2007)
3. GOConsortium. Creating the Gene Ontology resource: design and implementation. Genome Res. 11(8), 1425–1433 (2001)
4. Hartel, F.W., Coronado, S.d., Dionne, R., Fragoso, G., Golbeck, J.: Modeling a description logic vocabulary for cancer research. Journal of Biomedical Informatics 38(2), 114–129 (2005)

5. Jiménez-Ruiz, E., Grau, B.C., Horrocks, I., Llavori, R.B.: Building ontologies collaboratively using contentcvs. In: Grau, B.C., Horrocks, I., Motik, B., Sattler, U. (eds.) Description Logics. CEUR Workshop Proceedings, vol. 477 (2009), CEUR-WS.org
6. Lakhani, K.R., Wolf, R.G.: Why hackers do what they do: Understanding motivation and effort in free/open source software project. Technical Report Working Paper 4425-03, MIT Sloan School of Management (September 2003)
7. Mockus, A., Fielding, R.T., Herbsleb, J.D.: Two case studies of open source software development: Apache and mozilla. ACM Transactions Software Engineering Methodology 11(3), 309–346 (2002)
8. Muñoz García, O., Gómez-Pérez, A., Iglesias-Sucasas, M., Kim, S.: A Workflow for the Networked Ontologies Lifecycle: A Case Study in FAO of the UN. In: Borrajo, D., Castillo, L., Corchado, J.M. (eds.) CAEPIA 2007. LNCS (LNAI), vol. 4788, pp. 200–209. Springer, Heidelberg (2007)
9. Noy, N.F., Shah, N.H., Whetzel, P.L., Dai, B., Dorf, M., Griffith, N., Jonquet, C., Rubin, D.L., Storey, M.-A., Chute, C.G., Musen, M.A.: Bioportal: ontologies and integrated data resources at the click of a mouse. Nucleic Acids Research (2009), 10.1093/nar/gkp440
10. Raymond, E.S.: The Cathedral & the Bazaar: Musings on Linux and Open Source by an Accidental Revolutionary. O'Reilly Media, Sebastopol (2001)
11. Sebastian, A., Noy, N.F., Tudorache, T., Musen, M.A.: A generic ontology for collaborative ontology-development workflows. In: Gangemi, A., Euzenat, J. (eds.) EKAW 2008. LNCS (LNAI), vol. 5268, pp. 318–328. Springer, Heidelberg (2008)
12. Sioutos, N., de Coronado, S., Haber, M., Hartel, F., Shaiu, W., Wright, L.: NCI Thesaurus: A semantic model integrating cancer-related clinical and molecular information. Journal of Biomedical Informatics 40(1), 30–43 (2007)
13. Tempich, C., Simperl, E., Luczak, M., Studer, R., Pinto, H.S.: Argumentation-based ontology engineering. IEEE Intelligent Systems 22(6), 52–59 (2007)
14. Tu, S.W., et al.: A content model for the ICD-11 revision. Technical Report BMIR-2010-1405, Stanford Center for Biomedical Informatics Research (2010)
15. Tudorache, T., Noy, N.F., Musen, M.A.: Supporting collaborative ontology development in Protégé. In: Sheth, A.P., Staab, S., Dean, M., Paolucci, M., Maynard, D., Finin, T., Thirunarayan, K. (eds.) ISWC 2008. LNCS, vol. 5318, pp. 861–874. Springer, Heidelberg (2008)
16. von Krogh, G., Spaeth, S., Lakhani, K.R.: Community, joining, and specialization in open source software innovation: a case study. Research Policy 32(7), 1217–1241 (2003), Open Source Software Development

RDFauthor: Employing RDFa for Collaborative Knowledge Engineering

Sebastian Tramp, Norman Heino, Sören Auer, and Philipp Frischmuth

Universität Leipzig, Institut für Informatik, AKSW,
Postfach 100920, D-04009 Leipzig, Germany
lastname@informatik.uni-leipzig.de
http://aksw.org

Abstract. In this paper we present RDFauthor, an approach for authoring information that adheres to the RDF data model. RDFauthor completely hides syntax as well as RDF and ontology data model difficulties from end users and allows to edit information on arbitrary RDFa-annotated web pages. RDFauthor extends RDFa with representations for provenance and update endpoint information. RDFauthor is based on extracting RDF triples from RDFa annotations and transforming the RDFa-annotated HTML view into an editable form by using a set of authoring widgets. As a result, every RDFa-annotated web page can be made easily writeable, even if information originates from different sources.

1 Introduction

To a large extent the overwhelming success of the World Wide Web was based on the ability of ordinary users to author content easily. In order to publish content on the WWW, users had to do little more than to annotate text files with few, easy-to-learn HTML tags. Unfortunately, on the semantic data web the situation is slightly more complicated. Users do not only have to learn a new syntax (such as N3, RDF/XML or RDFa), but also have to get acquainted with the RDF data model, ontology languages (such as RDF-S, OWL) and a growing collection of connected RDF vocabularies for different use cases (such as FOAF, SKOS and SIOC).

Previously, many approaches were developed to ease the syntax side of semantic authoring [11,2]. In this paper we present an approach, which also hides the data model from ordinary users and thus allows absolute novices to create semantic representations easily.

The *RDFauthor* approach is based on the idea of making arbitrary XHTML views with integrated RDFa annotations editable. *RDFa* [1] is the W3C Recommendation, which allows to combine human and machine-readable representations within a single XHTML document. RDFauthor builds on RDFa by preserving provenance information in RDFa representations following the named-graph paradigm and by establishing a mapping from RDFa view representations to authoring widgets. On configurable events (such as the clicking of a button

P. Cimiano and H.S. Pinto (Eds.): EKAW 2010, LNAI 6317, pp. 90–104, 2010.

or moving over a certain information fragment with the mouse) the widgets will be activated and allow the editing of all RDFa-annotated information on the Web page. While editing, the widgets can access background information sources on the Data Web in order to facilitate the reuse of identifiers or to encourage the interlinking of resources. Our resource editing widget, for example, suggests suitable, previously defined resources derived from calls to the Sindice Semantic Web index [12]. Once editing is completed, the changes are propagated to the underlying triple stores by means of the SPARQL/Update language.

RDFauthor is not at all limited to editing semantic representations from a single source. An RDFa view made editable with RDFauthor can contain statements from a variety of sources, which can be edited simultaneously and in a wholly transparent manner for the user. Based on an extended RDFa markup supporting named graphs and SPARQL/Update endpoint information, simultaneous changes of several graphs from different sources will be dispatched to the respective SPARQL/Update endpoints. RDFauthor is implemented in JavaScript so that it works entirely on the browser side and can be used together with arbitrary Web application development techniques.

In particular with this paper, we make the following contributions:

- We define a light-weight extension of RDFa to accommodate named graphs and an RDF vocabulary to provide metadata on these graphs, such as provenance information.
- We develop the RDFauthor library, which can be used to make arbitrary RDFa representations editable. We provide a number of widgets for authoring common datatypes and define a mechanism for plugging in and automatically configuring additional editing widgets.
- We demonstrate the benefits of RDFauthor in three use cases: semantic authoring in OntoWiki, editing information from multiple sources in a combined vCard/publications view as well as collecting semantic data from any RDFa-enhanced page and pushing it to a personal RDF store.

As a result, RDFauthor radically simplifies the authoring of semantic information. Users can interact with Semantic Web applications without having to learn a new syntax or even having to get acquainted with the RDF data model or other knowledge representation formalisms. This advantage adds easy write support to Semantic Web applications, which can help them to enlarge their user bases significantly and to achieve generally a higher penetration of Semantic Web technologies.

The paper is structured as follows: We describe the requirements which guided the development of RDFauthor in section 2. We present our RDFa extension for representing named graphs and provenance in section 3. A description of our approach regarding architecture and implementation is given in section 4, while the approach is demonstrated on the basis of three use cases in section 5. Finally, we survey some related work in section 6 and conclude with an outlook on future work in section 7.

2 Requirements

In this section, we gather and describe the most important requirements, which guided the development of RDFauthor.

The idea behind the development of RDFauthor was to provide a general framework to edit data chunks (triple or multiple triples) in XHTML pages by means of small authoring components called editing widgets (or, as in the present paper, just widgets). The framework, which should be usable with arbitrary Web applications, has to provide edit functionality on top of RDFa-annotated web pages with only minor modifications of the existing markup, i. e. there should be no need to create special edit views. This mode will reduce the effort required for the development and maintenance of (Semantic) Web applications significantly. Judging from our experience with developing web application that focus on collaboration and interaction, we can assume that probably more than 50 % of the effort regarding the user interface creation is spent on implementing and maintaining edit functionality.

To allow mashing-up content from different sources, the framework should preserve the provenance of all content chunks, even if combined on a single resulting XHTML page. This possibility allows to hide even more complexity from the user, since she does not have to care about where to edit certain information or about switching between different editing views. To achieve this goal, we have to provide a vocabulary in order to connect RDFa fragments with updatable SPARQL/Update endpoints. RDFauthor should provide functionality not only to edit existing information, but also to create new data. The framework should also allow to distinguish between writeable and non-writeable information sources. In this way authentication and access control is easily combinable with RDFauthor, without increasing the complexity of the implementation for Web developers.

Moreover, in order to make the general editing framework as flexible as possible, the goal was to provide a number of authoring widgets for specific content types, such as resource references, dates, locations, images/files etc. The Web developer/designer should not be limited in her possibilities to create Web designs. RDFauthor should be as unobtrusive as possible and provide flexible editing widgets (or allow different configurations, e. g. via CSS definitions) for different use cases, such as inline editing, popup/overlay editing etc. RDFauthor should also retrieve background information (such as schema/vocabulary information with domain/range restrictions) required for the selection of appropriate widgets. Furthermore, it should facilitate the interlinking of information on the basis of the Linked Data paradigm and incorporate services, such as Sindice, DBpedia and Geonames, for establishing links.

3 Named Graphs and Provenance in RDFa

RDFa enables the annotation of information encoded in XHTML with RDF. This ability allows to extract a set of RDF triples from an RDFa-annotated XHTML page. RDFauthor makes these triples editable, but in order to store changes persistently in the triple store that was used to create the RDFa annotations, RDFauthor needs information about the data source (i. e. SPARQL and SPARQL/Update endpoint) regarding the named RDF graph from which the triples were obtained or where they have to be updated. In order to make this information available, we have defined a slight extension of the RDFa annotations.

To represent information about the information source, we follow the named graphs approach [4]. We created a vocabulary[1] to represent attributes and relations for the following purposes:

- In order to link certain RDFa annotations on the page to the respective querying/update services, namely SPARQL/Update and SPARQL endpoints, we propose the use of the `link` HTML tag with an `about`-attribute to identify the named graph, a `rel`-attribute with the value `update:updateEndpoint` and a `href`-attribute with the URL of the respective SPARQL/Update endpoint. Another option to declare graph metadata is the use of empty `span`- or `div`-elements together with the RDFa attributes inside the body of the page. This option is particularly useful, if the program, which generates the RDFa-enhanced HTML code from the RDF store, does not have access to the `head` of the page (which is typically true for small content plugins in CMS or CMS-like applications).
- For declaring which statements belong to which named graph, we propose the use of the `update:from`-attribute with the named graph as attribute value to which all nested RDFa annotations should belong. The `update:from`-attribute and the additional RDFa processing rules are inspired by [7]. The use of named graphs is optional and only required, if triples from multiple sources should be made editable.

The next listing is an example of an RDFa-enhanced XHTML snippet from the vCard and publications mashup (which we describe as a use case for RDFauthor more profoundly in section 5). All RDFa attributes as well as our update vocabulary extensions are highlighted.

```
<head xmlns:foaf="http://xmlns.com/foaf/0.1/"
  xmlns:update="http://ns.aksw.org/update/"
  xmlns:dc="http://purl.org/dc/elements/1.1/">[...]
</head>
<div update:from="http://showcase.ontowiki.net/"
     about="http://sebastian.dietzold.de/terms/me" typeof="foaf:Person">
  <img rel="foaf:depiction" src="http://aksw.org/img/..." />
  <b property="foaf:name">Sebastian Dietzold</b>
  <a rel="foaf:phone" href="tel:+49-341-9732366">tel:+49 341 9732366</a>
</div>
<div about="http://showcase.ontowiki.net/"
  rel="update:updateEndpoint" resource="http://trunk.ontowiki.net/sparul/" />
<div about="http://showcase.ontowiki.net/"
  rel="update:queryEndpoint" resource="http://trunk.ontowiki.net/sparql/" />
<div update:from="http://publications.aksw.org/">
```

[1] The RDFauthor vocabulary namespace is `http://ns.aksw.org/update/`. We use the prefix `update` for this namespace throughout this paper.

```
16 <p about="http://www2009.eprints.org/63/1/p621.pdf" typeof="foaf:Document">
17   <img rel="foaf:depiction" src="...">
18   <span rel="foaf:maker" resource="http://sebastian.dietzold.de/terms/me" />
19   <span property="dc:description">...</span>
20 </p>
21 </div>
```

After declaring all required namespaces in the page `head` (lines 1-4), two `div`-sections (starting in lines 5 and 15) contain RDFa annotations derived from two different named graphs. The graph URIs are specified by using the `update:from`-attribute. All nested RDFa annotations are parsed into RDF triples which belong to the given named graphs. The first graph contained in lines 4-10 consists of a vCard description of a `foaf:Person` and the second graph in lines 15-21 consists of information about a `foaf:Document` resource which is connected to the person using the `foaf:maker` relation. In addition to the FOAF vocabulary, properties from Dublin core and LDAP are used.

In order to annotate the named graph resources with the service locations, two more `div`-sections per graph are included (lines 11-14 associate one graph with two different endpoints for updates and queries). Here we use our `update`-vocabulary to link the SPARQL/update service (in this case an OntoWiki instance).

The XHTML listing above represents the simplified source code of the example screenshot from the mashup in figure 5. The XHTML page is parsed by the RDFauthor RDFa+named-graph parser into the triples (represented in N3 notation) shown in the following listing[2]:

```
<http://showcase.ontowiki.net/>
 update:updateEndpoint <http://trunk.ontowiki.net/sparul/>;
 update:queryEndpoint <http://trunk.ontowiki.net/sparql/>.

<http://showcase.ontowiki.net/> = {
 <http://sebastian.dietzold.de/terms/me> a foaf:Person;
  foaf:depiction <http://aksw.org/img/...>;
  foaf:name "Sebastian Dietzold";
  foaf:phone <tel:+49-341-97-32366>;
  #[...]
}.

<http://publications.aksw.org/> = {
 <http://www2009.eprints.org/63/1/p621.pdf> a foaf:Document;
  dc:description "Soren Auer, Sebastian Dietzold, [...]";
  foaf:maker <http://showcase.ontowiki.net/SoerenAuer>,
     <http://sebastian.dietzold.de/terms/me> .
}.
```

The extracted model consists of two named graphs and additional statements in the default graph. For both of these named graphs, update and query information is available. The RDFauthor widget library treats all statements from graphs without update information as read-only statements.

4 System Architecture and Implementation

In this section we describe the architecture and implementation of RDFauthor in more detail. The basic cycle of how web pages are edited with RDFauthor is

[2] For reasons of limited space, we omit the first lines with prefix definitions for `foaf`, `dc`, `update` and `ldap`.

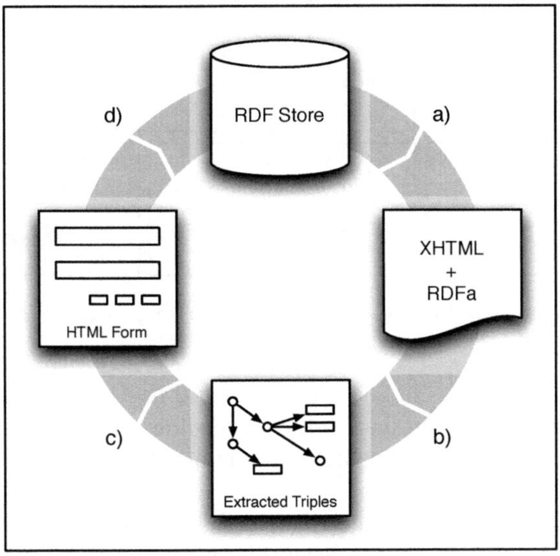

Fig. 1. Editing cycle for an RDFa-enhanced web page. The processes involved are a) page creation and delivery, b) client-side page processing, c) form creation and d) update propagation.

depicted in figure 1. It is composed of four distinct processes, three of which (b–d) are handled by RDFauthor components and are described in the subsequent sections.

Initiation of these processes can happen through a number of different trigger events. These events can be grouped into element-based events or page-wide events. In particular, the following triggers are supported:

- Clicking on an edit button next to an element containing the object of a statement,
- moving the pointer and hovering above an object element,
- an application-specified custom trigger similar to the button labelled "Edit Properties" in OntoWiki (see section 5),
- a bookmarklet which loads all RDFauthor components and runs all widgets at once,
- the universal edit button[3].

4.1 Client-Side Page Processing

Upon user interaction or a programmatic trigger, RDFauthor starts processing the current page by extracting all RDF triples and placing them in an *rdfQuery databank*[4] (cf. section 4.5); one for each named graph. Triples that

[3] `http://universaleditbutton.org`

[4] `http://code.google.com/p/rdfquery/wiki/RdfPlugin#Creating_a_Databank_by_Hand`

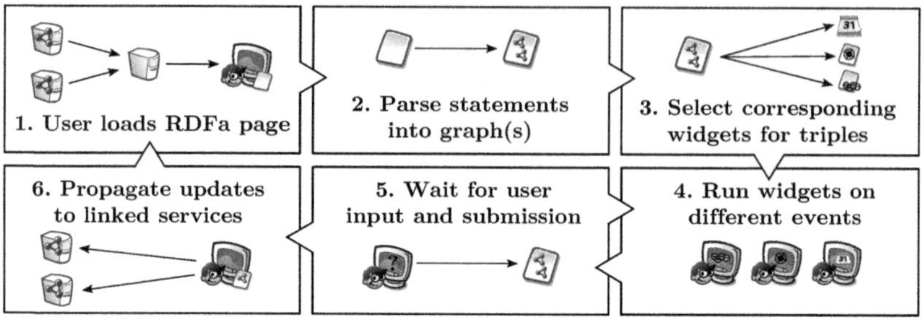

Fig. 2. Steps involved in the client-side processing of the page to be edited

describe the named graphs in the page by using the update vocabulary are excluded from editing. If no update information has been defined for a graph, it is considered non-editable, hence no form elements are created for the triples it contains.

Figure 2 depicts the default page processing procedure. Initially, the user loads an RDFa-annotated web page into her browser (1). She then triggers the parsing process by one of the possible edit triggers the developer of the page has decided to make available on his page (2). RDFa parsing and widget selection are performed lazily on the first of these events. For each statement on the page the corresponding widget is selected by an algorithm described in more detail in section 4.2 (3). An edit view is presented to the user in one of the ways described above. In which way it is shown is controllable by the author of the page (4). The user completes her editing tasks and submits her changes or cancels the whole process (5). In case of submission, the changes are propagated back to the services linked to each graph (6). In section 4.3 we describe this process in more depth.

4.2 Widget Selection and Form Creation

Widgets for editing existing statements are selected by exploiting the object's datatype and the property from the encoded RDFa model. If no datatype is present (plain literal or object property), a deployed selection cache of pre-calculated decisions is used.

For this cache, we analyzed 19 of the most frequently used namespaces listed by the *Ping the Semantic Web* service[5]. Together, these vocabularies describe 124 datatype properties and 176 object properties. For these 300 properties, we populated the widget selection cache with information on type and datatype of the properties used. This cache is made available as a JSON file. Most of the datatype properties requested a standard literal widget. Only 17 datatype properties had an integer range (float 8, date/time 4, boolean 2).

If the named graph from which the statement originates is linked to a SPARQL endpoint and neither the RDFa model nor our cache can provide useful hints as to which widget to use, RDFauthor tries to retrieve this information from

[5] `http://www.pingthesemanticweb.com/`

the SPARQL endpoint by querying the `rdf:type` and `rdfs:range` of the property.

The selected widgets are combined into an edit view and are displayed to the user. Depending on the type of trigger, this can be done in one of the following ways:

- A single-statement overlay,
- a single-statement widget injected into the page or
- a bulk overlay containing widgets for all editable statements.

4.3 Update Propagation

When the user finishes the editing process, all widgets involved are asked to update the respective named graph with their changes. The difference between the original and modified graphs are calculated (i. e. added statements, removed statements), yielding a diff graph. The associated store to each graph is then updated with the respective diff graph by means of SPARQL/Update [9] operations. By explicitly listing all inserted or deleted triples using `INSERT DATA` and `DELETE DATA` syntax, sophisticated SPARQL/Update support is not required. In addition, RDFauthor can cope with several access control scenarios. It, therefore, evaluates the server's response to SPARQL/Update requests. For instance, in the case of an HTTP 401 (unauthorized) or 403 (forbidden) status code, a login form is displayed.

4.4 Statement Adding Methods

In addition to modifying the triple content of a page, it is possible to add new statements. This can happen either based on existing triples used as templates or by adding entirely new statements. If existing triples are used as templates, three cases can be distinguished:

- Creating a new statement that shares subject and property with an existing statement. Our approach supports this case via a small button beside each statement.
- Creating a new statement that shares the subject with an existing statement. At the end of a subject description a small button is shown which lets the user add a new statement to the subject's description.
- Creating a new resource using an existing resource as a template. Widgets for all properties found on the template resource are available on the new resource.

4.5 Architectural Overview

Putting the processes described above into perspective, three components can be identified that are involved in the cycle depicted in figure 1.

- An XHTML page annotated with RDFa and a named graph extension as described in the previous section,
- for each named graph that is intended to be writable: a SPARQL/Update endpoint to which updates are sent and an optional SPARQL endpoint to gather additional information (see below),
- the RDFauthor API with a set of editing components (called widgets) and included libraries.

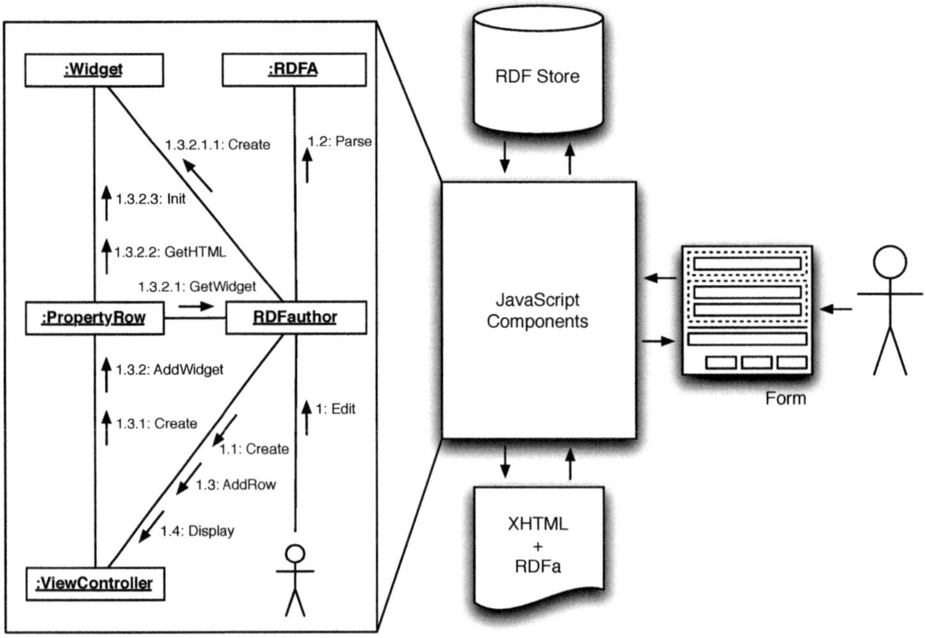

Fig. 3. RDFauthor architecture overview and UML communication sequence

In-page triple storage (databanks) and RDFa parsing are included from external projects. The JavaScript API has, thus, three components:

- RDFauthor JavaScript objects,
- an in-page RDF store based on the rdfQuery jQuery plug-in, developed by Jeni Tennison[6],
- an RDFa parser component obtained from the W3C RDFa JavaScript implementation page[7] (modified according to [7] in order to allow for parsing named graph attributes).

Our own contribution to this stack, namely the RDFauthor JavaScript objects, is a collection of scripts that allow the creation of an edit view and included

[6] `http://code.google.com/p/rdfquery/`
[7] `http://www.w3.org/2006/07/SWD/RDFa/impl/js/`

widgets. These widgets can be either included into the existing page or displayed as an overlay. The overlay approach provides sleek editing capabilities for even the most complex XHTML+RDFa markup, while the inline option can be used to integrate authoring functionalities seamlessly into existing pages.

5 Use Cases and Evaluation

In order to demonstrate the benefits of RDFauthor, we integrated the approach into two Semantic Web applications. Firstly, RDFauthor became the primary semantic authoring component in our Semantic Wiki OntoWiki. Secondly, we integrated RDFauthor into a text-based wiki application called WackoWiki, thus being able to demonstrate the simultaneous authoring of information from multiple sources. Finally, we describe a usage scenario facilitating the collection of RDF data from arbitrary RDFa-annotated websites.

5.1 OntoWiki

OntoWiki [2][8] is a tool for browsing and collaboratively editing RDF knowledge bases. It differs from other Semantic Wikis insofar as OntoWiki uses RDF as its natural data model instead of Wiki texts. Information in OntoWiki is always represented according to the RDF statement paradigm and can be browsed and edited by means of views, which are generated automatically by employing the ontology features, such as class hierarchies or domain and range restrictions. OntoWiki adheres to the Wiki principles by striving to make the editing of information as simple as possible and by maintaining a comprehensive revision history. It has recently been extended to incorporate a number of Linked Data features, such as exposing all information stored in OntoWiki as Linked Data as well as retrieving background information from the Linked Data Web. Apart from providing a comprehensive user interface, OntoWiki also contains a number of components for the rapid development of Semantic Web applications, such as the RDF API Erfurt, methods for authentication, access control, caching and various visualization components.

RDFauthor is used in OntoWiki both in the generic resource property view as well as in extensions which render resources in a domain-specific way (e. g. specific visualizations for SKOS concepts or FOAF persons). In order to perform the integration, we have extended OntoWiki in two ways:

1. We extended the default properties view for resources and all other views with RDFa attributes to annotate which data is presented as well as to link the graph to the internal update service. Since OntoWiki is entirely based on an RDF store, this extension was easy to implement. Likewise, all extension developers had to extend their views, e. g. for SKOS concepts.
2. We included RDFauthor by referencing it in the head of every OntoWiki page and adding JavaScript edit buttons on every page where data should be editable.

[8] Online at: `http://ontowiki.net`

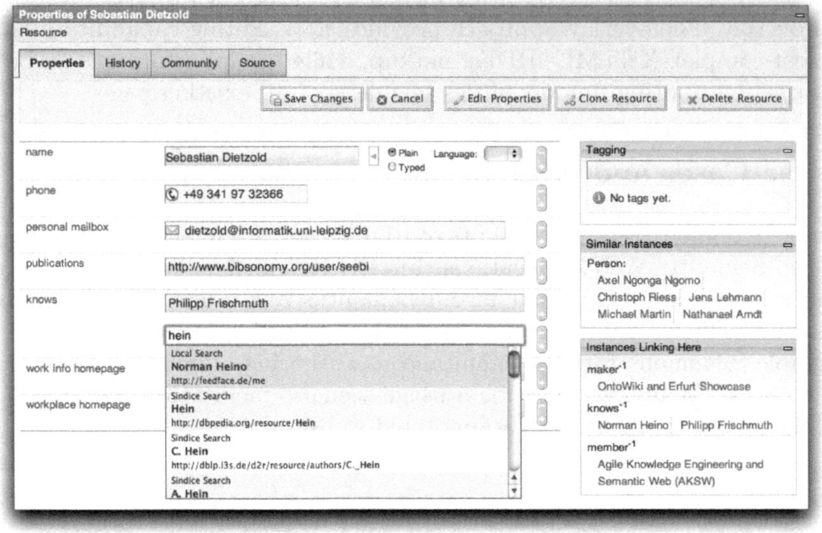

Fig. 4. OntoWiki with RDFauthor widgets in “inline mode”

The integration of RDFauthor into OntoWiki is displayed in figure 4. For all information displayed at the user interface, OntoWiki generates RDFa views which can be edited by using RDFauthor with a simple click on an edit button. In order to reuse previously defined resources as much as possible, we included a resource selector which searches for existing resources as the user is typing. A search for “Ber” would (amongst others) yield the DBpedia resource for Berlin[9].

Adding new properties to an existing resource is accomplished in two steps. First, the user chooses a property which she wants to use. She types a name or description fragment into the search input field of the property widget and RDFauthor searches for properties in the referenced SPARQL endpoint of the given named graph. Subsequently, the corresponding widget is selected from the library as described in section 4.2.

As a result of the RDFauthor integration, OntoWiki is now able to handle not only different visualizations for specific content, but it can also use these views as a base for independent editing widgets, thereby achieving a new level of content versatility.

5.2 vCard and Publication Mashup

In order to showcase the simultaneous authoring of information from multiple sources, we integrated RDFauthor into the text-based wiki application WackoWiki[10]. WackoWiki is often used in small and medium companies as well as in small organizations such as research groups.

[9] `http://dbpedia.org/resource/Berlin`

[10] `http://wackowiki.org`

The AKSW research group uses WackoWiki for its entire web page (`http://aksw.org`) and integrates external data sources by means of so-called WackoWiki actions. Actions are small scripts which prepare some content and output it at the given position in the wiki page. Actions are also able to fetch data from external resources, allowing us to use structured information on different places in the wiki, e. g. by presenting the last publications selected by author, project or topic.

Fig. 5. RDFa-enhanced FOAF vCard and publications mashup with statements from different named graphs. In addition to the plain literal and resource widgets, we developed widgets for the special URI schemes `tel:` and `mailto:`, which hide the URI syntax behind a plain input field.

While integrating and presenting this information is easy and covered by many applications and techniques, the read/write integration of such external resources is tackled by RDFauthor. By employing RDFauthor, users of our wiki are able to edit both the wiki page and the structured information in one place and avoid using different web applications for one edit task and with different data.

We have developed two actions for integrating two different resources: public vCard information and a publication database. Both sources are available as RDF data and accessible via SPARQL endpoints. The output of these actions included in the author's wiki page is displayed on figure 5.

The displayed page is a mashup of three sources: static wiki content, vCard RDF data and RDF data about publications using the FOAF vocabulary. The output describes two named RDF graphs with RDFa attributes as introduced in section 3. Both graphs are annotated with corresponding SPARQL/Update services. This annotation allows RDFauthor to pass the changes back to the databases from which they originate.

In doing so, a user who wants to edit her contact details (e. g. because she moved to another office room) can change this information directly where she notes the old and obsolete information.

5.3 Data Collection from RDFa Websites

Another interesting usage scenario, which is more concerned with collecting data instead of editing, is described in this section. Most of the RDFa-enabled pages on the web do not yet contain provenance and update information. However, RDFauthor also allows to use an arbitrary update endpoint, which does not necessarily have to match the originating endpoint.

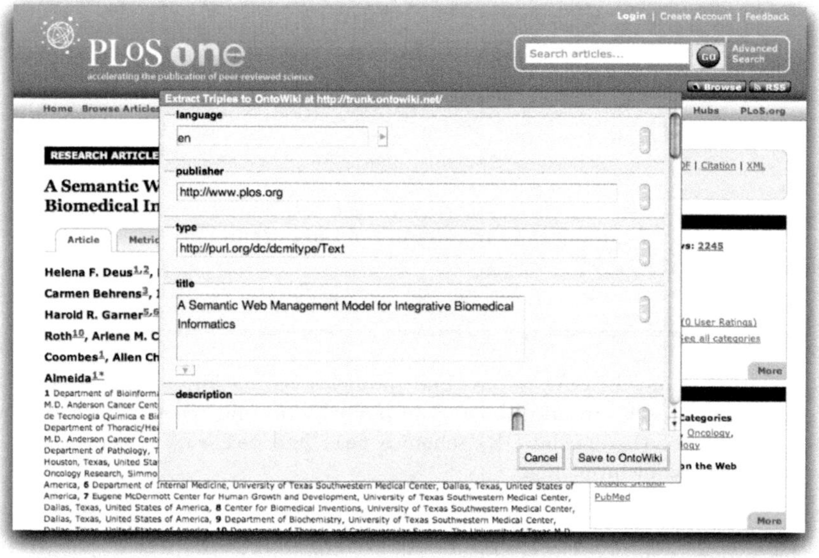

Fig. 6. An RDFauthor overlay view containing widgets for triples extracted from PLoS web page underneath

Since a SPARQL/Update-capable RDF store and a target graph is all the information required for using RDFauthor, it is easy to embed these into a bookmarklet used to initialize the editing process. In this case, the number of possible SPARQL/Update endpoints is limited to those under one's control. RDFauthor extracts the data from any page visited and displays the edit form. The data can be revised and unwanted statements can be removed from the view. Saving works, however, differently: instead of propagating the changed data back to the original source, it is sent to one's own RDF store and saved into the previously set-up graph.

6 Related Work

The problem of making Semantic Web content writable in an easy-to-use manner has been recognized by a number of authors. Pushback [6], for example, tackles this problem by providing a vocabulary and methodology for bi-directionally mapping Web 2.0 data sources and APIs to RDF. Since it relies on predefined vocabulary transformations from said sources into an RDF vocabulary describing edit forms (RDForms), its use is limited to cases where such a mapping already exists.

Earlier in [5] we presented a JavaScript API that allows the independent creation of editing widgets for embedded RDFa. The ideas in this paper build upon the concepts discussed there. [10] present a document-style editing model over RDF data, which, like RDFauthor, is based on commonly available HTML manipulation tools and rdfQuery, a JavaScript RDFa library, to maintain an RDF model embedded in the page. We use part of this work (the rdfQuery library) in our client-side JavaScript stack. Likewise, Tabulator [3] allows modification and addition of information naturally within the browsing interface and allows to relay changes to the server. However, due to Tabulator's nature of being a generic data browser, little effort is made to cater users unfamiliar with the RDF data model.

Loomp [8] aims at providing a user interface for both creating textual content as well as annotating this content by using semantic representations. However, the focus of Loomp is not on authoring RDF content in the first place, but only as annotations of texts.

7 Conclusion and Future Work

We presented RDFauthor, a pragmatic and light-weight approach to make arbitrary RDFa views editable. RDFauthor does not only simplify the syntactic editing of semantic representations, but it also allows to hide the RDF and related ontology data models from novice users completely. Thus, RDFauthor contributes to enabling more users to employ and interact with Semantic Web applications successfully. Since RDFauthor converts an RDFa-annotated view directly into an editable form, which is an additional benefit, the costs for the development and maintenance of (Semantic) Web applications can be significantly lowered.

Regarding future work, we aim at integrating RDFauthor into more (Semantic) Web applications and at establishing a repository of forms and widgets for common vocabularies and datatypes. Based on such a comprehensive repository of common vocabulary renderings, RDFauthor could evolve into a participatory semantic mashup technology.

References

1. Adida, B., Birbeck, M., McCarron, S., Pemberton, S.: RDFa in XHTML: Syntax and Processing. Recommendation, World Wide Web Consortium, W3C (October 2008), `http://www.w3.org/TR/rdfa-syntax/`

2. Auer, S., Dietzold, S., Riechert, T.: OntoWiki – A Tool for Social, Semantic Collaboration. In: Cruz, I., Decker, S., Allemang, D., Preist, C., Schwabe, D., Mika, P., Uschold, M., Aroyo, L.M. (eds.) ISWC 2006. LNCS, vol. 4273, pp. 736–749. Springer, Heidelberg (2006)
3. Berners-Lee, T., Hollenbach, J., Lu, K., Presbrey, J., Pru d'ommeaux, E., Schraefel, M.C.: Tabulator Redux: Writing Into the Semantic Web. Technical report, Electronics and Computer Science, University of Southampton (2007)
4. Carroll, J.J., Bizer, C., Hayes, P., Stickler, P.: Named graphs, provenance and trust. In: WWW 2005. ACM, New York (2005)
5. Dietzold, S., Hellmann, S., Peklo, M.: Using JavaScript RDFa Widgets for Model/View Separation inside Read/Write Websites. In: SFSW 2008, CEUR, vol. 368 (2008)
6. Hausenblas, M., et al.: Pushback – Write Data Back From RDF to Non-RDF Sources. ESW wiki (2009), `http://esw.w3.org/topic/PushBackDataToLegacySources`
7. Inkster, T., Kjernsmo, K.: Named Graphs in RDFa (RDFa Quads) (January 2009), `http://buzzword.org.uk/2009/rdfa4/spec`
8. Luczak-Roesch, M., Heese, R.: Linked Data Autoring for non-Experts. In: Workshop on Linked Data on the Web, Madrid (2009)
9. Seaborne, A., Manjunath, G.: SPARQL/Update: A language for updating RDF graphs. Technical Report Version 5: 2008-04-29, Hewlett-Packard (2008), `http://jena.hpl.hp.com/~afs/SPARQL-Update.html`
10. Styles, R., Shabir, N., Tennison, J.: A Pattern for Domain Specific Editing Interfaces Using Embedded RDFa and HTML Manipulation Tools. In: SFSW 2009, CEUR, vol. 449 (2009)
11. Tudorache, T., Noy, N.F., Tu, S., Musen, M.A.: Supporting Collaborative Ontology Development in Protégé. In: Sheth, A.P., Staab, S., Dean, M., Paolucci, M., Maynard, D., Finin, T., Thirunarayan, K. (eds.) ISWC 2008. LNCS, vol. 5318, pp. 17–32. Springer, Heidelberg (2008)
12. Tummarello, G., Delbru, R., Oren, E.: Sindice.com: Weaving the Open Linked Data. In: Aberer, K., Choi, K.-S., Noy, N., Allemang, D., Lee, K.-I., Nixon, L.J.B., Golbeck, J., Mika, P., Maynard, D., Mizoguchi, R., Schreiber, G., Cudré-Mauroux, P. (eds.) ASWC 2007 and ISWC 2007. LNCS, vol. 4825, pp. 552–565. Springer, Heidelberg (2007)

Pattern-Based Ontology Transformation Service Exploiting OPPL and OWL-API

Ondřej Šváb-Zamazal[1], Vojtěch Svátek[1], and Luigi Iannone[2]

[1]University of Economics, Prague
{ondrej.zamazal,svatek}@vse.cz
[2]School of Computer Science, University of Manchester, United Kingdom
iannone@cs.man.ac.uk

Abstract. Exploitation of OWL ontologies is often difficult due to their modelling style even if the underlying conceptualisation is adequate. We developed a generic framework and collection of services that allow to define and execute ontology transformation (in particular) with respect to modelling style. The definition of transformation is guided by transformation patterns spanning between mutually corresponding patterns in the source and target ontology, the detection of an instance of one leading to construction of an instance of the other. The execution of axiom-level transformations relies on the functionality of the OPPL processor, while entity-level transformations, including sophisticated handling of naming and treatment of annotations, are carried out directly through the OWL API. A scenario of applying the transformation in the specific context of ontology matching is also presented.

1 Introduction

The OWL ontology language, now in its more advanced version, OWL 2,[1] is a de facto standard for designing semantic web ontologies. However, with its relatively high expressivity, it often allows to express the same conceptualisation in different ways. This is an obstacle to using existing ontologies in more advanced semantic web scenarios, in particular:

- Two ontologies using different styles are difficult to *match* or to *import* to one another. Few matching systems support complex matching structures that bridge such heterogeneity, never mind considering schema merging and/or data migration.
- Opting for a style when designing an ontology may have dramatic impact on the usability and performance of *reasoners*, as some features cause performance problems for certain reasoners (for a specific reasoner, this has been investigated e.g. in [9]).

As a simple example of style heterogeneity let's consider the following:

[1] `http://www.w3.org/TR/2009/REC-owl2-overview-20091027/`

P. Cimiano and H.S. Pinto (Eds.): EKAW 2010, LNAI 6317, pp. 105–119, 2010.

Example 1. (In Manchester syntax[2]) In one 'conference' ontology,[3] the possibility of accepting or rejecting a paper can be expressed via *classes*:

PaperAcceptanceAct SubClassOf: ReviewerAct.
PaperRejectionAct SubClassOf: ReviewerAct.

In another ontology it can be captured using *object properties*:

accepts Domain: Reviewer. accepts Range: Paper.
rejects Domain: Reviewer. rejects Range: Paper.

A third possibility is the use of *enumerations*:

reviewerDecision Domain: Paper.
reviewerDecision Range: (EquivalentTo {acceptance, rejection}).

Obviously, such modelling choices can be captured using *ontology design patterns* [5], especially the language-specific and domain-neutral ones that are usually called 'logical patterns'. However, while common catalogues of ontology (design) patterns [1,2] aim at supplying human designers with best practices, for our purposes we do not distinguish whether the particular occurrence of a pattern in an ontology is an informed modelling choice (possibly based on one of these catalogues) or an unintentional one.

A transformation of an ontology fragment from one modelling style to another has to consider two (occurrences of) patterns: one in the *source* ontology and one in the *target* ontology. The two patterns plus the link between them can then be viewed as a *transformation pattern*. Therefore the first step in our workflow is the *detection* of pattern occurrence in the source ontology; it is followed by generation of *transformation instructions*, and, finally, the actual *transformation*, which is largely based on the OPPL pre-processor [4].

Section 2 briefly surveys OPPL as crucial pre-existing component of the whole approach. Section 3 then describes the workflow of ontology transformation and the RESTful services that implement it. Transformation patterns are presented in Section 4 in terms of general shape of patterns (Section 4.1), inclusion of naming patterns (Section 4.2), entity/axiom transformation operations generated (Section 4.3), and the execution of these operations using OPPL and OWL-API (Section 4.4). Finally, Section 5 illustrates the approach on an example within the ontology matching field. The paper is wrapped up with a brief survey of related work, and a Conclusions and Future Work section.

2 Overview of OPPL 2

OPPL [7] is a macro language, based on Manchester OWL syntax, for manipulating ontologies written in OWL. OPPL was introduced in [4] and applied in [3].

---

[2] `http://www.w3.org/TR/2009/NOTE-owl2-manchester-syntax-20091027/`

[3] A collection of such ontologies has been used in the OAEI ontology matching contest, see `http://nb.vse.cz/~svabo/oaei2009/`. We also refer to it in Section 5.

Its initial purpose was to provide a declarative language to enrich lean ontologies with automatically produced axioms. Its new version,[4] OPPL 2, differs from the previous one by allowing multiple variables in one script, and by aligning the OPPL syntax to the right level of abstraction.

A generic OPPL 2 script currently consists of three main sections, for variable declarations, queries and actions. *Variables* have types that determine the kind of entity each one may represent, i.e. named classes, data properties, object properties, individuals, or constants. A *query* is a set of axioms containing variables, plus an optional set of further constraints on such variables. An *action* may define the addition or removal of a single axiom containing variables.

In a nutshell, running a script consists of developing it into a set of variable-free changes to be applied to an ontology. This can summarised in the following steps: resolving the query, and instantiating the actions. *Resolving a query* means identify those values (OWL objects), which will make all the axioms and constraints in the query hold once they replace a given variable. The result of a query then is a set of bindings (variable assignments) that satisfy the query. Each axiom in the query could be evaluated against the *asserted model* only, or using a *reasoner*. OPPL 2 engines always try to use the current reasoner by default. If the OPPL 2 engine has not been initialised with any reasoner, or if the keyword `ASSERTED` is used before an axiom in the query, the matching will be performed on the asserted set of axioms of the ontology only.

As an example let us take the following OPPL 2 script:

```
?x:CLASS,
?y:OBJECTPROPERTY = MATCH("has((\w+))"),
?z:CLASS,
?feature:CLASS = create(?y.GROUPS(1))
SELECT ASSERTED ?x subClassOf ?y some ?z
BEGIN
REMOVE ?x subClassOf ?y some ?z,
ADD ?x subClassOf !hasFeature some (?feature and !hasValue some ?z)
END;
```

This script demonstrates most of what we described above. The purpose of the script is a simplified application of the Entity-Feature-Value Ontology Design Pattern.[5] For each subclass axiom asserting that a named class is the subclass of an existential restriction with a named filler, the script will:

- Create a ‘feature class’ using a portion of the original object property name;
- Link such feature to the original named class by means of a generic property `hasFeature` (created on demand, hence the ’!’ prefix);
- Specify that in the case of `?x` such a feature has a specific class of fillers, i.e. the filler of the original property.

---

[4] http://www.cs.man.ac.uk/~iannonel/oppl/

[5] http://www.gong.manchester.ac.uk/odp/html/Entity_Feature_Value.html

One of the advantages of employing the target pattern is the possibility to express features of a feature. Let us suppose that our initial ontology has a property `hasPrice` directly attached to the class `StockExchangeTitle`, with generic `MoneyAmount` kind of fillers. If we wanted to specify, for instance, when this price was last checked, or from what stock exchange index, we would have no choice but to overload our `MoneyAmount` class. However, from the modelling point of view this would not be the cleanest solution, as we would add features to a class that was originally designed to represent money amounts. What we really want is further characterise the feature of having a price. Hence, reifying it allows for adding other information to the mere feature without touching the class `MoneyAmount`, which might incidentally have been imported from a third party ontology and therefore should be better left untouched.

In the approach described in the rest of this paper, OPPL serves both as a baseline approach serving for inspiration (namely, its detection part) and as important computational component (its execution part). Detailed discussion is in Section 4.4.

3 Ontology Transformation Workflow

Figure 1 shows the three-step workflow of ontology transformation as currently implemented. Rectangle-shaped boxes represent the three basic (RESTful) services,[6] while ellipse-shaped boxes represent input/output data.[7]

The *OntologyPatternDetection* service outputs the binding of entity placeholders[8] in XML. It takes the transformation pattern (containing the source and target patterns) and a particular original ontology on input. The service internally automatically generates a *SPARQL query* based on the ontology pattern (the placeholders becoming SPARQL variables) and executes it. The structural/logical aspect is captured in the query structure, and the possible *naming constraint* is specifically dealt with based on its description within the source pattern. The service has only been partly implemented by now; its full implementation will leverage on Terp, a new syntax for querying OWL ontologies support[9], which is a combination of Turtle and Manchester syntax.

The *InstructionGenerator* service outputs particular transformation instructions, also in XML. It takes the particular binding of placeholders and the transformation pattern on input. Transformation instructions are generated according to the transformation pattern and the pattern instance.

The *OntologyTransformation* service outputs the transformed ontology. It takes the particular transformation instructions and the particular original on-

[6] All accessible via the web interface at `http://owl.vse.cz:8080/`.

[7] In colours, blue boxes represent RESTful services; yellow ones represent static input data; green ones represent dynamic input/output data; red ones represent output.

[8] The detection service is analogous to the first (pattern detection and action instantiation) phase of OPPL pattern application, and placeholders roughly correspond to OPPL variables. For reasons of not using OPPL here see Section 4.4.

[9] Available in the new release of Pellet, 2.1.

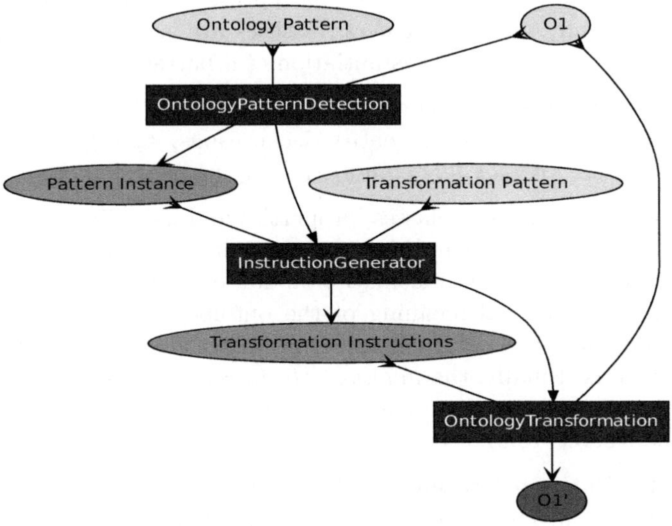

Fig. 1. Ontology transformation workflow; application workflow is depicted using line with normal head and dataflow is depicted using line with vee shape of head

tology on input. This service is based partly on OPPL and partly on our specific implementation over OWL-API.[10]

The intermediate products, pattern instance and transformation instructions, are assumed to be inspected and possibly edited by the user. In particular, the user can choose which pattern instances (from automatic detection) should be further used. However, there is also an aggregative *one-step Ontology Transformation service* that takes the original ontology, transformation pattern and pattern instance on input and returns the transformed ontology at once.

For the moment we do not specifically treat the status of the transformed ontology within the semantic web. In some contexts it can be used *locally*, as in an ontology matching scenario, while in some other it can be exposed with a unique identifier, as a new *ontology version* pointing to the pre-cursor one using the OWL 2 versioning mechanism.

4 Transformation Patterns and Operational Instructions

4.1 Transformation Pattern Representation

A *transformation pattern* includes two ontology patterns (the source one and the target one) and the schema of transformation of an instance of one to an instance of the other. Transformation patterns are serialized according to an XML schema.[11] The representation of *ontology patterns* is based on OWL 2. However,

[10] `http://owlapi.sourceforge.net/`

[11] `http://nb.vse.cz/~svabo/patomat/tp/tp-schema.xsd`

while an OWL ontology refers to particular entities, e.g. to class *Person*, in the patterns we generally use *placeholders.* Entities are specified (i.e. placeholders are instantiated) at the time of instantiation of a pattern.

Definition 1 (Ontology Pattern). Ontology pattern *is a triple* ⟨`E`, `Ax`, `NDP*`⟩, *such that* `E` *is a non-empty set of* entity declarations, `Ax` *a (possibly empty) set of* axioms, *and* `NDP*` *a (possibly empty) set*[12] *of* naming detection patterns.

Entity declarations[13] concern classes, properties and individuals (all at the level of placeholders). Properties can be object, data or annotation ones. Annotation properties enable to capture information about parts of ontology pattern that are not part of the logical meaning of the ontology. *Axioms* are facts about entities included in the transformation; we assume them to be OWL 2 axioms in Manchester syntax. Finally, the *naming detection pattern/s* capture the naming aspect of the ontology pattern for its detection (i.e. it is not used if the pattern is used in the 'target' role), see Section 4.2.

Definition 2 (Pattern Transformation). *Let* `OP1` *and* `OP2` *be ontology patterns. A* pattern transformation *from* `OP1` *(called source pattern) to* `OP2` *(called target pattern) is a tuple* ⟨`LI`, `NTP*`⟩, *in which* `LI` *is a non-empty set of* transformation links, *and* `NTP*` *is a (possibly empty) set of* naming transformation patterns. *Every* transformation link $l \in LI$ *is a triple* ⟨ `e`, `e'`, `R` ⟩ *where* $e \in OP1$, $e' \in OP2$, *and* `R` *is either a* logical equivalence *relationship or an* extralogical relationship *between* heterogeneous *entities.*

As *logical equivalence relationships* we consider standard OWL constructs declaring the equivalence/identity of two 'logical entities' of same type: classes, properties or individuals. An *extralogical relationship* can be 1) a relationship of type *eqAnn*, holding between a 'logical' entity and an annotation entity,[14] or, 2) a 'heterogeneous' relationships *eqHet*, holding between two 'logical entities' of different type. Extralogical relationships correspond to 'modelling the same real-world notion' as we saw in the motivating example in Section 1.

Naming transformation patterns capture the way how to name entities in OP2 with regard to entities in OP1, see Section 4.2.

Definition 3 (Transformation Pattern). Transformation Pattern `TP` *is a triple* ⟨`OP1`, `PT`, `OP2`⟩ *such that* `OP1`, `OP2` *are ontology patterns and* `PT` *is a pattern transformation from* `OP1` *to* `OP2`.

4.2 Naming Patterns within Transformation Patterns

The attention paid to naming patterns follows from the finding that untrivial and useful regularities can be observed in ontology entity naming [14]. While

---

[12] Our current implementation supports at most one naming pattern, in the form described in Section 4.2. However, multiple alternative naming patterns could be employed for detection of ontology pattern occurrence.

[13] Corresponding to axioms with *rdf:type* property.

[14] OWL 2 annotations may contain various interlinked entities in a separate 'space'; these are however excluded from the logical interpretation of the ontology.

OPPL supports naming operations at the level of regular expressions (as we saw in Section 2), for modelling style transformation (comprising e.g. part-of-speech alteration) we need a richer inventory of linguistic tools. Naming operations can be divided into *passive* ones, applied for checking purpose, and *active* ones, for naming a new entity.[15] While both can be plugged into naming transformation patterns, only passive operations can be used in naming detection patterns.

Definition 4. *A* naming detection pattern *is a set of passive naming operations, NDP=* $\{no_1, no_2, \ldots, no_n\}$*. All* no_i *have as operands entities from the ontology pattern to which NDP belongs, and constants.*

As an example of NDP with two operations we can take the following:[16]

{comparison(?B, head_term(?p)), exists(verb_form(?C))}

For instance, if ?B is 'Decision', ?p is 'hasDecision' (with 'Decision' as head term) and ?C is 'Acceptance' (with 'accept' as verb form) then the pattern succeeds.

Definition 5. *A* naming transformation pattern *is a set of pairs consisting of an entity and a naming operation, NTP=* $\{(e_1, no_1), (e_2, no_2), \ldots, (e_n, no_n)\}$*. All* no_i *have as operands entities from the source ontology pattern of the pattern transformation to which NTP belongs, and constants. All* e_i *are from the target ontology pattern of the pattern transformation to which NTP belongs.*

An example of NTP with one compound operation is the following:

{(?G, make_passive_verb(?C) + head_noun(?A))}

For instance, if ?A is bound with 'PresentedPaper' (with 'Paper' as head noun) and ?C with 'Rejection' (with 'Rejected' as passive verb form), the name of entity ?G in the transformed ontology will become 'RejectedPaper'.

Naming patterns can be generally defined on any lexical aspect of an ontology: URI of entities, its fragment, labels, comments etc. By default we consider naming patterns applied over fragments of URIs, otherwise it is stated in an attribute of the *ndp* or *ntp* element, e.g. *target="label"*.

The small collection of *implemented naming operations* is being gradually extended as needed for supported transformation patterns. Currently they include (we list together a passive and active variant where relevant):

- *delimiter* detection and change (e.g. underscore or camel-case)
- detection and derivation of *verb form* of a noun (using "derivationally related forms" resource from WordNet and the Stanford part-of-speech tagger[17])
- detection of *head noun* or its complement, for a noun phrase, and of *head term* for verb phrase, typically in a property name (only passive operation)
- construction of *passive form* of verb.

[15] A passive naming operation often has its active variant.

[16] The XML serialisation of this NDP and a superset of the following NTP is in the example in Section 5.

[17] `http://nlp.stanford.edu/software/tagger.shtml`

4.3 Entity and Axiom Transformation Operations

A transformation pattern, $\langle\langle \mathtt{E}_1, \mathtt{Ax}_1, \mathtt{NDP^*}_1\rangle, \langle \mathtt{LI}, \mathtt{NTP^*}\rangle, \langle \mathtt{E}_2, \mathtt{Ax}_2, \mathtt{NDP^*}_2\rangle\rangle$, is converted to transformation instructions for a particular ontology. Building blocks of these instructions are entity and axiom transformation operations.

At the level of *axioms* we consider two operations: *operation of removing of axiom* $REMOVE(a)$ and *operation of adding of axiom* $ADD(a)$.

At the level of *entities* we consider three operations:

- *operation of adding an entity* where we specify the type and name of the new entity: $ADD(e, t, n)$, where $e \in \mathtt{E}_1$, t is an entity type and $n \in \mathtt{NTP^*}$.
- *operation of removing an entity*: $REMOVE(e)$, where $e \in \mathtt{E}_1$,
- *operation of renaming an entity*, where we specify the new name of the entity: $RENAME(e, n)$, where $e \in \mathtt{E}_1$ and $n \in \mathtt{NTP^*}$.

As *removing* is a very sensitive operation with far-reaching effects, we distinguish three different strategies how to cope with this. They differ in the possibility of removing entities and/or axioms:

- *Conservative strategy* does not allow to remove anything. Obviously this is the safest strategy, avoiding undesirable changes in an ontology.
- *Progressive strategy* (used by default) does not allow to remove entities. However, it is possible to remove axioms.
- *Radical strategy* allows to remove both entities and axioms.

When we remove information from the logical content of the ontology, it is still possible to swap it into the *annotations*. For example, when we 'de-reify' a property (i.e. change a class expressing a relationship of multiple entities into an object property), we can put information about the third etc. argument of the relationship into annotations of the generated property. Capturing such 'leaked-out' information potentially allows reverse transformation. While we already consider annotation as a part of a transformation/ontology pattern, implementation of concrete reverse transformation support is left to future work.

In the following we specify several rules how *entity transformation operations* are derivable from a transformation pattern. For a naming transformation pattern NTP, let NTP(e) denote the function returning the result of a naming operation no such that $(e, no) \in \mathtt{NTP}$, and let TYPE(e) denote the function returning the meta-model type of a entity (placeholder) e.

1. If there is an equivalence correspondence between ?A $\in \mathtt{E}_1$ and $?B \in \mathtt{E}_2$ then the instance of ?B will be renamed accordingly, i.e. RENAME(?A, NTP(?B))
2. If there is an extralogical link *eqAnn* or *eqHet* between $?A \in \mathtt{E}_1$ and $?B \in \mathtt{E}_2$, then the instance of ?B will be named as NTP(?B), typed according to the kind of placeholder of ?B, and *in the case of radical strategy* ?A will be removed, i.e. ADD(?B, TYPE(?B), NTP(?B)), REMOVE(?A).
3. All entities from $\mathtt{E}_2$ that are not linked to an entity from $\mathtt{E}_1$ will be ADDed.
4. *In the case of radical strategy*, entities from $\mathtt{E}_1$ that are not linked to any entity from $\mathtt{E}_2$ will be REMOVEd.

For Rule 2 and conservative or progressive strategy, there is added an annotation property instance relating the new entity to the original entity. Furthermore, in any strategy we can still refer to the (heterogeneous) transformation link between the original entity and new one at the level of transformation pattern. For instance, in the transformation pattern for reducing a (reified) *n-ary relation* to binary[18] there is an extralogical link between class ?B and property ?q. According to Rule 2 it would lead to up to two operations:

ADD(?q, ObjectProperty, make_passive_verb(?B)), (*If radical:*) REMOVE(?B).

For instance, in the case of ?B = ReviewSubmission, it makes a new object property 'submitted' by verb derivation from the head noun of ?B. Assuming the conservative strategy (hence not removing ?B), an annotation property instance would relate the old and the new entity.

The *renaming operation* works on the naming aspect (entity URI, *rdfs:label* etc.) of an entity referred with placeholder. By default we process the URI fragment of an entity. Changing the URI fragment is however problematic because it, in principle, means creating a new entity. We can solve this problem by adhering to ontology versioning principles: retain the original entity (with original URI) in the ontology, annotate it as *deprecated*, and add an equivalence axiom between these two entities (i.e. between the original and new URI).

For deriving *axiom transformation operations* from a transformation pattern, there are only two simple rules:

1. remove all axioms within OP1 *in the case of progressive or radical strategy*
2. add all axioms within OP2

While removing of axioms is pretty straightforward, because it works on original entities, adding of axioms must be done in connection with entity operations, because it works on just added or renamed entities.

For instance, in ontology pattern 1 of transformation pattern dealing with restriction class[19] there is axiom '?A equivalentTo (?p value ?a)', e.g. 'PresentedPaper equivalentTo (hasStatus value Acceptance)' which can be swapped to annotations in ontology pattern 2: 'AcceptedPaper annotation:discr_property 'hasStatus'', 'AcceptedPaper annotation:value 'Acceptance''. As a result of that rule, there will be an instruction to remove (in the case of progressive or radical strategy) the original axiom and add two new axioms. The binding of placeholders and entity operations must be considered before.

4.4 Executing Transformation Instructions in OPPL and OWL-API

We base the execution of transformation on OPPL, and add some extensions using OWL-API in order to cover more specific features. We can divide the instructions currently unsupported by OPPL into three groups:

---

[18] `http://nb.vse.cz/~svabo/patomat/tp/tp_l-n-ary-relation.xml`

[19] `http://nb.vse.cz/~svabo/patomat/tp/tp_ce-hasValue.xml`

- Instructions not eligible for putting inside an OPPL script in principle. This regards entity level operations as OPPL is an axiom-level language; an exception is entity addition, which can be understood as axiom addition.
- Instructions that are possibly too specific for the transformation setting. This includes NLP-based operations such as making passive form of a verb.
- Instructions that are in the long-term implementation plan for OPPL, such as handling annotations.

Currently, we use OPPL for the operations on *axioms* and for *adding entities*. Renaming and naming entities according to naming transformation patterns, as well as adding annotations, is done using the OWL-API. As far as detection is concerned, the SELECT part of OPPL could be used to some extent; our naming constraints are however out of the scope of OPPL. Furthermore, in contrast to OPPL, we can take advantage of *decoupling* the process of transformation into parts, which enables user intervention within the whole workflow.

5 Complex Example for Ontology Matching Use Case

For the sake of brevity, we only show one complex example of transformation pattern usage, which addresses the ontology matching use-case: transforming an ontology, $O1$, to a form easier matcheable to another one, $O2$. In this experiment we want to match the *cmt* ontology[20] to the *ekaw* ontology,[21] both belonging to the *OntoFarm* collection[22] used in the OAEI matching contest.

Transformation Pattern Used. The *cmt* ontology will be transformed using the transformation pattern *tp_hasSome2*, which is based on the matching/detection pattern from [10], see Figure 2. This pattern captures the situation when some concept from $O2$ is not explicit in $O1$ and should be expressed as restriction. The pattern, containing the NDP and NTP from Section 4.2, looks as follows:[23]

- $OP1$: E={Class: ?A, Class: ?B, Class: ?C, ObjectProperty: ?p},
  Ax={?p Domain: ?A, ?p Range: ?B, ?C SubClassOf: ?B},
  NDP={comparison(?B, head_term(?p)), exists(verb_form(?C))}
- $OP2$: E={Class: ?D, Class: ?E, Class: ?F, Class: ?G, ObjectProperty: ?q},
  Ax={?q Domain: ?D, ?q Range: ?E, ?F SubClassOf: ?E, ?G EquivalentTo: (?q some ?F)}
- PT : LI={?A EquivalentTo: ?D, ?B EquivalentTo: ?E, ?C EquivalentTo: ?F, EquivalentProperties: ?p, ?q},
  NTP={(?G, make_passive_verb(?C) + head_noun(?A))}.

---

20 `http://nb.vse.cz/~svabo/oaei2009/data/cmt.owl`

21 `http://nb.vse.cz/~svabo/oaei2009/data/ekaw.owl`

22 Each ontology was designed by analysis of either a conference support tool or of the usual procedures of a concrete conference.

23 XML serialization is at: `http://nb.vse.cz/~svabo/patomat/tp/tp_hasSome2.xml`

Applying the rules from Section 4.3 we would get, at placeholder level, the following *entity operations*:

RENAME(?A, NTP(?D)), RENAME(?B, NTP(?E)), RENAME(?C, NTP(?F)), RENAME(?p, NTP(?q)), ADD(?G, owl:Class, NTP(?G)).

and *axiom operations*:

REMOVE(?p Domain: ?A), ADD(?q Domain: ?D),
REMOVE(?p Range: ?B), ADD(?q Range: ?E),
REMOVE(?C SubClassOf: ?B), ADD(?F SubClassOf: ?E),
ADD(?G EquivalentTo: ?q some F)).

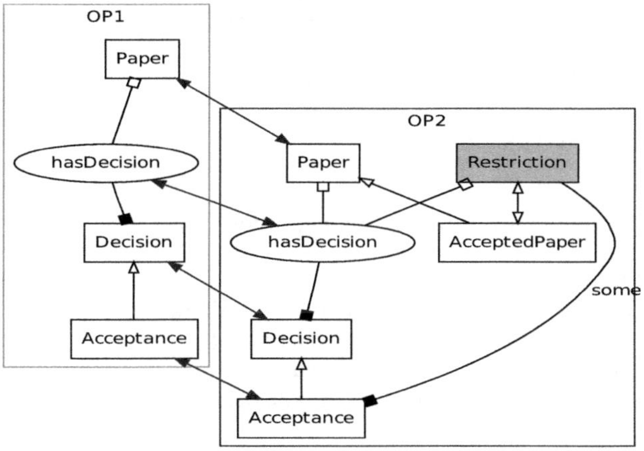

Fig. 2. Instantiated *tp_hasSome2* transformation pattern

Source Pattern Detection. OP1 is serialized as follows:

```
<op1>
  <entity_declarations>
    <placeholder type="ObjectProperty">?p</placeholder>
    <placeholder type="Class">?A</placeholder>
    <placeholder type="Class">?B</placeholder>
    <placeholder type="Class">?C</placeholder>
  </entity_declarations>
  <axioms>
    <axiom>?p domain ?A</axiom>
    <axiom>?p range ?B</axiom>
    <axiom>?C subClassOf ?B</axiom>
  </axioms>
</op1>
```

This is translated into a SPARQL query (omitting declarations of prefixes):

```
SELECT *
WHERE {
  ?p rdf:type owl:ObjectProperty.
  ?A rdf:type owl:Class. ?B rdf:type owl:Class. ?C rdf:type owl:Class.
  ?p rdfs:domain ?A;
     rdfs:range ?B.
  ?C rdfs:subClassOf ?B.
}
```

Furthermore, there are the specific naming constraints that filter out some query results:[24]

```
<ndp>
  <comparison threshold="1.0" measure="equal">
    <s1>?B</s1>
    <s2>head_term(?p)</s2>
  </comparison>
  <exist>verb_form(?C)</exist>
</ndp>
```

As a result, we have the binding of placeholders, e.g.:

```
<pattern_instance>
  <binding placeholder="?p">hasDecision</binding>
  <binding placeholder="?B">Decision</binding>
  <binding placeholder="?A">Paper</binding>
  <binding placeholder="?C">Acceptance</binding>
</pattern_instance>
```

This would be the output of the *OntologyPatternDetection* RESTful service.

Instruction Generation. In the second step, particular ontology transformation instructions are generated in XML serialization given the specific binding and the transformation pattern, especially its pattern transformation part:

```
<pt>
  <eq op1="?A" op2="?D"/>
  <eq op1="?B" op2="?E"/>
  <eq op1="?C" op2="?F"/>
  <eq op1="?p" op2="?q"/>
  <ntp entity="?G">make_passive_verb(?C)+head_noun(?A)</ntp>
  <ntp entity="?D">?A</ntp>
  <ntp entity="?E">?B</ntp>
  <ntp entity="?q">?p</ntp>
</pt>
```

In this case *entities* are just transferred to the target ontology under the same name. Most *axiom operations* just remove and then add the same axiom given the

[24] For explanation we can refer to Section 4.2.

equivalence of entities according to LI. An exception is the *addition* of a new axiom, `!AcceptedPaper equivalentTo (hasDecision some Acceptance)`, connected with creation of a new class, `AcceptedPaper`, according to Ax of *OP*2. No operations on *annotations* were needed, as there are no singular removals (without complementary additions).

The resulting *transformation instructions* are serialized as follows:

```
<instructions>
  <oppl_script>
    <remove>hasDecision domain Paper</remove>
    <remove>hasDecision range Decision</remove>
    <remove>Acceptance subClassOf Decision</remove>
    <add>hasDecision domain Paper</add>
    <add>hasDecision range Decision</add>
    <add>Acceptance subClassOf Decision</add>
    <add>!AcceptedPaper equivalentTo (hasDecision some Acceptance)</add>
  </oppl_script>
  <rename>
    <entity type="ObjectProperty" original_name="hasDecision">
      hasDecision
    </entity>
    <entity type="Class" original_name="Paper">Paper</entity>
    <entity type="Class" original_name="Decision">Decision</entity>
  </rename>
  <annotations/>
</instructions>
```

This would be the output of *InstructionGenerator* RESTful service.

Finally, the *cmt* ontology would be transformed, given the transformation instructions, using the *OntologyTransformation* RESTful service. Aside the mentioned enrichment with named entity 'AcceptedPaper', the interface to OWL-API also cares for adding information relating this new entity to the original entity.

Applying *ontology matching* on the *ekaw* ontology and the *transformed cmt* ontology we easily get, among others, the following *simple correspondence*:

`cmt#AcceptedPaper=ekaw#Accepted_Paper`

Although `AcceptedPaper` is not present in the original *cmt*, we can use the simple correspondence for getting a *complex correspondence* for the original *cmt*,

`(cmt#hasDecision some cmt#Acceptance) = ekaw#Accepted_Paper`

corresponding to the 'Class by Attribute Type' alignment pattern from [10,11].

6 Related Work

Several approaches to *ontology transformation* have recently been published. We refer here to two that look most relevant to our work (aside pure OPPL, to which we made a comparison along the paper). However, their principles and scope are still somehow different from our approach, so direct comparison is hard to make.

In [12] the authors consider *ontology translation* from the Model Driven Engineering perspective. The basic shape of our transformation pattern is very similar to their metamodel. They consider an *input pattern*, i.e. a query, an *output pattern* for creating the output, as well as variables binding the elements. However, the transformation is considered at the *data level* rather than at the *schema level* as (primarily) in our approach.

In comparison with the previous work the authors of [8] leverage the ontology translation problem to the generic meta-model. This work has been done from the *model management* perspective, which implies a generality of this approach. There are important differences to our approach. Although they consider transformations of ontologies (expressed in OWL DL), these transformations are directed into the generic meta-model or into any other meta-model such as that of UML or XML Schema. In contrast, in our approach we stay within one meta-model, the OWL language, and we consider transformation as a way of translating a certain representation into its modelling alternatives.

Our notion of heterogeneous links is also related to *heterogeneous matching* proposed in [6]. The authors propose a logical solution to this problem by extending *Distributed Description Logics* to allow a representation of relationship between classes and properties, for matching purpose. In our approach we use a more generic notion of heterogeneous relationship at extralogical level.

We should also mention prior work of the first two authors of the current paper [13], which was not based on OPPL and viewed ontology transformation primarily in the context of ontology matching, the transformation patterns having been closely associated with the *alignment patterns* from [11].

7 Conclusions and Future Work

We presented pattern-based ontology transformation based on OPPL and OWL-API, which includes ontology pattern detection, generation of instructions and finally transformation as such. All steps are implemented as RESTful services. We formally defined the notions related to transformation patterns and described the rules for generation of transformation instructions. Usefulness of the transformation was shown on a step-by-step example from ontology matching context.

Imminent future work lies in *full implementation* of pattern detection using SPARQL queries automatically generated from ontology patterns, and in enrichment and systematization of the *collection of naming patterns*. We also plan to experiment with detection procedures fine-tuned for the *matching scenario*; for instance, in the example in Section 5 we would instantiate the source ontology pattern so as to achieve a good degree of match to the other ontology. Furthermore, while currently the transformation patterns are designed by end user directly in XML serialization, we envision a *graphical editor* for this purpose. Our approach also definitely needs real *evaluation* in the ontology matching context, which is however difficult due to limited datasets available. Finally, we plan to work out *other use-cases* such as ontology importing and improved reasoning.

This research has been partially supported by the CSF grant no. P202/10/1825, "PatOMat – Automation of Ontology Pattern Detection and Exploitation".

References

1. Ontology design patterns. org (ODP), `http://ontologydesignpatterns.org`
2. Ontology design patterns (ODPs) public catalogue, `http://www.gong.manchester.ac.uk/odp/html/index.html`
3. Antezana, E., Egaña, M., Blondé, W., Mironov, V., Stevens, R., Baets, B.D., Kuiper, M.: The Cell Cycle Ontology: a step towards semantic systems biology. In: EKAW 2008 (2008)
4. Egaña, M., Stevens, R., Antezana, E.: Transforming the axiomisation of ontologies: The Ontology Pre-Processor Language. In: Proceedings of the Fifth OWLED Workshop on OWL: Experiences and Directions, OWLED 2008 (2008)
5. Gangemi, A., Presutti, V.: Ontology Design Patterns. In: The Handbook on Ontologies. Springer, Heidelberg (2009)
6. Ghidini, C., Serafini, L.: Reconciling concepts and relations in heterogeneous ontologies. In: Sure, Y., Domingue, J. (eds.) ESWC 2006. LNCS, vol. 4011, pp. 50–64. Springer, Heidelberg (2006)
7. Iannone, L., Aranguren, M.E., Rector, A.L., Stevens, R.: Augmenting the expressivity of the Ontology Pre-Processor Language. In: Proceedings of the Fifth OWLED Workshop on OWL: Experiences and Directions, OWLED 2008 (2008)
8. Kensche, D., Quix, C., Chatti, M., Jarke, M.: Gerome: A generic role based metamodel for model management. Journal on Data Semantics 8, 82–117 (2007)
9. Lin, H., Sirin, E.: Pellint - a performance lint tool for Pellet. In: Proceedings of the Fifth OWLED Workshop on OWL: Experiences and Directions, OWLED 2008 (2008)
10. Ritze, D., Meilicke, C., Šváb-Zamazal, O., Stuckenschmidt, H.: A pattern-based ontology matching approach for detecting complex correspondences. In: Ontology Matching Workshop, OM 2009 (2009)
11. Scharffe, F.: Correspondence Patterns Representation. PhD thesis, University of Innsbruck (2009)
12. Silva Parreiras, F., Staab, S., Schenk, S., Winter, A.: Model driven specification of ontology translations. In: Li, Q., Spaccapietra, S., Yu, E., Olivé, A. (eds.) ER 2008. LNCS, vol. 5231, pp. 484–497. Springer, Heidelberg (2008)
13. Šváb-Zamazal, O., Svátek, V., Scharffe, F.: Pattern-based ontology transformation service. In: International Conference on Knowledge Engineering and Ontology Development, KEOD 2009 (2009)
14. Svátek, V., Šváb-Zamazal, O., Presutti, V.: Ontology naming pattern sauce for (human and computer) gourmets. In: Workshop on Ontology Patterns (WOP 2009), CEUR (2009)

Experimenting with eXtreme Design

Eva Blomqvist, Valentina Presutti, Enrico Daga, and Aldo Gangemi

STLab, ISTC-CNR, via Nomentana 56, 00161 Rome, Italy
eva.blomqvist@istc.cnr.it,
{valentina.presutti,enrico.daga,aldo.gangemi}@cnr.it

Abstract. Ontology Design Patterns (ODPs) support reusability and use of best practices in ontology engineering. Previous studies have shown that Content ODPs, in particular, have some measurable beneficial effects on the produced ontologies. However, another conclusion was that methodology and tool support was needed. Now such support exist, in the form of the XD methodology and the XD Tools. In this paper we present a set of experiments for (i) confirming previous conclusions concerning the usefulness of Content ODPs, (ii) investigating the usefulness of the XD methodology, and (iii) investigating the usefulness of the XD Tools. Main conclusions are that we can confirm most of the previous results concerning the usefulness of Content ODPs, and certain negative effects observed previously are now mitigated by the new tool support. The tool is perceived as quite useful, however it also adds some overhead. The XD methodology is found to be a helpful means to organize the design process, and the main benefit shown through the experiments is the testing focus, resulting in a drastic decrease of certain frequent mistakes.

1 Introduction

Ontology Design Patterns (ODPs) are emerging as an important support for various ontology engineering tasks. Under the assumption that there exist classes of problems in ontology design that can be solved by applying common solutions (as experienced in software engineering), ODPs can support reusability on the design side. As described in [1] ODPs can be of several types e.g. focusing on logical language constructs, architectural issues, naming, or efficient provision of reasoning services. In this paper we focus on Content ODPs (CPs). CPs are small (or cleverly modularized) ontologies with explicit documentation of design rationales, representing modeling best practices, and can be used as building blocks in ontology design [2,3].

As an example we describe a CP that is called *AgentRole*. It represents the relation between agents, e.g., people, and the roles they play, e.g., manager, meeting chair, father, and friend, as well as the disjointness of agents and roles. Figure 1 shows the UML diagram (produced through TopBraid Composer[1]) of the OWL[2] building block representing this CP. CPs are collected in different

[1] For notation details, see tool documentation: http://www.topquadrant.com/products/TB_Composer.html

[2] http://www.w3.org/2004/OWL/

P. Cimiano and H.S. Pinto (Eds.): EKAW 2010, LNAI 6317, pp. 120–134, 2010.

catalogues, such as the *ODP portal*[3]. In addition to their diagrammatic representation CPs are described using a number of catalogue entry fields (c.f. software pattern templates), such as *name*, *intent*, *covered requirements*, *consequences*, and *building block* (linking to an OWL realization of the pattern).

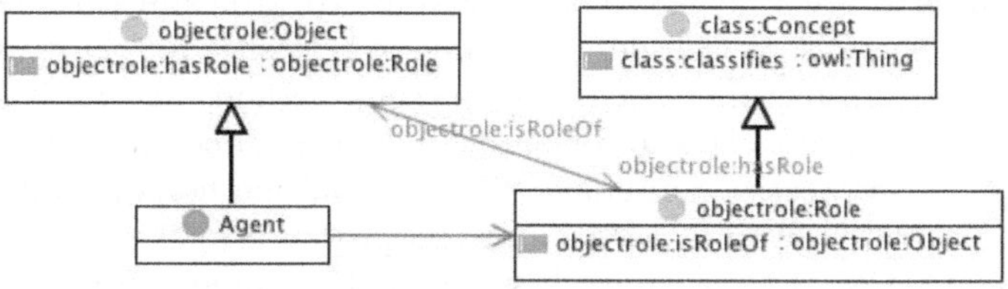

Fig. 1. The AgentRole Content ODP's graphical representation in UML

In [4] we presented the results of initial experiments on CP reuse, showing that CPs are indeed useful for constructing better and more (re)usable ontologies. However, we also concluded that additional method and tool support would be needed in order to truly benefit from CPs; common problems the participants experienced were to find the right CPs for their requirements, correctly specialize and compose them, as well as discover possible mistakes in the solutions. In response to the results of the study in [4] we have developed the XD Tools and a methodology (the eXtreme Design methodology - XD) for CP-based ontology design [5]. In this paper we present a new set of experiments with the following three aims; (i) to confirm the usefulness of CPs, (ii) to investigate the usefulness of the XD methodology, and (iii) to investigate the usefulness of the XD Tools. The novel contributions of this work include (1) a set of integrated tools called "XD Tools" for CP-based ontology design, and their user-based evaluation, (2) the evaluation of CP-based ontology design conducted with XD Tools, and comparison with results presented in [4], (3) the evaluation of the XD methodology.

The rest of the paper is structured as follows: Section 1.1 describes related work and in Section 2 we introduce the experimental setting, and evaluation criteria. Section 3 describes the XD Tools, and we analyze the results of the CP-based ontology design experiment as well as how XD Tools are perceived by the users. In Section 4, after a brief description of the XD methodology, we present its evaluation, and in Section 5 we discuss conclusions and future work.

1.1 Related Work

Early ontology engineering methodologies were [6], [7], and [8], while more recent ones focus on collaboration [9], or transfers popular software engineering processes to ontology engineering, e.g. the Unified Process [10]. The only pattern-based methodologies we are aware of are [11] (not considering collaboration, and patterns are assumed to be a non-evolving set) and [12] (tailored to ambient intelligence applications). When proposed, methodologies are commonly

[3] http://www.ontologydesignpatterns.org

not evaluated, only exemplified through use-cases as in [7] and [12], or analyzed through theoretical comparisons as in [10]. Instead, their later adoption in ontology engineering projects prove their usefulness. Methodology evaluation (for selection), as performed in software engineering (e.g. through NIMSAD [13]), has not been widely used in ontology engineering. Methodologies and tools have different focus and aims, hence, it is impossible to proclaim the 'best' tool or methodology if there is no well-defined frame of reference for the evaluation.

Currently, pattern-based ontology engineering methods and tools are present primarily on the logical level, e.g. for ontology learning and enrichment as in [2], the Ontology Pre-Processor Language (OPPL) and methods for applying it as a means for logical ODP reuse [14], and the proposal for a high-level pattern language in [15]. Use of ODPs have been present in some ontology engineering environments, such as the logical pattern templates in Protégé 3 (as explained in [16]), and the template wizard supporting OPPL pattern definitions in Protégé 4 [14], targeting mainly the use of Logical ODPs, although it supports the introduction of CPs in an ontology with a macro-like mechanism. The combination of Naming and Logical ODPs has also been proposed for supporting ontology refactoring in [17]. Benchmarking and evaluation has been more widely performed on the tool level, compared to the methodological level, e.g. through comparisons such as [18] and more recently in [19], and observational studies, as in [20].

2 Experimental Method

The focus is on evaluating the effectiveness of CP-based ontology design. We have conducted experiments in order to evaluate how CPs improve the quality of the results, i.e., the ontologies, and whether the XD Tools and methodology have an additional impact. Below we describe the experiment setting, the participants, and the criteria we have applied in order to analyze the resulting ontologies.

2.1 Experimental Setting

Similarly to [4] experiments were carried out during master and PhD courses. We divided the experiment into **two sessions**[4], each involving a different group of participants. The experimental variable of both sessions was to make the participants, who worked in pairs, first construct ontologies 'without using CPs', then 'with CPs and the XD Tools', and finally 'with CPs, the XD Tools and also following the XD methodology'. Furthermore, each participant (individually) filled out a questionnaire at the end of each task, as well as a background questionnaire at the beginning of the session[5]. The majority of the questions were propositions, where answers were selected from a 5-point Likert-scale, ranging from 'strongly agree' to 'strongly disagree'. Another common type was open questions, where participants explained their opinions freely.

[4] The sessions were separated in time and involved different sets of participants.

[5] All the questionnaires used can be downloaded at http://stlab.istc.cnr.it/documents/papers/QuestionnairesExperiment2010.zip

Both sessions were organized into three slots, as summarized in Table 1. Training in Slot 1 aimed at leveraging the previous knowledge of the participants, to limit the degrees of freedom of the setting. Tasks were expressed in terms of *Competency Questions* (CQs) [21], expressing the domain requirements to be addressed by the ontology. The two groups solved the same exercise as Task 1 (theater domain). For Tasks 2 and 3 the exercises were switched between the two sessions in order to reduce the impact of the task domain and participant maturation on the results, i.e., in the first session Task 2 was set in the music domain and Task 3 in the hospital domain, but in session two the exercises were switched. All tasks had the same number of CQs and contained approximately the same set of modelling issues, i.e., some n-ary relations, modelling of roles and time periods, etc.[6], so that the problems could be addressed by reusing a similar set of CPs from the catalogue (available for Task 2-3).

Table 1. Experimental setting

Slot 1	**Slot 2**	**Slot 3**
Background questionnaire		
Training (OWL modeling)	Training (CPs and XD tools)	Training (XD methodology)
Task 1: modeling without any insight into CPs (3 hours)	Task 2: modeling by using a catalogue of CPs, and XD Tools (3 hours)	Task 3: modeling by following the XD methodology (in addition to CPs and XD Tools) (3 hours)
Questionnaire 1	Questionnaire 2	Questionnaire 3

In both sessions the participants used the same ontology editor, i.e., TopBraid Composer[7]. The catalogue of CPs consisted of 56 patterns (i.e. all submissions available in the ODP portal). 32 of those were patterns addressing broad competency questions (e.g. modeling part-whole relations, or situations), while 17 belonged to the fishery domain, 6 to the biology and agriculture domains, and one to the business domain. Out of those 56 patterns, the tasks were constructed to cover problems matching the general requirements of 6 of the patterns. Additionally, 13 other patterns were applicable as alternatives to patterns in the set above, although the intents of these patterns were slightly different from the intent of the task descriptions. Each task also consisted of minor parts that could not be solved using any of the patterns included in the catalogue.

2.2 Participants

The total number of participants was 35, distributed over the two sessions (19 in the first and 16 in the second). Participants were mostly inexperienced ontology

[6] Details of the tasks can be found at http://ontologydesignpatterns.org/wiki/Training:PhD_Course_on_Computational_Ontologies_%40_University_ of_Bologna

[7] The reason for choosing this tool was that at the time of Session 1 it was the most stable Eclipse-based ontology editor compatible with the XD Tools plugin.

developers, an important target group of ODPs. The subjects of the first session were mainly master students in computer science and business informatics, without much experience in ontologies (except a course introducing information and data modelling). In the second session[8] the subjects were PhD students and junior researchers in mainly computer engineering, informatics, and law. In this group a few persons had more substantial experience developing ontologies, and already knew the basics of OWL, however, none had previously used ODPs.

2.3 Ontology Analysis Methods

To make the results comparable to [4], we used the same methods and measures to assess the characteristics of the output ontologies. Here we only give a brief summary of the measures, as they are explained in detail in [4]. The focus of the evaluation was on the functional and usability levels, as defined in [22]. The ontologies were analysed with respect to four aspects; 1) coverage of problem, 2) usability, 3) modelling mistakes/incomplete solutions, and 4) pattern usage.

Coverage of problem. Two different measures were used; terminological coverage and task coverage. 'Terminological coverage' measures the amount of the vocabulary of the domain problem, i.e. the terms (allowing for morphological variations or synonyms) used to express the CQs, that are represented in the solution. 'Task coverage' is a measure of the amount of the intended tasks, i.e. CQs, that is supported by the solution, i.e. the amount of CQs that can be executed as SPARQL queries on the model. Each CQ was classified either as 'excellently covered', 'covered with shortcomings', or 'not covered'. Shortcomings in this context can be that one has to know the implicit semantics of the property names in order to pose a correct query.

Usability. The usability, i.e. the clarity and understandability of the ontology, was measured using a set of usability profiling measures, and a set of structural aspects providing formal semantics, i.e. clarity of meaning, to the ontology. They are: the amount of (i) labels, (ii) comments, (iii) inverse relations, and (iv) disjointness axioms, as well as the (v) level of axiomatization, e.g. measured based on the number of complex class definitions.

Mistakes and patterns. Modelling 'mistakes' and the presence of CPs were both identified and analyzed through inspection of the solutions. We define, in this context, modelling 'mistakes' as incomplete solutions that attempt to solve a specific problem but that have shortcomings, see also above.

3 Tool Support for Ontology Design with CPs

The study presented in [4] pointed at the need for tool support for ODP-based ontology design. The main needs identified by users were support for finding

[8] Despite the difference in participant background we choose to present most results in this paper as averages over both groups, only in the cases when significant differences in the results were noted do we separate the presentation of results.

and selecting the right ODPs for their requirements, correctly specializing and composing them, and discovering possible mistakes in the resulting ontology. In order to address these requirements we have developed the eXtreme Design Tools (XD Tools)[9], a set of software components available as an Eclipse plugin, accessible through a *perspective* - eXtreme Design - compatible with Eclipse-based ontology design environments such as TopBraid Composer and the NeOn Toolkit[10].

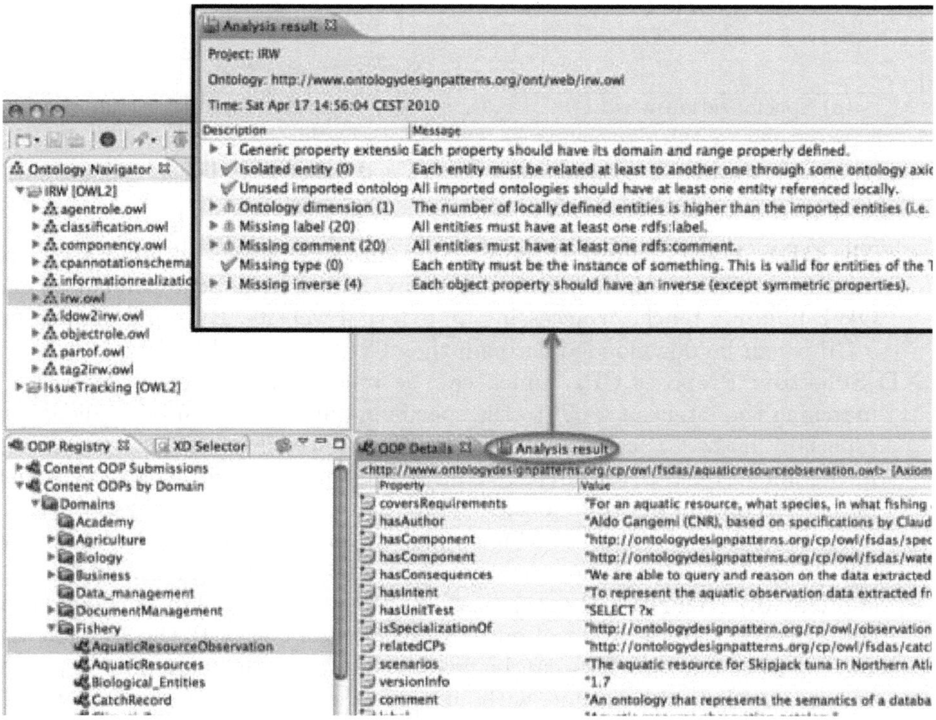

Fig. 2. XD Tools GUI in the NeOn Toolkit

3.1 Main Functionalities of XD Tools

Currently, XD Tools is comprised of five main components supporting pattern-based design. The overall view of XD Tools GUI is depicted in Figure 2. XD Tools' components are the following:

ODP Registry browser: Exposes sets of CPs to the user, in a tree-like view categorized by different aspects such as the domain of the CP (Figure 2 bottom-left). In this way users can access a set of reusable CPs without having them locally stored. The default registry is provided by the ODP portal.

[9] http://stlab.istc.cnr.it/stlab/XDTools
[10] http://neon-toolkit.org

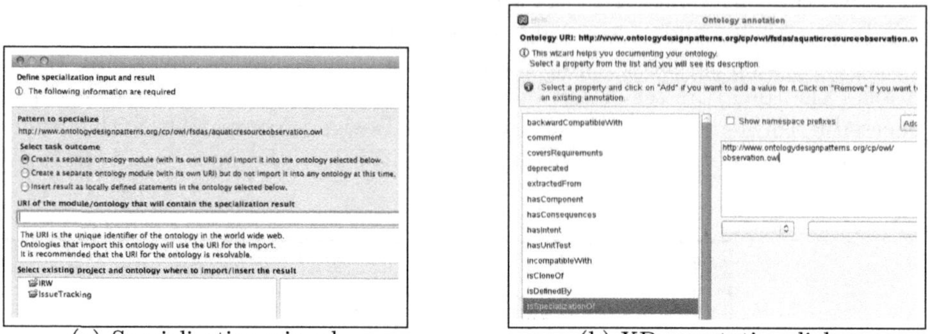

(a) Specialization wizard (b) XD annotation dialog

Fig. 3. XD specialization wizard and annotation dialog

The **ODP Details view** (Figure 2 bottom-right) shows all annotations of a selected CP. In this way CPs can be examined without downloading the OWL building block, or accessing an external website. By right clicking on a CP it can be downloaded through the "Get" command.

XD Selector: Proposes CPs, which can be reused, to the user. The task of matching the intent of a CP to the specific requirements can be challenging, especially if the CP catalogue is large. Since pattern selection is one of the most difficult tasks to automate, we have developed an extensible system that permits to plug in multiple services. Currently two services are available, i.e., search based on keyword indexing and latent semantic indexing, respectively. The suggested CPs can be downloaded through the "Get" command.

Specialization wizard: CP specialization, as the primary step of their reuse, concerns the specialization of ontology elements in the CP, through axioms such as subsumption. This can be challenging for an inexperienced user if it is done one element at a time, without guidance. From a user perspective, CP specialization has the following steps: (i) import the pattern into the working ontology, (ii) declare subClasses/subProperties for each of the (most specific) pattern elements needed, and (iii) add any additional axioms needed. The specialization wizard provided by XD Tools (Figure 3(a)) guides the user through this process, with some steps being optional and some required. The wizard is activated by right clicking on a CP and selecting "Specialize".

XD Annotation dialog: Supports annotation of ontologies, based on customized annotation vocabularies. The annotation properties already provided by OWL/RDF and vocabularies such as OMV [23] and the CP annotation schema[11] are provided by default[12].

XD Analyzer: Provides feedback to the user with respect to how 'best practices' of ontology design have been followed. The XD Analyzer has a

[11] http://ontologydesignpatterns.org/schemas/cpannotationschema.owl

[12] Since CPs are small ontologies the properties can be used for ontologies in general.

pluggable architecture, allowing to easily extend the set of heuristics expressing 'best practices'. Three levels of messages are produced; errors, warnings (identified 'bad practices'), and suggestions (proposals for improvement). An error is, for instance, a missing type, i.e., all instances should have a specified class they are instances of. Examples of warnings are missing labels and comments, and isolated elements that are not referred to by other elements. Proposing to create an inverse for each object property that has no inverse so far is on the level of suggestions. An example view of the Analyzer is shown at the top of Figure 2.

In addition, XD Tools provide several help functions, such as inline info boxes, help sections in the Eclipse help center, and cheat sheets.

3.2 Experimental Results: CP-Based Ontology Design

Four of the research questions posed in [4] are also the basis of the experimental setting described in this paper.

1. Are CPs perceived as useful by the participants?
2. Are the ontologies constructed using CPs 'better', in some modelling quality sense, than the ontologies constructed without patterns?
3. Are the tasks solved faster when using CPs?
4. What common modelling 'mistakes' can be identified, both when not using patterns and when using the available CPs?

Perceived usefulness (1). Table 2 compares the results observed in the two sessions with the ones obtained in the previous setting (see [4]). On average, the fraction of participants who perceive the CPs as useful has increased, with a decrease of those stating they were not useful. However, there is a significant difference between the two sessions. The only major difference (apart from the background of the participants that did not impact the results in [4]) between the two sessions, which in our opinion can explain the difference, is the tool support. While the first session had an initial version of the XD Tools, the second session had XD Tools in a stable version with full functionality.

Table 2. Perceived usefulness (percentage of participants who agreed or disagreed, the rest neither agreed nor disagreed)

Setting	Useful	Not Useful
Setting presented in [4]	67%	11%
Session 1	67%	8%
Session 2 (more stable tool support)	93%	4%

Result quality - Coverage (2). Table 3 compares terminological and task coverage of the ontologies resulting from the execution of Task 1 and Task 2, according to the ontology analysis method described in Section 2. For what concerns task coverage, the results are inconclusive, since the increase is very small.

While, with regard to terminological coverage the results have improved in the new setting, compared to [4]. In fact, in the previous setting, the terminological coverage decreased from Task 1 to Task 2, hence the ontologies were less complete from the terminological viewpoint. In the new setting the coverage keeps stable, which may be attributed to the new tool support.

Table 3. Terminological and Task Coverage. Percentages indicate an average over all ontologies (details on criteria in Section 2 and in [4])

	Termino-logical coverage	Task coverage	
		Covered (excellently or with shortcomings)	Covered excellently
Task 1	80%	69%	41%
Task 2	79%	70%	44%

Result quality - Usability (2). Table 4 compares the usability indicators between the two tasks. These results are comparable to [4], and confirm that usability is the aspect showing the clearest improvement when introducing CPs.

Table 4. Usability. Percentages indicate an average over all ontologies, e.g. in Task 1 on average 76% of classes and properties had labels, in Task 2 the average was 86%

	Labels	Comments	Disjoint classes	Inverse prop.	Complex class def.
Task 1	76%	0%	2%	6%	5%
Task 2	86%	35%	37%	42%	21%

Solving tasks faster (3). There is still no evidence that CPs support faster development, but as noted above the reduced coverage has now been remedied by introducing additional tool support. Hence, in this setting there is not any objective evidence for being slower either (as opposed to the previous study).

Modelling 'mistakes' (4). We have identified a set of frequent modelling mistakes in the ontologies of both tasks. The by far most frequent mistake (occurring in 93% of the ontologies of the first task and 80% of the ontologies of the second task) was missing n-ary relations, i.e., where the requirements clearly state a dependency between three or more elements but in the ontology these are modeled as binary relations, loosing the n-ary nature. Other frequent mistakes were failure to separate roles from persons, e.g., by stating that vocalist is a subclass of person it becomes difficult to state the time period when that role was held or in what band the person acted as vocalist, and missing or wrong datatype properties, e.g., declaring a class for time intervals but failing to add properties holding the actual start and end dates. The most frequent ones in the ontologies developed in Task 1, i.e., 6 types of mistakes, were all still present in the ontologies developed in Task 2 and we have used them to compare the results.

The fraction of ontologies showing these 6 types of ‘mistakes’, **decreased on average by 44% in Task 2**. The mistakes were not listed or discussed by the teacher between the sessions in order to reduce the effect of maturation. In addition, no new types of errors were introduced. A few of the mistakes did not show such a drastic decrease, e.g., problems when modeling n-ary relations only decreased with 14% even when having access to CPs dedicated to this issue.

In addition to the previous experiments we also anlayzed the modularity of the produced ontologies. In other words, we added one research question:

5. Do CPs increase the modularity of ontologies?

The results show that in Task 1 none of the ontologies are modularized, i.e. they are comprised of only one OWL-file, while in Task 2 the ontologies contain on average 7.5 modules, and all ontologies are comprised of more than one module. It has to be noted that no specific instructions on producing modular ontologies were given, hence, *the reuse of CPs inherently introduces a modular structure*. Although this may seem obvious, one should note that CPs can not only be used a components, imported and directly reused, but also as ‘inspiration’ and guidelines for creating your own solutions.

3.3 Experimental Results: Perception of the XD Tools

One major difference between the previous experiments [4] and the current setting was the introduction of the XD Tools. XD Tools was available for Task 2 and 3 in both sessions, however, in the first session XD Tools was still in a testing phase, i.e., contained several bugs and was not entirely stable and user friendly. During this experiment we aimed at answering the following questions:

1. How well is XD Tools perceived to support the process of *finding* CPs?
2. How well is XD Tools perceived to support the process of *specializing* CPs?
3. Does the XD Tools introduce too much overhead in the process, i.e., annoying the users?

These questions were addressed mainly by asking the participants to assess the usefulness of the different aspects of XD Tools when filling out the questionnaires, as well as asking directly if they felt that it introduced too much overhead. The responses (fractions of total number of responses) from both sessions can be seen in Figure 4. It should be noted that in Session 1 some pairs experienced technical problems with the tool, hence, all but one of the ‘not applicable’ responses originate in this session. In Session 2 technical problems were solved.

We note that 58% of the respondents agreed that the XD Tools was useful for finding CPs (only 5% disagreed), and 56% agreed that the tool was useful for reusing CPs (8% disagreed). Clearly, the majority of the participants found the tool useful, as opposed to browsing the ODP portal and specializing patterns without guidance (which was the alternative method presented to them). About 25% of the participants were unsure. A result that supports the conclusion that the tool was useful is the fact that in this new set of experiments terminological coverage did not decrease, which was the case when introducing CPs in the

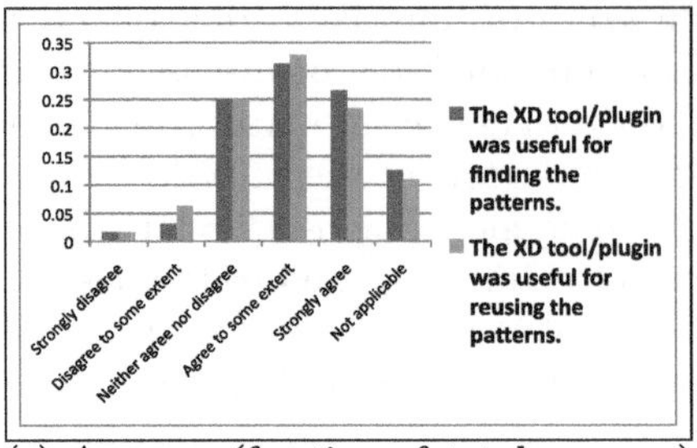

(a) Answers (fraction of total answers) to the propositions.

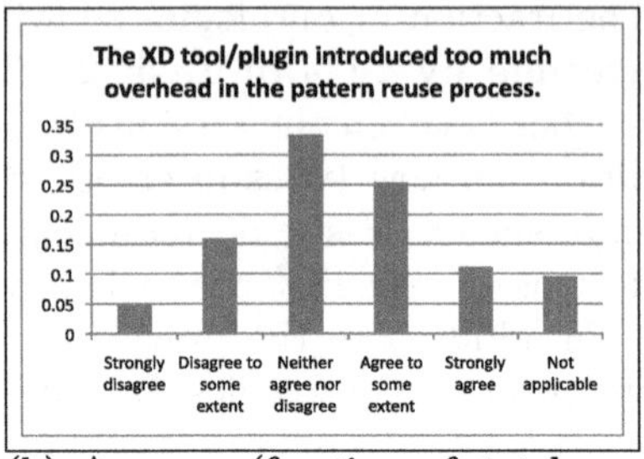

(b) Answers (fraction of total answers) to the proposition.

Fig. 4. Evaluation results for XD Tools

previous setting. Additionally, in the second session (using the stable version of XD Tools) we observed a much higher satisfaction with CPs than for the other session. In our opinion this supports the conclusion that the tool was helpful and reduced the effort for users to find and reuse CPs. Finally, more than one third of the participants (36%) agree that the tool does introduce too much overhead (while 33% of the participants are not sure). From informal discussions with the participants we conclude the need of finding a better balance between enforcing best practices on one hand, and providing shortcuts as users get more experienced on the other.

4 eXtreme Design

With the name eXtreme Design (XD) we identify an *agile*[13] approach to ontology engineering, a family of methods and tools, based on the application, exploitation, and definition of ODPs for solving ontology development problems [5]. Below we describe the part of XD targeted in this paper.

4.1 XD Methodology for CP Reuse

We focus on XD for CP reuse in ontology design (hereafter referred to simply as 'XD'), which is currently the most elaborated part of the XD family. In XD a development project is characterized by two sets: (i) the problem space, composed of the actual modeling issues (local problems), e.g., to model roles played by people during certain time periods; (ii) the solution space, made up of reusable modeling solutions, e.g., a piece of an ontology that models time-indexed roles (a CP). Each CP, as well as the local problem, is related to ontology requirements expressed as CQs or sentences, but on different levels of generality. If a local problem can be described, partly or completely, in terms of the CQs of a CP then that CP can be selected and reused for building the solution.

[13] We borrow the term *agile* from Software Engineering because XD is inspired by eXtreme Programming and Software Factories as described in [5] and brings the main principles of agile Software Engineering into Ontology Engineering.

XD is test-driven and task-focused, resulting in highly modular ontologies where each module solves a small set of requirements. Main principles of XD are pair design, the intensive use of CPs, and collaboration, for details see [5]. The iterative workflow of XD contains 12 steps, where the first four steps are concerned with project initiation, scoping, and requirements engineering (i.e. deriving the CQs from user stories), and the three final steps are concerned with the integration of modules into a final solution, hence, it is focused on the collaboration between the pairs. The evaluation of the collaborative part is ongoing work, hence, in these experiments we focus on the iteration by one design pair (creating and testing the modules), whereas the relevant steps include:

5. **Select a coherent set of CQs.** One or more of the CQs, i.e. a coherent set treating one modelling issue, are selected for a first development iteration.
6. **Match the CQs to CPs.** By matching the selected CQs to the requirements covered by CPs, candidate CPs for reuse are identified.
7. **Select CPs to use.** From the set of candidates the CPs that best fit the local problem without unnecessary overhead are selected.
8. **Reuse and integrate selected CPs.** Reusing CPs mean to import them into the ontology module to be built, specialize their classes and properties, and compose them, i.e., add properties or axioms that connect the CP specializations so that the module is able to answer the CQs.
9. **Test and fix.** The CQs are transformed into unit tests, e.g., SPARQL[14] queries, and test instances are added. Tests are run, and any errors discovered are fixed, before selecting a new set of CQs for the next iteration.

4.2 Experimental Results: The XD Methodology

In Task 3 the XD methodology was introduced. New questions were added to the questionnaires to record the participants' experience, but we performed the same analyses on the ontologies as for Task 1 and 2. Mainly we were trying to answer the following set of questions:

1. Is the XD methodology perceived as useful by the participants?
2. Is the XD methodology a 'natural' way to work with CPs?
3. Are the ontologies constructed using the XD methodology 'better', in some modelling quality sense, than the ontologies constructed 'only' using CPs?
4. Are the tasks solved faster when using the XD methodology, compared to 'only' using CPs?
5. What common modelling 'mistakes' can be identified and are they different from the ones noted when 'only' using CPs?

Usefulness of XD (1). That XD helped them to organize their work was proposed to the participants, and their answers can be seen in Figure 5(a). Only 6% of the participant claimed they did not follow XD closely, hence, we conclude that the XD methodology is perceived as useful for organizing your work.

[14] http://www.w3.org/TR/rdf-sparql-query/

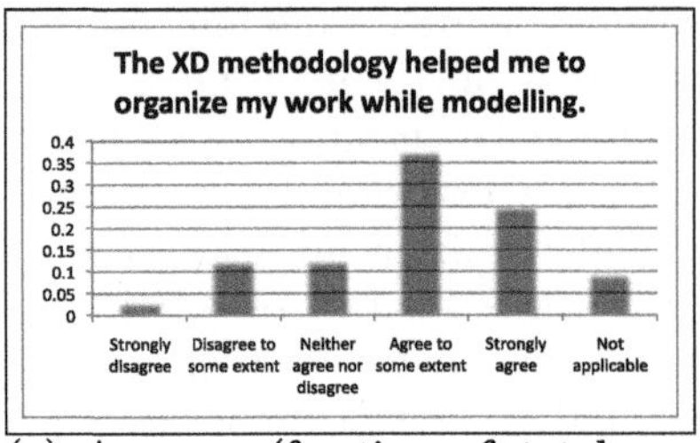

(a) Answers (fraction of total answers) to the proposition.

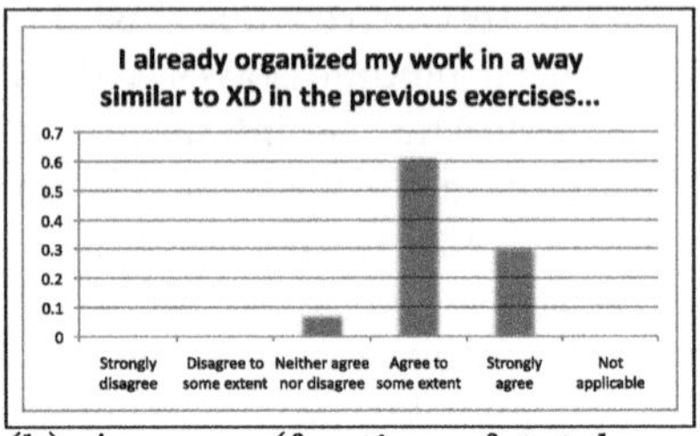

(b) Answers (fraction of total answers) to the proposition.

Fig. 5. Evaluation results for XD methodology

'Natural' way to work with CPs (2). Methodologies are sometimes perceived as awkward and restrictive by users, however, participants felt comfortable with XD, as can be seen in Figure 5(b). From this we conclude that XD is descriptive and pragmatic. This is not surprising since the methodology has been developed based on our own experience how to approach the problem.

Result quality (3). The terminological coverage of ontologies increased slightly (79% in Task 2 to 83% in Task 3), and the task coverage increased from 69% to 81%. The substantial increase seems to be in the task coverage. On the usability side, levels are similar for Task 2 and 3, only the disjointness axioms show a substantial increase (from 37% to 52%).

Solving tasks faster (4). While still applying the same time limit to solve a problem, task and terminological coverage increased (although the increase in terminological coverage is limited). Our opinion is that this is mainly due to that errors are found more easily (hence faster), although we have to consider some possible effects of participant maturation as well. We believe that XD helps designers to faster problem solving, still, we need to produce stronger evidence for supporting this claim in future studies.

Modelling 'mistakes' (5). The types of mistakes that are frequent are the same as in Task 2, but with a decrease of the occurrence of the top-6 common errors of 15%. Two types of errors decrease significantly more than the others, i.e. the problems in representing n-ary relations (decrease by 64%) and missing datatype properties (decrease by 46%). We believe that the decrease can be attributed to the test-driven nature of XD. By requiring ontology engineers to test their model in a structured fashion, errors that can easily be discovered through unit tests, e.g., missing properties, are indeed discovered.

5 Conclusions

In this paper we presented experiments on CP-related methods and tools. These experiments follow up on, and confirm the results of experiments presented in [4], as well as extend the scope to include experiments on the XD methodology and XD Tools. The aim of the new experiments was threefold; (i) confirming conclusions on the usefulness of CPs, (ii) investigating the usefulness of the XD methodology, and (iii) investigating the usefulness of the XD Tools.

We can confirm almost all of the results in [4]. However, terminological coverage kept stable in this setting while in the previous one it decreased. This can be easily explained by the new tool support, facilitating the reuse of CPs. The XD Tools was perceived as useful for finding and reusing CPs, however it needs a better balance between enforcing best practices and allowing for shortcuts in the workflow, since many participants felt that it added some overhead. The effects of the XD methodology can be seen mainly in the ontology quality, i.e., increased task coverage and particular previously frequent mistakes that drastically decreased. The frequent mistakes were all connected to missing parts, hence, we conclude that one main benefit of XD is its test-driven nature that forces the user to check every new module against the requirements. Additionally, we conclude that XD is perceived by users as a natural way of working with CPs, still, they felt the methodology was useful for guiding their modelling.

Future work contains further experiments on CPs and their relation to ontology quality, e.g. including other aspects and different groups of participants. For the XD methodology we already started investigating collaboration and integration aspect in some initial observations, but proper experiments are needed. More focused user testing of the XD Tools is also on the agenda, e.g., testing the different components separately, to get clearer indications on what parts of the user interaction can be improved. XD Tools will also be extended with more elaborate CP selection; we are currently working on methods for CQ-based CP selection rather than simple keyword search.

Acknowledgements. This research was partly funded by the European Commission through projects NeOn (FP6 IST-2005-027595) and IKS (FP7 ICT-2007-3/No. 231527).

References

1. Gangemi, A., Presutti, V.: Ontology Design Patterns. In: Handbook on Ontologies, 2nd edn. International Handbooks on Information Systems. Springer, Heidelberg (2009)
2. Blomqvist, E.: OntoCase-Automatic Ontology Enrichment Based on Ontology Design Patterns. In: Bernstein, A., Karger, D.R., Heath, T., Feigenbaum, L., Maynard, D., Motta, E., Thirunarayan, K. (eds.) ISWC 2009. LNCS, vol. 5823, pp. 65–80. Springer, Heidelberg (2009)
3. Presutti, V., Gangemi, A.: Content Ontology Design Patterns as practical building blocks for web ontologies. In: Li, Q., Spaccapietra, S., Yu, E., Olivé, A. (eds.) ER 2008. LNCS, vol. 5231, pp. 128–141. Springer, Heidelberg (2008)
4. Blomqvist, E., Gangemi, A., Presutti, V.: Experiments on Pattern-Based Ontology Design. In: K-CAP 2009. ACM, New York (2009)
5. Presutti, V., Daga, E., Gangemi, A., Blomqvist, E.: eXtreme Design with Content Ontology Design Patterns. In: Proceedings of the Workshop on Ontology Patterns (WOP 2009), collocated with ISWC 2009. CEUR Workshop Proceedings, vol. 516 (November 2009)

6. Grüninger, M., Fox, M.: Methodology for the Design and Evaluation of Ontologies. In: Proceedings of IJCAI 1995, Workshop on Basic Ontological Issues in Knowledge Sharing, April 13 (1995)
7. Uschold, M.: Building Ontologies: Towards a Unified Methodology. In: Proceedings of Expert Systems 1996, the 16th Annual Conference of the British Computer Society Specialist Group on Expert Systems, Cambridge, UK (December 1996)
8. Fernández, M., Gómez-Pérez, A., Juristo, N.: METHONTOLOGY: from Ontological Art towards Ontological Engineering. In: Proceedings of the AAAI 1997 Spring Symposium Series on Ontological Engineering (1997)
9. Pinto, H.S., Staab, S., Tempich, C.: DILIGENT: Towards a fine-grained methodology for DIstributed, Loosely-controlled and evolvInG Engineering of oNTologies. In: Proceedings of the 16th European Conference on Artificial Intelligence (ECAI 2004), Valencia, Spain (2004)
10. Nicola, A.D., Missikoff, M., Navigli, R.: A software engineering approach to ontology building. Inf. Syst. 34(2), 258–275 (2009)
11. Clark, P., Porter, B.: Building concept representations from reusable components. In: Proceedings of AAAI 1997, pp. 369–376. AAAI Press, Menlo Park (1997)
12. Maass, W., Janzen, S.: A Pattern-based Ontology Building Method for Ambient Environments. In: Proceedings of the Workshop on Ontology Patterns (WOP 2009), collocated with ISWC 2009, Washington D.C., USA, October 25. CEUR Workshop Proceedings, vol. 516 (2009)
13. Jayaratna, N.: Understanding and Evaluating Methodologies: NIMSAD, a Systematic Framework. McGraw-Hill, Inc., New York (1994)
14. Iannone, L., Rector, A., Stevens, R.: Embedding Knowledge Patterns into OWL. In: Aroyo, L., Traverso, P., Ciravegna, F., Cimiano, P., Heath, T., Hyvönen, E., Mizoguchi, R., Oren, E., Sabou, M., Simperl, E. (eds.) ESWC 2009. LNCS, vol. 5554, pp. 218–232. Springer, Heidelberg (2009)
15. Noppens, O., Liebig, T.: Ontology Patterns and Beyond - Towards a Universal Pattern Language. In: Proceedings of WOP2009 collocated with ISWC 2009, vol. 516 (November 2009), CEUR-WS.org
16. Stevens, R., Aranguren, M.E., Wolstencroft, K., Sattler, U., Drummond, N., Horridge, M., Rector, A.L.: Using OWL to model biological knowledge. International Journal of Man-Machine Studies 65(7), 583–594 (2007)
17. Sváb-Zamazal, O., Svátek, V., Scharffe, F.: Pattern-based Ontology Transformation Service. In: Dietz, J.L.G. (ed.) KEOD, pp. 42–47. INSTICC Press (2009)
18. Corcho, O., Fernández-López, M., Gómez-Pérez, A.: Methodologies, tools and languages for building ontologies. Where is their meeting point? Data & Knowledge Engineering 46(1), 41–64 (2003)
19. Mizoguchi, R., Kozaki, K.: Ontology Engineering Environments. In: Staab, S., Studer, R. (eds.) Handbook on Ontologies. International Handbooks on Information Systems, 2nd edn. Springer, Heidelberg (2009)
20. Dzbor, M., Motta, E., Buil, C., Gomez, J.M., Görlitz, O., Lewen, H.: Developing Ontologies in OWL: an Observational Study. In: Proc. of the OWLED 2006 Workshop on OWL: Experiences and Directions, vol. 216 (2006), CEUR-WS.org
21. Gruninger, M., Fox, M.S.: The role of competency questions in enterprise engineering. In: Proceedings of the IFIP WG5.7 Workshop on Benchmarking - Theory and Practice (1994)
22. Gangemi, A., Catenacci, C., Ciaramita, M., Lehmann, J.: Modelling Ontology Evaluation and Validation. In: Sure, Y., Domingue, J. (eds.) ESWC 2006. LNCS, vol. 4011, pp. 140–154. Springer, Heidelberg (2006)
23. Hartmann, J., Sure, Y., Haase, P., Palma, R., del Carmen Suárez-Figueroa, M.: OMV – Ontology Metadata Vocabulary. In: Welty, C. (ed.) Ontology Patterns for the Semantic Web Workshop, Galway, Ireland (2005)

Weaving a Social Data Web with Semantic Pingback

Sebastian Tramp, Philipp Frischmuth, Timofey Ermilov, and Sören Auer

Universität Leipzig, Institut für Informatik, AKSW,
Postfach 100920, D-04009 Leipzig, Germany
lastname@informatik.uni-leipzig.de
http://aksw.org

Abstract. In this paper we tackle some pressing obstacles of the emerging Linked Data Web, namely the *quality, timeliness and coherence* of data, which are prerequisites in order to provide direct end user benefits. We present an approach for complementing the Linked Data Web with a social dimension by extending the well-known Pingback mechanism, which is a technological cornerstone of the blogosphere, towards a Semantic Pingback. It is based on the advertising of an RPC service for propagating typed RDF links between Data Web resources. Semantic Pingback is downwards compatible with conventional Pingback implementations, thus allowing to connect and interlink resources on the Social Web with resources on the Data Web. We demonstrate its usefulness by showcasing use cases of the Semantic Pingback implementations in the semantic wiki OntoWiki and the Linked Data interface for database-backed Web applications Triplify.

Introduction

Recently, the publishing of structured, semantic information as Linked Data has gained much momentum. A number of Linked Data providers meanwhile publish more than 200 interlinked datasets amounting to 13 billion facts[1]. Despite this initial success, there are a number of substantial obstacles, which hinder the large-scale deployment and use of the Linked Data Web. These obstacles are primarily related to the *quality, timeliness and coherence* of Linked Data. In particular for ordinary users of the Internet, Linked Data is not yet sufficiently visible and (re-) usable. Once information is published as Linked Data, authors hardly receive feedback on its use and the opportunity of realising a network effect of mutually referring data sources is currently unused.

In this paper we present an approach for complementing the Linked Data Web with a social dimension. The approach is based on an extension of the well-known Pingback technology [9], which is one of the technological cornerstones of the overwhelming success of the blogosphere in the Social Web. The Pingback

[1] http://esw.w3.org/topic/TaskForces/CommunityProjects/LinkingOpenData/DataSets/Statistics

P. Cimiano and H.S. Pinto (Eds.): EKAW 2010, LNAI 6317, pp. 135–149, 2010.

mechanism enables bi-directional links between weblogs and websites in general as well as author/user notifications in case a link has been newly established. It is based on the advertising of a lightweight RPC service, in the HTTP or HTML header of a certain Web resource, which should be called as soon as a link to that resource is established. The Pingback mechanism enables authors of a weblog entry or article to obtain immediate feedback, when other people reference their work, thus *facilitating reactions and social interactions.* It also allows to automatically publish backlinks from the original article to comments or references of the article elsewhere on the Web, thus *facilitating timeliness and coherence* of the Social Web. As a result, the distributed network of social websites using the Pingback mechanism (such as the blogosphere) is much tighter and timelier interlinked than conventional websites, thus rendering a network effect, which is one of the major success factors of the Social Web.

With this work we aim to apply this success of the Social Web to the Linked Data Web. We extend the Pingback mechanism towards a Semantic Pingback, by adding support for typed RDF links on Pingback clients, servers and in the autodiscovery process.

When an RDF link from a Semantic Pingback enabled Linked Data resource is established with another Semantic Pingback enabled Linked Data resource, the latter one can be automatically enriched either with the RDF link itself, with an RDF link using an inverse property or additional information. When the author of a publication, for example, adds bibliographic information including RDF links to co-authors of this publication to her semantic wiki, the co-authors' FOAF profiles can be enriched with backlinks to the bibliographic entry in an *automated or moderated* fashion. The Semantic Pingback supports *provenance* through tracking the lineage of information by means of a provenance vocabulary. In addition, it allows to implement a variety of measures for *preventing spam.*

Semantic Pingback is completely downwards compatible with the conventional Pingback implementations, thus allowing to seamlessly connect and interlink resources on the Social Web with resources on the Data Web. A weblog author can, for example, refer to a certain Data Web resource, while the publisher of this resource can get immediately notified and `rdfs:seeAlso` links can be automatically added to the Data Web resource. In order to facilitate the adoption of the Semantic Pingback mechanism we developed three complementary implementations: a Semantic Pingback implementation was included into the semantic data wiki OntoWiki, we added support for Semantic Pingbacks to the Triplify database-to-RDF mapping tool and provide a standalone implementation for the use by other tools or services.

The paper is structured as follows: We describe the requirements which guided the development of Semantic Pingback in section 1. We present an architectural overview including communication behaviour and autodiscovery algorithms of our solution in section 2. A description of our implementations based on OntoWiki and Triplify as well as the standalone software is given in section 5. Finally, we survey related work in section 6 and conclude with an outlook on future work in section 7.

1 Requirements

In this section we discuss the requirements, which guided the development of our Semantic Pingback approach.

Semantic links. The conventional Pingback mechanism propagates untyped (X)HTML links between websites. In addition the Semantic Pingback mechanism should be able to propagate typed links (e.g. OWL object properties) between RDF resources.

Use RDFa-enhanced content where available. Since most traditional weblog and wiki systems are able to create semantically enriched content based on RDFa annotations[2], these systems should be able to propagate typed links derived from the RDFa annotations to a Semantic Pingback server without any additional modification or manual effort.

Downward compatibility with conventional Pingback servers. Conventional Pingback servers should be able to retrieve and accept requests from Semantic Pingback clients. Thus, widely used Social Web software such as WordPress or Serendipity can be pinged by a Linked Data resource to announce the referencing of one of their posts. A common use case for this is a Linked Data SIOC [4] comment which replies and refers to a blog post or wiki page on the Social Web. Such a SIOC comment typically uses the `sioc:reply_of` object property to establish a link between the comment and the original post[3].

Downward compatibility for conventional Pingback clients. Conventional Pingback clients should be able to send Pingbacks to Semantic Pingback servers. Thus, a blogger can refer to any pingback-enabled Linked Data resource in any post of her weblog. Hence, the conventional Pingback client should be able to just send conventional Pingbacks to the Linked Data server. Unlike a conventional Pingback server, the Semantic Pingback server should not create a comment with an abstract of the blog post within the Linked Data resource description. Instead an additional triple should be added to the Linked Data resource, which links to the referring blog post.

Support Pingback server autodiscovery from within RDF resources. The conventional Pingback specification keeps the requirements on the client side at a minimum, thus supporting the announcement of a Pingback server through a `<link>`-Element in an HTML document. Since the Semantic Pingback approach aims at applying the Pingback mechanism for the Web of Data, the autodiscovery process should be extended in order to support the announcement of a Pingback server from within RDF documents.

[2] This should be possible at least manually by using the systems HTML source editor, but can be supported by extensions as for example described in [6] for Drupal.

[3] Since SIOC is a very generic vocabulary, people can also use more specific relations as, for instance, `disagreesWith` or `alternativeTo` from the Scientific Discourse Relationships Ontology [5].

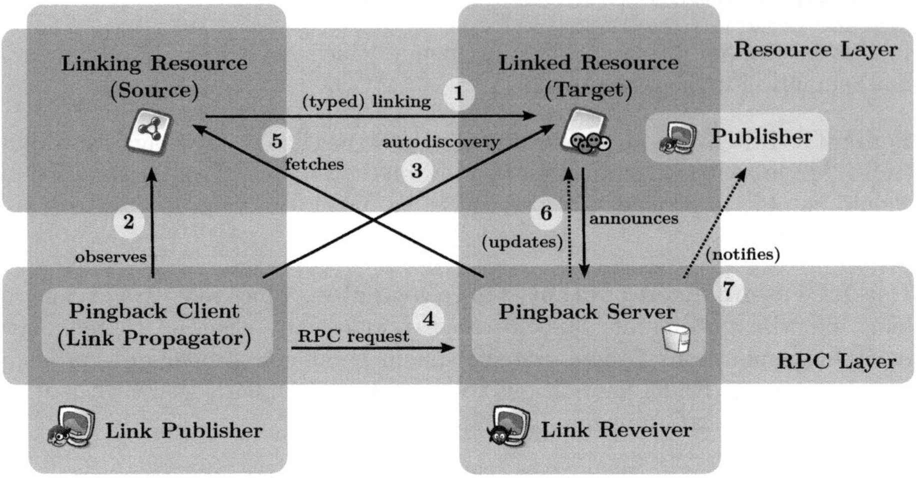

Fig. 1. Architecture of the Semantic Pingback approach

Provenance tracking. In order to establish trust on the Data Web it is paramount to preserve the lineage of information. The Semantic Pingback mechanism should incorporate the provenance tracking of information, which was added to a knowledge base as result of a Pingback.

Spam prevention. Another aspect of trust is the prevention of unsolicited proliferation of data. The Semantic Pingback mechanism should enable the integration of measures to prevent spamming of the Data Web. These measures should incorporate methods based on data content analysis and social relationship analysis.

2 Architectural Overview

The general architecture of the Semantic Pingback approach is depicted in Figure 1. A *linking resource* (depicted in the upper left) links to another (Data) Web resource, here called *linked resource* (arrow 1). The linking resource can be either an conventional Web resource (e.g. wiki page, blog post) or a Linked Data resource. Links originating from Linked Data resources are always typed (based on the used property), links from conventional Web resources can be either untyped (i.e. plain HTML links) or typed (e.g. by means of RDFa annotations). The *Pingback client* (lower left) is either integrated into the data/content management system or realized as a separate service, which observes changes of the Web resource (arrow 2). Once the establishing of a link was noted, the Pingback client tries to autodiscover a Pingback server from the linked resource (arrow 3). If the autodiscovery was successful, the respective Pingback RPC server is called (arrow 4), with the parameters linking resource (i.e. source) and linked resource (i.e. target). In order to verify the retrieved request (and to obtain information about the type of the link in the semantic case), the Pingback server fetches (or dereferences) the linking resource (arrow 5). Subsequently, the Pingback server can perform a number of actions (arrows 6,7), such as updating the linked resource (e.g. adding inverse links) or notifying the publisher of the linked resource (e.g. via email). This approach is compatible with the conventional Pingback specification [9], which illustrates the chain of communication steps with the help of a Alice and Bob scenario. This scenario as well as the general architecture introduce four components, which we now describe in more detail:

Pingback client. Alice's blogging system comprises the Pingback client. The Pingback client establishes a connection to the Pingback server on a certain event (e.g. on submitting a new blog post) and starts the Pingback request.

Pingback server. Bob's blogging system acts as the Pingback server. The Pingback server accepts Pingback request via XML-RPC and reacts as configured by the owner. In most cases, the Pingback server saves information about the Pingback in conjunction with the target resource.

Target resource. Bob's article is called the target resource and is identified by the *target URI*. The target resource can be either a web page or an RDF resource, which is accessible through the Linked Data mechanism. A target resource is called *pingback-enabled*, if a Pingback client is able to glean information about the target resource's Pingback server (see section 3.1 for autodiscovery of Pingback server information).

Source resource. Alice's post is called the source resource and is identified by the *source URI*. Similar as the target resource, the source resource can be either a web page or an RDF resource. The source resource contains some relevant information chunks regarding the target resource.

These information chunks can belong to one or more of the following categories:

- An *untyped (X)HTML link* in the body of the web page (this does not apply for Linked Data resources).
- A (possible RDFa-encoded) RDF triple linking the source URI with the target URI trough an arbitrary RDF property. That is, the extracted source resource model contains a *direct relation* between the source and the target resource. This relation can be directed either from the source to the target or in the opposite direction.
- A (possible RDFa-encoded) RDF triple where either the subject or the object of the triple is the target resource. This category represents *additional information* about the target resource including textual information (e.g. an additional description) as well as assertions about relations between the target resource and a third resource. This last category will most likely appear only in RDFa enhanced web pages since Linked Data endpoints are less likely to return triples describing foreign resources.

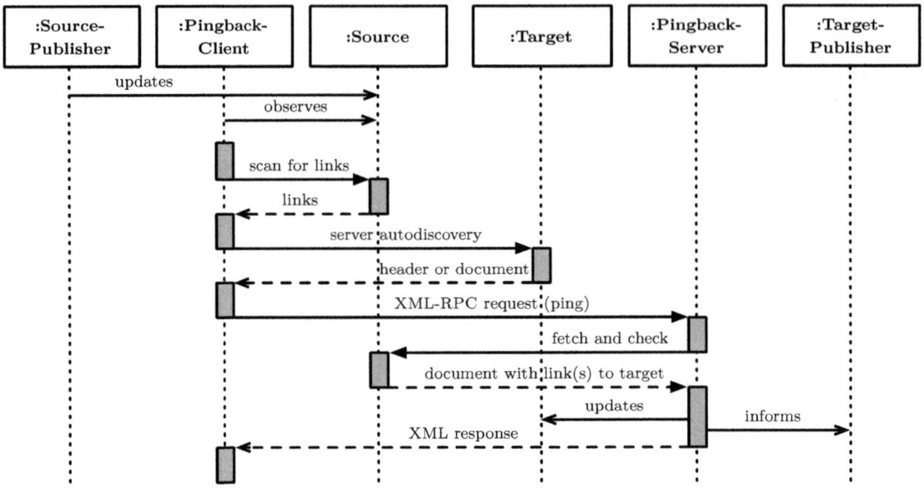

Fig. 2. Sequence diagram illustrating the (Semantic) Pingback workflow

Depending on these categories, a Semantic Pingback server will handle the Pingback request in different ways. We describe this in more detail later in section 4.

Figure 2 illustrates the complete life-cycle sequence of a (Semantic) Pingback. Firstly, the source publisher updates the source resource, which is observed by a Pingback client. The Pingback client then scans the source resource for links (typed or untyped) to other resources. Each time the client detects a suitable link, it tries to determine a Pingback server by means of an autodiscovery process. Once a Pingback server was determined, the client pings that server via an XML-RPC request. Section 3 contains a more detailed description of these steps. Since the requested Pingback server only receives the source and target URIs as input, it tries to gather additional information. At least the source document is fetched and (possibly typed) links are extracted. Furthermore the target resource is updated and the publisher of the target resource is notified about the changes. In section 4 the server behavior is described in more detail. Finally, the Pingback server responds with an XML result.

3 Client Behavior

One basic design principle of the original Pingback specification is to keep the implementation requirements of a Pingback client as simple as possible. Consequently, Pingback clients do not even need an XML/HTML parser for basic functionality. There are three simple actions to be followed by a Pingback client:

(1) Determine suitable links to external target resources, (2) detect the Pingback server for a certain target resource and (3) send an XML-RPC post request via HTTP to that server. Conventional Pingback clients would naturally detect (untyped) links by scanning HTML documents for `<a>`-elements and use the `href`-attribute to determine the target. Semantic Pingback clients will furthermore derive suitable links by examining RDFa annotated HTML or RDF documents. Both conventional and Semantic Pingback clients are able to communicate with a Semantic Pingback server, since the Semantic Pingback uses exactly the same communication interface. In particular, we did not change the remote procedure call, but we introduce a third possible autodiscovery mechanism for Semantic Pingback clients in order to allow the propagation of server information from within RDF documents. On the one hand, this enables the publisher of a resource to name a Pingback server, even if the HTTP header cannot be modified. On the other hand, this allows caching and indexing of Pingback server information in a Semantic Web application. Since a large number of Semantic Web applications store the data retrieved from other parties, they can take advantage of the embedded Pingback server information without requesting the data again, thus accelerating the discovery process.

3.1 Server Autodiscovery

The server autodiscovery is a protocol followed by a Pingback client to determine the Pingback server of a given target resource. The Pingback mechanism supports two different autodiscovery mechanisms which can be used by the Pingback client:

- an HTTP header attribute `X-Pingback` and
- a `link`-element in the HTML head with a relation attribute `rel="pingback"`.

Both mechanisms interpret the respective attribute value as URL of a Pingback XML-RPC service, thus enabling the Pingback client to start the request.

The `X-Pingback` HTTP header is the preferred autodiscovery mechanism and all Semantic Pingback server must implement it in order to achieve the required downward compatibility. We define an additional autodiscovery method for Linked Data resources which is based on RDF and integrates better with Semantic Web technologies.

Therefore, we define an OWL object property `service`[4], which is part of the Pingback namespace and links a RDF resource with a Pingback XML-RPC server URL. The advantage compared to an HTTP header attribute is that this information can be stored along with a cached resource in an RDF knowledge base. Another benefit is, that different resources identified by hash URIs can be linked with different Pingback servers. However, a disadvantage (as for the HTML link element too) is that Pingback clients need to retrieve and parse the document instead of requesting the HTTP header only.

---

[4] `http://purl.org/net/pingback/service`

4 Server Behavior

While the communication behavior of the server is completely compatible with the conventional Pingback mechanism (as described in [9]), the manipulation of the target resource and other request handling functionality (e.g. sending email notifications) is implementation and configuration dependent. Consequently, in this section we focus on describing guidelines for the important server side manipulation and request handling issues spam prevention, backlinking and provenance tracking.

4.1 Spam Prevention

At some point every popular service on the Internet, be it Email, Weblogs, Wikis, Newsgroups or Instant Messaging, had to face increasing abuse of their communication service by sending unsolicited bulk messages indiscriminately. Each service dealt with the problem by implementing technical as well as organizational measures, such as black- and whitelists, spam filters, captchas etc.

The Semantic Pingback mechanism prevents spamming by the following verification method. When the Pingback Server receives the notification signal, it automatically fetches the linking resource, checking for the existence of a valid incoming link or an admissible assertion about the target resource. The Pingback server defines, which types of links and information are admissible. This can be based on two general strategies:

- *Information analysis.* Regarding an analysis of the links or assertions, the Pingback server can, for example, dismiss assertions which have logical implications (such as domain, range or cardinality restrictions), but allow label and comment translations into other languages.
- *Publisher relationship analysis.* This can be based e.g. on the trust level of the publisher of the linking resource. A possibility to determine the trust level is to resolve `foaf:knows` relationships from the linked resource publisher to the linking resource publisher.

If admissible links or assertions exist, the Pingback is recorded successfully, e.g. by adding the additional information to the target resource and notifying its publisher. This makes Pingbacks less prone to spam than e.g. trackbacks[5].

In order to allow conventional Pingback servers (e.g. WordPress) to receive links from the Data Web, this link must be represented in a respective HTML representation of the linking resource (managed by the Pingback client) at least as an untyped X(HTML) link. This enables the server to verify the given source resource even without being aware of Linked Data and RDF.

[5] `http://en.wikipedia.org/wiki/Trackback`

4.2 Backlinking

The initial idea behind propagating links from the publisher of the source resource to the publisher of the target resource is to automate the creation of backlinks to the source resource. In typical Pingback enabled blogging systems, a backlink is rendered in the feedback area of a target post together with the title and a short text excerpt of the source resource.

To retrieve all required information from the source resource for verifying the link and gather additional data, a Semantic Pingback server will follow these three steps:

1. Try to catch an RDF representation (e.g. RDF/XML) of the source resource by requesting Linked Data with an HTTP `Accept` header.
2. If this is not possible, the server should try to gather an RDF model from the source resource employing an RDFa parser.
3. If this fails, the server should at least verify the existence of an untyped (X)HTML link in the body of the source resource.

Depending on the category of data which was retrieved from the source resource, the server can react in different ways:

- If there is only an *untyped (X)HTML* link in the source resource, this link can be created as an RDF triple with a generic RDF property like `dc:references` or `sioc:links_to` in the servers knowledge base.
- If there is at least one *direct link* from the source resource to the target resource, this triple should be added to the servers knowledge base.
- If there is any other triple in the source resource where either the subject or the object of the triple corresponds to the target resource, the target resource can be linked using the `rdfs:seeAlso` property with the source resource.

In addition to the statements which link the source and the target resource, metadata about the source resource (e.g. a label and a description) can be stored as well.

4.3 Provenance Tracking

Provenance information can be recorded using the provenance vocabulary [8][6]. This vocabulary describes provenance information based on data access and data creation attributes as well as three basic provenance related types: executions, actors and artefacts. Following the specification in [8], we define a *creation guideline* for Pingback requests, which is described in this paper, and identified by the URI `http://purl.org/net/pingback/RequestGuideline`. A specific Pingback request *execution* is then performed by a Pingback *data creating service*, which uses the defined creation guideline.

[6] The Provenance Vocabulary Core Ontology Specification is available at `http://trdf.sourceforge.net/provenance/ns.html`

The following listing shows an example provenance model represented in N3:

```
@prefix : <http://purl.org/net/provenance/ns#>.
@prefix rdf: <http://www.w3.org/1999/02/22-rdf-syntax-ns#>.
@prefix rdfs: <http://www.w3.org/2000/01/rdf-schema#>.
@prefix sioc: <http://rdfs.org/sioc/ns#>.
@prefix pingback: <http://purl.org/net/pingback/>.

[a rdf:Statement;
 rdf:subject <http://example1.org/Source>;
 rdf:predicate sioc:links_to;
 rdf:object <http://example2.org/Target>;
 :containedBy [
  a :DataItem;
  :createdBy [
   a :DataCreation;
   :performedAt "2010-02-12T12:00:00Z";
   :performedBy [
    a :DataCreatingService;
     rdfs:label "Semantic Pingback Service" ];
     :usedData [
      a :DataItem;
      :containedBy <http://example1.org/Source> ];
    :usedGuideline [a pingback:RequestGuideline ]
]];].
```

This provenance model describes a Pingback from `http://example1.org/Source` to `http://example2.org/Target`. The Pingback was performed Friday, 12 February at noon and resulted in a single statement, which links the source resource to the target resource using a `sioc:links_to` property.

5 Implementation and Evaluation

In this section we describe the implementation and evaluation of Semantic Pingback in three different scenarios. We implemented Semantic Pingback server and client functionality for OntoWiki in order to showcase the semantic features of the approach. Semantic Pingback server functionality was integrated in Triplify, thus supporting the interlinking with relational data on the Data Web. Finally, we implemented a standalone Semantic Pingback server (also available as service), that can be utilized by arbitrary resources that do not provide a Pingback service themselves.

5.1 OntoWiki

OntoWiki [2][7] is a tool for browsing and collaboratively editing RDF knowledge bases. Since OntoWiki enables users to add typed links on external resources, we integrated a Semantic Pingback client component. A recently added feature is the

[7] `http://ontowiki.net`

ability to expose the data stored in OntoWiki via the Linked Data mechanism. Based on that functionality, a Semantic Pingback server component was also integrated.

OntoWiki Pingback client. The Pingback client consists of a plugin that handles a number of events triggered when statements are added or removed from the knowledge base. Each time a statement is added or removed, the plugin first checks, whether:

- the subject resource is a URI inside the namespace of the OntoWiki environment,
- the subject resource is (anonymously) accessible via the Linked Data mechanism[8] and
- the object of the statement is a resource with an de-referenceable URI outside the namespace of the OntoWiki environment.

If the above steps are successfully passed, the plugin tries to autodiscover a Pingback server. This process follows the algorithm described in the original Pingback specification but adds support for target resources represented in RDF as described in section 3.1. If a server was discovered, an XML-RPC post request is send.

OntoWiki Pingback server. The OntoWiki Pingback server is an extension consisting of a plugin handling some request cycle related events, as well as a component that provides a Pingback XML-RPC service. The plugin is responsible for exposing the `X-Pingback` HTTP-header in conjunction with the URL of the RPC service.

The provided Pingback service initially checks, whether the target resource is valid, i.e. is inside the namespace of the OntoWiki environment and accessible via the Linked Data mechanism. If a valid target resource was passed, the service takes the following steps:

1. The server tries to request the target resource as RDF/XML. If an RDF/XML document is retrieved, all relevant triples are extracted.
2. If the above step fails or no relevant triples are found, the OntoWiki Pingback server utilizes a configurable RDFa extraction service (e.g. the W3C RDFa Distiller[9]), which dynamically creates an RDF/XML representation from a target Web page.
3. If the second step fails, the target resource is requested without an additional `Accept`-header. If an HTML document is retrieved, all links in the document are checked. If a link to the target resource is found, a generic triple with the property `sioc:links_to` is formed together with the source as subject and the target resource as object.

[8] This step is added to the process since OntoWiki is able to handle various access control mechanisms and we thus ensure that the Pingback server of the target resource is definitely able to access either the RDF or the (X)HTML representation of the source resource.

[9] `http://www.w3.org/2007/08/pyRdfa/`

Fig. 3. OntoWiki backlinks are rendered in the "Instances Linking Here" side box. The example visualises a personal WebID with three different backlinks using different relations.

Relevant triples are all triples that have either the source resource as subject and the target resource as object or vice versa. If no such statements were found, but the graph contains at least one statement that has the target resource as subject, a `rdfs:seeAlso` link is established from target resource to source resource.

All relevant statements are added to the knowledge base containing the target resource. By using the versioning functionality of OntoWiki, provenance information of statements added via Pingback requests can be determined, thus allowing the service to delete statements that are no longer contained by the source resource.

Backlinks that were established via the Pingback service are displayed in the standard OntoWiki user interface. The "Instances Linking Here" box shows all incoming links for a given resource in conjunction with the type of the link, as visualised in figure 3.

5.2 Triplify

Triplify [1] enables the publication of Linked Data from relational databases. It utilizes simple mappings to map HTTP-URLs to SQL queries and transforms the relational result into RDF statements. Since a large quantity of currently available web data is stored in relational databases, the number of available Linked Data resources increases. As people start to link to those resources, it becomes handy to notify the respective owner. Therefore, we integrated a Semantic Pingback server into Triplify, which exposes an `X-Pingback` HTTP header and handles incoming RPC requests.

The RPC service creates a new database table and stores all registered Pingbacks persistently. Pingbacks are unique for a given source, target and relation and hence can be registered only once. Each time the Pingback service is executed for a given source and target, invalid Pingbacks are removed automatically.

Triplify was extended to export statements for all registered Pingbacks regarding a given target resource along with the instance data. The following listing shows an excerpt of a Triplify export:

```
# ...

<post/1>
  a sioc:Post ;
  sioc:has_creator <user/1> ;
  dcterms:created "2010-02-17T05:48:11" ;
  dcterms:title "Hello world!" ;
  sioc:content "Welcome to WordPress. This is your..." .

# ...

<http://blog.aksw.org/2008/pingback-test/>
  sioc:links_to <post/1> .
```

5.3 Standalone Implementation

Since a large amount of available RDF data on the Web is contained in plain RDF files (e.g. FOAF files), we implemented a standalone Semantic Pingback server[10], that can be configured to allow Pingbacks also on external resources. Based on this implementation, we offer a Semantic Pingback service at: `http://pingback.aksw.org`. It is sufficient to add an RDF statement to an arbitrary web-accessible RDF document stating that the AKSW Pingback service should be used employing the `pingback:service` property. Once a Pingback was send to that service, the owner of the document gets notified via email. This works well for FOAF profiles, since the service can detect a `foaf:mbox` statement in the profile, which relates the WebID to a `mailto:`-URI. If no such statement is found, the service looks for statements that relate the target resource via a `foaf:maker`, `dc:creator`, `sioc:has_creator` or `sioc:has_owner` relation to a resource for which an email address can be obtained.

6 Related Work

Pingback [9] is one of three approaches which allow the automated generation of backlinks on the Social Web. We have chosen the Pingback mechanism as the foundation for this work, since it is widely used and less prone to spam than

[10] Available at: `http://aksw.org/Projects/SemanticPingBack`

for example Trackbacks[11]. Pingback supports the propagation of untyped links only and is hence not directly applicable to the Data Web.

The PSI BackLinking Service for the Web of Data[12] supports the manual creation of backlinks on the Data Web by employing a number of large-scale knowledge bases, as for example, data of the UK Public Sector Information domain. Since it is based on crawling a fixed set of knowledge bases, it cannot be applied for the entire Data Web. Another service that amongst others is integrated with the PSI BackLinking Service is SameAs.org[13] [7]. Other than the Semantic Pingback it crawls the Web of Data in order to determine URIs describing the same resources. OKKAM [3] is a system that aims at unifying resource identifiers by employing metadata about resources in order to match them on entities.

In [10] the authors introduce SILK as a link discovery framework for the data web. It enables the publisher of a dataset to discover links to other datasets, by employing various similarity metrics. Since SILK adds links in the local dataset only and does not inform the publisher of the target dataset, it could be enhanced with a Semantic Pingback client.

The approaches above support interlinking of resources employing centralised hubs, but do not support decentralised, on-the-fly backlinking, since they are based on crawling the Data Web on a regular basis. Consequently the primary goal of these approaches is to reveal resource identifiers describing the same entities, rather than interlinking different resources - a key feature of the Semantic Pingback approach.

7 Conclusion and Future Work

Although the Data Web is currently substantially growing, it still lacks a network effect as we could observe for example with the blogosphere in the Social Web. In particular coherence, information quality, and timeliness are still obstacles for the Data Web to become an Web-wide reality. With this work we aimed at extending and transferring the technological cornerstone of the Social Web the Pingback mechanism towards the Data Web. The resulting Semantic Pingback mechanism has the potential to significantly improve the coherence on the Data Web, since linking becomes bi-directional. With its integrated provenance and spam prevention measures it helps to increase the information quality. Notification services based on Semantic Pingback increase the timeliness of distributed data. In addition these different benefits will mutually strengthen each other. Due to its complete downwards compatibility our Semantic Pingback also bridges the gap between the Social and the Data Web. We also expect the Semantic Pingback mechanism to support the transition process from data silos to flexible, decentralised structured information assets.

[11] `http://www.sixapart.com/pronet/docs/trackback_spec`

[12] `http://backlinks.psi.enakting.org`

[13] `http://sameas.org`

Future Work. Currently the Semantic Pingback mechanism is applicable to relatively static resources, i.e. RDF documents or RDFa annotated Web pages. We plan to extend the Semantic Pingback mechanism in such a way, that it is also usable in conjunction with dynamically generated views on the Data Web - i.e. SPARQL query results. This would allow end-users as well as applications using remote SPARQL endpoints to get notified once results of a query change.

References

1. Auer, S., Dietzold, S., Lehmann, J., Hellmann, S., Aumueller, D.: Triplify – lightweight linked data publication from relational databases. In: Proceedings of the 17th International Conference on World Wide Web, WWW 2009 (2009)
2. Auer, S., Dietzold, S., Riechert, T.: OntoWiki - A Tool for Social, Semantic Collaboration. In: Cruz, I., Decker, S., Allemang, D., Preist, C., Schwabe, D., Mika, P., Uschold, M., Aroyo, L.M. (eds.) ISWC 2006. LNCS, vol. 4273, pp. 736–749. Springer, Heidelberg (2006)
3. Bouquet, P., Stoermer, H., Niederée, C., Mana, A.: Entity name system: The backbone of an open and scalable web of data. In: Proceedings of the 2th IEEE International Conference on Semantic Computing, ICSC 2008 (2008)
4. Breslin, J., Harth, A., Bojars, U., Decker, S.: Towards semantically-interlinked online communities. In: Gómez-Pérez, A., Euzenat, J. (eds.) ESWC 2005. LNCS, vol. 3532, pp. 500–514. Springer, Heidelberg (2005)
5. Ciccarese, P., Wu, E., Wong, G.T., Ocana, M., Kinoshita, J., Ruttenberg, A., Clark, T.: The swan biomedical discourse ontology. Journal of Biomedical Informatics 41(5), 739–751 (2008)
6. Corlosquet, S., Cyganiak, R., Polleres, A., Decker, S.: RDFa in Drupal: Bringing cheese to the web of data. In: Proc. of 5th Workshop on Scripting and Development for the Semantic Web at ESWC 2009 (2009)
7. Glaser, H., Jaffri, A., Millard, I.: Managing Co-reference on the Semantic Web. In: Proceedings of the Linked Data on the Web Workshop, LDOW 2009 (2009)
8. Hartig, O.: Provenance information in the web of data. In: LDOW 2009, Madrid, Spain, April 20 (2009)
9. Langridge, S., Hickson, I.: Pingback 1.0. Technical report (2002), `http://hixie.ch/specs/pingback/pingback`
10. Volz, J., Bizer, C., Gaedke, M., Kobilarov, G.: Silk – a link discovery framework for the web of data. In: Proceedings of LDOW (2009), `http://www4.wiwiss.fu-berlin.de/bizer/silk/spec`

Social People-Tagging vs. Social Bookmark-Tagging

Peyman Nasirifard, Sheila Kinsella, Krystian Samp, and Stefan Decker

Digital Enterprise Research Institute
National University of Ireland, Galway
IDA Business Park, Lower Dangan, Galway, Ireland
firstname.lastname@deri.org

Abstract. Tagging has been widely used and studied in various domains. Recently, people-tagging has emerged as a means to categorize contacts, and is also used in some social access control mechanisms. In this paper, we investigate whether there are differences between people-tagging and bookmark-tagging. We show that the way we tag documents about people, who we do not know personally, is similar to the way we tag online documents (i.e., bookmarks) about other categories (i.e., city, country, event). However, we show that the tags assigned to a document related to a friend, differ from the tags assigned to someone we do not know personally. We also analyze whether the age and gender of a taggee - a person, who is tagged by others - have influences on social people-tags (i.e., people-tags assigned in social Web 2.0 platforms).

Keywords: Tagging, People-Tagging, Folksonomy, Bookmark-Tagging, Social Media.

1 Introduction and Motivation

Tagging is a practice in knowledge management, which involves assigning arbitrary or closed terms to an object for various purposes [1]. Since the birth of Web 2.0 applications, tagging has been widely used and studied in various platforms, mainly for annotating online resources (e.g., photos, videos, bookmarks). Recently, people-tagging has emerged as a means to organize contacts, build user profiles and manage competencies, especially in large scale organizations [6,7,5]. People-tagging is simply the (online) tagging of human beings and is a mechanism that is currently used in platforms such as Fringe Contacts [7]. Some websites (e.g., blog.ca, tagalag.com, 43people.com) enable users to tag each other as well.

Tag recommenders for tagging online resources have been widely studied and are used in various platforms like delicious.com. Work by Rattenbury et al. [19] describes an approach for automatically identifying tags in Flickr which relate to locations and events. There exist also approaches like Tess [17] that recommends tags based on content of a document. To the best of our knowledge, a recommender for tagging human beings is not well studied. We hope a study of how people tag each other on social platforms can give us a starting point of how to recommend appropriate tags for people or to build recommender systems that use people-tags. We envision the application of such recommenders for enhancing the usability of access control mechanisms (e.g., information filtering mechanisms) that are built on top of annotating people [20,16,24].

P. Cimiano and H.S. Pinto (Eds.): EKAW 2010, LNAI 6317, pp. 150–162, 2010.

In this study, we plan to address two main research questions.

- *Q1*: Does the nature of tags of articles belonging to various categories (i.e., person, event, country and city) differ? In the first part of our analysis, we compare the tags associated to Wikipedia articles related to persons with the tags that have been assigned to articles of the other categories (i.e., city, country, and event).
- *Q2*: Does the nature of tags assigned to Wikipedia pages describing persons differ from the tags that are assigned to persons (i.e., friends) in online social network platforms?

Moreover, we also take a look at the roles of gender and age of taggees within social platforms. For the remainder of the paper, we will use the terms Person, Event, City and Country to refer to the subject of a Wikipedia article related to a person, event, city and country respectively; and Friend to refer to a contact on a social network site.

The rest of this paper proceeds as follows: First, we present related work in Section 2. In Section 3, we describe our method for extracting people-tags and also statistics related to data we collected. Next, in Section 4, we describe our methodology for analyzing the tags and we address the research questions we posed. We present results related to the age and gender of taggees in Section 5. Finally, we close the paper with the conclusion and have an overview of future work in Section 6.

2 Related Work

Previous research on document classification has shown that people use attributes that are subjective in the organization of personal documents [2]. Some researchers have studied various aspects of tag usage including the behavior of users of different types of tagging systems [12], motivations behind tagging [22], tag distribution, tag dynamics and tag-tag correlations [10], and the changes in user activity in tagging systems over time [9].

There exists previous work on classifying tags, both manually and automatically. Overell et al. [18] describe a method to automatically classify flickr.com tags using a vocabulary constructed from Wikipedia and WordNet. Bischoff et al. [4] compare tag characteristics between different types of resources: webpages (delicious.com), music (last.fm) and images (flickr.com). The classification is performed manually. Sen et al. [23] classify tags from a movie recommendation system as Factual, Subjective or Personal and study how these classes of tags are used, and how useful these tags are for user tasks. Xu et al. [25] present a taxonomy of tags, and use this taxonomy as a means of ensuring diversity in their tag suggestion system. Previous work comparing tagging for different resource types includes also [14], which studies bookmarks in systems for documents, for people, for blog entries, and for activity records, in an online corporate environment. They found that users' tagging behavior tended to differ between the systems. Koerner et al. [11] classified taggers into two broad groups: *categorizers*, who use a small set of tags similar to hierarchical classification schemes; and *describers*, who use more descriptive keywords for tagging resources. Then they applied semantic similarity measures to various partitions of a large data-set that were tagged by both *categorizers* and *describers* and concluded that describers are more effective for emergence of tag semantics.

Farrell et al. [7] analyze the people-tags that are assigned to people within an enterprise. Similarly, Muller et al. [15] present the results of an experiment, where a service was provided for people to apply tags to one another within an online corporate environment. They classified tag usage and found that users have a preference to apply tags related to expertise to themselves, and to apply tags related to roles to others. Bernstein et al. [3] showed that the initiative of people-tagging can be fun using social games.

Our work differs from the work listed above in that we compare the tag classifications inspired from [23] for different categories of Wikipedia articles (i.e., persons, places, and events). We also compare the tag classifications inspired from [23] for tags assigned to Wikipedia articles about famous people with those assigned by people to their friends within public social platforms.

3 Data Collection

Our first goal is to extract tags that were assigned to Wikipedia articles that are related to a particular type of category (i.e., Person, City, Country, Event). To this end, we used DBpedia[1], which is a community effort for extracting structured data from Wikipedia. DBpedia transforms Wikipedia pages into *categorized data*. There exist several end points for DBpedia data, which allow end users to query it using the SPARQL[2] query language. We used version 3.2 of DBpedia for our analysis. We extracted four different types of categories from DBpedia: person, city, country and event. For extracting the person data (i.e., links to Wikipedia pages related to persons), we used the complete set of instances in the DBpedia person data dump[3]. As there was no DBpedia data dump for other categories (i.e., city, country and event), we crafted SPARQL queries to extract links to Wikipedia pages. After gathering the Wikipedia links from DBpedia, we crawled delicious.com to get the tags associated to those Wikipedia articles[4]. Figure 1 shows a simplified view of our approach for extracting tags associated to a specific category. All tags are lower-cased. We retrieved only the tags associated to English Wikipedia pages. Table 1 shows properties of the data retrieved from four different categories of Wikipedia articles.

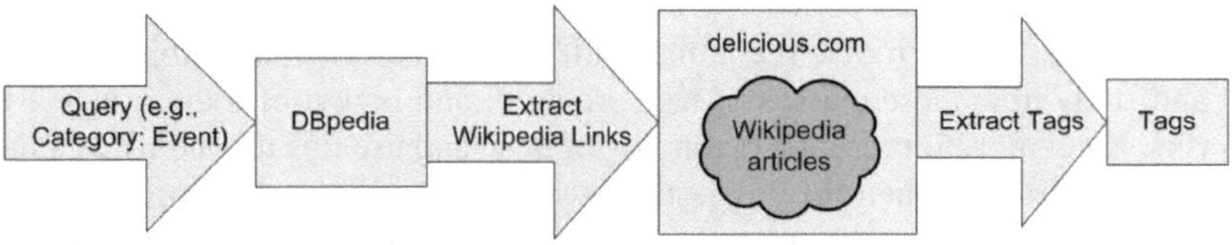

Fig. 1. Overall approach for extracting category-based tags

[1] `http://dbpedia.org`
[2] `http://www.w3.org/TR/rdf-sparql-query/`
[3] `http://wiki.dbpedia.org/Downloads32#persondata`
[4] We crawled delicious.com in June 2009.

Table 1. Properties of Wikipedia article collection

Type	Items	Tagged	Untagged	Total Tags	Unique Tags
Person	20284	4031 (19.9%)	16253 (80.1%)	75548	14346 (19%)
Event	7601	1427 (18.8%)	6174 (81.2%)	8924	2582 (29%)
Country	1734	638 (36.8%)	1096 (63.2%)	13002	3200 (25%)
City	40197	1137 (2.8%)	39060 (97.2%)	4703	1907(40%)

Table 2. Properties of social sites tag collection

Site	Users	Tagged	Untagged	Total Tags	Unique Tags
blog.co.uk	1474	553 (37.5%)	921 (62.5%)	3509	2665 (75.9%)
blog.ca	429	100 (23.3%)	329 (76.7%)	569	492 (86.5%)
blog.de	5836	2035 (34.8%)	3801 (65.2%)	11966	7626 (63.7%)
blog.fr	962	239 (24.8%)	723 (75.2%)	1082	803 (74.2%)
Aggregation	8701	2927 (33.6%)	5774 (66.4%)	17126	10913 (63.7%)

For our second goal, extracting social people-tags, we used four distinct but related social websites[5]. The main purpose of these sites is to blog, but they allow also users to maintain social networks and tag each other. Two websites are in English, one in German and one in French. In order to unify the people-tags, we used the Google translator API[6] to translate non-English tags. As the context of the people-tags were not present in those websites, using the Google API was a good alternative to using a native human translator for top tags, which were mostly one-term tags. Note that in non-English websites, some people used English tags as well. Table 2 shows properties of the people-tags crawled from those websites. The number of users in Table 2 indicates the total number of registered users on the sites[7].

4 Experiments

In this section, we address the research questions we posed in section 1, i.e., do tags of Persons differ from tags of other topics? And do tags of Friends differ from tags of Persons? In order to answer these questions we first examined the distribution of the tags. We used WordNet [13] to categorize the tags and compared them. We also used a manual method inspired from [23] to categorize the top-100 tags for each topic. Towards this direction, we defined the following categories:

- Objective: Objective tags are those tags that identify the facts about somebody or something. For example, locations, concepts, somebody's role and expertise are categorized as objective tags. Name Entities (NE) fall into this category (e.g., london).

[5] `http://www.blog.de, http://www.blog.ca, http://www.blog.co.uk/, http://www.blog.fr/`

[6] `http://code.google.com/apis/ajaxlanguage/`

[7] We crawled the websites in June 2009.

- Subjective: Subjective tags are those tags that reflect the personal opinion and feedback about someone or something. For example, the opinions about physical and behavioral characteristics of somebody are categorized as subjective tags (e.g., jealous).
- Uncategorized: We asked our participants to assign those tags that could not fit well into one of above categories, or their meaning/usage were ambiguous, to this category (e.g., abcxyz).

We tried to keep the categories as clear and simple as possible, as we did not want to make the categorization task difficult for our participants. In total, 25 persons, who were mainly from computer science and IT backgrounds participated in our study. Each of the 25 participants was assigned the top-100 tags for one category and was asked to categorize them based on our scheme. The participants were free to search for the meaning of the tags on the Web.

4.1 Research Question 1 (Q1) - Does the Nature of Tags of Articles Belonging to Various Categories of Wikipedia Articles Differ?

Table 3 shows the top-20 tags assigned to Wikipedia articles related to various categories (i.e., Person, City, Country, and Event) plus their frequencies. What we observed from the nature of top tags of Wikipedia articles was the fact that *Persons* on Wikipedia were mostly tagged with the concepts that they are famous for (e.g., music, politics, poetry). Most of the top tags associated to *Events* were related to *war* (e.g., ww2, battle, war). The *Countries* were likely tagged with their continents, their historic background or the name of the country itself (e.g., europe, empire, japan). The *Cities* were mostly tagged with the countries that they are located in (e.g., spain, germany, uk). The distribution of the tags among four categories follows Zipf's law [21]. That means most tags occurred rarely, whereas a small subset of tags have been used a lot (see Figure 2).

Figure 3 demonstrates the linguistics categories of the tags based on WordNet classifications. We normalized the values. As illustrated in Figure 3, most tags for all four resource types, that were categorized by WordNet, were nouns; while verbs, adjectives and adverbs followed respectively.

After getting the results from our participants, we ran a Repeated Measures Analysis of Variance (ANOVA) [8] with between-subject factor. The ANOVA statistical method is commonly used in fields such as sociology or human-computer interaction to analyze data obtained from human participants in controlled experiments. This method allows us to determine if differences between results are statistically significant. In our study each participant received top-100 tags for one Wikipedia resource type (i.e., Country, City, Event, or Person) and had to categorize them into three groups: objective, subjective or uncategorized. Consequently, the between-subject factor was *wikipedia-resource-type* (i.e., Country, City, Event, and Person) and the within-subject factor was the *tag-category* (i.e., objective, subjective, and uncategorized).

Note that Friend as a resource type was not included here. The dependent variable was the number of occurrences of a *tag-category* within top-100 tags for a *wikipedia-resource-type*. There was no significant main effect of *wikipedia-resource-type*, as the mean number of tag occurrences for each resource type was always the same (i.e., 100

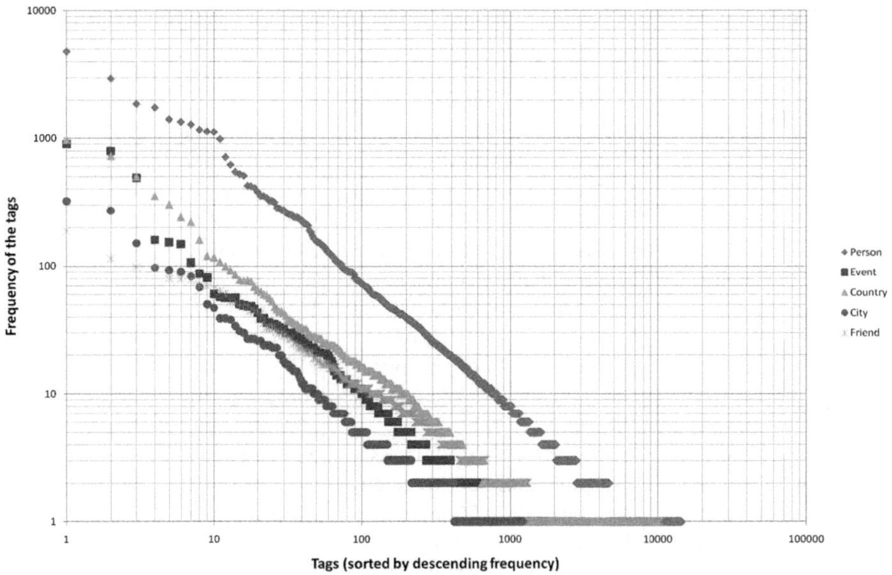

Fig. 2. Distribution of the tags assigned to various types of Wikipedia articles and also Friends on blog-related websites based on a log-log scale. 64% of the tags assigned to Friends on blog-related websites were unique, whereas only 19% of the tags assigned to Persons on Wikipedia were unique.

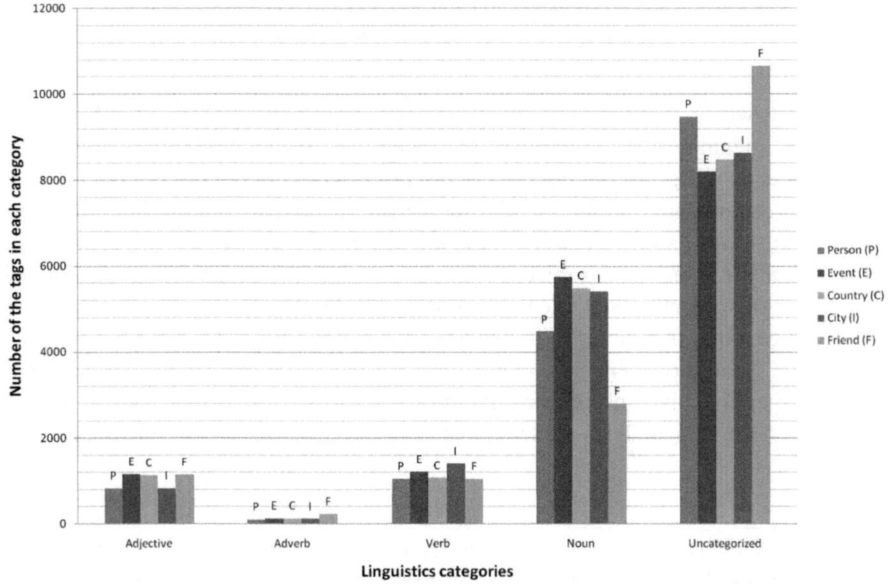

Fig. 3. Normalized linguistics categories of the tags assigned to various types of Wikipedia articles and also Friends on blog-related websites

Table 3. Top-20 tags associated to various Wikipedia categories and their frequencies

Person	F.	Event	F.	Country	F.	City	F.
wikipedia	4776	history	904	wikipedia	972	travel	322
people	2941	war	791	history	727	wikipedia	273
philosophy	1856	wikipedia	488	travel	500	italy	151
history	1737	ww2	160	geography	354	germany	97
wiki	1404	politics	153	africa	303	history	93
music	1341	wiki	148	culture	242	london	90
politics	1279	military	106	wiki	222	uk	83
art	1164	battle	87	reference	161	wiki	68
books	1130	wwii	81	europe	120	places	50
literature	1119	iraq	60	country	117	england	47
science	984	reference	57	countries	108	geography	39
biography	708	ajalugu	56	world	100	scotland	39
reference	618	wars	56	politics	93	europe	38
authors	543	olympics	56	research	86	brazil	34
author	522	civilwar	50	empire	78	slow_italy	31
research	508	usa	49	islands	77	city	30
film	424	wwi	48	information	77	information	27
toread	420	vietnam	48	india	76	japan	27
artist	409	russia	46	info	69	barcelona	27
psychology	380	iraqwar	43	japan	65	spain	26
poetry	353	china	39	island	63	berlin	26
religion	352	music	39	china	60	cities	24
culture	342	300	36	asia	59	photography	24
design	325	research	36	australia	56	reference	24
writing	324	ww1	35	germany	53	switzerland	23

tags). There was a significant main effect of *tag-category* ($F(1.48, 23.7) = 270.3$, $p < .001$)[8] meaning that the numbers of subjective, objective and uncategorized tags differed. Lack of significant interaction effect between *tag-category* and *wikipedia-resource-type* indicated, however, that the ratios of objective, subjective and uncategorized tags were similar across *wikipedia-resource-types*. Pair-wise comparisons[9] showed that the number of subjective tags was smaller than objective ones and that the number of subjective and uncategorized tags did not differ from each other. These results suggest that people tag Wikipedia resources the same way regardless of the resource type using more objective than subjective tags. Figure 4 shows the distribution of subjective, objective and uncategorized tags for different resource types. Note that Figure 4 contains tag analysis related to Friend as well, as we refer to it in the following subsection.

[8] The ANOVA's assumption of sphericity for tag-category was violated as indicated by Mauchly's test. In such a situation, it is necessary to use one of the corrections for degrees of freedom. To this end, we used Greenhouse-Geisser correction ($\epsilon = .74$).

[9] For pair-wise comparisons we used Bonferroni adjustment to preserve familywise significance level.

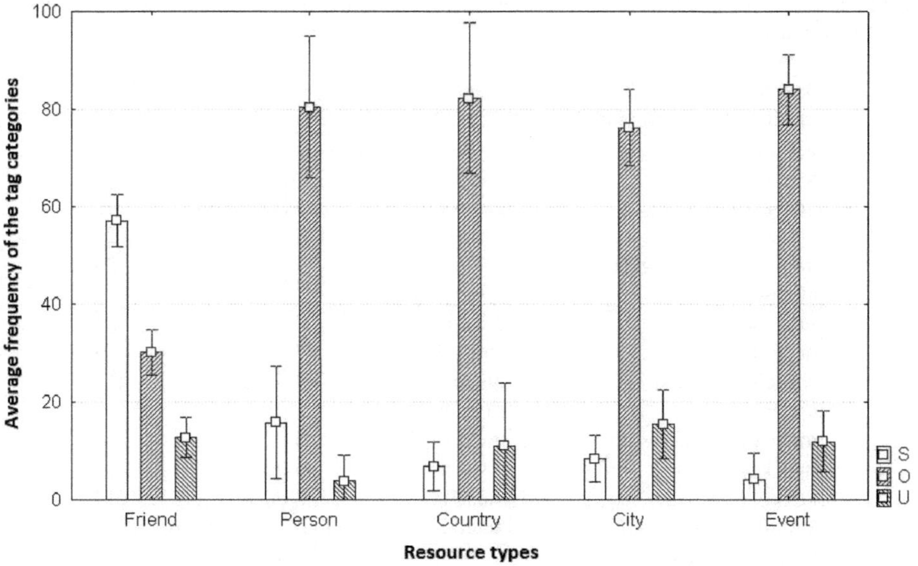

Fig. 4. Average frequencies (+/- standard deviations) of subjective (S), objective (O) and uncategorized (U) tags as a function of resource type. For Person, Country, City and Event resource types tags are mostly objective (Q1), while for Friend tags are mostly subjective (Q2).

4.2 Research Question 2 (Q2) - Does the Nature of Tags Assigned to Wikipedia Pages Describing Persons Differ from the Tags That Are Assigned to Persons (i.e., Friends) in Online Social Network Platforms?

To answer Q2, we compared the people-tags assigned in social platforms with the tags that were assigned to Persons on Wikipedia. Table 4 shows the top-15 people-tags extracted from previously mentioned blog-related websites, their translation and also the frequencies. We observed that top tags assigned to people in social media were *attributes* and mostly related to physical characteristics and hobbies (e.g., music junkie, pretty, sweet, nice, honest). This was also proved by mapping the tags to WordNet. The mapping showed that among those people-tags that could be categorized by WordNet, the frequency of adjectives and adverbs in social media were higher than for Wikipedia articles related to persons (i.e., Person), whereas the frequency of nouns was lower (see Figure 3 for a normalized comparison). The distribution of Friend people-tags follows Zipf's law as well, but with a longer tail, meaning that 64% of the tags assigned to Friends on blog-related websites were unique, whereas only 19% of the tags assigned to Persons on Wikipedia were unique (see Figure 2).

After getting the results from our participants, we ran the same type of ANOVA with the difference that the *resource-type* factor had 2 levels: Person and Friend. Again, there was no significant main effect of *resource-type*. There was a significant main effect for

Table 4. Top-15 people-tags in different languages from blog-related websites, their translation and frequencies

blog.de	F.	blog.fr	F.	blog.ca & .co.uk	F.
musikjunkie (music junkie)	188	art (art)	19	funny	34
nett (nice)	81	politique (politics)	14	music	32
leben (live)	77	musique (music)	14	life	31
lustig (funny)	73	gentil (kind)	9	kk friend	29
lieb (dear)	69	adorable (adorable)	8	funky	25
intelligent (intelligent)	66	amour (love)	7	friendly	23
huebsch (pretty)	61	sympa (sympa)	7	lovely	22
sexy (sexy)	59	dessin (drawing)	7	cool	22
liebe (love)	58	amiti (friendship)	7	sexy	19
ehrlich (honest)	56	digne de confiance (trustworthy)	7	love	18
interessant (interesting)	48	bon (good)	6	art	16
musik (music)	45	histoire (history)	6	poetry	16
kreativ (creative)	45	vie (life)	6	nice	14
humorvoll (humorous)	42	humour (humor)	6	photography	13
freundlich (kind)	41	sensible (sensitive)	5	barking	13

tag-category ($F(1.33, 13.3) = 69.6, p < .001$)[10] meaning that the numbers of subjective, objective and uncategorized tags differed. This time, there was a significant interaction effect ($F(2, 20) = 67, p < .001$) indicating that the ratios of objective, subjective and uncategorized tags differed for both *resource-types*. For pair-wise comparisons we used dependant and independent t-tests. The number of subjective tags for Friend was higher than for Person (independent samples t-test, $t(10) = 8.5$, $p < .00001$). The number of objective tags for Friend was lower than for Person (independent samples t-test, $t(10) = -8.7, p < .00001$). Also, the number of uncategorized tags was higher for Friend than for Person (independent samples t-test, $t(10) = 3.29$, $p = .008$). For Person, the number of objective tags was higher than subjective ones (dependent samples t-test, $t(4) = -5.6, p = .005$); there were more objective tags than uncategorized ones (dependent samples t-test, $t(4) = 9.2$, $p < .001$), but the number of subjective and uncategorized tags did not differ from each other. For Friend, the number of subjective tags was higher than objective ones (dependent samples t-test, $t(6) = 7.9$, $p < .001$); there were more subjective tags than uncategorized ones (dependent samples t-test, $t(6) = 14.2, p < .0001$) and more objective than uncategorized (dependent samples t-test, $t(6) = 6.5$, $p < .001$). These results suggest that people use different tags for their friends compared to resources describing other persons. Friends are mostly assigned subjective tags while other persons objective ones.

4.3 Random Tags

We also wished to investigate whether the properties of a random set of tags were similar to the properties of the most popular tags that we used in our experiments. Many of

[10] Again, as the data for *tag-category* was non-spherical, we used Greenhouse-Geisser correction ($\epsilon = .67$).

the tags in delicious.com and people-tags within social platforms are part of the long tail (i.e., tags with lower frequencies) and it is possible that these tags have different usage patterns to the top tags. Therefore, we also created one set of random-100 people-tags (i.e., associated with Friends) and one set of random-100 Wikipedia tags for each category (i.e., Person, Event, City and Country) and asked each of the 25 participants in our experiments to categorize them based on our scheme. For the Wikipedia articles, the result showed that even for random tags on average more objective tags are assigned than subjective. But for Friend, the amount of subjective and objective tags were statistically equal, taking into account that more than 40% of the tags could not be categorized by our participants. The participants mentioned that some tags were strange, as they could not understand the meaning of them. Thus, they assigned them to the uncategorized group. We speculate that our participants were not aware of the context that the people-tags were assigned. In other words, among friends, there are usually lots of events and issues that only those friends are aware of and can be used as tags (i.e., subjective), but from a participant point of view, they could not be categorized.

Finally, we calculated the inter-annotator agreement of the random-100 sets and the top-100 sets. The average inter-annotator agreement for random-100 tags was 76%, whereas for top-100 tags it was 86%. The long-tail tags do not have as clear a meaning as the top tags, and therefore are probably less useful in applications such as information filtering.

5 Age and Gender

The data on social blog sites contains age and gender of taggees as well. Although this was not the main focus of this paper, the data gave us useful input for further analysis. Towards this direction, we conducted an additional experiment. We prepared three sets of top tags ($A1$,$A2$, and $A3$) assigned to various age ranges (age ≤ 25, $25 <$ age ≤ 50, and age > 50) respectively; and for the second part of the experiment, we prepared two sets of top tags ($G1$ and $G2$) assigned to the male and female genders respectively. Note that we removed tags that refer to a specific gender for this experiment. Table 5 shows the top-15 tags of $A1$, $A2$, $A3$, $G1$, and $G2$. We asked 10 participants to a) take a look at the first three sets and let us know, if they could predict the possible age range of taggees for each set; and b) take a look at the second two sets and let us know if they could justify whether one set is more suitable for a specific gender. We asked these questions in order to determine whether there were perceptible differences between the tag sets. All participants agreed that $A1$ is used for younger people, due to existence of some tags that are mostly used for teens and young people (e.g., naive, music junkie, sexy, freak, dreamy). These tags were categorized as subjective tags. Most participants did not see any major differences between $A2$ and $A3$, and they mentioned that it was extremely difficult to distinguish between them, but they claimed that both sets are more likely used for older people, due to existence of some tags like politics, art, and poetry (i.e., objective tags). For the second part of the experiment, there was a consensus indicating that no major differences exist between $G1$ and $G2$. Most participants claimed that both sets suit both genders.

Table 5. Top-15 tags for varying age ranges and gender of taggees

≤ 25	> 25 and ≤ 50	> 50	Male	Female
music junkie	funny	kk friend	music junkie	music junkie
pretty	music junkie	funky	funny	love
nice	nice	funny	music	pretty
love	music	politics	nice	nice
sweet	live	love	politics	funny
funny	love	kunst	intelligent	sexy
music	intelligent	live	sexy	live
sexy	sexy	kind	love	dear
crazy	dear	music	live	sweet
dear	cool	friendly	kind	honest
honest	humorous	helpful	reliable	intelligent
intelligent	interesting	art	dear	crazy
creative	honest	humor	sports	interesting
interesting	kind	sensitive	sweet	music
thoughtful	creative	honest	art	cool

6 Conclusion and Future Work

In this paper, we presented the result of experiments related to people-tagging and bookmark-tagging. We showed that the pages related to persons on Wikipedia are tagged the same as other types (i.e., events, cities, and countries) - in terms of subjective/objective/uncategorized categories. People use more objective tags for tagging Wikipedia articles related to aforementioned article types. However, the tags assigned to a web-page related to a person on Wikipedia differs from the way we tag a friend on a social website. Friends on social websites are mostly tagged with subjective tags. In addition, we found that in social media, younger taggees are primarily assigned with more subjective tags, whereas older ones are also assigned with some objective tags. We plan to explore the possibility of using the result of this study for building a social people-tag recommender for our access control framework. As taggers tend to use more subjective tags for their friends within social platforms, this brings new challenges for recommending appropriate people-tags. It will be necessary to find some ways to handle or eliminate the subjectivity of people-tags (e.g., by defining and using controlled or semi-controlled vocabularies based on the top used people-tags), in order to increase the precision of people-tag-based recommenders and thus, usability of information filtering frameworks that are built on top of people-tags [20,16,24].

Recently, Twitter[11] introduced a feature called *Twitter Lists* that enables users to assign each other to various lists. This feature is normally used for grouping like-minded or similar people (in terms of affiliation, interest, expertise, etc.) and can be perceived as a way of tagging them. As Twitter is the fastest growing social networking service on the Web[12] and Twitter data (e.g., friends, followers, Twitter lists) are also public (for

[11] `http://twitter.com`

[12] `http://eu.techcrunch.com/2010/01/26/opera-facebook-largest-\mobile-social-network-twitter-fastest-growing`

public accounts), we envision getting more real-world (people-tag) data by crawling Twitter and perhaps building an information filtering recommender based on Twitter lists.

Acknowledgments

This work is partially supported by Science Foundation Ireland (SFI) under Grant No. SFI/08/CE/I1380 (Lion-2 project). We appreciate Conor Hayes for his valuable comments. We also thank anonymous reviewers for their valuable inputs.

References

1. Ames, M., Naaman, M.: Why we tag: motivations for annotation in mobile and online media. In: CHI 2007, pp. 971–980. ACM Press, New York (2007)
2. Bergman, O., Beyth-Marom, R., Nachmias, R.: The user-subjective approach to personal information management systems. Journal of the American Society for Information Science and Technology 54(9), 872–878 (2003)
3. Bernstein, M., Tan, D.S., Smith, G., Czerwinski, M., Horvitz, E.: Collabio: a game for annotating people within social networks. In: UIST 2009, pp. 97–100. ACM, New York (2009)
4. Bischoff, K., Firan, C.S., Nejdl, W., Paiu, R.: Can all tags be used for search? In: CIKM 2008: Proceeding of the 17th ACM conference on information and knowledge management, pp. 193–202. ACM, New York (2008)
5. Braun, S., Kunzmann, C., Schmidt, A.: People tagging & ontology maturing: Towards collaborative competence management. In: 8th International Conference on the Design of Cooperative Systems, COOP (2008)
6. Farrell, S., Lau, T.: Fringe contacts: People-Tagging for the enterprise. In: Proceedings of the Collaborative Web Tagging Workshop at WWW 2006 (2006)
7. Farrell, S., Lau, T., Nusser, S., Wilcox, E., Muller, M.: Socially augmenting employee profiles with people-tagging. In: UIST 2007, pp. 91–100. ACM, New York (2007)
8. Freedman, D., Pisani, R., Purves, R.: Statistics. W.W. Norton & Co. (2007)
9. Golder, S.A., Huberman, B.A.: Usage patterns of collaborative tagging systems. Journal of Information Science 32(2), 198–208 (2006)
10. Halpin, H., Robu, V., Shepherd, H.: The complex dynamics of collaborative tagging. In: WWW 2007: Proceedings of the 16th International Conference on World Wide Web, pp. 211–220. ACM, New York (2007)
11. Koerner, C., Benz, D., Hotho, A., Strohmaier, M., Stumme, G.: Stop thinking, start tagging: tag semantics emerge from collaborative verbosity. In: WWW 2010: Proceedings of the 19th International Conference on World Wide Web, pp. 521–530. ACM, New York (2010)
12. Marlow, C., Naaman, M., Boyd, D., Davis, M.: Ht06, tagging paper, taxonomy, flickr, academic article, to read. In: HT 2006: Proceedings of the Seventeenth Conference on Hypertext and Hypermedia, pp. 31–40. ACM, New York (2006)
13. Miller, G.A.: Wordnet: A lexical database for english. Communications of the ACM 38(11), 39–41 (1995)
14. Muller, M.J.: Comparing tagging vocabularies among four enterprise tag-based services. In: GROUP 2007, pp. 341–350. ACM, New York (2007)
15. Muller, M.J., Ehrlich, K., Farrell, S.: Social tagging and self-tagging for impression management. Tech. rep., IBM Watson Research Center (2007)

16. Nasirifard, P., Peristeras, V.: Uncle-share: Annotation-based access control for cooperative and social systems. In: OTM Conferences (2), pp. 1122–1130 (2008)
17. Oliveira, B., Calado, P., Pinto, H.S.: Automatic tag suggestion based on resource contents. In: Gangemi, A., Euzenat, J. (eds.) EKAW 2008. LNCS (LNAI), vol. 5268, pp. 255–264. Springer, Heidelberg (2008)
18. Overell, S., Sigurbjörnsson, B., van Zwol, R.: Classifying tags using open content resources. In: WSDM 2009: Proceedings of the Second ACM International Conference on Web Search and Data Mining, pp. 64–73. ACM, New York (2009)
19. Rattenbury, T., Good, N., Naaman, M.: Towards automatic extraction of event and place semantics from flickr tags. In: SIGIR 2007, pp. 103–110. ACM, New York (2007)
20. Razavi, M.N., Iverson, L.: Improving personal privacy in social systems with people-tagging. In: GROUP 2009, pp. 11–20. ACM, New York (2009)
21. Reed, W.J.: The pareto, zipf and other power laws. Economics Letters 74(1), 15–19 (2001)
22. Santos-Neto, E., Condon, D., Andrade, N., Iamnitchi, A., Ripeanu, M.: Individual and social behavior in tagging systems. In: HT 2009: Proceedings of the 20th ACM Conference on Hypertext and Hypermedia, pp. 183–192. ACM, New York (2009)
23. Sen, S., Lam, S.K., Rashid, A.M., Cosley, D., Frankowski, D., Osterhouse, J., Harper, F.M., Riedl, J.: Tagging, communities, vocabulary, evolution. In: Proceedings of the 20th Anniversary Conference on Computer Supported Cooperative Work, pp. 181–190. ACM, New York (2006)
24. Wang, Q., Jin, H.: Selective message distribution with people-tagging in user-collaborative environments. In: CHI Extended Abstracts, pp. 4549–4554 (2009)
25. Xu, Z., Fu, Y., Mao, J., Su, D.: Towards the semantic web: Collaborative tag suggestions. In: Proceedings of the Collaborative Web Tagging Workshop at WWW 2006 (2006)

FOLCOM or the Costs of Tagging

Elena Simperl[1], Tobias Bürger[2], and Christian Hofer[3]

[1] Karlsruhe Institute of Technology, Karlsruhe, Germany
elena.simperl@kit.edu
[2] Salzburg Research Forschungsgesellschaft mbH, Salzburg, Austria
tobias.buerger@salzburgresearch.at
[3] University of Innsbruck, Innsbruck, Austria
c.hofer@student.uibk.ac.at

Abstract. This paper introduces FOLCOM, a FOLksonomy Cost estimatiOn Method that uses a story-points-approach to quantitatively assess the efforts that are cumulatively associated with tagging a collection of information objects by a community of users. The method was evaluated through individual, face-to-face structured interviews with eight knowledge management experts from several large ICT enterprises interested in either adopting tagging internally as a knowledge management solution, or just in tangible evidence of its added value. As a second theme of our evaluation, we calibrated the parameters of the method based on data collected from a series of six user experiments, reaching a promising prediction accuracy within a margin of $\pm 25\%$ in 75% of the cases.

1 Motivation and Main Contributions

Capitalizing on their popularity on the public Web – through Web 2.0-style platforms such as del.icio.us, Flickr and YouTube – folksonomies gradually enter the enterprise arena with the promise to provide a lightweight, easy-to-use means to manage and share knowledge in a collaborative environment [6,14,20]. Nevertheless, to sustain this trend, and to have a strong case in favor of knowledge-based technologies, CIOs and CTOs are yet seeking for instruments to accurately analyze the costs and benefits associated with the adoption of tagging, and the creation and maintenance of folksonomies, within enterprises. A study done by McKinsey in 2008 on the usage of Web 2.0 technologies within companies confirms this state of affairs – the most important barrier impeding the mainstream adoption of tagging, wikis, social networks, to name just a few, at the corporate level lays within the fact that the benefits of these technologies are not tangible, or yet poorly investigated [13]. Furthermore, the study identifies a number of additional open issues in this regard: Web 2.0 projects often lack commitment at the management level, are rarely fully compliant with the corporate culture, and overlook the importance of setting in place the proper incentive schemes to ensure the durable involvement of a critical mass of enterprise users. Supported by these findings, we argue that instruments to analyze the real costs and benefits of tagging are a must to provide businesses with the right arguments in favor of the usage of Web 2.0 technologies, and to encourage large-scale, sustainable take-up.

P. Cimiano and H.S. Pinto (Eds.): EKAW 2010, LNAI 6317, pp. 163–177, 2010.

This paper introduces FOLCOM, which offers such an instrument. FOLCOM, which stays for **FOL**ksonomy **C**ost estimati**O**n **M**ethod, uses a story-points-approach to quantitatively assess the efforts that are cumulatively associated with tagging a collection of information objects by a community of users. We surveyed well-established approaches to cost estimation in software and knowledge engineering, in particular along the themes of agile development, and open source and community-driven development, which share many commonalities with the tagging scenario from a procedural point of view. Based on the findings of this survey, we designed a method by which the time required to annotate a collection of information objects by a community of users can be estimated in relation to the size of this collection, the complexity of the content it contains, and the expertise of the community contributing to this effort. The method was evaluated using individual, face-to-face structured interviews with eight knowledge management experts from several large ICT enterprises interested in either adopting tagging internally as a knowledge management solution, or just in tangible evidence of its added value. In addition, we calibrated the parameters of the method by collecting data from a series of six user experiments, reaching an adequate prediction accuracy within a margin of $\pm 25\%$ in 75% of the cases.

Applications of FOLCOM include planning and controlling of knowledge management projects. The results of the method can be transferred into financial outputs based on the employee-salary/time relation. Furthermore, the estimates offer a quantitative means to compare the added value of folksonomies with alternative approaches to organize and structure knowledge (e.g., ontologies) in terms of effort and costs. Finally, by monitoring the efficiency of tagging one could identify specific difficulties and challenges of the tagging process, and consider automated tool support for those aspects.

2 Folksonomies and Tagging in a Nutshell

The term "folksonomy" was first coined by Thomas Vander Wal in 2004 as the *"result of personal free tagging of information and objects (anything with a URL) for one's own retrieval."*[1] Typically, folksonomies emerge in Web-based, collaborative environments in which users produce, consume and share information. They are lightweight forms of knowledge management, unconstrained in the choice of the keywords they include, openly structured, and inclusive.[2]

The process of creating a folksonomy is conceived and understood as a continuous, iterative effort in which a loosely defined community of users describe or annotate information objects through tags, according to their knowledge management needs. The operations which can be executed in the course of this process can be divided into two distinct categories: (i) *add*, through which a user assigns a tag to an object; and (ii) *remove*, through which the user deletes a tag previously assigned to an object. Changes, such as modifications of the keywords used within a tag, can be modeled as sequences of add and remove operations [8].

[1] `http://vanderwal.net/folksonomy.html`

[2] Folksonomies are inclusive in the sense that tags assigned to knowledge resources and objects do not exclude each other.

Vander Wal differentiates between two styles of folksonomy creation:[3] *collective* and *collaborative*. In the collective case the folksonomy reflects the individual perspectives of the user community with respect to the objects being described or annotated. In other words, the folksonomy is merely the collection of tags contributed by the users throughout the tagging process. In contrast, in the collaborative case the tags are agreed within the community, and the resulting folksonomy represents the consensual view of the contributors with respect to the vocabulary that should be used for tagging. Another distinction is made between *broad* and *narrow* folksonomies.[4] A broad folksonomy is typically created by many users freely assigning tags to information objects. The same tag can be used multiple times by different users to describe the same object. This type of folksonomy is delivered, for instance, by the del.icio.us platform. In del.icio.us a large user community tags bookmarks based on their own vocabulary, while network effects are crucially reinforced by automatically suggesting popular tags. The emerging folksonomy is acknowledged to be a useful means to build a shared vocabulary, and to select the preferred terms to describe specific content. In narrow folksonomies objects are tagged by a comparatively lower number of users. Users can not re-use externally contributed tags of the same information object – though they can, of course, use the same keywords to describe or annotate them. The resulting, much more focused folksonomy is useful for information retrieval, in particular for types of content that are not easily findable using traditional (e.g., full-text-based) search technology. A prominent example thereof is Flickr. In Flickr each information object is associated with a low number of tags, contributed mainly by the author, and by other users who are in possession of adequate rights. The author can add, remove and change the tags related to the content she uploads, and can grant access rights to other users to do so. The resulting folksonomy is an effective means to find Flickr photos.

In the next sections we will explain how FOLCOM can be used to accurately predict the efforts associated to creating such folksonomy structures within a community of users. First, we introduce the story-points method, the cost estimation approach which is at the core of FOLCOM, and then FOLCOM itself.

3 The Story-Points Method

The story-points method has its origins in agile software development [3,4].

3.1 Why Story Points?

We selected it after conducting a comprehensive literature survey of some of the most important cost estimation methods in software and knowledge engineering published in the last two decades – software engineering as an archetypal area in which cost estimation has a long-standing tradition both among researchers and industry; and knowledge engineering as it bears many similarities in the type of artifacts produced, which are in both cases knowledge models. We examined these approaches with respect to their applicability to the folksonomy creation process. In this paper we can only sketch the

[3] `http://www.personalinfocloud.com/2008/03/getting-to-know.html`

[4] `http://www.personalinfocloud.com/2005/02/explaining_and_.html`

main rationales for choosing this particular method due to space limitations, but a full account of the findings is available in [1].

In brief, from a procedural point of view folksonomy creation exhibits a number of features which make the application of well-established cost estimation methodologies, methods and techniques from classical software engineering unfeasible, but there are some parallels to agile and open-source software development [11]. Among these we highlight the open, evolving nature of the overall process, the lack of a clearly defined process model – including phases, activities and tasks, as well as roles, skills and expertise associated with them. The unavailability of empirical data from historical projects introduces additional constraints, as many approaches in cost estimation heavily rely on it to calibrate the underlying prediction model.

In agile software engineering, requirements, technology and team capabilities evolve in the course of a project. The development is highly iterative and incremental, and new features are continuously released. There are several proposals on how to tackle cost estimation for this particular type of projects [5,12,15,18,19], and story points are one of the most popular approaches among them. We selected it because it offers a number of key advantages: it produces continually-updated estimates throughout the entire development life cycle, it does not make assumptions on a particular work breakdown structure, involves the entire development team, and relies on prior known information acquired from previous iterations of the same project.

In the knowledge engineering area, cost estimation has received comparatively less attention. In our previous work we have introduced ONTOCOM, which estimates the costs of developing ontologies [17,16]. ONTOCOM is based on similar premises as the software-engineering approaches just mentioned, thus not addressing highly evolving, open development scenarios which are specific to folksonomy creation. Other proposals have emerged in the context of ontology reuse [2], semantic wikis [21], Semantic Web Services [22], and knowledge-based systems [7], providing either quantitative methods which typically require calibration based on historical data, or analytical considerations which have not been proven empirically. Furthermore, the procedural models they assume (implicitly or explicitly) are not compatible to folksonomy creation, which, as already mentioned, shows similarities rather with agile software engineering.

3.2 Basic Idea and Assumptions

The story-points approach is based on two core parameters: (i) the future workload (the so-called "user stories") expressed in imaginable units of complexity (termed "story points"), and (ii) the skills of the development team (termed "velocity"). The number of story points are estimated collaboratively within the development team; the velocity is measured in the course of a controlled experiment once the total number of story points is determined.

The estimated effort delivered by the story-points method is given in "ideal time". The ideal time denotes the amount of time that something takes when all peripheral activities are stripped off [4]. Additional costs – for instance related to technical infrastructure, system administration staff, and training – are not taken into account. Schedules can be derived from the effort estimates, provided information about the team productivity is available.

Each task in the project is assigned a number of story points, accounting for the impact of the task – or specific features thereof – on the overall development effort. Examples of such features are the size, the complexity, and the risk of the task. Story points are *relative* measures, in the sense that a ten-point story should be twice as large, complex or risky as a five-point story, and half as large, complex or risky as a twenty-point story. They provide a consistent variable that, together with the "velocity" of the team, provides a projection of when the target functionality will be delivered – or what functionality will be completed at a specific deadline. There are various guidelines and best practices on how to optimally assign story points to stories in an agile project [5,18]. Most of the them involve the entire development team, and some Delphi-like methodology to foster effective consensus-finding [10].[5] Empirical findings recommend the usage of the Fibonacci sequence $(1, 2, 3, 5, 8, 13, \cdots)$ or powers of 2 $(1, 2, 4, 8, 16, \cdots)$ in order to facilitate effective and consistent estimations.

The velocity is determined through average productivity measurements within a "project iteration". The effort estimated for the remainder of the project can then be computed based on the total number of story points divided by the velocity. The theoretic principle underlying this formula is that the sum of the independent samples from any distribution converges towards a normal distribution. Thus, the velocity measurements from one iteration form an adequate basis for predicting the velocity of future iterations [3]. The method can be applied at various stages of the project, once its two core parameters are determined.

3.3 Example

We will illustrate the usage of the story-points method through a simple example. Assuming we would like to estimate how much time it will take to clean our apartment. The apartment consists of a living room, a bedroom, a bathroom, and a kitchen, whereas the size of the bedroom and of the kitchen are 60% the size of the living room, and the bathroom is half the size of the kitchen. According to the story-points method we first have to assign each individual room a number of story points, reflecting the relative "complexity" of the cleaning job. The dimensions of the rooms are likely to be an important relevant in this context, the furnishing as well. Based on such considerations, we come up with the following estimates for the four rooms previously mentioned: living room (5), kitchen (4), bedroom (3), bathroom (2). The kitchen story points are arguably more than 60% of the story points assigned to the living room, as the size of the room is not the only factor to take into account here; kitchens tend to be more complex on average to clean due to the high number of appliances and alike. The total number of story points is thus 14.

To determine the value of the velocity parameter one would have to measure the average time spent in cleaning, for instance, the bathroom. If cleaning the bathroom (accounting for 2 story points) takes one hour, we can estimate that the rest of the apartment will be finished after 6 more hours of work (for $14 - 2 = 12$ story points). Of

[5] See, for instance, `http://kanemar.com/2006/01/28/story-points-as-spicy-ness-using-rsp-to-estimate-story-points/` and `http://www.planningpoker.com/`

course, we can improve the accuracy of this projection by performing further measurements later in the process. If we see that, for instance, cleaning the bedroom took two hours, we can adjust our average velocity parameter based on this new evidence, and obtain a better time prediction for the bedroom and the living room.

We now turn to applying the story-points method to folksonomy creation.

4 FOLCOM: Applying Story Points to Folksonomy Creation

Our aim is to design a method that predicts the time that is cumulatively invested by a community of users in tagging a collection of information objects. Taken into account the folksonomy creation aspects discussed in Section 2, it is expected that this effort will depend on (i) the characteristics of the collection of objects to be tagged, such as the number of objects in the collection, and the complexity of the tagging task for particular types of objects; (ii) the number of tags assigned to each object by each user (single- vs multi-tagging); (iii) the degree to which the tags are assumed to be consensual, thus implying additional overhead (collaborative tagging); and (iv) the size and dynamicity of the tagging community.

The scenario investigated in our work can be summarized as *"tagging a collection of information objects"*. This scenario is certainly simple. Still, it is representative for a wide range of Web 2.0-based knowledge management applications, and allows us to design a baseline cost estimation approach for folksonomies, which will be adjusted and extended to more advanced tagging scenarios as part of our future work. Examples of such advanced scenarios include collaborative tagging, collections of information objects of various modalities and complexity, or folksonomy maintenance in terms as, for instance, tag mapping and tag cleansing activities.

The estimates, just as for the original story-points method, are in terms of "ideal time". It is assumed that the time spent for activities immediately associated with tagging can be monitored. A GOMS[6]-like analysis of folksonomy creation, in which tagging is subdivided into interaction costs, such as mouse clicks, button presses, and typing, and attention switching costs – moving attention from one window to another – can be applied for this purpose [9]. It is also assumed that a tagging tool providing users with an interface to assign tags to information objects is available. This tool should be used by a representative sample of the folksonomy contributors in a project iteration in order to determine the tagging velocity. Ideally, it should include functionality for logging the tagging time; alternatively, one could use a stopwatch to measure it.[7]

4.1 Algorithm

FOLCOM consists of three steps that are executed in sequential order: (i) story-points estimation; (ii) velocity measurement; and (iii) effort estimation.

[6] http://en.wikipedia.org/wiki/GOMS

[7] If the technical support changes – for instance, new features are added to the tagging interface – the velocity parameter needs to be re-estimated. The total number of story-points stays the same.

Story-points estimation. First one estimates the total number of story points associated to creating a folksonomy describing and annotating a collection of information objects. Each object in the $Collection := \{o_1, o_2, \cdots, o_n\}$ represents a tagging "story" and the number of story points of the collection is calculated cumulatively. To estimate these values effectively, one typically builds groups of similar objects according to their types and characteristics. One dimension is certainly the modality of the content (textual documents, images, videos), a second, orthogonal dimension is the size of the information object (expressed in modality-specific metrics such as number of words in a document, length of a video). Other aspects which could be taken into account are, for instance, multi-linguality or familiarity with the content. Independently of these considerations, it is important to understand story points as relative measures of complexity. They stand for challenges associated to accessing, reading, viewing, browsing and comprehending the content of an information object, and identifying tags that meaningfully reflect it. In the following, $complexity(o)$, denotes the function which returns the complexity value of object o assigned by the estimator in this first step.

As soon as each object has got its size/complexity value, the story points for the whole object collection sp_{col} can be computed as the sum of the complexity values of all the objects in the collection.

$$sp_{col} := \sum_{i=1}^{n} complexity(o_i) \tag{1}$$

where $n := |Collection|$ is the number of objects in the collection, and $o_i \in Collection$. In case objects are grouped in $Groups := \{g_1, g_2, \cdots, g_n\}$, the computation can be simplified by multiplying the complexity values of each group with the number of objects in the group and then adding up these values.

$$sp_{col} := \sum_{i=1}^{n} (complexity(g_i) * |g_i|) \tag{2}$$

where $n := |Groups|$ is the number of groups, $g_i \in Groups$, $complexity(g_i)$ returns the complexity value of group g_i, and $|g_i|$ returns the number of objects in group g_i.

Velocity measurement. Velocity relates time information to story points (e.g., 2 minutes per story point), therefore allowing to map the project size expressed in story points to effort. Typically not all members of the community contributing to a folksonomy are known in advance; for estimation purposes, however, one has to select a representative share of this community, for instance based on the types of skills and expertise which are beneficial (or expected to be available) for each group of information objects.

During a project iteration the time invested by all users in tagging-related activities, in other words in adding, removing and changing tags, is measured. As discussed earlier in the paper, peripheral activities are not taken into account. The $Samples_{it} := \{s_1, s_2, \cdots, s_n\}$ gathered during this iteration are triples of the type $sample := (o, taggingTime, user)$, where o denotes an object in the collection which was tagged during the iteration, $user$ is the user who tagged o and $taggingTime$ is the time $user$ needed for tagging o.

The total tagging effort $totalEffort_{it}$ is computed by adding up the individual tagging times for all samples:

$$totalEffort_{it} := \sum_{i=1}^{n} (taggingTime_i) \tag{3}$$

where $n = |Samples_{it}|$ is the number of samples, and $taggingTime_i \in TaggingTimes_{it}$. Here $TaggedObjects_{it}$ represents all information objects tagged during the iteration, and the multi-set $TaggingTimes_{it}$ represents the tagging times measured for each object, tag and user.

In a folksonomy where each object is tagged exactly by one user (i.e., single-tagging), the calculation of the completed story points value sp_{it} is done via the following formula:

$$sp_{it_{single}} := \sum_{i=1}^{n} (complexity(o_i)) \tag{4}$$

where $n = |Samples_{it}|$ is the number of samples and $o_i \in TaggedObjects_{it}$. For multi-tagging the formula considers how many times each object has been tagged:

$$sp_{it_{multi}} := \sum_{i=1}^{n} (complexity(o_i) * times\_tagged(o_i)) \tag{5}$$

where $n = |Samples_{it}|$ is the number of samples, $o_i \in TaggedObjects_{it}$ is an information object tagged during the iteration, and $times\_tagged(o_i)$ returns the number of users tagged the object o_i during the iteration.

The velocity is then calculated as the total effort spent per iteration divided by the total number of story points.

$$velocity := totalEffort_{it}/sp_{it} \tag{6}$$

where sp_{it} is $sp_{it_{single}}$ for single-tagging or $sp_{it_{multi}}$ for multi-tagging.

Additionally, a factor $multiTagFactor$ must be computed, which captures the increase in value of one story point due to the possibility that a single object can be tagged by multiple users:

$$multiTagFactor := sp_{it}/sp_{it_{single}} \tag{7}$$

Alternatively multi-tagging could be modeled as the average number of tags assigned to an information object as in the formula 8 This, however, does not consider the different levels of complexity of specific groups of information objects.

$$multiTagFactor := |Samples_{it}|/|TaggedObjects_{it}| \tag{8}$$

where $|Samples_{it}|$ is the number of samples gathered during the iteration (each sample corresponds to one user which tagged an object) and $|TaggedObjects_{it}|$ is the number of objects tagged in the iteration.

Effort estimation. To estimate the effort to be invested to complete the project, one first determines the remaining number of story points using formula 9.

$$sp_{rem} := sp_{col} - sp_{it} \tag{9}$$

The effort estimate is then calculated as the number of story points multiplied by the velocity measured in the previous step.

$$effortEstimation_{rem} := multiTagFactor * sp_{rem} * velocity \tag{10}$$

For single-tagging, the $multiTagFactor$ in formula 10 is equal to 1. For multi-tagging scenarios one uses formula 7.

As the community who creates the folksonomy evolves over time, both the multi-tagging factor and the velocity are likely to change, as contributors will improve their tagging skills. The second step of the method should be repeated at regular intervals to compensate for these changes. The story-points estimation needs to be revisited only if the collection of information objects radically changes – for instance, by adding new types of content or information objects which significantly vary in their tagging-related complexity.

4.2 Experimental Evaluation

FOLCOM was evaluated on a slightly adapted version of the ONTOCOM evaluation framework [17] as listed in Table 1.

The evaluation of the non-calibrated method met was performed by conducting face-to-face structured interviews with eight knowledge management experts from three large-scale corporations in the sectors telecommunications and operators, ICT consultancy, and software development. Three of the participants of business managers with an extensive background in enterprise knowledge management; the other participants were technical consultants and IT practitioners who have been actively developing

Table 1. The FOLCOM evaluation framework

No	Criterion	Description
1	Definition	- clear definition of the estimated and the excluded costs - clear definition of the decision criteria used to specify the cost factors - intuitive and non-ambiguous terms to denominate the cost factors
2	Objectivity	- objectivity of the cost factors and their decision criteria
3	Constructiveness	- human understandability of the predictions
4	Detail	- refers to the work breakdown structure used by the method, not applicable
5	Scope	- usability for a wide class of tagging scenarios
6	Ease of use	- easily understandable inputs and options - easily assessable ratings based on the decision criteria
7	Prospectiveness	- applicability early in the project
8	Stability	- small differences in inputs produce small differences in outputs
9	Parsimony	- lack of highly redundant cost factors - irrelevant factors
10	Fidelity	- reliability of predictions

knowledge management solutions. Participants were given a one hour overview of the FOLCOM approach, followed by the individual interviews covering the quality criteria of the framework previously mentioned. This part of the evaluation resulted largely in positive qualitative feedback, and we summarize the most important findings in the following:

Definition. One expert remarked that it is not totally clear how specific characteristics of the tagging scenario, be that with respect to the artifacts being tagged or the community of users, are influencing the parameters of the method. In particular, the issue of tag quality was identified as particularly important and will be taken into account in future versions of the model in the velocity determination formulas. More extensive experiments covering larger, more heterogeneous collections of information objects will lead to a refinement of the story-points-estimation guidelines summarized in Section 4.1, which have been created in response to these comments.

Objectivity. Experts requested additional clarification about the rationales to use the Fibonacci sequence or powers of 2 as story points scales. The scales should provide a framework for effective and consistent estimation; based on empirical findings in agile software development, confirmed by our own user experiments, a higher level of precision is typically neither possible, nor required to deliver accurate predictions.

Constructiveness. The experts agreed that the predictions of the method can be understood and reproduced by its users.

Scope. The applicability to arbitrary tagging scenarios is one of the main advantages of our method. The method does neither depend on the object domain, nor on the tagging interface. These aspects were appreciated by the evaluators.

Ease of use. Inputs and options of the method were easily comprehended by all experts, though concerns were raised with respect to estimating story points for heterogeneous collections of objects. We have as a result extended our method to cover groups of objects reflecting various modalities, however more user experiments would be needed to obtain a better understanding of tagging challenges in general, and to compare the complexity of this task for text, audio, images and video. This could be achieved, for instance, through an analysis of the data collected in approaches such as Games with a Purpose.[8]

Prospectiveness. There were no special concerns regarding prospectiveness as the description of our method clearly states that FOLCOM can be applied throughout a project once data from a project iteration is available.

Stability. There were no concerns regarding the stability criterion from the expert team. As shown in the experimental evaluation, the quality of the predictions improves with larger samples of tagging time data.

Parsimony. No redundant cost factors were identified.

Fidelity. This aspect was evaluated during a series of six user experiments, which are discussed in the following.

[8] `http://www.gwap.com/`

Experimental setup. Our experiments were based on the same collection of 200 images collected through Web crawls tagged in single-tagging mode. Tags were assigned to images with the help of self-developed folksonomy tool, which included time logging and auto-completion features. Each experiment involved at least 30 participants, who were asked to perform tagging tasks randomly assigned to them – we assigned images to participants until every image in the object collection of an experiment was tagged successfully.

Table 2 lists the six user experiments including the experiment id, the tagging interface used, the number of images in the experiment object collection, and the maximum number of recommended tags per object.[9]

Table 2. Experimental setup

Experiment	Tagging interface	Number of images	Maximum number of tag recommendations
beta	t2t	100	0
gs1	t2t	200	0
oc1	t2t+ac	200	0
mm1	t2t+ac+tr	200	20
gs2	t2t+ac+tr	200	20
pw1	t2t+tr	200	20

The outcomes of the experiments. To measure the accuracy of FOLCOM, we compared the actual effort value, directly measured by our folksonomy tool during the experiment, with the estimates delivered by our method based on a number of 30 tagging samples measured automatically during the experiments. The estimation error is defined as the difference between the actual and the estimated effort values.

Table 3. Experimental results

Experiment	Actual total effort	Estimate after 30 samples
beta	39.05 minutes	38.28 minutes
gs1	71.27 minutes	71.33 minutes
oc1	60.77 minutes	70.11 minutes
mm1	63.33 minutes	92.11 minutes
gs2	52.22 minutes	57.00 minutes
pw1	40.92 minutes	48.00 minutes

Figure 1 presents the estimation errors of our method (in percent) for each experiment for the first 30 tagging-time long entries. The only estimates within an error margin larger than 25% were observed in experiment *mm1*. This behavior can be traced back to an above average tagging time for images 15 to 50 in this particular experiment.

[9] The abbreviations used for the tagging interfaces are: t2t (type to tag, manual tagging) tr (tag recommendation, users can accept a recommendation by typing in the corresponding tag), ac (tag auto-completion). For the most complex interface covering all three features we performed two experiments with different sets of users in order to increase the accuracy of the observations.

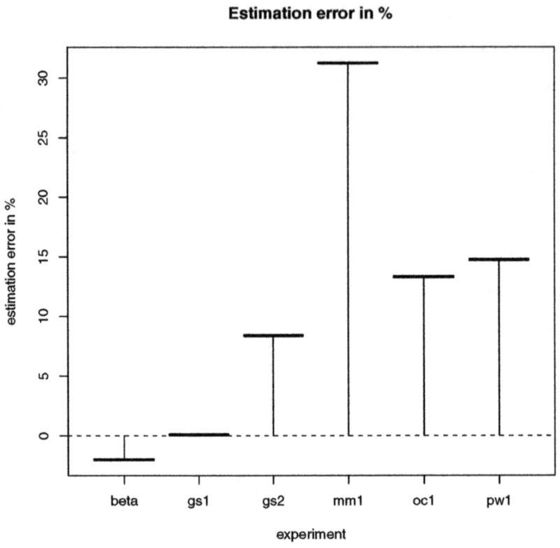

Fig. 1. FOLCOM's accuracy based on the first 30 tagging time samples

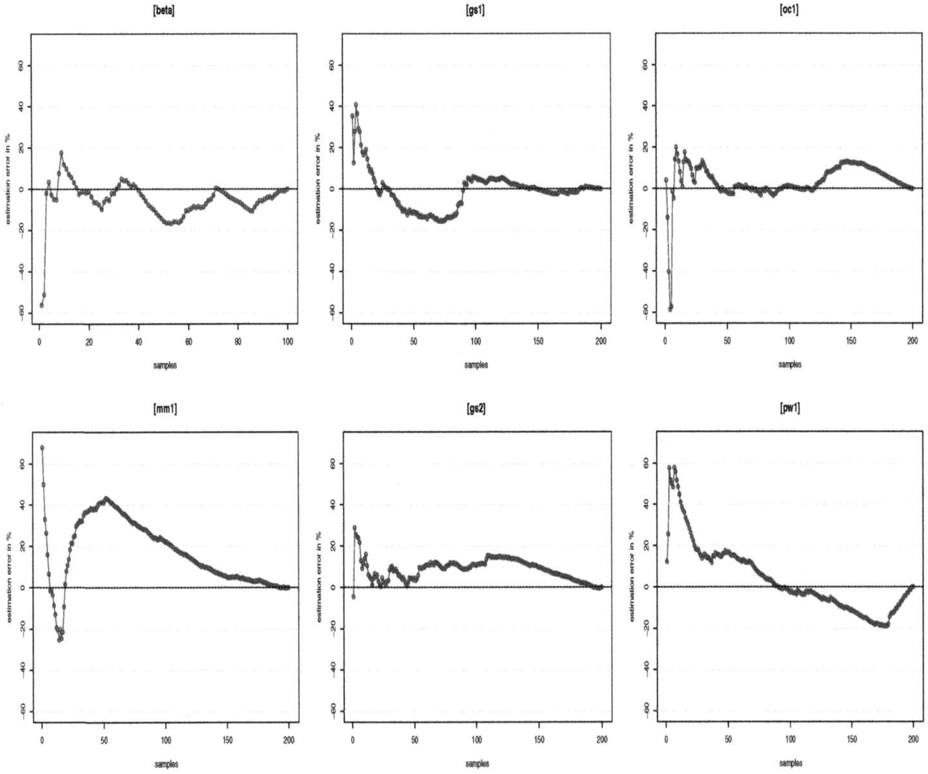

Fig. 2. Method prediction accuracy

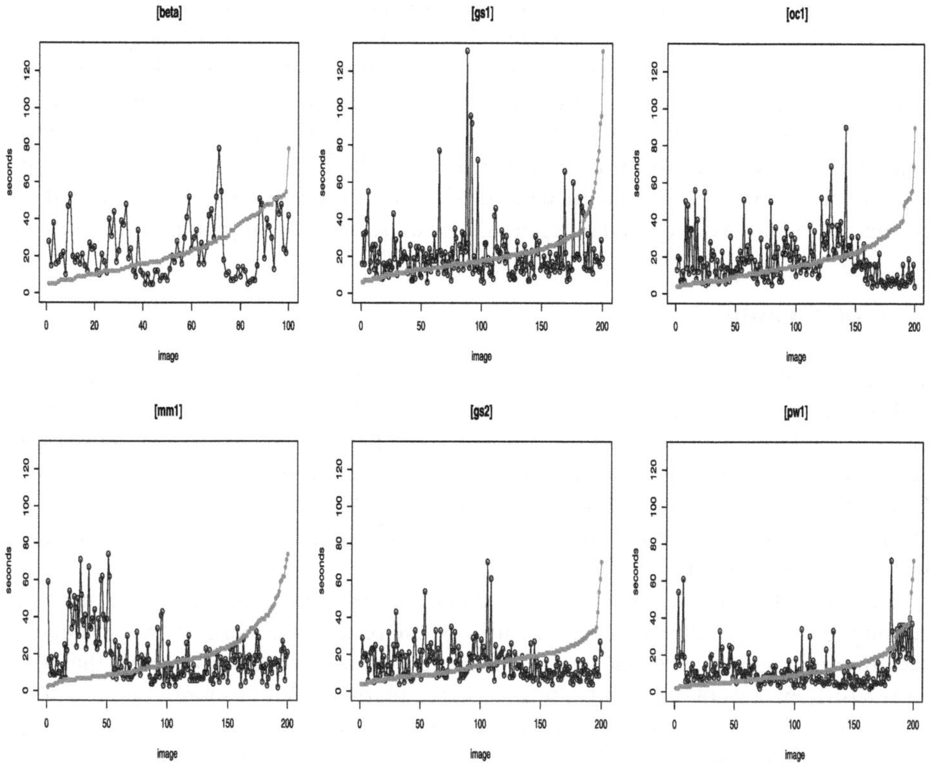

Fig. 3. Tagging times

It is furthermore interesting to see how the estimation accuracy of the method varies in relation to the number of samples taken as input. Figure 2 illustrates this relation: the x-axis displays the number of samples used to compute the estimates, and the y-axis shows the corresponding estimation error in %.

The fluctuations in Figure 2 can be explained by analyzing the tagging times displayed in Figure 3, where the x-axis of denotes the number of images and the y-axis the corresponding tagging times. The blue line corresponds to the tagging times as they were chronologically measured during the experiments. The green line plots the same tagging times, but this time in ascending order. The sum of tagging times gives the actual total effort required to tag the entire collection of images within an experiment. Since our method derives the estimates from the average of the tagging time samples given as input, a significant deviation of the average of the given samples from the average of the tagging times of the overall experiment leads to a bad estimate. This also explains the rather slow adaptation of the method's estimates to the sample fluctuations. A good example is experiment *mm1*. As illustrated in Figure 3 the tagging times for images 15 to 50 are relatively high; leading to a higher prediction error as demonstrated in Figure 2.

The experiments reveal an adequate prediction accuracy within a margin of $\pm 25\%$ in 75% of the cases. This is an indicator that the method could be reliably applied in productive environments of larger scale and diversity, though a more in-depth study of the specificities of enterprise tagging is surely needed in order to substantiate these preliminary positive results. Aspects which are likely to be of relevance include information objects such as Word documents (of tens to hundreds of pages), slides, tables and databases, but also the influence of classification practices based on controlled vocabularies and taxonomies, and in relation to incentives, the quality of the contributions.

5 Conclusions

The sustainable adoption of Web 2.0 technologies by the industry depends on the availability of reliably instruments to predict and analyze their costs and benefits, as well as on a critical level of commitment at the management level, a compatible corporate culture, and appropriate incentive schemes supporting enterprise-wide user involvement. In this paper we presented FOLCOM, a story-points-based method to predict the costs of tagging. To the best of our knowledge, this is the first folksonomy cost estimation method available so far.

The method has been evaluated by eight knowledge management experts experts according to several evaluation criteria with positive results. Furthermore, we conducted six different tagging experiments, in which the method was able to predict the effort with sufficient accuracy (within the 25% error margin). While more comprehensive experiments are needed to increase the reliability of the method, these first findings indicate that the approach works and is able to provide accurate estimations. The tagging experiments were also used to compare different tagging interfaces with different tagging features. The results hint at the fact that the tag recommendation feature can reduce tagging times per word in general and hence improve tag production. The autocomplete feature, however, seemed to be rejected by the users and/or did not lead to any positive tagging effects.

In the near future we will continue to evaluate FOLCOM along two dimensions. One of them is surely multi-tagging. Estimating the efforts implied by creating broad folksonomies is more complicated, since it involves a multi-tag factor. The behavior of this factor over time is largely unknown and additional empirical evidence is needed to determine it. In addition, more experiments are needed to allow for a more careful analysis of the types of automatic tag recommendation functionality and their effect on tagging costs. Finally, FOLCOM should take into account the quality of tags created by users, as as additional parameter to be taken into account when determining the velocity parameter.

Acknowledgements

The research leading to this paper was partially supported by the European Commission under the contract FP7-215040 "ACTIVE".

References

1. Bürger, T., Popov, I., Simperl, E., Hofer, C., Imtiaz, A., Krenge, J.: Calibrated predictive model for costs and benefits. Deliverable D4.1.2, ACTIVE (February 2010)
2. Cohen, P.R., Chaudhri, V.K., Pease, A., Schrag, R.: Does prior knowledge facilitate the development of knowledge-based systems? In: AAAI/IAAI, pp. 221–226 (1999)
3. Cohn, M.: User Stories Applied For Agile Software Development. Addison-Wesley, Reading (2004)
4. Cohn, M.: Agile Estimating and Planning. Robert C. Martin Series. Prentice Hall PTR, Englewood Cliffs (November 2005)
5. Cohn, M.: Agile Estimation and Planning. Prentice-Hall, Englewood Cliffs (2005)
6. Cook, N.: Enterprise 2.0: How Social Software Will Change the Future of Work. Gower Publishing Ltd. (2008)
7. Felfernig, A.: Effort estimation for knowledge-based configuration systems. In: Proc. of the 16th Int. Conf. of Software Engineering and Knowledge Engineering SEKE 2004 (2004)
8. Heymann, P., Garcia-Molina, H.H.: Collaborative creation of communal hierarchical taxonomies in social tagging systems. Technical Report 2006-10, Stanford InfoLab (2006)
9. Hong, L., Chi, E., Budiu, R., Pirolli, P., Nelson, L.: Spartag.us: a low cost tagging system for foraging of web content, pp. 65–72. ACM, New York (2008)
10. Linstone, H.A., Turoff, M.: The Delphi Method: Techniques and Applications. Addison-Wesley Educational Publishers Inc., Reading (1975)
11. Martin, R.C.: Agile Software Development. Principles, Patterns, and Practices. Prentice-Hall, Englewood Cliffs (2002)
12. McConnell, S.: Software Estimation: Demystifying the Black Art (Best Practices (Microsoft)). Microsoft Press, Redmond (2006)
13. McKinsey. Building the web 2.0 enterprise: Mckinsey global survey results (July 2008)
14. Morrison, J.: Tagging and searching: Search retrieval effectiveness of folksonomies on the world wide web. Information Processing & Management 44(4), 1562–1579 (2008)
15. Lavanya, R., Chandrasekaran, S., Kanchana, V.: Multi-criteria approach for agile software cost estimation model. In: Proceedings of the International Conference on Global Manufacturing and Innovation in Engineering, GMICIT (2006)
16. Simperl, E., Popov, I., Bürger, T.: ONTOCOM Revisited: Towards Accurate Cost Predictions for Ontology Development Projects. In: Aroyo, L., Traverso, P., Ciravegna, F., Cimiano, P., Heath, T., Hyvönen, E., Mizoguchi, R., Oren, E., Sabou, M., Simperl, E. (eds.) ESWC 2009. LNCS, vol. 5554, pp. 248–262. Springer, Heidelberg (2009)
17. Simperl, E., Tempich, C., Sure, Y.: ONTOCOM: A Cost Estimation Model for Ontology Engineering. In: Cruz, I., Decker, S., Allemang, D., Preist, C., Schwabe, D., Mika, P., Uschold, M., Aroyo, L.M. (eds.) ISWC 2006. LNCS, vol. 4273, pp. 625–639. Springer, Heidelberg (2006)
18. Steindl, C., Krogdahl, P.: Estimation in agile projects. Presentation at IBM Academy of Technology Best Practices in Project Estimation Conference (2005)
19. Stellman, A., Greene, J.: Agile Software Project Management. O'Reilly, Sebastopol (2005)
20. Van Damme, C., Coenen, T., Vandijck, E.: Turning a corporate folksonomy into a lightweight corporate ontology. In: Proceedings of the 11th International Conference on Business Information Systems, BIS 2008 (2008)
21. Völkel, M., Abecker, A.: Cost-benefit analysis for the design of personal knowledge management systems. In: Proceedings of 10th International Conference on Enterprise Information Systems (ICEIS 2008), pp. 95–105 (2008)
22. Wolff, F., Oberle, D., Lamparter, S., Staab, S.: Economic reflections on managing web service using semantics. In: EMISA, pp. 194–207 (2005)

Epiphany: Adaptable RDFa Generation Linking the Web of Documents to the Web of Data

Benjamin Adrian[1], Jörn Hees[2], Ivan Herman[3], Michael Sintek[1], and Andreas Dengel[1,2]

[1] Knowledge Management Department, DFKI GmbH, Kaiserslautern, Germany
[2] CS Department, University of Kaiserslautern, Kaiserslautern, Germany
[3] Centre for Mathematics and Computer Sciences (CWI), Amsterdam, The Netherlands

benjamin.adrian@dfki.de, j_hees@cs.uni-kl.de, ivan.herman@cwi.nl, michael.sintek@dfki.de, andreas.dengel@dfki.de

Abstract. The appearance of Linked Open Data (LOD) was an important milestone for reaching a Web of Data. More and more RDF data sets get published to be consumed and integrated into a variety of applications. Pointing out one application, Linked Data can be used to enrich web pages with semantic annotations. This gives readers the chance to recall Semantic Web's knowledge about text passages. RDFa provides a well-defined base, as it extends HTML tags in web pages to a form that contains RDF data. Nevertheless, asking web authors to manually annotate their web pages with semantic annotations is illusive. We present Epiphany, a service that annotates Linked Data to web pages automatically by creating RDFa enhanced versions of the input HTML pages. In Epiphany, Linked Data can be any RDF dataset or mashup (e.g., DBpedia, BBC programs, etc.). Based on ontology-based information extraction and the dataset, Epiphany generates an RDF graph about a web page's content. Based on this RDF graph, RDFa annotations are generated and integrated in an RDFa enhanced version of the web page. Authors can use Epiphany to get RDFa enhanced versions of their articles that link to Linked Data models. Readers may use Epiphany to receive RDFa enhanced versions of web pages while surfing. We analysed results of Epiphany with Linked Data from BBC about music biographies and show a similar quality compared to results of Open Calais. Epiphany provides annotations from a couple of Linked Data sets.

1 Introduction

Motivated by the Linked Open Data (LOD) Initiative [1] more and more domain-specific Linked Data gets published in RDF format into the growing LOD cloud,[1] which is the emerging Web of Data. Following the Semantic Web idea, it is necessary not only to create links across different data sets, but also to link text

[1] http://richard.cyganiak.de/2007/10/lod/

P. Cimiano and H.S. Pinto (Eds.): EKAW 2010, LNAI 6317, pp. 178–192, 2010.

```
<!DOCTYPE html PUBLIC "-//W3C//DTD XHTML+RDFa 1.0//EN"
"http://www.w3.org/MarkUp/DTD/xhtml-rdfa-1.dtd">
<html xmlns:rdfs="http://www.w3.org/2000/01/rdf-schema#"
      xmlns:dbpedia="http://dbpedia.org/resource/" ...>
<head>...
<link rel="meta" type="application/rdf+xml"
          href="epiphany/rdf?url=http://www.dfki.de"
          title="EPIPHANY's RDF">
</head><body>...
<span about="dbpedia:DFKI" property="rdfs:label">DFKI</span>
```

Listing 1. Excerpt of a web page, enriched by Epiphany. It contains a link to relevant RDF resources and RDFa annotations about their occurrences in the text. For example, it annotates the term 'DFKI' as `rdfs:label` and links it to the DBpedia HTTP URI `dbpedia:DFKI`.

sequences of web pages to existing LOD resources. Technically, the HTML extension RDFa [2] provides functionalities to allow web authors annotating their content with semantic markup and thus link their unstructured text into the world of machine understandable data. In addition to Microformats [3], which is another semantic markup language, RDFa is not constrained to tag text with properties such as names or phone numbers, but also allows linking these properties to existing real world instances of LOD data sets via HTTP URIs. Both, RDFa and Microformats, gain tool support from browser extensions such as Operator,[2] Semantic Radar,[3] or Ozone Browser [4]. Web authors[4] and web developers (see Drupal plug-in [5]) get more and more excited about the possibility to enrich their static or dynamic web sites with semantic markup. Even Google's [6] and Yahoo's [7] web crawlers start analyzing semantic markup in web sites. However, creating these annotations with RDFa (in style of Listing 1) or Microformats manually is cumbersome. Furthermore, manually created RDFa annotations are static. Thus they might not represent those properties and instance references the reader is currently interested in.

We present Epiphany,[5] a service that automatically generates RDFa annotations. Epiphany uses Linked Data as input to annotate HTML content with those properties and reference to those LOD resources [8] the user or group is currently interested in. Epiphany generates RDFa as shown in Listing 1. The service provides the following functionalities:

- Epiphany is adaptable and can be configured with any existing Linked Data model. Currently it is configured with data from DBpedia and BBC.
- Authors can generate RDFa annotations for their dynamic web pages.

[2] `http://www.kaply.com/weblog/operator`
[3] `http://www.sioc-project.org/firefox`
[4] E.g., Ivan Herman's homepage `http://www.ivan-herman.net`
[5] Please lookup Epiphany at `http://projects.dfki.uni-kl.de/epiphany/`

Fig. 1. Screenshot displaying Epiphany generated RDFa annotations

- Readers can generate RDFa annotations on demand for existing web pages (see screenshot in Fig. 1). These annotations are visualized with lighting boxes that provide additional background information about the resource (e.g., in case of dbpedia:DFKI, listing the abstract, the company logo, web page, etc.) they refer to. Readers also obtain links to common Linked Data Browsers, i.e., Tabulator, Marbles, Zitgist (see screenshot in Fig. 2).
- Web crawlers can be extended to generate Epiphany's RDFa annotations for crawled web pages.

In the following, we start with discussing related work. Afterwards, Epiphany's functionalities, visualizations, user interactions and provenance aspects are explained. The ontology-based information extraction facilities for generating RDF are outlined. An evaluation based on data from BBC music artist biographies confirms the quality of Epiphany. We show that Epiphany's results are comparable to those of Open Calais on the same data set. In addition to Open Calais that is specialized on the news domain, Epiphany may be configured with any domain that is published as Linked Data. After discussing evaluation results, and summarizing Epiphany's functionalities, we present future activities.

2 Related Work

Even before Linked Open Data, annotation systems like S-Cream [9] annotated web pages with instances or datatype properties from domain ontologies, semi-automatically. S-Cream did not provide its annotations in machine-readable

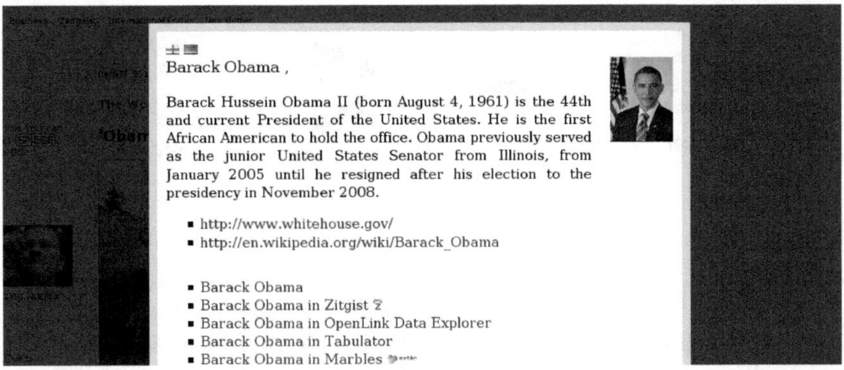

Fig. 2. Screenshot of Epiphany's lighting box for a single RDFa annotation

format, but highlighted annotations to users or stored annotations back into a domain ontology. S-Cream and Epiphany use different kinds of information extraction (IE) techniques. Epiphany uses the ontology-based information extraction facilities that can be trained on any RDF domain model. S-Cream uses Amilcare, a traditional IE system without any ontology support. In consequence, S-Cream had to map non-ontological results (e.g., entities) from Amilcare to properties, classes, and instances of the domain ontology. Epiphany's incorporation of RDF domain knowledge into the IE process provides advantages, i.e., disambiguating possible instance candidates with similar labels, using SPARQL for specifying which entities to extract, or extracting new facts as RDF triples [10].

The Firefox plug-in Piggy Bank allows IE from web sites by screen scrapers. Results are stored in a local or global RDF store [11]. A screen scraper is a piece of Javascript code that extracts RDF information from within a web page's content. Similar approaches are GRDDL [12] and Monkeyformats.[6] GRDDL allows users to add references to XSLT scripts to web page headers that transform XML data on that page into RDF. Monkeyformats are userscripts for the Firefox plugin Greasemonkey [13].[7] These Javascripts search for patterns of DOM elements inside certain websites for adding Microformats into the DOM Tree.

Open Calais[8] services provide named entity recognition (NER, e.g., *Angela Merkel* as a person's name), instance recognition (e.g., *Angela Merkel* as a *person* with an HTTP URI) and facts with a couple of predefined properties (e.g., *Angela Merkel* is *chancellor*) with focus on News content. Open Calais is ontology-based, returns extraction results in RDF, and maintains Linked Data covering common sense instances (cities, countries, persons, companies, etc.). The coverage of instances that possess links to other Linked Data sets is very small. We

[6] `http://monkeyformats.org`
[7] `http://www.greasespot.net`
[8] `http://www.opencalais.com`

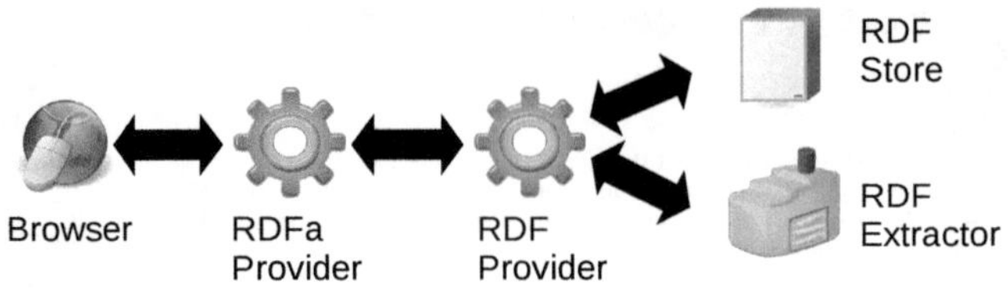

Fig. 3. Epiphany's RDFa generation process

could not find any cross links for recognized persons or music groups.[9] The Gnosis Firefox plugin[10] performs NER about web pages, highlights results in text, and also lists entities grouped by types (e.g., person, city) in a sidebar. Gnosis renders tooltips while hovering over highlighted text passages with the mouse cursor that contain links to search the highlighted text passages in Wikipedia, Google, or the Reuters database. Gnosis does not perform instance recognition nor does it return data in RDF or Microformats.

Zemanta [14] is a web service for building web mashups. It finds relevant web links or images about blog entries. Zemanta also spots for labels of DBpedia[11] or Freebase[12] resources in web pages. The API can return results in RDF format.

Compared to these systems, Epiphany's characteristic features are *adaptivity* by changing Linked Data models used for annotating, *machine-readability*, as Epiphany annotates web pages with RDFa, and finally *usability* as Epiphany renders visualizations that link text with RDF resources from Linked Data.

3 The Epiphany Approach

Epiphany is a web service[13] that recognizes relevant instances and properties of a Linked Data model in web pages. It returns a version of the web page that contains RDFa annotations about these properties and instances, and a link to an RDF graph that summarizes these. We provide an overview about Epiphany's annotation process, provenance aspects, its data interface, and visualizations.

3.1 RDFa Generation

Figure 3 shows an overview of Epiphany's annotation process. Epiphany ties together Linked Data models and the content of web pages. It depends on Linked Data [8] to ensure that the user is able to request more information about an RDFa annotated text phrase via HTTP URIs. Figures 1 and 2 show an example where DBpedia is taken as Linked Data model. By using ontology-based information extraction methods, Epiphany extracts an RDF graph (called scenario

[9] An online discussion about Calais' linking coverage: `http://www.opencalais.com/forums/known-issues/linked-data-how-much-linking`

[10] `http://www.opencalais.com/Gnosis`

[11] `http://dbpedia.org`

[12] `http://www.freebase.com`

[13] `http://projects.dfki.uni-kl.de/epiphany/`

graph) that consists of recognized instances with datatype property values that match with text content, and known object property values between these instances (see Section 4 for details). The scenario graph is stored in an RDF store as Named Graph. This facilitates caching different RDF content about the same text resource. Epiphany's RDFa Provider (see Fig. 3) parses a web page and compares datatype property values of the scenario graph with the page's text nodes. It returns a transformed version of the web page that contains positive matches for semantic annotations in RDFa:

- The HTML or XHTML document type definition of the original web page is replaced with W3C's XHTML+RDFa document type definition.
- In the HTML header a URI linking to the scenario graph is added as meta information (see Listing 1). If RDF is generated from the RDFa inside the website, the `<link rel="meta"...>` statement adds an extra triple referring to the scenario graph. This reinforces the Linked Data aspect of the whole process: Users can find extra information, not necessarily present on the page itself, by consulting that scenario graph.
- Inside the page's body, each match between scenario graph and text content creates an RDFa annotation, i.e., HTML `span` elements (see Listing 1).
- Epiphany adds CSS information to the RDFa enhanced web page that highlights RDFa content with colored borders (see screenshot in Fig. 1).
- In addition, added Javascript functions render a lighting box (see screenshot in Fig. 2) when clicking on RDFa content with the mouse cursor. This lighting box contains configurable text and image information about the annotated instance taken from the domain model published as Linked Data.

Epiphany's RDF Provider manages persistence, access, and creation of RDF scenario graphs about web pages. Each scenario graph is stored as a named graph in an RDF store (an OpenLink Virtuoso Server). Accessing scenario graphs is done in Linked Data style, as every graph is identified by an HTTP URI that leads to the RDF document.[14]

3.2 Provenance

The RDF Provider enriches extracted scenario graphs with additional meta information. These are used to determine whether an existing scenario graph about a dynamic web is still up-to-date with respect to page changes or different Linked Data models in Epiphany. In addition, meta data contains optional information about the user or group who triggered the creation of the scenario graph. The Vocabulary of Interlinked Datasets (VOID [15]) is used to describe the version of Epiphany's underlying Linked Data model. The Dublin Core Metadata Element Set (DC [16]) is used to describe the web page the scenario graph is about (dc:subject), the last modified date of the web page (dc:modified), creation date of scenario graph (dc:created), and user or group identifiers (dc:audience). The

[14] Please refer to `http://projects.dfki.uni-kl.de/epiphany/db`

```
PREFIX dc: <http://purl.org/dc/terms/>
PREFIX oc: <http://s.opencalais.com/1/pred/>
ASK { GRAPH ?g {
  ?s dc:subject PAGE_URI;
     dc:audience USER_URI;
     dc:created ?creation;
     oc:score ?confidence.
  PAGE_URI dc:modified ?modified.
FILTER (
  xsd:float(?confidence) >= xsd:float(THRESHOLD) &&
  xsd:integer(?modified) >= xsd:integer(CURRENT_TIME_STAMP))
}}
```

Listing 2. Epiphany's SPARQL ASK query pattern querying the RDF store for an existing scenario graph with given provenance information. Variable names written in capitals are configurable or dynamically replaced.

score property defined by Open Calais[15] is used to describe the minimum confidence value an extracted instance or fact has inside a scenario graph.
Based on this provenance information, by executing the SPARQL ASK query in Listing 2, the RDF Provider can decide if a scenario graph exists inside the RDF store. If no graph exists, Epiphany creates a new one.

3.3 Epiphany's Data Interfaces

Epiphany provides four data interfaces to create RDFa annotations:

1. Web authors can use a web form to generate RDFa for text snippets. These RDFa annotated text snippets can be used as static content in web pages. Scenario graphs about text snippets are not persisted in the RDF store.
2. Web surfers can configure their browsers to use an HTTP-Proxy to call the Epiphany service for web pages. Modern browsers allow the setup of proxies with white- or blacklists of Internet domain names to control proxy requests. Using proxies ensures preserving the original URL of the web page.
3. Web surfers can also use a bookmarklet, which allows to encapsulate arbitrary Javascript code into a bookmark. At will, the users can click on the bookmarklet, which can then
   - redirect to an Epiphany URL quoting the current web page
   - directly replace parts of the page's DOM with RDFa annotated content from Epiphany. This approach also preserves the original URL, but requires the browser to interpret the parameter `AccessControl-AllowOrigin *` in HTTP response headers[16] in order to allow cross site scripting for this domain.

[15] `http://s.opencalais.com/1/pred/score`
[16] See W3C working draft at `http://www.w3.org/TR/access-control`

Fig. 4. Epiphany's lighting box rendering process

The bookmarklets are implemented by Epiphany's RESTful API.[17] To enhance usability even more, the Firefox plugin WebSmartyPants is provided and can be downloaded under Epiphany's website.

4. As soon as the W3C RDFa working group publishes an RDFa DOM API[18] in a definite form, it is planned to provide a conforming Epiphany Javascript API.

3.4 Epiphany's RDFa Visualizations

Without any browser plugin support, existing RDFa content in web pages remains hidden to users. Existing RDFa visualizations, such as Ozone Browser [4], or W3C's RDFa Bookmarklets[19] visualize information rather technically. In Epiphany, lighting boxes are used to visualize additional information about annotated text passages (see screenshot in Figure 2).

According to Figure 4, the Javascript event onmouseclick on an RDFa span leads to an AJAX request to the Information Agent, passing the subject's URI of the RDFa span. The Information Agent requests the RDF graph of the given HTTP URI, parses it, and then filters RDF triples for specified properties. These properties can be grouped by template categories listed in a configuration file (see Table 1). The lighting box is a simple HTML template with slots that correspond to existing template categories. These slots can be designed by CSS documents that define CSS classes with the category as name.

Table 1. Categories with RDF properties used to populate the lighting box in Figure 2

Template Category	RDF Property List
label	`foaf:name`, `rdfs:label`
image	`foaf:depiction`, `dbpedia:thumbnail`
description	`rdfs:comment`, `dbprop:abstract`
reference	`foaf:homepage`, `foaf:page`

4 Ontology-Based Information Extraction

Epiphany's generated RDFa annotations are based on scenario graphs, which are generated by ontology-based information extraction (OBIE) methods [17].

[17] See the API description at `http://projects.dfki.uni-kl.de/epiphany/api`

[18] See agenda at `http://www.w3.org/2010/02/rdfa/`

[19] `http://www.w3.org/2006/07/SWD/RDFa/impl/js/`

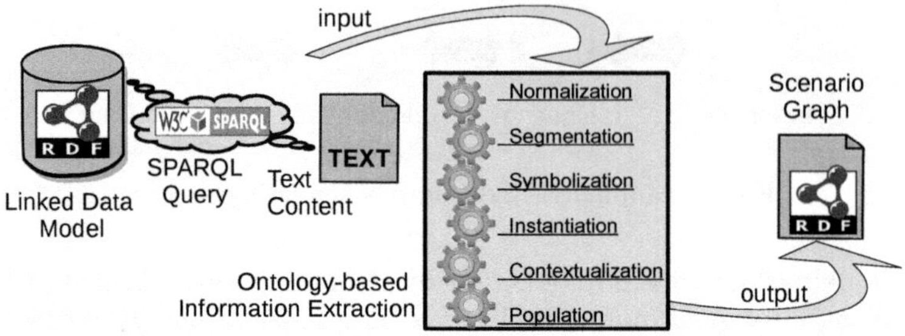

Fig. 5. Usage scenario of Epiphany's OBIE system: Based on an RDF model, a user asks a SPARQL query about a text document. Taking the RDF model, text, and query as input, Epiphany's extraction pipeline creates a weighted RDF scenario graph.

Epiphany's OBIE facility incorporates domain-specific RDF data into the IE pipeline [10] (see Fig. 5) and returns extracted results in RDF format by reusing the RDFS schema of the input data. The IE pipeline is designed to support optional SPARQL queries as input which specify the types of entities and relations to extract from text. By changing the RDF model, the user is allowed to "ask" different queries covering other domains and receive different IE results. The following system description summarizes (OBIE) tasks used in Epiphany. More detailed information are given in [10,17].

4.1 Preprocessing the RDF Domain Model

In a preprocessing step Epiphany analyzes the input RDF model consisting of instances, classes, datatype property values (e.g., `foaf:name`) and object property values (e.g., `foaf:knows`). Datatype property values are converted to efficient data structures (e.g., Suffix Arrays) for pattern matching on character strings. RDF Properties are represented as adjacency lists and stored in bit vectors.

4.2 Extraction Pipeline

The RDF model preprocessor returns a so-called extraction session. Based on this session, Epiphany's OBIE pipeline is ready to extract model-specific information from text. This comprises six major process steps (see Fig. 5) covering necessary IE tasks. Each task generates a set of hypotheses weighted with confidence values that are combined by using Dempster-Shafer's belief function [18].

Normalization transforms a document into a textual representation. Here, plain text content and existing metadata (e.g., title, author) are extracted based on the Aperture framework.[20]

Segmentation partitions the plain text content into units of tokens and sentences. The implementation token and sentence detection is based based on regular expressions. In steps of sentences, each token is classified by a *POS*

[20] `http://aperture.sourceforge.net`

tagger.[21] Noun phrases (that are sequences of tokens) are detected by a Noun phrase chunker that is implemented as conditional random field. These noun phrases are stored and finally sorted in a suffix array.

Symbolization recognizes datatype property values in text. It matches the noun phrases in text that are stored inside the suffix array and sorted values of datatype properties inside the domain model. (e.g., assuming the existence of the triple (`:_ foaf:label 'DFKI'.`), in text: *DFKI was founded in 1988*, 'DFKI' is recognized as content symbol of type `foaf:label`).

Instantiation resolves instances of the domain-specific data model for each recognized datatype property value (e.g., assuming the existence of the triple (`dbpedia:DFKI foaf:label 'DFKI'.`) and text snippet: *DFKI was founded in 1988*, '*DFKI*' is resolved as `foaf:label` of instance `dbpedia:DFKI`). An instance candidate recognition resolves possible candidates for recognized datatype property values. Here, ambiguities may occur if more than one instance possesses the same datatype property values (e.g., first names of *Helmut Kohl* and *Helmut Schmidt*). Candidates are disambiguated by counting resolved instances in the domain model that are related directly with an object property[22] or indirectly via another instance of the domain model.[23] As result, the ambiguous instance with a higher count of related and recognized instances is taken.

Contextualization extracts facts (RDF triples) about resolved instances. At first, a fact candidate extraction computes all possible facts between resolved instances. Then, a set of fact selectors rates these facts according to heuristics. Currently Epiphany contains a known fact selector and a spreading activation based fact selector. The known fact selector increases rates of extracted facts that exist as triples inside the domain model.

The **Population** task collects results from the previous extraction tasks and stores them as RDF triples inside scenario graphs. (which is technically-seen a named graph). Thus, a scenario graph contains URIs of resolved instances with those datatype property values that match with text sequences and RDF triples about object properties between these resolved instances. The minimal confidence value of all contained hypotheses is represented by the confidence value of the scenario graph.

4.3 Usage in Epiphany

Currently, Epiphany uses a configuration of the OBIE pipeline which focuses on text annotation. It covers text extraction, tokenization, content symbol recognition, instance recognition and disambiguation, fact extraction and known fact selection, and finally the population of scenario graphs. Epiphany uses the generic SPARQL query as template for scenario graphs: `SELECT * WHERE {?s ?p ?o}`. For future work, it is planned to let Epiphany even recommend domain specific new instances for given Linked Data.

---

[21] `http://opennlp.sourceforge.net`

[22] E.g., `dbpedia:Helmut_Kohl rdf:type dbpedia:Chancellor`

[23] E.g., `dbpedia:Helmut_Kohl dbprop:politicalParty dbpedia:CDU` and `dbpedia:Angela_Merkel dbprop:politicalParty dbpedia:CDU`

Table 2. (a): Cardinality statistics of BBC corpus values, (b): Frequent music group names extracted by Epiphany

Facet	Cardinalities
web pages	12,462
words	5,530,477
`mo:MusicGroup`	12,462
`mo:SoloMusicArtist`	31,429
`<> foaf:name <>.`	36,397
`<> mo:member <>.`	32,104

Music group name	Frequency
Off	3,991
Free	5,715
Contact	12,461
Fin	12,461
Food	12,461
Sport	12,461

5 Evaluation

The evaluation proved that the quality of Epiphany's extraction results (and finally of the generated RDFa annotations) is comparable to results from Open Calais. An advantage of Epiphany is its adaptability. It is not tied to the News domain like Open Calais. The Epiphany service is initialized with multiple Linked Data models called sessions. It generates different RDFa for each session.

We decided to evaluate Epiphany by analyzing the quality of extracted scenario graphs, as these graphs form the base of the generated RDFa annotations. Furthermore, we compared RDF graphs generated by Epiphany with those generated by Open Calais.

5.1 Experimental Setup

Three essential things were identified for evaluating Epiphany as domain-adaptive and ontology-based information extraction system:

1. A document corpus is needed. The content of each document should cover a single domain and refer to multiple instances and facts.
2. These instances and facts should be explicitly listed for each document. Ideally, RDF graphs exist for each document, that formalize its content.
3. This RDF data should be formalized clearly by using a set of ontologies. Ideally, these ontologies should be commonly used in Linked Data.

As data basis, we used web pages from `bbc.co.uk/music`[24] describing biographies about music groups. For each biography on a web page, BBC provides metadata in form of a Linked Data model.[25] The ontologies FOAF, Music Ontology (MO), and Dublin Core are used to describe music groups and their members. The RDF graphs were used as baseline. Extracted RDF graphs from Epiphany for a given web page are compared against corresponding metadata by BBC.

[24] `http://www.bbc.co.uk/music/developers`

[25] E.g., BBC's Linked Data graph about the `mo:MusicGroup` Queen: `http://www.bbc.co.uk/music/artists/0383dadf-2a4e-4d10-a46a-e9e041da8eb3.rdf`

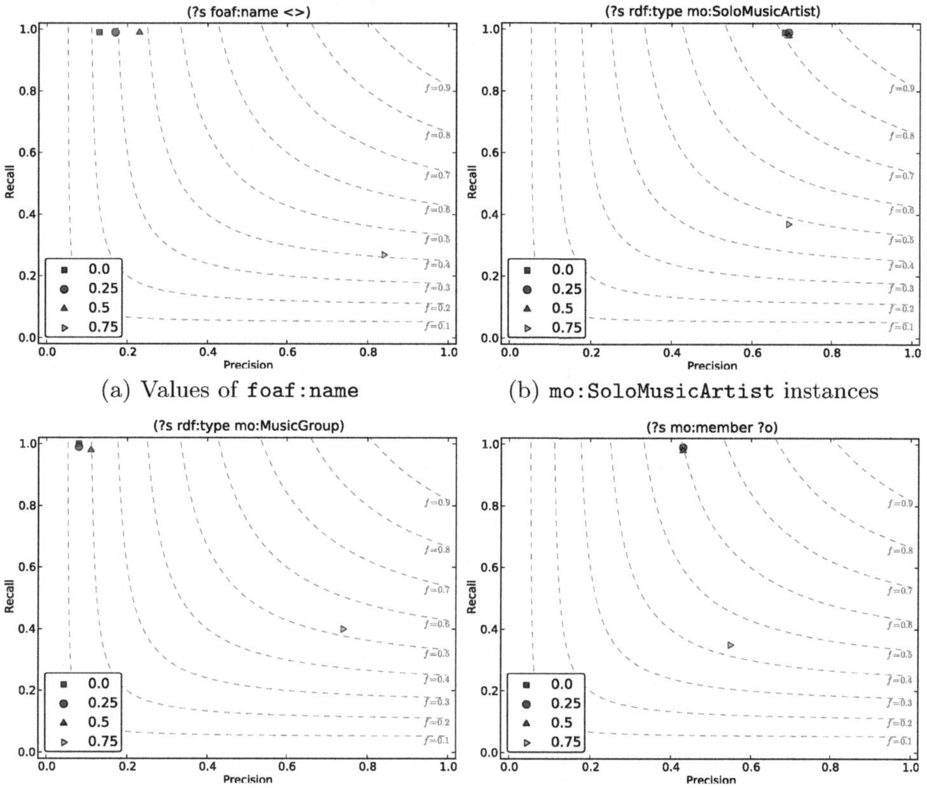

(a) Values of `foaf:name` (b) `mo:SoloMusicArtist` instances

(c) `mo:MusicGroup` instances (d) `mo:member` relations.

Fig. 6. Diagrams about Epiphany's extraction results. Four measured values represent the scenario graphs possessing a higher confidence than the labeled threshold.

HTTP URIs of music group members refer to additional Linked Data. We collected all RDF graphs about music groups that could be found by querying BBC's backstage SPARQL endpoint[26] and added the RDF graphs of all group members. The resulting mashup was used as domain-specific Linked Data input for Epiphany. Table 2(a) lists statistics about the amount of documents and tokens inside the test corpus. It also lists the count of properties about music groups and their solo music artist members inside the mashup.

We evaluated the quality of the following extraction results: (Fig. 6.a) all extracted instances with `foaf:name` values, (Fig. 6.b+c) just extracted instances with `foaf:name` values of type `mo:MusicGroup` and `mo:SoloMusicArtist`, (Fig. 6.d) `mo:member` relationships between `mo:MusicGroups` and `mo:SoloMusicArtists`. Therefore we checked, if certain RDF triples (Fig. 6.a+d) or RDF molecules (Fig. 6.b+c) inside baseline RDF graphs were extracted and thus exist in Epiphany's scenario graphs.

[26] `http://api.talis.com/stores/bbc-backstage`

5.2 Comparing Epiphany's Scenario Graph with BBC's Baseline

Figure 6 describes evaluation results for each extracted instance or fact. Four measure points (≥ 0.75, ≥ 0.5, ≥ 0.25, and ≥ 0.0.) summarize the extracted scenario graphs having confidence values higher than the given decimal value. Measure points are rated by precision and recall. Curves inside diagrams represent layers of harmonic F-measure ratios. Three points show that Epiphany extracts instances and facts with recall ratios above 96.0% for thresholds up to ≥ 0.5. Precision values except for extracted `mo:SoloMusicArtist` instances stay below 35%. Extracted instances of `mo:SoloMusicArtist` gained precision values above 65%. In general, an increase of threshold up to ≥ 0.75 leads to precision values higher than 50%. The distribution of precision can be explained by some `foaf:name` values of `mo:MusicGroups` (see Table 2(b)) which occur in nearly all web pages in a different language context.

5.3 Comparing Results from Open Calais and Epiphany

We compared results obtained from Open Calais and Epiphany about the same data set. Open Calais is not domain-specific, thus extracted more types of instances than we needed. It also uses its own RDFS vocabulary[27] to represent RDF results. So, we had to filter results, transformed the classes `oc:Person` and `oc:MusicGroup` to `mo:SoloMusicArtist` and `mo:MusicGroup`, and transformed the properties `oc:name` and `oc:match` to `foaf:name`. This allowed comparing Calais' RDF to BBC's baseline. Calais could not extract group member relationships. The diagrams in Figure 7 are structured as Figure 6, but also contain results of Open Calais. For instances with `foaf:name` values and those of type `mo:MusicGroup`, Open Calais' results gained higher precision values compared to Epiphany's measure points with thresholds below ≥ 0.75. In general, Epiphany's results were rated with higher recall values. Epiphany reached better precision values for measure points ≥ 0.75.

5.4 Result Discussion

Comparing results of Epiphany and Open Calais shows, that Epiphany is able to annotate existing instances and facts of the input Linked Data if the web page refers to these. Epiphany even achieved slightly better Recall results than Open Calais. One reason is that Epiphany's data base is much more related to the web pages content than the generic data base of Open Calais. Open Calais gained better precision values than Epiphany because Open Calais' domain model did not cover such a huge amount of music group names as they exist in BBC Programs. (Especially not the ambiguous band names listed in Table 2 b.) For dealing with ambiguous instance labels, we plan to look for a contextual analysis that re-ranks extraction results based on how they are interrelated inside the domain model. Also consider that compared to Open Calais, Epiphany is domain adaptable and supports more than just one domain model.

[27] `http://d.opencalais.com/1/type/`

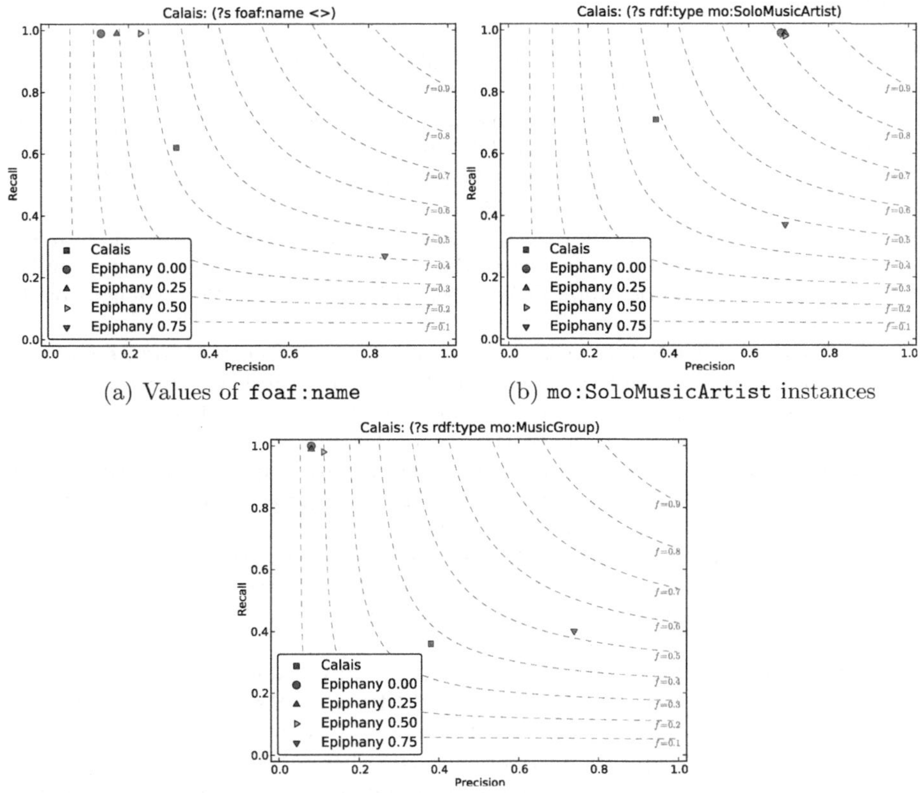

(a) Values of `foaf:name` (b) `mo:SoloMusicArtist` instances

(c) `mo:MusicGroup` instances

Fig. 7. Comparing results from Epiphany's OBIE component and Open Calais

6 Summary and Outlook

We described Epiphany, a web service that annotates web pages with RDFa which is linked to a Linked Data model (e.g., DBpedia , BBC programs, etc.). The service is published at `http://projects.dfki.uni-kl.de/epiphany/` and provides Bookmarklets, an HTTP proxy server, a RESTful API, and the Firefox plugin WebSmartyPants. Epiphany provides Linked data from DBpedia and BBC programs for being annotated as RDFa to web pages. The evaluation confirmed that the coverage of extracted instances from web pages is comparable between Epiphany and Open Calais. Epiphany is adaptable and can be configured to support different Linked Data models for annotating web pages with additional Linked Data content. Current activities comprise a Javascript API, the use of Epiphany in web crawlers, the support of the Good Relations ontology, and an integration into Virtuoso's Spongers technologie via REST URIs.
Acknowledgements This work was financed in part by the BMBF project Perspecting (Grant 01IW08002).

References

1. Bizer, C., Heath, T., Berners-Lee, T.: Linked Data – the story so far. Int. Journal on Semantic Web and Information Systems, IJSWIS (2009)
2. W3C: RDFa in XHTML: syntax and processing rules for embedding rdf through attributes. W3C working draft, W3C (2010)
3. Khare, R.: Microformats: The next (small) thing on the semantic web? IEEE Internet Computing 10(1), 68–75 (2006)
4. Burel, G., Cano, A.E., Lanfranchi, V.: Ozone browser: Augmenting the web with semantic overlays. In: Proceedings of the 5th Workshop on Scripting and Development for the Semantic Web SFSW 2009. CEUR Workshop Proceedings, vol. 449 (2009)
5. Corlosquet, S., Delbru, R., Clark, T., Polleres, A., Decker, S.: Produce and Consume Linked Data with Drupal! In: Bernstein, A., Karger, D.R., Heath, T., Feigenbaum, L., Maynard, D., Motta, E., Thirunarayan, K. (eds.) ISWC 2009. LNCS, vol. 5823, pp. 763–778. Springer, Heidelberg (2009)
6. Google: Help us make the web better: An update on Rich Snippets (2009), `http://googlewebmastercentral.blogspot.com/2009/10/help-us-make-web-better-u%pdate-on-rich.html`
7. Yahoo! Inc.: SearchMonkey Guide - A Manual for SearchMonkey Developers and Publishers (2008), `http://developer.yahoo.com/searchmonkey/smguide`
8. Bizer, C., Cyganiak, R., Heath, T.: How to publish linked data on the web. Web page (2007), `http://www4.wiwiss.fu-berlin.de/bizer/pub/LinkedDataTutorial`
9. Handschuh, S., Staab, S., Ciravegna, F.: S-CREAM - Semi-automatic CREAtion of Metadata. In: Gómez-Pérez, A., Benjamins, V.R. (eds.) EKAW 2002. LNCS (LNAI), vol. 2473, pp. 358–372. Springer, Heidelberg (2002)
10. Adrian, B.: Incorporating ontological background knowledge into information extraction. In: Maynard, D. (ed.) ISWC 2009 Doctoral Consortium (2009)
11. Huynh, D., Mazzocchi, S., Karger, D.: Piggy bank: Experience the semantic web inside your web browser. Web Semantics 5(1), 16–27 (2007)
12. W3C: Gleaning resource descriptions from dialects of languages (GRDDL). W3C rec., W3C (2007)
13. Pilgrim, M.: Greasemonkey Hacks: Tips & Tools for Remixing the Web with Firefox (Hacks). O'Reilly Media, Inc., Sebastopol (2005)
14. Tori, A.: Zemanta Service (2008)
15. Alexander, K., Cyganiak, R., Hausenblas, M., Zhao, J.: voiD Guide - Using the Vocabulary of Interlinked Datasets (2009), `http://rdfs.org/ns/void-guide`
16. Dublin Core Metadata Initiative: DCMI Metadata Terms (2006), `http://dublincore.org/documents/dcmi-terms`
17. Adrian, B., Hees, J., van Elst, L., Dengel, A.: iDocument: using ontologies for extracting and annotating information from unstructured text. In: Mertsching, B., Hund, M., Aziz, Z. (eds.) KI 2009. LNCS (LNAI), vol. 5803, pp. 249–256. Springer, Heidelberg (2009)
18. Adrian, B., Dengel, A.: Believing finite-state cascades in knowledge-based information extraction. In: KI. LNCS (LNAI). Springer, Heidelberg (2008)

Scaling Up Question-Answering to Linked Data

Vanessa Lopez[1], Andriy Nikolov[1], Marta Sabou[1], Victoria Uren[2], Enrico Motta[1], and Mathieu d'Aquin[1]

[1] KMI. The Open University, MK76AA, UK
{v.lopez,a.nikolov,r.m.sabou,e.motta,m.daquin}@open.ac.uk
[2] The University of Sheffield, S14DP, UK
v.uren@dcs.shef.ac.uk

Abstract. Linked Data semantic sources, in particular DBpedia, can be used to answer many user queries. PowerAqua is an open multi-ontology Question Answering (QA) system for the Semantic Web (SW). However, the emergence of Linked Data, characterized by its openness, heterogeneity and scale, introduces a new dimension to the Semantic Web scenario, in which exploiting the relevant information to extract answers for Natural Language (NL) user queries is a major challenge. In this paper we discuss the issues and lessons learned from our experience of integrating PowerAqua as a front-end for DBpedia and a subset of Linked Data sources. As such, we go one step beyond the state of the art on end-users interfaces for Linked Data by introducing mapping and fusion techniques needed to translate a user query by means of multiple sources. Our first informal experiments probe whether, in fact, it is feasible to obtain answers to user queries by composing information across semantic sources and Linked Data, even in its current form, where the strength of Linked Data is more a by-product of its size than its quality. We believe our experiences can be extrapolated to a variety of end-user applications that wish to scale, open up, exploit and re-use what possibly is the greatest wealth of data about everything in the history of Artificial Intelligence.

Keywords: question answering, link data, fusion, semantic web, natural language.

1 Introduction

The SW has expanded rapidly, offering a wealth of semantic data that can be used for experimental purposes, for example to enhance keyword search technologies. A prominent example is the amount of web data in the Linked Data [2] cloud. It is possibly, the largest Knowledge Base (KB) about everything in the history of Artificial Intelligence. Till now, most KBs covered specific domains and were created by relatively small groups. Yet, this is starting to change and we are reaching the critical mass required to realize the vision of large scale, distributed SW, with real-world datasets, representing real community agreement, and leading to astonishing research possibilities that can exploit and reuse these freely available data. For instance, the DBpedia project [3] extracts structured information from Wikipedia. The DBpedia

P. Cimiano and H.S. Pinto (Eds.): EKAW 2010, LNAI 6317, pp. 193–210, 2010.

ontology describes 170 classes in a shallow subsumption hierarchy, and more than 900 properties[1]. DBpedia has a high degree of conceptual overlap with other datasets, and it is increasingly becoming the central interlinking hub. The web of data around DBpedia covers 4.7 billion pieces of information about domains such as geography, people, companies, films, music, genes, amphibians, books and publications.

Ultimately, by integrating and connecting data on the web, Linked Data, and DBpedia in particular, as stated in [3] "can be used to answer quite surprising queries about a wide range of topics". E.g., by failing to link the content one can obtain films directed by Francis Ford Coppola but not what actors have played in any of his movies. However, while back end technologies and semantic applications can be robust at the small or medium scale, they may not be suitable when applying them to a real-world scale of heterogeneous web data. In other words, while Linked Data datasets literally may contain the answers to millions of questions, locating and exploiting the relevant information to extract these answers from them is a major challenge. In fact, most tools analyzed in Section 2 only perform a shallow exploitation of these data. Thus, in this paper we analyze the practicability of this ambition from the end-user application side, by looking at the scalability issues when integrating our multi-ontology QA system, PowerAqua, which uses state of the art methods from computational linguistics, ontology mapping, and data fusion, with some of the large general purpose data offered by the Linked Data community: DBpedia, the BBC backstage data whose scope is TV broadcasts and music [6], umbel[2] and musicBrainz.

Kaufmann and Bernstein [5] demonstrated, via a usability experiment comparing four query interfaces to an ontology, that casual users preferred the interface that used full NL queries to those using keywords, partial sentences and a graphical interface. Furthermore, the intuition that it would be easier to obtain answers from structured data than open text had lead to much interest in open NL interfaces that build and query their own massive trusted comprehensive factual KBs about the world (e.g., commercial ventures such as Powerset, START, Wolfram Alpha or True Knowledge[3]). Hence, it is worth considering an open NL interface for the end user to locate and query the Linked Data content on the web.

PowerAqua [9] takes a NL query from the user and retrieves answers from heterogeneous semantic data repositories. In particular, PowerAqua is able to integrate, on the fly, statements drawn from different sources to generate integrated answers to questions. Knowledge can be aggregated to complete information partially presented in single sources, fusing similar answers and filtering irrelevant ones. Furthermore, the most accurate answer(s), in terms of their relevance to the query and the varying levels of quality, popularity and trust, are elicited from different sources [8]. As such, PowerAqua supports users in locating, reusing and querying the open SW or organizations with large semantics intranets, where the information is distributed across independent departmental sites and external semantic sources. However, the SW has

---

[1] Plus a dataset of 8000 property types for which there is no formal ontology (as November 2009).

[2] Derived form OpenCyc and which consists of 20,000 classes (http://www.umbel.org/backbone.html)

[3] http://www.powerset.com/, http://start.csail.mit.edu/, http://www.wolframalpha.com/index.html and http://www.trueknowledge.com/ respectively.

been rapidly evolving during the development of PowerAqua. PowerAqua was first envisioned in 2006 as a shift between the first generation of closed domain semantic systems, akin to smart KB applications, and the next generation of open SW applications to exploit the increasing amounts of semantic markup data, which is heterogeneous with respect to both the ontology characterization and provenance. Again, now, we can distinguish a new turning point in the evolution of the SW driven by the emergence of Linked Data. Querying Linked Data brings up a new scenario, the differentiating characteristics of which (detailed in Section 4) are:

I. Scalability is not only in the number of ontologies but also on their size (number of ontological elements). E.g., more than 2.9 million things are described in DBpedia.
II. From specific domain ontologies to large generic ontologies about everything, with a wider coverage of relationships across entities from a variety of domains.
III. Ontologies are decentralized, containing redundant and heterogeneous terminology, and connected to each other creating a network or cloud of ontologies.

In what follows, we look at the abilities of existing tools that handle the sheer amount of multi-domain data offered by Linked Data to provide easy access to the end user (Section 2). Then we briefly describe PowerAqua (Section 3), and present the major issues (Section 4) that we faced to scale up PowerAqua to take advantage of Linked Data's potential to answer queries. The feasibility of the solutions presented (in Section 5) is assessed through initial experiments that measure the QA performance before and after using the main representative Linked Data set, DBpedia (Section 6). We finish by drawing some conclusions (Section 7). We believe that the lessons learned obtained with our experiments can be extrapolated to a large proportion of semantic tools that wish to retrieve, use and combine these large, rich multi-domain semantic data on the fly.

2 Motivations: Current Interfaces for Linked Data and Limitations

The database and SW communities had developed back-end technologies for managing large amounts of web data. Various RDF stores can scale over large amounts of data originating from different sources, such as Virtuoso or the Talis platform[4]. Search engines such as Watson [10] and Sindice [11] come also with features for indexing data from the SW. Linked Data sources usually offer a SPARQL endpoint for their dataset(s)[5]. Alternatively, they also provide RDF data dumps to build and query your own store[6]. However, users can hardly know which identifiers and properties are used in the KBs and hence can be used for querying. Consequently, they have to be guided when building queries, e.g., through the suggestion of reasonable alternatives. Creating innovative ways to interact with Linked Data is crucial and even envisioned as a potential "killer app".

---

[4] Virtuoso: http://virtuoso.openlinksw.com and Talis: http://www.talis.com/platform/
[5] A more complete list of SPARQL Endpoints at: http://esw.w3.org/topic/SparqlEndpoints
[6] Jena http://jena.hpl.hp.com/wiki/TDB; Sesame http://www.openrdf.org; 4store http://4store.org;

Nonetheless, to find a trade-off between the complexity of the querying process and the amount of data it can use and integrate is still an open problem for ontology-based approaches. Semantic search models that have proved to work well in specific domains still have to undertake further steps towards an effective deployment on a decentralized, heterogeneous and massive repository of content about a potentially unlimited number of domains. Here we present a state of the art of the available user interfaces that can, in principle, scale enough to explore the Linked Data.

- Triple query builder interfaces: a Query Builder allows users to query the KB by means of multiple triple patterns. For each triple pattern variable, identifiers or filters for the subject, predicate and object can be defined. The user needs to follow the terminology and structure of the ontology to pose queries, e.g., the DBpedia Leipzig query builder [1]. However, for each typed identifier name a look ahead search proposes suitable options in a (in some cases long) drop down menu that helps the user to create complex queries, e.g.: <?x, rdf:type, db-ont:Person> <?x, notablePrize, Nobel_Peace_Prize>. Graph-based visualizations, on the contrary, in which all property values of the selected instances are analyzed for facet-filtering, are more resource demanding [1].
- Relationship finder: i.e., the DBpedia relationship finder [7] explores connections between objects. DBpedia is treated as an undirected graph and given two objects, the relationship finder looks for a path between them (not necessarily the shortest).
- Keyword lookup: e.g., the DBpedia URI Lookup Index and OpenLink Software[7] find the most likely matches (URIs) for a given term. The service combines Lucene's string similarity based ranking with a relevance ranking similar to PageRank. The OpenLink Software builds a text, label and URI lookup service upon a larger collection of sources, but it limits the number of results to only those containing an exact mapping of the input keyword and the search can be refined by specifying URIs of classes, properties or values, but usability is limited (e.g., 1358 classes are associated to the keyword "actor").
- Data aggregators and mash-ups: e.g., in Sig.ma (http://sig.ma/) the user enters a keyword and is able to explore all the aggregated data coming from the search engine Sindice (including synonyms and approximate mappings). Although mash-up technologies provide support for large-scale indexing and aggregating heterogeneous information, they do not attempt to disambiguate or rank between different interpretations, however, in Sig.ma the user can filter out the irrelevant sources.
- Linked Data browsers: they bring a way to browse RDF data on the web (data should be in RDF/XML or embedded in web documents using microformats). Examples are Tabulator and Disco[8]. Given a dereferenceable URI (i.e. an application can look up a URI over the HTTP protocol), these browsers render all information that they can find about that URI. All aggregated data across sources is viewed in a tabular form and the user can navigate through interlinked sources. However, it does not aggregate unconnected entities with different URIs representing the same individual.

[7] http://lookup.dbpedia.org/ and http://lod.openlinksw.com

[8] http://www.w3.org/2005/ajar/tab and http://sites.wiwiss.fu-berlin.de/suhl/bizer/ng4j/disco/

- DBpedia Faceted search[9]: it allows the user to easily ask queries like “recent films about Buenos Aires”, by typing the keyword “Buenos Aires” and then applying an intelligent filtering base on the underlying ontology, in this case by the item type “Film”. The interface guides the user to filter objects according to facets (properties) and range of values. Nevertheless, the user needs to familiarize herself to some extent with the vocabulary and the structure of the KB, e.g., lexically related words like “Movie” are not understood. This applies not only to undefined terms, but also when there is not a straight mapping between the user query and the way the knowledge is structured in the ontology. For example, the query “Give me the husbands of Elizabeth Taylor” cannot be easily formulated if the user does not know that the relevant relation “spouse” is defined only for the entities representing Elizabeth Taylor’s husbands, whose ontological type is “Actor”, and it is neither defined for the instance “Elizabeth Taylor”, nor for the types “Person” or “Artist”. As the system is unable to map “husband” to the relation “spouse”, the only solution left is to manually explore among all the results that contain a match for “Elizabeth Taylor”.

Research on user interfaces for Linked Data is a open-ended area, each of the above paradigms have different abilities to handle the sheer amount of multi-domain data and the following limitations according to the criteria presented in Table 1:

1) Usability: if the input of the system is a URI or is some of the components of a triple, usability is limited to knowledgeable users, familiar with semantic source contents.
2) Expressivity: if the system builds upon keywords, then it provides limited capabilities to grasp and exploit the conceptualizations involved in user needs, with limitations such as the inability to account for relations between terms, or to cope with complex queries.
3) Scalability: if the system is restricted to one or a set of domains to maintain performance then it cannot scale to a truly open environment.
4) Mapping: the vocabulary that the system can understand is limited to that used in the ontology, the input is controlled and if a term has more than one sense, disambiguation is done manually by the user. Although these guided interfaces solve the old habitability problem (a mismatch between the user expectations and the abilities of the system), the burden or responsibility to formulate the queries is shifted from the system to the user.
5) Fusion: if the system has limited abilities to merge heterogeneous facts or multiple different answers (representing the same individual) across different semantic sources.
6) Ranking: the lack of ranking algorithms to cope with large-scale information sources.

The existing querying approaches for Linked Data are restricted, among all of them, only facets and query builder interfaces provide an efficient way to pose complex and expressive queries to a large repository, with varying levels of usability depending on the query complexity and the number of filtered options presented on the drop menus, as end-users can get lost in large-scale information spaces. In fact, a common

[9] http://dbpedia.neofonie.de/browse

Table 1. Limitations of the existent paradigms according to 6 criteria

Criteria	Query Builder	Rel. Finder	Term Lookup	Mash-ups	Browsers	Facets
Usability	√	√	√	√	--	√
Expressivity	√	--	X	X	X	√
Scalabilty	√	√	√	√	√	√
Mapping	X	X	--	--	X	X
Fusion	X	X	X	--	--	X
Ranking	X	X	--	X	X	X

drawback of all these systems is that the user, not the application, is the one who has the responsibility and burden to reformulate the query in a way that can be understood. Another open issue concerns the usability of menu views and facets over multiple heterogeneous sources. Only keyword-based mash-ups (and lookup services to some extent) can aggregate information across sources, but they do not attempt to fuse similar results, nor do they have enough context to interpret and elicit the best answers. What is achievable on small/medium scale data by querying interfaces (in particular sophisticated NL ones) has until now not been achieved on large Linked Data. In this paper, we aim to go one step beyond the state of the art, by adapting the mapping and fusion techniques required by a particular NL interface, PowerAqua, to the Linked Data scenario.

3 PowerAqua: An Open NL Interface over Structured Data

Contrary to existing ontology-based NLI systems (see [5] for an example) whose scope is limited to one or a set of a-priori selected medium size ontologies at a time, PowerAqua dynamically selects and combines information drawn from multiple and heterogeneous ontologies in order to interpret and answer a query, making it worth investigating whether it can be successfully used to exploit the metadata offered by Linked Data. We briefly explain PowerAqua through the illustrative example "Find me university cities in Japan", a linguistically simple query that nevertheless, to be answered requires knowledge fusion across different sources. PowerAqua follows a pipeline architecture, the query is first transformed by the linguistic component[10] into a triple based intermediate format called Query-Triples (QTs): <university cities, ?, Japan>. At the next step, the QTs are passed on to the PowerMap mapping component, which identifies potentially suitable semantic entities in various ontologies that are likely to describe QT terms and answer a query, producing initial element level mappings. For example, PowerMap selects 81 mappings over 23 ontologies for the query term "Japan". PowerMap maximizes recall by searching for approximate mappings (e.g., "CountryJapan" in the TAP ontology) as well as exact mappings. These are jointly referred to as equivalent mappings. PowerMap also uses both WordNet and the SW itself (*owl:sameAs)* to find synonyms, hypernyms, derived words, meronyms and hyponyms (e.g., "Japanese islands", "Nippon", etc). In the third step, the Triple Similarity Service (TSS), exploring the relations of these entities, matches the QTs to

[10] The linguistic component uses GATE (www.gate.ac.uk) to transform into triples factual queries formed with wh-terms (which, what, who, when, where) or commands (give, list, show, tell,..).

ontological expressions or ontology based triple patterns specific to each of the considered semantic sources, producing a set of Onto-Triples (OTs), from which answers are derived as a list of entities matching the given triple patterns in each semantic source.

The algorithm iteratively refines candidates only as needed, analyzing most likely solutions first, and using more expensive but broader techniques last, if the previous steps fail to obtain a solution. First, the TSS chooses, whenever possible, the ontologies that better cover the user query and domain (i.e., it first searches for OTs in the ontologies that have potential mappings for at least two of the terms in a given QT). In our example, as PowerMap does not find any covering ontology with mappings for both arguments in the QT: "university cities" and "Japan", the TSS algorithm reiterates again by splitting the compound term "university cities", and consequently modifying the QT into: <cities / universities, ?, Japan> and creating a new QT for the compound <university, ?, cities>. For the QTs obtained in this second iteration, the TSS extracts, by analyzing the ontology relations, a small set of ontologies containing the valid OTs that jointly cover the user query and produce an answer. The resultant OTs are partially presented in Table 2.

Table 2. Triple Mapping Tables returned by PowerAqua for the example query

QT_1: <cities / universities, ?, Japan>	
Agrovoc	OT_1 <*city, generic-location, Japan*> 27 answers: Ibaraki, Kyoto, kushiro-shi, etc.
SWETO	OT_1 <*city, attribute-country, Japan*> 30 answers: Chuo-ku Tokyo, Chuo-ku Osaka, etc.
KIM	OT_1 <*city, locatedIn, Country_T JA (Japan)*> 290 answers: Mishima, Kodaira, Soka, etc.
TAP	OT_1 <*city, locatedIn, CountryJapan*> 30 answers: CityChitose, CityKyoto, etc.
DBpedia	OT_1 <*RadioStation, city, Japan*> 2 answers: FM802, J-Wave.
QT_2: <university, ?, cities>	
DBpedia	OT_3 <*PopulatedPlace, city, University*> 7177 answers: Madrid (Polytechnic_University_of_Madrid), Kyoto (Kyoto_University), etc.

Finally, because each resultant OT only leads to partial answers, they need to be combined into a complete answer. The fourth component merges and ranks the various interpretations produced in different ontologies. In our example, 19 final answers are selected (e.g.: Kyoto (Kyoto_University), Fukushima (Fukushima_University)), by intersecting the answers from both QTs to obtain as a final set of answers those shared between the 7177 answers of *cities with a university* from DBpedia, and the more than 500 answers about *cities in Japan* derived from 8 ontologies (agrovoc, KIM, TAP, ATO, DBpedia, nepomuk, mid-level, and SWETO). Among other things, merging requires the system to identify similar entities across ontologies, e.g., "Kyoto" in DBpedia and "CityKyoto" in TAP. Furthermore, ranking (based on the quality and popularity of the mappings and answers) can be applied to sort the answers. E.g., a ranking measure is capable of providing a lower confidence to the noisy answers derived from the DBpedia OT: <*RadioStation, city, Japan*>. Although, in this case all answers derived after fusion are correct (as irrelevant answers only appear in one triple). As we show in [8], merging and ranking algorithms enhance the quality of the results.

To scale our model to a truly open web environment implies exploiting all the increasingly available semantic metadata in order to provide a good coverage of topics.

To address this, PowerAqua is coupled with: a) the Watson SW gateway [10], which collects and provides fast access to the increasing amount of online available semantic data, and b) its own internal mechanism to index and query selected online ontological stores[11], as an alternative way to manage large repositories, like those offered by the Linked Data community, often not available in Watson due to their size and format (RDF dumps available for download as compressed files). One of the main issues for PowerAqua is to keep real time performance in a scenario of perpetual change and growth. The time needed to answer a query depends on: (1) the number of calls required to the Watson API or to query the repositories and the indexes, and (2) the response times to these calls. The total number of calls depends directly on the number of semantic sources and mappings that take part in the answering process. The response times to these calls depend on the complexity of the (SPARQL-alike) query and the size of the ontology. PowerAqua algorithms are optimized to reduce the number of expensive calls in the following way:

- The algorithm operates in a sequential fashion, by first collecting all candidate ontological entities for the terms in a query, and then identifying relevant relationships between them. However, the algorithm can re-iterate through the two different phases in order to look only for the mappings needed in the first instance. As such, the algorithm looks for mappings for terms forming a compound, e.g., "university cities", only if the first iteration, without splitting the compound, fails to produce results.
- The time consuming process of analyzing indirect relationships between two entities (i.e., relationships which require two triples to be joined, as the length of the path is limited to one mediating concept) is only carried out when no satisfactory is-a or ad-hoc direct relationships between any of the candidate entities within the ontology are found.
- The number of mappings returned by Watson is reduced through a functionality used to restrict the mappings for a given term to the ontologies that also contain mappings for another given term. E.g., in our query PowerMap retrieves hits for "university", "cities", or any of its lexical variations, from ontologies that also contain mappings for "Japan".

4 Before and After Linked Data: A New Dimension in QA

We have identified three crucial factors that give a new perspective and draw a new line in the scope of SW applications before and after Linked Data, therefore, challenging Linked Data's potential in the QA context.

4.1 Scaling to Highly Populated and Dense Ontologies

A well-known limitation of the SW is its sparseness, as stated in [13], without a well populated SW, developing semantic search systems is only an intellectual exercise. Only a reduced number of topics were covered entirely or partially by an existing ontology (domain sparseness), and added to this, sparseness at the level of instances

[11] Using Lucene indexes and a common API to access and query ontologies (currently in sesame).

and relation (model complexity) was also found [4, 10]. However, Linked Data initiatives are producing a critical mass of semantic data, and it is likely that soon we will have so much data that the core issues would not be so much related to sparseness as to scalability and robustness.

Furthermore, as reported in an analysis of 25,500 ontologies and semantic documents collected by Watson [10] in 2007: "the SW is characterized by a large number of small, lightweight ontologies and a small number of large-scale, heavyweight ontologies", the biggest one at that time containing more than 28,000 entities. By contrast, an obvious characteristic of Linked Data is that it is very large, DBpedia alone consists of more than 103 million RDF triples, and describes more than 2.9 million entities. Also, as analyzed in [7] the DBpedia dataset is densely connected. As ever, the links between entities are more important than the entities themselves because that's where the context lives. Exploring these connections between entities, e.g., through SPARQL queries, is the major bottleneck. Scale matters since the response time of the calls to query the ontologies depends directly on the size of the ontology, in particular when a query involves one or more classes with lots of instantiated data. Therefore, to query Linked Data mapping algorithms need to be able to explore the relevant connections while trying to avoid expensive computations.

4.2 Mapping Query Terms to Large Generic Ontologies about Everything

The really challenging aspects of these Link Datasets appeared to be not only their scale but also their heterogeneity: new challenges are introduced by simultaneously querying not only a large number of domain specific ontologies but also a few very large populated ontologies about everything.

The first version of PowerAqua was developed to work on an initial, sparsely populated SW. Therefore, PowerAqua algorithms were designed to maximize recall in order to bridge the gap between user terminology and terms used in the ontologies. Nevertheless, to keep up with the continuous and rapidly growth of the SW and to avoid analyzing an unfeasibly large space of solutions, the algorithms are iterative, and try to find an answer by augmenting the search space in each re-iteration until either an answer is found or all possibilities have been analyzed. The algorithm is based on the assumption that the ontologies that better cover a query (i.e. contain matches for most of the elements on a QT) are likely to represent better the domain(s) of the query and contain an answer. The algorithm uses this coverage criterion to restrict the mappings to be analyzed to those in the covering ontologies, extending the search space only if no answers are found.

However, the main distinctive feature of DBpedia, apart from its size, is that it is a repository about everything. Therefore, even in the cases where the answer to the user query is not contained in DBpedia, this dataset is frequently selected as relevant, and often contains a huge number of potential ontological hits, from a large number of domains, for one or more of the terms in the user query. Consequently, this coverage criterion to filter ontologies, ergo candidate mappings, becomes insufficient when most of the lexical matches for a user query belong to just one large open domain KB and often have different meanings than the one intended by the user. For instance, DBpedia alone contains more than 1000 mappings for an apparently unambiguous keyword like "Russian"*:* e.g., the exact mappings Russia (instance) & russia (property); the synonyms Soviet_Union (instance) & USSR (instance); the hypernym country (class); the approximate instances: Russian_empire, president_of_russia, MTV_Russia, Rocket_to_Russia, Russia_Today, Anastasia_of_Rusia, etc. Analyzing the ontological context of all potentially relevant hits, to select the ones containing an answer, would result in unacceptably slow response time for a run time algorithm. Therefore, new filtering heuristics are needed.

4.3 Fusion across the Heterogeneous and Decentralized Cloud of Ontologies

When searching multiple collections together, knowledge needs to be shared and reused through fusion techniques. Redundant information or partial results from different sources need to be either combined and merged together or ranked in terms of their relevance to the query and the confidence in the answers derived from different sources.

Fusion requires matching at the schema level as well as entity reconciliation at the data level; it assigns the individuals returned as answers from different ontologies into subsets of answers that represent identical entities. A decision about the equivalence of two answers is made based on string similarity metrics applied to their labels, local names, and, in case of uncertainty, other datatype attributes. Pairwise comparison of entities would make the complexity of the procedure N^2 with respect to the input set size. In order to avoid this, candidate matches are selected using a search over the indexes and the comparison focuses only on the entities that appear among the search results. This makes the complexity linear with respect to the answer set size, but in cases where the answer set is formed by thousands of partial answers, further heuristics to improve efficiency are needed.

5 Solutions to Challenges and Lessons Learned

Next, we report on the solutions adopted by PowerAqua to solve the challenges outlined above. Our experiments also give us an insight on the quality of the datasets and a better understanding of the concrete issues encountered when handling large-scale data.

5.1 Large Scale Data: Shifting Focus onto Precision for Mapping and Fusion

DBpedia contains a large number of instances across domains, and as said before, it can produce a large number of diverse mappings for a single query term. Strategies to select the most likely mappings to answer a query and filter the least promising ones are crucial to keep run time performance especially when querying a huge amount of semantic data.

These strategies start with a quick filtering mechanism based on scores (not processing), returned by Lucene **string similarities**, to ensure that the mappings for a given term, within one single repository, have a minimum quality and their number does not go over a given threshold. This favors precision and can negatively affect recall, however, it is a necessary measure to ensure that all questions can be answered in real time. Secondly, the number of mappings is reduced according to **heuristics to filter out** the least promising individual mappings. These heuristics are not based on a

PageRank-like algorithm (i.e., the popularity of the entity within the ontology)[12] but rather on the context of the query. The reason behind this is that we do not want to penalize searches in which the user is interested in the unique meaning (not the popular meaning) of the word. For instance, the meaning of Turkey is clear when asking for "Give me books written in Turkey" or "which wine is good for a meal based on Turkey?". Based on the **coverage criterion** ontologies about geography or food would be selected respectively. However, a dataset like DBpedia contains both meanings of Turkey (*Turkey_(bird)* and *Turkey*) plus several mappings for "books" and "wine". Before the time consuming process of analyzing the relationships between the mappings to obtain the interpretation that better translates the query in a given ontology, further heuristics to reduce the number of mappings within an ontology are applied. These heuristics are **based on the syntactic relevance** of the mappings: (1) the quality: exact vs. approximate; (2) the semantic relation: equivalent, synonyms, hyper(hypo)rnyms, or meronyms. Next, more expensive semantic mechanisms based on the **ontology taxonomy** are applied, i.e. to discard redundant mappings by selecting those that are higher in the same ontology hierarchy (e.g., the class "wine" selected over its subclasses "rose-wine", "white-wine", "sugary-wine", etc). Also, **unconnected mappings** with no ontological context, in the form of ad-hoc or is-a relations, are discarded.

These strategies applied by PowerMap mapping algorithms to increase precision, and consequently performance, require making certain assumptions about the quality of the semantic sources, without making any unreasonable or a-priori assumption. As explained in Section 5.2, if the heuristics are too strict recall is affected and valid answers are missed, in particular for the heterogeneous and general datasets such as DBpedia. The mapping finishes with, the TSS iterative algorithms [9] that exploit the **ontological relationships** between the candidate entities to translate the user query (starting with the most straightforward solutions and executing expensive steps last, if no solution is found).

In order to improve the efficiency of the fusion procedure, our approach is to balance the quality of the resulting set of the answers and the expected time cost. When the number of answers, which have to be processed by the fusion module is large, our procedure tries to minimize the number of index search calls. The input of the fusion procedure is a set of answers retrieved from one or more ontologies $o_i, i=1...n$. Let A_i denote a set of answers $\{a_{i1}...a_{im}\}$ coming from the ontology o_i. By default, for each a_{ij} we searched the index using as keywords the label and local name of a_{ij} together with their synonyms extracted from WordNet. Instances a_{kx} which were retrieved by the search, and at the same time belonged to the original set of query answers, were considered as candidates for fusion. In the new version of the algorithm, we introduced two thresholds for $|A_i|$. The first regulates the use of WordNet synonyms in search: if $|A_i|> \lambda$, then WordNet synonyms are not used when searching for instances similar to $a_{ij} \in A_i$. The second one excludes the whole set A_i from search: if $|A_i|> \mu$, then the module does not try to search for instances similar to any $a_{ij} \in A_i$. Thus, if there is an instance a_{kx} belonging to an ontology o_k such that $a_{kx} \equiv a_{ij}$, they can only be merged if a search for a_{kx} returns a_{ij}, which potentially leads to lower

[12] Popularity measures are used only to rank the final answers obtained across ontologies [8].

recall of the fusion procedure. However, this potential loss of recall is justified when we are dealing with very large answer sets.

5.2 Heterogeneity and Duplicated Terms: Filtering Based on Quality and Semantics

In DBpedia, the most valuable contents extracted from Wikipedia are the *infoboxes*. However, different infobox templates use different names for the same attribute (e.g., *birthplace* and *placeofbirth*). The DBpedia project deals with this situation by using two different extraction approaches in parallel: a *generic* one that aims at a high coverage, and a *mapping-based* one that aims at high data quality by mapping Wikipedia terms to a manually created ontology [3]. However, the latest covers only 350 Wikipedia templates.

One of the filtering heuristics to favor precision is to consider the quality and semantic relation of the mappings. However, the presence of duplicated entities within the same semantic source limit the effectiveness of this criterion. Consider the example: "Give me the husbands of Elizabeth Taylor", the keyword "husbands" produce several mappings in DBpedia, the approximate equivalent instances: Clifford_Husbands, Commuter_Husbands, Dead_Husbands, Husbands_and_Wives, Young_Husbands, etc; the exact equivalent properties: husbands, husband, etc; and the exact hypernyms: spouse, spouses, partner, etc. The equivalent properties representing "husband(s)" do not produce any valid OTs with the entity "Elizabeth Taylor". The answer is encoded in the hypernym property "spouse". Therefore, hypernyms can be as relevant as equivalent mappings. With this kind of dataset, in which different terms have the same semantics, heuristics need to be flexible. First, exact mappings, if any, independent of their semantic relation, are selected over approximate mappings. Furthermore, exact mappings are a requirement in cases where the type of the mapping is not the expected one. E.g., in "who won a Nobel prize" the linguistic relation "won" is mapped to the instance "Won_James_Won", this approximate mapping is discarded before analyzing how it relates to the subject and object of the triple.

The TSS ultimately establishes the semantic validity of the candidate mappings by analyzing the ontological context, which is translated in many SPARQL-like queries to find the OTs. However, for queries that are particularly expensive, heuristics based on the semantic relation (synonym, hyper(hypo)nym) together with the quality of the mapping (exact, approximate) are also applied to minimize the number of those expensive queries. In large ontologies like DBpedia, searching for both *ad-hoc relationships* (1:1) between two highly populated classes and *indirect relationships* with one mediating concept (1:2) are expensive computations. In these two cases, to favor precision when looking for relationships among the mappings, only pairs in which at least one candidate mapping is exact and equivalent are analyzed (singulars and plurals are considered exact mappings). In this way for the query "which languages are spoken in a country?" the TSS avoids searching for relations between DBpedia matches such as "text", an hypernym of "language", and "land", a synonym of "country".

Finally, heterogeneity is not only present in the vocabulary but also in the granularity of the data (i.e., entities modeled with different degrees of richness). For instance, the deepness that characterizes the YAGO hierarchy [12] and its conjunctive schema classes (used in DBpedia classification), which encode too much information in one class, e.g., "MultinationalCompaniesHeardquarteredInTheNetherlands", make the processing of the labels too difficult for automatic QA understanding.

5.3 Lack of Semantics or Formal Ontology: Light-Weight Reasoning

PowerAqua is able to scale thanks to the various strategies and filtering heuristics that keep the number of mappings and queries to the semantic sources more or less constant, even when adding large semantic sources or a large number of them. However, as said in Section 3, performance also depends on the size of the ontologies, which influences the response time of the calls (SPARQL or Serql) to query them. The effectiveness of these queries, which use the ontology semantics to perform basic light-weight inferences based on the taxonomy and relationships, also relates to the quality of the sources they are querying.

In DBpedia the properties defined in the namespace http://dbpedia.org/ontology belong to the data generated by the mapping-based approach. In this approach, fine-grained rules are applied to define the target datatype and ignore additional text that may be present in the attribute value. However, although the percentage of properties pointing to other DBpedia entities is much higher in the mapping-based dataset (53%) than in the generic dataset (25.6%) [3], the coverage is lower (843,000 compared to 1,462,00 entities). In the generic approach, http://dbpedia.org/property/, coverage of all infoboxes is complete but synonymous attribute names are not resolved, and there is a high error rate to determine the datatype of a value. The effectiveness of finding answers in the generic approach is limited with respect to the mapping approach and it has an important impact on query performance.

a) Domain and range: In the mapping approach OTs can be extracted with reasonable performance by querying the schema (domain and range). However the answer can be encoded in a property defined within the generic approach, where properties do not map to a schema. The lack of domain and range information, results in either sending expensive SPARQL / SeRQL queries or missing connections between the analyzed entities. To balance performance and recall, domain and range information is crucial in cases where we are looking for indirect relationships, or ad-hoc relations between two classes or a class and a literal. For example in "give me languages used in Islamic countries?" the query is translated into OTs representing "languages spoken in a country" and "countries that are Islamic", domain and range are used to get all possible relations among the two classes "language" and "country", because it is not feasible to check all the instances of languages to find ad-hoc relations with any instance of country in real time, particular for highly populated classes. Therefore, the answers encoded in the OTs formed with the KB relation "http://dbpedia.org/property/states" are not found, but it finds answers for the schema relation: <language, http://dbpedia.org/ontology/states, country>. Furthermore, domain and range information is also needed in order to complete a triple when the relation is mapped but not the subject of the triple. E.g., the query "in which region is Cantonese spoken?" is mapped to the OT: <PopulatedPlace (domain of region), region, Cantonese> with 12 answers (Hong Kong, Macau, etc). Because an instance can instantiate a relation with thousands of other instances, schema information is needed to model the OT.

b) Inference of relationships: When looking for relationships between two entities, the ontology is treated as an indirect graph, and all direct and inverse relations are retrieved. Inheritance of relations is considered: if the ontological platform does not offer schema inferencing (as it is the case for Postgres repositories in Sesame 2), then complex *SeRQL* queries need to be generated to consider the relationships defined for the superclasses of the classes involved. In our previous example, domain and range information is used to find instantiated relations between the classes "language" and "country", or any of their superclasses. If looking for indirect relations inherency is also considered, but the search is restricted to candidate mediated concepts with relations defined in the schema, looking for indirect inverse relations is avoided as it is computationally expensive to search for relations to and from highly populated mediated concepts. Also, inferences cannot be done with instances whose type is defined in another ontology.

c) Literals and good enough labels: a literal has no structure and the meaning is given just by its label. E.g, the unprocessed value for the property "states" in the instance "Tamil language" ("*India, Sri Lanka and Singapore, where it has an official status; with significant minorities in Canada, {..}*") is too complex to automatically infer answers.

6 Initial Experiments and Discussion

Despite using community driven large scale knowledge obtained from sources that are heterogeneous, redundant and not always complete or well formed, the SW technology is mature enough to interpret and answer NL user queries. In this section, we present some example queries[13] to justify our claim that we can obtain answers to queries directly from the DBpedia semantically rich information – even in its current form. The solutions in Section 5 had allowed us to improve PowerAqua mapping and fusion algorithms to exhibit better performance, measured in terms of speed or seconds to answer a query, by shifting the focus on precision while minimizing the loss in recall. We have made an initial comparative study between PowerAqua efficiency before and after adding DBpedia dataset and the heuristics to favor precision, by using the semantic data and a subset of queries from previous evaluations [9, 8, 4]. This semantic data consists of 700 semantic documents distributed in 130 repositories, 3GBs data in which the biggest source (SWETO and SWETO-DBLP) is not more than 1GB (over 3 million triples). A sample of 16 queries can be seen in Table 3, where the last 6 queries can only be answered if DBpedia is included in the query dataset. As shown, the average time for the mapping algorithms to translate a query increases from 32 to 48 secs when using the same queries and datasets but adding DBpedia, even with the use of filtering heuristics. However, the resulting number of valid answers obtained after applying the fusion algorithm (which has a precision of 94%[15]) rises from 64 to 370 on average. The average mapping time with DBpedia increases to 52 secs when adding complex queries like Q_{11} and Q_{12} that require fusing partial translations from DBpedia and other datasets to obtain a complete one. While this is acceptable for a research demo, work still has to be done to improve the speed.

[13] More demo queries at: http://kmi.open.ac.uk/technologies/poweraqua

In any case, it shows that semantic data can be handled in modest projects, our demo runs in one reasonable sized server (a 3GHz Intel Pentium dual core with 8GB RAM).

The reasons behind the decrease in speed are not so much because of the increase of the number of resultant hits obtained when querying more and larger repositories. Heuristics that balance precision and recall reduce SeRQL calls by more than 40% (352/587) and even keep them lower (540) when mapping complex queries into multiple facts. However, speed falls because of a suboptimal performance at the back end, where the response times to calls to the repositories increases for single large datasets, in particular for expensive queries to find: (1) relationships between instances of highly populated classes (domain-range information is limited and inherency is take into account); (2) indirect relationships; (3) relationships involving literal values. The first fact explains that Q_1 is executed faster than Q_{12}, even if it implies twice as many (*SeRQL*) calls, because there are 47,821 actors starring in films in DBpedia while there are just 3,224 languages related to a country. The second and third facts explain why Q_9 is the slowest query, because answers are obtained in DBpedia through 21 indirect OTs, with mediating concepts such as airlines, company, person, military conflict, that relate to both DBpedia entities "island" and "spain", plus the SWETO ontology contains multiple literal values for "spain" (corresponding to instances of Spanish cities) that need to be analyzed. Nevertheless, we are optimistic that PowerAqua (and other query-intensive interfaces) can scale to a huge amount of semantic information, as long as the semantic software it is based on can efficiently respond to the growth of the semantic sources. Furthermore, if the quality of ontologies improves and more semantic data becomes available, it should be easier to find more precise mappings with answers.

Table 3. Examples of queries after and before using the DBpedia dataset + heuristics (precision)

(Q_i) NL Query: After DBpedia / Before Dbpedia	**N°Ont**	**Answ.**	**Secs**	**Calls**
Q_1: How many languages are used in Islamic countries?	2/ 2	170/ 0	95.2/ 34.5	1078/ 419
Q_2: Which Russian rivers end in the Black Sea	3/ 1	4/ 1	41.3/ 27.3	639/ 428
Q_3: Who lives in the white house	4/ 3	12/12	17.9/ 13.7	310/ 144
Q_4: Give me airports in Canada	2/ 1	156/155	23/ 14.22	157/ 40
Q_5: List me Asian countries	6/ 6	64/ 72	15.3/ 67.4	298/ 1308
Q_6: Give me the main companies in India	2/ 2	710/ 386	17.4/ 43.9	298/ 588
Q_7: Give me movies starring Jennifer Aniston	3/ 2	28/ 23	10.7/ 4.5	94/ 22
Q_8: Which animals are reptiles?	9/ 8	2518/ 23	42.8/ 7.1	165/ 49
Q_9: Which islands belong to Spain	3/ 3	13/ 7	206/ 104	387/ 2617
Q_{10}: Find all the lakes in California	2/ 2	37/ 2	13.6/ 12.9	103/ 258
Average (10 queries) – after / before DBpedia	**3.6/3**	**371/68**	**48.3/32**	**352/587**
Q_{11}: Find me university cities in Japan	7/-	19/-	68/-	1087/-
Q_{12}: Tell me actors starring in films directed by Francis Ford Coppola	3/-	135/-	120/173	574/-
Q_{13}: Show me Spanish films with Carmen Maura	1/-	2/-	30.5./-	477/-
Q_{14}: Give me English actors that play in Titanic	1/-	4/-	144/-	3340/-
Q_{15}: Give me tennis players in France	1/-	29/-	14.7/-	113/-
Q_{16}: Television shows created by Walt Disney	1/ -	8/ -	9.4/ -	137/ -
Average (16 queries) – after DBpedia	**3.1**	**244.3**	**54.3**	**578.5**

Table 4. Fusion with DBpedia – after precision heuristics / before precision heuristics

	Q1	Q2	Q3	Q4	Q5	Q6	Q7	Q8	Q9	Q10	Q11	**Avg**
Secs	16.5/516	6.7/25	1.8/2	0.3/77	50.9/30	55.7/219	0.1/6.5	74.43/255	3.6/2.3	1.6/3	126/940	30.7/188
Calls	11/771	16/177	14/16	1/311	131/138	370/1148	44/53	19/2803	14/26	38/40	579/3792	112/843

We do not always have enough ontological context to focus on precision when, because of heterogeneity, there are many alternative translations. Take the query Q_{14}, which requires an unusual number of calls (3340) to find the OTs that translate to the QTs <actors/ English, play, Titanic> and <English, ?, actors>. There are 31 OTs in DBpedia for the first QT linking the class "Actor" to 7 instances of "Titanic" (Cinematic_Titanic, Titanic_1943_film, Titanic_1953_film, Titanic_1997_film, Titanic_TV_miniseries, etc), through several ad-hoc relations (starring, director, producer, academyawards, etc.), because the matches for the linguistic relation "play" (the properties: play, plays and show) turn out not to be relevant for the query. Similarly, the second QT is mapped to 18 DBpedia OTs formed with various ad_hoc relations (residence, ethnicity, location, hometown, deathPlace, etc, and the duplicated properties: birthplace, birthPlace and born) between the class "Actor" and the instance "England". Moreover, the keyword "English" alone produces several mappings that had to be analyzed to determine or not their relevance (e.g., English language, English people, English channel, English actor, English football, etc).

Yet, the needed filtering heuristics impose a toll in recall, e.g., new DBpedia answers are obtained for Q_5 but the answers from one ontology (KIM) are missed, producing a loss in total answers (64/72). Moreover, in Q_{13}, relevant films are missed because the mapping "spanish_language" was not selected and only OTs formed with the mapping "Spain" were retrieved. Notwithstanding, generally, we cannot see any negative effect on recall if we compare the total number of final answers with the previous version of PowerAqua but quite the contrary (371/68), in fact, many of the missed mappings were imprecise (and in any case filtered after fusion), like the city "Mammoth Lake" as an answer for Q_{10}, or their answers were already obtained from other ontologies.

Table 4 compares the average fusion times before and after applying the fusion heuristics to reduce the number of calls to the indexes, and therefore improve efficiency. The average fusion times have been reduced from 188 secs to 30.7 secs. We could not see any loss in recall due to the new fusion heuristics in this query sample.

Nevertheless, there are many open grounds for exploration of techniques to: (1) lead to better mappings, e.g., "British actors in Titanic" translates into multiple OTs but with no answers after fusion, because British is not mapped to England, and the resultant answers like "Kate Winslet" are related to England but not to Britain; (2) improve the selection of mappings by trust mechanisms and user feedback; (3) we have not yet fully exploited the explicit linkage for bridging data in the Linked Data world, e.g., if no ontology offers a complete translation of a single QT, instead of obtaining partial translations, explicit connections stated across different sources (*owl: sameAs*) can be use to efficiently search for cross ontology connections across entities as if they were part of the same graph.

7 Conclusions and Future Work

In the early stages of development, sparseness overshadowed the potential for QA using semantic data [4], however the transition from restricted domains to real world scale structured datasets stimulated by Linked Data, adds a new dimension of scalability for both applications and back-end technologies that aim to exploit the SW, opening new QA possibilities, beyond prototypes and proof of concepts. In this paper, we analyzed the implications of fusion and mapping techniques for querying large scale Linked Data content across multiple domains in NL, which allow us to extract useful lessons for the Linked Data community and developers in the wider SW community.

Existing techniques focusing simply on effectiveness may not scale to large amounts of data. To scale to a large amount of data, applications need to leverage precision and recall needs with the potential of scaling up through parallelization and adaptive load balancing. Although still more work needs to be done in our back end infrastructure to cover not just a subset but all Linked Data available, in this paper we analyzed the implications from the front-end (application) perspective on the way the query process should be realized to efficiently extract answers from large and highly heterogeneous community-driven open data, beyond any particular implementation, and in particular, the issues that we have addressed in order to scale our mapping and fusion techniques to millions of triples.

Currently, evaluation initiatives that would allow formal evaluations and direct comparison between systems are being investigated, e.g., in the SEALS (semantic evaluation at large scale) project. In this work our aim is to present some examples and initial experiments to justify our claim that we can obtain answers to queries from the huge amount of semantically rich information extracted from DBpedia – even in its current form.

QA over Linked Data opens the way to ambitious future research directions. For instance, DBpedia entities are also being used to annotate web content, i.e., DBpedia is being used as the controlled vocabulary to annotated BBC news. In this way, stories across different BBC domains are linked together through DBpedia data [6]. As the number of annotated sites increases, the answers to a question extracted by PowerAqua in the form of lists of entities (e.g., from DBpedia), that can be used as a valuable resource for discovering classic web content that is related (annotated) with those entities. Our future goal is to complement the answers given by PowerAqua with web pages to enhance the expressivity of traditional search engines with semantic information. Summing up, PowerAqua aims to provide a service that extends capabilities from querying a large number of unconnected sources to more interlinked ecosystems of data, in response to a user demand.

References

1. Auer, S., Lehmann, J.: What have Innsbruck and Leipzig in common? Extracting Semantics from Wiki Content. In: Proc. of the 4th European Conference on the Semantic Web, Austria (2007)
2. Bizer, C., Heath, T., Berners-Lee, T.: Linked Data – The Story So Far. Int. Journal on Semantic Web and Information Systems 5(3) (2009)
3. Bizer, C., Lehmann, J., Kobilarov, G., Auer, S., Becker, C., Cyganiak, R., Hellman, S.: DBpedia. A Crystallization Point for the Web of Data. Journal of Web Semantics 7(3) (2009)
4. Fernandez, M., Lopez, V., Sabou, M., Uren, V., Vallet, D., Motta, E., Castells, P.: Semantic Search meets the Web. In: Proc. of the Int. conference on Semantic Computing, California (2008)

5. Kaufmann, E., Bernstein, A.: How Useful Are Natural Language Interfaces to the Semantic Web for Casual End-Users? In: Proc. of the ISWC/ASWC, Korea (2007)
6. Kobilarov, G., et al.: Media Meets Semantic Web — How the BBC Uses DBpedia and Linked Data to Make Connections. In: Aroyo, L., Traverso, P., Ciravegna, F., Cimiano, P., Heath, T., Hyvönen, E., Mizoguchi, R., Oren, E., Sabou, M., Simperl, E. (eds.) ESWC 2009. LNCS, vol. 5554, pp. 723–737. Springer, Heidelberg (2009)
7. Lehmann, J., Schüppel, J., Auer, S.: Discovering unknown connections – the DBpedia relationship finder. In: Proc. of the 1st SABRE Conference on Social Semantic Web, Germany (2007)
8. Lopez, V., Nikolov, A., Fernandez, M., Sabou, M., Uren, V., Motta, E.: Merging and Ranking answers in the Semantic Web: The Wisdom of Crowds. In: Proc. of the ASWC, China (2009)
9. Lopez, V., Sabou, M., Uren, V., Motta, E.: Cross-Ontology Question Answering on the Semantic Web – an initial evaluation. In: Proc. of the KCAP Conference, California, USA (2009)
10. d'Aquin, M., Baldassarre, C., Gridinoc, L., Angeletou, S., Sabou, M., Motta, E.: Characterizing knowledge on the semantic web with Watson. In: Proc. of 5th Int. EON Workshop, Korea (2007)
11. Oren, E., Delbru, R., Catasta, M., Cyganiak, R., Stenzhorn, H., Tummarello, G.: Sindice.com: A document-oriented lookup index for open linked data. Journal of Metadata, Semantics and Ontologies 3(1) (2008)
12. Suchanek, F.M., Kasneci, G., Weikum, G.: YAGO: A Large Ontology from Wikipedia and WordNet, Web Semantics. In: Proc. of the WWW, vol. 6 (3) (2008)
13. Uren, V., Sabou, M., Motta, E., Fernandez, M., Lopez, V., Lei, Y.: Reflections on five years of evaluating semantic search systems. Journal of Metadata, Semantics and Ontologies 5(2) (2010)

Using Semantic Web Resources for Data Quality Management

Christian Fürber and Martin Hepp

E-Business & Web Science Research Group, Werner-Heisenberg-Weg 39, 85577 Neubiberg, Germany
christian@fuerber.com, mhepp@computer.org

Abstract. The quality of data is a critical factor for all kinds of decision-making and transaction processing. While there has been a lot of research on data quality in the past two decades, the topic has not yet received sufficient attention from the Semantic Web community. In this paper, we discuss (1) the data quality issues related to the growing amount of data available on the Semantic Web, (2) how data quality problems can be handled within the Semantic Web technology framework, namely using SPARQL on RDF representations, and (3) how Semantic Web reference data, e.g. from DBPedia, can be used to spot incorrect literal values and functional dependency violations. We show how this approach can be used for data quality management of public Semantic Web data and data stored in relational databases in closed settings alike. As part of our work, we developed generic SPARQL queries to identify (1) missing datatype properties or literal values, (2) illegal values, and (3) functional dependency violations. We argue that using Semantic Web datasets reduces the effort for data quality management substantially. As a use-case, we employ Geonames, a publicly available Semantic Web resource for geographical data, as a trusted reference for managing the quality of other data sources.

Keywords: Semantic Web, Ontologies, Data Quality Management, Ontology-Based Data Quality Management, Metadata Management, SPARQL, Linked Data, Geonames, Trust.

1 Introduction

Data is the source for almost every business transaction or decision and also has become increasingly important for our social activities. With the current evolution of the internet from a "Web of Documents" to a "Web of Data", huge amounts of business-relevant data is being published on the Web. That data may be used to increase automation of business operations and supporting processes of our social activities. Hence, it becomes critical to manage the correctness and reliability, i.e., the quality of data on the Web. It is a well-known fact that when using data for business cases, data quality problems can influence the satisfaction of customers and employees, produce unnecessary costs, and cause missed revenues [1]. Eventually,

P. Cimiano and H.S. Pinto (Eds.): EKAW 2010, LNAI 6317, pp. 211–225, 2010.

performing business processes based on poor data can be very expensive. Yet in 1998, the average total costs of poor data quality have been estimated to be 8 – 12 % of a company's revenues [2]. In the meanwhile, the automation of business processes and likewise the production and consumption of data have increased. Thus, the impact of poor data quality will likely be even higher today. Despite its importance to the overall success for the adaption of the Semantic Web, data quality is currently missing in the well-known Semantic Web layer cake diagram published by the World Wide Web Consortium (W3C) [3]. At present, there are only a few research approaches addressing data quality management with the use of Semantic Web technologies. Even less approaches provide means for quality management of data published on the Semantic Web.

In this paper, we (1) define typical problems that may occur on the data instance level in Semantic Web resources, (2) describe how to identify data quality problems of literal values in the Web of Data, and (3) show how we can use Semantic Web technology and datasets for data quality management of knowledge bases or local relational sources. As part of our proposal, we present SPARQL queries for data quality checks that can be executed completely within the Semantic Web technology stack.

2 Data Quality Management on the Semantic Web

In data quality research, high data quality is often described as data that is "fit for use" [4]. This definition relies on the subjective judgment of data quality by data consumers. Usually data consumers consider data to be of high quality and, therefore, "fit for use", when data meets their requirements. *Wang, et al.* have analyzed this perspective in more detail and identified 15 essential dimensions of data quality for data consumers, such as accuracy, completeness, accessibility, and relevance [4]. The perspective of a data consumer on data quality is of high practical relvance, in particular during data presentation.

From the technical perspective, high quality data is data that is "free of defects" [5]. Several typologies have been developed to classify respective defects in data [6-10]. These categorizations of data quality problems are especially suitable for the development of algorithms for the identification and improvement, as they provide insight into their technical characteristics. Because we aim at automated tools for data quality management and because the context of data consumption is often not immediately available on the Web of Data, we adopt the technical perspective on data quality to develop algorithms for the identification of data quality problems in knowledge bases. For a summary of instance-related data quality problems found in single-source scenarios, we refer to our previous work published in [11]. In the following, we summarize the most important types of defects for Semantic Web data.

2.1 Missing Literal Values

Missing values are values of certain properties that are missing, even though they are needed, either in general or within a certain context. For instance, the literal value for the property `country` might always be mandatory in address data, while the literal values for the property `state` might only be required for instances with the literal value "USA" in the datatype property `country`. In other words there are at least two types of missing values: (1) values that must not be missing at all, and (2) values that must not be missing in certain contexts. In Semantic Web data, missing literal values can be either in the form of (1) an empty literal attached to a datatype property, or by (2) the absence of a particular datatype property for a certain instance. Solution algorithms for the identification of missing values in Semantic Web scenarios have to consider both patterns. The first case will often be found when RDF data is derived automatically from relational sources and no sanity checks for empty attributes are included in the transformation process. The popular Semantic Web repository at http://loc.openlinksw.com/sparql, for instance, includes more than 3 Million triples from more than 44,000 RDF graphs with an empty literal as the object of at least one triple.

It is important to note that (1) standard database-style cardinality constraints cannot be modeled in neither RDFS nor OWL, and that (2) the constraints in real-world settings are often more subtle than simple validity intervals for the frequency of a particular property.

2.2 False Literal Values

False literal values are either (1) imaginary values that do not have a corresponding state in reality, (2) values that may exist in reality, but do not represent the correct state of an object, (3) values that are supposed to represent the current state of an object, but use the wrong syntax or are mistyped, and (4) values that represent an outdated real-world state of an object. In cases where values are part of functional dependencies, false values may be discovered by the use of queries for the identification of functional dependency violations (see below). Other cases require a separate set of query elements that can identify illegal states solely by the definition of legal or illegal states for an object. In many cases, the actual set of valid values is a small subset of the lexical space defined by the standard datatype (e.g. xsd:string or xsd:int).

Checks for false literal values can be performed with different levels of accuracy by (1) the definition of legal values or value ranges, (2) the definition of illegal values or value ranges, (3) the definition of syntax patterns for legal or illegal values, e.g. by the use of regular expressions, or (4) the definition of valid time ranges for sufficiently current values (only applicable in cases where time data about the actuality of values is available). In this paper, we focus on the use of legal value lists for the identification of illegal values. The identification of legal but outdated values is part of our future work, because it requires meta-data about the temporal properties of the datasets.

2.3 Functional Dependency Violations

Functional dependencies can be defined as dependencies between the values of two or more different properties [12], e.g. the value for the datatype property `prop:city` may depend on the value for datatype property `prop:zipcode`. More formally we can express a functional dependency between the literal x for datatype property A and the dependent literal y for the datatype property B as shown in (1).

$$A(x) \rightarrow B(y) \quad (1)$$

$$FDV: \{y \mid y \notin V_c\} \quad (2)$$

A functional dependency violation (FDV) occurs when the dependent literal y obtains a value outside of the correct value set V_c. Thereby, V_c can consist of exactly one correct value or a set of correct values. In a lot of real world cases, literal values are not unique, even when they aim at uniquely representing only one real-world entity. This circumstance is mainly caused by the existence of homonyms and other forms of lexical variety (e.g. British vs. American English). For example, the same city name may have different legal zip codes if the city name is a homonym, which is used for multiple different cities around the world. The city name "Neustadt", for instance, which is used for at least 48 different cities according to Geonames data[1]. Accordingly, it may have way more than 48 different valid zip codes. The theoretical problem underlying such cases is that literal values in RDF data cannot be mapped easily to a single conceptual entity, because this disambiguation is regularly prohibitively expensive in real-world settings.

In short, homonymous literal values may have a set of legal dependent values even if the individual entity can only obtain a single correct value. Likewise, different countries may assign identical zip codes for different cities since there is no global authority that enforces unique zip codes worldwide. Hence, zip codes may also be homonyms on a global scale, unless we use a strict prefix system.

Thus, the identification of illegal combinations of literal values has to be tolerant to homonyms. The major drawback of this tolerance to homonyms is that we will be unable to spot values that are within the set of valid lexical representations, but incorrect in that particular case.

In section 3.5, we show how functional dependency violations can be identified using trusted knowledge bases, e.g. Semantic Web datasets, as references. We will provide queries that minimize undiscovered incorrect value combinations and are tolerant to homonymous literal values.

3 Identification of Data Quality Rule Violations in the Web of Data

In the Semantic Web technology stack, there are multiple options to identify data quality problems. For instance, it is possible to use the formal semantics of an underlying ontology [cf. 14], such as disjointness axioms, to identify data quality problems in knowledge bases referring to that ontology. On the other hand, data quality problems can be identified by the definition of queries in SPARQL[2], the query language for Semantic Web data. Additionally, we could define conceptual elements in the ontology for the annotation of data to enable data quality problem identification algorithms through SPARQL. In this paper, we focus on the second option. The other two options are subject to our future work.

---

[1] http://www.geonames.org/

[2] http://www.w3.org/TR/2008/REC-rdf-sparql-query-20080115/

3.1 Methodology for Improving Data Quality

Data and information quality management has been addressed in database-oriented research for nearly two decades. Total Data Quality Management (TDQM) as proposed by *Wang* [13] is one of the most prominent methodologies for managing data quality. Based on the principle that the quality of data needs to be managed similar to the management of product quality, it describes an adjusted lifecycle of quality management suitable for data. The TDQM methodology encompasses four phases, namely (1) the definition phase, (2) the measurement phase, (3) the analysis phase, and (4) the improvement phase. In the definition phase, the requirements that constitute high quality data are defined regarding the different perspectives of data stakeholders, i.e. consumers, manufacturers, suppliers, or managers. Based on these requirements, metrics are developed and executed in the measurement phase. The analysis phase covers the examination of potential data quality problems identified through the metrics in the measurement phase. Possible alternative solutions have to be identified in order to resolve the data quality problems at its origin. Besides the simple correction of data values, the resolution of problems can also require the correction of business processes. Eventually, the best solution is executed during the improvement phase. Since business processes and thereby data manufacturing underlies changes, the TDQM lifecycle needs to be repeated over time.

In this paper, we focus on the definition and measurement phase of TDQM when applying DQM techniques to the Semantic Web. We define a set of data quality requirements through SPARQL queries that can be executed during the measurement phase and are useful for the subsequent analysis of the data quality problems and their causes. At the moment, we do not define key performance indicators (KPI) for the judgment of data and information quality, which can also be part of TDQM.

3.2 Architecture

As a major goal of our approach, we aim at defining generalized data quality rules, i.e. metrics for the identification of data quality problems, solely with the use of technologies provided by the Semantic Web technology stack. Therefore, we use the SPARQL query language extended by elements of Jena's ARQ language[3] due to its high expressivity. Hence, our data quality rules are transparent to the user and applicable to knowledge bases throughout the Web of Data. Besides official W3C specifications, we use D2RQ[4] for wrapping relational data sources into the Resource Description Framework (RDF[5]). Moreover, with the use of Jena ARQ's SERVICE keyword[6], we are able to execute federated SPARQL queries over the Semantic Web and remotely retrieve linked data available from public SPARQL endpoints in real time.

In the following, we present our generic SPARQL data quality problem identification queries for the identification of missing literals, illegal literals, and functional dependency violations in Semantic Web knowledge bases. Parameters that need to be substituted by real ontology elements before the execution of the query are put into angle brackets.

---

[3] http://jena.sourceforge.net/ARQ/
[4] http://www4.wiwiss.fu-berlin.de/bizer/d2rq/
[5] http://www.w3.org/TR/2004/REC-rdf-syntax-grammar-20040210/
[6] http://jena.sourceforge.net/ARQ/service.html

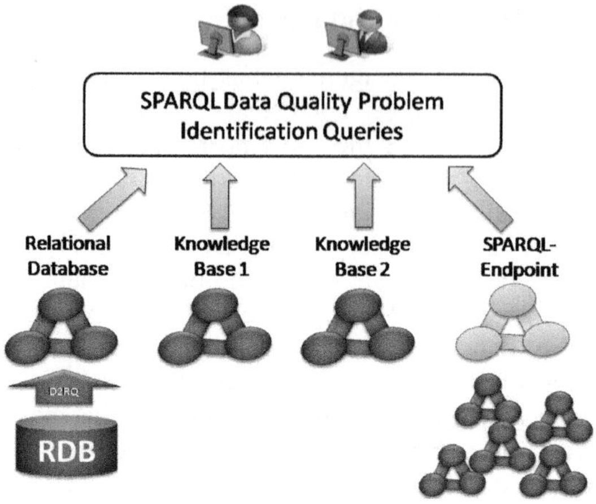

Fig. 1. Using SPARQL for data quality problem identification in the Web of Data

3.3 Identification of Missing Literals

In section 2.1, we explained the different types of missing values which can occur in Semantic Web scenarios. In [11], we defined a query that identifies datatype properties that have missing literal values for a single, known datatype property. In this paper, we (1) extend this query by enabling the additional detection of missing (but required) datatype properties attached to instances of particular classes, and (2) define a query for the identification of literals that are missing on the basis of a functional dependency, e.g. datatype properties that are mandatory within certain literal value combinations.

Table 1. SPARQL queries for the identification of missing literals

Data Quality Problem	Generalized SPARQL Query

Missing literal or datatype property	SELECT ?s
	WHERE{{
	?s a <class1> .
	?s <prop1> "" .}
	UNION{
	?s a <class1> .
	NOT EXISTS {
	?s <prop1> ?value}}}

Functionally dependent missing literal or datatype property	SELECT ?s
	WHERE{{
	?s a <class1> .
	?s <prop1> <value1> .
	NOT EXISTS{
	?s <prop2> ?value2 .
	}
	}UNION{
	?s <prop1> <value1> .
	?s <prop2> "" .
	}}

In case one, we select all instances `?s` of class `<class1>` that have an empty literal value for the datatype property `<prop1>` and/or that do not have the datatype property `<prop1>`. The second query returns all instances `?s` of class `<class1>` that have a datatype property `<prop1>` with the literal value `<value1>` and do not have the datatype property `<prop2>` at all or simply no literal value for it. Hence, the latter query only checks for missing literal values or datatype properties in instances with the value `<value1>` for datatype property `<prop1>`. Thus, it can be used to check literals that are only mandatory when another datatype property of the same instance obtains a certain literal value. E.g. the property `prop:state` may only be mandatory in cases where the property `prop:country` has the literal value `"USA"`. Note that the queries shown in here still require the substitution of the parameters in the angle brackets by real ontology classes, properties, and literal values.

3.4 Identification of Illegal Literal Values

In this section, we focus on the identification of incorrect values of a single datatype property without the use of any relationships from the knowledge base at hand. Without any semantic relationships to other literal values of an instance, the concise identification of false values is a difficult task that requires a precise definition of the allowed values for a datatype property. This can be done approximately by defining (1) the syntactical pattern for valid values or (2) a range of legal values. Accurately, illegal values can be identified by the definition of (3) all allowed values for a datatype property. The latter option can be very costly to implement since it may require manual effort to define or obtain an exhaustive list of legal values. In cases where there is a trusted reference, e.g. a knowledge base on the Semantic Web or a relational data source with a corresponding attribute that contains a nearly complete

Table 2. Identification of illegal values with the use of a trusted knowledge base

Data Quality Problem	Generalized SPARQL Query

Listed values of <prop2> are legal	SELECT ?s
	WHERE {
	?s <prop1> ?value .
	OPTIONAL {
	?s2 <prop2> ?value .
	} .
	FILTER (!bound(?s2)) .
	}

Listed values of <prop2> are illegal	SELECT ?s
	WHERE {
	?s <prop1> ?value .
	OPTIONAL {
	?s2 <prop2> ?value .
	} .
	FILTER bound(?s2) .
	}

list of legal values, the manual effort can be minimized. Moreover, it can be promising to (4) define all illegal values for a certain datatype property. Depending on the ratio of legal vs. illegal literals, one option may be more efficient than the other. Often, it is unfeasible to define all illegal values without constraining the ability of the system to deal with innovation and dynamics in the domain; thus, option (4) should only be applied on the subset that is already retrieved through option (3) in order to identify strictly forbidden literal values and, therefore, reduce the amount of manual checks. Table 2 below shows the queries for options (3) and (4) that utilize literal values of a trusted reference indicating legal or illegal values respectively.

Note that the queries shown in here still require the substitution of the parameters in the angle brackets by real datatype properties. The OPTIONAL clause in here is meant to be used against the trusted knowledge base.

3.5 Identification of Functional Dependency Violations

In [11], we proposed an algorithm for the identification of functional dependency violations, which required the manual definition of legal combinations of literal values of two dependent datatype properties. Similar to false values it is also possible to check functional dependent literal values against a trusted knowledge base that already contains information on these dependencies. This latter option may save a lot of manual work, but requires the availability of trusted data sources that contain the

Table 3. SPARQL queries for the identification of functional dependency violations

Data Quality Problem	Generalized SPARQL Query

Functional dependency check tolerant to homonyms, n-ary literal value combinations, and missing datatype properties	`SELECT ?s`
	`WHERE {`
	`    ?s a <class1> .`
	`    ?s <prop1> ?value1 .`
	`    ?s <prop2> ?value2 .`
	`NOT EXISTS {`
	`    ?s2 a <class2> .`
	`    ?s2 <prop3> ?value1 .`
	`    ?s2 <prop4> ?value2 .`
	`}}`

Functional dependency check that enforces the existence of datatype properties	`SELECT ?s`
	`WHERE {{`
	`    ?s a <class1> .`
	`NOT EXISTS{`
	`    ?s <prop1> ?value1 .`
	`    ?s <prop2> ?value2 .}}`
	`UNION{`
	`    ?s a <class1> .`
	`    ?s <prop1> ?value1 .`
	`    ?s <prop2> ?value2 .`
	`NOT EXISTS{`
	`    ?s2 a <class2> .`
	`    ?s2 <prop3> ?value1 .`
	`    ?s2 <prop4> ?value2 .}}}`

required literal combinations. In Table 3, we provide two different algorithms for the identification of functional dependency violations. Each of the algorithms requires a trusted reference source. The first algorithm presented in Table 3 returns all instances `?s` that do not have an identical value combination in the trusted knowledge base for the literal value combinations of `<prop1> ?value1` and `<prop2> ?value2`. The semantics of datatype property `<prop1>` should thereby be equivalent to `<prop3>`, and likewise `<prop2>` to `<prop4>` in order to obtain the required literal value sets.

Although the first query returns functional dependency violations that are not defined in the trusted reference, it does not return functional dependency violations in which the whole datatype property of the tested knowledge base is missing. Therefore, we have extended the first query by additionally defining the triples for the datatype properties `<prop1>` and `<prop2>` to be mandatory. Thus, the second query returns all functional dependency violations that are not listed in the trusted knowledge base and all instances of the tested knowledge base that have missing datatype properties involved in the functional dependency (`<prop1>` and `<prop>`).

Both queries tolerate multiple assignments of the same literal value to more than one literal value of the dependent datatype property as the reference holds these combinations. As already stated in section 2.3, this must be tolerated due to the existence of homonymous values and n-ary relationships between literal values of different datatype properties. The drawback of this approach is that an incorrect instance will not be identified by the queries if the instance contains a legal combination that is still incorrect in the further context. For example, the combination of the datatype property `prop:city "Neustadt"` and the datatype property `prop:country "DE"` could be identified as correct, although the instance actually intends to represent the Austrian city `"Neustadt"`. Such detection errors can be minimized by integrating more than two datatype properties into the functional dependency check, thus enhancing the probability of the identification of illegal value combinations, e.g. the zip code of our knowledge base may clearly indicate that the country has to be "AT". Accordantly, the generalized SPARQL queries as proposed in Table 3 may be extended by additional dependent datatype properties and their literal values if the trusted reference provides those properties and literals. Note that the queries shown in Table 3 still require the substitution of the parameters in the angle brackets by real ontology classes and properties.

3.6 Options for Integrating Trusted Knowledge Bases into Quality Checks

Assuming that our knowledge base is stored locally, we have at least two basic options how to integrate Semantic Web resources as trusted data sources in our data quality identification metrics, namely (1) by replicating the data into local data sources, or (2) by querying linked data remotely, e.g. by including SPARQL endpoints remotely by means of the SERVICE function for query federation from Jena's ARQ language[7]. Moreover, with wrapping technologies, such as D2RQ[8], it is

[7] http://jena.sourceforge.net/ARQ/service.html

[8] http://www4.wiwiss.fu-berlin.de/bizer/d2rq/

Table 4. Checking the existence of city names of a local knowledge base in DBPedia

Federated SPARQL Query

```
PREFIX dbo:<http://dbpedia.org/ontology/>
SELECT *
WHERE {
?s1 stockdb:location_CITY ?city .
OPTIONAL{
SERVICE <http://dbpedia.org/sparql>{
?s2 a dbo:City .
?s2 rdfs:label ?city .
FILTER (lang(?city) = "en") .
}}
FILTER(!bound(?s2))
}
```

also possible to use non-Semantic-Web data as a reference for quality management purposes in the Semantic Web technology stack.

4 Evaluation

In the following, we evaluate our proposal. First, we analyze the data quality problem identification techniques presented in the previous section. The techniques for the identification of illegal values and functional dependency violations are evaluated by comparison of a local knowledge base against the publicly available data dumps from Geonames[9], a Semantic Web knowledge base for geographical data. The techniques for the identification of missing literal values and datatype properties have been sufficiently evaluated on a local knowledge base and are not considered in here. In a second phase, we evaluate the quality of Geonames itself.

4.1 Evaluation of Data Quality Techniques

We tested our queries against a local knowledge base that contains manually created address data. We thereby used a locally installed replication of Geonames as the trusted knowledge base for values and value combinations on geographical data. We checked whether the city names also occur in Geonames and are, therefore, considered legal, and whether all instances of our knowledge base have correct combinations of city and country names. We thereby used the city-country-combinations in Geonames as a trusted reference.

It must be noted that solely the existence of a certain city-country-combination was tested by our algorithm. It was not tested whether the combination is correct in further context of the data, although the used query is flexible enough to consider a third literal value or even more, if appropriate.

Since Geonames only supplies the ISO-3166 2-letter country code to indicate the country, we had to adjust the queries slightly to convert the country codes into

[9] http://download.geonames.org/export/dump/

Table 5. Evaluation of functional dependency algorithms

No.	City	Country Property	Country	1st Algorithm	2nd Algorithm
1	Nantes2	Yes		X	X
2	Stavern	Yes	Norway		
3	Neubiberg	No			X
4	Neubiberg	Yes	USA	X	X
5	San Rafael	Yes	US	X	X
6	Melbourne	Yes	Australia		
7	Las Vegas	Yes	France	X	X

country names by using matches to literals of other datatype properties of Geonames that are connected to a full country name. Table 5 shows the results of the two queries for the identification of functional dependency violations from Table 3. The "X" indicates that the literal combination was detected as illegal by the algorithm. The data set for No. 3 had a missing datatype property for the country name. Thus, it was only detected by the second algorithm of table 3.

The test data contained the seven instances shown in Table 5. The queries were executed on an AMD QuadCore CPU with 4 GB RAM. Due to the small size of the test data, the execution time of the queries was not part of our evaluation. We also evaluated the first query from Table 2 using Geonames' full city labels ("`asciiname`") as a legal reference for evaluating the correctness of our city names. The algorithm identified that "Nantes2" is not known by Geonames. To enable the detection of incorrect literals, such as country names used as values for the property for city of the tested knowledge base, the trusted reference (Geonames) should be filtered to names of category "P" (city, village) when querying for illegal values.

4.2 Identification of Quality Problems in Geonames

To evaluate whether we can trust in the quality of a knowledge base, it is appropriate to apply quality problem identification metrics on the trusted knowledge base itself. Therefore, we applied algorithms for identifying a functional dependency violation and missing literals to the Geonames dataset itself. To evaluate the quality of the property "population", we defined an illegal combination between instances classified as populated places, such as country, state, region (fclass "A"), or city, village (fclass "P") that have a population of "0". Surprisingly, we observed that 93.3 % of all populated places in Geonames indicate a population of zero. If the value "0" means that the information about the accurate population is not available, then the value might be correct, but is still misleading to anyone who is not aware of this meaning. The other quality checks have shown that the properties `fclass`, `fcode`, `asciiname`, `country`, and `timezone` have only a few missing literals relative to the whole data set. Hence, for our quality checks it seems to be suitable to use the `asciinames` property from Geonames as a reference for legal location names.

Table 6. Quality metrics applied to Geonames (in literals)

Data Quality Problem	# of Occurences	Total #	Defect Ratio in Percent
Populated places (fclass P or A) without population (0)	2,626,026	2,814,701	93.30 %
Missing classification (fclass)	134,155	7,069,329	1.90 %
Missing classification (fcode)	135,253	7,069,329	1.91 %
Missing asciiname	604	7,069,329	0.01 %
Missing country	10,579	7,069,329	0.15 %
Missing timezone	29,312	7,069,329	0.41 %

4.3 Limitations

Although the algorithms of the latter two sections may identify false values and functional dependency violations very accurately without the investment of much manual effort, the use of Semantic Web resources as trusted references has one major weakness, which is that the reference data must be (1) complete and (2) reliable. If the reference dataset is incomplete, correct values in the data will be marked as incorrect. If the reference dataset contains illegal values, corresponding defects in the data to be analyzed will not be found. It is likely that there is at least a partial overlap between defects found in Semantic Web resources and relevant local datasets. For example, we have to expect the same common typos in DBPedia, derived from Wikipedia content, and local databases. One possible solution approach to this problem is the utilization of data quality problem identification techniques, e.g. as presented in [11], on the trusted source itself before starting the use of Semantic Web resources as a trusted reference for quality checks on local knowledge bases.

5 Related Work

Despite its importance, data quality has not yet received a lot of attention by Semantic Web researchers. A frequent misconception is that trust and data quality were the same. However, it is obvious that many of the data quality problems that we discuss in this paper are not directly related to the identity of the publisher of the data, nor to the lack of access control or authentication. For instance, there will be a lot of public datasets from the governments suffering from quality issues, despite the fact that the origin of the data and the integrity of the transformation and transportation is not in doubt. In the following, we summarize relevant related work.

Hartig and Zhao proposed a framework to assess the information quality of web data sources based on provenance information [15]. In addition, *Hartig* proposed an extension for the definition of trust values within Semantic Web data [16]. *Bizer and Cyganiak* described a framework to filter poor information in Web-based information systems according to user defined quality requirements [17]. Although these approaches are very promising, they do not provide much help to cure data quality problems in Semantic Web data sources or local data. Additionally, they are focused on the subjective assessment of data quality by users which may be occasionally not accurate enough or even wrong.

Lei, et. al. proposed an approach to identify data quality problems in semantic annotations. This approach utilizes Semantic Web data to identify incorrect classifications [18]. The proposed approach rather focuses on the quality of semantic annotations during its creation, but not on the quality of knowledge bases at instance level.

Other approaches use Semantic Web technology to identify and correct data quality problems in information systems. *Brüggemann and Grüning* have used ontologies to annotate incorrect data, e.g. redundant instances or incorrect attribute value combinations, to train detection algorithms for automated identification of data quality problems in cancer registries and data sources from the energy industry. Furthermore, they proposed to use domain ontologies to populate commonly accepted data quality rules within the domain [19]. However, they focus on a small set of data quality problems of information systems and neither use the potential of data already published on the Semantic Web, nor attempt to identify quality problems within the Semantic Web. Moreover, none of the above approaches solely utilizes the expressivity and functionality of SPARQL as a widely established pillar of the Semantic Web technology stack.

The database and data quality research community has provided several proposals to identify, avoid, and cleanse data quality problems primarily for relational data sources [20]. However, those cannot be applied directly to data on a Web of Data, nor do they utilize Semantic Web datasets as references.

6 Conclusion and Outlook

The usefulness of knowledge representation strongly depends on the underlying data quality. Likewise, the success of the Semantic Web will depend on the quality of the published data. It is clear that the Semantic Web itself will never be a complete nor consistent knowledge representation, and that every consumer will have to apply filtering and cleansing techniques prior to using Semantic Web data. However, the ratio of noise and errors on one hand and the technical effort for filtering and cleansing the data for a given purpose will highly affect the value of Semantic Web data. Thus, it is very important to address data quality issues on a Web scale as part of the core Semantic Web technology stack. Unfortunately, there is currently a very limited amount of research on data quality on and for the Semantic Web.

In this paper, we have presented an approach to evaluate the quality of knowledge bases solely by using SPARQL queries. We provided generic queries for the identification of (1) missing literal values or datatype properties, (2) illegal literal values, and (3) functional dependency violations. Queries for the latter two data quality problems were built to make use of already available knowledge bases as a trusted reference. Including access of knowledge published in the Semantic Web in the data quality management process seems very promising for reducing the manual effort for data quality management. The major drawback of our approach is the uncertainty about the quality of the used knowledge bases available in the Semantic Web. Thus, we started to evaluate the quality of Geonames and have identified several data quality problems.

Our future work will address the extension of the evaluation of Geonames and other Semantic Web resources, such as DBPedia. Moreover, we plan to evaluate the quality of geographical data in DBPedia by using Geonames as a trusted knowledge base, and vice versa. We also plan to apply our approach for the quality assurance of master data of a local information system. To gain insight into the practical usefulness of Semantic Web resources for data quality management, we also plan to develop information quality scoring approaches built on top of our existing queries.

References

1. Redman, T.C.: Data quality for the information age. Artech House, Boston (1996)
2. Redman, T.C.: The impact of poor data quality on the typical enterprise. Communications of the ACM 41, 79–82 (1998)
3. Brett, S.: World Wide Web Consortium (W3C), `http://www.w3.org/2007/Talks/0130-sb-W3CTechSemWeb/layerCake-4.png` (retrieved on March 8, 2010)
4. Wang, R.Y., Strong, D.M.: Beyond accuracy: what data quality means to data consumers. Journal of Management Information Systems 12(4), 5–33 (1996)
5. Redman, T.C.: Data quality: the field guide. Digital Press, Boston (2001)
6. Rahm, E., Do, H.-H.: Data Cleaning: Problems and Current Approaches. IEEE Data Engineering Bulletin 23(4), 3–13 (2000)
7. Oliveira, P., Rodrigues, F., Henriques, P.R., Galhardas, H.: A Taxonomy of Data Quality Problems. In: Proc. 2nd Int. Workshop on Data and Information Quality (in conjunction with CAiSE 2005), Porto, Portugal (2005)
8. Oliveira, P., Rodrigues, F., Henriques, P.R.: A Formal Definition of Data Quality Problems. In: International Conference on Information Quality (2005)
9. Leser, U., Naumann, F.: Informationsintegration: Architekturen und Methoden zur Integration verteilter und heterogener Datenquellen. Dpunkt-Verlag, Heidelberg (2007)
10. Kashyap, V., Sheth, A.P.: Semantic and Schematic Similarities Between Database Objects: A Context-Based Approach. Very Large Data Base Journal (5), 276–304 (1996)
11. Fürber, C., Hepp, M.: Using SPARQL and SPIN for Data Quality Management on the Semantic Web. In: 13th International Conference on Business Information Systems (BIS 2010), Berlin, Germany. LNBIP. Springer, Heidelberg (2010) (forthcoming)
12. Olson, J.: Data quality: the accuracy dimension. Morgan Kaufmann/Elsevier Science, Oxford (2003)
13. Wang, R.Y.: A product perspective on total data quality management. ACM Commun. 41, 58–65 (1998)
14. Gruber, T.R.: A Translation Approach to Portable Ontology Specifications. Knowledge Acquisition 5, 199–220 (1993)
15. Hartig, O., Zhao, J.: Using Web Data Provenance for Quality Assessment. In: First International Workshop on the role of Semantic Web in Provenance Management (Co-located with the 8th International Semantic Web Conference, ISWC 2009, Washington DC, USA (2009)
16. Hartig, O.: Querying Trust in RDF Data with tSPARQL. In: Aroyo, L., Traverso, P., Ciravegna, F., Cimiano, P., Heath, T., Hyvönen, E., Mizoguchi, R., Oren, E., Sabou, M., Simperl, E. (eds.) ESWC 2009. LNCS, vol. 5554, pp. 5–20. Springer, Heidelberg (2009)

17. Bizer, C., Cyganiak, R.: Quality-driven information filtering using the WIQA policy framework. Web Semant 7, 1–10 (2009)
18. Lei, Y., Nikolov, A.: Detecting Quality Problems in Semantic Metadata without the Presence of a Gold Standard. In: EON, vol. 329, pp. 51–60 (2007), CEUR-WS.org
19. Brüggemann, S., Grüning, F.: Using Ontologies Providing Domain Knowledge for Data Quality Management. In: Pellegrini, T., Auer, S., Tochtermann, K., Schaffert, S. (eds.) Networked Knowledge - Networked Media, pp. 187–203. Springer, Heidelberg (2009)
20. Batini, C., Scannapieco, M.: Data quality: concepts, methodologies and techniques. Springer, Berlin (2006)

Using Ontological Contexts to Assess the Relevance of Statements in Ontology Evolution

Fouad Zablith, Mathieu d'Aquin, Marta Sabou, and Enrico Motta*

Knowledge Media Institute (KMi), The Open University
Walton Hall, Milton Keynes, MK7 6AA, United Kingdom
{f.zablith,m.daquin,r.m.sabou,e.motta}@open.ac.uk

Abstract. Ontology evolution tools often propose new ontological changes in the form of statements. While different methods exist to check the quality of such statements to be added to the ontology (e.g., in terms of consistency and impact), their relevance is usually left to the user to assess. Relevance in this context is a notion of how well the statement fits in the target ontology. We present an approach to automatically assess such relevance. It is acknowledged in cognitive science and other research areas that a piece of information flowing between two entities is relevant if there is an agreement on the context used between the entities. In our approach, we derive the context of a statement from online ontologies in which it is used, and study how this context matches with the target ontology. We identify relevance patterns that give an indication of relevance when the statement context and the target ontology fulfill specific conditions. We validate our approach through an experiment in three different domains, and show how our pattern-based technique outperforms a naive overlap-based approach.

1 Introduction

Ontologies are conceptual representations of defined domains. Consequently, they are subject to constant updates and evolution to keep-up with domain changes. Ontology evolution is a painstaking and time-consuming task. Thus we observe an increase in the availability of tools that automatically suggest new additions to be applied to ontologies in the form of statements [2,8,11,19]. Nevertheless, although such tools help by automatically identifying ontology changes, they have introduced a new burden on users: inspecting the quality of a large number of proposed statements in terms of consistency and relevance with respect to the ontology.

There exist many tools that can be used to manage and preserve the consistency of an ontology after adding new statements [7,15]. However, assessing the relevance of a statement with respect to an ontology is not a trivial task, and is usually left to the user. For example, introducing *Concert* as a type of *Event* in an academic related ontology might not result in any logical conflict

* Work funded by the NeOn project under EC grant number IST-FF6-027595.

P. Cimiano and H.S. Pinto (Eds.): EKAW 2010, LNAI 6317, pp. 226–240, 2010.

to the ontology, however, such an addition is not particularly relevant to the ontology, where events are mainly about conferences, seminars, workshops, etc. We understand statement relevance with respect to an ontology as an indication of how well it fits in the ontology.

Relevance is a core subject of interest in various domains including Artificial Intelligence, Cognitive Science [16,17] and Information Retrieval [1,9]. However, this problem is not very well explored in the domain of ontology evolution. As Wilson and Sperber noted in their work on relevance theory [16], two entities communicating and in exchange of knowledge, require a kind of agreement on the choice of context in which the conversation occurs. Moreover, they argue that "an input is relevant to an individual when it connects with background information he has available to yield conclusions that matter to him." [16]

Based on these key ideas, we present an approach towards automatically assessing the relevance of statements with respect to an ontology. Our process starts by identifying the context of a statement, by finding an online ontology in which it appears (Section 3). This context is matched to the ontology to derive the shared concepts. We initially investigate a naive overlap approach that takes into account the number of shared concepts. It is based on the idea that the more shared concepts exist between the target ontology and the external ontology defining the context of a statement, the more relevant a statement is. With the various limitations of this technique, we point out the need for a more sophisticated approach that takes into account not only the shared entities, but also the structure surrounding them. We accomplish this by identifying a set of patterns (Section 4), where each pattern has specific application conditions and a confidence value. When a pattern occurs at the intersection area of the statement context and the target ontology, a certain degree of confidence can be calculated. We back our work by an experiment in three domains (Section 5), showing that the pattern-based technique outperforms the naive overlap approach in terms of precision and recall, and can be used to support users in the selection of relevant statements during the process of ontology evolution (Section 6).

2 Related Work and Motivation

Our previous experiment conducted in the context of the Evolva ontology evolution tool, showed that a significant amount of statements proposed automatically to be added to a target ontology are irrelevant [19]. Within Evolva, currently users have to manually identify such statements (e.g., in the academic domain *Concert* is a type of *Event*) and select relevant ones (e.g., *Tutorial* is a type of *Event*). However with many statements to check, this can be a time-consuming task by itself. Thus having a mechanism that automatically gives an indication of the statements' degree of relevance would be of added value to the ontology evolution process.

Besides Evolva, there exist tools, e.g. SPRAT [8] and Text2Onto [2], which extract information from text documents, and convert them into ontological entities. Such tools mostly rely on the TF.IDF statistical measure to check the relevance of terms with respect to the corpus used. This of course assumes that the corpus has been selected to represent precisely the intended domain. In particular, if the extracted entities are intended to be used in or in conjunction with an existing ontology, this ontology is not currently taken into account in calculating the confidence degree of the extracted elements.

Automatically finding ontology changes is important for ontology evolution, however maintaining the consistency and quality of the ontology is equally significant. Thus several approaches have emerged recently that focus on evaluating the impact of statements on the ontology they are added to. For example in [13], a solution is suggested to highlight what is gained or lost as a result of adding an axiom (i.e., a statement) to an ontology. The aim here is to present the effect of a statement to the user, in order to make a more informed judgment in implementing the change and preserving conceptual consistency. Another approach proposes the evaluation of changes in ontology evolution using an impact function, which computes the cost involved in performing the change [12]. Tools such as RaDON [7] that check the consistency of the ontology after adding statements, are commonly used to evaluate the impact of the statements, in particular in evolution tasks. While these techniques provide valuable support to the users in assessing the impact of statements on their ontologies, to our knowledge there is still no solution to support them in assessing the relevance of such statements.

3 Overview of the Relevance Assessment Process

We understand the *relevance* of a statement s with respect to a target ontology O_t as an indication of how well s fits in O_t. An ontology is a set of statements, which we manipulate as a graph. A statement s is of the form $< subject, relation, object >$. We focus in this paper on the scenario in which the target ontology is extended by introducing statements that have one part (i.e. *object*) that already exists in O_t. The *relation* of s can be either of taxonomic type (*sub-class*, *super-class*), or other named relations. For now, we focus on the taxonomic relations, as they are less ambiguous than the named ones, of which relevance is much harder to assess even by users.

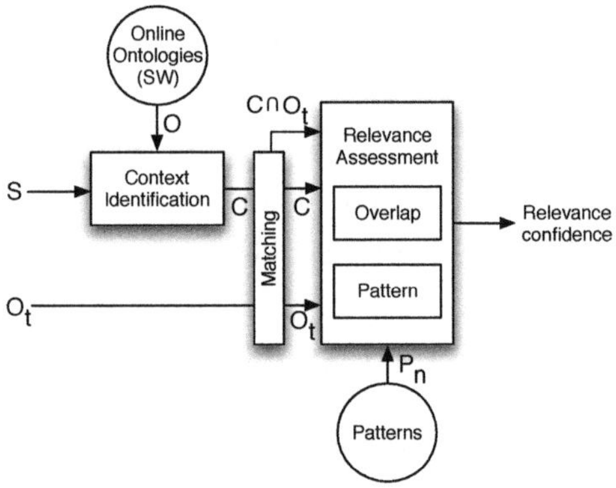

Fig. 1. Checking the relevance of statement s with respect to ontology O_t

The relevance assessment process (Figure 1) starts with identifying a context C for s from online ontologies. Subsequently, the context C is matched to the target ontology O_t to identify shared concepts, which result from the intersection of the graphs C and O_t, and used for the relevance assessment.

Identifying the Context of a Statement. Similarly to other tools that exploit the open Semantic Web for performing a variety of tasks [5], our approach uses online ontologies as background knowledge to provide contextual information for a statement. To find online ontologies in which the statement appears, we use Scarlet, a relation discovery engine on the Semantic Web [14]. Scarlet uses the Semantic Web gateway Watson [4], and automatically selects and explores online ontologies *to discover relations between two given concepts.* For example, when relating two concepts labeled *Tutorial* and *Event*, Scarlet 1) identifies online ontologies that can provide information about how these two concepts inter-relate and then 2) combines this information to infer their relation. To find online ontologies in which s appears, we use the *subject* and *object* of s as input to Scarlet, which returns a list of relations that exist between the two entities, along with information about the source ontologies from where the relations have been identified.

Matching the Statement Context with the Target Ontology. The statement context is matched to the target ontology to detect their shared concepts. Our approach is independent from the ontology matching technique to use. In our implementation, we perform the matching between the concepts' names using the Jaro-Winkler string similarity metric [3]. We define the function $e(G)$ to extract the set of nodes n_i that exist in the graph G. We use the matching to generate the intersection of the statement context and the target ontology: $e(C) \cap e(O_t) = \{n_i \mid n_i \in e(C) \wedge n_i \in e(O_t)\}$.

We developed a tool for visualizing how the context matches with the target ontology. This tool proved to be very useful during our experiments, as it makes understanding the matching process easier. It has customizable parameters that enable for example only to display the shared nodes with their connected entities up to a certain depth, and hide or show the target or online ontology. Matching nodes between the graphs are represented by star shaped nodes as shown in Figure 2, a visualization of the context of $< proposal, subClass, document >$ extracted from the online OntoSem ontology[1], and the SWRC target ontology[2].

Assessing Relevance Based on Overlap Analysis. We investigate a first naive approach based on the idea that the more overlapping the statement context and ontology are, the more relevant the statement is. The relevance confidence in this case is based on the ratio of the number of shared concepts, to the number of concepts in O_t, as calculated using the following formula:

$$conf_{overlap}(s, C, O_t) = \frac{|e(C) \cap e(O_t)|}{|e(O_t)|}$$

For example in Figure 2, with the string similarity threshold value of 0.96, there are 18 shared concepts between the context of $< proposal, subClass, document >$, and the SWRC ontology that includes 71 concepts. Thus the confidence of the overlap in this case is 0.2535 (i.e., $\frac{18}{71}$).

[1] http://morpheus.cs.umbc.edu/aks1/ontosem.owl

[2] http://kmi-web05.open.ac.uk:81/cache/6/98b/5ca1/94b45/7e29980b0f/dfc4e24088dffe851

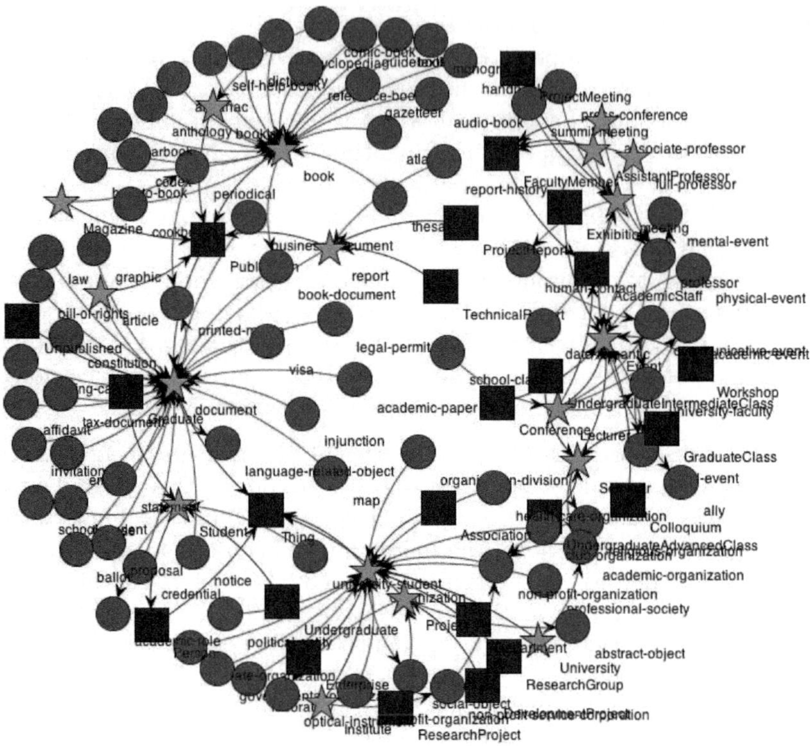

Fig. 2. Visualization of the overlap section between the OntoSem context of $< proposal, subClass, document >$ and the target SWRC ontology, where the star shaped nodes are shared, round nodes belong to the statement context, and square nodes belong to the target ontology

The drawback of this approach is that it does not take into consideration how the ontological entities connect with each other, as it focuses on the number of shared nodes only, without any additional analysis. As a side effect, all the statements used in the context will be treated with the same relevance confidence. With big ontologies that are not domain focussed such as OntoSem or Cyc (www.cyc.com), it will cause the overlap technique to misjudge relevance. For example the statement $< capture, subClass, event >$ is extracted from OntoSem as well, but not relevant to add to the SWRC ontology. However, it has the same confidence value as the relevant statement $< proposal, subClass, document >$.

4 Pattern-Based Relevance Assessment

Given the limitations of the naive overlap technique, a more sophisticated approach is needed, which takes into account not only the overlap at the level of entity names, but also the way these entities are structured, giving a better indication of how the context fits in the ontology. Our preliminary work based on the analysis of some graph examples, highlighted the presence of patterns that reflect the relevance of statements [18]. Such *relevance patterns* identify specific structural conditions, supported by a confidence value.

In this section, we discuss next how we collect our experimental data (Section 4.1). Then we show how we refine the generation of the statements' context (Section 4.2), and finally present the relevance patterns (Section 4.3).

4.1 Gathering Experimental Data

To refine our initial approach and discover further relevance patterns, we needed a gold standard of statements assessed in terms of relevance that would serve as the basis of our analysis and tests. As such a gold standard does not exist yet, we created a set of statements evaluated by experts for relevance in three different domains: academic, music and fishery. The assessed statements played a major role in defining and discovering our relevance patterns.

Data collection of experts' evaluation was accomplished through a web interface. It supplied experts with a visualization of the target ontology, along with the options to select whether a statement is relevant, irrelevant or if relevance can not be judged from the given information ("Don't Know"). Experts were also given guidelines[3] describing the evaluation process, with some clarifications on what is meant by relevance supported by examples.

We use Evolva, our ontology evolution tool, to generate the set of statements to add to the ontologies of each domain. We parametrize Evolva to use online ontologies as a source of background knowledge, which link new concepts extracted from text to existing ones in the ontology in the form of statements.

In the academic domain, we randomly pick 30 news articles published on the Knowledge Media Institute's website (KMi). For the fishery domain, we extract 108 online web documents that include information about fishes and fishery stock. For the music domain, we extract 20 music blog pages that have on average seven blog post headers each. Table 1 lists the domains, the target ontology to evolve, the corpus used and the total number of statements suggested.

Table 1. Statements generation setup

Domain	**Target Ontology**	**Corpus**	**Total** *s*
Academic	SWRC: http://kmi-web05.open.ac.uk:81/cache/6/98b/5ca1/94b45/7e29980b0f/dfc4e24088dffe851	KMi_News: http://news.kmi.open.ac.uk/	251
Fishery	Biosphere: http://kmi-web06.open.ac.uk:8081/cupboard/ontology/Experiment1/biosphere?rdf	Fishery_Website: http://fishonline.org/	124
Music	Music: http://pingthesemanticweb.com/ontology/mo/musicontology.rdfs	Music_Blog: http://blog.allmusic.com/	341

We apply a filter on the generated statements to 1) select only the taxonomic relations (cf. Section 3), and 2) remove generic relations, as our previous investigations show that statements linked to generic terms (e.g. *thing*, *object*, etc.) are

[3] http://evolva.kmi.open.ac.uk/experiments/statementrelevance/guidelines.php

mostly irrelevant [19]. We generate random selections of 100 statements in each domain to form the data-sets for experts to evaluate. We assign three different experts for each data-set, with two academic data-sets, given the expertise and availability of our evaluators in this area, and one data-set for each of the music and fishery domains.

4.2 Statement Context Generation Revisited

A first improvement we introduce, following the analysis of the naive overlap approach, concerns the context generation. Instead of dealing with the ontology as a whole to define the context, we generate the context of the statement based on the surrounding entities of the statement up to a certain depth. This will help in focussing the usage of the statement by analyzing the close entities only. For that, we use $context(s, O, d) = C$, a recursive function that generates a sub-graph, formed of nodes related through taxonomic and other types of relations to the *subject* and *object* of s in O, up to a depth d (set to 1 in our implementation). This function is similar to the Prompt ontology view extraction [10] or some ontology modularization techniques [6]. The sub-graph generated forms the context C of the statement in the specified ontology.

4.3 Relevance Patterns

Another improvement comes at the level of introducing patterns for relevance detection. Relevance patterns are structural situations of interlinked nodes. When the surrounding entities in the matching graph around s trigger such patterns, a degree of relevance can be identified. This lifts the problem of the overlap that only matches the concepts' names, by providing further elements to analyze and hence a better relevance judgement. For example, a shared concept that is a sibling of an entity in s has a better influence on the relevance of s, than a shared concept which is not related to the elements of s. We create relevance patterns to detect such conditions and help deducing relevance. A clear visualization of the context and its intersection with the ontology (as shown in Figure 2), helped in identifying the relevance patterns that we discuss in this part. The statement relevance evaluation based on expert users in concrete domains contributed to spotting further undetected relevant statements, which improved our selection and definition of patterns.

Each pattern has specific *application conditions*, supported by a *confidence value*. Application conditions are defined in a way that makes the patterns mutually exclusive, thus facilitating their performance analysis. Based on our analyzed data, we identified five different patterns visualized in Figure 3, where the statement to assess is in the dashed oval, round and square nodes belong to the context and target ontology respectively, and star nodes are the ones shared by both. At a glance, Pattern 1 identifies direct shared siblings of the *subject* in s; Pattern 2 detects whether s introduces a new leaf to the ontology; Pattern 3 identifies shared ancestors of the *object* of s; and Pattern 4 detects shared siblings that occur at different levels of depth in the context and the target ontology. As per our analysis, shared ancestors (Pattern 3) gave better relevance indications

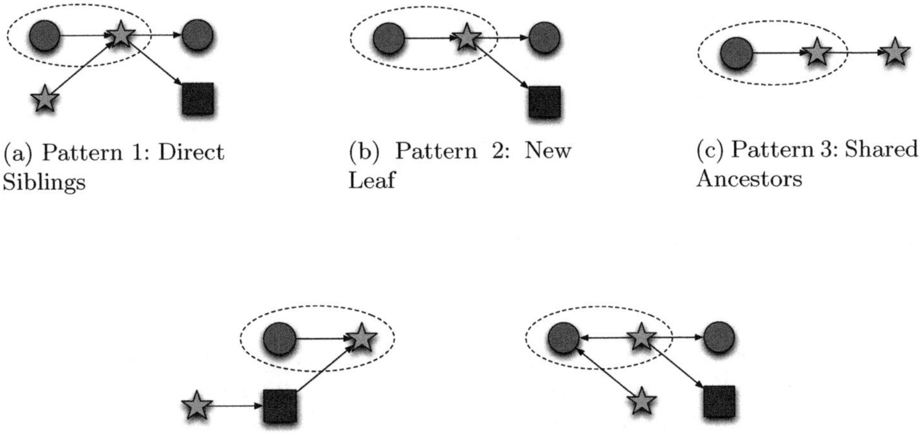

(a) Pattern 1: Direct Siblings

(b) Pattern 2: New Leaf

(c) Pattern 3: Shared Ancestors

(d) Pattern 4: Granularity Mismatch

(e) Pattern 5: New Parent

Fig. 3. Relevance patterns for detecting the relevance of statement s represented in the dashed oval, star nodes denote shared concepts, round and square nodes belong to C and O_t respectively. The arrows depict sub-class relations

then the other patterns, thus our application conditions are defined in a way to favour Pattern 3 over Patterns 1, 2 and 4. The last pattern, Pattern 5, is applied when s introduces a new parent in the target ontology.

Pattern 1: Direct Siblings. One core indication of relevance is when a new concept to add to the target ontology is surrounded by shared siblings between the statement context and target ontology. Shared siblings show that the concept in focus is missing in the target ontology, giving the statement adding it a high relevance. Pattern 1, shown in Figure 3a, detects shared siblings of the introduced concept. This is illustrated in Figure 4, where the statement in focus is $< tutorial, subClass, event >$ (in the dashed oval), in the context of the ISWC ontology[4]. This context shares with the SWRC target ontology the concepts *workshop* and *conference*. Those concepts show that the new concept *tutorial* is important to add to the SWRC ontology. *Application conditions*:

1. $\exists\, n_a \mid n_a \in e(C) \cap e(O_t) \wedge\ < n_a, subClass, object > \in C \cup O_t$
2. $\neg\exists\, n_b \mid n_b \in e(C) \cap e(O_t)\ \wedge C \models <\ object, subClass, n_b >$

Condition 1 ensures that the *subject* of s has direct siblings, while Condition 2 checks that there are no shared ancestors, thus prioritising Pattern 3. The *pattern confidence* formula is:

$$conf_{p1}(s, C, O_t) = \frac{|dSubC(object, C) \cap dSubC(object, O_t)|}{|dSubC(object, C)| - 1}$$

[4] http://annotation.semanticweb.org/ontologies/iswc.owl

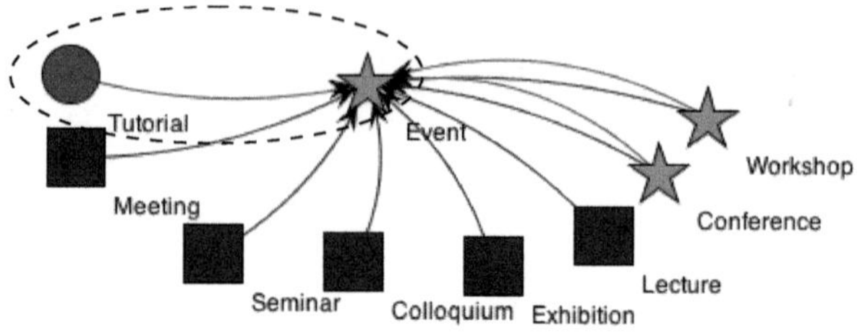

Fig. 4. Pattern 1 detected on $s = < tutorial, subClass, event >$, $C = ISWC.owl$ and $O_t = SWRC.owl$

where $dSubC(n, G) = \{x_i \mid < x_i, subClass, n > \in G\}$, is a function to extract the direct sub-classes of a node in a graph. The confidence in this case is the ratio of the number of shared siblings (the numerator in the $conf_{p1}$ formula), to the total number of siblings in the context of s. If we apply the formula on $s_1 = < tutorial, subClass, event >$ in Figure 4, the confidence is:

$$conf_{p1}(s_1, ISWC, SWRC) = \frac{|\{Workshop, Conference\}|}{|\{Workshop, Conference, Tutorial\}| - 1} = 1$$

Even though Pattern 1 is one of the most intuitive patterns, it occurred on average only 11.25% of the statement cases (including relevant and irrelevant), in our four testing datasets.

Pattern 2: New Leaf. As Pattern 1 relies on the shared siblings of the *subject* of *s*, it will fail when the *object* of *s* is a leaf in the target ontology, because there will be no shared siblings in this case. This is where Pattern 2 (Figure 3b) called *New Leaf* comes in place, to detect the *subject* added as a new leaf to the target ontology. This pattern happened to be common in detecting relevant statements in the music domain, where many statements introduce new ontology levels, for example statements $< duet, subClass, performer >$ and $< quartet, subClass, performer >$[5] link *duet* and *quartet* as sub-classes to *performer*, an existing leaf in the target ontology. On average, this pattern occurred 10.25% of the cases in our tested statements. *Application conditions*:

1. $\neg\exists\, n_a \mid < n_a, subClass, object > \in O_t$
2. $\neg\exists\, n_b \mid n_b \in e(C) \cap e(O_t) \wedge C \models < object, subClass, n_b >$

Condition 1 ensures that the *object* of *s* does not have children (i.e it's a leaf in the target ontology), and Condition 2 confirms that the *object* doesn't have common ancestors. With the absence of close relatives (i.e., shared parents, ancestors and siblings), the confidence of the new leaf pattern is based on the overlap ratio of the target ontology cut to a specified depth around the *object* of *s*, and the context of *s*. Thus the *pattern confidence* formula is:

$$conf_{p2}(s, C, O_t) = \frac{|e(C) \cap e(context(s, O_t, d))|}{|e(context(s, O_t, d))|}$$

[5] Statement contexts extracted from: http://maciej.janik/test

Pattern 3: Shared Ancestors. The *Shared Ancestors* pattern (Figure 3c) relies on the condition that the relevance of a statement with respect to a target ontology increases if the shared *object* in s has shared ancestors between the target ontology and the context in which it is used. This situation was very common in the fishery domain, where Pattern 3 applied to 50% of the statements identified. For example, for the statement $< cod, subClass, fish >$, $fish$ has the ancestor *animal* in C, which is shared with O_t. This reflects a degree of common representations of animal species in online ontologies, where top levels in many ontologies tend to be more aligned than in the other domains. On average this pattern occurred in 20% of our analyzed dataset cases. *Application condition*:

1. $\exists\, n_a \mid n_a \in e(C) \cap e(O_t) \;\wedge C \models < object, subClass, n_a >$

The *pattern confidence* formula is:

$$conf_{p3}(s, C, O_t) = \frac{|aSupC(object, C) \cap e(O_t)|}{|aSupC(object, C)|}$$

based on the ratio of shared ancestors of the *object* of s, to the total number of ancestors of *object* in C. $aSupC(n, G) = \{x_i \mid G \models < x_i, superClass, n >\}$ extracts all the (direct and inferred) super-classes of a node n in a graph G.

Pattern 4. Granularity Mismatch. As ontologies are used in different application contexts, design decisions such as the level of granularity often vary from an ontology to another. This affects the performance of Pattern 1, which checks only the *direct* shared siblings of the *subject* in s. Pattern 4 (Figure 3d), called *Granularity Mismatch*, identifies such situations. With the highest occurrence of 41.75% of the cases, this pattern shows that granularity differences in concept representation when designing ontologies is a very common case. With our tests performed on the datasets, we have set this pattern to be applied as a last resort if Patterns 1, 2, and 3 are not detected. *Application conditions*:

1. $\neg\exists\, n_a \mid n_a \in e(C) \cap e(O_t) \wedge < n_a, subClass, object > \in C \cup O_t$
2. $\exists\, n_a, n_b \mid n_a \in e(C) \cap e(O_t) \;\wedge n_b \in e(C) \ominus e(O_t) \wedge n_b \in aSupC(n_a, C) \wedge n_b \in aSupC(n_a, O_t) \wedge object \in aSupC(n_a, C) \wedge object \in aSupC(n_a, O_t)$
3. $\neg\exists\, n_a \mid n_a \in e(C) \cap e(O_t) \wedge < object, subClass, n_a > \in C$

where Condition 1 is for ruling out the presence of Pattern 1, and Condition 2 checks for the presence of shared siblings (including the inferred ones) that fall at different levels in depth with respect to the *object* of s through a non-shared concept (i.e., a concept in the symmetric difference of C and O_t denoted by the symbol $\ominus$). Condition 3 rules out the presence of shared ancestors, for which Pattern 3 should be applied. This *pattern confidence* is:

$$conf_{p4}(s, C, O_t) = \frac{|aSubC(object, C) \cap aSubC(object, O_t)|}{|aSubC(object, C)|}$$

which takes the ratio of all the shared sub-classes of *object* in C and O_t, to the total number of all sub-classes of *object* in C. The function $aSubC(n, G)$ extracts all (direct and inferred) sub-classes of a concept n in G.

Pattern 5. New Parent. In cases where s links *subject* to *object* through a super-class relation, i.e. s is introducing *object* as a new parent to the ontology, Pattern 5 is applied (Figure 3e). There is indication of relevance in this case if *object* is a parent of other shared concepts between the statement context and the target ontology. The *application condition* of this pattern is solely limited to checking whether the type of relationship linking *subject* to *object* is super-class. The *pattern confidence* is based on the following formula:

$$conf_{p5}(s, C, O_t) = \frac{|aSubC(subject, C) \cap e(O_t)|}{|aSubC(subject, C)|}$$

The numerator in the fraction detects the number of shared concepts between C and O_t that are children of *subject* in C.

As per our tests, the number of statements with super-class relations is much lower than the sub-class relations. On average, only 16.75% of the total number of statements are super-classes. Furthermore, the percentage of relevance judgment correctness of this pattern is high in the four data-sets. Thus one pattern dealing with super-class relations proved to be enough for our domains.

5 Evaluation

In order to evaluate the discussed approaches, we analyze and compare the performance of the naive overlap approach, versus the pattern-based approach. We use the experts' statements evaluation data-sets in the three domains as the basis of our evaluation, which we present in this section.

5.1 Experiment Measures

Statement relevance being in many cases subjective, we made sure that each statement is evaluated by three experts per domain, having in total 12 experts for the four datasets. Based on the intuition that "relevance is not just an all-or-none matter but a matter of degree" [16], we use a measure to assess the overall relevance of each statement. To achieve this, we assign a score for each answer type from the experts: 1 for *relevant*, 0.5 for *don't know* and 0 for *irrelevant* (cf. Section 4.1). We use the sum of these values as an overall relevance score:

$$overall_{rel}(s, d) = \sum_{i=1}^{3} score(e_i, s, d)$$

where $overall_{rel}(s, d)$ is a function that returns the overall relevance score of a statement s in a data-set d, and $score(e_i, s, d)$ is the score given by expert e_i to s in d. For example, if the evaluation of a statement s is *relevant*, *relevant* and *don't know* by experts A_d, B_d and C_d respectively, the overall relevance value of

s is 2.5. We set two thresholds to handle the overall relevance measure outcome: a *relevance threshold* sets the limit above which s is considered relevant and an *irrelevant threshold* below which s is irrelevant. If the overall relevance value falls between the two thresholds, the relevance can not be determined in this case, as the experts are undecided.

Concerning the naive overlap and pattern-based algorithms output, a threshold is set to determine relevance based on the confidence value for each algorithm, i.e., when the overlap or a pattern is applied with a confidence degree higher than the specified threshold, the corresponding statement is classified as relevant, otherwise it is irrelevant. Given the different ways that each pattern calculates confidence, we use a separate threshold for each pattern (displayed in Table 2). As the goal of this experiment is to check the feasibility of the pattern-based approach, we empirically set the combination of thresholds that obtained the highest performance.

Table 2. Employed thresholds selected empirically to provide the highest average relevance and irrelevance F-measure in each data-set

Threshold	Academic-1	Academic-2	Fishery	Music
User Relevance	2	2	2	2
User Irrelevance	1	1	1	1
Overlap	0.2	0.29	0.4	0.05
Pattern 1	0.2	0.1	1	0.08
Pattern 2	0.8	1	0.5	1
Pattern 3	1	1	0.01	0.05
Pattern 4	0	0.4	1	0
Pattern 5	1	0.4	0.05	0.02
Pattern 6	1	0.01	0.03	1

We use *Precision*, *Recall* and *F-measure* to evaluate the performance of the relevance algorithms. We define 4 sets REL_{ed}, IRR_{ed}, REL_{ad} and IRR_{ad}: REL_{ed} is the set of all statements evaluated as relevant by the experts in dataset d; IRR_{ed} the set of irrelevant statements as judged by experts in d; REL_{ad} and IRR_{ad} the sets of relevant and irrelevant statements as classified by the algorithm a (i.e. pattern or overlap), in dataset d. We use the following formulas:

$$P_{rel}(d,a) = \frac{|REL_{ed} \cap REL_{ad}|}{|REL_{ad}|} \qquad R_{rel}(d,a) = \frac{|REL_{ed} \cap REL_{ad}|}{|REL_{ed}|}$$

where $P_{rel}(d,a)$ and $R_{rel}(d,a)$ compute the precision and recall of relevance respectively, in data-set d as judged by algorithm a. We use the usual *F-measure* computation based on precision and recall. In the case of irrelevance, the formulas are similar to the ones of relevance, but replaced with sets related to irrelevance (i.e. IRR_{ed} and IRR_{ad}).

5.2 Results

The main conclusion of our experiment, as shown in Table 3, is that the pattern-based approach performs better than the naive overlap approach. By simply comparing the precision and recall in each data-set, patterns are able to identify more correct relevant statements as classified by experts, with a better precision than then overlap approach. Overall, the overlap relevance F-measure is in the range of [7.41%, 58.06%], while the range is higher for the pattern-based relevance F-measure [43.75%, 69.05%]. In terms of irrelevance, the range is [60.87%, 85.71%] for the overlap approach, compared to the [74.74%, 92.48%] F-measure range using the pattern-based irrelevance detection. This is mainly due to the presence of large ontologies online that tend to highly overlap with target ontologies in general, and the fact that the overlap technique treats all statements coming from such ontologies equally, leading to lower precision and recall.

Table 3. Evaluation results for relevance assessment

		Overlap		**Patterns**	
		Relevance	Irrelevance	Relevance	Irrelevance
Academic-1	Statements	18	82	13	87
	Precision	05.56%	83.72%	46.15%	91.95%
	Recall	11.11%	87.80%	66.67%	93.02%
	F-measure	07.41%	85.71%	**54.52%**	**92.48%**
Academic-2	Statements	15	85	16	84
	Precision	26.67%	81.18%	43.75%	90.00%
	Recall	25.00%	86.25%	43.75%	85.71%
	F-measure	25.81%	83.64%	**43.75%**	**87.80%**
Fishery	Statements	57	43	59	41
	Precision	47.37%	74.42%	55.39%	90.24%
	Recall	75.00%	55.17%	91.67%	63.79%
	F-measure	58.06%	63.36%	**69.05%**	**74.74%**
Music	Statements	57	43	35	65
	Precision	29.82%	81.40%	42.86%	83.08%
	Recall	73.91%	48.61%	65.22%	75.00%
	F-measure	42.49%	60.87%	**51.73%**	**78.83%**

Note that identifying irrelevant statements is equally important as identifying relevant ones. Moreover, our experiment shows that in most data-sets, the proportion of irrelevant statements is higher than the one of relevant statements. Thus having a high precision and recall on the bigger portion of the datasets (formed of irrelevant statements) reflects that the pattern-based approach would successfully act as a filter of irrelevant statements, reducing the workload on the user in the process of statement selection during ontology evolution.

To put the results in perspective, we rank the outcomes based on the confidence values of the overlap and pattern-based approaches, and compare them to the randomly ordered statements by Evolva (Figure 5). Due to the pattern specific threshold and confidence calculations, a direct ranking based on the confidence is not possible. Thus we normalize the pattern-based confidence values to a target unified threshold of 0.5, based on which we perform the ranking. As Figure 5 shows, the ranking based on the pattern technique groups relevant statements more towards the top of the list, meaning that ontology engineers could more confidently select most of the top statements, while safely discard most of the lower ranked ones. It is interesting to test in the future how these results would combine with other statement evaluation techniques (i.e., in terms of consistency, impact, etc).

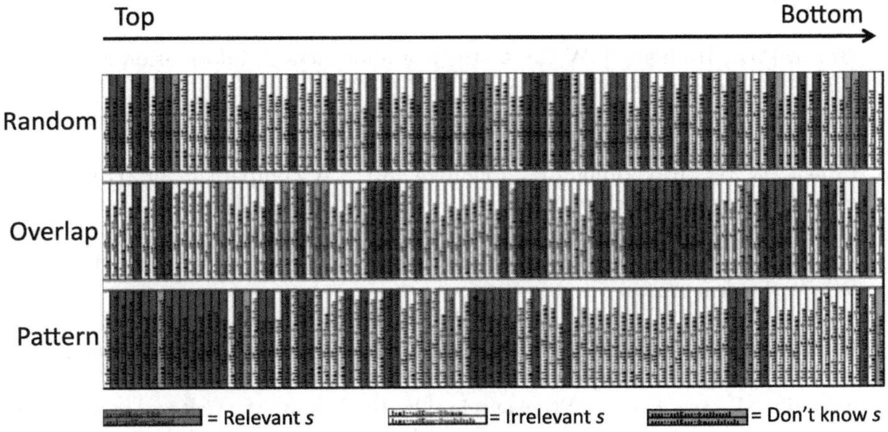

Fig. 5. Visualized ranking from left to right of 100 statements in the fishery domain, comparing the results of the random order on the top, overlap approach in the middle and pattern-based approach at the bottom

6 Conclusion and Future Work

In this paper, we presented an approach towards the automatic assessment of the relevance of statements with respect to ontologies. This approach is based on the analysis of the context in which the statement occurs, and how it compares to the considered ontology. A set of relevance patterns in the graph merging the context with the ontology are identified, which provide indications of the level of relevance of the statement, by showing how the context fits in the ontology. The evaluation experiment demonstrates the feasibility of our pattern-based approach and how it outperforms a naive technique of measuring the overall overlap between the context and the ontology.

Even though the evaluation of our approach shows promising results, we identify potential improvements that will be part of our future work. Firstly, we plan to extend and identify further relevance patterns, in addition to test the combination of patterns rather than having them mutually exclusive. Secondly, instead of using the first online ontology returned by Scarlet as the statement context, we plan to devise a method to select the context with the highest relevance confidence. Thirdly, our future plans include a technique to automatically identify the relevance thresholds, which is crucial when our work is integrated in ontology evolution tools. One potential way to do so is to take the set of statements that have been lately added to the ontology under evolution as a base case of the threshold values calculation. The idea is that such statements are already assessed relevant by the user once added. Fourthly, a particular point to investigate is at the level of the user interaction with the tool. We foresee that our visualization tool that shows how the context of the statement matches with the target ontology, would be of added value to the user as a validation support of the assessed relevance.

References

1. Bruza, P.D., Huibers, T.W.C.: A study of aboutness in information retrieval. Artificial Intelligence Review 10(5), 381–407 (1996)
2. Cimiano, P., Volker, J.: Text2Onto - a framework for ontology learning and data-driven change discovery. In: Proc. of (NLDB) (2005)
3. Cohen, W.W., Ravikumar, P., Fienberg, S.E.: A comparison of string distance metrics for name-matching tasks. In: Proc. of (IIWeb) (2003)
4. d'Aquin, M., Baldassarre, C., Gridinoc, L., Sabou, M., Angeletou, S., Motta, E.: Watson: Supporting next generation semantic web applications. In: Proc. of WWW/Internet (2007)
5. d'Aquin, M., Motta, E., Sabou, M., Angeletou, S., Gridinoc, L., Lopez, V., Guidi, D.: Toward a new generation of semantic web applications. IEEE Intelligent Systems 23(3), 20–28 (2008)
6. d'Aquin, M., Schlicht, A., Stuckenschmidt, H., Sabou, M.: Criteria and evaluation for ontology modularization techniques. In: Modular Ontologies: Concepts, Theories and Techniques for Knowledge Modularization, pp. 67–89. Springer, Heidelberg (2009)
7. Ji, Q., Haase, P., Qi, G., Hitzler, P., Stadtmuller, S.: RaDON-repair and diagnosis in ontology networks. In: Proc. of (ESWC) (2009)
8. Maynard, D., Funk, A., Peters, W.: SPRAT: a tool for automatic semantic pattern based ontology population. In: Proc. of (ICSD) (2009)
9. Mizzaro, S.: Relevance: the whole history. Journal of the American Society for Information Science archive 48(9), 810–832 (1997)
10. Noy, N.F., Musen, M.A.: Specifying ontology views by traversal. In: McIlraith, S.A., Plexousakis, D., van Harmelen, F. (eds.) ISWC 2004. LNCS, vol. 3298, pp. 713–725. Springer, Heidelberg (2004)
11. Ottens, K., Hernandez, N., Gleizes, M.P., Aussenac-Gilles, N.: A Multi-Agent system for dynamic ontologies (October 2008)
12. Palmisano, I., Tamma, V., Iannone, L., Payne, T.R., Doran, P.: Dynamic change evaluation for ontology evolution in the semantic web. In: Proc. of (WI-IAT) (2008)
13. Pammer, V., Serafini, L., Lindstaedt, M.: Highlighting assertional effects of ontology editing activities in OWL. In: Proc. of the ISWC International Workshop on Ontology Dynamics (IWOD) (2009)
14. Sabou, M., d'Aquin, M., Motta, E.: Exploring the semantic web as background knowledge for ontology matching. Journal on Data Semantics (XI) (2008)
15. Sirin, E., Parsia, B., Grau, B.C., Kalyanpur, A., Katz, Y.: Pellet: A practical OWL-DL reasoner. Journal of Web Semantics 5(2), 51–53 (2007)
16. Sperber, D., Wilson, D.: Relevance (1986)
17. Sternberg, R.J.: Metaphors of mind (1990)
18. Zablith, F., d'Aquin, M., Sabou, M., Motta, E.: Investigating the use of background knowledge for assessing the relevance of statements to an ontology in ontology evolution. In: Proc. of the ISWC International Workshop on Ontology Dynamics (IWOD) (2009)
19. Zablith, F., Sabou, M., d'Aquin, M., Motta, E.: Using background knowledge for ontology evolution. In: Proc. of the ISWC International Workshop on Ontology Dynamics (IWOD) (2008)

What Is Concept Drift and How to Measure It?

Shenghui Wang[1,2], Stefan Schlobach[2], and Michel Klein

[1] Department of Communication Science
[2] Department of Computer Science
Vrije Universiteit Amsterdam

Abstract. This paper studies concept drift over time. We first define the meaning of a concept in terms of intension, extension and label. We then introduce *concept drift* over time and two derived notions: *(in)stability* over a time period and *concept shift* between two time points. We apply our framework in three case-studies, one from communication science, on DBPedia, and one in the legal domain. We describe ways of identifying interesting changes in the meaning of concept within given application contexts. These case-studies illustrate the feasibility of our framework in analysing concept drift in knowledge organisation schemas of varying expressiveness.

1 Introduction

Knowledge organisation systems (KOS), such as formal ontologies (*e.g.* modelled in OWL), thesauri or taxonomies (*e.g.* described in SKOS) or other term classification schemes, play an crucial role in providing semantic interoperability in many domains and use cases. They have become critical to the Web of Data, for structured access of documents in libraries or patient records based on diagnostic information, and many more applications. In almost all modern types of KOS, *concepts* are the central constructs that are used to describe sets of objects with shared characteristics. Although it is widely recognised to be an oversimplification most current systems consider their underlying KOS to be stable over time. For many applications, this starts to be a critical problem, and this paper attempts to provide a first step towards a better understanding of what we call *concept drift*.

Problem description: As the world is continuously changing, concepts also change over time. That is, for example, a concept refers to different objects at different points in time. The term Government of the Netherlands refers to different people in 1999 and in 2009. Consider the concept Middle class which is interpreted very differently in various periods of time.[1]

To our knowledge there has been no formalisation of what concept drift actually means and implies. In order to identify different types of changes in concepts

[1] This drift in meaning occurs not only over time, but also over location, culture, *etc.* For ease of presentation we will mostly refer to drift in time, but significant parts of the framework should extend to other kinds of "contexts."

P. Cimiano and H.S. Pinto (Eds.): EKAW 2010, LNAI 6317, pp. 241–256, 2010.

and to understand the impact of concept drift, such a formalisation is critical. Therefore, this paper focuses on the following research questions:

RQ1 What is concept drift, and how to formalise it?
RQ2 Can we identify the impact of concept-drift?

Methodology: We provide a generic formalisation of the meaning of concepts in terms of label, intension and extension. These definitions are not intended to provide new philosophical insights, but aim at making existing accepted notions applicable in practice. For each of the three elements of concept meaning we define *concept drift* and study two important consequences: the *(in)stability* over a time period and *concept shift* between time points (where part of the meaning of a concept shifts to some other concept).

Experiments: We instantiate our framework in three case-studies, studying concept drift in a SKOS vocabulary used by communication scientists for political analysis, a general purpose RDFS ontology, DBpedia and a legal OWL ontology, LKIF-Core. We investigate the introduced mechanisms for studying concept drift in these three different KR models. Our experiments show the feasibility of both the formalisation and identification mechanisms by pointing to some examples of concept (in)stability and shift which were identified as relevant by collaborating domain experts.

Contributions: The paper should be read as an attempt to turn established (philosophical) insights into a general pragmatic framework. We believe that we also contribute to a better understanding of temporal change of meaning in formal knowledge organisation schemes and its impact in practical applications.[2] We motivate and define the crucial notions of *drift, shift* and *stability.* In three case-studies we show that our findings are relevant, most particular in our main case-study in communication science.

2 A Theory of Concept Drift

The meaning of concepts changes over time. Let us first commit to some basic definitions regarding the meaning of concepts. The *intension* of a concept are the properties implied by it, the *extension* the set of things it extends to. We also consider the *labelling* as a part of the meaning of a concept, as the way people reference a concept is crucial in studying concept drift. Labels do not refer to a unique identifier but to a natural language description used to convey the meaning of a concept from one human to another.[3]

[2] Discussions with "only" philosophical relevance will usually be dealt with in footnotes to improve the flow of the story-line.

[3] We try to be consistent with common philosophical approaches. We apply and formalise the standard distinction between intension and extension which goes back to [1]. We include, somewhat more unconventionally, the labelling in the meaning of a concept (in the tradition of the *signifier* [2]).

The meaning of concepts. Our definition of the meaning of a concept, and its drift, should be generic enough to be applied in different ontological frameworks. In this paper, we apply our idea to a set of concepts used for annotating documents in communication science as well as one RDFS ontology and one OWL ontology. We start out from a set of objects referred to as the universe of the domain, and a set of properties (unary predicates). Both universe and properties depend on the application and the formalism used.

Definition 1. *The* meaning of a concept *C is a triple $(label(C), int(C), ext(C))$, where $label(C)$ is a string, $int(C)$ a set of properties (the* intension *of C), and $ext(C)$ a subset of the universe (the* extension *of C).*

All elements of the meaning of a concept can change. Still it makes sense to talk about a concept being the same over time. Our solution to this problem is based on the rigid part of the intension of concepts.[4] Formally, we assume that the intension of a concept C is the disjoint union of a rigid and a non-rigid set of properties (*i.e.* $(int_r(C) \cup int_{nr}(C)))$. This separation between rigid and non-rigid properties does not need to be explicitly specified, but rigidity is crucial for *identity* of a concept over time. Intuitively, this amounts to the assumption that a concept is uniquely identified through some core properties that do not change over time.[5]

Definition 2. *Two concepts C_1 and C_2 are considered identical if and only if, their rigid intension are equivalent,* i.e. , $int_r(C_1) = int_r(C_2)$.

Identity allows us to compare two variants of the same concept at different moments in time even if the meaning (either label, extension or the non-rigid part of its intension) has changed. We will assume that there is always only one variant of a concept at each moment in time, *i.e.* , only one concept at a moment can be identical to a concept at another moment.

Concept drift. If a concept at different times has the same meaning, there is no concept drift. A more subtle notion of concept drift, however, requires notions of similarity of meaning, which can be decomposed into intensional similarity, sim_{int}, which is calculated between sets of predicates, extensional similarity, sim_{ext}, between sets of objects, and label similarity, sim_{label}, between strings. Each similarity is a function with the range [0, 1], and a similarity value of 1 indicates an equality.

---

[4] Rigidity is discussed in Ontoclean [3] in a slightly different way. There rigidity is a meta-property of a concept that modellers should make explicit. We use it in a stronger way as an intrinsic and the only stable part of the meaning of a concept which otherwise can drift in various ways.

[5] This assumption implies that if the rigid core of a concept changes, the new concept will be a *different* concept. An example is demagogue which used to denote the concept of political leaders. The concept of a populist now referred to by the label "demagogue" is a different concept.

Definition 3. *A concept has extensionally drifted in two of its variants*[6] C' *and* C''*, if and only if,* $sim_{ext}(C', C'') \neq 1$*. Intensional and label drift are defined similarly.*

Concept shift and (in)stability. Concept drift happens regularly and even if it can be measured it is often difficult to grasp its impact. Therefore, we define other notions: *(in)stability* and *concept shift.* Both can be used to identify more drastic concept drift. The more the meaning of a concept drifts, the more *unstable* it becomes. Although there is no indication of when an unstable concept becomes *critically* unstable, instability can still be an interesting notion. First, one could define a threshold based on experience. Label similarity is often defined using edit distance and one could define lexically instability in terms of a high edit-distance. Another way of analysing concept drift over time is to compare the (average) stability of concepts. As a *relative* measure, it does not require any priori commitment (such as a threshold).

A special case of instability is when a concept becomes so unstable, that part of its meaning is more representative for a different concept rather than for itself. We call this *concept shift.*

Definition 4. *The meaning of a concept extensionally shifts between two of its variants* C' *and* C'' *if the extension of* C'' *is more similar to the extension of a non-identical concept rather than to the extension of* C'*. Intensional and label shift are defined similarly.*

Concept shift can have drastic consequences on the use of a concept in an application as some other concept has basically taken over its meaning.

Applying the framework. To apply our framework for concept drift in a specific use-case, the following steps are required:

1. to define intension, extension and a labelling function.
2. to define similarity functions over intension, extension and labels

Given that the mission of the Semantic Web includes giving meaning to resources on the Web, it could come as a suprise that defining intensions, extensions and even labelling functions is by no means trivial. The usual model-theoretic notions of extension and intension, *e.g.* for RDF(S) or OWL semantics are slightly misleading here, as they refer to specific models, whereas ontologies usually represent classes of models. In practice, one needs to define the relevant notions per use-case, where each such definition is an ontological commitment. In the following section, we will give such commitments for 3 different case-studies. It should be understood that such a commitment is never uncontroversial.

---

[6] This means that C' and C'' are identical but have different meaning at different moments in time.

3 Case-Studies

3.1 Case Study 1: Concept Shift in Political Reporting

Communication scientists annotate various media content with concepts from controlled vocabularies (of increasing expressiveness) in order to quantitatively study the influence of the Media on the political processes. Such controlled vocabularies have recently been represented using the SKOS model [4]. Each concept has a preferred Label and possibly a few alternative Label which are the synonyms of this concept. One concept can be linked to the others using skos:broader, skos:narrowed and skos:related.

In this case study, we focus on five variants of a SKOS vocabulary of political concepts used during five most recent Dutch national election campaigns. All newspaper articles on Dutch politics during these campaign periods were manually annotated with the concepts from the particular variant of that year. In our case, these articles can be considered as the instantiation of the abstract political concepts.

Political concepts and their meaning. We now formally define our problem: for each election campaign $t \in \{1994, 1998, 2002, 2003, 2006\}$ we have a set Δ_t of sentences annotated by concepts from a SKOS vocabulary V_t.

The label of a concept is obtained using the SKOS Core labelling property skos:prefLabel. The extension $ext_s(C_t)$ of a concept $C_t \in V_t$ at time t is the set of all sentences annotated by C_t, *i.e.* ,

$$ext_s(C_t) = \{s \in \Delta_t \mid \mathsf{annotatedBy}\ C_t\}.$$

It is more difficult to formally define the intension of a concept, as there is no explicit intensional definition of the concepts available. We construct an explicit intension based on co-occurrence of concepts in annotations. For each concept C, we calculate the top K concepts $topKuse(C)$ which co-occur the most in the sentences they code in one moment in time. The properties we use to define the intension are based on "topicality", *i.e.* , a property $P_C(D)$ is true if, and only if, D is in the $topKuse$ relation with C. The intension of C is then the set of properties $int_s(C) = \{P_C(D) = \text{true}\}$, *i.e.* , the intension is in fact determined by all associated concepts.

Similarity of intension, extensions and labels. Similarity of labels can be determined through standard Levenshtein edit distance. In our case we define similarity as 1 minus the hyperbolic tangent of the original edit distance. For each concept C, we average over the Levenshtein edit distance $ed(label_s(C_t), label_s(C))$ between the preferred labels of all its variants C_t in each year.

Extensional similarity is usually determined by calculating the overlap of the extensions. In our case, this is not possible, as the set of sentences in different years are disjoint. In order to use disjoint extensions to measure the similarity of concepts from different years, we applied the mapping tool which was developed in [5]. For each sentence in Year1, the mapping tool first looks for the most

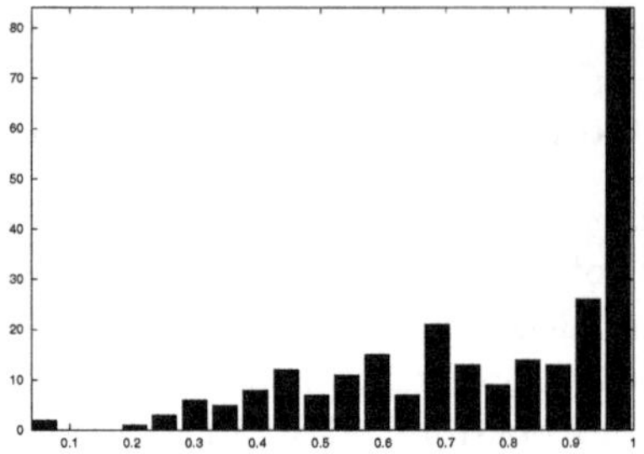

Fig. 1. Label stability: The X-axis gives the average label similarity over the years; the Y-axis the number of concepts with this average.

similar sentence in Year2. Then this sentence of Year1 is considered to be coded by the concept(s) with which its most similar sentence of Year2 is coded. In this way, two disjoint extensions become dually annotated, and we then measure the similarity between two concepts in terms of their common extensions.

Since the intension of a concept is determined by its associated concepts, the intensional similarity between two concepts is therefore determined by the set similarity between the sets of concepts with which they are associated. We use the Jaccard similarity for this purpose.

For each concept C, we calculated the above three kinds of similarity between all pairs of variants C_t in each year. We take the average as the measure of the corresponding *stability* of this concept over time, noted as S_{label}, S_{int} and S_{ext}.

Note that these similarity measures can only provide relative ranking whether one concept is more stable than another. A lower similarity indicates a higher instability. In the following experiments, we use automated methods to evaluate instability. Concept shift, on the other hand, is harder to quantify and we study it using selected examples.

Experiments to study concept drift in our political ontology. The identity problem is solved, in our case, by the manual concept mapping provided by a communication science expert, based on the rigid part of the intention. In this way, we are sure whether two concepts in different years are actually the two variants of a single concept. This enables us to investigate the concept drift in terms of the labels, intension and extension.

Identifying label instability and shift. Since the domain expert has indicated identical concepts across different years, our question is to see whether these "intensionally" identical concepts have "stable" labels.

Figure 1 shows the histogram of the label stability values, indicating that most (over 80) concepts have very stable labels ($S_{label}(C) = 1$) over these years. For example, all five variants of the concept Asielzoekers (asylum seekers) has exactly the same label. However, some concepts do have very unstable labels. According to the domain expert, the following 6 concepts are intensionally identical:

1994_sjo_creawetsto → 1998_wcorruptie (corruption) → 1998_rbeursfraude (stock fraud) →2002_belangenverstrengeling (conflict of interest) →
2003_corruptie (corruption)→ 2006_fraude_en_corruptie (fraud and corruption)

The instability of its label over the years is striking, and it results in a label stability value of $S_{label} = 0.47$.

Obviously, concepts with the same label across different years can have different intensions or, more precisely, the difference of their non-rigid parts of intension is so big that the whole concept shifts to another concept with a different label, which we call *label shift*. For example, when newspapers used "openbaarheid" (openness) in 2002, they meant "public sphere," which is an area in social life where people can get together and freely discuss and identify societal problems, and through that discussion influence political action. While, in 2003, they uses the same label to mean "open government" in particular. These two concepts with the same label are actually different concepts. Therefore, Concept 1994_openbaarheid has a shift in label as its label shifts to another concept, according to Definition 4. Therefore we claim that the meaning of Concept openbaarheid shifts between 1994 and 1998.

Identifying extensional shift. As stated before, by looking at the extension of the concepts, we can detect whether the extension of one concept shifts over time or whether two concepts shift towards each other. For one concept, we calculate the similarity between its extension and the extension of the concepts from the following year. The concept with the highest similarity is considered to be the *extensionally identical* one. If this identity is consistent with the intensional identity provided by the domain experts, then there is no concept shift; otherwise, the concept has shifted to some other concept(s).

In Table 1, we compare the "extensionally" identical concepts and the "intensionally" identical ones. The first column gives the number of concepts which have found their extensionally identical concepts and also have an "intensionally" identical concept according to our domain expert. The second column is the number of concepts when extensional and intensional identities are consistent. As it shows, the consistency between these two identities is rather low.

We have to take into account the reliability of the calculated extensional similarity. Since it uses an approximation of the real extension, we therefore relax the criterion of identity consistency by introducing the parameter K: if the intensionally identical concept is within the top K most extensionally similar concepts, then we consider the two identities to be consistent. The third column

Table 1. Extensional shift vs intensional stability

Year	Extensional	Consistent	Consistent_at_5
1994–1998	41	8	19
1998–2002	43	9	16
2002–2003	23	8	11
2003–2006	92	35	58

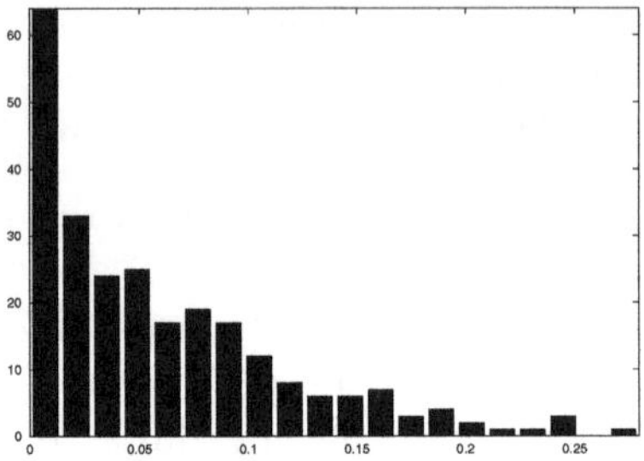

Fig. 2. Intensional stability: the X-axis lists the average intensional similarity between variants of a concept The Y-axis shows the number of concepts with this average.

gives the number of consistent concepts if $K = 5$. The degree of consistency increases, however, there is still a big inconsistency between these two identities.

As said, the validity of this identity is unfortunately not guaranteed. The traditional evaluation method is to compare it with some gold standard provided by human experts. However, it is not applicable here since both identities are under investigation in our study. Because of the lack of reliable extensional identity, we could not measure the (in)stability at the concept level as we did in terms of labels.

Although an automated stability analysis is not possible, we can still manually identify some real extensional shift. For example, according to the domain expert, 2003_kinderopvang (childcare) is the same as 2006_kinderopvang. However, 2006_gratis_kinderopvang (free childcare) is more similar to 2003_kinderopvang in terms of their extension. In this case, we say 2003_kinderopvang has shifted its meaning towards a more specific topic, namely free childcare. This is also confirmed by the post-hoc analysis of our domain experts.

Identifying intensional stability and shift. As we described earlier, we use the association to other concepts of the same year as an indicator of the intension of a concept. By measuring the similarity between such associations, we can get some information about how intensionally stable one concept is over the years.

Figure 2 gives the histogram of the measure of intensional stability (S_{int}). Now most concepts have a rather unstable intension over the years. On one hand, comparing to the label stability (Figure 1), few concepts have a stable intension, which suggests that the label of concepts is more stable then their intension. On the other hand, the instability of intension is far beyond our expectation, which suggests that we should look for another way of formalising concept intension, as the reliability of the results provided by the current formalisation is doubtful.

Nevertheless, Figure 3 and Figure 4 respectively give an example of very unstable and very stable concepts.[7] Here, the red links are the intentionally identical concepts provided by domain experts, the black links are the association links (*i.e.* , the concepts which co-occur the most to annotated sentences) and

[7] For convenience, we translate all the Dutch labels into English.

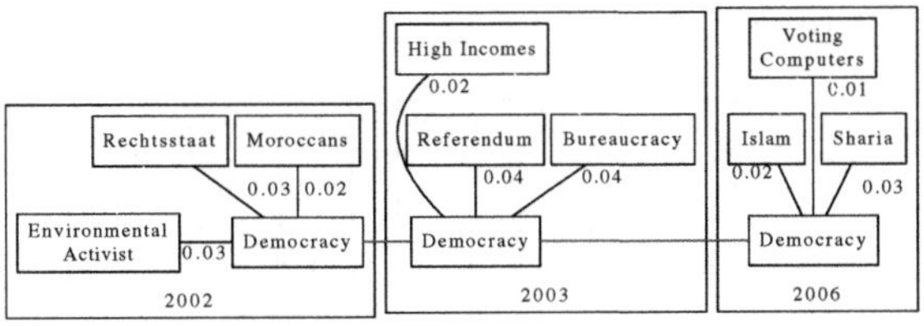

Fig. 3. Intension of concept Democracy in 3 years, with average drift of ($S_{int} = 0.02$)

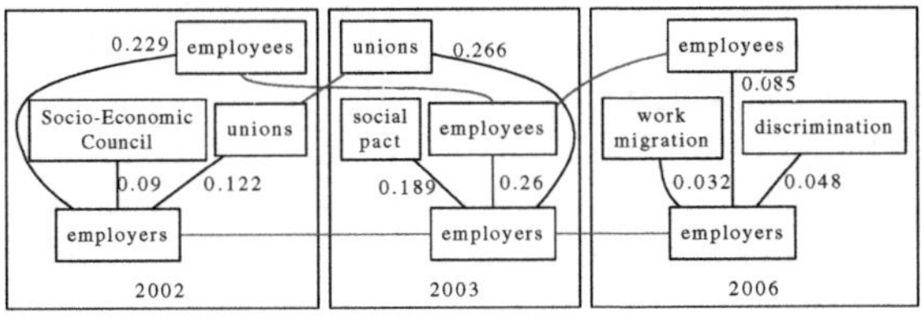

Fig. 4. Intension of concept Employers in 3 years, with average drift of ($S_{int} = 0.15$)

the number next to the links are the strength of the association. As the S_{int} value indicates, Concept Employers is rather stable over the years, while Concept Democracy seems to shift its meaning in different years. This observations are also consistent with the political reality. An interesting point observed from these two figures is that, when one concept is stable, its closely associated concepts tend to be stable too, while the concepts closely associated with an unstable concept tend to be also unstable.

3.2 Case-Study 2: Concept Drift in DBpedia

DBpedia[8] is probably the most successful ontology currently linked within the Linked-Open Data (LOD) cloud. It combines a hand-crafted class hierarchy with automatically generated instance data taken from the Wikipedia effort. Through its high quality and huge coverage DBpedia is now the most strongly linked dataset within the LOD. For the sake of this research we consider the the DBpedia ontology in RDFS [6], *i.e.* , we ignore the (very few) OWL operators used in the model. RDF(S) and its underlying semantics is a very common modeling framework, which makes DBpedia an interesting object of study as it is almost exclusively modeled in RDF(S).

RDF(S) concepts and their meaning. RDFS comes with a specific labeling relation rdfs:label. Furthermore, RDF is equipped with a rdf:type relation that relates objects with classes. It seems natural to define the extension of an RDF class to be the set of all instances in the rdf:type relation. The intension of a class is on the other hand not specifically defined in RDF(S). We have chosen a simple

[8] `http://wiki.dbpedia.org/`

Table 2. Four version of the DBpedia ontology

Version	#Concept	#Resource
3.5	255	1,477,377
3.4	204	1,161,678
3.3	174	1,054,199
3.2	174	875,273

approach which focusses on the "semantic" operators in RDFS with fixed semantics, more precisely rdfs:subclass, rdfs:range, rdfs:domain. The intension of a concept C is then simply the set of all triples with C in the subject or object position of these three types of triples.

Let us define the meaning of a DBpedia concept formally. We will call the combination of the DBpedia terminology T[9] and the explicit type information as well as the relations translated from Wikipedia, the DBpedia ontology.

Definition 5. *Let O be the DBpedia ontology,* i.e. *a set of triples (s, p, o), and O^* the semantic closure of O. The* rdf-label $lab_r(C)$ *of C is defined as the object of the $(C$,rdfs:label$, o)$. The* rdf-extension $ext_r(C)$ *of C is defined as the set of resources r such that (r* rdf : type *$C) \in O^*$. The* rdf-intension $int_r(C)$ *of C is defined as the set of all triples $(C, p, o) \in O^*$ in O where $p =$*rdfs:subclass *and (s, p, C), where $p \in \{$*rdfs:subclass, rdfs:domain, rdfs:range*$\}$.*

Please note that this definition is just one possible choice of ontological commitment regarding the meaning of a concept in RDF(S).

Similarity relations between labels are defined on the basis of string similarity. Similarity between intension and extension, which are just sets of resources and triples respectively, can easily be defined through the set similarity (*e.g.* Jaccard).

Experiments to study concept drift in DBpedia. We studied the four latest versions of the same DBpedia ontology, namely, 3.5, 3.4, 3.3 and 3.2. The Table 2 gives some general information of these four versions. These versions were uploaded into independent RDF repositories.

The identity problem is solved by the use of unique URI references that remain stable over these versions. Our basic assumption is that two concepts in different versions are actually the two variants of a single concept. This enables us to investigate concept shift and instability in terms of their labels, intension and extension.

Although most DBpedia concepts define their label using rdfs:label, these labels are mostly equivalent to the local-names of their URIrefs. These abels are strongly related to identify, and thus less interesting to study label drift.

For each concept C at year t, we built its extension $ext_r C_t$ (*i.e.* , the set of instances) and the intension $int_r C_t$ (*i.e.* , the set of related triples). The Jaccard similarity[10] was measured between the intension and extension of the different

[9] The terminology is called differently in the different DBpedia versions, but usually something like `dbpedia-ontoloy.owl`.

[10] `http://en.wikipedia.org/wiki/Jaccard_index`

Table 3. The top 5 most stable and ustable DBpedia concepts in terms of their extension and intension (of the 167 concepts present in all four versions)

Rank	Extensional	Intensional	Rank	Extensional	Intensional
1	Planet	SportsEvent	163	OfficeHolder	Vein
2	Road	FormulaOneRacer	164	Politician	BasketballPlayer
3	Infrastructure	WineRegion	165	City	EthnicGroup
4	Cyclist	Cleric	166	College	Band
5	LunarCrater	WrestlingEvent	167	ChemicalCompound	BritishRoyalty

variants of the same concept. In the end, we calculate the measure of intensional stability ($S_{int}(C)$) and extensional stability ($S_{ext}(C)$). Table 3 gives the top 5 most stable and the last 5 least stable concepts from these two aspects.

Concept Politician is considered extensionally very unstable. This can easily be confirmed by the change of the sheer amount of instances. In Version 3.2, it has only 476 instances, while in Version 3.5, it has already 19,285 instances. The extension of this concept clearly has expanded significantly. However, low stability not necessarily leads to concept shift. For example, although growing, the extension of Politician is always the most similar to the extension of its following variant.

Concept City is also very unstable extensionally. In Version 3.4 it has indeed shifted to another concept in Version 3.5, Settlement. These two concepts share more than 73% instances, which causes a high extensional similarity between them, which is higher than the similarity between the two variants of City. We found that Settlement appeared only in version 3.5. For some reason, most of the instances of City in version 3.4 have been transferred to Settlement. This poses an interesting question to the modeler whether this is intentional or by mistake.

Similarly, studying the intensional stability and shifts also gives insight to the evolution of the intensional semantics of a concept. For example, the intensionally very unstable concept, EthnicGroup, has been involved in the rdfs:domain and rdfs:range of a continuously changing set of properties. This indicates this concepts are related to different concepts in different versions, which contributes to the intensional instability. Furthermore, real shifts happened to some concepts. The identified extensional shift, from City to Settlement is also found to be an intensional shift, that is, these two concepts not only share a lot of instances, but their intensional definitions are very similar too. This double-confirmation is valuable because it may well indicate a genuine concept shift.

3.3 Case-Study 3: Concept Drift in LKIF-Core

In this section we look at the evolution of concepts in the LKIF-Core, an OWL ontology of basic legal concepts.[11] This ontology has also been continuously developed, and uses most of OWL's expressiveness.

[11] `http://ontology.leibnizcenter.org/trac/wiki/LKIFCore`

OWL concepts and their meaning. The formal meaning of a concept in an OWL DL ontology is often far more explicitly defined than in other formalisms. The intension of a concept could potentially be defined as the set of all possible DL concepts that are equivalent to it *wrt.* the ontology. Unfortunately, this is only possible in so-called definitorical terminologies, and difficult to calculate even if possible. We will approximate this set in our experiments (rather coarsely) by using the OWLIM[12] interpretation of LKIF, and consider finite sets of consequences (triples-chains). As OWL ontologies are specifications of sets of possible models, there is no unique notion of the extension of concepts. However, once committed to a particular model, DL semantics provide the formal instance-of relation to specify the extension of a concept.

The LKIF ontology does not come with instances, so that we do not consider extensional drift in this paper.

Let us define the meaning of concepts in LKIF.

Definition 6. *Let O to be the LKIF-OWL ontology and O^* denote the OWLIM inferred semantic closure. The owl-label $lab_o(C)$ of C is defined as the object of the $(C, \mathsf{rdfs{:}label}, o)$. The owl-intension $int_o(C)$ of C is defined:*

1. *all triples $(C, p, o) \in O^*$ and $(s, p, C) \in O^*$*
2. *all triples in chains $\{(C, p_1, o_1) \circ (s_2, p_2, o_2) \circ \ldots, \circ(s_n, p_n, o_n)\}$ where $s_k = o_k - 1$, plus*
3. *all triples in chains $\{(s_1, p_1, o_1) \circ (s_2, p_2, o_2), \circ, \ldots, \circ(s_n, p_n, C)\}$ where $s_{k+1} = o_k$ being blank nodes.*

Again, the above definition is only one possible ontological commitment regarding the meaning of an OWL concept. Based on such definition, the similarity of label and intension can be calculated using set similarity, as done for the DBpedia case.

Experiments to study concept drift in LKIF. We studied 4 major versions of LKIF, namely, 1.0, 1.0.2, 1.0.3 and 1.1. Similarly, the local-name in the URI reference is used as the identity of one concept. Unfortunately, the rdfs:label actually was rarely used; only 4 concepts specify their labels which stay constant for all variants. Therefore, we focus on the intensional stability and shift, which we calculate as before based on Jaccard similarity. All concepts were ranked according to its intensional stability. The ranked list has been confirmed by one of the developer of LKIF to be consistent with his expectations.

By comparing the intension of concepts between different versions, we were also able to find true concept shifts, listed in Table 4.

As Table 4 shows, some intensional shift corresponding to shifting in modules, for example, Speech_Act is no longer a general action, instead it belongs to the expression module for describing, propositions and propositional attitudes (belief, intention), qualifications, statements and media. While the other kind of shift, for example, Mental_Concept to Mental_Entity, were confirmed to be a renaming operation.

[12] `http://www.ontotext.com/owlim/`

Table 4. Examples of confirmed intensional shift in LKIF-Core

lkif1.0:action.owl#Speech_Act	lkif1.0.2:expression.owl#Speech_Act
lkif1.0:action.owl#Termination	lkif1.0.2:process.owl#Termination
lkif1.0.2:lkif-top.owl#Mental_Concept	lkif1.0.3:lkif-top.owl#Mental_Entity
lkif1.0.2:lkif-top.owl#Physical_Concept	lkif1.0.3:lkif-top.owl#Physical_Entity

Our three case studies have shown the feasibility of both the formalisation and identification mechanisms in analysing concept drift in knowledge organisation schemas of varying expressiveness.

4 Related Work

Let us first look at research in other domains that is related to our notion of *concept drift*. In historical linguistics, *semantic shift* describes the evolution of word usage. Each word has multiple senses and connotations which can be added, removed or altered over time. Semantic change is a change in one meaning of a word. Semantic shift can be triggered by different forces and have different types [7], but this interpretation of "semantic" does not say anything about the meaning and change of the underlying concepts.

In machine learning *concept drift* addresses a similar problem [8]. The term *concept* refers to the quantity that a learning model is trying to predict, *i.e.* the variable. *Concept drift* is the situation in which the statistical properties of the target concept change over time. This requires regular updates in the predicting model itself. A special case is *virtual concept drift* [9] (or *sampling shift*), in which the meaning of a concept does not change, while in the latter case only the data distribution changes. An example is the concept "spam", for which the meaning does not change, but the data distribution (*i.e.* the relative frequency of the properties) is changing.

In 1994, Klenner and Hahn [10] discuss exactly the problem of concept drift because of evolving notions over time, however, not in the context of Semantic Web applications but for technical standards. As a mechanism for updating static value restrictions or integrity constraints, they propose an automatic procedure. This generates a generational stratification of the underlying level of generic concepts in terms of concept versions; single instances are then related to their associated concept version. The procedure exploits a so called progress model—provided by an expert—which describes in qualitative terms the regularities of foreseeable changes of attributes in a domain. Versions are then detected by measuring the change in values of attributes of instances.

With the goal of detecting concept drift and the occurrence of new concepts in a domain, Fanizzi *et.al.*describe the use of a conceptual clustering technique based on unsupervised learning [11]. In their approach, a clustering method is used to hierarchically organize groups of similar instances. Concept drift is detected by finding new individuals that are too far apart from existing clusters, but that together do not form a new cluster. If the unclustered instances do form a cluster, a new concept has occurred.

Takahira Yamaguchi also discusses concept drift in the context of ontologies [12]. This paper focuses on constructing domain ontologies starting from a hierarchically structured set of domain concepts without concept definitions (machine readable dictionary). This initial ontology is then refined by adding domain-specific knowledge; the places in the ontology that have to change because of this new knowledge are seen as places where concept drift occurs. Two specific strategies for such changes are presented. The paper does not define concept drift but merely uses this term for a step in an ontology construction methodology.

In the Semantic Web community, the problem addressed here is related to a broader problem of *ontology change*, which refers to the "problem of deciding the modifications to perform upon an ontology in response to a certain need for change as well as the implementation of these modifications and the management of their effects in depending data, services, applications, agents or other elements" [13]. The existing research on ontology evolution and versioning mainly addresses this problem at the macro ontological level, that is, the effect of certain change operations over the ontology elements, including concepts, relations and instances, as well as the interoperability issue between different variants (versions) over time. For example, [14] formally defines ontology perspectives, which describe the relation between versions of an ontology and its extension. An exception might be the work of [15] who study the intensional change of concepts in different versions of ontologies,

On the specific meaning of change for specific concepts not much has been done. In [16] a series of "concept signatures" extracted from the textual definitions of the same concept at different time are used detect drifts. This definition-based method is applicable if there is rich definitions of concepts and the definitions are constantly modified. In the Ontoclean framework [3] the meta-properties identity and rigidity are defined with relate to the stability of a concept. In [17], a distinction is made between the "specification" and the "conceptualisation" of a concept.

5 Conclusion

More and more applications critically depend on some kind of concept schemes for the semantic interoperability of their data. However, although it is recognised by many as a critical problem, the continuous change in meaning of concepts (called drift in this paper) has not yet received the attention it deserves in the ontology modelling community. Despite the significant efforts that have gone into topics such as ontology evolution, semantic versioning or temporal modelling and reasoning, most tools are still based on static representations. The existing ontology versioning frameworks focus on the interoperability between versions and data. There is not yet a formal framework for concept drift, nor an implementation for identifying significant concept drift.

This paper attempts to close this gap by introducing a theoretical foundation for the notions **drift, shift** and **stability** over time. We show that the proposed mechanisms are useful in practical applications modeled in SKOS, RDFS and OWL respectively. The results of our evaluation are preliminary, but encouraging: although intensional drift is difficult to study because the concepts are often not formally defined, the detected concept shift and stability ordering on concepts gives useful information for the domain experts.

Future research will be directed in two directions: first, in cooperation with Communication Scientists working on political reporting and legal experts we will apply the proposed methods in more in-depth studies on meaning change. With the experience that will be gained in at least one of these additional use-cases we plan to create a generic implementation for analysing concept drift.

References

1. Frege, F.L.G.: über sinn und bedeutung. Zeitschrift für Philosophie und philosophische Kritik 100, 25–50 (1892)
2. Saussure, F.D.: Course in General Linguistics. Open Court Classics (1986) (reedition)
3. Guarino, N., Welty, C.: Evaluating ontological decisions with ontoclean. Commun. ACM 45, 61–65 (2002)
4. Isaac, A., Summers, E.: SKOS Primer. W3C Group Note (2009)
5. Schopman, B., Wang, S., Schlobach, S.: Deriving concept mappings through instance mappings. In: Proceedings of the 3rd Asian Semantic Web Conference, Bangkok, Thailand (2008)
6. W3C: RDFS, `http://www.w3.org/TR/rdf-schema/`
7. Bloomfield, L.: Language. Allen and Unwin (1933)
8. Tsymbal, A.: The problem of concept drift: definitions and related work. Technical Report TCD-CS-2004-15, Computer Science Department, Trinity College Dublin, Ireland (2004)
9. Widmer, G., Kubat, M.: Effective learning in dynamic environments by explicit context tracking. In: Brazdil, P.B. (ed.) ECML 1993. LNCS, vol. 667, pp. 227–243. Springer, Heidelberg (1993)
10. Klenner, M., Hahn, U.: Concept versioning: A methodology for tracking evolutionary concept drift in dynamic concept systems. In: Proc. of ECAI 1994, pp. 473–477. Wiley, Chichester (1994)
11. Fanizzi, N., d'Amato, C., Esposito, F.: Conceptual clustering and its application to concept drift and novelty detection. In: Bechhofer, S., Hauswirth, M., Hoffmann, J., Koubarakis, M. (eds.) ESWC 2008. LNCS, vol. 5021, pp. 318–332. Springer, Heidelberg (2008)
12. Yamaguchi, T.: Constructing domain ontologies based on concept drift analysis. In: IJCAI 1999. Workshop on Ontologies and Problem-Solving Methods (1999)
13. Flouris, G., Manakanatas, D., Kondylakis, H., Plexousakis, D., Antoniou, G.: Ontology change: classification and survey. Knowledge Eng. Review 23, 117–152 (2008)

14. Heflin, J., Pan, Z.: A model theoretic semantics for ontology versioning. In: Third International Semantic Web Conference, pp. 62–76. Springer, Heidelberg (2004)
15. Huang, Z., Stuckenschmidt, H.: Reasoning with multi-version ontologies: A temporal logic approach. In: Gil, Y., Motta, E., Benjamins, V.R., Musen, M.A. (eds.) ISWC 2005. LNCS, vol. 3729, pp. 398–412. Springer, Heidelberg (2005)
16. Gulla, J.A., Solskinnsbakk, G., Myrseth, P., Haderlein, V., Cerrato, O.: Semantic drift in ontologies. In: Proceedings of 6th International Conference on Web Information Systems and Technologies, Valencia, Spain (April 2010)
17. Klein, M.: Change Management for Distributed Ontologies. PhD thesis, Vrije Universiteit Amsterdam (August 2004)

Mobile Cultural Heritage Guide: Location-Aware Semantic Search

Chris van Aart[1], Bob Wielinga[1,2], and Willem Robert van Hage[1]

[1] VU University Amsterdam, The Netherlands
[2] Universiteit van Amsterdam, The Netherlands
cj@vanaart.com, b.j.wielinga@uva.nl, wrvhage@few.vu.nl

Abstract. In this paper we explore the use of location aware mobile devices for searching and browsing a large number of general and cultural heritage information repositories. Based on GPS positioning we can determine a user's location and context, composed of physical nearby locations, historic events that have taken place there, artworks that were created at or inspired by those locations and artists that have lived or worked there. Based on a geolocation, the user has three levels of refinement: pointing to a specific heading and selection and facets and subfacets of cultural heritage objects. In our approach two types of knowledge are combined: general knowledge about geolocations and points of interest and specialized knowledge about a particular domain, i.e. cultural heritage. We use a number of Linked Open Data sources and a number of general sources from the cultural heritage domain (including Art and Architecture Thesaurus, Union List of Artist Names) as well as data from several Dutch cultural institutions. We show three concrete scenarios where a tourist accesses localized information on his iPhone about the current environment, events, artworks or persons, which are enriched by Linked Open Data sources. We show that Linked Open Data sources in isolation are currently too limited to provide interesting semantic information but combined with each other and with a number of other sources a really informative location-based service can be created.

1 Introduction

In this paper we explore the use of location aware mobile devices for searching and browsing large collections of general and cultural heritage information repositories using minimal interaction. Given a particular geolocation we provide cultural heritage resources for an end user. The material origins from the MultimediaN E-Culture project which deployed large virtual collections of cultural-heritage resources [7]. These resources are imbedded in the Linked Open Data (LOD) cloud [6].

Current smart phones such as the iPhone, Blackberry, HTC or Android have continuous access to internet, know about their geographic location and even know what direction the user is looking at. These capabilities are being used for a number of applications that show the user a map of his/her current location with possible places of interest marked on the map (Linked Geo Data browser, Google Maps,

P. Cimiano and H.S. Pinto (Eds.): EKAW 2010, LNAI 6317, pp. 257–271, 2010.

Layar, WikiTude, Mobile DBpedia [4]) or they provide the user with detailed information about a particular aspect of the current location, such as interesting architectural structures to be seen. These applications use two categories of knowledge: general knowledge about geolocations and points of interest (POIs), and/or specialized knowledge about a particular domain. The first category of knowledge is present in the LOD cloud, the second category of knowledge may be available from sources not represented in the LOD cloud. Google Maps (and applications based on Google Maps) particularly show POIs and links to a website on a map, but does not provide related specialized knowledge related to a POI.

In our approach these two types of knowledge are combined: general knowledge about geolocations and points of interest (as represented in GeoNames, Linked-Geodata, Freebase and DBPedia) and specialized knowledge about the cultural heritage domain (Art and Architecture Thesaurus, Union List of Artist Names, Thesaurus of Geographic Names) as well as data from several cultural institutions (Netherlands Institute for Art History and Rijksmuseum Amsterdam).

The challenges that we have to resolve to reach the goal are: to enrich location data by constructing an "enriched local map" of nearby Points of Interest enriched with additional information, such as e.g. events, persons and artworks. Next we find a way to present this information to a user on a mobile device, taking into account the constraints of a mobile device and the limited span of attention of that user. We show three concrete scenarios where a tourist can access localized information on his iPhone about locations, artworks, events and persons.

2 Domain: Tourist Guides and Cultural Heritage

The profession of tourist guide is almost as old as tourism and is defined as: *a person who guides visitors in the language of their choice and interprets the cultural and natural heritage of an area...* [13]. Those who cannot afford a guide, or those who want to explore on their own can make use of guide books, such as provided by the companies: "Lonely Planet" and "Rough Guides". The self-made tourist or the active tourist finds satisfaction in the process of composing his/her own program for the day [5]. Guide books include information about hotels, restaurants, travel, city life (e.g. culture, economy, environment, etc.), arts (literature, theater, music, cinema, etc.), architecture (e.g. building styles), history and walking tours. When actually visiting a foreign place, the active tourist has questions such as: "What do I see?", "How did artists look at this location?", "What is the history?", "What kind of stories are related?", "Which events have taken place?", "Which persons were involved in this place?", "What is my next stop?", etc.

Current smart phone and internet technology has the power of providing answers on these questions in the form of digital tourists guides. A lot of these applications deal with finding locations of interest nearby and guide navigation, e.g. TomTom, Garmin and Navico. Most of these applications rely on own proprietary maps or on public sources such as Google Maps or Open Street Map.

At this moment there are a few mobile applications that make use of the Semantic Web, e.g. DBpedia mobile [4]. However, for enriched storytelling, one needs fast searching mechanism for selecting information and presentation format relevant to the user, based on his/her preferences and the current context [5]. An example is Google Goggles for searching the web, based on pictures from a unified picture library [10], but this application mainly provides names of places of interest, not background information.

The MultimediaN E-Culture project has harvested 200,000 objects from six collections (including Netherlands Institute for Art History and Rijksmuseum Amsterdam) about the cultural heritage of Amsterdam [7]. These collections include digital representations of oil paintings, photographs, artists styles and artists information. These object are annotated with a range of thesauri and proprietary controlled keyword lists adding up to 20 million triples. Several Semantic Web technologies (such as lexical analysis, several conversions, enrichments, alignments) and ontologies (AAT, ULAN, TGN) are applied to convert all this data in to a consistent RDF representation. This is stored in the RDF store of the Semantic Web search engine `ClioPatria` [7]. `ClioPatria` can be accessed via SPARQL and a JSON-REST API. The aim of the current paper is to show how a combination of data from the LOD cloud combined with the E-Culture data can provide interesting, in-depth information about a certain location. A comparable project is SMARTMUSEUM (`http://smartmuseum.eu/`).

3 Concepts: Mobile Tourist Guide

Day trips and walking tours described in printed sources, such as the Lonely Planet and Rough Guides, are rather static. We envision a mobile Tourist Guide application able to dynamically combine navigation, information provision and a form of entertainment: *navitainment*. Based on a geolocation and filtering criteria given by the tourist, the app can constructs a dynamic walking tour [1]. Typical cultural filtering criteria are: architecture, paintings (how are artists inspired by a geolocation), photographs (capturing of historical moments), historical locations, etc. The idea is that the tourist starts with an initial criterion, e.g. paintings and can alter his criterion during the tour.

In order to construct dynamic tour guides, we need semantic annotated geolocations. In order to navigate the tourist we need intuitive ways of representing navigation data. Typically for a overview of POIs we can use a table, where each rows describes the name (e.g. Van Gogh Museum), type (e.g. Museum) and distance (e.g. 350m). To navigate we can use a map, showing the current location of the tourist and the path to the selected POIs, see Fig. 1. For this we have selected facets of cultural heritage objects (location, event, artwork or people) and subfacets (e.g.: painting, photograph, book, artist, musician, politician, sport and conflict). Next we need techniques to present the annotated data, such as background descriptions, representations of paintings, art and photographs.

Fig. 1. Impressions of table, map and augmented reality-based interfaces

4 Approach: from Geolocation to Real-World Annotation

Our approach is composed of a number of steps. Figure 2 shows the task structure implemented in the system. In the first subtask ("harvest locations") we gather data about locations nearby the user's current location. This results in a set of RDF triples about nearby locations. The second step ("merge and align") is to identify sets of triples that describe the same location. The result is a reduced set of unique locations. Next, for each unique location a semantic enrichment task is performed that searches various sources (a.o. the Dutch Wikipedia and the Eculture data cloud) to find additional information such as events, persons, artworks etc associated with the location. Finally each enriched location is classified in terms of the facet hierarchy. The result is a set of RDF statements that can be sent to a mobile device. Below we will describe the four subtasks in more detail.

Besides the Eculture data cloud and an RDF database about Dutch historical buildings, the system uses the ontologies of the Linkedgeodata initiative (LGDV), the ontology of DBpedia and a set of mapping rules. In total the database consists of almost 12M triples. RDF statements from LOD sources,

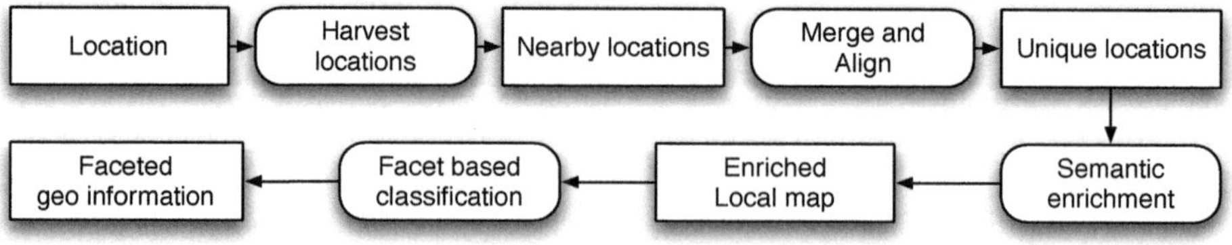

Fig. 2. Task structure

Wikimapia and Wikipedia are retrieved on line using various server API's. This process can be somewhat slow (for the Spui, a square in Amsterdam, the entire process takes some 50 seconds). This is not a big problem when the user sends a request to the server when approaching the location of interest. Furthermore, intermediate results can directly be shown, while processing happends in the background. The performance of the communication between back-end and the iPhone is related to the quality of the Internet connection.

4.1 Harvesting Nearby Locations

Figure 3 shows the reasoning process performed to harvest nearby locations. We start with a geolocation, represented by a point received from a mobile device: $s = \langle lat, long \rangle$ (e.g. $s = \langle 52.3638611, 4.88944 \rangle$ for the Spui square in Amsterdam). Using s, we determine the ontological characterization of the surroundings of the user's current location, such as the features found in geo-knowledgeable LOD repositories such as GeoNames and LinkedGeoData, while using relations such as `owl:sameAs`, `skos:exactMatch` and `skos:closeMatch` properties in the gathered RDF to obtain information about the entire equivalence classes of the nearby features. This includes crawling DBpedia entries. The crawling is done with the space package's `space_crawl_url` predicate [3]. In addition to the data harvested from the LOD sources, we use WikiMapia [1] which not only offers point coordinates, but also polygon and line information about locations such as buildings and streets. Wikimapia also provides links to Wikipedia pages in various languages. These links are followed using the crawling engine.

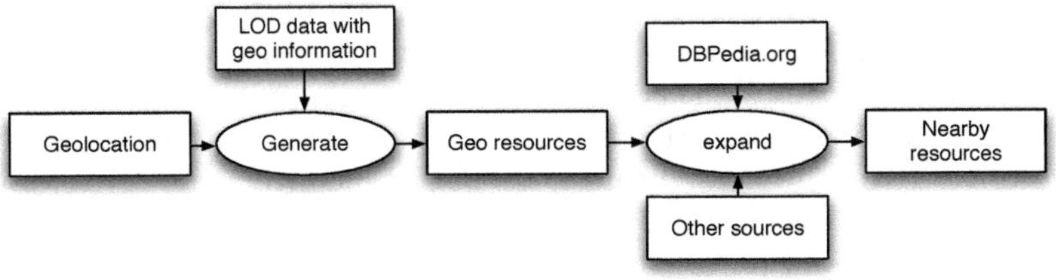

Fig. 3. Method: Harvest Locations

This process results in an RDF database of locations and points of interest near the user with additional information, such as names, descriptions and type. Typical results for a user located at the Spui square in Amsterdam from Linked Geo Data include `Spui25`, `Het Lieverdje`, `Nieuwezijds Voorburgwal`, from DBpedia: `Spui (Amsterdam)`, `Universiteit van Amsterdam`, from GeoNames: `Lutherse Kerk`, `Begijnhof`. In addition quite a few historical buildings are found. For the Spui we find 304 URIs related to that square while searching within a 150 meter radius. These 304 URIs are associated with 2467 RDF triples and 678 geographical shape definitions. Due to the crawling process the system will also find places that are further removed than the search radius. Only 103 URIs (with 973 RDF triples and 264 shape descriptions) represent locations that have an actual distance from the user which is less than 150 meters.

[1] http://wikimapia.org/

4.2 Merge and Align Locations

The URIs that were gathered in the harvesting process by no means correspond to unique locations. Many points of interest have several locations associated with them. In the "Merge and Align" process we try to combine the different results into an "aligned local map", see Fig. 4. This process involves both spatial reasoning and alignment techniques.

Fig. 4. Method: Merge and Align Locations

We encountered typical Semantic Web challenges, such as different schemas, different labeling conventions, different geodata (e.g. square `Spui` in Amsterdam has at least 5 different coordinates in LOD), errors in geodata and in human annotation and conflicts in typing (e.g. `Begijnhof rdf:type way`, `Begijnhof rdf:type area`, and `Begijnhof rdf:type building`).

We developed a number of mapping rules to align the different vocabularies and schema's. First, vocabularies such as Wikimapia tags and Wikipedia categories were mapped onto the LGDV ontology, which was slightly extended with a number of relevant concepts. Second, the LGDV top level concepts were mapped onto the facet ontology. In total some 200 mapping rules were ceated by hand.

The first step in the merging process is to find candidate URIs that could possibly refer to the same physical location. From the list of candidates we select a root URI, preferably one that has a spatial description in the form of a polygon. Using the `space_nearest` predicate in the spatial reasoning package ([3]), we retrieve those URIs that are within a small distance from the URI we are investigating. We have found that the inaccuracy of the geodata requires a range of at least 35 meters in order to find all possible candidates. Subsequently the candidate locations will be matched with the root location in terms of type and name. The type matching requires some ontological mappings since the URIs come from different sources which have different schema's. The name matching requires a normalization of labels, since many sources have conventions to qualify labels with tags like language, city or even more specific qualifications (e.g. "Maagdenhuis", "Maagdenhuis (nl)", "Universiteit van Amsterdam: Maagdenhuis"). Normalizing labels is not a guarantee that different names of the same object will be mapped onto the same location. In our example dataset the URI "http://dbpedia.org/resource/University_of_Amsterdam" falls within the location of the Maagdenhuis (the administrative centre of the University of Amsterdam), but the URI describes the University of Amsterdam in general and name matching fails. In such cases a "skos:relatedTo" relation will be added.

A second step concerns the alignment of resources. When a number of URIs have been identified as pointing to equivalent locations the information of each URI will have to be integrated. A new (unique) URI will be generated with a type that conforms to the LGDV ontology with our own extensions. The new URI will contain provenance information about its sources, the normalized label will be used as new skos:prefLabel, original labels will be used as skos:altLabel and scope notes will be copied from all sources. Integrating the spatial information is a bit more difficult. A set of URIs may have associated points, lines or polygons. Our current alignment algorithm takes the largest polygon that encompasses the most points in the locations and discards points that are outside this preferred polygon. In addition the centroid of the polygon is added as the point coordinates of the location. More sophisticated spatial reasoning could be employed here, for example we could use the fact that crowd-sourced coordinate data may be subject to a discrepancy between a camera location and the actual location of the object being photographed. In addition we could use type and location information to constrain certain location interpretations, e.g. it is unlikely that a pub is located within the administrative centre of a university. The current system does not implement these constraints. The result of this subtask is a set of URIs that represent unique physical locations with their integrated and aligned properties.

4.3 Semantic Enrichment

In this subtask, we start a "semantic crawling" process by using the labels found in the previous subtask as key for several search engine queries.

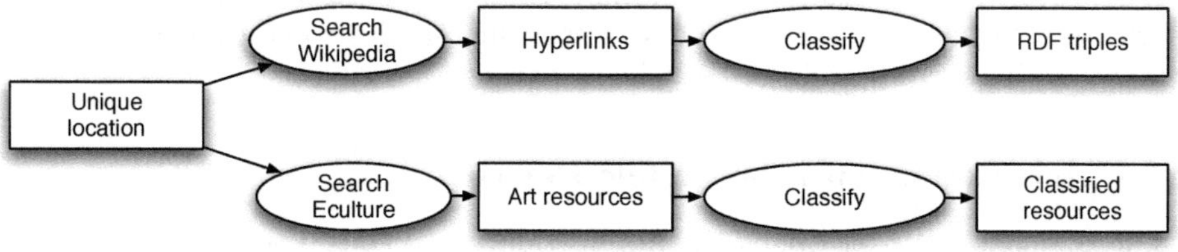

Fig. 5. Method: Semantic Enrichment

Figure 5 shows the reasoning steps that will enrich the data acquired in the previous processes. We use two sources for semantic enrichment: the Dutch Wikipedia server and the ECulture data cloud server. Both servers are queried with keywords derived from the label fields of the locations combined with background knowledge. For example, the label "Het Lieverdje" is converted into a query (`spui+lieverdje`) to the Cliopatria search engine to find artworks relevant to the location.

The results can yield new keywords (such as the name of a person) for further crawling. Where DBpedia does not give any results, Wikipedia pages are retrieved and basic information is extracted from the HTML source, such as geo-coordinates, category information and (href) links to other topics. Since this crawling process can –in principle– continue indefinitely, we put a pragmatic limit to the length of the link paths followed. This limit depends on the facet selection that the user has made, and is usually set to 3.

Data that have been retrieved in the semantic enrichment process are in general not annotated with a type that can be related to the facets. Dutch Wikipedia pages have a category that essentially is a string. We use mapping rules to classify the Wikipedia categories to WordNet classes. For example, the Dutch string "Nederlands architect" (Dutch architect) is mapped to the concept architect in WordNet. The data from the cultural institutions generally use literal terms to describe subjects of art works. Using simple lexical matching and some mapping rules we map the subject terms to WordNet concepts. For example the Dutch word "bezetting" (occupation –of a building–) will be mapped to the WordNet concept `occupation-3`.

4.4 Classification of URIs

The URIs collected in the previous steps come from many different schema's and use different ontologies. For example, for the Spui square the enriched location set of URIs contains 43 different values for the `rdf:type` property (a.o. restaurant, shop, building, church, place_of_worship, university, way, bequinage, market, marketplace). Each of these types has to be classified in terms of the facets and subfacets. Most of these types occur in the (extended) linked geo data ontology (LGDV). The hierarchy of the facets and LGDV are mapped onto each other such that each type maps to a facet-subfacet pair. In addition to location types, the RDF database contains URIs pointing to persons, organisations, artworks, events etc. We use the WordNet hierarchies to construct a mapping between these types and the facet hierarchy.

4.5 Interaction with the Mobile Device

The moment the user opens the application we already know the geolocation. The mobile device can then send a request to the server to create an RDF database, which is subsequently send back. After the mobile device has recieved the RDF triples that were collected at the server, the results have to be presented to the user. From there the user can use three levels of refinement: (1) pointing to a specific heading, where $h = [0..359]$, (2) select facets of resources relevant to the current geolocation and heading, where cultural related facets are location, event, artwork and people, and (3) select subfacets of the selected facet, e.g. painting, photograph, book, artist, musician, politician, sport or conflict.

5 Architecture: A Light Weight Client with a Heavy Endpoint

In order to find an intuitive way to present the enriched data, we apply a number of constraints. We already know a lot about the users: they are mobile, they want to be able to see useful content immediately without too much configuration and they need to be able to accomplish things with just a few taps [9]. Furthermore, a mobile device, such as an iPhone is limited by bandwidth, computing and power capacity. Therefore we need to develop a light weight client for user interaction. The GUI of this device is limited: 7 ± 2 items is about what a smart phone can display and be controlled by Fingertip or stylus-based touching. The 7 Fingertip-Size Targets is similar to the Magical Seven defined by he psychologist George Miller. He stated that human short-term memory has a short-term memory span of approximately seven items plus or minus two [2]. End-user interaction is handled by a mobile device, in our case an iPhone 3GS (with GPS capabilities, a digital compass and assuming an internet subscription).

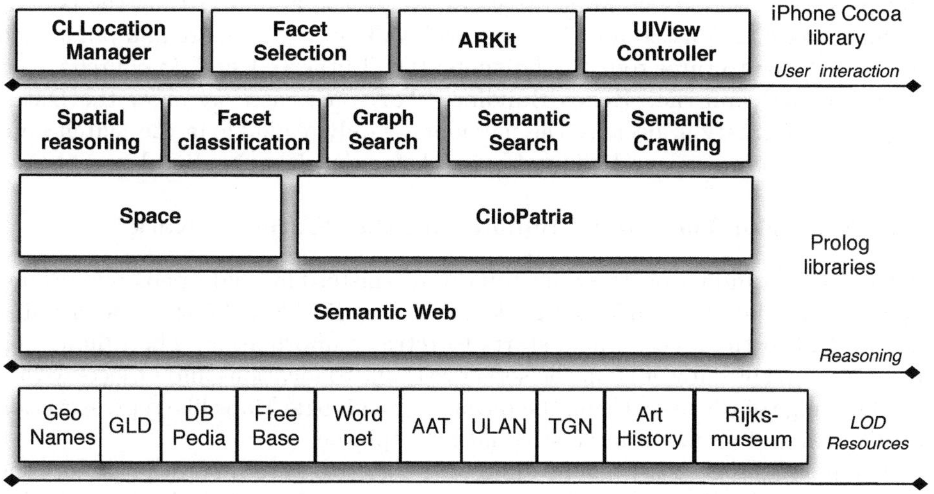

Fig. 6. 3-Tier layer architecture: user interaction on the iPhone, reasoning with Prolog on the Back-end server and LOD resources in the Semantic Web

Most iPhone applications uses the `UIView Controller`: one of the basic packages to display content and handle user interaction. To make an intuitive location selection, we use augmented reality[2], for which we adopted the open source `ARKit` package, which is able to display real world vision via the phone's camera and put labels and controls over this [11].The `CLLocation` package tells the application the geolocation expressed in WGS 84 and heading in degrees [12]. Finally, facet selection show the user two layers of selections: the main facets and subfactes. When choosing a main facet, the sub facets will adapt accordingly, see Figs 7,8 a and b. The iPhone communicates via a REST interface with the back-end server.

[2] A live direct or indirect view of a physical real-world environment whose elements are merged with (or augmented by) virtual computer-generated imagery - creating a mixed reality, see `http://en.wikipedia.org/wiki/Augmented_reality`

We also know a lot about the cultural heritage domain. There are several sources, such as the Dutch Art History resource and Rijksmuseum Amsterdam resource, centrally accessible via `ClioPatria` [7]. Diverse LOD resources are accessible via SPARQL or via our web services which we access with semantic crawling method described in section 4. We used several existing Prolog packages, able to access LOD resources and perform graph search [8,3]. This resulted in a three tier architecture: user interaction, reasoning and LOD resources, see Fig. 6.

6 Use Cases: Displaying POIs

In this section we present three use cases, where the user is visiting the famous "Spui" square in Amsterdam. The user will walk over the square and point with his/her iPhone to three touristic hotspots: the "Lutherse Kerk" (a church), "het Maagdenhuis" and the "Helios Building". For some cases we show the Dutch language information, because the metadata is only available in the Dutch Language. The metadata can be found here: "http://eculture2.cs.vu.nl/spuitest".

6.1 Scenario: The "Spui" Square and the "Lutherse Kerk"

A tourist is standing on the Spui square in Amsterdam and opens our iPhone app. The application sends the geolocation $s = \langle 52.2237, 4.5333\rangle$ and heading $h = 182.23$ to the server which starts to retrieve information. The iPhone app receives an RDF dataset from the server relevant to locations and objects within a 150m range of the user. Using the place facet a Google Maps like representation of the area and points of interest could be displayed.

The next step is to use the heading of the user to determine what object the user's iPhone is directed at. This turns out to be the "Oude Lutherse kerk", a church. Assuming that the user has selected the artwork/painting facet, the system will launch a search request (`spui+lutherse+kerk`) to the ClioPatria engine, which returns a set of pointers to paintings relevant to the place. One of the paintings is selected and additional information about the painting is retrieved. The results are projected on the screen of the iPhone, see Fig. 7.

6.2 Scenario: The "Maagdenhuis" Building

The "Maagdenhuis" was built in 1783 and served as an orphanage for girls until 1953. Since then it is the administrative centre of the University of Amsterdam. In 1969 the "Maagdenhuis" became famous and an icon for student protest: it was occupied 5 days by students demanding influence in university affairs. Since then it has been occupied around ten times. Searching the ECulture engine with the key "maagdenhuis+amsterdam" results in about 100 hits of objects (paintings, ceramics, other types of objects) about this place. When we filter these results on the "event" facet, 5 photographs remain that are part of the

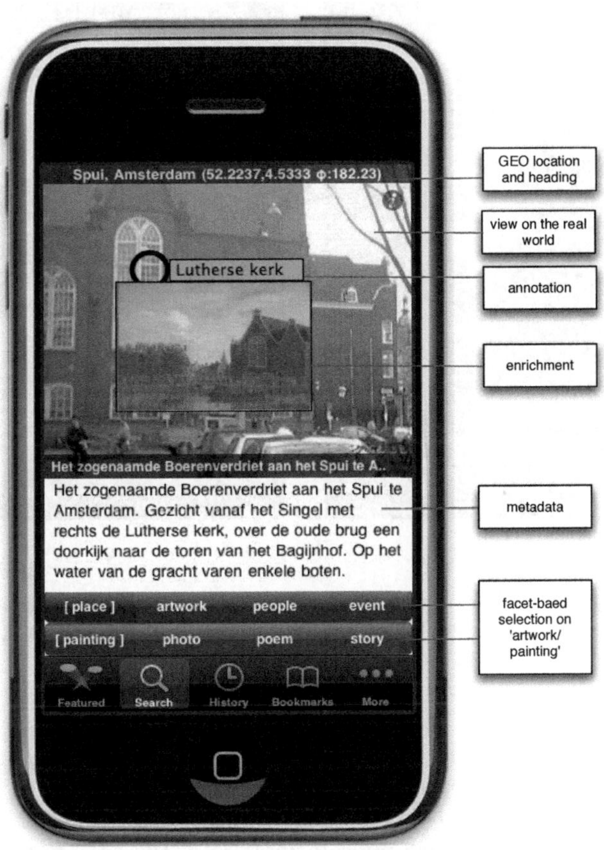

Fig. 7. On the left: Augmented reality view on "Lutherse Kerk" (church) with selection: [artwork/painting], combined with annotation (in Dutch) and the facet-based selection [artwork/painting]. On the right explanation of the components of the GUI

collection of the Amsterdam Historical Museum and depict the student occupation of 1969 (Fig. 8 a).

6.3 Scenario: The "Helios Building"

When the user chooses the selection [people/artist] the system will attempt to find relevant persons, for example architects. In this case, this results in a description of "Gerrit van Arkel", the architect of the famous "Helios Building" at the Spui square (Fig. 8 b). The Helios building and its architect could also have been found on the basis of user coordinates and bearing. Data about this building are also found using the location data and the semantic enrichment process, resulting in the retrieval of the Wikipedia page of "Gerrit van Arkel".

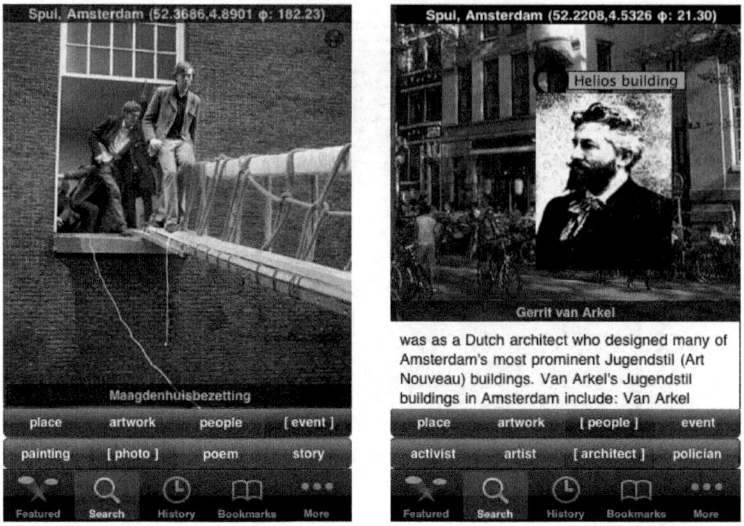

a b

Fig. 8. (a): Photograph of the ending of the Maagdenhuis occupation. (b): Augmented reality view on the "Helios building", showing the architect with selection [people/artist].

7 Discussion

There are countless ways to encode location on the web. There is GML, KML, GeoRSS, the vCard and hCard microformats, etc. We have found that GeoRSS is the most promising of these. Both the Open Geospatial Consortium and the World Wide Web Consortium support GeoRSS and it allows a gradual dumbing down from (partial) GML shape support to simple points (see the Geospatial Vocabulary[3]). The periodically updated World Geodetic System is the only viable coordinate system that works in a uniform way throughout the world. The accuracy might not be sufficient for many indoor augmented reality application, but for outdoor guides like the one presented in this paper it is more than sufficient.We have found that if you want to reason about geospatial concepts, it is important to represent shapes as first-class citizens. This makes conversion between various geospatial formats on the web much easier, as well as allowing you to add support for new types of shapes (e.g. polygons, polygons with holes, geometry collections) in the future if they eventually turn out to be relevant for your project. Also, it is important to draw the boundary between the representation of geospatial and semantic objects at the URI of the geofeature, i.e., e.g. not to represent shapes using RDF triples or `rdfs:subClassOf` relations in GML. This way you can benefit the most from the current standards provided by the OGC and W3C.

[3] `http://www.w3.org/2005/Incubator/geo/`

While using various sources with geo data information we found that significant discrepancies exist between coordinates for the same location. In many cases these discrepancies exceed a distance of 20m, in some cases even hundreds of meters. Our system could be used to identify such discrepancies and point crowd-sourcing users to possible corrections to be made in the open source data.

Table 1. Numbers of URIs and RDF statements for different schema's of the location data for the Spui

Schema	URIs	RDF statements
dbpedia.org	3	153
linkedgeodata.org	21	162
nl.wikipedia.org	6	53
rdf.freebase.com	1	15
rijksmonumenten.wikia.com	227	1619
sws.geonames.org	10	117
wikimapia.org	42	401

Tabel 1 shows the statistics for the location data of the Spui location. The major part of the data comes from non-LOD sources. In addition a significant amount of other data comes from the Eculture sources. Therefore we conclude that the Linked Open Data sources in isolation are currently too limited to provide interesting semantic information but combined with each other and with a number of other sources a really informative location-based service can be created.

Matching the many "synonymous" geofeatures and their types on the web is a challenge for the near future. In both the semantic web and geospatial community this is current research, respectively named ontology alignment or conflation. Another challenge for the future is to provide guided tours through the city-based on the semantics of the surroundings. For example, if you are struck by a building with an interesting style of architecture, it would be great if your mobile device could route you through town along related buildings, telling the story behind their commonality along the way.

8 Conclusions

In this paper we explored the use of location aware mobile devices for acquiring knowledge from, searching and browsing large collections of general and cultural heritage information repositories using minimal interaction. We showed that given a particular geolocation, current Semantic Web data and technology and the constraints of a mobile device, we can find interesting material for an active tourist, providing dynamic information in favor of a classical travel guide.

We presented a novel user interface design, where a combination of location, heading and facet-based filtering provides a user with a dedicated smart phone application. The challenges that we solved in its development are: determining the ontological characterization of the current location, by mapping a geolocation represented by a point to the ontological characterization of that location. We constructed a 'mental map' of nearby points of interest with their direction, by taking a range and finding objects of interest within a circular shape. Next we crawled for other information relevant to these locations, using semantic crawling. It turns out that the interplay of sources from the LOD cloud, WikiPedia and cultural heritage data can provide a very rich knowledge base about a certain topic that is machine processable. Semantic crawling resembles the process of a human using Google to find information, using a cycle of key word selection, inspection of results, interpreting and (possibly generating new queries on the basis of this interpretation. Finally, we use augmented reality in combination with facet selection to present this information to a user on a mobile device.

Next to mobile devices, there are also a number of other common devices that become connected to the Web, such as televisions, cars, and other devices in houses (or domotics). All these devices have a form of limitation, such as a remote control for a television or a dashboard, but also an advantage for determining a user's context, for example watching a certain movie or driving in a certain direction. Semantic crawling can be applied to find background information about movies and actors or locations on the road.

We found that the Linked Open Data sources in isolation are currently too limited to provide much interesting semantic information, but combined with each other and with a number of other sources (for example sources from the cultural heritage domain) a really informative location-based service can be created. Semantic crawling is a major improvement over the current state of the art applications such as Google Maps), which only show labels of resources near a given location, instead of the background knowledge associated with the location. We feel that the power of the Semantic Web concept has clearly been demonstrated in the application we have described. In isolation the currently available repositories provide limited knowledge, but combining a large number of sources and using a semantic crawling approach that accesses many of the Semantic Web services that have become available, yields a reality that is approaching the original Semantic Web vision. In some ways, knowledge acquisition has moved from acquiring knowledge from human experts to the enterprise of acquiring and integrating knowledge from the rich sources of knowledge on the World Wide Web.

Acknowledgments

This work has been partially supported by the EU project NoTube (ICT-231761), the Poseidon project (supported by the Dutch Ministry of Economic Affairs under the BSIK03021 program) and the Agora project (funded by NWO in the CATCH programme, grant 640.004.801).

References

1. Bloem, J., van Aart, C.: On Digital (Mobile) Humanism: helping understand it, engineer its future and ensure its social benefit. In: WebScience 2010 (2010)
2. Miller, G.A.: The magical number seven, plus or minus two: Some limits on our capacity for processing information. Psychological Review 63(2), 81–97 (1956)
3. van Hage, W.R., Wielemaker, J., Schreiber, A.T.: The Space package: Tight Integration Between Space and Semantics. Transactions in Geographical Information Systems 14(20), 131–146 (2010)
4. Becker, C., Bizer, C.: DBpedia Mobile: A Location-Enabled Linked Data Browser. In: Linked Data on the Web, LDOW 2008 (2008)
5. Evjemo, B., Akselsen, S., Schurmann, A.: bTourist Guides Lessons Learnt from Two Field Studies. In: HCI 2007. LNCS, vol. 4550, pp. 746–755. Springer, Heidelberg (2008)
6. Bizer, C., Heath, T., Berners-Lee, T.: Linked Data - The Story So Far. International Journal on Semantic Web and Information Systems, 1–22 (2009)
7. Schreiber, G., Amin, A., Aroyo, L., Van Assem, M., De Boer, V., Hardman, L., Hildebrand, M., Omelayenko, B., Van Osenbruggen, J., Tordai, A., Wielemaker, J., Wielinga, B.: Semantic annotation and search of cultural-heritage collections: The MultimediaN E-Culture demonstrator. Journal of Web Semantics 6, 243–249 (2008)
8. Van Ossenbruggen, J., Amin, A., Hardman, L., Hildebrand, M., van Assem, M., Omelayenko, B., Schreiber, G., Tordai, A., De Boer, V., Wielinga, B., Wielemaker, J., De Niet, M., Taekema, J., Van Orsouw, M., Teesing, A.: Searching and Annotating Virtual Heritage Collections with Semantic-Web Techniques. In: Museums and the Web 2007, April 11-14 (2007)
9. iPhone Human Interface Guidelines, `http://developer.apple.com/iPhone/library/documentation/UserExperience/Conceptual/MobileHIG/Introduction/Introduction.html`
10. Google goggles, `http://www.google.com/mobile/goggles/#landmark`
11. Open source augmented reality package: ARKit, `http://code.google.com/p/iphonearkit`
12. CLLocation Class Reference:incorporates the geographical coordinates and headving of a devices location, `http://developer.apple.com/iphone/library/documentation/CoreLocation/Reference/CLLocation_Class/CLLocation/CLLocation.html`
13. CEN: European Committee for Standardization, `http://www.cen.eu`

Semantic Scout: Making Sense of Organizational Knowledge

Claudio Baldassarre, Enrico Daga, Aldo Gangemi, Alfio Gliozzo,
Alberto Salvati, and Gianluca Troiani

Semantic Technology Laboratory of ISTC (CNR-Italy)

Abstract. Knowledge takes many forms in large organizations, and a unique opportunity exists to perform substantial integration of heterogeneous knowledge through semantic technologies. We present a sustainable method to create and maintain a data cloud that provides added value to an organization, while not interfering with existing practices. Our method shows one of the first application of knowledge-centric data access, following a web 3.0 paradigm. A use case has been implemented in a large research organization, based on explicit requirements. RDF-OWL datasets generated on the basis of a highly modular, pattern-based ontology are created, enriched by means of inferences and NLP techniques, and are integrated with linked open data. They are presented in different interaction modes that embrace important tasks such as navigation and search of organizational knowledge from any point, expert finding, competence matching etc. The tools implemented have been submitted to end-users for a task-based evaluation.

1 Introduction

An information system for organizations is traditionally thought as a mere technical tool for automation and management of administrative activities. In a scenario where semantic technologies are consistently proving that this idea is too restrictive, we want to reinforce the semantic web vision of *aggregative* information systems. We present the *Semantic Scout*, a software framework that offers semantic support to functionalities such as competence finding, social network discovery, etc.

The need for the *Semantic Scout* is motivated by the quest to provide a flexible decision making support within large organization, and in particular to support expert finding and project management. This is a common requirement within any organization with many stakeholders who are required to work in synergy, and to exploit internal resources, before looking for external competences. The hypothesis at the basis of this work is that the use of semantic technology, and in particular semantic search, automatic text categorization, linked data and ontologies, can make that requirement more easily achievable. In principle, the hypothesis is sensible for two reasons: firstly because semantic technology decouples knowledge from implemented systems, so that data can be consumed in ways closer to specific requirements or new scenarios; secondly, because semantic technology explicitly represents the entities of an organization, which gather an own identity: such identity enables simple and effective data aggregation procedures, and nicely matches the way humans *refer* to relevant things in their environment. A conceptual level that is close to human knowledge management is additionally provided by explicit *conceptual schemata* for the data (ontologies) [3].

P. Cimiano and H.S. Pinto (Eds.): EKAW 2010, LNAI 6317, pp. 272–286, 2010.

In general, semantics improves the flexibility and adaptability of the systems, reducing the problems related to legacy and inconsistent data access, while augmenting the overall productivity. For example, the system described in our use case can be adapted to new requirements by simply changing the way the data are accessed, in a fully transparent and system-independent way.

Part of this work builds upon the results presented in [4], where the authors introduce an approach to migrate legacy data, in the domain of a large research institution, to a format that fosters interoperability and re-usability (RDF/OWL). Consistently with [4] we analyze the case of the *Italian National Research Council* (CNR)[1], and capitalize the capability acquired to integrate information from different databases into an OWL knowledge base (KB). At the same time, we redefine the target goal from [4], expanding the request for tools that supports *organizational research management* both for internal needs, and for opening organizational assets and data to the external world. By *asset* we mean humans, departments, research programs, scientific production (publications, patents), dissemination activities, etc. The objectives pursued by this work include:

- to describe a methodology that spans from an easy and rationalized integration of existing information sources in a variety of formats and media, to appropriate ways to consume the new integrated datasets;
- to improve information exchange and retrieval within and outside of an existing organization;
- to develop a powerful cognitive support for strategic decision makers;
- to reinforce collaboration within the organization.

In section 2 we depict the software architecture of our system when applied to the CNR use case, together with an explanation of the main aspects of the methodology to implement the *Scout* framework. The following sections reflect a more detailed presentation of our general methodology as illustrated by Figure 1. Firstly, we identify the data sources and analyze them in order to figure out the proper ontology able to semantically describe their content; this is described in section 3. Then we perform a reengineering process on the data, as described in section 4. The next step is publishing data, texts and ontologies developed so far on the semantic web, by following the linking open data paradigm: this is described in section 5. Once the data have been represented semantically, it is easy to design applications exploiting data according to different requirements. This is described in a section about data consumption 6. Finally we present an evaluation of the *Semantic Scout* (sec. 7), the related works (sec. 8) and the conclusions (sec.9).

2 Methodology and Software Architecture

The CNR organization presents a fairly complex network of information sub-systems (e.g. accounting, personnel-related, scientific projects and publications, administration documentation, etc.) maintained by different parties. Moreover, there are a number of internal services/procedures (e.g. plan management, contracts repository, activity economic balance etc.) that hardly integrate and interoperate. In [4] the authors explain

[1] http://www.cnr.it

a possible way to overcome these limitations, by designing an OWL knowledge base dense with relations among the main concepts of the CNR domain. We introduce here another aspect: the heterogeneity of user groups like administration, researchers, technicians, executives etc. People belonging to any of these job roles require mechanisms for fetching the information that fits their working style and daily tasks.

The analysis of the CNR user contexts led to the formulation of five core functional requirements to be addressed in order to successfully tackle the problem of managing organizational knowledge supported by semantic technologies:

1 - Browsing the network of organizational resources: requires the capability to traverse the entire collection of resources seamlessly crossing different domains (e.g. human resources, research programs, scientific production, dissemination activities etc.)

2 - Expert Finding: requires the capability to materialize, on demand and in one place, the relevant information about who in CNR is involved in some research or technological context. This activity can be assimilated to performing a sub-network extraction from the network of organizational resources (1).

3 - Semantic search of organizational resources: requires the capability to perform a keyword based search, closer to a classical Google-style search, against the resources in the organization KB (1). In other words, the search results for the user consist in *entities whatsoever* rather than documents only.

4 - Enriching the network of relations among the resources: requires the capabilities to discover degrees of similarity among the resources in the organization (e.g. researchers, institutes, competences, research fields), and to instantiate new relations among them. This requirement extends and supports (1) (2) and (3).

5 - Linking the organizational resources to Web resources: requires the capabilities to instantiate relations between entities belonging to the organization, and entities belonging to knowledge bases available on the Web (e.g. DBpedia[2]).

For what we presented so far (i.e. scenario description and user requirements), we can wrap our concerns into two main requests: (i) on the one hand we are required to make data interoperable, and (ii) on the other hand we are required to keep a sufficient level of specialization when designing information access for a wide range of data consumers, human or machine agents. Such an articulated context includes a spectrum of aspects ranging from systems for persistent data storage, to the tools provided to each user group in order to consume the data relevant to their activity. Figure 1 depicts the five types of methods applied to design and implement the Semantic Scout. The methods are described herewith:

Sources: sources to be reengineered include: (i) *legacy databases*, which are reengineered by following mainstream components for schema transformation and ontology population from databases, as well as specialized patterns for schema exception handling (realistic databases are far less clean than in the idealized situation); (ii) *large textual records* within databases, which deserve to be treated differently, e.g. creating specialized ontology entities to represent them: large textual records are

[2] http://www.dbpedia.org

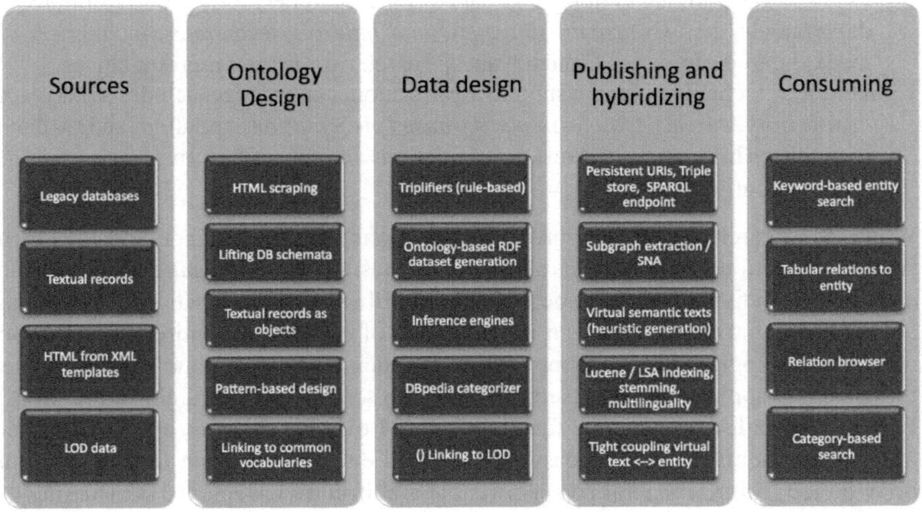

Fig. 1. Semantic Scout Methodology

specially important to build *textual representatives* of the entities, and to facilitate the hybridization of ontology engineering and information retrieval techniques; (iii) *HTML structures* from XML templates, which are a primary source for up-to-date user-oriented views over database data: these are specially useful for ontology design; (iv) *Linked Open Data* [5] from the Web, to be later linked to organizational ontologies and data.

Ontology Design: the methods used for ontology design include: (i) *HTML scraping* in order to derive user-oriented views over data and schemata; (ii) *DB schema lifting* in order to generate the backbone ontology for DB data; (iii) *textual records boosting* in order to create textual objects that will be linked to organizational entities, and used to perform semantic search; (iv) *pattern-based design* in order to create a modular ontology that fits the modelling requirements requirements, e.g. coming from the scraped HTML templates; (v) *linking to common vocabularies* in order to make the organizational ontology interoperable with external ontologies.

Data Design: methods used for data design include: (i) rule-based *rdf-izers* to convert legacy data to RDF, according to the OWL ontology patterns and modules created during ontology design; (ii) *inference engines* such as DL classifiers, rule and SPARQL engines, etc. in order to generate novel RDF triples; (iii) a *text categorizer* to create associations between (the textual representatives of) organizational entities and topics, e.g. DBPedia categories; (iv) *linked data matchers* to link organizational data to linked open data at the data level.

Data Publishing: techniques for publishing and hybridizing data include: (i) *URI schemes, triple stores, SPARQL endpoints* to maintain semantic datasets; (ii) *subgraph extraction and social network analysis* in order to provide synthetic views over the semantic graph induced by the linked RDF-OWL datasets; (iii) *heuristical generation of textual representatives* in order to maintain a textual counterpart to key organizational entities, e.g. papers for researchers, official descriptions for departments, etc.; (iv) *(multi-)linguistic and indexing techniques*, including LSA indexing, to perform basic and advanced search over textual representatives.

Consuming: technology for consuming organizational knowledge includes: (i) *keyword-based entity search*; (ii) *table- or matrix-based presentation* of relations and attributes of entities; (iii) *graphical browsing* of relations among entities; (iv) *category-based search* of entities.

While the research aspects in figure1 give directions along the methodological dimensions, the functional requirements also drive the design of the *Semantic Scout* software architecture. In figure 2 we have depicted the distribution of the functional components among the architectural layers: an infrastructure of components entirely based on semantic technologies, where we move from the idea of a single data source designed for one client application, as presented in [4], to a service oriented architecture (SOA). Web services allow to integrate functionalities of existing systems, and to build new lightweight clients that enable easy fetching and data consumption from a same underlying KB. From a general perspective, the architecture is deployed considering the three logical layers typically used by any application to organize the functional components of the system: data layer, engineering layer and UI layer. This distinction reflects a good practice in software engineering following the actual trend in semantic web applications [6].

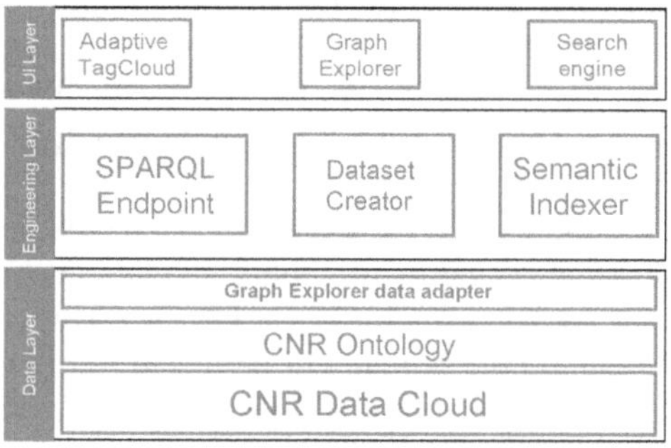

Fig. 2. Architecture

Next sections from 3 to 6 reflect the organization of methods given in figure1, and contain the description of how we achieved the realization of the functional components in Fig. 2.

3 Sources

Although during the analysis of the organization information systems we have run through different ways to expose data, from Internet web portals, to text based documents, the original sources of these data mostly reside in database structures. The databases are hosted in a distributed fashion, inside the departments to which their maintenance is assigned. The domains that they cover are categorized as:

Organizational: Departments and Institutes inner structure information; Basic activities, Laboratories, Research Units, and International activities. In this set there are also International projects and Partnerships description, for example Spin-offs. This set of repositories belong to the intranet application for structures data management (called "Gestione Istituti", "Gestione Dipartimenti");

Research activities: Institutional research projects and products of research (e.g. journal articles, papers, books, patents etc.). This set of repositories belong to the application for managing the research plans ("Piano di gestione preliminare"), research results ("Consuntivi") and of the research activities ("GeCo - Gestione Commesse").

Administration Contracts, and Statistics; this set of repository belong to the administration management systems.

People: Employeers, Researchers, Technologists, Administratives; Collaborators, and Consultants. This set of repositories belong to the Employeer's management system.

Textual descriptions: Missions of departments, project descriptions, CVs, competence resumes, patent abstracts, publication abstracts.

Not all the data contained in these repositories are relevant to the objectives of producing an integrated organizational management system, hence we need data preparation to produce table views to be further queried. The consistent adoption of the same technology for the databases allowed to extract the data adopting template-based scripts using SQL language. On the other hand, the semantic interpretation of extracted data relies on the analysis of the existing interaction patterns by which the users access and consume the data (e.g. forms in the web portal); this is detailed in section about ontology desing.

4 Ontology Design

The first component of our system performs the reengineering of CNR databases containing administrative and financial data, research organization data, project, publication, and personal data. This component implements the ontology layer of the architecture (Fig. 2).

The reengineering process consists of four major steps: schema reengineering, script-based extraction, dataset generation, and KB evolution. A parallel enrichment process consists of: (1) inference-based dataset generation; (2) datasets created out of NLP-based extraction of implicit associations, and (3) datasets created from semi-automatic linking to Linked Open Data datasets.

A crucial phase in porting databases to semantic datasets is the extraction of the schema. Although several automated procedures exist to transform database schemas to ontologies, the results are usually quite poor when applied to databases that have been evolving for years in large organizations. The reasons for that low quality include the independent evolution of the physical schema of the database with respect to the conceptual schema used at design time, and the "pragmatic" tuning operated on the physical schema in order to solve local issues emerging during the use of the database. In order to overcome this problem, some methods (e.g. [2] propose to "embed" ad-hoc queries to databases into annotations to the elements of an ontology.

While in a distributed context such ontology can be provided for particular tasks, or even on-the-fly, in case of a single organization like CNR, it is advisable to attempt the construction of a shared ontology. However, since the physical schemas of CNR databases are degraded, we have applied a method for *requirement-based ontology design* that focuses on the actual user consumption of the databases.

In the case of CNR, user consumption is currently ensured by means of HTML pages that are generated on-the-fly by running dedicated scripts on the databases, and by filling 61 dedicated HTML templates with the extracted data. Those scripts play the same role as the embedded queries to databases, and can therefore be reused for porting databases to semantic datasets.

Pattern-based ontology design [7] tries to define the boundaries of an ontology on the basis of explicit requirements provided by users or extracted from reference resources. Requirements are normalized and used as *competency questions*, and an ontology "pattern" is built for each competency question, and has been used as a module of the CNR ontology. In the case of CNR, each HTML template has been considered as a requirement.

HTML templates are structurally and conceptually similar to microformats, consequently, for each HTML template, we have tried to encode a module of the CNR ontology. As usual in realistic projects, the requirements have been massaged in order to obtain a modularization that complies to dependency issues:

- When a strong mutual dependency between two templates has been found (e.g. *departments* and *subdivision in programmes*), we have considered the union of them as a unique requirement
- When a template depends on another (e.g. *research lines* on *programmes*), we have considered the first as a specialization of the second
- When concepts are very general and occur sparsely in several templates (e.g. *localizations*, *subdivisions*, *categories*, etc.), they have been put into "upper" modules that are imported by most of the other modules

The final result is a network of OWL(DL) ontologies, currently consisting of 28 modules, partially ordered in an `owl:import` graph. The whole network includes 120 classes, 162 object properties, 134 datatype properties, 309 restrictions, 543 taxonomic axioms.[3]

5 Data Publishing and Hybridizing

Two rationales have guided the dataset creation according to the approach explained in 4:

1. Each dataset must be focused on collecting the instantiation of a single OWL property (i.e. obtaining an property-centric dataset);
2. A network of datasets is preferred to a monolithic collection of data materialized in a single file.

[3] http://www.ontologydesignpatterns.org/ont/cnr/cnr.owl

After the first rationale, we have generated more then 200 RDF datasets, each of them instantiating the value for a single property. All the collections have been made persistent in files with conventional names, so that the path to an RDF file is composed of a static base address *http://www.cnr.it/rdfgen/*; the prefix of the namespace of the property; the name of the property:

```
Path: base/ns-prefix/property-name.rdf
Ex: owl:ObjectProperty -> commesse:modulo,
Path to the RDF file: http://www.cnr.it/rdfgen/commesse/modulo.rdf
```

With the second rationale, we have generated we have a network of RDF datasets, using the `owl:imports` mechanism. A file containing a "bottom" ontology includes the import closure over the 200 datasets.

This approach has several benefits. First, the granularity of the extraction makes the work easier for debugging and testing w.r.t. to the original data schemas. Additionally, it is easy to manage user access policies, which can have several levels of privacy and sensitivity.

The property-centric organization of datasets support also the lifecycle of reengineered data because it is easier to identify smaller clusters of data to synch, than running the script mechanism on the entire data set, even when we know that a value for the properties is not going to change.

6 Consuming Data

The set of functional components, together with the CNR data cloud, and the CNR ontology, are used as the *toolkit* for the Semantic Scout. This section is dedicated to *unfolding* each tool and to explain how and why they fit into the kit. In addition, we present the use cases where they are daily used by CNR people.

The Semantic Scout infrastructure includes an information retrieval engine. As described in section 2, starting from a known interaction pattern is beneficial to the users. Figure 3 shows the result page for the query:

```
{ ethics, sociology, collaboration, social network, reputation }.
```

Traditional information retrieval is performed on, and retrieves, only information objects, typically documents. The variety of semantic search performed by the Scout is still performed on documents, but retrieves *entities*.

Internally, the search engine (traditionally) indexes selected texts, which are however *textual representatives* of entities, generated at data design time by means of regular SPARQL CONSTRUCT queries over the heuristically relevant text data from datatype values in the RDF datasets (for example, publication titles and abstracts for persons). Heuristics is based on context, task, and available data.

This search design pattern is based on a semiotic assumption: each entity can have a typical, although context-dependent, textual representation.

The search engine is able to index both Italian and English text, and implements two types of search, Basic (i.e. keyword based) or Latent (i.e. based on statistical methods to

Fig. 3. CNR Semantic Scout - Search Engine

represent texts into a cluster based representation similar to Latent Semantic Indexing). The user has the possibility to choose the desired modality of search before performing the query. In order to implement the multilingual search, we have used two different stemming algorithms for different languages (implemented by the Snowball Analyzer embedded in the standard distribution of Lucene). Latent search is based on Semantic Vectors[4].

In other words, the semantic search design pattern adopted by the Scout tightly couples information retrieval technology for basic search, and ontology design plus linked data to data management, reasoning, and actual consumption of data.

An additional functionality enables the Scout to enrich the emergent semantic social network of CNR with topics, and to link CNR data to DBpedia [1].

We categorize entities with topics by using a (novel, yet unpublished) text categorization system whose goal is to link documents to categories selected from the more than 500,000 categories present in DBPedia, which then provide a rich set of distinctions for the scientific subjects of interest in the CNR case study. The output of the categorizer has been represented in RDF by using the `subject` relation from the SKOS vocabulary, e.g.:

```
<> <http://www.w3.org/2004/02/skos/core#subject>

   <http://dbpedia.org/resource/Category:Knowledge_representation> .

<> <http://www.w3.org/2004/02/skos/core#subject>

   <http://dbpedia.org/resource/Category:Artificial_intelligence> .
```

The categorization data generated so far have been loaded in a dedicated dataset, and used to enrich the knowledge base. This is an example of the application of statistical techniques to enrich the knowledge base. In section 6.1 we show the usefulness of the categorization data for expert finding and semantic browsing of data. The *Semantic Scout* networks the entities of an organization, besides content objects. It is crucial that this approach is backed by tools that can support a proper presentation, and can

[4] `http://code.google.com/p/semanticvectors/`

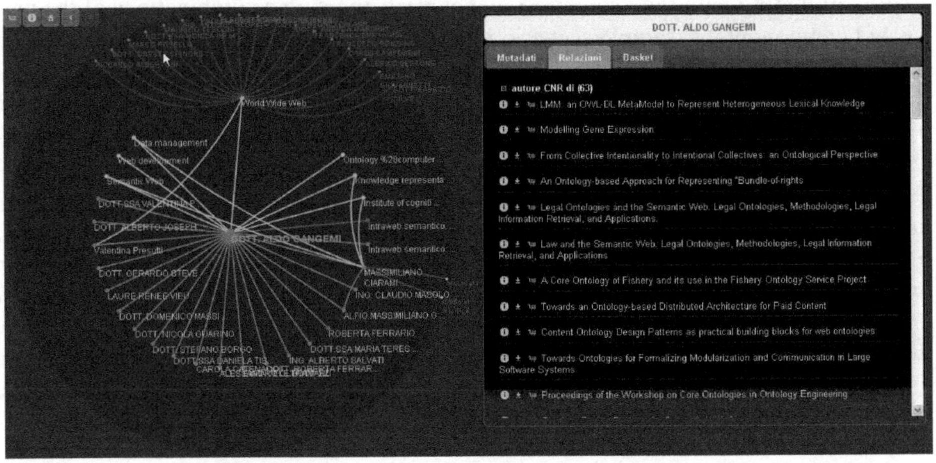

Fig. 4. CNR Semantic Scout - Graph Explorer

be coherent with the idea of linked data. The *Graph Explorer* (figure 4) is our choice for the prototype to effectively tackle the presentation of, and the interaction with, the datasets for our targeted user groups. Suppose a user looks for CNR researchers that have competence in the topic *Semantic Web*. A search can be performed with different sets of keywords, but once entities are shown, a user can browse the rich knowledge e.g. in terms of relations between researchers and departments, other researchers, topics, publications, etc. This allows a deeper understanding of who is doing what, explaining how a researcher is involved in the Semantic Web. In addition, it allows us to find additional associated information. Most likely, this information will be very relevant to the user. Figure 4 shows an example of the *Graph Explorer*, with the focused node describing the researcher Aldo Gangemi connected to other researchers, the projects he is/was involved in, research topics, and belonging research institute. A panel on the right gives a description of the focused node.

We stress the idea of exploring, as opposed to searching, since the former leads to targeted resources along multiple paths, which could be previously unknown to the user; this is emphasized by the graph based representation.

6.1 Expert Finding

Research on expert finding is typically performed on curated data or massive social web data. Our lightweight approach is based on the ability to materialize on demand, and in one place, the relevant information about who in CNR is involved in some academic or technological context. In [4] we explained how to enrich an initial set of relations between researchers, publications, workplaces, conferences, etc. to a much denser set of linking properties. The application of the hybridization processes explained in section 4 is intended to delegate almost most of the complexity of data matching, typical of a process of expert finding, to a reasoning procedure made at design time over the CNR datasets.

Expert finding with the *Semantic Scout* consists in using a combinations of the presented components. A sample scenario includes Carmelo Russo, a project manager in one of the CNR institutes, who is involved in a project on Social Knowledge for e-Governance. Carmelo has been introduced to the problems affecting the area and that the project is expected to solve: "*Reputation is a social knowledge, on which a number of social decisions are accomplished. Regulating society from the morning of mankind becomes more crucial with the pace of development of ICT technologies, dramatically enlarging the range of interaction and generating new types of aggregation. Despite its critical role, reputation generation, transmission and use are unclear. The project aims to an interdisciplinary theory of reputation and to modeling the interplay between direct evaluations and meta-evaluations in three types of decisions, epistemic (whether to form a given evaluation), strategic (whether and how interact with target), and memetic (whether and which evaluation to transmit).*"

Carmelo has been asked to acquire more information about possible researchers, consultants, showcase technologies, and publications related to the project topics.

Identifying the Main Topics of Research. Carmelo needs to focus his attention on a few research topics, and to use them as entry points in the network of resources of CNR. Analyzing the text from the the scenario description, an initial step consists in finding out what categories, e.g. from DBpedia, the project scenario can be associated with. Carmelo submits the text from the description to the *Text Categorizer*, and automatically finds the following main topics: *Ethics, Sociology, Collaboration, Social network, Reputation.*

Searching the CNR Network of Resources. The extracted topics are representative key-terms of the problem description; they can be used to trigger a search in the CNR datasets by using the *Semantic Scout* search engine (see sec.6). Carmelo needs to find people involved in any of the areas named by topics, and preferably people who have experience of past collaborations directly (e.g. working on the same activity), or indirectly (e.g. publishing on the same research subject), and might belong to the same group (e.g. same department, institute). He can then trigger a search with input keys: { `Ethics, Sociology, Collaboration, Social network, Reputation` }, which returns a number of results faceted by **Persone**[5](e.g. researchers, consultants, directors), **Attività**[6] (e.g. projects, workpackages, tasks), and **Strutture CNR**[7]. The faceting of results increases Carmelo's capability to select the scope of the results, and to set the entry points to browse the CNR network of resources, as explained in the next section.

In order to respond to a request for building a team of experts on the topics identified in 6.1, Carmelo needs to explore who, among CNR staff members, and how, is networked through them. The *Graph Explorer* exposes a network not just among people, but among the whole set of organizational assets. Since Carmelo is not familiar with any of the names listed in the **Persona** facet, or in the **Strutture CNR** one, he decides to enter the graph of CNR resources from the **Attività** facet, and chooses the item *Il Circuito dell'Integrazione: Mente, Relazioni e Reti Sociali. Simulazione Sociale e Strumenti di Governance* that looks relevant to his search.

[5] People.

[6] Activities.

[7] CNR administrative units.

Figure 4 depicts the graph of connections among the activity (central node) selected by Mario, and other CNR resources. Dr. Rosaria Conte holds a relation with the activity to be its key person (i.e. responsible). When the node of Dr. Rosaria Conte is selected to the center, her social network of co-authors is revealed. Starting from the network of names, Carmelo goes back to the **Persona** facet, to investigate those who have a higher score against the search performed in 6.1; the exploration makes it emerge the following list:

```
KEY PEOPLE (ranked): Dr. Rosaria Conte, Ing. Jordi Sabater,
Dott. Mario Paolucci, Samuele Marmo, Daniele Denaro,
Gennaro Di Tosto, Walter Quattrociocchi,
Francesca Giardini, Dott. Paolo Landri.
```

Checking the Quality of Results. The people selected during the previous step have been found relevant to the keyword based search, and connected to a key person (Dr. Rosaria Conte), because she's their co-author in some publication; we expect that all of them share some research topic, and that they match the keywords used in the search. When opening the tabular views about each person (see 5), it is possible to read the subject of research associated with them; in the following we report some:

```
Ing. Jordi Sabater: Cognitive Science;
Dott. Mario Paolucci: Sociology, Psichology;
Gennaro di Tosto: Artificial Intelligence;
Walter Quattrocchi: Interdisciplinary Fields;
```

Most of those people cover research areas that are relevant to the search. On the other hand, some of the topics/keywords from the search remain uncovered. The same process from searching to quality checking is performed using only those topics/keyword found uncovered; the results found are:

```
Giuseppe Castaldi: Ethics;
Aldo Gangemi: Semantic Web, Knowledge representation.
```

By combining a few tools, Carmelo has been capable to collect information about researches and research leaders. A set of relevant publications is also available through the results in the **Attività** facet.

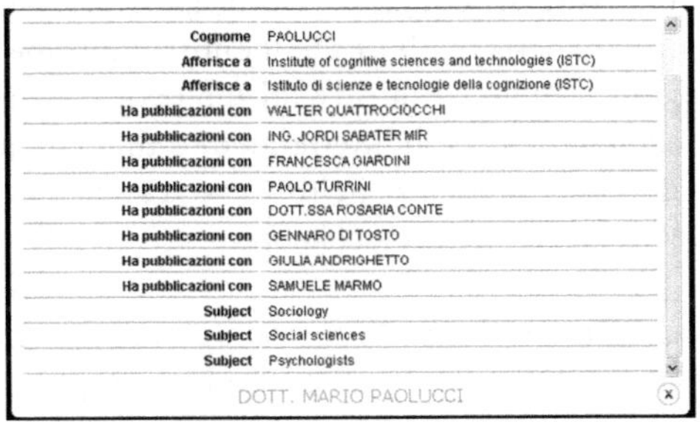

Cognome	PAOLUCCI
Afferisce a	Institute of cognitive sciences and technologies (ISTC)
Afferisce a	Istituto di scienze e tecnologie della cognizione (ISTC)
Ha pubblicazioni con	WALTER QUATTROCIOCCHI
Ha pubblicazioni con	ING. JORDI SABATER MIR
Ha pubblicazioni con	FRANCESCA GIARDINI
Ha pubblicazioni con	PAOLO TURRINI
Ha pubblicazioni con	DOTT.SSA ROSARIA CONTE
Ha pubblicazioni con	GENNARO DI TOSTO
Ha pubblicazioni con	GIULIA ANDRIGHETTO
Ha pubblicazioni con	SAMUELE MARMO
Subject	Sociology
Subject	Social sciences
Subject	Psychologists

DOTT. MARIO PAOLUCCI

Fig. 5. Tabular view of data about CNR staff member Dr. Mario Paolucci

7 Functional Evaluation

The scenario exemplified in section 6.1 is in fact an existing project named "eRep" ended in March 2009, and whose web portal is available on line[8]. In the eRep project researchers of CNR have been active. We decided to adopt the description of a real case, in order to have a golden standard to compare the results when testing the *Semantic Scout*. This test was performed without an a-priori knowledge of the team from CNR involved in the eRep project, in order to avoid any kind of bias.

The CNR staff members involved in eRep are listed online[9], and out of 10 CNR researchers, we could match 6 people, among which the project coordinator (Dott. Mario Paolucci), plus a project member affiliated with another institution (Jordi Sabater Mir).

In the following, we analyze the aspects that we consider positively qualifying the *Semantic Scout*, and the reasons for missed matching of the remaining people in the list.

Accuracy: All the retrieved people scored among the first 10 in the result from the search engine; we remind that the search was performed with keywords considered topics relevant to the scenario/project description. Their relevance was proved when the same names where found to be part of the social network of Dr. Rosaria Conte, the leader of an activity considered of interest for Carmelo Russo, and returned among the results of the search.

Benefit of integrated data cloud: The entry point to the network of CNR resources has been an activity considered of interest for Carmelo Russo, and returned among the results of the search. In fact, reading the title of the activity triggered a cognitive process of spotting out similarity with the scope and aims of eRep project. This kind of workflow is made available thanks to the information hybridized in the CNR network of resources, as explained in section 4.

Accessibility and Interaction: Carmelo Russo was able to quickly identifying all the key people, by investigating the social network of Dr. Rosaria Conte through the Graph Explorer. The expert finding with the *Semantic Scout* starts with a keyword based search 6.1, and continues by navigating the faceted results, and the data cloud of CNR generated by integrating the distributed data sources 3. The access to this network of resources is critical to the success of our approach in making sense of organizational knowledge. The Graph Explorer provides here the support for a good level of accessibility and interaction with the data network.

Completeness: The first search retrieved CNR member staff whose field of application was only partially covering the topics/keywords used as input. Carmelo Russo task was to build a team of experts in all of the identified disciplines, without knowing he already acquired the names of mostly all the people involved in eRep project. Since CNR staff members are explicitly related to their subject topics, it has been easy to determine the complementary fields to be searched in order to complete the expertise set needed to cover the project scope.

Reasons for Unmatched Researchers. When comparing the result of the expert finding with the list of CNR members who participated in eRep, we have discovered that

[8] http://bit.ly/8mOr7Z

[9] http://megatron.iiia.csic.es/eRep/?q=node/36

four people have not been included in our result set. One of them (Antonietta Di Salvatore) scored below the first 10 people in the list; the other three are Giulia Andrighetto, Marco Capenni, and Stefano Picascia. Giulia Andrighetto is not listed among the people relevant to the query, but belongs to the social network of Dr. Rosaria Conte. Both Marco Capenni and Stefano Picascia are known to our system, but they are neither reported among the people relevant to the search query, nor belong to the network of any of the other researchers. The reason is that they do not share any publications with them, most probably because they have a technician profile. We can safely conclude that the key players in a "dream team" for Carmelo Russo have been found by the Semantic Scout.

8 Related Work

Although this work is not meant to compete with existing corporate knowledge management systems, either distributed or integrated, we notice that all of the technologies we mentioned exist as isolated technological examples, and none of them is intended to cover the same class of problems we are interested in; similarly, the motivations and the objectives underlying those works are different from ours. We intended to prove that it is possible to employ off-the-shelf semantic components, and with a little integration effort, to obtain a nice prototypical toolkit for exploring the information assets of a big organization. It is anyhow worth mentioning that if possible competitors are not present in the open software world, there is a commercial framework called Vivisimo[10] that features a job assistant called *Mr. Stan*. *Mr. Stan* has functionalities similar to what we propose here. We have discovered this only recently. A closer look to *Mr. Stan* assistant shows that in fact it is not empowered with any semantic technologies, which does not make it a direct competitor to our approach. Moreover it has no sign of being a distributed system accessible via services and different kinds of clients.

9 Conclusions and Future Work

We have presented the practices, methods, and implemented components of a framework for integrating existing data and user requirements with semantic technologies in a large organization. The use case is provided by the largest Italian research organization, CNR. Pattern-based ontology engineering and linked open data methods seem to be adequate to generate added value knowledge, simple decoupling of data gathering and consumption layers, and openness to data external to an organization. Among the critical issues, we mention privacy and provenance aspects, which are typically interlaced with internal practices and hierarchical responsibilities in an organization. Those complex interrelations are being studied for the linked open data initiative, where they prove to be non-trivial. On the other hand, within the intraweb of an organization, the same policies that apply to legacy data can be taken as received practices. Nonetheless, the increased dynamics and openness of organizational data pose specific problems, which will be extremely interesting to monitor in the next future, in the context of the

[10] http://vivisimo.com/

NetwOrK project, sponsored by the CNR technology transfer office in order to increase the links between the CNR scientific network, and the industrial or business networks outside of it. Future work has two main objectives; evaluating in detail the user and functional tests, and enriching the number of components that can satisfy requirements such as: (i) social refinement of the CNR datasets through semantic wikis or content management systems, and social bookmarking, (ii) enriching the CNR datasets with new relations inferred from linking to other external data, and finally (ii) extending the capability of matching offer and public request for CNR competences.

Acknowledgements

This work has been supported by the CNR program *Semantic IntraWeb*, the *Semantic Scouting* project funded by the CNR Technology Transfer Office, as well as by the EU projects *NeOn*, funded within the 6th Framework Programme, and *IKS*, funded within the 7th FP.

References

1. Bizer, C., Lehmann, J., Kobilarov, G., Auer, S., Becker, C., Cyganiak, R., Hellmann, S.: DBpedia – A Crystallization Point for the Web of Data. Journal of Web Semantics 7, 154–165 (2009)
2. Calvanese, D., De Giacomo, G., Lembo, D., Lenzerini, M., Poggi, A., Rosati, R., Ruzzi, M.: Data integration through dl-lite ontologies. In: Schewe, K.-D., Thalheim, B. (eds.) SDKB 2008. LNCS, vol. 4925, pp. 26–47. Springer, Heidelberg (2008)
3. Gangemi, A., Presutti, V.: Ontology design for interaction in a reasonable enterprise. In: Rittgen, P. (ed.) Handbook of Ontologies for Business Interaction. IGI Global, Hershey (November 2007)
4. Gliozzo, A., Gangemi, A., Presutti, V., Cardillo, E., Daga, E., Salvati, A., Troiani, G.: A Collaborative Semantic Web Layer to Enhance Legacy Systems. In: Aberer, K., Choi, K.-S., Noy, N., Allemang, D., Lee, K.-I., Nixon, L.J.B., Golbeck, J., Mika, P., Maynard, D., Mizoguchi, R., Schreiber, G., Cudré-Mauroux, P. (eds.) ASWC 2007 and ISWC 2007. LNCS, vol. 4825, pp. 764–777. Springer, Heidelberg (2007)
5. Hausenblas, M.: Exploiting linked data for building web applications (2009), `http://sw-app.org/pub/exploit-lod-webapps-IEEEIC-preprint.pdf` (Stand 12.5.2009)
6. Heitmann, B., Hayes, C., Oren, E.: Towards a reference architecture for SemanticWeb applications. In: Proceedings of the 1st International Web Science Conference (2009)
7. Presutti, V., Gangemi, A.: Content Ontology Design Patterns as Practical Building Blocks for Web Ontologies. In: Li, Q., Spaccapietra, S., Yu, E., Olivé, A. (eds.) ER 2008. LNCS, vol. 5231, pp. 128–141. Springer, Heidelberg (2008)

Authoring Technical Documents for Effective Retrieval

Jonathan Butters and Fabio Ciravegna

Department of Computer Science, University of Sheffield, Regent Court,
211 Portobello Street, S1 4DP, Sheffield, UK
{j.butters,f.ciravegna}@dcs.shef.ac.uk

Abstract. In this paper we outline the design considerations and application of a methodology to author technical documents in order to improve retrieval. Our approach is firmly aimed at large organizations where variations in terminology at personal, national and international scales often impede retrieval of relevant knowledge. We first present the difficulties in performing entity extraction in technical domains and the role variation in terminology has in the information extraction task before outlining and evaluating a methodology that allows for effective retrieval.

1 Introduction

Effective Knowledge Management (KM) within large organizations relies on the capability to *capture*, *locate* and *exchange* relevant knowledge in a *timely* manner, howeverknowledge work is often a time consuming and expensive process [1], to draw conclusions from corpora requires the ability to accurately identifyrelevant knowledge within documents. To facilitate this, knowledge workers 1) *formulate* a search query– not necessarily using their own terms 2) *retrieve* relevant documents – in accordance with some metric, 3) *assimilate*information– assuming that their comprehension matches the document author's intentions, and 4)*assess* whether the knowledge is relevant to their situation – classify the document.

At each of these stages errors are introduced;systemsonly retrieve documents that contain the query string, real-world document recall is never 100%, comprehension of the document requires recognition of the concepts referred to by heterogeneous terms, and the degree of relevancy requires the identification of complex relations between entities. Large organizations are prone to the effects of *sublanguage* [2], where different groups of people use different subsets of language. In addition to this as people in technical domains are confronted with a large number of *specifications* (such as convergence towards a terminological standard based on geographical locatione.g. *'hpcstage 5 shaft'*Vs.*'l5drum, mod 31'*) and *standards* (including S1000D/ATA Spec 100/internal naming conventions e.g. *'72-31-53'* Vs. *'FK12345'* Vs *'HP Compressor stage 5 disc'*). The large number of valid terms, along with the inevitable list of distortions and variations (word order, misspellings, morphological variations, e.t.c.) that ariseduringtheir use (Table 1) mean thatterms vary both within and across documents and corpora.This further compounds the information retrieval task, as in order to increase recall, queries must be expanded to include a multitude of synonyms that may or may not exist within documents.

P. Cimiano and H.S. Pinto (Eds.): EKAW 2010, LNAI 6317, pp. 287–300, 2010.

Table 1. Examples of typical term variation for an *'LP2Turbine Blade'* concept

"Low Pressure Turbine Stage 2 Rotor Blade" *"LP2 Blade"* *"FK42164"* *"LPT 2 Blade"* *"72-41-12"* *"T800 LP Turbine Blade Stage 2"* *"Turbine Blade"* *"72-41-12-400"* *"Blade, Turb l2"* *"Blade, LPT"* *"TurbinneBladee"* *"FK12548"*	

By accurately capturing information and relations at the point of data creation, knowledge can be accessed more precisely and be comprehended in the manner the author intended.

The most precise method of capturing data at the point of creation involves the annotation of entities and their relations by domain experts, this is a complex and expensive [3], low recall operation [4] and when performed manually proves to be a bottleneck [5]. Methods that support the user through the annotation processreduce the time taken to annotate documents [6] and can be adapted to new domains (adaptive IE systems [7]) but are limited by their capability to extract named entities (perform NER). Extraction based on shallow NLP methods [8] may not be directly applicable due to the *deviant grammars*sublanguagesfrequently used[2], and also as many entities can appear with little context or no context at all (as a search keyword or within a sparse table for example). The current trend for automatic Named Entity and Relation Extraction in *open world* domains make use of lexical resources such as WordNet [9], Wikipedia [10, 11, 12, 13] and Google [14]. These resources are less practical in more technical and restricted domains such as *Aerospace*, *Biomedical* and *Automotive*where coverage is sparse. It is for these reasons that, Named Entity and Relation Extraction efforts in restricted technical domains tend to involve supervised [15,16] or semi-supervised [17] machine learning techniques coupled with bootstrapping algorithms [18] where manually extracted entities are used as seeds in order to learn generalized extraction rules which in turn identify further seeds. These approaches are significantly affected by the annotation bottleneck and variationsin terminology; the annotation bottleneck governs the number (and quality) of annotated documents where-asvariations in terminology reduce the number of examples per class and negatively affects the benefits of bootstrapping.

Other methods to capture data at the point of creation involve authoring documents as a form where each field is linked to an ontological concept [19]. Although this method mitigates the need for information extraction on a document level,instances of concepts still need to be recognized – for example, the terms *'comp drum'* and *'hp shaft'*may be applied as the concept 'part_removed'within two different documents, however these terms are synonymous and should be recognized as such. The inclusion of free-text boxes where authors are able toinsert paragraphs of text means information extraction is sometimes still necessary.

Terminology Recognition is the ability to recognize the semantic class[1] and concept[2] referred to given a term, allowing a dereferencable URI[3] to be assigned. Terms vary for many reasons: use of *sublanguage*, *morphology*, *acronyms*, *abbreviations*, *lexical differences*, *word order* and *misspellings* [2]. We performed experiments on approximately 40000 Aerospace jet engine component terms linked to Part numbers. The resultsshow that the number of synonymous terms used to refer to a particular part number increases in accordance with a power law with the popularity of that part number (Figure 1), this means that for any given conceptit is unlikely that a gazetteer list of all valid termscould be compiled *a priori*. Terminology recognition systems therefore need the capability to identify term forms that have never been encountered before. This allows authors own terms to be usedat a *document* level and conceptURIsat a *metadata* level.

Due to term variation, Information Retrieval (IR) is a more involved task. Basic keyword search usually only returns documents that contain the query term, shrewd users often reformulate [20] their query (sublanguage) to use more popular terms or term variations indicative of a corpora they wish to target. More sophisticated search systems can account for linguistic features such as *affixes,morphology* and simple *synonyms*. A more effective search solution isbeable to retrieve documents based on *conceptual similarity* [21], in this regime a URIis generated from the query term (the query URI uniquely identifies the concept referenced to by the query term). The query URI is then compared against URIs generated for indexed entities. A match indicates conceptual similarity even though terms used may have a high string distance[4].

In this paper we present a terminology aware, ontology-driven methodology for extracting knowledge from free-text at the point of creation. We utilize Terminology Recognition in order to recognize ontological concepts within thedocument in real time as it is authored. Ontological relationships are suggested and displayed between relevant collocated concepts. Cross media resources and external information is drawn together and presented to the user in order to make the identification of correct URIs and relations as non-intrusive as possible. Positive and negative examples of concepts and relations are fed back in order to improve the entity and relation extraction task. Entities and relations are then recorded in an unambiguous and machine-readable format and are directly useable by downstream processes such as search engine indexer.

2 Requirements

The primary objective of our methodology is to provide a support capabilityfor technical domain document authors in order to facilitate more effective document retrieval. We do this by applying Terminology Recognition as the document is authored

[1] Semantic Class – The type of entity, for example; 'part', 'feature' or 'mechanism'.

[2] Concept – A particular instance of a semantic class. Concepts may be referenced to by many synonymous terms for example 'FK12345', 'HPC5 blade', 'HP Comp stg.5 blade'.

[3] URI – Uniform Resource Identifier; a unique string of characters used to identify a resource. Allows knowledge workers access to concept across corpora no matter how the concept is represented in text.

[4] String Distance – String distance metrics cost the number of character edits required to transform one string into another. A high string distance indicates a pair of dissimilar strings.

in order to identifyentities, concepts andrelationswithin free-text. If Terminology Recognition is able to identify both the entity[5] and concept[6] from a term, no further action is required from the authoras the term can be uniquely represented with the concept's URI. If on the other hand Terminology Recognition identifies an entity but not the concept, the author is required to specify the concept in order for the term to be uniquely identified. Concepts may not be identified for two reasons:

1. The author underspecified the term – for example *'bolt'* as opposed to *'combustor case lower bolt'* –in which case the author should use a more descriptive term or manually apply the URI of the concept they are referring to.
2. Terminology Recognition fails to classify the concept's URI, in which case Terminology Recognition requires further training.

The complexity in the entity, concept and relation identification taskstems from the largenumber of ways in which entities, concepts and relations can be expressed. However, by recognizing variations in terminology, sublanguage may be used freely within the documents without compromising the ability to retrieve the document.

We will now present some design considerations and requirements for a system that is able to identify entities and relations by recognizing the terminology used.

Entity Extraction: The primary requirement is the ability to identify entities and recognize term variation. This differs from a typical Named Entity Recognition (NER) task as it not only entails the identification of semantic type (i.e. Date/Person/Organization/etc) but also requires the identification of the concept (i.e. *"McDonalds"* = *"MCD"* = *"Mac-Donnallds"*[sic] = *"Golden Arches"*). This allows the assignation ofa URI that facilitates the identification of the concept across corpora and databases.

Resources: The poor coverage of technical domains within lexical resources such as WordNet, Wikipedia and Google means that these resources cannot be used for entity, concept or relation extraction. Pre-existing resources such as gazetteer lists, parts catalogues and taxonomic breakdownsshould be leveraged in order to construct domain ontologies that provide basic relations such as holonym, meronym and hypernyms as well as domain specific concepts and relations.

Provide Feedback: If a concept can be uniquely identified (i.e. a URI can be assigned), no further user interaction is required. On the other hand, if no unique concept can be identified, the entity's term iseither ambiguous (applicable to multiple concepts), may not reference a concept in the ontology, or Terminology Recognition may have failed to apply a URI. In other words, further action is required to identify the concept. The user should be alerted that the concept cannot be uniquely identified and that further action is required.

Information regarding relations should also be fed back to the user, when an entity is extracted, Terminology Recognition identifies collocatedentities with which a relation may exist (in accordance with the domain ontology) and classifies the relation as appropriate. This must be displayed to the user.

Real Time: The approach must process documents in real time; entities and their relations should be extracted as the author types.

---

[5] e.g. 'Part' | 'Feature' | 'Date'.

[6] e.g. 'Part Number 123' | 'Standard Feature # 12' | '1997-07-16T19:20:30+01:00'.

Large Scale and Maintainable: The approach must be maintainable, cost effectiveand scalable across large organisations. As the number of term variations increases with the number of authorsin accordance to a power law (Figure 1) the need to decentralize the term management task becomes apparent. Devolvingthe term management task to document authors themselves allows a greater number ofmorphological differences, acronyms, abbreviations, lexical diversity, misspellings and differences in word orderto be identified, this information can in turn be analyzed and used to better identify further term variations. By using the approach across a large organization it would be possible to conflate different sublanguages, this can be used to improve information extraction from legacy documents where terminology variation is a major difficulty when performing entity recognition.

Non-intrusive: The approach must be fast and non-intrusive, and operate in a similar manner to a spell-checker.In order to reduce the 'annotation bottleneck' the time taken to assign URIs to concepts must be kept to a minimum, this should be achieved by reducing the annotation task to a correction task wherever possible.

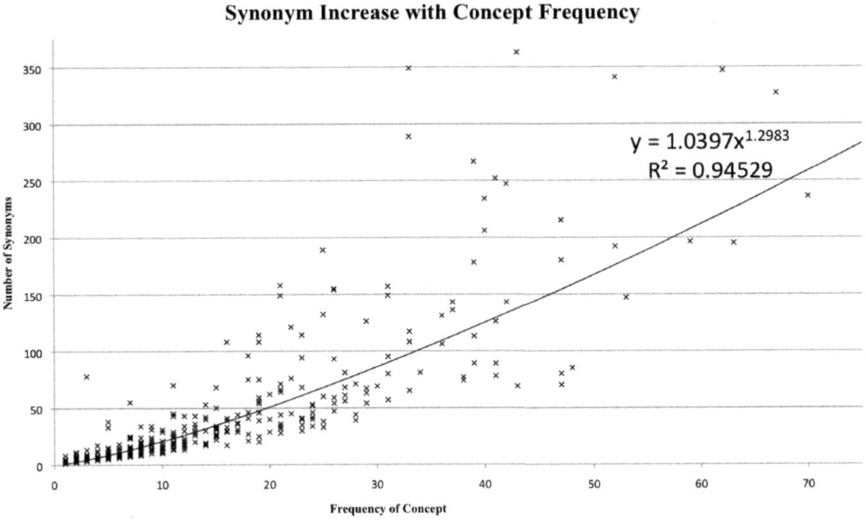

Fig. 1. Number of synonyms increase with the frequency of concept occurrence in accordance with a power law

3 Resources

3.1 Ontology

We developed an aerospace jet enginedomain ontologysourcing a large amount of information from the Rolls-Royce official engine parts catalogue. The ontology describes the relations between components (such as *meronyms* and *holonyms*) as well as providing *hypernyms*. We manually added concepts and relations for:

- Features – Afeature is a location on a component. Components may have multiple features e.g. a blade has a*'leading edge'*, a *'face'* and a *'root'*.Although the number of aerospace jet engine features is finite, comprehensive component-feature lists do not currently exist.
- Deterioration Mechanisms – Adeterioration mechanism is a process that causes a component or feature's condition to deteriorate. Examples are*crack*, *rub* and*dent*.
- Service Bulletins – A Service Bulletin is a type of report that discusses the condition of one or more components. Given any particular component it is useful for engineers to be able to retrieve relevant service bulletins in order to identify common faults.Service Bulletins are identified by their report number.
- Technical Variances – A Technical Variance is a type of report issued when an in-use component is found to be outside of design tolerances. Rolls-Royceproduce the report which advises whether the component is safe to fly or not.Technical Variances are identified by their report number.

The ATA100 Spec[7] is an aerospace industry standard numbering specification used by aviation manufacturers, suppliers and airlines to identify aircraft systems. Rolls-Royce has extended this numbering specification to identify individual components within jet engines. The virtue of using the extended ATA100 Spec to refer to components rather than part numbers is that as components are improved/redesigned they are given a new part number (even though the component fulfills the same task), whereas the ATA number will remain the same, for this reason we use the R-R extended ATA100 Spec to form component URIs.

3.2 Terminology Recognition

We have developed a Terminology Recognition (TR)system thatis in the process of being patented by Rolls-Royce(unfortunately therefore we cannot disseminate technical details yet). Terminology Recognition builds on the functionality of typical Named Entity Recognition (NER) system by identifying term variations such as acronyms, abbreviations, lexical, morphological, and syntactic differences.

Terminology Recognition does not require context in order to extract entities from text. This is because TR was designed to extract entities in different situations, in some cases there will be very little surrounding text (in a search query scenario for example, where there may only be one entity), in other cases there may bemany collocated entities (a paragraph of text or an entire document). When context is present, TR makes use of surrounding terms in order to disambiguate underspecified and ambiguous concepts in order to apply a URI. When applied to text, TR outputsa list of entities associated with URIsalong with entity offset information. If no single URI can be assigned to a given entity, a list of URIs is provided along with a probability for each. Each semantic class of entity TR extracts is linked to a concept within the domain ontology.

To be unambiguous, an aircraft engine component term needs to include: 1) an object(i.e. hypernym), 2) the type of object, and 3) the system the objectis attached to.

[7] http://en.wikipedia.org/wiki/Air_Transport_Association

Several terms require positional modifiers on systems and objects (such as *'Stage 4 Compressor'* or *'rear case'*). To illustrate this, the term "High Pressure Compressor speed sensor", refers to a 'sensor' object with type 'speed' (i.e. the sensor senses speed), and the 'speed sensor' is attached to the 'HPC' system. Terminology Recognition models terms using its own ontological representation (term ontology), the relationships between the systems, types and positions are identified such that if one is missing, Terminology Recognition is capable of identifying why a term is underspecified.

4 User Interaction

As a document is authored, entities and relations are extracted and presented to the user,mal-extracted entities, concepts and relations are corrected by the author who ensures they match their intention. Through this interaction:1) documents are writtenusing the author's sublanguage (i.e. without forcing the author to use alternate terms) while allowing the retrieval of the document based on concepts rather than terms, and 2) provides training data in order to better classify mal-extracted entities, conceptsand relations.

The interaction scheme is depicted in Figure 2and is described in detail in the following sections.

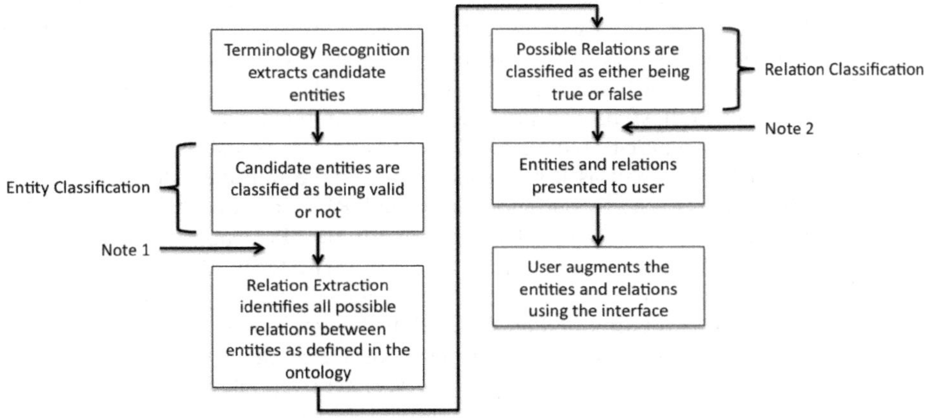

Fig. 2. Interaction scheme

4.1 Knowledge Capture

We developed a prototype interface utilizing Terminology Recognition in the process depicted in Figure 2.

A. Entities

As a document is authored,Terminology Recognition (TR) extracts candidate entities, as further context is added TR is able to better identify whether a candidate entity is an instance of an ontological concept or not. For example, the term *'man'* is used in some contexts as a reference to 'EGCC[8]' the term may also occur freely in text with other senses. In order to classify entities based on context TR uses an SVM classifierwith features including words immediately surrounding the entity along with information about the candidate entity itself such as canonical form and semantic type.

If the entity persists once context is taken into consideration a second classifier attempts to assign a URI. This classifier returns a list of possible URIs along with a confidence value for each. The confidence values are used to determine whether a URI should be automatically assigned or if the author should be notified that further action is required to disambiguate the entity. When a URI is assigned, the entity is uniquely identified, allowing the system to establish a link to references of the concept within other databases. In order to assist the author in choosing the correct URI (ATA100 code) the system queries the Rolls-Royce illustrated parts catalogue to display an image of the component referenced by the URI. Other databases that can be drawn together by the ATA100 code include list of materials and list of common faults, this information is displayed within a tool-tip when the author hovers over an entity. The system notifies the user that an entity has been uniquely identified by using a distinct text color based on the entity type.

If TR identifies an entity but does notassign a URI (as confidence values are too low), the entity text is highlighted with the entity type color, this indicates to the user that further interaction is required in order to uniquely identify the concept. This may be remedied by either modifying the entity text to include a more detailed description, or manually selecting one of the lowerconfidenceURIs. Underspecified entities are a common issue within aerospace domain technical documents. For example, there are many blades within an aerospace gas turbine, blades are situated within six different systems, three of these systems have multiple stages (up to a total of eight). The term *'IPC Stage 3 blade'* is fairly descriptive as it indicates the system, and position (stage) of the blade, the highest probability URI classified by Terminology Recognition (http://www.k-now.co.uk/r-r.owl#72-32-32-170) scores a probability of 86.53% (in this case this URI is correct as it references the 3rd stage intermediate pressure compressor blade concept). The second most probable URI scores a probability of 12.36% and references a component physically connected to the IPC stage 3 blade, the 3rd, 4th and 5th suggestion each score a probability <0.05%. The term *'Blade'* is clearly less descriptive,it does not indicate which blade is being referred to. The highest ranking classification suggests the Engine Fan Blades(http://www.k-now.co.uk/r-r.owl#72-32-32-170) - the largest and most prominent blades on the engine - with a confidence of 40.16%, the 2nd, 3rd 4th and 5th suggestions are various other blades in different positions across different systems each with a confidence value of approximately 10%. As extra characters are added to the termTerminology Recognition reclassifies the termin real time allowing the user to see whether enough information has been added to uniquely identify the concept.

In technical domain documentsendophoric references (typically anaphoric) are commonly made.For example, when a component is described in one paragraph and then discussed in more detail in the following. *"The outlet guide vane case appeared to be in a serviceable condition. </P>The case was then removed for an intrascope inspection procedure"*. It is from situations like these that mostunder specified terms (and therefore low confidence URIs) are generated – This situation can be mitigated

[8] EGCC – The International Civil Aviation Organization (ICAO) airport code for Manchester Airport, UK.

by resolving co-references. It is also important to recognize that the two entities 'outlet guide vane' and 'case' are co-referential as two sets of relations could be assigned to the entities, when it is more accurate to realize all relations occuron the same entity. Terminology Recognition attempts to establish ontological 'same_as' relations between co-referential concepts. Authors can manually establish and break same_as relations by right clicking an entity and selecting the 'Resolve Coreference' submenu, other entities with a same semantic type are suggested as possible co-references (both anaphoric and cataphoric within a window of 300 characters).

B. Relations

As the author continues to create the document,Terminology Recognitionidentifies pairs of entities between which the domain ontology specifies a relation may exist. These relations indicated to the user asarcsdawn within the interface connecting the subject and object entities. The arcs appear when the user hovers over either subject or object entity. As each relation is represented with a <subject><predicate><object> triple, it is therefore possible to construct a sentence fragment (e.g. "*combustor case*-has_damage*crack*") for each relation. These fragments are displayed within the tooltip as the user hovers over an entity, and provide an easy to digest test.

Terminology Recognition classifies all possible relations as either positive or negative using an SVM based classifier. The classifier uses features including the distance and words (tokenized on white space) between the subject and object entity, the relation predicate, context words surrounding the subject and object entity, as well details about the two entities themselves, such as any classified URIs. Positively classified relation is indicated with a more pronounced arc where as negative relations become faded.

Relations between entities may also be specified by the user, when an entity is selected, relations are read from the ontology. Appropriate entities from within a window of text (collocated within 300 characters of the entity) are suggested, the cardinality of the predicate within the ontology determines whether the relation may be established between multiple entities.

Within technical documents, the leastambiguous entities include part numbers, serial numbers, ATA 100 codes, Technical Variance numbers and Service Bulletin numbers.As these entities usually follow a strict syntax they can be identified with very high precision and recall. Part numbers can be used to identify components

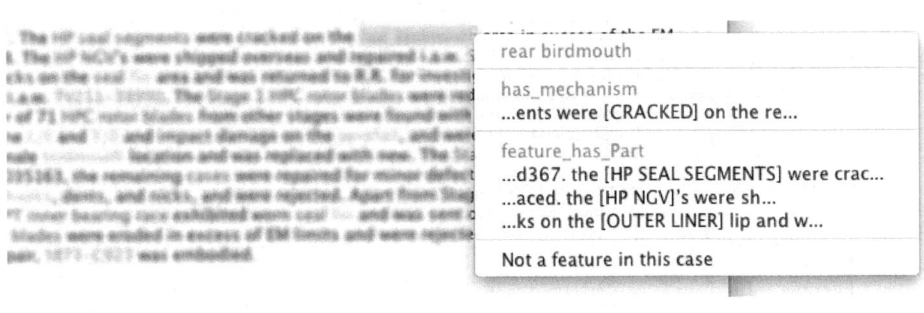

Fig. 3. The interface. Author is establishing relations for the concept 'rear birdmouth' (Text has been blurred due to data confidentiality).

within otherdata sources (such as a parts catalogue or bill of materials),this information can then be used to accurately identify hypernyms, holonyms and meronyms.It is likely that an entity collocated with a reference number will share the same concept and Terminology Recognition uses this information as features in order to better classify entity URIs.

4.2 Learning

Normal author interaction is leveraged at every stage in order to provide training examples to improve entity extraction, coreference resolution and relation extraction. As the author corrects automatically classified entities and relations the features required for each task are recorded. The classifiers can them be retrained offline using both the existing and new training data.

5 Evaluation

We ran a series of experiments in order to assess how our methodology assisted authors at the document generation stage –in particular, we focused on evaluating the methodology's performance in supporting authors generate semantically rich documents.

The experiments are set in the Aerospace jet engine domain. As no gold standard annotated corpora for this domain exists, we divided our evaluation into a number of separate tasks each to evaluate separate processes of our methodology individually.

Table 2. Precision and Recall across different corpora

	Corpus A			Corpus B		
	Pre	**Rec**	**F1**	**Pre**	**Rec**	**F1**
TF-IDF	12.00%	8.54%	9.98%	14.62%	7.32%	9.76%
Termex	41.69%	18.02%	25.16%	49.82%	21.30%	29.84%
C-Value	52.87%	34.86%	42.02%	62.40%	41.85%	50.10%
TR	69.03%	97.12%	80.70%	92.77%	98.30%	95.45%

	Corpus C			Corpus D		
	Pre	**Rec**	**F1**	**Pre**	**Rec**	**F1**
TF-IDF	16.33%	5.83%	8.59%	13.59%	6.21%	8.52%
Termex	41.34%	25.34	81.35%	51.43%	22.73%	31.53%
C-Value	60.29%	39.93%	48.04%	64.76%	43.86%	52.30%
TR	94.49%	98.10%	96.26%	85.14%	94.03%	89.36%

	Corpus E			Corp F		
	Pre	**Rec**	**F1**	**Pre**	**Rec**	**F1**
TF-IDF	12.99%	7.24%	9.30%	16.65%	11.02%	13.26%
Termex	43.56%	22.10%	29.32%	35.23%	31.54%	33.28%
C-Value	59.43%	41.11%	48.60%	53.36%	42.40%	47.25%
TR	94.32%	95.40%	94.86%	97.35%	98.21%	97.78%

Rolls-Roycesupplied two datasets; data set 1 comprised a collection of 88213 report summaries spanning three corpora. The summaries originated from the structured tables included within the header of each report, and so for each report summary we were able to accurately extract fields such as date, part number, ATA100 number, component term. Data set 2 comprised 4394 complete documents randomly selected from across 6 corpora.

We first assessed our methodology's ability to identify entities within free-text. As a document is authoredentities must be identified, we evaluated Terminology Recognition (without the contextual classifier), *'Termex'* [22] and *'C-Value'*[23]ATR algorithms against TF-IDF as a baseline. In order to generate the statistical measures for the ATR algorithms we first considered each corpus individually, then split the documents 40% training, 60% testing, we used the training split to generate statistics for *domain pertinence*, *domain consensus* and *lexical cohesion* (Termex), *document frequency* (C-Value), and *inverse document frequency* (TF-IDF), before extracting entities from the test set. The ability to identify entities within the test corpus was measured in terms of precision and recall. In this experiment, *precision* represents the fraction of identified entities that were correct, if an entity was partially identified we counted this as a half correct extraction. *Recall* represents the fraction of entities that were identified by the algorithm.

Our second experiment evaluated Terminology Recognition's ability to assign a correct ATA100 code (and therefore URI) given an entity term. Using data set 1 we first filtered out blank, malformed and invalid ATA100 codes using the official engine parts catalogue this resulted in 39034 high quality term-ATA pairs. TR's URI classifier was trained using a 40% training split and evaluated on the remaining terms. Terminology Recognition assigned the correct ATAwith a precision of 87.64%.

Our third experiment evaluated the capability to learn and extract relations by measuring the precision and recall of automatically predicted relationsat regular intervals (after 5, 10, 20, 40 and 80 documents).We manually asserted relations for the first five documents, then used the positive and negative training examples to train the classifier, we then evaluated the classifier while confirming correctly classified relations, asserting missed relations and removing incorrect relations in the following five documents, after which we retrained the relation classifier on the ten marked up documents. We continued until the classifier achieved a *recall* greater than 75%.

Our final experiment simulated the task of producing semantically rich technical documents.We evaluated the time taken to identify entities and relations within a sample of 20 documentsfrom data set 2 using TR to identify entities and relations in contrast to manually identifying and asserting entities and relations.

Table 3. Number of documents required to achieve a recall > 75%

Relation Type	Number of Training Documents	Precision	Recall	F-Measure
Part_has_mechanism/ Mechanism_has_part	20	83.43%	78.35%	80.81%
Part_has_feature/ Feature_on_part	40	88.41%	75.20%	81.27%
SB_has_part	5	100%	94.21%	97.02%
TV_has_part	5	100%	98.40%	99.19%

Table 4. Manual extraction Vs TR Assisted extraction

		Precision	Recall	F-measure	Annotator Agreement
Entities	**TR**	98.74%	99.43%	99.08%	99.49%
	Manually	98.62%	99.01%	98.81%	84.37%
Relations	**TR**	96.21%	92.81%	94.48%	99.21%
	Manually	94.38%	91.34%	92.84%	92.37%

Table 5. Time taken to annotated documents manually and with TR assistance

	Time taken per document (seconds)
TR assisted	494
Manually	1239
Average length of document = 1552 words.	

Our experiments show that time taken to semantically mark up documents is significantly reduced when variations in terminology are identified, and that entity and relation extraction across corpora within a large organization can be improved through non-intrusive identification of entities. In our first experiment we showed that Terminology Recognition outperforms both the C-Value and Termex ATR algorithms in identifying entities across different corpora within the Aerospace domain. C-Value outperformed Termex across all corpora as it is more capable at extracting multi-wordterms (typically component terms which occured frequently).The terms Termex identified tended to be single word feature, and mechanism entities. Once an entity text has been identified, Terminology Recognition can identify the concept and assign the correct URI 87.64% of the time.

Our third experiment demonstrated that for most relation types, very few training documents were required to achieve a reasonable precision and recall. The relation needing most documents to train are the symmetric relations part_has_feature and feature_has_part, this is mostly due to the amount of variation in how these relations are expressed within the documents, the relationships SB_has_part& TV_has_partrequired very few training examples due to the very regular way they are expressed.Our final experiment showed recognizing variation in terminology can dramatically reduce the amount of time taken to semantically enrich documents, we achieved a 60.13% reduction in the time taken to assign URIs and establish relations.

6 Discussion and Conclusions

Applying rich semantic information to documents allows documents to be retrieved and consumed in the manner the author intended. Unfortunately, the task of annotating technical documents is extremely complex and expensive and open domain solutions based on WordNet, Wikipedia and Google are not directly applicable due to poor coverage. Our experiments show that by recognizing variations in terminology,we can achieve a 60% decrease in the time taken to identify entities and relations in aerospace domain documents. In this paper we outlined requirements in order to author technical domain documents for effective retrieval, our methodology:

1. Identifies entities and relations within free text affording a semantically searchable ontological representation of the knowledge within the document. Identified entities and relations are indicated to the author allowing them to ensure the classification matches their intention.
2. Operates in real time, allowing authors to mark up their document as it is written.
3. Is applicable across different corpora within large organizations, and improves in performance as the system is used.
4. Operates in a similar manner to a spellchecker without disrupting the authoring process.

One concern that arises from our experiments is that as authors become more and more familiar with the automatically extracted entities and relations authors may begin to trust and accept Terminology Recognition's suggestions without examining whether they are correct or not and as these entities and relations are used as training examples the feedback provides further strength to the misclassification.

Acknowledgements

This work was carried out in association with Rolls-Royce plc. Sponsored by the UK Engineering and Physical Sciences Research Council Case Studentship number 0800133X.

References

1. Just-in-Time Delivery Comes to Knowledge Management. Harvard Business Review 80(7) (July 2002)
2. Kittredge, R., Lehrberger, J.: Sublanguage: Studies of Language in Restricted Semantic Domains. deGruyter (1982)
3. Engelson, S.P., Dagan, I.: Minimizing manual annotation cost in supervised training from corpora. In: Proceedings of the 34th Annual Meeting on Association for Computational Linguistics (1996)
4. Wilson, T., Wiebe, J., Hoffmann, P., et al.: Recognizing contextual polarity in phrase-level sentiment analysis. In: Proceedings of the conference on Human Language Technology and Empirical Methods in Natural Language Processing (2005)
5. Schlueter, S., Dong, Q., Brendel, V.: GeneSeqer@PlantGDB: gene structure prediction in plant genomes. Nucleic Acids Research 31(13), 3597–3600 (2003)
6. Grishman, R.: Adaptive Information Extraction and Sublanguage Analysis. In: Proceedings of IJCAI Workshop on Adaptive Text Extraction and Mining, pp. 77–79 (2001)
7. Ciravegna, F., Dingli, A., Petrelli, D., Wilks, Y.: User-System Cooperation in Document Annotation based on Information Extraction. In: Gómez-Pérez, A., Benjamins, V.R. (eds.) EKAW 2002. LNCS (LNAI), vol. 2473, p. 122. Springer, Heidelberg (2002)
8. Ciravegna, F.: Adaptiveinformationextractionfromtextbyruleinductionandgeneralisation. In: Proceedings of the 17th International Joint Conference on Artificial Intelligence, IJCAI 2001 (2001)
9. Culotta, A., Sorensen, J.: Dependency tree kernels for relation extraction. In: Proceedings of 'the 42nd Annual Meeting of the Association for Computational Linguistics, ACL 2004 (2004)

10. Zhang, Z., Iria, J.: A Novel Approach to Automatic Gazetteer Generation using Wikipedia. In: Proceedings of the ACL 2009 Workshop on Collaboratively (2009)
11. Ponzetto, S.P., Strube, M.: Exploiting semantic role labeling, wordnet and wikipedia for coreference resolution. In: Moore, R.C., Bilmes, J.A., Chu-Carroll, J., Sanderson, M. (eds.) HLT-NAACL. ACL (2006)
12. Strube, M., Ponzetto, S.P.: Wikirelate! computing semantic relatedness using wikipedia. In: AAAI, pp. 1419–1424. AAAI Press, Menlo Park (2006)
13. Toraland, A., Munoz, R.: A proposal to automatically build and maintain gazetteers for Named Entity Recognition by using Wikipedia. In: Workshop on New Text, 11th Conference of the European Chapter of the Association for Computational Linguistics (2006)
14. Pantel, P., Pennacchiotti, M.: Espresso: Leveraging generic patterns for automatically harvesting semantic relations. In: ACL (2006)
15. Feldman, R., Rosenfeld, B., Soderland, S., Etzioni, O.: Self-supervised relation extraction from the web. In: ISMIS, pp. 755–764 (2006)
16. Agichtein, E.: Confidence estimation methods for partially supervised relation extraction. In: SDM 2006 (2006)
17. Chen, J., Ji, D.-H., Tan, C.L., Niu, Z.-Y.: Semi-supervised relation extraction with label propagation. In: HLT-NAACL (2006)
18. Riloff, E., Wiebe, J.: Learning extraction patterns for subjective expressions. In: EMNLP 2003 (2003)
19. Bhagdev, R., Chakravarthy, A., Chapman, S., Ciravegna, F., Lanfranchi, V.: Creating and Using Organisational Semantic Webs in Large Networked Organisations. In: Proceedings of the 7th International Semantic Web Conference, Karlsruhe, Germany (October 2008)
20. Liu, H., Lieberman, H., Selker, T.: GOOSE: A Goal-Oriented Search Engine With Commonsense. In: De Bra, P., Brusilovsky, P., Conejo, R. (eds.) AH 2002. LNCS, vol. 2347, p. 253. Springer, Heidelberg (2002)
21. Giunchiglia, F., Kharkevich, U., Zaihrayeu, I.: Concept search. In: Aroyo, L., Traverso, P., Ciravegna, F., Cimiano, P., Heath, T., Hyvönen, E., Mizoguchi, R., Oren, E., Sabou, M., Simperl, E. (eds.) ESWC 2009. LNCS, vol. 5554, pp. 429–444. Springer, Heidelberg (2009)
22. Sclano, F., Velardi, P.: Termextractor: a web application to learn the shared terminology of emergent web communities. In: Proceedings of the 3rd International Conference on Interoperability for Enterprise Software andApplications, I-ESA 2007 (2007)
23. Frantzi, K.T., Ananiadou, S.: The c/nc value domain independent method for multi-word term extraction. Journal of Natural Language Processing utilization in the Information Search and Delivery System for IBM Technical Support. IBM Systems Journal 43(3), 546–563 (2003)

A Methodology towards Effective and Efficient Manual Document Annotation: Addressing Annotator Discrepancy and Annotation Quality

Ziqi Zhang[1], Sam Chapman[2], and Fabio Ciravegna[1,2]

[1] Department of Computer Science, University of Sheffield, UK
[2] K-Now, UK
z.zhang@dcs.shef.ac.uk, sam@k-now.co.uk,
f.ciravegna@dcs.shef.ac.uk

Abstract. Manual document annotation is an essential technique for knowledge acquisition and capture. Creating high-quality annotations is a difficult task due to inter-annotator discrepancy, the problem that annotators can never agree completely on what and exactly how to annotate. To address this, traditional document annotation involves multiple domain experts working on the same annotation task in an iterative and collaborative manner to identify and resolve discrepancies progressively. However, such a detailed process is often ineffective despite taking significant time and effort; unfortunately, discrepancies remain high in many cases. This paper proposes an alternative approach to document annotation. The approach tackles the problem by firstly studying annotators' suitability based on the types of information to be annotated; then identifying and isolating the most inconsistent annotators who tend to cause the majority of discrepancies in a task; finally distributing annotation workload among the most suitable annotators. Tested in a named entity annotation task in the domain of archaeology, we show that compared to the traditional approach to document annotation, it produces larger amounts of better quality annotations that result in higher machine learning accuracy while requires significantly less time and effort.

Keywords: inter annotator disagreement, annotator discrepancy, document annotation, knowledge acquisition, machine learning, named entity recognition.

1 Introduction

Manual document annotation is the basis to provide data for training and evaluating a supervised machine learning system. It has been recognised that the annotation process is often laborious and costly, and has been the major bottleneck to the development and adaptation of knowledge acquisition systems [6][22]. Crucial to the annotation process is resolving annotator discrepancies and achieving reasonable inter-annotator agreement, the problem stems from annotators behaving differently and inconsistently for the same annotation task. This is due to the differences in their skills, knowledge and experiences, and issues such as workload and tiredness. The problem affects the quality of annotation and therefore, the learning accuracy of a

P. Cimiano and H.S. Pinto (Eds.): EKAW 2010, LNAI 6317, pp. 301–315, 2010.

system [2][29]. For this reason, the typical annotation process requires a number of domain experts to work in an iterative and collaborative manner in order to discover and resolve discrepancies progressively. Usually in each iteration, a set of documents are duplicated across all annotators, who are required to annotate the same documents for the same types of information (e.g., person and place names) independently. Outputs from different experts are then cross-checked, discussed, validated, consolidated and a sophisticated annotation guideline is documented, followed, and refined [10][17][24] in following iterations. The process is repeated as much as possible until the level of discrepancies is reduced to a satisfactory level. Such a repetitive process often requires months and even up to years of work from experienced researchers [2][29], yet discrepancies can never be eliminated [14] and the resulting annotations and guidelines are often application-specific and non-generalisable. Given such an ineffective and inefficient process, the tremendous cost from key experts means that it is inapplicable in many practical situations such as industries, due to resource limitations (e.g., finance, time and personnel) [15]. A more effective and efficient approach is required.

Essentially, the majority of discrepancies among annotators are caused by the differences in their knowledge and experiences [14]. The traditional annotation process identifies these differences and aims to minimise them iteratively, eventually producing an output that best matches the subtly varying viewpoints across a community. We argue that, these differences result in different levels of annotators' suitability for an annotation task or sub-tasks. In most cases, no candidates are perfectly suitable for all tasks; however, one can be more suitable for particular tasks than others (e.g., based on the classification scheme in an entity classification task). Therefore, the key to improving annotation quality is not correcting the differences revealed by the repetitive checking process at the maximum effort, but rather identifying annotators' suitability and suitability-based task assignment. Inconsistent annotators unsuitable for a task should be identified and isolated such that the annotation quality is not compromised.

This paper details an alternative approach to document annotation based on the analysis of annotators' suitability for annotation tasks and annotator selection based on their suitability. We illustrate the approach using a typical annotation task; named entity annotation and classification, in which annotators' suitability analysis and annotator selection are carried out on the per-entity-class basis, namely, the type of information to be annotated. The studies reveal different levels of discrepancy and individual inconsistency for different classes of entities, suggesting the task be split and treated differently in the annotation process. The nature of task specialisation allows one to assign specific sub-tasks to the most suitable, mutually consistent annotators, among whom workload may be distributed. A set of experiments are designed and performed to show improved quality of annotations compared to those obtained by the traditional approach; whilst the time required for annotation is significantly reduced, but the total amount of annotations produced is largely increased.

The rest of this paper is organised as the follows: Section 2 gives an insight to the difficulties of document annotation and the prevailing problems of annotator discrepancy. It then reviews the typical document annotation process adopted in most scientific research and summarises important lessons learnt from these work. Section 3 proposes our alternative method to manual document annotation, and describes the study carried out in a large archaeology named entity annotation task, with details on our experiment design, results and findings. Section 4 is a further discussion of the results and other problems noted in this study, and finally concludes the paper.

2 Isn't It Easy to Annotate?

In the past few decades extensive amount of research has been dedicated to automate the process of knowledge acquisition, in which creating manual annotations for training or testing an automated system is an essential step. Typically in the field of Machine Learning, high quality and sufficient quantity of annotations are required for an automated system to be able to learn accurately. Unfortunately, the process of creating the necessary annotations has never been an easy or rewarding experience.

2.1 Annotator Discrepancy

Research has shown human annotators can never agree completely with each other on what and how to annotate [14], and they even tend to disagree with themselves in some situations [7]. The first case is often referred to as *inter*-annotator "agreement", "consistency" or "discrepancy". The second case is referred to as *intra*-annotator "agreement", "consistency" or "discrepancy". Inter-annotator discrepancies are often caused by the differences in annotators' knowledge and experiences, their understanding and reasoning of the corpora [17]. Intra-annotator discrepancies exist because annotators' level of interest and motivation may drop and level of fatigue rises as the annotation process continues [12], as a result, annotators make mistakes. This paper focuses on the *inter*-annotator issue only.

Inter-annotator discrepancy is a prevailing issue in the research of knowledge acquisition. It has been noted in many relevant fields, such as Word Sense Disambiguation (WSD) [23], Speech Recognition [12], Information Retrieval [1], event recognition [17] and Named Entity Recognition (NER) [10][28][29]. Depending on the difficulty of the annotation task, the inter-annotator agreement can vary significantly. For example, [27] indicated that the agreement between human annotators varied between 40% and 75% for different tasks. Most reports of inter-annotator discrepancy are found in the field of NER, which concerns recognising and classifying atomic texts into pre-defined categories. Research by [10] and [8] has shown that in NER, discrepancies typically arise due to three types of difficulties in annotating entities. Firstly, it is difficult to choose the right category (e.g., Ben Nevis can refer to person or a mountain in the UK); secondly, it is difficult to select the candidate texts and delimitation boundaries (e.g., should we annotate proper nouns only, or also pronouns and definitional descriptions); thirdly, how to annotate homonyms, e.g., "England" may refer to a location or a football team. These problems become even harder to resolve within specialised domains such as bioinformatics and engineering, due to the intrinsic complexity of terms in these domains including multi-word expressions, complex noun phrase compositions, acronyms, ambiguities and so on [28]. Typically, the inter-annotator agreement in NER found in these domains is between 60% and 80% [29][5][21].

From all these studies, it is evident that perfect agreement between annotators is difficult to reach, and it is also difficult to obtain a high level of inter-annotator consistency, especially in specialised domains. However, researchers advocate that consistency highly increases the usefulness of a corpus for training or evaluation purposes, and it is crucial to the success of machine learning algorithms [2][29]. Therefore, studies have been conducted to research scientific methodology for creating high quality annotations, addressing inter-annotator consistency. In the following, a list of these literature is described.

2.2 How to Annotate Properly: What Have We Learnt?

The typical process of annotating a corpus often involves a group consisting of a number of domain experts and ideally also linguists working on a same range of annotation tasks in an iterative and collaborative approach aimed at resolving discrepancies. For example, in NER, multiple domain experts are required to annotate a corpus for the same sets of entity classes. In each iteration, a duplicated set of documents are annotated by each domain expert independently. Then, their output is cross-checked; discrepancies are discussed and resolved as much as possible. The entire process and decision making logic is documented to form a guideline for the annotation task, which is to be followed in future exercises. Due to the nature of the work, it is always a lengthy and costly process. The guidelines are often subject to the specialised domain and not generalisable to other problems.

For example, Brants [2] reports their work on creating syntactic annotations (part-of-speech and structural information) on a German newspaper corpus. The activity involves trained annotators performing the annotation tasks at sentence level independently, then cross-checking and discussing together to resolve discrepancies. They report that a trained annotator needs on average 50 seconds per sentence, with average of 17.5 tokens; however, the total annotation effort including the consolidation activity increases to 10 minutes per sentence. Pyysalo et al. [26] annotates a corpus of 1100 sentences from abstracts of biomedical research articles for biomedical named entities, relationships between entities and syntactic dependencies. They also adopt a repetitive process, which took 15 man-months of effort. Wilbur et al. [29] conduct experiments to investigate inter-annotator agreement in a text annotation task in biomedical domain and identify factors that can help improve consensus. Their experiment involves twelve annotators annotating the same set of 101 sentences. Multiple iterations were conducted in a period of over one year, during which they develop and refine a guideline considered applicable for similar annotation problems. The resulting inter-annotator agreement stayed between 70% and 80%. They conclude that annotators must have a good understanding of the language and experience in reading scientific literature, and must be properly trained in order to deliver high quality annotations. Also, they indicate the presence of a clear, well developed annotation guideline as critical.

Other researchers have also recognised the necessity for a clear annotation guideline. Kim et al. [17] show by experiments that high level of discrepancy will form without annotation guidelines even if the task is carried out by well-educated domain experts. Their studies on event annotation on the Genia corpus [24] took 1.5 years of effort of five graduate students and two coordinators. Whenever new annotators joined the project, they had to be trained using previously annotated examples and follow the guideline. Colosimo et al. [5] and Tanabe et al. [28] also conduct corpus annotation in the biology domain and conclude that clear annotation guidelines are important, and the annotations should be validated by proper inter-annotator-agreement experiments.

Even if well-prepared guidelines are available for annotation problems, they are not the ultimate answer to the problem. Firstly, most guidelines are lengthy documents and are difficult to read. For example, Ferro et al. [9] design guidelines for annotating temporal information, which has 57 pages. The entity recognition task defined by ACE [18] is accompanied with a guideline of over 70 pages for annotating only five classes of entities [25]. Secondly, interpretation of the guideline documents differs from annotator to annotator; as a result, some annotation criteria remain problematic and can cause discrepancies [10]. For example, the event annotation on the Genia corpus by [17] only achieves 56% inter-annotator agreement with strict match [20] even though all annotators have been trained and educated using example annotations and guidelines.

2.3 The Reality Check

The conclusion of previous research advocates for clear definition of annotation guidelines to be followed, well-educated domain experts with proper training in document annotation, careful study of inter-annotator agreement and iterative attempts to address the issues revealed by the study and to resolve discrepancies, all of which demand costly investment. Many scientific research tracks such as MUC [11] present a scenario in which the cost of such effort is not considered important [6]. However, the scenario breaks as the technology is to be adopted by various specialised domains, in which the cost is a serious issue [22]. Industries and businesses are not willing to invest resources (personnel, finance and time) into lengthy document annotation exercises [15]; annotators feel overwhelmed by the scale of monotonous annotation tasks expressing a strong reluctance to doing them. They want a shortcut.

One exception to this is the domain of bio-informatics, where well-curated resources are richly available and users are more familiar with the benefits that can follow from annotation. Unfortunately, these resources are hardly re-usable across domains because they address specific issues in bio-informatics; and demands for similar resources in other specialised domains such as aerospace engineering, astronomy and arts and humanity are equally high, these however are scarcely addressed [15][21][16].

Recognising the urgency of this issue, in the last decade there has been an enormous amount of research dedicated to weakly-supervised learning methods [22] and domain-adaptation for Machine Learning [19] in order to reduce a learning system's dependence on manually annotated data. Unfortunately, evidence of these methods applied to specialised domains is scarce. Their applicability in these areas is questionable given the intrinsic complexity of language and decreased availability of knowledge resources in these areas.

Given the complexity of these problems and the inadequacy of existing technologies, this work has identified a strong demand for more effective, efficient and practical approaches to manual document annotation. In the following, we propose a new method to manual document annotation to achieve this goal.

3 Towards a New Document Annotation Approach

In this section, we propose a new approach towards effective and efficient manual document annotation. We present the details using a case study of named entity annotation in the domain of archaeology; however, the methodology is generic and can be applied to other annotation problems. Following the traditional named entity annotation process, in each iteration, domain experts are required to annotate a set of documents for the same set of entity classes. Then for each entity class, all annotations are cross-checked, and discrepancies are identified, discussed and resolved as much as possible. In contrast, our method is based on the hypothesis that the different levels of knowledge and experiences of annotators lead to different levels of suitability for an annotation task, or sub-tasks. This is reflected by different levels of discrepancies they demonstrate in annotating different classes of entities. Therefore, annotator discrepancies and suitability must be studied on per-entity-class basis, and only the most suitable annotators should be selected for annotating specific entity classes other than all classes.

The method contains three phases. In the first phase, we follow the traditional approach to manual document annotation to create sufficient amount of annotations that sample the level of discrepancy in this task. The size of this corpus is properly controlled such that efforts required from annotators are minimised to an acceptable level and the annotations created are just adequate for studying the inter-annotator agreement. In the second phase, a set of experiments are carried out to evaluate machine learning accuracy using these annotations. The results together with the inter-annotator agreement studies in phase one are used to evaluate annotators' suitability of annotating the documents for a particular class of entity, and then specific annotators (*best-fit-annotators*) are chosen to annotate the classes of entities (*best-fit-class*) for which they are most suitable. In the third phase, the final set of documents to be annotated is selected. Then for each class of entity, the documents are split equally between each member of the *best-fit-annotators* to annotate just for that class, i.e., their *best-fit-class*. This ensures all documents are annotated by the most consistent annotators for all entity classes, while no annotators perform redundant work. Compared to the traditional approach, this is a desirable feature since the distributional nature of work in the final phase allows workload to be reduced and total output to be increased. A set of experiments are then carried out to evaluate the machine learning accuracy obtainable on this corpus.

3.1 The Archaeology Domain

The domain of modern archaeology is a discipline that has a long history of active fieldwork and a significant amount of legacy data dating back to the nineteenth century and earlier. Despite fast-growing large corpora existence, little has been done to develop high quality meta-data for efficient access to the contained information in these datasets, and there is a pressing need for knowledge acquisition technologies to bridge the gap [16]. Manual document annotation in archaeology is a challenging task because of the complexity of language characterised by ambiguities, uncertainties, long and composite terms, changing language use over the extended timeframe of the corpora, acronyms and so on. As a result, low inter-annotator agreement has been noted in related work [3].

Our work deals with archaeological entity extraction from un-structured legacy data, which mostly consist of full-length archaeological reports archived by the Arts and Humanities Data Service (AHDS[1]). The reports vary from five to over a hundred pages. According to [16], three classes of entities are most useful;

- Subject - topics that reports refer to, such as findings of artifacts and monuments. It is the most ambiguous class because it covers various specialised domains such as warfare, architecture, agriculture, and machinery. For example "Roman pottery", "spearhead", and "courtyard".
- Temporal terms - archaeological dates of interest, which are written in a number of ways, such as years "1066 - 1211", "circa 800AD"; centuries "C11", "the 1st century"; concepts "Bronze Age", "Medieval"; and acronyms such as "BA" (Bronze Age), "MED" (Medieval).
- Location of interest - place names of interest, such as site addresses and site types related to a finding or excavation. In our study, these typically refer to UK-specific places.

3.2 The First Phase – Sampling Annotator Discrepancy in NER for Archaeology

Overview of the Procedure. In this phase, five documents were randomly selected from the AHDS archive. Each document varied from five to thirty pages, containing much more content than standard datasets used in MUC and abstracts used in bioinformatics NER. The size of the corpus was decided by the domain experts, who considered the workload to be acceptable. Meanwhile, the selection of documents was ensured such that there were sufficient contents for annotation (as indicated by the *tag density* and number of annotations revealed in the post-annotation statistical analysis). The total number of words in this corpus was 47,101, and the average *tag density* (the percentage of words tagged as entities) by all annotators was 8.7%, compared to MUC7 11.8% and Genia 33.8% [21]. The average total number of annotations for all three classes was approximately 2,100. This corpus is referred to as "*trial corpus*". It was then to be annotated by five full-time archaeology researchers in three iterations following the traditional document annotation approach.

Throughout phase one, two annotators were constantly involved in all meetings with knowledge acquisition (KA) experts to provide feedback from all annotators and design simple annotation guidelines and ensure they are followed. The annotation process consisted of four mini-iterations. In the first iteration, two annotators made trial attempts at annotating two medium sized documents from the *trial corpus*. Discrepancies were identified at this early stage and were discussed and resolved in the meeting with the KA experts. The output of this process were some guidelines for annotation, which were then provided to all five annotators in the second iteration,

[1] http://ahds.ac.uk/

during which each annotated 1 ~ 2 documents. The purpose of this exercise is again to identify as many discrepancies as possible at low costs. By studying these annotations, the guideline for annotation was further refined and enriched. In the third iteration, all five annotators were required to follow the guideline to re-annotate the *trial corpus* independently and fully in a series of intensive workshops. In the final iteration, one annotator undertook final validation by checking 10% of all annotations to correct obvious mistakes that violated the guidelines. These corpora are used to study inter-annotator consistency and machine learning accuracy.

Cost of the Process. Thanks to the size of the sample corpus, according to the annotators' estimation, the first iteration of phase one took 2 person-days of work; the second iteration took 5 person-days of work; the third iteration took 5 person-days of work; and the final iteration took 2 person-days of work. The total estimated cost in terms of person-days work is 14.

Inter-Annotator Agreement. Many different measures are available for computing inter-annotator agreement, and the most popular is the κ-statistics [4]. However, it is not suitable for entity recognition tasks [26]. We adopt the *F-measure* proposed by [13], which allows computing pair-wise inter-annotator agreement using the standard *Precision*, *Recall* and the harmonic *F-measure* in information studies by treating one annotator as gold standard and the other as predictions. Table 1 shows the pair-wise agreement for each entity class.

Comparing the figures, it is evident that even with reasonable effort from well-trained and skilled archaeology professionals devoted to developing annotation guidelines and resolving discrepancies in several iterations, the task of annotating domain specific entities remained difficult and the level of discrepancy remained

Table 1. Pair-wise inter-annotator-agreement *F-measure*. A, B, C, D, E are identifiers of domain-expert annotators

Location						**Temporal**					
	A	*B*	*C*	*D*	*E*		*A*	*B*	*C*	*D*	*E*
A	1	0.8	0.69	0.77	0.66	*A*	1	0.83	0.77	0.79	0.77
B	0.8	1	0.72	0.75	0.75	*B*	0.83	1	0.67	0.77	0.83
C	0.69	0.72	1	0.69	0.7	*C*	0.77	0.67	1	0.78	0.71
D	0.77	0.75	0.69	1	0.69	*D*	0.79	0.77	0.78	1	0.77
E	0.66	0.75	0.7	0.69	1	*E*	0.77	0.83	0.71	0.77	1

Subject					
	A	*B*	*C*	*D*	*E*
A	1	0.55	0.65	0.63	0.62
B	0.55	1	0.51	0.53	0.49
C	0.65	0.51	1	0.51	0.51
D	0.63	0.53	0.51	1	0.5
E	0.62	0.49	0.51	0.5	1

high. Annotating *Subject* is a much harder task than the other two classes of entities. This is expected because *Subject* spans across multiple specialised domains and terms are characterised by a high level of ambiguity and heterogeneity. Most discrepancies were due to identifying the boundaries of composite noun phrase entities, acronyms and identifiers (object codes, ID's). Also for every class of entities, we can always identify sub-groups of annotators that are more mutually consistent than with other annotators. This raised the issue of annotator suitability and the question that it is beneficial to eliminate in-consistent annotators from an annotation task to reduce discrepancies.

3.3 The Second Phase - Evaluating Machine Learning Accuracy and Annotator Selection

In order to gain a different view of the quality of the annotations produced in such an iterative way, two sets of experiments were conducted to evaluate how well a machine can learn from these annotations. In the first set of experiments, we created a corpus including annotations from all annotators to reflect the high level of discrepancy in the annotations. Annotations produced by the five annotators were selected randomly, whilst ensuring the five documents are covered in full and roughly proportional annotations were selected from each annotator. This corpus is referred to as *consolidated-trial-corpus*. In the second set of experiments, we used each individual annotator's corpus separately, thus there were five corpora for testing and they are referred as *individual-trial-corpus*. On each of these six corpora, an SVM[2]-based named entity tagger was trained and evaluated in a five-fold cross validation experiment, in which annotations are randomly split to 5 complementary subsets[3], and the learning algorithm learns from four subsets and is then validated on the other one subset. The process is repeated for 5 iterations, where each time different subsets are used for training and validation and the final performance is the average of the performance figures obtained in all iterations. Throughout the experiment we kept consistent settings (parameters, features, etc.) for the learning algorithm in order to fairly compare the effect of corpus quality.

Firstly, we applied the experiment on the *consolidated-trial-corpus*, which had inter-annotator inconsistency as discussed in the previous section. We refer to this as *collective-annotator-learning*. Next, we applied the experiment on each *individual-trial-corpus* that was annotated by a single annotator. Since there was only one annotator for each corpus, this is equivalent to perfect inter-annotator agreement. We refer to this as *intra-annotator-learning*. Results of these are shown in Table 2.

Results of this set of experiments show interesting findings. Given no inter-annotator issues in each individually annotated corpus, one would expect higher levels of consistency and better annotation quality, which translate to better machine learning accuracy. This was mostly true compared to results obtained on the *consolidated-trial-corpus*. However, exceptions were noticed for annotator A on *Location* (2 percent lower), and E on *Temporal* (1 percent lower). Also, comparing across different entity types for each annotator, the entity tagger had the lowest

---

[2] http://www.support-vector-machines.org/

[3] To cope with varied document lengths we split documents into sections of sentences.

Table 2. F-measure of entity taggers obtained from individual-trial-corpus

Annotator	Subject	Temporal	Location
A	0.73	0.78	0.62
B	0.66	0.78	0.65
C	0.76	0.74	0.69
D	0.78	0.84	0.7
E	0.79	0.67	0.75
Consolidated-trial-corpus	0.53	0.68	0.64

performance on *Location* among four annotators (A, B, C, D), possibly indicating the lower quality of annotations and that it was the hardest task among all three classes. Whereas, for the annotations created by person E, the learning algorithm performed badly for *Temporal*, possibly indicating person E had more inconsistency at annotating *Temporal.* Comparing across different annotators for each entity class, we noticed that most annotators produced fairly good annotations for *Temporal* but person E, of whom the result in *F-measure* was even lower than that obtained from the *consolidated-trial-corpus*; and similar exception of person B was noted for *Subject*, and person A for *Location*. We believe that the results so far have revealed several conclusions that are useful for document annotation. Firstly, inter-annotator discrepancy has a major impact on the quality of corpus and therefore, machine learning accuracy. High level of discrepancy damages the quality of annotations, and decreases obtainable machine learning accuracy on a corpus. On the other hand, given uniform settings for a learning algorithm, different accuracies obtained from similar corpora may indicate different levels of quality of the corpora; secondly, annotators may have different skill levels for annotating different classes of entities, possibly due to the difference in the focus of their knowledge. This has caused varying levels of inconsistencies in an annotator's annotations, depending on the specific entity class. Therefore, there is the need for considering annotator's suitability for a task and isolating inconsistent annotators from a task. In line with the conclusion from Table 1, these results foster the motivation of identifying and selecting most suitable annotators (mutually consistent) for each entity-class annotation task.

Annotator Selection. Using these analyses, we split the document annotation task by entity-class and select *best-fit-annotators* for specific *best-fit-class* annotations. For each class of entity, we selected three most consistent annotators based on the experiment results. However, depending on the availability of annotators, the workload and inter-annotator consistency analysis, one can select more or fewer annotators if needed. In the simplistic form, we can select annotators with the highest average agreement in *F-measure* for each entity type. To do so, we simply add up the scores for each row in Table 1 (excluding him/herself) and divide the total by four, results of which are shown in Table 3. However, as concluded from Table 2, certain annotators had high levels of in-consistency in annotating a particular class of entity as indicated by the machine learning accuracy (*F-measure*) tested on their annotations, possibly due to gaps in their knowledge. Therefore, we believe it is important to exclude these annotators and their contributions to the calculation of inter-annotator agreement. As a result, for each class of entity, we eliminated those annotations on which the learner obtained the lowest *F-measure*, particularly those below that from the *consolidated-trial-corpus*. This caused person A eliminated from *Location*, person B eliminated from *Subject* and person E eliminated from *Temporal*. Re-calculating the average agreement using figures in Table 1, we obtained "revised" scores, as indicated in the columns of "Revised" in Table 3.

Table 3. Average agreement in F-measure for each entity type

Annotator	Subject	*Revised Subject*	Temporal	*Revised Temporal*	Location	*Revised Location*
A	0.61	*0.63*	0.79	*0.8*	0.73	-
B	0.52	-	0.78	*0.76*	0.76	*0.74*
C	0.55	*0.56*	0.73	*0.74*	0.7	*0.7*
D	0.54	*0.55*	0.78	*0.78*	0.73	*0.71*
E	0.53	*0.54*	0.77	-	0.7	*0.713*

With these figures, we simply selected three annotators that have the highest scores, that is, persons A, C, D for annotating *Subject*; persons A, D, B for annotating *Temporal* and persons B, E, D for annotating *Location*, as shown in Table 4.

Table 4. Selected annotators and annotation task

Annotator	Subject	Temporal	Location
A	O	O	
B		O	O
C	O		
D	O	O	O
E			O

3.4 The Third Phase – Final Corpus Annotation

The annotation exercise continued next by selecting the final corpus of 25 full-length documents from the AHDS archive, and giving them to the selected annotators for annotation. However, unlike in the first phase, no duplicate documents were given to different annotators, and annotators were only required to annotate entities that they were chosen for, as indicated by the "O" in Table 4. For each class of entities, the documents were split into equal portions among different *best-fit-annotators*. For example, the 25 documents are split into three sets and each set was given to an annotator (A, C, or D) for annotating *Subject* entities. In the end, all annotations were merged into a single collection of 25 documents. This is based on the assumption that mutually consistent annotators will continue annotating consistently for the same annotation problem and the same type of corpus even without the process of consolidation and discrepancy resolution. Therefore, we can distribute the workload among different but consistent annotators for a particular entity-class annotation task, expecting equal level of consistency in the annotations they jointly create. The annotation activity was performed in a series of intensive workshops, during which annotators were free to raise questions and discuss about discrepancies. However, generally speaking, this kind of process is much more cost-saving and workload for each annotator is much lighter than if done in the traditional way as in phase one.

Cost of the Process and Quality of Annotation. The annotation process of phase two took roughly 10 - 15 person-days of work, although in practice it was spread across a couple of weeks to minimise fatigue to ensure annotators have the highest level of concentration during the work. The final annotated corpus (*final-corpus*) was also used for a 5-fold cross validation experiment. The final experiment results in *F-measure* are shown in Table 5.

Table 5. Results on the *final-corpus* in *F-measure*

	SUB	TEM	LOC
Final-corpus	*0.68*	*0.83*	*0.71*
Consolidated-trial-corpus	0.53	0.68	0.64
Best result on individual-trial-corpus	0.79	0.84	0.75

As shown in Table 5, compared against results obtained on the *consolidated-trial-corpus*, the machine learning algorithm produced much better results on the *final-corpus*, which can be attributed to fewer discrepancies and therefore high quality of the annotations. Compared against the best results obtained on the *individual-trial-corpora*, which we consider the top ceiling performance under zero inter-annotator discrepancy, the machine learning system achieved very good results. The relatively smaller improvement on *Subject* is believed due to the heterogeneity of information encompassed by the entity class, which would have increased the difficulty of reaching agreement, as indicated by the inter-annotator agreement studies before. We believe these results are strong evidence supporting the applicability and technical soundness of our methods for annotator selection and task assignment in document annotation and yet producing high quality annotations in a much more effective and efficient way.

4 Discussion and Conclusion

This paper addresses manual document annotation in knowledge acquisition. Document annotations are crucial resources for knowledge acquisition and capture applications. However, creating high-quality annotations is a difficult task due to the inter-annotator discrepancies caused by differences in annotators' knowledge and experiences. Consequently, the process of document annotation typically requires significant amount of effort and time from multiple domain experts to work iteratively and collaboratively to identify and resolve discrepancies. The process is often expensive and time-consuming, preventing its application to practical scenarios.

To address this issue, this paper has proposed an effective and efficient alternative approach to document annotation based on the idea of identification of annotator suitability, task specialisation and annotator selection for specific annotation tasks. Illustrated using a typical named entity annotation scenario, the method starts by sampling the annotator discrepancy problem using the traditional document annotation process on a small corpus; the annotations are then used to evaluate machine learning accuracy to gain an insight to the annotator discrepancies in the task. Results of these experiments show that even with reasonable effort following the traditional annotation approach, high-level discrepancy may still remain, and can lead to low machine learning accuracy. Further analysis reveals that annotators may have different skill levels for annotating different classes of entities, suggesting the need for considering annotators' suitability in specialised annotation tasks. Using this information, thc annotation task is split according to entity-classes and sub-tasks are treated differently where the most suitable candidates are chosen for specific annotation tasks. Essentially, matching *best-fit-annotators* to *best-fit-classes* allows distribution of workload, which reduces workload per annotator, but increases the potential amount of annotations that can be produced whilst retaining high quality of annotations. Shown by the experiments, the approach produced a final annotated corpus of five times of the size of the corpus created using the traditional approach (phase one). The machine learning accuracy obtained on these annotations is far better than that obtained from the annotations created in the traditional way, and is very close to the best result obtained under zero inter-annotator discrepancy in the *intra-annotator-learning* experiments.

In terms of the time required for this annotation process, the method has significantly shortened the process required in the traditional document annotation approach. The first phase of the experiment that follows the traditional approach was estimated to cost 14 person-days to annotate 5 documents; whereas, the last phase of the experiment that follows our method was estimated to cost only 10-15 person-days to annotate 25 documents. In total, the annotation exercise undertook less than 1 person month, yet produced high quality annotations for machine learning purposes.

Although applied to the named entity annotation problem, the method can be generalised and applied to other document annotation tasks. Essentially, the key is to sample the discrepancy issue based on which the task can be specialised, annotators' suitability can be evaluated and annotators selected. For example, in document classification, the problem may be analysed based on the topics of documents (e.g., science, entertainment) since some annotators maybe more suitable for dealing with certain kinds of topics than others, especially when they have different academic backgrounds; in WSD, the analysis may be performed from the angle of word classes, or contexts (e.g., different documents) in which words appear; and likewise the different types of events in event recognition.

However, several inadequacies can be further investigated in future research. Firstly, intra-annotator agreement has been isolated from this study due to unavailability of resources. Studying intra-annotator agreement will reveal valuable details of annotators' skills in an annotation task, and evidence should be combined with results from *intra-annotator-learning* to make stronger support for annotator selection. Secondly, our annotator selection criteria can be improved. Ideally, figures from the experiments should be combined in a mathematical formula to transform the numbers into an appropriate measure of the annotator suitability. Lastly, the method proposed splits an annotation task from the angle of entity-class and base the studies of annotator suitability and selection on this type of task specialisation. On the other hand, an annotation task could also be specialised according to the characteristics of documents, such as structured and un-structured documents. Although these characteristics were not evident in our testing corpora, it may prove useful in other scenarios. In the future, our work will concentrate on these areas.

Acknowledgement. This work was funded by the Archaeotools project that is carried out by Archaeology Data Service, University of York, UK and the Organisations, Information and Knowledge Group (OAK) of the Department of Computer Science, University of Sheffield, UK. This work was further supported by Knowledge Now Limited, Sheffield, UK.

References

1. Bermingham, A., Smeaton, A.: A Study of Inter-Annotator Agreement for Opinion Retrieval. In: Proceedings of SIGIR 2009 (2009)
2. Brants, T.: Inter-annotator agreement for a German newspaper corpus. In: Proceedings of the Second International Conference on Language Resources and Evaluation, LREC (2000)
3. Byrne, K.: Nested Named Entity Recognition in Historical Archive Text. In: Proceedings of International Conference on Semantic Computing (2007)
4. Carletta, J.: Assessing agreement on classification tasks: the kappa statistic. Computational Linguistics 22(2), 249–254 (1996)
5. Colosimo, M., Morgan, A., Yeh, A., Colombe, J., Hirschman, L.: Data preparation and internannotator agreement: BioCreAtIvE Task 1B. BMC Bioinformatics (2005)
6. Ciravegna, F., Lavelli, A., Satta, G.: Bringing information extraction out of the labs: the Pinocchio Environment. In: Proceedings of the 14th European Conference on Artificial Intelligence (2000)
7. Cucchiarini, C., Strik, H.: Automatic transcription agreement: An overview, pp. 347–350 (2003)
8. Ehrmann, M.: Les entites nommees, de la linguistique au TAL: statut theorique et methods de desambiguisation. Ph.D. thesis, Univ. Paris (2008)
9. Ferro, L., Mani, I., Sundheim, B., Wilson, G.: TIDES Temporal Annotation Guidelines. Draft Version 1.0. MITRE Technical Report MTR 00W0000094 (October 2000)
10. Fort, K., Ehrmann, M., Nazarenko, A.: Towards a methodology for named entities anntoation. In: Proceedings of the Third Linguistic Annotation Workshop, ACL-IJNLP, pp. 142–145 (2009)
11. Grishman, R., Sundheim, B.: Message understanding conference - 6: A brief history. In: Proceedings of International Conference on Computational Linguistics (1996)
12. Gut, U., Bayerl, P.S.: Measuring the Reliability of Manual Annotations of Speech Corpora. In: Proceedings of Speech Prosody (2004), Nara, pp. 565–568 (2004)

13. Hripcsak, G., Rothschild, A.: Agreement, the F-measure and Reliability in Information Retrieval. Journal of the American Medical Informatics Association, 296–298 (2005)
14. Hripcsak, G., Wilcox, A.: Reference standards, judges, and comparison subjects: roles for experts in evaluating system performance. J. Am. Med. Inform. Assoc., 1–15 (2002)
15. Iria, J.: Automating Knowledge Capture in the Aerospace Domain. In: Proceedings of the Fifth International Conference on Knowledge Capture, pp. 97–104 (2009)
16. Jeffrey, S., Richards, J., Ciravegna, F., Chapman, S., Zhang, Z.: The Archaeotools project: Faceted Classification and Natural Language Processing in an Archaeological Context. In: Special Theme Issues of the Philosophical Transactions of the Royal Society A, Crossing Boundaries: Computational Science, E-Science and Global E-Infrastructures (2009)
17. Kim, J., Ohta, T., Tsujii, J.: Corpus annotations for mining biomedical events from literature. In: BMC Bioinformatics (2008)
18. Linguistic Data Consortium, Automatic Content Extraction (ACE) (2008), `http://projects.ldc.upenn.edu/ace/`
19. Minkov, E., Wang, R., Cohen, W.: Extracting Personal Names from Email: Applying Named Entity Recognition to Informal Text. In: Proceedings of HLT/EMNLP 2005 (2005)
20. Morante, R., Asch, V., Daelemans, W.: A memory–based learning approach to event extraction in biomedical texts. In: Proceedings of the Workshop on BioNLP: Shared Task, pp. 59–67 (2009)
21. Murphy, T., McIntosh, T., Curran, J.: Named entity recognition for astronomy literature. In: Australian Language Technology Workshop (2006)
22. Nadeau, D.: PhD Thesis: Semi-Supervised Named Entity Recognition: Learning to Recognize 100 Entity Types with Little Supervision (2007)
23. Ng, H., Lim, C., Foo, S.: A Case Study on Inter-Annotator Agreement for Word Sense Disambiguation. In: Proceedings of the ACL SIGLEX Workshop on Standardizing Lexical Resources SIGLEX 1999, pp. 9–13 (1999)
24. Ohta, T., Tateisi, Y., Kim, J.: The GENIA corpus: an annotated research abstract corpus in molecular biology domain. In: Proceedings of the Second International Conference on Human Language Technology Research, pp. 82–86 (2002)
25. Olsson, F.: PhD thesis: Bootstrapping Named Entity Annotation by Means of Active Machine Learning: A Method for Creating Corpora (2008)
26. Pyysalo, S., Ginter, F., Heimonen, J., Björne, J., Boberg, J., Järvinen, J., Salakoski, T.: BioInfer: a corpus for information extraction in the biomedical domain. BMC Bioinformatics (2007)
27. Saracevic, T.: Individual differences in organizing, searching, and retrieving information. In: Proceedings of the 54th Annual ASIS Meeting, pp. 82–86 (1991)
28. Tanabe, L., Xie, N., Thom, L., Matten, W., Wilbur, W.: GENETAG: a tagged corpus for gene/protein named entity recognition. BMC Bioinformatics (2005)
29. Wilbur, W., Rzhetsky, A., Shatkay, H.: New directions in biomedical text annotation: definitions, guidelines and corpus construction. Bioinformatics (2006)

Towards Better Ontological Support for Recognizing Textual Entailment

Andreas Wotzlaw

Fraunhofer Institute for Communication, Information Processing and Ergonomics FKIE
Neuenahrer Str. 20, 53343 Wachtberg, Germany
andreas.wotzlaw@fkie.fraunhofer.de

Abstract. Many applications in modern information technology utilize ontological knowledge to increase their performance, precision, and success rate. However, the integration of ontological sources is in general a difficult task since the semantics of all concepts, individuals, and relations must be preserved across the various sources. In this paper we discuss the importance of combined background knowledge for recognizing textual entailment (RTE). We present and analyze formally a new graph-based procedure for integration of concepts and individuals from ontologies based on the hierarchy of WordNet. We embed it in our experimental RTE framework where a deep-shallow semantic text analysis combined with logical inference is used to identify the logical relations between two English texts. Our results show that fine-grained and consistent knowledge coming from diverse sources is a necessary condition determining the correctness and traceability of results. The RTE application performs significantly better when a substantial amount of problem-relevant knowledge has been integrated into its inference process.

1 Introduction

The utilization of ontological background knowledge is of increasing importance for many applications in modern information technology. This applies in particular to the applications from the Semantic Web, e.g., entity- and fact-oriented Web search [1,2], but also to other domains. For instance, machine translation exploits lexical knowledge [3], document classification uses ontologies [4], whereas question answering [5], information retrieval [6], and textual entailment [7] rely strongly on background knowledge. Furthermore, ontological knowledge structures play an important role in information integration in general [8].

Unfortunately, the existing applications today use typically only one source of background knowledge, e.g., WordNet [9] or Wikipedia. They could boost their performance if a huge ontology with knowledge from several sources were available. Such knowledge base would have to be of high quality and accuracy comparable with that of an encyclopedia. It should include not only ontological concepts and lexical hierarchies like those of WordNet, but also a great number

P. Cimiano and H.S. Pinto (Eds.): EKAW 2010, LNAI 6317, pp. 316–330, 2010.

of named entities (here also referred to as individuals) like, e.g., people, geographical locations, organizations, events, etc. Also other semantic relations between them, e.g., who-was-born-when, which-language-is-spoken-in, etc. should be comprised. Here, we mean by ontology any set of facts and/or axioms comprising potentially both individuals (e.g., Berlin) and concepts (e.g., city).

2 Supporting Recognizing Textual Entailment

We discuss now the importance of background knowledge for *recognizing textual entailment* (RTE, see [10,11]). In RTE we try to identify the type of a logical relation between two input texts. In particular, we are interested in proving the existence of an entailment between them. The concept of *textual entailment* indicates the situation in which the semantics of a natural language written text can be inferred from the semantics of another one. RTE requires a processing at the lexical, as well as at the semantic and discourse level. Fine-grained and consistent knowledge computed for an RTE problem is a necessary condition determining the correctness of results. This requires, however, the preservation of semantic concepts, individuals, and relations across various knowledge sources. RTE is without doubt one of the ultimate challenges for any natural language processing (NLP) system. If it succeeds with reasonable accuracy, it is a clear indication for some thorough understanding of how language works.

We try to solve a given RTE problem by applying a *model-theoretic* approach where a *formal semantic representation* of the RTE problem is computed and used in the further analysis. In our setting, we want to recognize, by means of *logical inference*, the relation between two English texts. The following definition specifies more formally the inference problems we consider in RTE [12,13].

Definition 1. *Let T be a text consisting of several sentences and H a hypothesis expressed by a short sentence. Given a pair $\{T, H\}$, find answers to the following, mutually exclusive conjectures with respect to the background knowledge relevant both for T and H:*

1. *T entails H,*
2. *$T \wedge H$ is inconsistent, i.e., $T \wedge H$ contains some contradiction, or*
3. *H is informative with respect to T, i.e., T does not entail H and $T \wedge H$ is consistent (contains no contradiction).*

To demonstrate how crucial the integration of background knowledge from various ontological sources for RTE is, we integrate two knowledge sources into our experimental framework for semantic text analysis which we present briefly in Sect. 3. In particular, we use the huge and highly precise semantic knowledge base YAGO (Yet Another Great Ontology, see [14]) parallel with the more efficient but lexically limited WordNet. In Sect. 4 we define formally the generation of background knowledge and analyze its integration into the RTE problem. Here, a special attention is given to the preservation of consistency across many knowledge sources and lexicons. To this end, we introduce a new graph-based procedure for combining ontologies based on the WordNet lexical hierarchy and show how its usage can improve the quality and the success rate of RTE.

Related work. As a generic problem, RTE has many applications in NLP which have been studied extensively in the last few years [6]. Our model-theoretic approach for RTE was inspired by the ideas given in [12,15]. For a good overview of a combined application of deep and shallow NLP methods we refer to [16,17]. The application of logical inference methods, which are using a dynamic approach for NLP based on the *Discourse Representation Theory* (DRT, see [18]), was elaborately presented in [19,20,21,7,15]. In [22] a new knowledge representation model and a logic proving setting with axioms on demand was proposed for RTE. A detailed discussion on the importance of WordNet as a source of background knowledge for RTE can be found in [21,7]. Furthermore, a new approach for RTE using *natural logics* was presented in [23]. The authors propose there an alternative, annotation-based model of natural language inference which identifies valid inferences by their lexical and syntactic feature, without full semantic interpretation. Finally, there is also a number of huge ontology projects like, e.g., Suggested Upper Model Ontology (SUMO) [24], DBpedia [25], or the Linking Open Data Project [26] which aim is to extract and to combine ontological data from many sources. Since YAGO is a part in those ontology projects, is should be possible to integrate them (at least partially) into the RTE application by applying the integration procedure presented here.

3 Framework for Solving RTE Problems

We introduce now our experimental *framework for semantic text analysis* which we use for solving RTE problems given formally by Definition 1. The framework (see Fig. 1) is build on deep-shallow techniques for syntactic and semantic text analysis combined with logical inference for RTE. Its purpose is to make the realization of a linguistically motivated large-scale semantic text analysis as flexible, robust, and modular as possible. It was designed to give a good support not only to RTE, by also to other NLP tasks like, e.g., syntactic and semantic analysis of English texts, or (multilingual) information extraction.

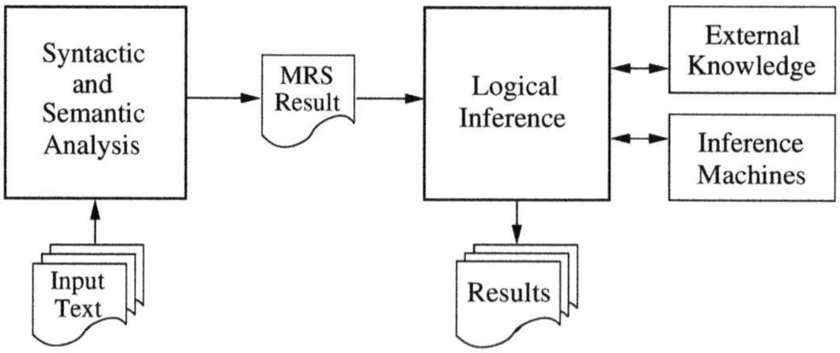

Fig. 1. Main modules of the framework for semantic text analysis

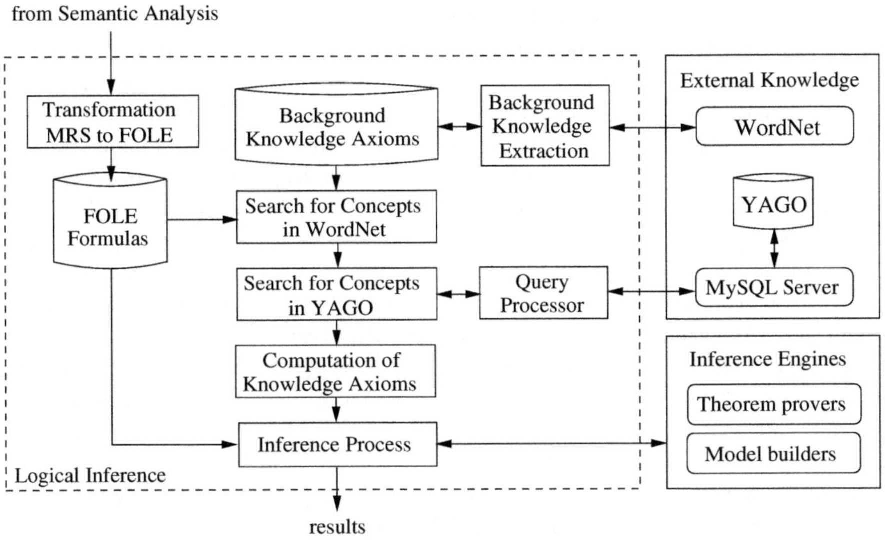

Fig. 2. Logical inference with external inference machines and background knowledge

In order to solve a given RTE problem, the texts representing T and H (see Definition 1) go first through the syntactic processing and semantic construction where their first-order representations in form of *Minimal Recursion Structures* (MRS, see [27]) are computed. This task is performed by the first module of the framework (see Fig. 1). It is build on the XML-based middleware architecture *Heart of Gold* [16] centered around the English Resource HPSG Grammar (ERG, see [28]). It allows for a flexible integration of shallow and deep linguistics-based and semantics-oriented NLP components like, e.g., the statistical part-of-speech tagger TnT [29], the named entity recognizer SProUT [30], or the deep HPSG parser PET [31]. The results of the semantic analysis in form of specified MRS combining deep-shallow predicates are sent to the module for logical inference (see Fig. 2), where they are translated into another, semantic equivalent representation of *First-Order Logic with Equality* (FOLE). This logical form with a well-defined model-theoretic semantics was already applied for RTE [12,15].

An adequate representation of a natural language semantics requires an access to a vast amount of common sense and domain-specific knowledge. As already clearly indicated in [20], RTE systems need problem-relevant background knowledge to support their proofs. To this end, the module for logical inference supports integration of external knowledge sources and by using them it extends automatically the locally stored FOLE formulas with problem-relevant knowledge in form of *background knowledge axioms* (see Sect. 4).

As already mentioned in Sect. 2, we integrate here exemplarily two huge sources of external knowledge. We use WordNet 3.0 as a lexical database for synonymy, hyperonymy, and hyponymy relations. It helps the logical inference process to detect entailments between lexical units from the text and the hypothesis. It serves also as a database for individuals but rather a very small one when compared to the second source. For efficiency purposes, it was integrated directly into the module (see Fig. 2). Conceptually, the hyperonymy/hyponymy relation in WordNet spans a directed acyclic graph (DAG) with the root node `entity` [9,14]. This means that there are nodes representing various concepts or individuals in the WordNet graph that are direct hyponyms of more than one concept. For that reason the knowledge axioms which are generated later from the WordNet graph may induce inconsistencies between the input problem formulas and the extracted knowledge. This can be very harmful for the subsequent logical inference process. In Sect. 4 we discuss this problem more formally and present several strategies that can deal with this restriction.

YAGO, the second source we use, is a large and arbitrarily extensible ontology with high precision and quality. Its core was assembled automatically from the category system and the infoboxes of Wikipedia, and combined with taxonomic relations from WordNet [14]. Similar to WordNet, the concept and individual hierarchy of YAGO spans a DAG. Thus, we must proceed carefully when integrating data from that source into the RTE problem, too (see Sect. 4). To access YAGO, we use a dedicated query processor (see Fig. 2) with its own query language, similar to that of [14]. The query processor first normalizes the shorthand notation of the query, and after translating it into SQL, sends it to the MySQL-Server. The incoming results are first preprocessed by the query processor, so that only those concepts are sent back for integration which are consistent with WordNet concept hierarchy, i.e., which include the prefix `wordnet_`.

After the computation of relevant background knowledge and its integration into the input RTE problem is finished, the resulting *extended* RTE problem is solved by the inference process (see Fig. 2). To check which logical relation for the extended RTE problem holds, we use external automated reasoning tools like *finite model builders* (e.g., Mace4 [32]) and *theorem provers* (e.g., Prover9 [33]). While theorem provers are designed to prove that a formula is valid (i.e., the formula is true in any model), they are generally not good at deciding that a formula is not valid. Model builders are designed to show that a formula is true in at least one model. The experiments with different inference machines show that solely relying on theorem proving is in most cases insufficient due to low recall. Indeed, our inference process incorporates model building as a central part of the inference process. Similar to [15], we exploit the complementarity of model builders and theorem provers by applying them *in parallel* to the input RTE problem in order to tackle with its *undecidability* more efficiently. More specifically, the theorem prover attempts to prove the input whereas the model builder simultaneously tries to find a model for the negation of the input.

4 Combining Knowledge from Various Sources

In the following we describe our *two-phase* integration procedure which we apply for the integration of ontological knowledge from two sources, WordNet and YAGO, into the logical inference process of RTE. In particular, we show how we can combine problem-relevant individuals and concepts from YAGO with those from WordNet so that the consistency of background knowledge axioms is preserved whereas the original logical properties of the input RTE problem do not change. Since the input problem itself may be consistent and our goal is to prove it, the knowledge we integrate into it must not make it inconsistent.

To make our presentation as comprehensible and self-explanatory as possible, we apply our procedure to a small RTE problem which we augment with relevant background knowledge axioms in the course of this section. More specifically, we want to prove that the text T:

> *Leibniz was a famous German philosopher and mathematician born in Leipzig. Thomas reads his philosophical works while waiting for a train at the station of Bautzen.*

entails the hypothesis H:

> *Some works of Leibniz are read in a town.*

In order to prove the entailment above, we must know, among other things, that *Bautzen* is a town. We assume that no information about *Bautzen*, except that it is a named entity (i.e., an individual), were yielded by the deep-shallow semantic analysis. However, we expect that this missing information can be found in the external knowledge sources. The search for relevant background knowledge begins after the first-order representation of the problem is computed and translated into FOLE (see Sect. 3). At this stage, the RTE problem has already undergone syntactic processing, semantic construction, and anaphora resolution in our framework which together have generated a set of semantic representations of the problem in form of MRS. The translation of the specified MRS into FOLE for the hypothesis H from our example above produces the following formula with a neo-Davidsonian event representation [34]:

```
some(X3,and(
    work_n_2(X3),
    some(X7,and(and(
        named_r_1(X7),and(
        leibniz_per_1(X7),
        of_r_1(X3,X7))),
        some(X8,and(
            town_n_1(X8),
            some(E2,and(
                event_n_1(E2),and(and(
                read_v_1(E2),
                patient_r_1(E2,X3)),
                in_r_1(E2,X8)))))))))).
```

The integration procedure is composed of two phases. In the first phase we search for relevant knowledge in WordNet, whereas in the second phase we look for additional knowledge in YAGO which we combine afterwards with that found in the first phase. Finally, we generate from the knowledge we have found and successfully combined background knowledge axioms and integrate them into the set of FOLE formulas representing the input RTE problem.

4.1 First Phase: Integration of WordNet

At the beginning of the phase, we list all predicates, i.e., concepts and individuals from the input FOLE formulas. They will be used for the search in WordNet. In the current implementation we consider as *search predicates* all nouns, verbs, and named entities, together with their sense information which is specified for each predicate by the last number in the predicate name, e.g., sense 2 in `work_n_2`. In WordNet, the senses are generally ordered from most to least frequently used, with the most common sense numbered `1`. Frequency of use is determined by the number of times a sense was tagged in the various semantic concordance texts used for WordNet [9]. Senses that were not semantically tagged follow the ordered senses. For our small RTE problem we can select as search predicates, e.g., `work_n_2`, `read_v_1`, or `leibniz_per_1`. It is important for the integration that the sense information computed during the semantic analysis matches exactly the senses used by external knowledge sources. This ensures that the semantic consistency of background knowledge is preserved across the semantic and logical analysis. However, this seems to be an extremely difficult task, which does not seem to be solved fully automatically yet by any current word sense disambiguation technique. Since in WordNet but also in ERG the senses are ordered by

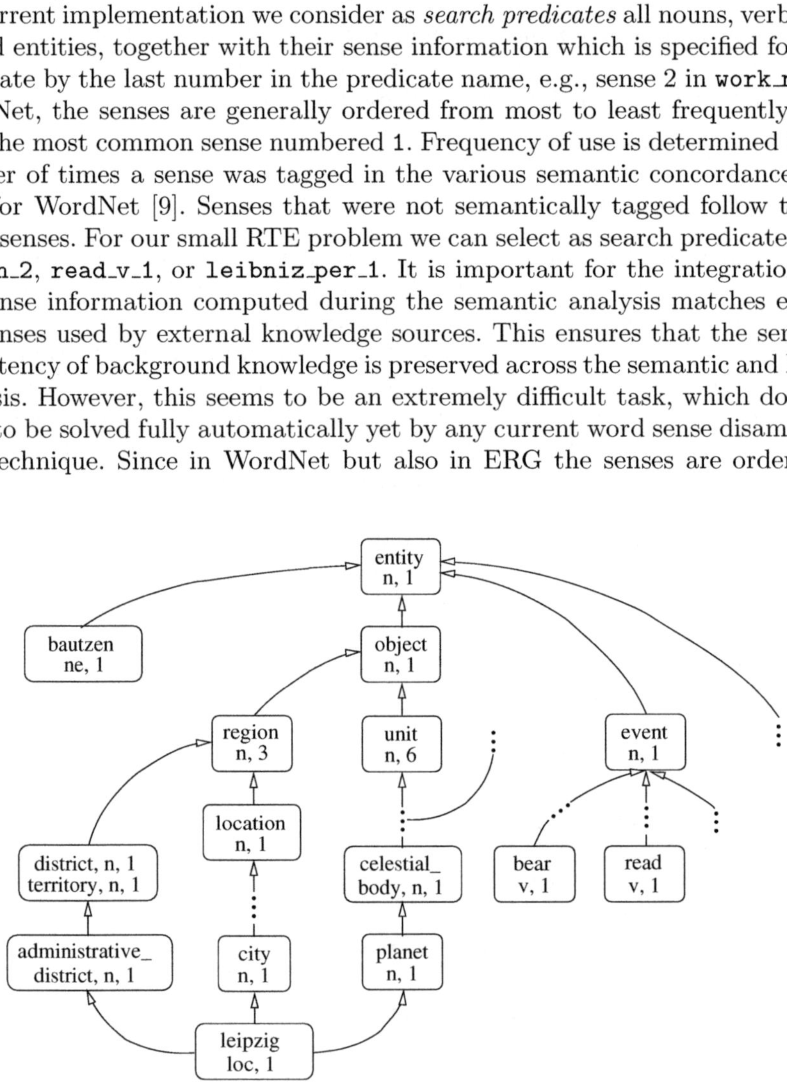

Fig. 3. Fragment of knowledge graph G_W after the search in WordNet

their frequency, we take for semantic representations generated during semantic analysis the most frequent concepts from ERG.

Having identified the search predicates, we try to find them in WordNet and, by employing both the hyperonymy/hyponymy and synonymy relations, we obtain a *knowledge graph* G_W. A small fragment of such a knowledge graph for text T of our example is given in Fig. 3. In general, G_W is a DAG with leaves represented by the search predicates, whereas its inner nodes and the root are concepts coming from WordNet. The directed edges in G_W correspond to the hyponym relations, e.g., in Fig. 3, the named entity `leipzig` is a hyponym of the concept `city`. Note that in the opposite direction they describe the hyperonym relations, e.g., the concept `city` is a hyperonym of the named entity `leipzig`. Each synonymy relation is represented in G_W by a *complex node* composed of synonymous concepts $C_1, ..., C_n$ induced by the relation (i.e., all concepts represented by a complex node belong to the same synset in WordNet), e.g., the complex node with concepts `district` and `territory` in Fig. 3.

Furthermore, it can be seen in Fig. 3 that the leaf representing individual `leipzig` has more than one direct hyperonym, i.e., there are three hyponym relations for leaf `leipzig` with concepts `administrative_district`, `city`, and `planet`. As already indicated in Sect. 3, this property of graph G_W may cause inconsistencies when the background knowledge axioms are later generated from it and integrated into the input FOLE formulas. We address this problem more carefully now. We begin with the explanation how the background knowledge axioms are generated. The method we use for it is an extension of the heuristic presented in [15] and can be defined formally as follows:

Definition 2. *There are three types of background knowledge axioms:* `IS-A`, `IS-NOT-A`, *and* `IS-EQ`. *They can be generated from a given knowledge graph G by traversing its nodes and edges and applying the following rules:*

1. *Let U and V be two different (complex) nodes from G, and C_i and C_j two arbitrary concepts or individuals represented by U and V, respectively. If C_i is a direct hyponym of C_j (i.e., there is an edge from U to V in G), then generate an* `IS-A` *axiom $\forall x(C_i(x) \rightarrow C_j(x))$.*
2. *Let V be a (complex) node from G and $U = \{U_1, ..., U_n\}$ a set of all children of V in G. All concepts and individuals represented by (complex) nodes from U are direct hyponyms of the concepts or individuals represented by V. The sets of concepts and individuals represented by nodes from U are pairwise disjoint. For every pair (i, j) such that $i = 1, .., n-1$ and $j = i, ..., n$ generate an* `IS-NOT-A` *axiom $\forall x(C_i(x) \rightarrow \neg C_j(x))$ where C_i and C_j are two arbitrarily chosen concepts or individuals represented by U_i and U_j, respectively.*
3. *Let U be some complex node from G and $C = \{C_1, .., C_n\}$ a set of synonymous concepts represented by U. For every pair (i, j) such that $i = 1, .., n-1$ and $j = i, ..., n$ generate an* `IS-EQ` *axiom $\forall x(C_i(x) \leftrightarrow C_j(x))$.*

Since all concepts and individuals represented by a given complex node are synonymous, Rule 1 and Rule 2 from Definition 2 need to be applied only to one arbitrarily chosen concept or individual represented by that node. By applying the rules from Definition 2 to graph G_W from Fig. 3, the following axioms can be generated (not a complete list here):

$$\begin{aligned} \texttt{IA-A:}\ & \forall x(object\_n\_1(x) \rightarrow entity\_n\_1(x)) \\ \texttt{IS-NOT-A:}\ & \forall x(region\_n\_3(x) \rightarrow \neg unit\_n\_6(x)) \\ \texttt{IS-EQ:}\ & \forall x(district\_n\_1(x) \leftrightarrow territory\_n\_1(x)) \end{aligned}$$

Furthermore, note that the set of all background knowledge axioms A_K generated for knowledge graph G_W according to Definition 2 is a finite set of first-order formulas without free variables restricted to unary predicate symbols and no function symbols. This monadic fragment of the first-order logic is known to be *decidable* for logical validity [35]. However, to show the consistency (i.e., the absence of contradictions) of A_K generated for an arbitrary knowledge graph G_W, we need to show that A_K is *satisfiable*. We conjecture here that every A_K is satisfiable in some finite model. To prove this, one need to give, for instance, some method which describes formally the construction of a finite model for every set of axioms A_K generated for an arbitrary knowledge graph G_W according to Definition 2. Since the predicate calculus of first order is complete [35], one can also proceed in a purely syntactical way by showing that there is no formula f such that both f and its negation are provable from axioms A_K under its associated deductive system. In the further research we examine our conjecture more carefully, i.e., we will try either to prove it or to deliver some counterexample.

Theorem 1. *Let F be a set of FOLE formulas representing semantically an RTE problem P, and A_K a set of background knowledge axioms computed for P according to Definition 2. Furthermore, let f be a formula $\exists x(C_k(x) \wedge ...)$ from F and $A = \{A_1, A_2, A_3\} = \{\forall x(C_i(x) \rightarrow \neg C_j(x)), \forall x(C_k(x) \rightarrow C_i(x)), \forall x(C_k(x) \rightarrow C_j(x))\}$ a set of one* `IS-NOT-A` *and two* `IS-A` *axioms. If $A \subseteq A_K$, then $F \cup A_K$ is inconsistent.*

Proof. Note that the three axioms from A reflect the situation depicted in Fig. 4. To show the inconsistency of $F \cup A_K$, we need to prove its unsatisfiability. To prove the theorem, we show first that $\{f\} \cup A$ is unsatisfiable. To this end we transform $\{f\} \cup A$ into an equivalent conjunctive normal form. The resulting set of clauses $\{\{f\}, \{A_1\}, \{A_2\}, \{A_3\}\}$ is unsatisfiable if and only if there exists a

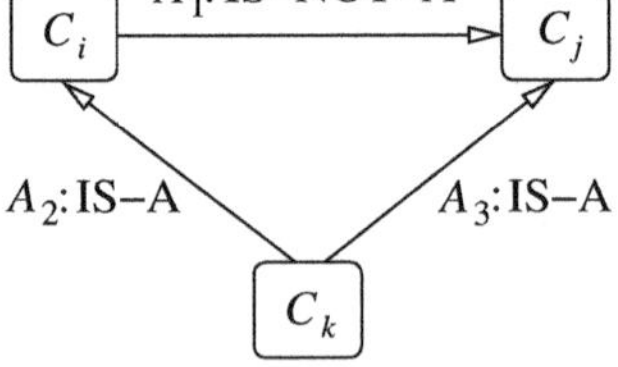

Fig. 4. Three background knowledge axioms leading into inconsistency

derivation of the empty clause using alone the resolution rule. By doing this, it can be shown that the empty clause can be derived. Thus, $\{f\} \cup A$ is unsatisfiable and since $\{f\} \cup A \subseteq F \cup F_K$, the claim follows. □

According to Theorem 1, we cannot in general integrate all background knowledge axioms A_K generated from knowledge graph G_W by the rules given in Definition 2 into the RTE problem when its original logical property (i.e., consistency or inconsistency) has to be preserved. To deal with that problem, we propose two strategies:

1. Only Rule 1 and Rule 3 from Definition 2 are used for the generation of knowledge axioms from knowledge graph G_W.
2. Some edges from knowledge graph G_W are removed, so that afterwards each concept or individual from G_W is hyponym of concept(s) of at most one (complex) node, i.e., every child node in G_W has only one father node.

Both strategies can cause some loss of effectivity of the entire RTE inference process. By using the first strategy, no `IS-NOT-A` axioms are generated and the situation described in Theorem 1 does not hold. However, the generated background knowledge is not as precise as before (there are no uniqueness constraints for concepts). The elimination of conflicting edges from G_W by the second strategy results in loss of knowledge, too, e.g., in Fig. 4 either the edge for axiom A_2 or the edge for axiom A_3 will be removed. To overcome this restriction and to make use of all knowledge from G_W, we could integrate all available hyponym relations into the RTE problem separately, one after the other. However, this would result in many parallel entailment problems (one for each reading), which we must solve and evaluate separately. Furthermore, we observed that for now it is difficult to automate the task for selecting edges for removal from G_W.

In our implementation we follow the second strategy and transform knowledge graph G_W into knowledge tree T_K with root node `entity`, the most general concept in WordNet [9]. Currently, the edges for removal can be selected either manually by the analyst from the list of proposals made by the framework, or automatically by leaving only concepts with the most frequent senses. Here, we use a variant of Lesk's WSD algorithm [36]. Fig. 5 shows a fragment of tree T_K for our example. The construction of the tree was optimized so that only those concepts from G_W appear in T_K which are directly relevant for the inference problem, e.g., only search predicates can serve as leaves in T_K, or every non-branching node between two other nodes is removed. Thus, all knowledge which will not add any inferential power is removed from T_K.

One can see in Fig. 5 that not all search predicates were recognized enough precisely during the first phase. More specifically, the named entity `bautzen` was not classified as a town as we would expect that. Since a suitable individual was not found in WordNet, the named entity `bautzen_ne_1` was assigned directly to the root of tree T_K. Clearly, without having more information about `bautzen`, we *cannot* prove the entailment.

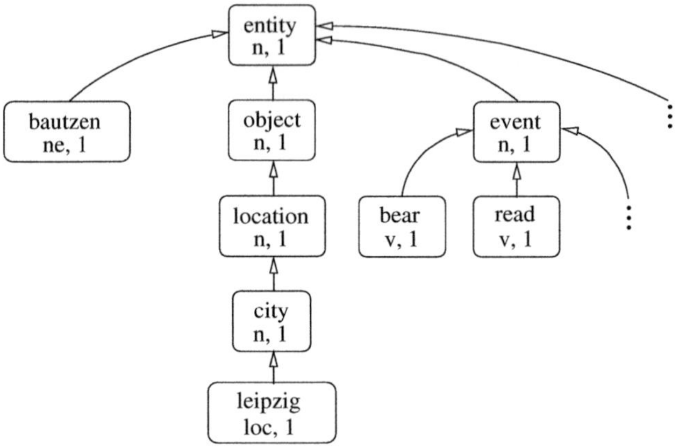

Fig. 5. Fragment of knowledge tree T_K after optimization.

4.2 Second Phase: Integration of YAGO

In this phase we consult YAGO about search predicates that were not recognized in the first phase. We formulate for each such predicate an appropriate query and send it to the query processor (see Fig. 2). To this end, we use relation `type`, one of the build-in ontological relations of YAGO [14]. For our small RTE problem, we ask YAGO with a query `bautzen type ?` of what type (or in YAGO nomenclature: of what class) the named entity `bautzen` is. If succeed, it returns knowledge graph G_Y with WordNet concepts which classify the named entity. Fig. 6 depicts graph G_Y for our example. We can see that `bautzen` was now classified more precisely, among other things, as a town.

In general, each graph G_Y is a DAG composed of partially overlapping paths leading (with respect to the hyperonymy relation) from some root node (i.e., the most general concept in G_Y, e.g., node `object` in Fig. 6) to the leaf representing the search predicate (e.g., the complex node `bautzen` in Fig. 6). Observe that there is one and only one leaf node in every graph G_Y. Since the result of every YAGO-query is in general represented by a DAG, we cannot integrate it completely into the knowledge tree T_K (see discussion above). According to

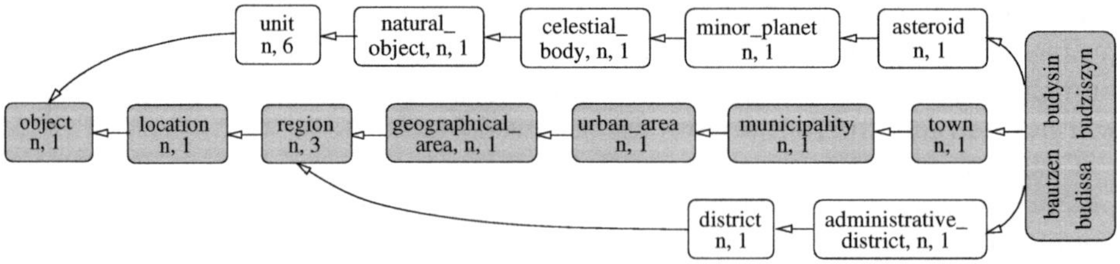

Fig. 6. Knowledge graph G_Y with results of two queries to YAGO

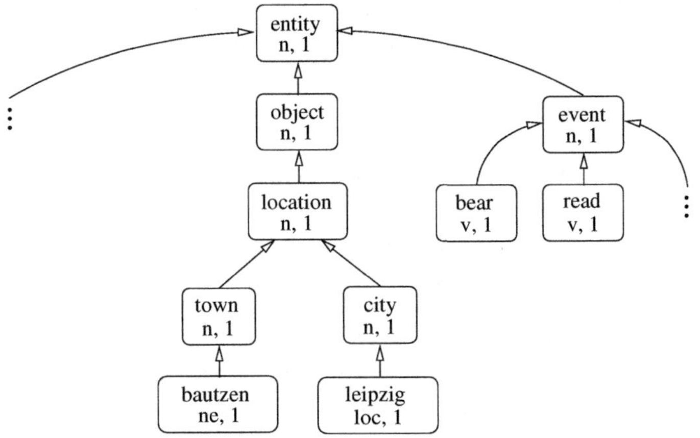

Fig. 7. Fragment of knowledge tree T_K after integration of results from YAGO

the leaf of G_Y in Fig. 6, the named entity `bautzen` can also be classified as an asteroid or an administrative district.

In order to preserve the correctness of results, we select for the integration into tree T_K only those concepts, individuals, and relations from G_Y which lay on the longest path from the most general concept in G_Y to one of the direct hyperonyms of the leaf, and which has the most common nodes with the knowledge tree T_K from the first phase. In Fig. 6 the concepts and individuals on the gray shaded path were chosen by our heuristic for the integration into T_K. After the path has been selected, it is optimized and integrated into the knowledge tree T_K. Fig. 7 depicts the knowledge tree T_K after the gray shaded path from Fig. 6 was integrated into it.

The selection of a relevant path could also be done manually by some analyst with sufficient knowledge about the problem. A fully automatic selection turns out to be a much more difficult task. Another strategy is to integrate all available paths separately, one after the other. Here, however, this would result in three parallel entailment problems, which we must solve and evaluate separately.

Observe finally that the integration of selected parts of graph G_Y into tree T_K is performed sequentially for each search predicate which was not classified in the first phase (note that each search generates its own knowledge graph G_Y).

Additionally to the first query to YAGO, we can also formulate a second one like `bautzen isCalled ?`, in which we ask what are the names of the named entity in other languages. In Fig. 6 we can see four different names for this entity. This complementary information can be combined afterwards into the FOLE formulas of the RTE problem as new predicates, e.g.,

$$...\exists x((bautzen(x) \leftrightarrow \boldsymbol{budysin}(x) \leftrightarrow \boldsymbol{budissa}(x) \leftrightarrow \boldsymbol{budziszyn}(x)) \wedge ...)...$$

After the second phase of the integration procedure is finished and the final knowledge tree T_K has been computed, the background knowledge axioms are generated from T_K according to Definition 2. The resulting axioms are added into the FOLE formulas of the input RTE problem. Such an extended input problem is passed over to the inference process (see Fig. 2) and solved correspondingly.

5 Conclusion and Future Work

In this paper we presented a new integration procedure which can be used to combine different background knowledge sources in order to support RTE. The correctness of our two-phase procedure was discussed formally and its functionality was explained in detail with several examples.

For now, it is still impossible to measure its exact semantic accuracy as there is no corpus with gold standard representations which would make such a comparison possible. Measuring semantic adequacy could be done systematically by running the system on controlled inference tasks for selected semantic phenomena. To this end, we have embedded the procedure into our experimental system for semantic text analysis and preliminarily evaluated it with RTE problems from the development sets of the past RTE Challenge [37]. A systematic evaluation against existing approaches will be part of further investigations. Because of a huge coverage of YAGO, it was almost always possible, to find information we needed for the proof. Here, it is interesting to look at the inconsistent cases of the inference process. They were caused by errors in presupposition and anaphora resolution, incorrect syntactic derivations, and inadequate semantic representations. They give us good indications for further improvements. Here, the word sense disambiguation problem plays a decisive role for matching the set of senses of the semantic analyzers with multiple, and likely different, sets of senses from the different knowledge resources.

Furthermore, for our work-in-progress, we plan to extend the set of query types for YAGO. Not only ontological relations like, e.g., `type`, `subClassOf`, or `isCalled`, but also temporal ones such `during`, `since`, or `until` should be considered, e.g., for the implementation of some temporal calculus. Finally, we plan to extend further the external knowledge resources by integrating OpenCyc [38] and DBpedia [25].

Acknowledgment. I wish to thank Matthias Hecking and the anonymous reviewers for many valuable comments on the preliminary version of the paper.

References

1. Cafarella, M.J., Re, C., Suciu, D., Etzioni, O.: Structured querying of web text data: A technical challenge. In: Proceedings of the Third Biennial Conference on Innovative Data Systems Research (CIDR), pp. 225–234 (2007)
2. Milne, D.N., Witten, I.H., Nichols, D.M.: A knowledge-based search engine powered by wikipedia. In: Proceedings of the 16th ACM Conference on Information and Knowledge Management (CIKM), pp. 445–454 (2007)

3. Chatterjee, N., Goyal, S., Naithani, A.: Resolving pattern ambiguity for English to Hindi machine translation using WordNet. In: Workshop on Modern Approaches in Translation Technologies (2005)
4. Ifrim, G., Weikum, G.: Transductive learning for text classification using explicit knowledge models. In: Proceedings of the 10th European Conference on Principles and Practice of Knowledge Discovery in Databases, PKDD (2006)
5. Hunt, W., Lita, L., Nyberg, E.: Gazetteers, wordnet, encyclopedias, and the web: analyzing question answering resources. Technical Report CMU-LTI-04-188, Language Technologies Institute, Carnegie Mellon (2004)
6. Bentivogli, L., Dagan, I., Dang, H.T., Giampiccolo, D., Magnini, B.: The fifth PASCAL recognizing textual entailment challenge. In: TAC 2009 Workshop, Gaithersburg, Maryland (2009)
7. Bos, J., Markert, K.: When logical inference helps determining textual entailment (and when it doesn't). In: Proceedings of the Second PASCAL Challenges Workshop on Recognizing Textual Entailment, Venice, Italy (2006)
8. Noy, N.F., Doan, A., Halevy, A.Y.: Semantic integration. AI Mag. 26(1), 7–9 (2005)
9. Fellbaum, C. (ed.): WordNet: An Electronic Lexical Database. The MIT Press, Cambridge (1998)
10. Dagan, I., Dolan, B., Magnini, B., Roth, D.: Recognizing textual entailment: Rational, evaluation and approaches. Natural Language Engineering. Special Issue on Textual Entailment 15(4), i–xvii (2009)
11. Herrera, J., Peñas, A., Verdejo, F.: Techniques for recognizing textual entailment and semantic equivalence. In: Marín, R., Onaindía, E., Bugarín, A., Santos, J. (eds.) CAEPIA 2005. LNCS (LNAI), vol. 4177, pp. 419–428. Springer, Heidelberg (2006)
12. Blackburn, P., Bos, J.: Representation and Inference for Natural Language. A First Course in Computational Semantics. CSLI (2005)
13. Van der Sandt, R.A.: Presupposition projection as anaphora resolution. Journal of Semantics 9(4), 333–377 (1992)
14. Suchanek, F., Kasneci, G., Weikum, G.: YAGO - a large ontology from Wikipedia and WordNet. Elsevier Journal of Web Semantics 6(3), 203–217 (2008)
15. Curran, J.R., Clark, S., Bos, J.: Linguistically motivated large-scale NLP with C&C and boxer. In: Proceedings of the 45th Annual Meeting of the ACL on Interactive Poster and Demonstration Sessions, Prague, Czech Republic, pp. 33–36 (2007)
16. Schäfer, U.: Integrating Deep and Shallow Natural Language Processing Components – Representations and Hybrid Architectures. PhD thesis, Saarland University, Saarbrücken, Germany (2007)
17. Bos, J., Markert, K.: Combining shallow and deep NLP methods for recognizing textual entailment. In: Proceedings of the First PASCAL Challenges Workshop on Recognising Textual Entailment, Southampton, UK, pp. 65–68 (2005)
18. Kamp, H., Reyle, U.: From Discourse to Logic. Introduction to Modeltheoretic Semantics of Natural Language. In: Formal Logic and Discourse Representation Theory. Kluwer Academic Publishers, Dordrecht (1993)
19. Blackburn, P., Bos, J., Kohlhase, M., Nivelle, H.D.: Automated theorem proving for natural language understanding. In: Problemsolving Methodologies with Automated Deduction (Workshop at CADE-15) (1998)
20. Bos, J., Markert, K.: Recognising textual entailment with logical inference. In: Proceedings of the 2005 Conference on Empirical Methods in Natural Language Processing (EMNLP), Vancouver, Canada, pp. 628–635 (2005)
21. Bos, J.: Towards wide-coverage semantic interpretation. In: Proceedings of the 6th International Workshop on Computational Semantics IWCS-6, pp. 42–53 (2005)

22. Tatu, M., Moldovan, D.: A logic-based semantic approach to recognizing textual entailment. In: Proceedings of the COLING/ACL on Main Conference Poster Sessions, Morristown, NJ, pp. 819–826 (2006)
23. MacCartney, B., Manning, C.D.: An extended model of natural logic. In: Proceedings of the 8th International Conference on Computational Semantics (IWCS-8), pp. 140–156 (2009)
24. de Melo, G., Suchanek, F., Pease, A.: Integrating YAGO into the Suggested Upper Merged Ontology. In: Proceedings of the 20th IEEE International Conference on Tools with Artificial Intelligence, ICTAI (2008)
25. Auer, S., Bizer, C., Kobilarov, G., Lehmann, J., Cyganiak, R., Ives, Z.: DBpedia: A nucleus for a web of open data. In: Aberer, K., Choi, K.-S., Noy, N., Allemang, D., Lee, K.-I., Nixon, L.J.B., Golbeck, J., Mika, P., Maynard, D., Mizoguchi, R., Schreiber, G., Cudré-Mauroux, P. (eds.) ASWC 2007 and ISWC 2007. LNCS, vol. 4825, pp. 722–735. Springer, Heidelberg (2007)
26. Bizer, C., Heath, T., Berners-Lee, T.: Linked data: Principles and state of the art. In: Proceedings of the 17th World Wide Web Conference, WWW (2008)
27. Copestake, A., Flickinger, D., Pollard, C., Sag, I.A.: Minimal recursion semantics: An introduction. Research on Language and Computation 3, 281–332 (2005)
28. Flickinger, D.: On building a more efficient grammar by exploiting types. Natural Language Engineering 6(1), 15–28 (2000)
29. Brants, T.: TnT – a statistical part-of-speech tagger. In: Proceedings of the Sixth Applied Natural Language Processing Conference ANLP 2000, Seattle, WA, pp. 224–231 (2000)
30. Drożdżyński, W., Krieger, H.U., Piskorski, J., Schäfer, U., Xu, F.: Shallow processing with unification and typed feature structures – foundations and applications. Künstliche Intelligenz 18(1), 17–23 (2004)
31. Callmeier, U.: PET – a platform for experimentation with efficient HPSG processing techniques. Natural Language Engineering 6(1), 99–108 (2000)
32. McCune, W.: Mace4 Reference Manual and Guide. Argonne National Laboratory, IL (2003)
33. McCune, W.: Prover9 manual (2009), `http://www.cs.unm.edu/~mccune/prover9/manual/2009-11A/`
34. Dowty, D.: On semantic content of the notion of "thematic role". In: Barbara Partee, G.C., Turner, R. (eds.) Properties, Types and Meaning, vol. 2, pp. 69–129. Kluwer, Dordrecht (1989)
35. Boolos, G.S., Burgess, J.P., Jeffrey, R.C.: Computability and Logic. Cambridge University Press, Cambridge (2002)
36. Banerjee, S., Pedersen, T.: An adapted Lesk algorithm for word sense disambiguation using WordNet. In: Proceedings of the 3rd International Conference on Computational Linguistics and Intelligent Text Processing, London, UK, pp. 136–145 (2002)
37. Giampiccolo, D., Magnini, B., Dagan, I., Dolan, B.: The third PASCAL recognizing textual entailment challenge. In: Proceedings of the ACL-PASCAL Workshop on Textual Entailment and Paraphrasing, Prague, Czech Republic, pp. 1–9 (2007)
38. Matuszek, C., Cabral, J., Witbrock, M., DeOliveira, J.: An introduction to the syntax and content of Cyc. In: Proceedings of the 2006 AAAI Spring Symposium on Formalizing and Compiling Background Knowledge and Its Applications to Knowledge Representation and Question Answering, Stanford, CA (2006)

Making Sense of Design Patterns

Rinke Hoekstra[1,2] and Joost Breuker[1]

[1] Leibniz Center for Law
Faculty of Law
University of Amsterdam
{hoekstra,breuker}@uva.nl
[2] Department of Computer Science
Faculty of Exact Sciences
VU University Amsterdam
hoekstra@few.vu.nl

Abstract. This paper discusses the way in which design patterns may improve the current practice of ontology engineering. It presents five requirements that go beyond the current state of the art of collecting and curating design patterns. We build on the thesis outlined in [17] that design patterns should be one of several possible outcomes of a fundamental *design decision*. We emphasise their relation to structures in cognition rather than domain dependence. This to improve our understanding of what ontology design patterns are, and how they relate to (modelling) expertise. We provide a definition of structural design patterns, give a number of examples, and discuss further work.

1 Introduction

An ontology is not just *any* terminological knowledge base as it embodies a specific definitional perspective. Terminological knowledge representations are based on Minsky's notion of a frame [23] – concepts are defined by context. An ontology refines this notion and needs to distinguish between the inherent and accidental properties of concepts [8,16,3]. For instance, although a typical property such as 'position' is clearly relevant from a knowledge engineering perspective, ontologically speaking it is usually a side issue: changing the position of an object does not make it intrinsically different.

This *epistemological promiscuity* of terminological knowledge representation has led to the formulation of several design principles (cf. [17] for an overview). Over the years several design principles have been cast in ontology engineering methodologies to improve the quality of ontology development. Also, the widespread availability of ontologies on the web has opened the door to the adoption of pre-existing general ontologies. By providing an initial structure and a set of basic concepts and relations, these ontologies can be a valuable jump start for more specific ontology development.

A more recent development is the identification of *design patterns* that are meant to overcome some of the limitations in the use of existing ontologies and

P. Cimiano and H.S. Pinto (Eds.): EKAW 2010, LNAI 6317, pp. 331–340, 2010.

design principles. In this paper we explore a set of requirements for ontology design patterns, which emphasise their relation to structures in cognition rather than domain dependence.

Related Work. Ontologies are frequently quite large and heavyweight; they are hard to mould and extend to a usable domain ontology. Design principles can be quite abstract and difficult to translate into concrete definitions. Design patterns offer a middle ground between the two, where the methodological principles are made concrete in manageable building blocks [13,27, a.o.]. Furthermore, these patterns can assist in tackling problems related to the ontology representation language of choice [18, a.o.]. For instance, the OPPL language [20] functions as a macro language for authoring ontologies at pattern level.

In the context of ontology development, work on Ontology Design Patterns (ODPs) is based on the notion of *knowledge pattern* [10].[1] Ontology design patterns are typically categorised as either *logical* of *content* patterns [13,27], where logical patterns do not introduce domain dependence. The ODP portal is a community effort to build a catalog of high quality ontology design patterns[2] Patterns undergo a peer-review based on a set of criteria before they become 'certified'. These criteria are based on [12] and include the availability of an OWL representation and coverage of requirements in terms of competency questions: a pattern is a solution to one or more use cases. The content pattern should be a small, autonomous ontology, that covers a core of cognitively relevant components, allows some form of reasoning and reflects best practices.[3]

An initial evaluation of content pattern-based ontology construction [2] shows that participants feel that patterns help, and that using design patterns results in 'better' ontologies. Unfortunately this is only preliminary work, most subjects were not very experienced knowledge engineers, and the set of available design patterns was limited to 22. Also, the evaluation concerned the ontology engineering process rather than the design patterns themselves, making it hard to assess how the quality of these patterns contributed to the evaluation results.

The cognitive perspective of [13] has received little attention in practice: patterns are mainly considered to be engineering artefacts, and essentially form a collection of best practices. Indeed this is very useful, but in this paper we aim to delve somewhat deeper and improve our understanding of what ontology design patterns are, and how they relate to (modelling) expertise.

In light of this exercise we explore several requirements that support this perspective. Admittedly these requirements differ from the criteria of the ODP portal as they are not aimed to optimise categorisation and publication in a catalog. We build on the thesis outlined in [17] that design patterns are *language*

---

[1] We will use the terms 'ODP', d'esign pattern' and 'pattern' interchangeably throughout this paper.

[2] See `http://www.ontologydesignpatterns.org`

[3] See `http://ontologydesignpatterns.org/wiki/index.php?title=Odp:EvaluationPrinciples&oldid=1714`. These criteria apply only to *content* patterns ([27], and 2.3).

dependent and should emphasise *structure* rather than content. We expound the intuition that these structures should be *recurrent*, sufficiently *complex*, and that they should be applicable and query-able *across domains*. In short, the pattern should be one of several possible outcomes of a fundamental *design decision*. We discuss these five requirements, provide a definition of structural design patterns (section 2.3), give a number of examples (subsection 2.5), and discuss further work (section 3).

2 Requirements for Design Patterns

2.1 Design Patterns are Language Dependent

Most requirements and principles for ontology construction are described at the knowledge level [24]; they pertain to what van Heijst et al. [28] called *knowledge modelling*: they are conceptual and independent of the language in which the ontology is eventually specified. However, an ontology itself is a *design model*, where the design is subject to *design principles* that guide the expression of the conceptual model in a formal language. The distinction between the two types of models dates back to e.g. the KADS [7] and role limiting [9] approaches that tried to maximise the reusability of expert knowledge.

Design patterns can help to bridge the gap between the two levels. They reflect a choice for a set of *design decisions* needed to translate a knowledge model into a concrete knowledge representation. These decisions fall into two categories. First, a design pattern involves a commitment to a particular view on the structure of the world (see also section 2.2). Secondly, the choice of a representation language, and in particular its expressiveness, determines what parts of the ontology as conceptual model can be represented.

The trade-off between expressiveness on the one hand and decidability and computational efficiency on the other played an important role in the specification of description logics [21]. It is reflected by an ontological trade-off: not all ontologically relevant features can always be represented in OWL DL, and some features can be represented in multiple ways, each with its own benefits.

The encoding of an ontology is therefore not only the result of ontological choices, but also of a design decision for a particular knowledge representation language. As a consequence, design patterns are specific to a particular language, but solve a conceptual modelling problem that exists independently of it.

2.2 Design Patterns Are Recurring Structures

Syntactically, definitions of concepts in a formal language do not differ much from descriptions of terms in natural language. In both cases an expression is a combination of symbols that follows certain grammatical rules. The way in which we combine words in linguistic expressions follows basic, cognitive rules and suggests the existence of fundamental concepts in thought [26]. Pinker [26] describes the atypical behaviour of some verbs in the dative form. While most transitive verbs can be used both in a propositional dative form (subject-verb-'to'-recipient) and a double-object form (subject-verb-recipient-thing), this cannot be extracted to a general rule. For instance, whereas we *can* say:

- 'Give a muffin to a moose' and 'Give a moose a muffin', we *cannot* say:
- 'Biff drove the car to Chicago' and 'Biff drove Chicago the car'

Idiosyncrasies such as this indicate that the two constructions are not synonymous, but in fact follow differing underlying patterns. Whereas the propositional dative matches the pattern "cause to go", as in '*cause a muffin to go to a moose*', the double-object dative matches "cause to have", as in '*cause a moose to have a muffin*'. A plethora of other constructions such as these exists. For example, to indicate a distinction between direct and indirect causation as in '*dimming the lights*' when sliding a switch and '*making the lights dim*' when turning on the toaster. It is these patterns that are used to construct metaphors such as the *container* and *conduit* metaphors where ideas are things, knowing is having, communicating is sending and language is the package: "*We* gather *our ideas* put *them* into *words, and if our verbiage is not* empty *or* hollow, *we might* get *these ideas* across *to a listener, who can* unpack *our words to* extract *their* content." [26, p.60].

According to Pinker, the basic concepts in a language of thought correspond to the kinds of concepts that fit the slots of grammatical constructions. The grammar rules of language reflect the structure of our conceptualisation of the world around us. It shows the restrictions on the ways in which we can combine concepts to create meaningful categories: the position of a term in a sentence is indicative of its meaning, and the general category it belongs to. Although every language has a different grammar, each of them has a mechanism for expressing the same set of basic notions. Linguistic expressions follow frequently recurring patterns that can be re-applied to new circumstances to create new meaning (e.g. in metaphors). These patterns are design patterns, and depending on *which* pattern we apply, we create a different meaning or shift emphasis.

Can the way in which we apply grammatical patterns to construct meaning teach us something about ontology design patterns? If we follow Pinker – and let's do so for now – then design patterns are *recurring* structures that capture a fundamental understanding of the world. Arguably, recurrence is a useful selection criteria when collecting and curating patterns.[4]

2.3 Design Patterns Are Applicable Across Domains

The examples in section 2.2 show that patterns have to somehow 'fit': applicability is determined by the (in)compatibility between that which a pattern is meant to express about it, and the meaning of the word. This incompatibility is not a priori evident in knowledge engineering. In linguistics, we can do pattern learning by analysing a corpus of text and search for metaphors. Not so in knowledge

[4] The linguistic patterns in the ODP portal, and the FrameNet repository (`http://framenet.icsi.berkeley.edu/`) referred to by [27], can be a valuable resource for identifying these deeper recurrent structures.

engineering, where the meaning of a concept is a posteriori, and *follows from* the application of a pattern in a knowledge representation language.

At its heart, knowing which pattern to apply where is a specific case of the general problem of knowledge acquisition: extracting expert knowledge about a domain, and casting it into a model. The focus on larger structures takes out some of the difficulties in having to deal with the primitives of a representation language, but it does not solve the larger problem unless design patterns have some way of indicating to which types of concepts they can be applied. Too strong a connection to a particular category of concepts has a negative impact on their applicability to other domains. Furthermore, there should be some mechanism in place that allows us to check whether a pattern is correctly implemented in an ontology.

Signalling by Content or Structure. Content ontology design patterns are mini-ontologies, and their utility lies in the fact that many ontologies cover parts of the same or overlapping domains. [12] require that the implementation of a content pattern should preserve *downward taxonomic ordering*: the concepts in the ontology are subsumed by the concepts of the pattern.[5] However, this restriction reduces pattern reusability to ontology reuse. This is problematic because of the *ontology interaction problem*: the general problem that if an ontology reuses another, its ontological commitments may affect the commitments of the reused ontology [17]. Because languages such as OWL 2 DL are too expressive to determine the *safe reuse* of imported axioms in an ontology [14], there is no way to guarantee correct implementation of the pattern. Indeed, if no formal representation of the content pattern is available, then the restriction on downward taxonomic ordering is merely a call to pattern designers to use generic categories to better indicate applicability of the pattern.

[10] define knowledge patterns as theories whose axioms are not part of the knowledge base that implements it. The implementation of a pattern occurs by importing its axioms, and mapping the symbols of the implementation to symbols in the pattern's signature. This mapping is given by a *morphism* that maps every non-logical symbol in the pattern to a corresponding symbol in the knowledge base. The implementation of a knowledge pattern is not structure-preserving: multiple classes in the pattern can be mapped onto a single class in the ontology. Both the pattern and the mapping are required to be external to the knowledge base, and no formal method of guaranteeing correct implementation exists.

Although *logical design patterns* have a more structural character than content patterns [12], they suffer from the same limitations as knowledge patterns. Axioms in the implementation are *typed* according to the meta-categories defined by the logical pattern. In model theoretic terms, the part of an ontology that implements a logical pattern should be a valid model of the pattern. As a consequence, logical patterns expressed in OWL cannot be enforced using a

[5] Note that this does not exclude the possibility of having a partial order of patterns themselves [27].

description logics classifier; they are limited to OWL Full. Furthermore, implementing meta level statements is not structure preserving either; multiple positions in the pattern may be instantiated by the same class.

The limitations of these approaches has been recognised in the community, most notably by the OPPL Protege plugin of [20]. It guides the implementation of ontology design patterns expressed in OPPL into an OWL ontology.

Structure Patterns and Metaphors. What sets the knowledge pattern and logical pattern apart from content patterns, is that the mapping between pattern and implementation is not subject to ontological restrictions: they do not assume an ontological relation between the symbols in either signature. Both pattern types are intended to be *structure patterns*, that try to ensure the transposition of the *structure* of the pattern to categories in the implementation. A proper *structure pattern* is an ontology design pattern for which the mapping function is *injective* – there is a one-to-one correspondence between elements of the pattern and the implementing ontology – and no ontological requirements hold on elements of the signatures.

Even though the implementation of a structure pattern does not explicitly involve an *ontological* commitment, it may still incorporate certain other, less strict commitments. Firstly, structure pattern implementations signal an *intended interpretation* for that part of the ontology; i.e. they may have an *epistemological* commitment (c.f. [3]). For instance, an OWL implementation of the n-ary relation pattern of the SWBP [25] signals that even though it *is not* an n-ary relation according to the OWL semantics, it should be interpreted as such.[6] This works in exactly the same way that the presence of OWL constructs signal the applicability of OWL semantics.

Secondly, even without an explicit ontological commitment, they do convey a certain ontological 'message': design patterns may transpose the stereotypical structure of ontological categories to new domains. In other words, structure patterns can be used to construct *metaphors*. The strength of the metaphor depends on the strength of the ontological relation between a pattern and its implementation [17]. The properties of an implementing ontology should be at least (conceptually) sub properties of corresponding properties in the pattern. For instance, the conduit metaphor from section 2.2 cannot be implemented as content pattern, but can be a metaphoric use of a structure pattern. The former requires words to literally *be* containers for ideas, and the latter merely signals a connotation. The relational character of metaphoric use corresponds to the role of verbs in natural language metaphors [26], and the prototypical representation of verbs as properties [4].

Structure patterns relax the ontological restrictions of content patterns, but strengthen the structural requirements of logical and knowledge patterns. Furthermore, if a structure pattern is implemented as metaphor, the implementation can still be queried at pattern-level (i.e. in terms of the pattern) and checked for consistency.

[6] SWBP: Semantic Web Best Practices and Deployment Working Group. See `http://www.w3.org/TR/swbp-n-aryRelations/`

2.4 Design Patterns are Complex Structures

In order for design patterns to be of use, they should assist in creating an adequate knowledge representation of a domain. This means that they may be small, but should be complex enough to take work out of the hands of an ontology engineer: not just quantitatively, but qualitatively as well. It is nice if a pattern reduces the number of mouse clicks needed to create a certain part of the ontology, but the real challenge lies in addressing the time and depth needed to come up with a particular modelling solution. Of course, complexity is a rather imprecise notion: it may reside both in the combination of constructs of the knowledge representation language, as well as in the domain.

2.5 Design Patterns Capture Fundamental Design Decisions

In the preceding sections we observe that the recurrence and cross-domain applicability of design patterns are some of their key attributes. These attributes are reflected by the ability of structure patterns to construct metaphors. Given these characteristics, there are a number of relatively influential examples that come to mind.

First, there is Allen's general theory of time [1]. In this theory, time consists of a series of *intervals* that are only defined by their position *relative* to other intervals. This approach can be juxtaposed against the more commonly used *absolute* time, that commits to fixed time *points*.[7] The distinction between the two perspectives is well known, as are their benefits (i.e. expressiveness vs. conciseness), but they cannot be mixed. Choosing one over the other is a fundamental design decision.

What makes Allen's theory into a design pattern? Not its way of treating time, but rather its way of *structuring* reality. In fact, the pattern has been successfully applied in a theory of relative places [11]: the same relations defined by Allen could be used in defining the position of places relative to one another.[8] Again, the perspective can be juxtaposed against a theory of *absolute* space, which is arguably more practical when building a house.

Two contrasting patterns that have found their way into knowledge representation languages are the binary and n-ary relations (cf. [25,17]). Although these are often regarded as mere language features, they convey a commitment to a particular structure of reality. Although n-ary relations seem more expressive, they hide away the structure that must be made explicit if one does without [17]. Again, choosing one option over the other is an important design decision: no Semantic Web language supports n-ary relations, and only in highly expressive knowledge one can reify an n-ary relation into its individual components.

For instance, an exchange binds two processes by reciprocity (cf. [18]). This is particularly reflected by identity and other constraints on roles in the two

[7] Though we are using the same terms here, we are not referring to absolute vs. relative time as in Newton vs. Einstein.

[8] Both theories were used in the LKIF Core ontology as part of the space-time module. See [17].

constituting processes. In a heat exchange between two objects, the heat emitted by one object should be in balance with respect to the heat absorbed by the other. The pattern underlying exchanges can be used in a position metaphor, e.g. goods and money are said to *trade places*. The same metaphor holds in a legal context for the exchange of ownership: ownership is a *legal* position, a right [19]. Legal positions themselves involve reciprocity as well: the right to own is balanced by a duty to pay. The choice here is between a representation of exchange as either an N-ary relation, as a 'spider' or as a more complex, layered structure. Again, the three variants result in an progressing cognitively precise representation of reality. For instance, response time research suggests that thematic roles exist at three distance levels from an action [5].

3 Discussion and Future Work

The preceding sections list five requirements for ontology design patterns. Design patterns are:

1. *language dependent*, they bridge the gap between a conceptual model and its implementation in a knowledge representation language; they are
2. *recurring structures* that can be re-applied to new circumstances as metaphors and create meaning; they are
3. *applicable across domains*, because they emphasise structure over content; they are
4. *complex structures* that alleviate the burden of knowledge engineers, both quantitatively and qualitatively; and, they
5. *capture fundamental design decisions* between alternate, disjoint ways of looking at the world.

Some of these requirements are not readily in accord with the guidelines of the ODP portal listed in the introduction. The portal requires submitted patterns to be language independent, where we argue for language dependence.[9] Secondly, we deemphasise the domain dependence of design patterns.[10] The portal is a commendable initiative to make a significant paradigm shift in the way we construct ontologies. Collecting design patterns is indeed the only way to make this happen. And in fact, similar initiatives have been launched several times: the Ontolingua server [15] and the WonderWeb library that sparked DOLCE [22]. However, it seems that the way in which patterns are currently being curated could benefit from a more principled approach. First of all, design patterns should be recognised as being a key part in bridging the knowledge acquisition bottleneck. Rather than being only a means to facilitate the representation of complex structures in a knowledge representation formalism, design patterns can also work the other way around, and provide insight in the structure of expert

[9] In fact the ODP portal does require content patterns to be accompanied with at least a representation in OWL.

[10] The ODP portal is ongoing work and its aim is to cater for all types of design patterns.

knowledge. Secondly, the evaluation of design patterns should move beyond the methodological question as to whether pattern-based ontology engineering is at all a good idea. If individual patterns are subject to evaluation in the context of the modelling problem they were designed for, and *others*, this will allow us to assess and study patterns in their own right. What are the properties of design patterns that make them more or less desirable?

Furthermore, if design patterns truly capture a unique perspective on the world, they are prime candidates as an index of existing ontologies. The CommonKADS library of expertise models (mainly related to problem solving) was indexed by a suite of problem types [6]. These problem types were carefully selected to create a concise, generic categorisation of problems that covered the entries in the libraries. A similar selection of design patterns could fulfil the same role for ontologies on the web.

In this paper we have tried to emphasise that there is a *reason* why certain patterns are more useful than others. Selecting design patterns is therefore not merely a question of peer reviewing freely submitted patterns, but rather a quest for the different, alternate ways in which we can and do structure the world. Such a quest can build not only on existing domain theories (e.g. temporal logic, thermodynamics) but should rely on insights from linguistics and cognitive science to lay bare our own conceptualisations. This way, we hope to ensure that a suite of design patterns can move beyond a collection of modelling tips and tricks, however useful they are.

References

1. Allen, J.: Towards a general theory of action and time. Artificial Intelligence 23, 123–154 (1984)
2. Blomqvist, E., Gangemi, A., Presutti, V.: Experiments on pattern-based ontology design. In: Proceedings of K-CAP 2009. ACM, New York (2009)
3. Bodenreider, O., Smith, B., Burgun, A.: The ontology-epistemology divide: A case study in medical terminology. In: Varzi, A.C., Vieu, L. (eds.) Proceedings of FOIS (2004)
4. Brachman, R.J., McGuiness, D.L., Patel-Schneider, P.F., Resnick, L.A., Borgida, A.: Living with CLASSIC: When and how to use a KL-ONE-like language. In: Sowa, J.F. (ed.) Principles of Semantic Networks: Explorations in the Representation of Knowledge, pp. 401–456. Morgan Kaufmann, San Francisco (1991)
5. Breuker, J.A.: Availability of Knowledge. PhD thesis, COWO, University of Amsterdam (1981)
6. Breuker, J.A.: A Suite of Problem Types. In: CommonKADS Library of Expertise Modelling, pp. 57–88. IOS-Press/Ohmsha, Amsterdam/Tokyo (1994)
7. Breuker, J.A., Wielinga, B.J.: Knowledge acquisition as modelling of expertise: the KADS-methodology. In: Addis, T., Boose, J., Gaines, B. (eds.) Proceedings of EKAW, Reading GB, pp. 102–110. Reading Press (1987)
8. Breuker, J., Hoekstra, R.: Epistemology and ontology in core ontologies: FOLaw and LRI-Core, two core ontologies for law. In: Gangemi, A., Borgo, S. (eds.) Proceedings of the EKAW Workshop on Core Ontologies in Ontology Engineering, CEUR (2004)

9. Bylander, T., Chandrasekaran, B.: Generic tasks for knowledge-based reasoning: The "right" level of abstraction for knowledge acquisition. International Journal of Man-Machine Studies 26(2), 231–243 (1987)
10. Clark, P., Thompson, J., Porter, B.: Knowledge patterns. In: Cohn, A., Giunchiglia, F., Selman, B. (eds.) Proceedings of the 7th International Conference KR 2000, pp. 591–600. Kaufmann, San Francisco (2000)
11. Donnelly, M.: Relative places. Applied Ontology 1(1), 55–75 (2005)
12. Presutti, V., et al.: A library of ontology design patterns: reusable solutions for collaborative design of networked ontologies. Technical Report D2.5.1, NeOn Project (2008)
13. Gangemi, A.: Ontology design patterns for semantic web content. In: Gil, Y., Motta, E., Benjamins, V.R., Musen, M.A. (eds.) ISWC 2005. LNCS, vol. 3729, pp. 262–276. Springer, Heidelberg (2005)
14. Ghilardi, S., Lutz, C., Wolter, F.: Did i damage my ontology? a case for conservative extensions in description logics. In: Doherty, P., Mylopoulos, J., Welty, C.A. (eds.) KR, pp. 187–197. AAAI Press, Menlo Park (2006)
15. Gruber, T.R.: A translation approach to portable ontology specifications. Knowledge Acquisition 5(2), 199–220 (1993)
16. Guarino, N., Welty, C.: Evaluating ontological decisions with OntoClean. Communications of the ACM 45(2), 61–65 (2002)
17. Hoekstra, R.: Ontology Representation – Design Patterns and Ontologies that Make Sense. Frontiers of Artificial Intelligence and Applications, vol. 197. IOS Press, Amsterdam (June 2009)
18. Hoekstra, R., Breuker, J.: Polishing diamonds in OWL 2. In: Gangemi, A., Euzenat, J. (eds.) EKAW 2008. LNCS (LNAI), vol. 5268, pp. 64–73. Springer, Heidelberg (2008)
19. Hohfeld, W.: Fundamental Legal Conceptions as Applied in Legal Reasoning. Yale University Press (1919); Cook, W.W. (ed.): fourth printing (1966)
20. Iannone, L., Rector, A., Stevens, R.: Embedding knowledge patterns into owl. In: Aroyo, L., Traverso, P., Ciravegna, F., Cimiano, P., Heath, T., Hyvönen, E., Mizoguchi, R., Oren, E., Sabou, M., Simperl, E. (eds.) ESWC 2009. LNCS, vol. 5554, pp. 218–232. Springer, Heidelberg (2009)
21. Levesque, H.J., Brachman, R.J.: Expressiveness and tractability in knowledge representation and reasoning. Computational Intelligence 3, 78–93 (1987)
22. Masolo, C., Borgo, S., Gangemi, A., Guarino, N., Oltramari, A.: WonderWeb ontology library. Deliverable D18, version 1, ISTC-CNR, Italy (2003)
23. Minsky, M.: A framework for representing knowledge. In: Winston, P.H. (ed.) The Psychology of Computer Vision. McGraw-Hill, New York (1975)
24. Newell, A.: The knowledge level. Artificial Intelligence 18(1), 87–127 (1982)
25. Noy, N., Rector, A.: Defining n-ary relations on the semantic web. Working group note, W3C (April 2006), `http://www.w3.org/TR/swbp-n-aryRelations/`
26. Pinker, S.: The Stuff of Thought. Penguin Books (2007)
27. Presutti, V., Gangemi, A.: Content ontology design patterns as practical building blocks for web ontologies. In: Li, Q., Spaccapietra, S., Yu, E., Olivé, A. (eds.) ER 2008. LNCS, vol. 5231, pp. 128–141. Springer, Heidelberg (2008)
28. van Heijst, G., Schreiber, A.T., Wielinga, B.J.: Using explicit ontologies for kbs development. International Journal of Human-Computer Studies 46(2/3), 183–292 (1997)

Acquiring and Modelling Legal Knowledge Using Patterns: An Application for the Dutch Immigration and Naturalisation Service

Patries Kordelaar, Freek van Teeseling, and Edwin Hoogland

Pharosius, Netherlands
patries@pharosius.nl
Be Informed, Linie 620, 7325 DZ Apeldoorn, Netherlands
{f.vanteeseling,e.hoogland}@beinformed.nl

Abstract. The Dutch Immigration and Naturalisation Service is replacing its existing paper based case system with a fully electronic system with integrated decision support based on ontologies. In nature a large proportion of the organisations knowledge is based on law and regulations. In acquiring this legal knowledge for modelling we faced the classic knowledge acquisition bottleneck due to communication problems between experts from different background. To overcome this bottleneck a methodology was developed to transfer these laws in semantic knowledge models, based on legal patterns. In this paper we describe different archetypes of law and how these are transformed in models with the help of patterns. The patterns are thereby used for both translation of the true meaning of the law and for inclusion in the semantic models for automatic execution.

Keywords: Legal Patterns, Knowledge Representation, Semantics, Acquisition, Methodology.

1 Introduction

The Dutch Immigration and Naturalisation Service (IND) [8] decided, as a reaction to a review of its processes by the Dutch Court of Audit [3], to completely replace its existing (mostly) paper based case system and some form of decision support (decision trees). The new application had to be an electronic case system with integrated decision and process support for the internal knowledge worker, including a directly connected front office for clients [9]. The case system consists of a Siebel workflow system communicating within a SOA architecture with intelligent components for the decision and process support made with the knowledge-based platform Be Informed (www.beinformed.nl). The core functionality of Be Informed is a semantic modelling environment in which models can be made that are used by the inferencer for classification, calculation and decisions tasks. The new application replaces the current operational cluster of systems, of which the ICT maintenance costs are way too high.

The IND is responsible for enforcing Immigration Law in the Netherlands and handles around 255.000 permit applications per year. Since the IND is an enforcement

P. Cimiano and H.S. Pinto (Eds.): EKAW 2010, LNAI 6317, pp. 341–349.

organisation the main body of knowledge to include in the new IND application consists of legal knowledge. In acquiring and modelling this legal knowledge we faced a knowledge acquisition bottleneck. Actors with different backgrounds, legal experts and knowledge engineers, had to work together to make sound models. However, while the legal experts could not see how a piece of text was not sufficient to be machine-interpreted, the semantic engineers could not understand the interpretations of the legal experts. One of the main challenges of the project was getting the two groups closer to each other. Therefore we decided to standardize the communication between legal experts and knowledge engineers by introducing legal patterns as a means for exchanging information. Thereby it was important for the IND that the patterns would be intuitive and easy to use by the legal experts, since they are the most scarce resource within the IND. As an answer we came up with legal patterns based on legal theory. Practice has shown that these patterns could be easily used by the legal experts and that, as a side-effect, they could also be used for finding defects in the legislation.

In this paper we describe the development of the legal patterns. First we show where in the modelling process the patterns play a role. Next we shortly position the legal patterns in the light of existing literature on patterns. Then we turn our attention towards legislation. What is the nature of legislation and how did we use that nature in constructing our legal patterns. We conclude this paper with some concluding remarks and plans for future research.

2 Legal Patterns in the Modelling Process

The process of implementing legislation in the IND application is shown in figure 1.

Interpretation of legislation plays a role in the phases: analyzing the legal source texts, formulating the IND interpretation of these texts and modelling the interpretation. In these phases over 20 knowledge engineers, many domain experts and other stakeholders participated. The modelling domain consists of over 30.000 concepts and a multitude of relations. On that scale it is clear that there is a strong need to structure the modelling process.

Before the introduction of the legal patterns we encountered a major delay in the modelling process transforming the interpretation to semantic models. The IND interpretation of the legal source was laid down by the legal experts in a natural language representation, with a form of cross-linking between fragments, and the representation is accompanied by a reference to the original source text. For the knowledge engineers it was not straightforward to get from the interpretation in natural language to the much more restricted language of Be Informed (a restriction that is essential for the automatic execution of the model). The knowledge engineers still had a lot of questions about the right interpretation of the text in natural language and many times had to disambiguate the text themselves before they could model it. The (free format) textual representation and cross-links proved not to be explicit nor structured enough. Not being legal experts the engineers turned to the legal experts for the answers to their questions. Like in many organizations, legal experts are a scarce resource and the modelling process was severely delayed by these extra iterations. In response to this we developed the solution to standardize the patterns used in the communication between legal experts and knowledge engineers. This resulted in the legal patterns described in section 3.3.

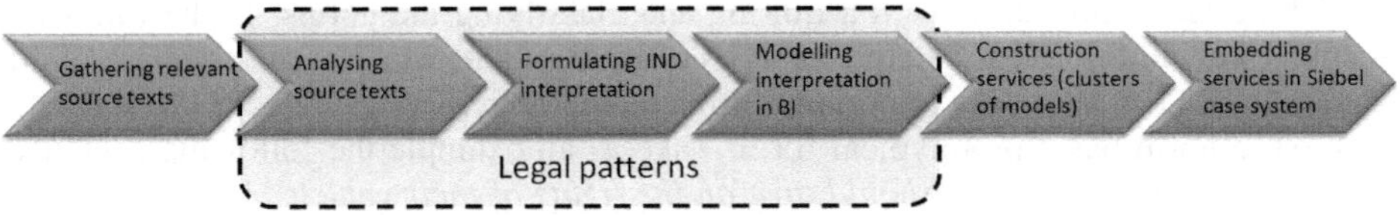

Fig. 1. Stages in the modelling chain

In the new process the developed legal patterns were introduced and used during the interpretation of the legislation. The patterns form the "glasses" with which the legal experts look at the legislation. When they recognize a norm in the legislation they make an IND interpretation of the norm (with accompanying definitions and fictions) and represent this in a structure according to a pattern. They highlight and name the different elements of the norm (and the different types of definitions, references and fictions) as agreed upon in the legal pattern. This representation is taken by the knowledge engineers to make a Be Informed model. Using the patterns, the legal interpretation was easily transformed into the semantic models. These models are used by the Be Informed inferencer for automatic reasoning tasks such as classification, calculation and deciding.

The patterns we describe in this paper have strong similarities to the patterns mapped to legal problems, like described by Gangemi [4]. His ODPs focus on legal tasks, one of which is knowledge extraction. The legal patterns we have developed for the IND can be seen as specific instances of patterns used within a broader pattern for knowledge extraction such as Gangemi's. The approach of Gangemi is towards automatic extraction. In contrast, our patterns have been used for acquisition purposes by humans, but as we will discuss in our concluding remarks our legal patterns certainly have the potential to be used for automatic knowledge extraction. Human readability however remains an important issue if the patterns are to be used in an acquisition task. Like most other ODP approaches Gangemi uses the patterns for ontology design rather than for supporting the knowledge acquisition process. This might be the reason that most formulations of ODP's are rather technical, making them unfit for use by legal experts. Graphs, and even more syntax like OWL or RDF or the Be Informed models appear to legal experts as "programming" language which they consider technical and very abstract and they found it very hard to map this to their text based world of legal knowledge. We therefore decided to turn to legal theory as the basis for the formulation of our legal patterns, instead of the final ontology design, trying to stay as close as possible to the vocabulary of legal experts. In doing this, our approach resembles the lexico-syntactic branch of ODP development like described by Aguado et. al. [1], although they have a more didactical purpose.

In the next chapter we describe how we developed the legal patterns using legal theory. Following, examples of the patterns are given.

3 Developing Legal Patterns Based on Legal Theory

3.1 Characterizing Legislation

Norms are the core element of legislation. A norm says which behaviour is allowed or forbidden. A norm can also say which situation may exist and which may not.

Modelling legislation starts with acquiring and classifying the norms. In the following sections we will discuss a systemic analysis of legal norms, which forms the base of our patterns. Two key issues are important; form and typology.

First, a norm has a prototypical form. Take as an example the following sentence: "*As the sun sets car-drivers should turn on the lights of their vehicle*" [13]. This norm sentence bears all the constituting elements of the prototypical norm (see also figure 2):

- *Subject* or addressee of the norm: to whom is the rule directed (in the example "car-drivers");
- *Objective* or action part of the norm: What behaviour or situation does it allow or prohibit (in the example the phrase "turn on the lights of the vehicle")
- *Deontic Operator* of the norm: What is the normative type of the rule, is it a prohibition or a permission (in the example presented by the word "should")
- *Condition* of the norm: Under what circumstances does the rule apply (in the example the phrase "as the sun sets")

When the norm sentence is without flaws we can find all the elements mentioned above in the norm.

Since our legal patterns rely heavily on the prototypical norm structure, we must make sure that all norm elements are recognizable in the norm. This means that the legal experts have the task to make the norms complete and designate the different parts. The legal patterns help them to identify omissions in the norm, so that they can repair these. Given that we aim at making models that can be automatically executed, all other defects must be repaired. As a final resort some vagueness can be handed over for interpretation to the end-user (but we have to be sure then that the end-user has the competencies to make the interpretation).

Next to the typical form of norms, there are also several types of norms. Sartor [15] for instance distinguishes norms that forbid behaviour, that allow behaviour, that state that persons x should do y in situation z, state that people under certain conditions are entitled to z, etc. Literature contains a lot of different divisions in types of norms, [2,10, 12, 13, 14, 15]. For the development of our legal patterns we have used a combination of these theories. In this manner we could produce a typology of norms that was:

- well understood by the legal experts of the IND because they resemble closely the vocabulary they are normally using;
- detailed enough to be able to construct patterns that result in semantic models that can be used with the Be Informed inferencers.

As a first division we used the theory of Larenz [10] about independent and dependent legal rules. The independent rules are the norms as stated above. They can function as a separate rule by themselves. Dependent rules clarify parts of the norms. For instance a rule defining the concept of a car-driver in our example norm is a dependent rule in the sense of Larenz. Dependent rules cannot function as a separate rule but get meaning only in combination with an independent rule. This does not mean that dependent rules are not normative, but that we can only make sense of the dependent rule in the context of an independent rule. Larenz mentions as dependent rules definitions, references and fictions. As a result we made not only patterns for norms, but also for definitions, references and fictions[1].

[1] In this paper we only discuss the norm patterns. For research about patterns for definitions and references we refer to [11, 12].

Analyzing the literature we derived a major distinction in norm types between duties and permissions. Duties reflect the imposing side of the law. They state what is prohibited and what should be the case. Permissions on the other hand express what is permitted; we recognize dispensations and approvals (a right is a 'strong" approval). Another distinction that is important in our construction of legal patterns is that norms can see upon conduct and upon situations (tun-sollen and sein-sollen [14]). Taking all these distinctions into account we came up with legal patterns for conduct and situations for all kind of duties and permissions. In section 3.3 we give some examples of the legal patterns.

3.2 The Representation Language of Be Informed

Our source language is legislation where the goal representation is the semantic Be Informed representation language. All examples given in the following sections will thus be illustrated by graphically represented semantic models, native to Be Informed. The reader is trusted with the possibilities of using the very same patterns in any semantic standard, like for instance OWL and RDF(S). For clarity we briefly describe the elements of the Be Informed representation language.

The Be Informed knowledge representation formalism can be characterized as a triples-based semantic network. Concepts and strong typed relations are the main elements of the language. If needed, these concepts and relationships can be further specified with formula and conditions. The concepts that are important within a (e.g. legal) domain are represented in Be Informed concepts. Often these are nouns or noun-groups. A concept can typically have a Boolean value, but can also be a number, date, or string. A concept is defined once and only once in the model with relations to other concepts, formula and conditions. Once a concept is defined, this concept can be referred to from any other concept in the model. Among the relations the Be Informed reasoner reasons with are taxonomical relations (e.g. instance-of) as well as causal relations (e.g. requires). Typical tasks that the out-of-the-box inferencers of Be Informed automatically perform are classification, decision and calculation. The inferencers are based on propositional logic and use backward chaining mechanisms.

Before we turn to examples of the legal patterns we developed we have to take one last issue into account. An organization like the IND, and certainly employees of the IND with different roles, can apply norms from several distinctive viewpoints. A decision-maker for instance can apply the norms answering the question whether a person is compliant with the norms (only then the person gets the entrance permit) or whether a person violates the norms (this sanction is issued only if that person violates the rule). A legislator however might only be interested in what the norm is, without applying the norm (an informative position). In constructing the legal patterns we also have to take the viewpoint of the user into account.

3.3 Examples of Norm Patterns in Be Informed

We start with our fictitious exemplary norm: *As the sun sets car-drivers should turn on the lights of their vehicle.* This norm is a *command* stating which behaviour a car-driver must exhibit in case the condition(s) hold. Suppose we are interested in knowing whether someone has *violated* this rule (viewpoint). The representation in natural language, highlighting the different parts of the norm is shown in figure 2.

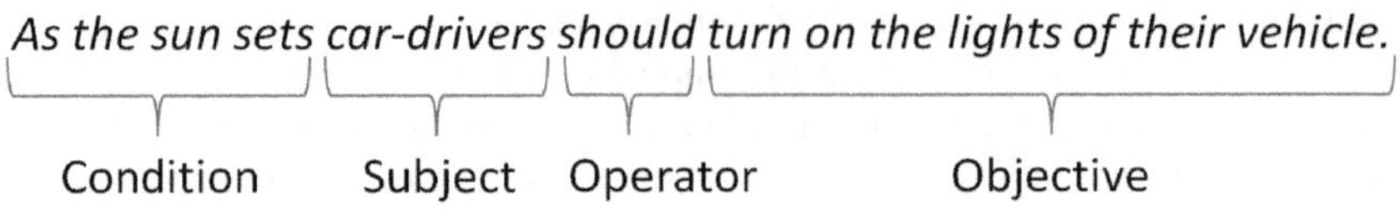

Fig. 2. Natural language representation of a command

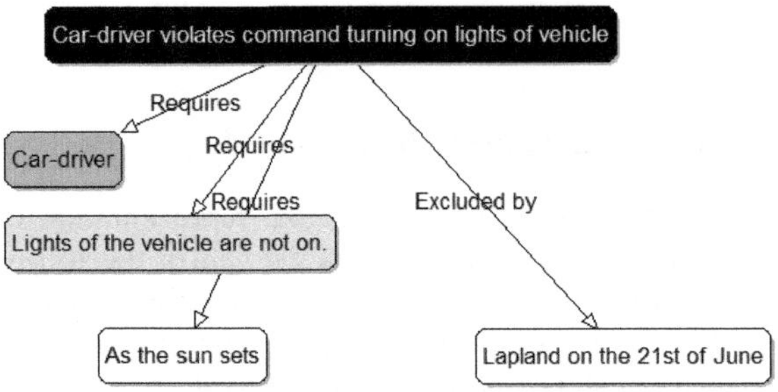

Fig. 3. Be Informed model representing a commanding norm

The corresponding Be Informed model is shown in figure 3.

The central concept of the model (car-driver violates command "turning on the lights of the vehicle") reflects the question we're interested in. This concept also makes clear that the norm is a command. It is a Boolean concept, so in this case the question is either answered with a "yes" or "no". The other concepts determine the value of the central concept. The central concept becomes true when:

- the *subject* at hand really is a car-driver (behind this concept other models that define the notion of a car-driver can be placed),
- the *condition* " as the sun sets" is fulfilled; and when
- the negation of the *object* is true (the lights of the vehicle are *not* on).

In the final model we recognize all the elements of the norm that were already highlighted in the natural language representation.

If we extend this rule with an exception, for instance "the rule holds except in Lapland on the 21st of June", we add in the model an exception concept (see also figure 5). The relation between this concept and the central concept is another causal relation in Be Informed: "Excluded by".

The natural language representation of a second example, taken from the "*Wet tot vaststelling van bepalingen betreffende het opium en andere verdovende middelen*", 1928, section 2" (translation by the authors), is shown in figure 4.

We look at this norm now from an informative point of view (suppose you are a legislator interested in what the current norm is). The model is shown in figure 5.

Notice that in this model the norm-object only plays a role in the central concept (more or less the "then" part of the rule), not in the conditional part of the model.

de model, ex lacks the norm-object completely, . This makes sense because from an informative perspective the user of the models is not interested in what happened in reality only in the "artificial" norm. Again we recognize in the resulting model the basic elements from the natural language representation of the norm.

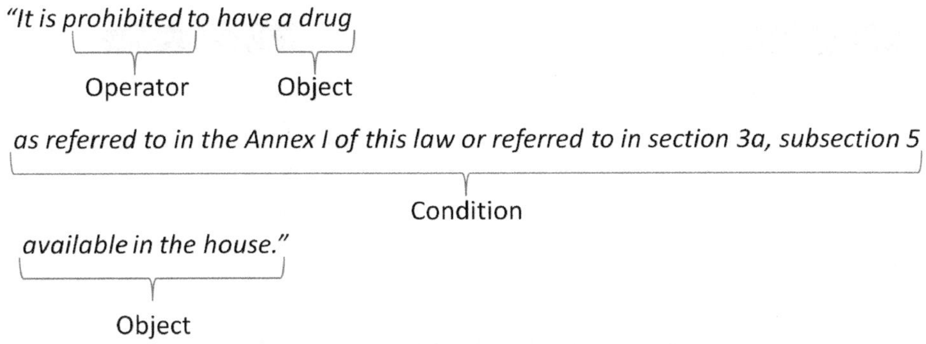

Fig. 4. Natural language representation of a prohibition[2]

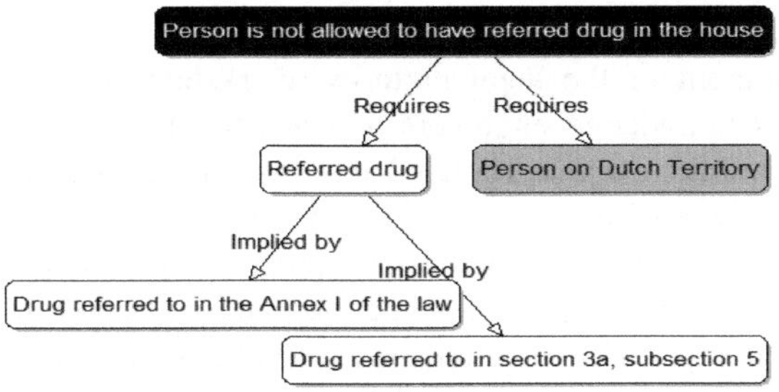

Fig. 5. Informative pattern

3.4 Towards Generic Patterns

Figure 6 shows the abstract legal patterns of both "type of norm –perspective" combinations discussed in the examples. We see that in both cases with the help of the elements of a norm recognized in section 3.1 we can make a translation from the natural language text to a Be Informed model. We found that the same pattern can be applied every time we encounter the same "type of norm-perspective" combination. As long as the elements of a norm can be recognized (and that's where the experts come in) it is not difficult to make the translation into models with the help of the patterns.

We have constructed legal patterns for all "types of norms – perspective combinations". All legal patterns could be made using only the form and the type of the norm as well as the viewpoint of the user. In using the patterns we have found that the patterns cover all the norms we encounter so far in the Immigration legislation. At this moment legal experts as well as knowledge engineers are using the legal patterns in their acquisition and modelling processes.

---

[2] Notice that the subject group is not mentioned in the rule (the norm is incomprehensively stated), we assume here that the group that is addressed consists of the persons that are located within the Dutch borders.

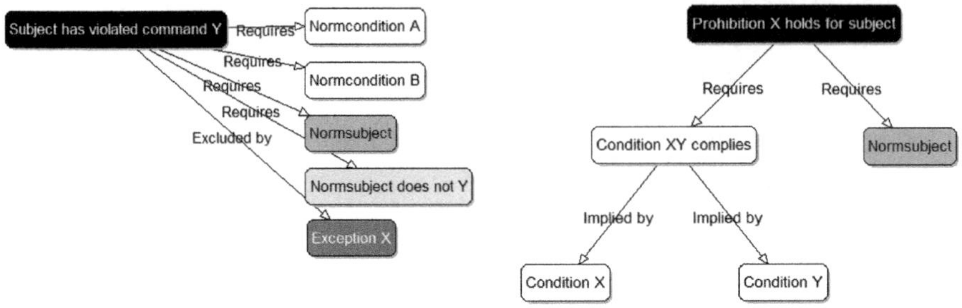

Fig. 6. Abstract legal patterns of the examples

4 Concluding Remarks and Future Research

After the development of the legal patterns, workshops have been given to legal experts as well as knowledge engineers to learn them how to work with the legal patterns. At the moment about 10 legal experts and 20 knowledge engineers are using the patterns. Legal experts prove to find the patterns very intuitive. According to their evaluating statements the patterns represent the essence of legislation quite well. This is of course not surprising since the patterns find their origin in legal theory. Also the legal experts have better means to check their representation for comprehensiveness. Omissions which would lead to incomplete knowledge models are found at an early stage and can be repaired by making additional policy rules. The knowledge engineers find the representation more understandable now and also much more complete. For the knowledge engineers it is not difficult to use the patterns because they are stated in the elements they already know quite well, the Be Informed modelling elements. At this moment the first major delivery of the system is finalized and will be implemented, replacing part of the existing IND systems, in the second half of this year.

Currently, other legal based projects have started using the patterns with similar success. Mayor effort will be put in incorporating the legal patterns, used for acquisition, in the Be Informed Implementation methodology, which has already been put to the test in numerous projects, and is common practice in the company and her partners. Adding legal knowledge acquisition as described here will benefit all these and future projects. At the same time we try to further speed up the modelling process by using the patterns for automated model generation. Another interesting approach is currently investigated by developing a text based knowledge editor, which will integrate with the graphical representations in Be Informed. This will allow (legal) experts to write down their interpretation in a specified (domain specific) syntax (possibly based on the legal patterns) which directly corresponds with the semantic models (in contrast to having to translate between the two representations) again eliminating another step in the process.

References

1. Aguado, G., Gómez-Pérez, A., Montiel-Ponsoda, E., Suárez-Figueroa, M.C.: Natural Language-Based Approach for Helping in the Reuse of Ontology Design Patterns. In: Gangemi, A., Euzenat, J. (eds.) EKAW 2008. LNCS (LNAI), vol. 5268, pp. 32–47. Springer, Heidelberg (2008)
2. Boer, A.: Legal Theory, sources of law and the semantic web. IOS Press, Amsterdam (2009), diss.
3. Dutch Court of Audit (Algemene Rekenkamer) Audit Report, `http://www.courtofaudit.com/english/News/Audits/Bronnen/2005/09/Immigration_and_Naturalisation_Service`
4. Gangemi, A.: Introducing Pattern based Design for Legal Ontologies. In: Breuker, J., et al. (eds.) Law, Ontologies and the Semantic Web, pp. 65–85. IOS Press, Amsterdam (2009), doi:10.3233/978-1-58603-942-4-53
5. Heller, R., van Teeseling, F.: Knowledge Applications for Life Events. In: The Semantic Web: Research and Applications: 6th European Semantic Web Conference, ESWC 2009 Heraklion, Crete, Greece, May 31-June 4 (2009)
6. Heller, R., van Teeseling, F., Gülpers, M.: A Knowledge Infrastructure for the Dutch Immigration office. In: 7th Extended Semantic Web Conference, ESWC 2010 Heraklion, Crete, Greece, May 30-June 3 (2010)
7. Hoekstra, R.: Ontology Representation: design patterns and ontologies that make sense. IOS Press, Amsterdam (2009), diss.
8. IND, Dutch Immigration and Naturalisation Service, `http://www.ind.nl`
9. IND Verblijfwijzer, `http://www.verblijfwijzer.nl`
10. Larenz, K.: Methodenlehre der Rechtswissenschaft. Springer, Berlin (1975)
11. de Maat, E., Winkels, R., van Engers, T.: Automated detection of reference structures in law. In: van Engers, T.M. (ed.) Legal Knowledge and Information Systems. Jurix 2006: The Nineteenth Annual Conference. Frontiers in Artificial Intelligence and Applications, vol. 152, pp. 41–50. IOS Press, Amsterdam (December 2006)
12. de Maat, E., Winkels, R.: Categorisation of norms. In: Lodder, A.R., Mommers, L. (eds.) Legal Knowledge and Information Systems. Jurix 2007: The Twentieth Annual Conference Annual Conference. Frontiers in Artificial Intelligence and Applications, vol. 165, pp. 79–88. IOS Press, Amsterdam (December 2007)
13. Ruiter, D.W.P.: Bestuursrechtelijke Wetgevingsleer. Van Gorcum, Assen (1987)
14. Van Kralingen, R.W.: Frame-Based Conceptual Models of Statute Law, Rijksuniversiteit Leiden (1995), diss.
15. Sartor, G.: Fundamental Legal Concepts: A Formal and Teleological Characterisation. In: GS 2006 AI Law Normative Ontology Springer.tex (2006)

A Model-Driven Approach for Using Templates in OWL Ontologies

Fernando Silva Parreiras, Gerd Gröner, Tobias Walter, and Steffen Staab

WeST — Institute for Web Science and Technologies, University of Koblenz-Landau
Universitaetsstrasse 1, Koblenz 56070, Germany
{parreiras,groener,walter,staab}@uni-koblenz.de

Abstract. Integrating model-driven development and semantic web resulted in metamodels and model-driven tools for the semantic web. However, these metamodels or tools do not provide dedicated support for dealing with templates in ontology engineering. Templates are useful for encapsulating knowledge and modeling recurrent sets of axioms like ontology design patterns. We propose an extension of existing metamodels and tools to support ontology engineers in modeling ontology templates. Our approach allows ontology engineers to keep template specifications as first-class citizens, reducing complexity and increasing reusability in ontology engineering. We demonstrate our approach with templates for ontology design patterns and well-known problems like domain closure.

1 Introduction

As OWL ontologies get more complex, approaches that use abstraction to encapsulate complexity emerge. For example, ontology engineers may use macros and annotations to represent ontology design patterns (ODPs) [1], key artifacts for reuse in ontology engineering.

Nevertheless, these approaches do not consider the abstraction mechanism as first-class citizens to encapsulate complexity. For instance, the development of ODPs relies on the usage of macros [2] or annotations [3] to represent the structure of these patterns. Ontology engineers should be able to encapsulate reusable sets of axioms that capture well known modeling practices in templates. In other words, ontology engineers need declarative specifications of templates and tools to test these template specifications and realizations.

The usage of templates is a well-known technique in software engineering areas like generative programming for some decades to encapsulate complexity, leading indeed OMG to add support to templates in UML [4]. For ontology engineers, the main advantages of using templates are increase in reliability, since templates comprise reliable sets of axioms developed by domain experts.

Providing a declarative specification of templates and support to template realization enables ontology engineers to handle templates as first-class citizens instead of having template descriptions embedded in ontologies as annotations or using pre-processing macros. Moreover, a dedicated approach for handling

P. Cimiano and H.S. Pinto (Eds.): EKAW 2010, LNAI 6317, pp. 350–359, 2010.

templates would enable ontology engineers to explore the full expressiveness of template declarations and to analyze template realization scenarios.

Current approaches [3, 2, 5] have limited expressiveness and are tool-oriented instead of generic, i.e., they do not allow ontology engineers to choose freely tools and representation notations for templates. Moreover, current ontology metamodels and model-driven tools do not provide those constructs [6, 7, 8].

Templates should be first-class citizens in a higher abstract level than annotations, i.e., in the ontology metamodel. Such an approach allows the following: (1) extending the usage of templates to other OWL-related languages like SWRL [9], SAIQL [10], or SPARQL-DL [11]; (2) using different modeling notations, including graphical languages; and (3) extending the usage of templates beyond individuals, classes and properties to literals and class expressions.

The contribution of this paper is twofold: (1) we present an approach for modeling ontology templates applicable to different OWL metamodels and extensible to a family of OWL-related languages like SWRL, SPARQL-DL and SAIQL; (2) we introduce graphical notations containing dedicated constructs to specify templates and to bind them with domain ontologies, enabling ontology engineers to design and test templates as first-class citizens.

We present our approach in this paper as follows. Section 2 gives a scenario motivating template design. We give an example of our approach and describe the graphical notations and the main constructs of our approach in Sect. 3. Section 4 presents applications of templates to accomplish different tasks. Section 5 presents an analysis of existing approaches and Sect. 6 concludes the paper.

2 Running Example

As running example, we consider an ontology for capturing music records as domain ontology. For this domain ontology, we want to reuse existing knowledge from three resources: ontology design patterns (ODP), SWRL rules and domain closure.

To represent the role of performers, we use the *AgentRole* design pattern from the ontology design pattern collection [12]. The intention of this ODP is to represent agents and their roles. A `Role` is a subclass of the class `Concept`, i.e. a `Role` is a specialization of `Concept`. An `Agent` is a specialization of the class `Object`. The property `hasRole` assigns `Roles` to `Objects`, whereas the inverse property `isRoleOf` assigns `Objects` to `Roles`.

Additionally, we want to propagate the genre of a musical group to a record, i.e., we want to assert that the style of the record is the same as the style of the group. Thus, we reuse a SWRL rule (in this case a DL rule) to move the property values from one individual to a related individual.

Furthermore, we want to consider the knowledge about genres as complete. In general, OWL models realize the open-world assumption (OWA), i.e. the represented knowledge base is considered as incomplete. However, in certain applications, it is more appropriate to consider a knowledge base as complete. If complete knowledge is assumed, the set of all individuals in the knowledge base must be equivalent to the set of individuals declared.

The following knowledge base (TBox and ABox) describes our simple domain ontology about music records. *Beatles* and *RollingStones* are instances of *Group*. A *Group* has *Performer* as a member. A *Performer* plays a role in a *Group*. The *Group* belongs to a *Genre* and produces *Records*. In our knowledge base, there are only four genres: Rock, Blues, Country and Samba.

$$Group \sqsubseteq \exists hasMember.Performer \sqcap \exists hasStyle.Genre$$
$$\sqcap \exists creatorOf.Record \tag{1}$$
$$Record \sqsubseteq \exists stylePeriod.Genre \tag{2}$$
$$Performer \sqsubseteq \exists hasRole.Position \tag{3}$$
$$Genre(Rock, Blues, Country, Samba), Record(LetItBleed) \tag{4}$$
$$Group(RollingStones), Performer(Mick), Position(Vocalist) \tag{5}$$
$$hasRole(Mick, Vocalist), creatorOf(RollingStones, LetItBleed) \tag{6}$$
$$hasMember(RollingStones, Mick) \tag{7}$$
$$hasStyle(RollingStones, Rock), Group(Beatles) \tag{8}$$
$$hasStyle(Beatles, \neg Blues), hasStyle(Beatles, \neg Country) \tag{9}$$
$$hasStyle(Beatles, \neg Samba) \tag{10}$$

Based on this knowledge base, a user may be looking for all rock bands as described by the following DL query: $\exists hasStyle.\{Rock\}$. If we consider an incomplete knowledge base, the result of this query contains only the individual *RollingStones*. If we assume a complete knowledge base though, the result also includes the group *Beatles*.

There are different strategies for closing the domain of a class. In this paper, we only make the class *Genre* equivalent to the set of existing individuals of the class *Genre*, i.e., $Rock, Blues, Country, Samba$.

Additionally, we want to assert that the genre of a record is the same as the genre of the group:

$$Performer(?a) \wedge Genre(?s) \wedge Record(?c) \wedge hasStyle(?a, ?s) \tag{11}$$
$$\wedge\ creatorOf(?a, ?c) \rightarrow\ stylePeriod(?c, ?s)$$

For other ontologies, ontology engineers might want to reuse these resources, since these resources represent modeling guidelines and best practices identified by domain experts. Thus, it makes sense to encapsulate these axioms, identifying generic pieces, i.e., to create a *template*. We consider templates as parameterized generic sets of axioms that can be combined with different specifications to produce a variety of artifacts like domain ontologies and queries.

One might try to use inheritance to encapsulate reusable axioms and define a super class of Genre which is equivalent to a list of existing individuals of this type, and the SWRL rule to propagate the genre to records. However, this super class and rule would not be reusable for other types of art like poetry, painting, acting and would work only for music.

In summary, the usage of a template has the following advantages:

- Templates work as interfaces to encapsulate axioms and expose only the constructs to be used as parameters. Thus, ontology engineers know exactly which concepts and roles are needed for applying the ontology design pattern.
- Ontology engineers can reuse repeatedly templates in other ontologies or in other pieces of the same ontology.
- Ontology engineers can easily bind and unbind templates to see different results, e.g, using the open world or closed domain assumption.
- Templates are reliable, since ontology experts derive templates from well known sets of axioms.
- Templates can realize macros when inheritance is not enough for encapsulating reusable axioms.

3 A Model-Driven Approach for Specifying Templates

In this section, describe the main constructs of our metamodel extension and the different notations. We have implemented our solution in the TwoUse Toolkit and it is available for download together with the examples used in this paper on the project website[1].

Figure 1 depicts the running example using the OMG UML Profile for OWL 2 with support to templates in OWL 2 ontologies. A template agent-role represents the agent role ODP [12]. This template has the two parameters – Agent and Role – to be bound in order to adopt this pattern.

A template closed-domain defines a class X which is equivalent to a list of individuals {}. Both class X and class expression {} are template parameters and are bound to the class Genre and to the class expression {Rock Blues Country Samba} of the ontology music records.

Finally, the third template shows an ontology with a SWRL rule asserting that the genre of an artist is the same as the genre of a record. When realizing these template bindings, the result is set of axioms (1-11) presented in Sect. 2.

3.1 Extending the OWL Metamodel with Templates

In this section, we define a metamodel for templates that can be used with any of the current available metamodels for OWL (OMG OWL Metamodel [6], the Neon OWL Metamodel [7] and the OWL 2 Structural Specification [8]). Afterwards, we extend it to different OWL-related languages like SWRL [9] and query languages like SPARQL-DL Abstract Syntax [11] and SAIQL [10].

UML class-based modeling and OWL comprise some constituents that are similar in many respects like classes, associations, properties, packages and instances [6]. UML [4] allows software developers to design templates of packages and classes. With templates, software developers describe reusable structures with unbound parameters. In order to use these templates, developers have to bind package templates to actual classes or properties to create real structures.

[1] `http://code.google.com/p/twouse`

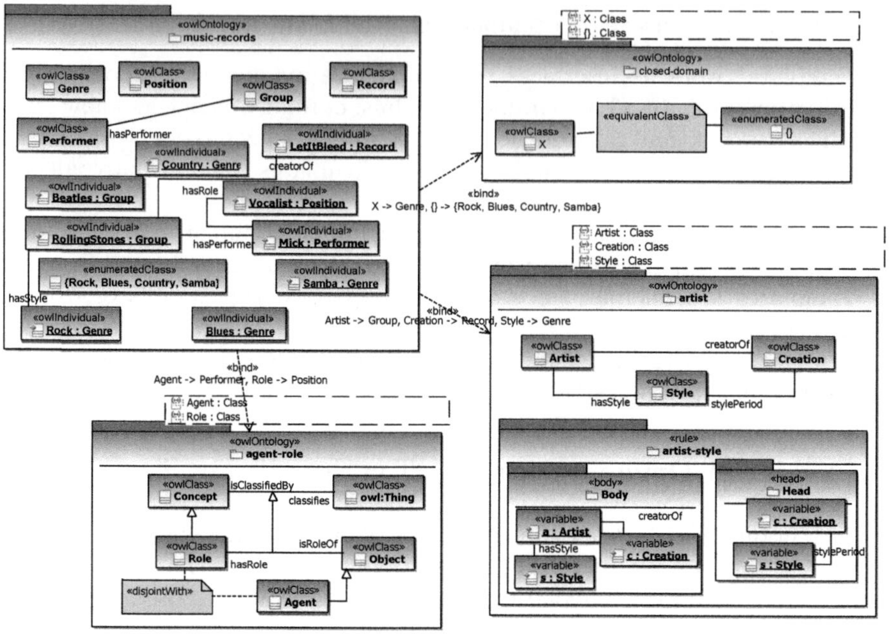

Fig. 1. Modeling the Running Example with OMG UML Profile for OWL and UML Profile for SWRL

By binding template parameters to actual values, developers apply, for example, software design patterns to software model.

UML packages and UML ontologies are similar structures (cf. [6]). While UML package templates allow classes, interfaces and datatypes as parameterable elements, we define ontology templates as templateable elements and allow classes, properties, datatypes, literals and class expressions as parameterable elements.

In the following, we explain each of these metamodel elements as addressed in our solution and present the relationships between them in Fig. 2.

- *TemplateableElement:* A templateable element is an element that can optionally be defined as a template. When a template is used, a *template binding* is created describing the replacement of template parameters with actual parameters. Examples of templateable elements are ontologies and queries.
- *Ontology:* The class Ontology specializes TemplateableElement to specify an ontology template. We apply the same rationale to queries (SPARQL-DL::Query and SAIQL::Query). For example, in Fig. 1, closed-domain, artist and agent-role are ontology templates.
- *TemplateSignature:* A template signature wraps the set of template parameters for a templateable element. In Fig. 1, the signature of closed-domain is a bundle containing the parameters X and {}.

- *TemplateParameter:* A template parameter exposes a parameterable element as a template parameter of a template. For example, in the template signature closed-domain, X and {} are representations of the parameterable elements with the same names.
- *ParameterableElement:* A parameterable element is an element that can be exposed as a template parameter for a template or be specified as an actual parameter in a binding of a template. In Fig. 2, we show only some parameterable elements like ObjectProperty, Class and Individual. Other parameterable elements include DataProperty, ClassExpression and Literal. For Example, in Fig. 1, the class X and the class expression {} are template parameters while the class Genre and the class expression {Rock Blues Country Samba} are actual parameters in the template binding.
- *TemplateBinding:* A template binding represents a relationship between a templateable element and template parameters. A template binding specifies the substitutions of actual parameters for the template parameters of the template. In Fig. 1, the template binding is represented by the association linking the ontology music-records with the templates artist, agent-role and closed-domain using the keyword << *bind* >>.
- *TemplateParameterSubstitution:* A template parameter substitution relates the actual parameter(s) to a template parameter as part of a template binding.

The metamodel for ontology templates depicted in Fig. 2 is independent of the ontology metamodel. Although we have considered the OWL 2 metamodel for

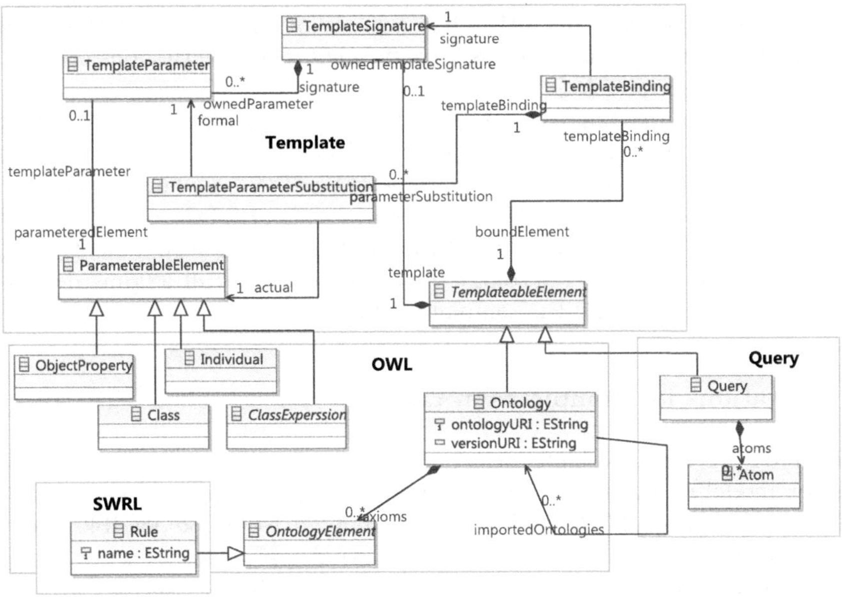

Fig. 2. Metamodel for ontology templates

our implementation, implementers can use any OWL metamodel of choice or other ontology metamodels like RDF. Implementers must then specialize the class ParameterableElement with the elements that can be used as parameters, e.g., RDFSClass.

To write description logic rules, ontology engineers rely on the structure provided by the SWRL metamodel which connects with the OWL metamodel through the class Rule. Please refer to [13] for the complete specification of the SWRL metamodel.

In order to have query templates, we specialize the class TemplateableElement with the class Query and the class ParameterableElement with variables. Thus, we can specify templates of queries and give variables as parameters.

3.2 Semantics of Templates

We treat templates as generators, i.e. templates for generating axioms. Thus, reasoners cannot inspect the contents of templates until a transformation *realizes* the template bindings by generating an effective OWL ontology.

One issue when creating templates is to ensure that they are consistent, i.e., that there exists at least one possible valid binding. A mechanism for doing this is to realize the template by automatically generating an ontology and the respective bindings. Thus, the effective OWL ontology can be tested with any standard reasoning for satisfiability and consistency.

The template mechanics do not add to the complexity of the OWL ontology. The complexity of the effective OWL ontology is composed of the complexity of the template and the complexity of the ontology bound to the template. For example, if the template definition has expressivity $\mathcal{SHON}$ and the ontology bound to the template has expressivity $\mathcal{ALCIQ}$, the effective ontology would have expressivity $\mathcal{SHOINQ}$.

The outcome of realizing the template bindings is an effective OWL ontology that can be normally checked by reasoners. When realizing template bindings, actual parameters replace template parameters and the remaining elements are copied. Consequently, the template definition is not part of the effective ontology document (the generated one), but of the implicit ontology document based on our approach. The implicit ontology document contains all axioms defined by the ontology engineers and the template definitions.

3.3 Notations for Templates in OWL

With Model-Driven Development, we are able to provide easily different notations for modeling ontology templates: our OWL 2 graphical syntax and the OMG ODM UML Profile for OWL. Additionally, it would be possible to extend the approach to support OWL 2 concrete textual syntaxes.

In Fig. 1, we show the running example modeled using the OMG UML Profile for OWL and the UML Profile for SWRL [13]. It relies on package templates natively supported by UML.

4 Analysis of Templates in Ontology Engineering

The requirements of using templates in OWL ontologies and SPARQLAS are based in our experience in building core ontologies in the past years [14, 15, 16] and in modeling software artifacts with OWL. In this section, we analyze the application of our approach.

Many versions of ontologies. We can, at the low maintenance cost of a template binding, generate many versions of an ontology. For example, one might want to have two versions of the artist ontology: one with the open-world assumption and another with the closed-domain assumption on class Genre. In some domains like software engineering, it is usual to assume complete knowledge. We can generate variations of ontologies simply by changing the bindings.

Ontology design patterns. Ontology design patterns (ODPs) are key artifacts for reuse in ontology engineering. Applying templates in ODPs provides demands specialized support to ODP constructs.

We have applied our approach in the development of domain ontologies that use core ontologies like the COMM ontology [14], the Event-Model-F Ontology [15] and the M3O ontology [16]. We are able to model all ODPs of these ontologies (three of COMM, six of Event-Model-F, four of M3O), which pointed at advantages and limitations of our approach.

Introducing templates raises the level of abstraction by allowing ontology engineers to identify quickly the requirements for using a given ODP. For example, in the COMM ontology, the semantic annotation design pattern involves at least 12 concepts and six roles to represent that a multimedia data is annotated with a label. The concepts are grounded by upper level ontologies like DOLCE. In this case, we use templates for creating an *interface* for semantic annotations, i.e. we expose only two classes – label and multimedia-data – as parameters.

In comparison with textual templating systems, the main advantage of our approach is portability. Because we handle templates at the platform-independent level, we can easily develop plug-ins for ontology editors like Protégé or Neon Toolkit. Moreover, we can generate OWL annotations for templates to keep compatibility with existing templating approaches like [3].

4.1 Limitations

The usability of the tool is a fact to consider when working with templates. Although we used existing standards for UML profiles for OWL and SWRL created to popularize OWL among software developers, there is limited tool support for those. Our implementation works with all eclipse-based UML editors, but not with non-eclipse UML editors.

One way to remedy this shortcoming is to provide multiple notations and plug-ins for various ontology editors, which should be fortunately easier with model-driven development, as discussed above. Providing additional support to widely used tools is crucial for effective uptake of our approach.

Another issue is transparency. Because templates work as generators, their results are not always apparent. Therefore, using templates requires attention about possible unsatisfiability or inconsistency caused by properties or concepts added to the effective ontology.

5 Related Work

Relevant work related to this paper cover mainly the engineering of ontology design patterns from three perspectives: macros, annotations and language dependency.

Relevant research about the engineering of ontology design pattern is analyzed in [3, 2, 5]. In [3] a pre-processor language is used to specify knowledge patterns to allow modeling on a more general pattern level than directly in the OWL ontology. This is a tool-oriented application with some procedural constructs like ADD and REMOVE. Our approach is completely declarative and supports different notations and tools.

Vrandecic analyzes the usage of macros in ontologies in [2]. These macros allow the specification of design patterns for OWL ontologies. In a preprocessing step, a macro is transformed to a set of axioms in the OWL ontology. However, the authors do not provide a concrete specification language for macros.

In [5] semantic patterns are described in RDF. These semantic patterns are transformed into the target language. The target language is not restricted to a certain language; therefore, the semantic patterns are more general. Although general, this approach does not provide constructs to handle patterns as first-class citizens as our approach does.

The creation of ontology design patterns from existing ontologies is considered in [17]. The most similar creation methods to our approach are the re-engineering from other (conceptual) data models and the extraction method from reference ontologies.

In comparison with related work, we provide an approach that is flexible, since it supports different syntaxes (including the widely used UML), extensible, as it comprises different OWL metamodels and related languages like SWRL, SPARQL and SAIQL, and platform independent, since templates are tackled at the modeling level and not at the language specific level.

6 Conclusion

We have presented an approach that raises the level of abstraction in the ontology development process by providing formalism-independent specifications of templates. The prime benefit of this approach is that it is based on pre-existing metamodels and profiles and therefore enhances the utility of previous work. Moreover, our approach is generic enough to enable model-driven tools to support different ontology metamodels of OWL-related languages.

References

[1] Gangemi, A.: Ontology Design Patterns for Semantic Web Content. In: Gil, Y., Motta, E., Benjamins, V.R., Musen, M.A. (eds.) ISWC 2005. LNCS, vol. 3729, pp. 262–276. Springer, Heidelberg (2005)

[2] Vrandecic, D.: Explicit Knowledge Engineering Patterns with Macros. In: Proceedings of the Ontology Patterns for the Semantic Web Workshop (2005)

[3] Iannone, L., Rector, A., Stevens, R.: Embedding Knowledge Patterns into OWL. In: Aroyo, L., Traverso, P., Ciravegna, F., Cimiano, P., Heath, T., Hyvönen, E., Mizoguchi, R., Oren, E., Sabou, M., Simperl, E. (eds.) ESWC 2009. LNCS, vol. 5554, pp. 218–232. Springer, Heidelberg (2009)

[4] OMG: Unified Modeling Language: Superstructure, version 2.1.2. Object Modeling Group (November 2007)

[5] Staab, S., Erdmann, M., Maedche, A.: Engineering Ontologies using Semantic Patterns. In: IJCAI 2001 Workshop on E-business and the Intelligent Web (2001)

[6] OMG: Ontology Definition Metamodel. Object Modeling Group (May 2009)

[7] Brockmans, S., Volz, R., Eberhart, A., Löfler, P.: Visual modeling of OWL DL ontologies using UML. In: McIlraith, S.A., Plexousakis, D., van Harmelen, F. (eds.) ISWC 2004. LNCS, vol. 3298, pp. 198–213. Springer, Heidelberg (2004)

[8] Motik, B., Patel-Schneider, P.F., Parsia, B.: OWL 2 Web Ontology Language: Structural Specification and Functional-Style Syntax

[9] Horrocks, I., Patel-Schneider, P.F., Boley, H., Tabet, S., Grosof, B., Dean, M.: SWRL: A Semantic Web Rule Language Combining OWL and RuleML. W3C Member Submission (May 21, 2004)

[10] Kubias, A., Schenk, S., Staab, S., Pan, J.Z.: OWL SAIQL - an OWL DL query language for ontology extraction. In: OWLED 2007 – OWL: Experiences and Directions Third International Workshop, Innsbruck, Austria, June 6-7 (2007)

[11] Sirin, E., Parsia, B.: SPARQL-DL: SPARQL Query for OWL-DL. In: OWLED 2007 – OWL: Experiences and Directions Third International Workshop, Innsbruck, Austria, June 6-7 (2007)

[12] Gangemi, A., Presutti, V.: Ontology Design Patterns. In: Handbook of Ontologies, 2nd edn. Springer, Berlin

[13] Brockmans, S., Haase, P., Hitzler, P., Studer, R.: A Metamodel and UML Profile for Rule-Extended OWL DL Ontologies. In: Sure, Y., Domingue, J. (eds.) ESWC 2006. LNCS, vol. 4011, pp. 303–316. Springer, Heidelberg (2006)

[14] Arndt, R., Troncy, R., Staab, S., Hardman, L., Vacura, M.: COMM: Designing a Well-Founded Multimedia Ontology for the Web. In: Aberer, K., Choi, K.-S., Noy, N., Allemang, D., Lee, K.-I., Nixon, L.J.B., Golbeck, J., Mika, P., Maynard, D., Mizoguchi, R., Schreiber, G., Cudré-Mauroux, P. (eds.) ASWC 2007 and ISWC 2007. LNCS, vol. 4825, pp. 30–43. Springer, Heidelberg (2007)

[15] Scherp, A., Franz, T., Saathoff, C., Staab, S.: F–a model of events based on the foundational ontology dolce+DnS ultralight. In: K-CAP 2009, pp. 137–144. ACM, New York (2009)

[16] Saathoff, C., Scherp, A.: Unlocking the Semantics of Multimedia Presentations in the Web with the Multimedia Metadata Ontology. In: WWW 2010 Proceedings. ACM, New York (2010)

[17] Presutti, V., Gangemi, A.: Content Ontology Design Patterns as Practical Building Blocks for Web Ontologies. In: Li, Q., Spaccapietra, S., Yu, E., Olivé, A. (eds.) ER 2008. LNCS, vol. 5231, pp. 128–141. Springer, Heidelberg (2008)

Specialization and Validation of Statecharts in OWL

Gerd Gröner and Steffen Staab

WeST — Institute for Web Science and Technologies,
University of Koblenz-Landau, Germany
{groener,staab}@uni-koblenz.de

Abstract. It is germane in the engineering process of knowledge bases to represent a model on different abstraction levels, developed and refined by different engineers. Hence, they are initially described at a level of coarse granularity and then refined into a more specific representation. Given two behavior models like statecharts, it is a challenging task to decide whether one statechart is still a valid specialization of the other, more abstract model. We use OWL to model statecharts and to validate statechart specializations.

1 Introduction

Statecharts, finite automata and process models are well established for representing knowledge of dynamic applications and the behavior of systems. As described in [10], the understanding of behavior and functionality of artifacts is a key issue in (domain) knowledge representation. This includes a representation of actions, effects and behavior conditions of artifacts and their functionality. Bryant describes in [7] the need in knowledge management to capture and represent knowledge by behavioral and dynamic models rather than by structural models to understand and represent complex systems.

Knowledge engineering aims at providing means for domain experts to author their knowledge directly [2]. This implies that models and knowledge bases are often described on different levels of abstraction involving different engineers that create and maintain knowledge and knowledge based systems. E.g., knowledge engineers design on a high level of abstraction, using generic descriptions for the core aspects of the knowledge base. Domain experts provide more specific descriptions for a certain domain enriched with additional informations of the domain. However, a specific knowledge base that is (probably independently) modeled and specialized by a domain expert has to satisfy all constraints and restrictions that are given by the more abstract model.

This problem is quite hard to solve, since knowledge engineering is often a continuous process in which a knowledge base is stepwise specialized, modified and enriched on different abstraction levels (cf. [24]). Once, a specialization is recognized as invalid, it might be adequate to go just one step back instead of doing the whole specialization process again. We refer to this as the spiral

P. Cimiano and H.S. Pinto (Eds.): EKAW 2010, LNAI 6317, pp. 360–370, 2010.

development methodology. Hence, it is a necessary task to validate whether a more specific and detailed knowledge base is a valid specialization of an abstract knowledge base, according to given specialization definitions.

There is related work to tackle the problem of representing behavioral knowledge on different abstraction levels and with different granularity. In [10] an ontology-based methodology for functional knowledge modeling is described. They represent concepts of functionality. The (logical) separation of domain knowledge and the knowledge formulation for planning engines is analyzed for planning technologies in artificial intelligence in [14]. However, none of these approaches consider the validation of model specializations with respect to an abstract behavior model by semantic means, i.e. different syntactical representations may describe the same meaning (behavior) of a statechart.

In this paper, we use the Web Ontology Language (OWL) to represent behavior models. As an underlying graphical formalism we use statecharts. The contribution of this work is threefold. (i) We present modeling principles and design decisions for statechart modeling in OWL. (ii) Specialization relations between different statecharts are defined. We distinguish between refinement and extension. These definitions are based on existing work in action and situation calculus. We demonstrate how our approach captures these different types of specializations. (iii) A reduction algorithm in combination with standard OWL reasoning services is applied in order to validate specialized models with respect to a more abstract statechart.

2 The Problem of Statechart Specialization

UML Statecharts [1] are a kind of finite automata, their notation has been developed by Harel (cf. [9]). They provide a hierarchical structuring of states. We define a statechart as a five-tuple $M = (\mathcal{S}, \Sigma, \mathcal{T}, s, \mathcal{F})$ as follows: $\mathcal{S}$ is a finite and non-empty set of states, Σ is a finite set of actions and events (alphabet), $\mathcal{T}$ is a finite set of transitions, triggered by events ($E \subseteq \Sigma$), $s \in \mathcal{S}$ is the initial state or start state and $\mathcal{F} \subseteq \mathcal{S}$ is a set of end states.

An abstract model may be specialized in several ways. The statechart in Fig. 1(a) describes the behavior of an online reservation system. The state *ItemSelected* is the initial state. This is indicated by the circle. The final state is *Ordered*. This is depicted by the double-lined circle. The statechart from Fig. 1(a) is modified to a more specific statechart (Fig. 1(b)).

The state $ItemOffered$ is decomposed into two substates $InternalSupplier$ and $ExternalSupplier$. The incoming and outgoing transitions (edges) remain in the superstate $ItemOffered$. A superstate that consists of substates is also called a composite state. The state *Ordered* is also decomposed into two substates *Domestic* and *Abroad*, both contain state conditions. The state *Pending* is added to the statechart with two outgoing transitions. One reaches a new final state via transition *abort* with the transition guard *stalled*, the other transition $re - select$ with guard *item chosen* leads back to the state *ItemSelected*.

As described in Sect. 1, the abstract model is usually created by a knowledge engineer on an abstract level, while the more specific model is designed and

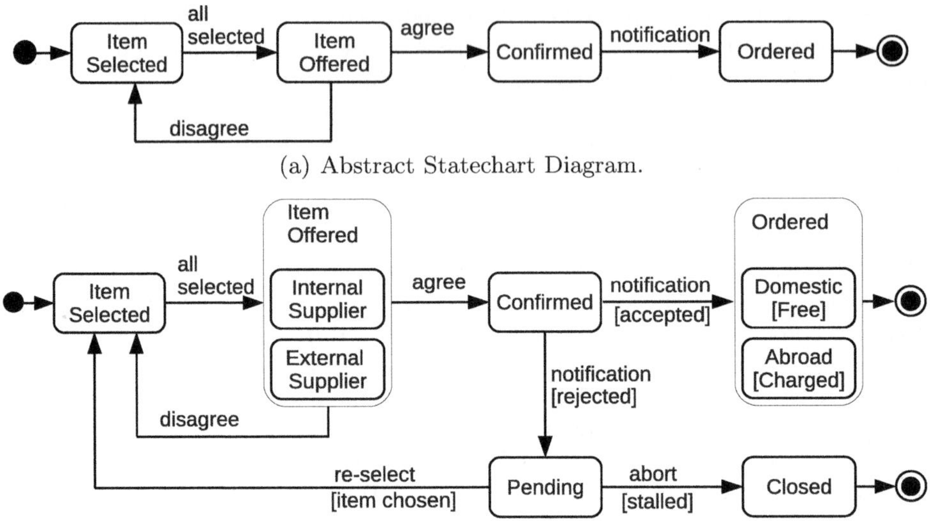

(a) Abstract Statechart Diagram.

(b) Modified and specialized Statechart Diagram.

Fig. 1. Statechart Modification

specialized independently with more details of the domain. However, the more detailed and specialized statechart has to be a valid specialization. A specialized statechart is a valid specialization of an abstract model if all instances of the specialized model are also instances of the more abstract model. Specializations have to satisfy certain consistency criteria (cf. [25] and Sect. 4).

A challenge in such a scenario is to identify whether a modified statechart is a valid specialization of a more abstract model. As demonstrated in this example, there are different means to specialize a model like the decomposition of a state into substates, adding transitions, state conditions and additional states. Hence, the validation has to account for these different kinds of specializations.

3 Transformation to OWL

In this section, we describe how to model UML statechart primitives in OWL DL allowing for the exploitation of Description Logics (DL) [4] reasoning in order to validate statechart specializations. We use a standard DL notation.

Each (notational) state A of a statechart is described by a state label S_A. The state label S_A of a state A is defined by a class expression collecting all valid system states as instances, constrained by transitions and state conditions. Likewise, transitions T_a are represented by intersecting class expressions standing for source, target, event and guard of a transition T_a. We distinguish the set of states and transitions by introducing disjoint superclasses $State_i$ and $Transition_i$.

No. 1 in Table 1 depicts a transition from state A to B. The state A is represented in OWL by the state label S_A that is defined by the intersection of class A

Table 1. Transformation for Modeling Statechart Primitives

No.	Description	Diagram	DL Representation - TBox
1	Transition	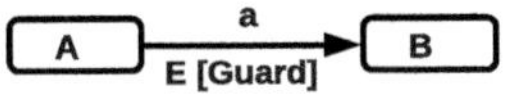	$S_A \equiv A \sqcap \exists sourceOfTransition.T_a$ $S_B \equiv B \sqcap \exists targetOfTransition.T_a$ $T_a \equiv a \sqcap \exists event.E \sqcap \exists prec.Guard$ $\sqcap \exists source.S_A \sqcap \exists target.S_B$
2	Substate (complete)	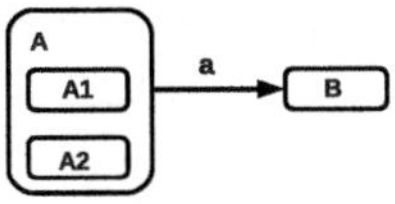	$S_A \equiv A \sqcap (S_{A_1} \sqcup S_{A_2}) \sqcap \exists sourceOfTransition.T_a$ $S_{A_1} \equiv A_1$ and $S_{A_2} \equiv A_2$ $S_{A_1} \sqsubseteq S_A$ and $S_{A_2} \sqsubseteq S_A$ $S_B \equiv B \sqcap \exists targetOfTransition.T_a$ $T_a \equiv a \sqcap \exists source.S_A \sqcap \exists target.S_B$
3	Conditions	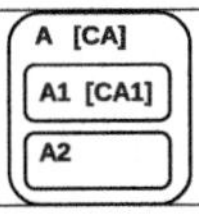	$S_A \equiv A \sqcap CA \sqcap (S_{A_1} \sqcup S_{A_2})$ $S_{A_1} \equiv A_1 \sqcap CA_1$ $S_{A_2} \equiv A_2$ $S_{A_1} \sqsubseteq S_A$ and $S_{A_2} \sqsubseteq S_A$
4	Loop	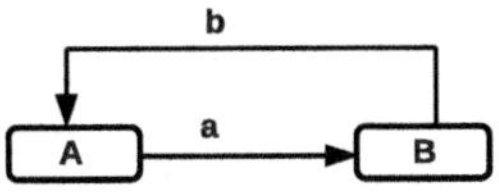	$S_A \equiv A \sqcap \exists sourceOfTransition.T_a$ $\sqcap \exists targetOfTransition.T_b$ $S_B \equiv B \sqcap \exists sourceOfTransition.T_b$ $\sqcap \exists targetOfTransition.T_a$ $T_a \equiv a \sqcap \exists source.S_A \sqcap \exists target.S_B$ $T_b \equiv b \sqcap \exists source.S_B \sqcap \exists target.S_A$
5	Start and End State	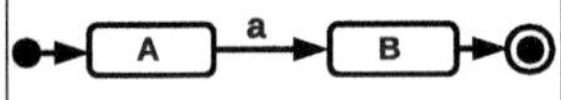	$S_A \equiv A \sqcap \exists\ sourceOfTransition.T_a$ $S_B \equiv B \sqcap \exists\ targetOfTransition.T_a$ $S_A \sqsubseteq Start$ and $S_B \sqsubseteq End$ $T_a \equiv a \sqcap \exists source.S_A \sqcap \exists target.S_B$

and the outgoing transition T_a ($\exists sourceOfTransition.T_a$). No. 2 specifies how to translate substates with a transition. A_1 and A_2 are substates of A and are modeled by the state labels S_{A_1} and S_{A_2}. Conditions are represented as classes CA and CA_1 in the intersection of the state definition (No. 3). No. 4 represents a loop. The state A has the outgoing transition T_a and the incoming transition T_b. Start and end states (No. 5) are modeled as subclasses of the pseudo-states *Start* and *End* that cannot be refined. The property *source* is an inverse property of *sourceOfTransition*, and *target* is the inverse of *targetOfTransition*.

There are approaches that map events to fluents (conditions that change over time) as ABox assertions like [5,8,26,27]. However, the semantics of state and transition description in our model is to restrict state traces by state descriptions A, conditions CA and possible transitions are restricted by guards and the set of all possible events. Therefore, we model events as concepts in the TBox.

4 Statechart Specializations

In this section, we define (atomic) specialization relations between statecharts. We start with statechart extensions followed by refinements. This general distinction is adopted from [23,25]).

An extension adds additional states and transitions with respect to the more abstract statechart. State and transition extensions are realized as follows.

E1: Add a transition to an existing source state, the target is a new state.
E2: Add a transition to an existing target state, the source is a new state.

E3: A transition T is replaced by a new added state and two new transitions (T_a, T_b). One of the new transitions is the incoming transition of the new state, the other is the outgoing transition.

E4: Add a transition T between two existing states.

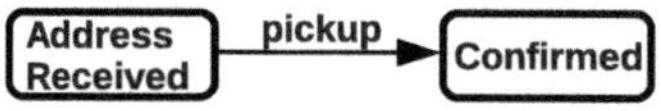

Fig. 2. Before Extension E3

Fig. 3. After Extension E3

Fig. 2 and 3 display an example of extension E3. A new state (*AddressChecked*) is added between two states (*AddressReceived* and *Confirmed*). The transition *pickup* is replaced by two transitions *verify* and *load* which are both modeled as subtransitions (subclasses in OWL).

The statechart refinement is either a restriction on states with respect to state conditions and decompositions or a restriction on transitions. The refinements R1 - R7 refine states by conditions, substates and condition movement.

R1: A condition is added to a state or to a substate.

R2: A condition is moved from a substate to its superstate.

Fig. 4 and 5 depicts the move of a condition to the superstate (R2). This condition move (e.g. *Insured*) restricts all the instances of this state, whereas a condition in the substate (Fig. 4) only restricts instances of this substate. After the move, the superstate is characterized by *Ordered* ⊓ *Insured*. All instances of S_{A_1} (Fig. 4) are also instances of $S_{A_1'}$ (Fig. 5) and vice versa.

$S_A \equiv Ordered \sqcap (S_{A_1} \sqcup S_{A_2})$

$S_{A_1} \equiv Domestic \sqcap Free \sqcap Insured$

$S_{A_2} \equiv Abroad$

$S_{A_1} \sqsubseteq S_A$ *and* $S_{A_2} \sqsubseteq S_A$

Fig. 4. Condition in the Substate

$S_{A'} \equiv Ordered \sqcap Insured \sqcap (S_{A_1'} \sqcup S_{A_2'})$

$S_{A_1'} \equiv Domestic \sqcap Free$

$S_{A_2'} \equiv Abroad$

$S_{A_1'} \sqsubseteq S_{A'}$ *and* $S_{A_2'} \sqsubseteq S_{A'}$

Fig. 5. Condition moved to Superstate

Refinements R3 - R5 decompose a state and change the internal structure of the state. We distinguish between three different kinds of refinements concerning the internal structure of the refined state.

R3: A state (Fig. 6) is partitioned into substates, that are a complete partition of the state (Fig. 7).
R4: A state is partitioned into an incomplete partition of the superstate.
R5: A state is partitioned into substates that are connected by internal transitions, i.e. the connected substates build a substatechart.

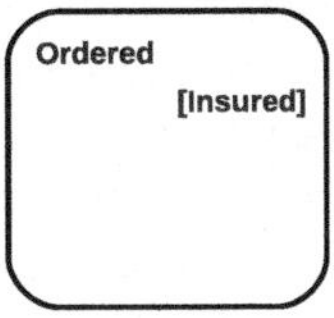

$$S_A \equiv Ordered \sqcap Insured$$

Fig. 6. State without Substates

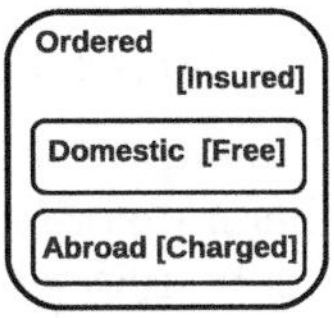

$$S_{A'} \equiv Ordered \sqcap Insured \sqcap (S_{A_1'} \sqcup S_{A_2'})$$
$$S_{A_1'} \equiv Domestic \sqcap Free$$
$$S_{A_2'} \equiv Abroad \sqcap Charged$$
$$S_{A_1'} \sqsubseteq S_{A'} \text{ and } S_{A_2'} \sqsubseteq S_{A'}$$

Fig. 7. Complete State Partition

Fig. 6 depicts the abstract state. The more specific state (Fig. 7) is a complete partition, i.e. each instance of $S_{A'}$ is either an instance of $S_{A_1'}$ or of $S_{A_2'}$. If there are transitions from substates that reaches other (super-) states, the source (or target) of the transition can be moved from the substate to its superstate (R6 and R7). The transition refinements R8 and R9 restrict transitions. In R8, a further expression, e.g. $\exists prec.Guard$ is added to the class definition of the transition label T, e.g. $T \equiv a \sqcap \exists prec.Guard$. A more restrictive guard is represented in OWL by a subclass of the original guard.

R6: Move of at least one outgoing transition from a substate (internal state) to its superstate (composite state).
R7: Move of at least one incoming transition from a substates to its superstate.
R8: A guard (condition) is added to an existing transition T or replaced by a more restrictive guard.
R9: An event is added to an existing transition T.

5 Validation of Statechart Specializations

The input of the validation is an abstract and a specialized model. The output is a decision whether it is a valid specialization w.r.t. the atomic specializations of Section 4. We adopt the notion of observation consistent specialization from action and situation calculus, i.e. if added features are ignored and refined features are considered as unrefined, the same behavior is given by the specific model.

5.1 Basic Definitions and Propositions

A specialization may consist of an arbitrary number of atomic specializations that affect the statecharts as characterized by the Theorems 1 and 2.

Theorem 1. *In each of the described atomic refinements R1 - R7, exactly one state of the pre-refined statechart is refined to substate(s) that is (are) a specialization in OWL of the state in the pre-refined statechart. In the refinements R8 and R9 exactly one transition is refined and is a specialization in OWL.*

Proof. The refinements R1 - R5 add conditions to a particular state, move conditions to the superstate or decompose the state into substates. Each refinement restricts the states by further (or more restrictive) expressions in the definition. If a transition is moved (R6 and R7), the affected superstate is more restrictive due to the additional expression ($\exists sourceOfTransition.T$). Adding guards and events (both are classes in OWL) to a transition (R8 and R9), leads to a more restrictive definition (additional expression).

Theorem 2. *In each (atomic) extension E1 - E4, the source and target state of the new transition is either a new state or is a specialization of this state compared to the pre-extended (more abstract) statechart.*

Proof. After each extension, the already existing state is a specialization in OWL compared to the pre-extended model. In extension E1, E2 and E4 the outgoing (or incoming) new transition T is added to the state S_A. This is realized in OWL by a further class expression in the conjunction of the definition of S_A, e.g. $\exists sourceOfTransition.T$ which leads to a more restrictive state. In E3, the expression $\exists sourceOfTransition.T$ in the definition of state S_A is replaced by the more restrictive expression $\exists soureOfTransition.T_1$ and is modeled as a subtransition (subclass in OWL), e.g. $T_1 \sqsubseteq T$.

5.2 Reasoning for Validation

We exploit the following modeling principles: (i) Each atomic refinement R1 - R7 and every atomic extension E1 - E4 results in at least one more specific state (Theorems 1 and 2) . (ii) The atomic refinements R8 and R9 lead to one more specific transition (Theorem 2). (iii) The characterizations of states A and transitions a, conditions CA, guards and events, are the same in both statecharts and are disjoint from each other. (iii) States and transitions of the pre- and post-specialized model are distinguishable by the labels S, T. (iv) All state and transition labels are subclasses of the superclass $State_i$ and $Transition_i$. *PreMod* denotes the pre-modified and *PostMod* denotes post-modified statechart. For each state $S\prime$ of *PostMod* one of the following conditions hold:

1. There is a state S in *PreMod*: $S\prime \sqsubseteq S$
2. There is no state S in *PreMod* : $S\prime \sqsubseteq S$ and the following conditions hold:
   - if there is an outgoing transition $T\prime$ of $S\prime$ in *PostMod*
     $S\prime \sqsubseteq \exists sourceOfTransition.T\prime$ then
     $T\prime$ has to be removed or replaced by its supertransition T of *PreMod*

– if there is an incoming transition T' of S' in $PostMod$
  $S' \sqsubseteq \exists targetOfTransition.T'$ then
  T' has to be removed or replaced by its supertransition T of $PreMod$

The first condition has to hold for all refinements and the second condition is imposed for extensions. The validation consists of two steps: (1) The states and transitions of the post-specialized model $PostMod$ are reduced according to $PreMod$. (2) The reduced sets of states and transitions are compared with the states and transitions of $PreMod$.

Reduction: The reduction is realized by the Reduce-Algorithm, described in Fig. 8. The result is a set of states $\mathcal{S}''$ that is a reduction of the states of $PostMod$ that only consist of states of $PreMod$ or specializations of them. The set $\mathcal{T}''$ consist of all transitions that are either in $PreMod$ or specializations.

Algorithm: Reduce(Statechart $PreMod$, Statechart $PostMod$)
Input: A pre-modified statechart $PreMod$ and a modified statechart $PostMod$
Output: Reduced sets of states $\mathcal{S}''$ and transitions $\mathcal{T}''$ of $PostMod$
begin

```
 1: Set⟨State⟩𝒮 = getStates(PreMod)
 2: Set⟨State⟩𝒮'' = Set⟨State⟩𝒮' = getStates(PostMod)
 3: Set⟨Transition⟩𝒯 = getTransitions(PreMod)
 4: Set⟨Transition⟩𝒯'' = Set⟨Transition⟩𝒯' = getTransitions(PostMod)
 5: for all State S' ∈ 𝒮' do
 6:     if there is no state S in 𝒮 : S' ⊑ S then
 7:         𝒮''.remove(S')
 8:         for all incoming and outgoing transitions T' of 𝒯' do
 9:             𝒯''.remove(T')
10:             if there is a supertransition T in 𝒯 : T' ⊑ T then
11:                 𝒯''.add(T)
12:             end if
13:         end for
14:     end if
15: end for
16: Return 𝒮'' and 𝒯''.
```

Fig. 8. The Reduce-Algorithm

The Reduce-Algorithm (Fig. 8) works as follows. Sets for states and transitions of the pre-modified (line 1,3) and post-modified (line 2,4) statechart are created. Here, we exploit the property that all states are subclasses of the superclass $State_i$ and all transitions are subclasses of $Transition_i$. The result sets ($\mathcal{S}''$ and $\mathcal{T}''$) are initialized with the states and transitions from $PostMod$ ($\mathcal{S}'$ and $\mathcal{T}'$). Each state of the post-specialized statechart S' that is not subsumed by a state of $PreMod$ is removed from the result set $\mathcal{S}''$ (line 6,7) Transitions are either replaced by supertransition (line 10,11) or removed (line 9).

Subsumption of States and Transitions: $\mathcal{S}''$ is the set of reduced states from *PostMod* and $\mathcal{T}''$ the set of reduced transitions form *PostMod* with respect to the pre-specialized model *PreMod*. *PostMod* is a valid specialization of *PreMod* if the following conditions hold:

1. For all states $S'' \in \mathcal{S}''$ there is a state $S \in \mathcal{S}$: $S'' \sqsubseteq S$
2. For all transitions $T'' \in \mathcal{T}''$ there is a transition $T \in \mathcal{T}$: $T'' \sqsubseteq T$

6 Evaluation

We randomly created 30 (3×10) pre-modified statecharts. Each statechart is specialized into 6 more specific statecharts, three of them are valid, the other are wrong specializations. The statecharts are represented in OWL DL with DL-expressivity $\mathcal{ALCI}$. We used the Pellet 2.0.0 reasoner in Java 1.6 on a computer with 2.5 GHz CPU and 2 GB RAM. The result is depicted in Tab. 2. Column two contains the number of states in the pre-specialized models, the number of states in the post-specialized statecharts is given in columns three and four. We distinguish between reduction time (Reduce-Algorithm) and time for state and transition subsumption checking. The last two columns describe the time for subsumption checking for the reduced states and transitions.

Table 2. Evaluation Result

No.	Statechart Size pre-mod.	Statechart Size post-mod.		Reduction Time		Subsumption Time	
		Av.	Max.	Av.[msec.]	Max.[msec.]	Av.[msec.]	Max.[msec.]
1	20	32.4	44	516	548	332	356
2	40	61.6	82	806	846	574	593
3	80	105.7	118	1653	1714	981	1013

7 Related Work and Conclusion

In [16] and [22], an implementation of statecharts in temporal logics and the validation with the model checker SPIN is described in order to provide a modeling framework for statechart modeling in temporal logics. Likewise in [15], a representation of statecharts in a tool for specification of reactive systems is given. However, the validation of relations between statecharts is not considered there. Description Logics are used for modeling of actions in [12]. Description Logics are extended by temporal logics and operators in [3,13]. More general reasoning tasks on UML class diagrams is considered in [6]. None of these works consider specializations and validations.

Behavior and communication systems in mathematical calculus, containing descriptions for states, transitions and activities are described in [19,17,18,21]. The calculus gives foundations for definitions, modeling principles and for expressing the equivalence of behavior systems like bisimulation. However, there is no implementation to (automatically) validate statecharts and relations between them. Statechart formalization and refinement is presented in [28] without validation. In [11,20] certain specification like reachability and error checks are validated using a model checker ([20]) or by using a theorem prover in [11]. However, these works do not provide definitions of specializations and are not focused on the validation of specializations.

In this paper, we presented modeling and specialization patterns for statecharts and specializations of them for knowledge engineering and representation of behavior systems. Based on existing work on action and situation calculus, we defined refinements and extensions of statecharts in OWL. Statechart specializations with respect to these definitions are validated using reasoning services. After a state and transition reduction, the validation of statechart specializations is reduced to standard OWL subsumption checking.

References

1. OMG Unified Modeling Language (OMG UML) Superstructure Version 2.2 (2009), `http://www.omg.org/spec/UML/2.2/Superstructure/PDF`
2. Stuart Aitken, J., Curtis, J.: A Process Ontology. In: Gómez-Pérez, A., Benjamins, V.R. (eds.) EKAW 2002. LNCS (LNAI), vol. 2473, pp. 108–113. Springer, Heidelberg (2002)
3. Artale, A., Franconi, E., Wolter, F., Zakharyaschev, M.: A Temporal Description Logic for Reasoning over Conceptual Schemas and Queries. In: Flesca, S., Greco, S., Leone, N., Ianni, G. (eds.) JELIA 2002. LNCS (LNAI), vol. 2424, pp. 98–110. Springer, Heidelberg (2002)
4. Baader, F., Calvanese, D., McGuinness, D.L., Nardi, D., Patel-Schneider, P.F.: The Description Logic Handbook, 2nd edn. Cambridge University, Cambridge (2007)
5. Baader, F., Lutz, C., Milicic, M., Sattler, U., Wolter, F.: Integrating Description Logics and Action Formalisms: First Results. In: Proc. of AAAI 2005 (2005)
6. Berardi, D., Calvanese, D., De Giacomo, G.: Reasoning on UML Class Diagrams. Artificial Intelligence 168(1-2), 70–118 (2005)
7. Bryant, A.: Chinese Encyclopaedias and Balinese Cockfights - Lessons for Business Process Change and Knowledge Management. In: Dieng, R., Corby, O. (eds.) EKAW 2000. LNCS (LNAI), vol. 1937, pp. 274–287. Springer, Heidelberg (2000)
8. Drescher, C., Thielscher, M.: Integrating Action Calculi and Description Logics. In: Hertzberg, J., Beetz, M., Englert, R. (eds.) KI 2007. LNCS (LNAI), vol. 4667, pp. 68–83. Springer, Heidelberg (2007)
9. Harel, D.: Statecharts: A Visual Formalism for Complex Systems. Science of computer programming 8(3), 231–274 (1987)
10. Kitamura, Y., Mizoguchi, R.: Ontology-Based Functional-Knowledge Modeling Methodology and its Deployment. In: Motta, E., Shadbolt, N.R., Stutt, A., Gibbins, N. (eds.) EKAW 2004. LNCS (LNAI), vol. 3257, pp. 99–115. Springer, Heidelberg (2004)
11. Krupp, A., Mueller, W., Oliver, I.: Formal Refinement and Model Checking of an Echo Cancellation Unit. In: Proceedings of the Conference on Design, Automation and Test in Europe, vol. 3. IEEE Computer Society, Los Alamitos (2004)
12. Lutz, C., Sattler, U.: A Proposal for Describing Services with DLs. In: Proceedings of the 2002 International Workshop on Description Logics (2002)

13. Lutz, C., Wolter, F., Zakharyaschev, M.: Temporal description logics: A survey. In: Int. Symposium on Temporal Representation and Reasoning, pp. 3–14 (2008)
14. McCluskey, T.L., Simpson, R.M.: Knowledge Formulation for AI Planning. In: Motta, E., Shadbolt, N.R., Stutt, A., Gibbins, N. (eds.) EKAW 2004. LNCS (LNAI), vol. 3257, pp. 449–465. Springer, Heidelberg (2004)
15. Mikk, E., Lakhnech, Y., Petersohn, C., Siegel, M.: On Formal Semantics of Statecharts as Supported by STATEMATE. In: Workshop, Ilkley, Citeseer, vol. 14, p. 15 (1997)
16. Mikk, E., Lakhnech, Y., Siegel, M., Holzmann, G.J.: Implementing statecharts in PROMELA/SPIN. In: Proc. of 2nd IEEE Workshop on Industrial Strength Formal Specification Techniques, p. 90 (1998)
17. Milner, R.: A Calculus of Communicating Systems. LNCS. Springer, Heidelberg (1980)
18. Milner, R.: Communication and Concurrency. Prentice-Hall, Englewood Cliffs (1989)
19. Ng, M.Y., Butler, M.: Towards Formalizing UML State Diagrams in CSP. In: 1st International Conference on Software Engineering and Formal Methods, pp. 138–147. IEEE Computer Society, Los Alamitos (2003)
20. Roscoe, A.W., Wu, Z.: Verifying Statemate Statecharts Using CSP and FDR. In: Liu, Z., He, J. (eds.) ICFEM 2006. LNCS, vol. 4260, pp. 324–341. Springer, Heidelberg (2006)
21. Sangiorgi, D.: Bisimulation for Higher-Order Process Calculi. Information and Computation 131, 141–178 (1996)
22. Schäfer, T., Knapp, A., Merz, S.: Model Checking UML state Machines and Collaborations. Electronic Notes in Theor. Comp. Science 55(3), 357–369 (2001)
23. Schrefl, M., Stumptner, M.: Behavior Consistent Refinement of Object Life Cycles. In: Embley, D.W., Goldstein, R.C. (eds.) ER 1997. LNCS, vol. 1331, pp. 155–168. Springer, Heidelberg (1997)
24. Studer, R., Benjamins, V.R., Fensel, D.: Knowledge Engineering: Principles and Methods. Data & Knowledge Engineering 25(1-2), 161–197 (1998)
25. Stumptner, M., Schrefl, M.: Behavior Consistent Inheritance in UML. In: Laender, A.H.F., Liddle, S.W., Storey, V.C. (eds.) ER 2000. LNCS, vol. 1920, pp. 527–542. Springer, Heidelberg (2000)
26. Thielscher, M.: From Situation Calculus to Fluent Calculus: State Update Axioms as a Solution to the Inferential Frame Problem. Artificial Intelligence 111(1), 277–299 (1999)
27. Thielscher, M.: FLUX: A Logic Programming Method for Reasoning Agents. Theory and Practice of Logic Programming 5(4-5), 533–565 (2005)
28. Uselton, A., Smolka, S.A.: A Process Algebraic Semantics for Statecharts via State Refinement. In: PROCOMET 1994. Elsevier, Amsterdam (1994)

Temporal Knowledge Acquisition and Modeling

Cyril Faucher[1], Charles Teissèdre[2,3], Jean-Yves Lafaye[1], and Frédéric Bertrand[1]

[1] L3i – University of La Rochelle, France
{cyril.faucher,frederic.bertrand,jean-yves.lafaye}@univ-lr.fr
[2] MoDyCo – UMR 7114 - Paris Ouest Nanterre La Défense University – CNRS, France
[3] Mondeca – 3, cité Nollez, Paris, France
charles.teissedre@mondeca.com

Abstract. The objectives of this paper are to present, describe, and explain the foundations and the functionalities of a temporal knowledge acquisition and modeling solution workflow, which aims at acquiring temporal knowledge from texts in order to populate a constrained object model. We are using several models for temporal data, one of which is generic and employed as a pivot model between a linguistic representation and a calendar representation. The approach we propose is generic and has been tested against a real use case, in which input data is made of temporal properties defining when a given location (a theater, a restaurant, a shopping center, etc.) is open or closed. Most expressions entered are expressed in intension. Our models provide a core support to the system that linguistically analyses data entries, transforms them into extensive calendar information and allow users to control the quality of the system's interpretation.

Keywords: Temporal Knowledge Acquisition, Temporal Data Modeling, Linguistic Annotation, Model Driven Engineering.

1 Introduction

With the surge of Semantic Web applications, many fields of knowledge are now subject to semantic browsing and querying. Time is a common feature that appears in many pieces of information, whatever the domain. Hence, the need of models and standards to deal with temporal issues; either for querying, visualizing, updating or reasoning, i.e.: processing temporal data. Useful standard specifications already exist: ISO19108 [1], OWL-Time [2], iCalendar [3]. Leaving apart the heterogeneity of time reference systems which is extensively and rather satisfactorily addressed in the literature, processing temporal information remains a challenge, and open practical questions are still key issues. Temporal expressions enounced in natural language can be complex. In fact, a huge amount of knowledge about time and calendar shared by people is still out of the scope of concrete time related information systems because information is neither accessible nor exploitable.

This paper describes an integrated approach with corresponding models and software components that fulfill a part of users' needs. The comprehensive applicative context concerns a knowledge base about event's occurrences. In the simplest case, a

P. Cimiano and H.S. Pinto (Eds.): EKAW 2010, LNAI 6317, pp. 371–380, 2010.

user queries the system to get the dates when an event occurs, or alternately, he queries for the event set that happen during a given period.

These typical use cases assume that prior functionalities are to be offered, for instance: extracting temporal information from original information sources, recording significant issues in appropriate formats, recording metadata as well, and providing means for data management, including data consistency checking.

Our proposal aims at providing constrained generic models and some tools that can be reused and adapted to various applicative contexts and domains. Nevertheless, we shall here focus on some examples stemming from tourism leisure. The main questions in this specific context concern the opening or closing hours for registration, the schedule of a show, and so on. The set of time assertions below, are instances of the kind of information we intend to process.

(1) The museum is open every day except Tuesday and the following French holidays: December 25, January 1, May 1, and August 15. Opening hours: Monday, Thursday, Saturday, Sunday: from 9 a.m. to 6 p.m. Wednesday, Friday: from 9 a.m. to 10 p.m.
(2) Opening times: Monday to Friday: Lunch (12 noon to 2 p.m.) Dinner (6.30 p.m. to 11 p.m.). Saturday: Dinner (6.30 p.m. to 11 p.m.)
(3) Opened every day from 10:00 to 18:00, except Tuesdays.

We shall pay a special attention to first: the extraction process of temporal information from English texts, second: the specification of an Object Model that stands as a pivot representation for temporal information being either intensional [4] or extensional, and third: the connection between the two. Indications will be given about some ways to check data consistency and achieve data visualization. The entire workflow interoperates between technical spaces, i.e. texts, linguistic models, object models and user interfaces. Our contribution pertains to Model Driven Engineering (MDE, [5]) which explicitly references common metamodels and standards.

The next section gives an overview of related work. Section 3 and 4 respectively describes the architecture of our proposal and provides excerpts of the Object Model. Section 5 is dedicated to temporal knowledge acquisition and presents the steps going from an English text up to a set of structured well identified temporal expressions. We also present a formal grammar which can be used as a controlled language to edit the model instances. We conclude by listing the key issues of our work and outline the future developments.

2 Related Work

One purpose of developing Natural Language Processing (NLP) resources and services for temporal data capture is to ease the process of populating a knowledge base. Within the Semantic Web community and in the context of knowledge acquisition, an important issue is to automate (partly or completely) the process that captures information provided in texts, in order to make it computable for software components [6]. Many research projects take more specifically interest in temporal information expressed in texts, designing annotation tagsets that describe their semantics, such as the TimeML project [7]. A challenging task tackled by many research projects is to transform calendar expressions found in texts into a structured and computable format, such as iCalendar or ISO 8601 standards: for instance, they aim at anchoring the situations described in texts on a timeline [8], [9], [10].

Our process explicitly distinguishes the linguistic representation of time from the calendar representation of temporal data. Indeed, the linguistic representation of time is external to its social representation [11], which, in a rationalizing effort, progressively stabilized itself in the standard calendar representation that uses concrete dates and describes temporal intervals. Natural language can define periodic references (*"on Mondays"*) or vague references (*"somewhere around mid March"*). Moreover, expressions like complex aggregates can build a new temporal reference on top of another (e.g.: *"on the 1st Wednesday of every Month"*, *"two days later"*) or in link with the enunciation process (e.g.: *"today"*, *"this week-end"*). OWL-Time [2] took interest in modeling calendar references, without reducing them only to their numeric representation. This formal ontology can model complex temporal aggregates and periodic references. A significant aspect of our approach, in front of existing standards [2] and models, is that it clearly distinguishes different modeling layers, each addressing different users and roles: a linguistic modeling of temporal references for natural language processing, business-case models for end-users applications, and a generic pivot model to map them all [12].

The calendar expressions' linguistic model reused here is presented in [13] and [14]. It describes the semantics of temporal adverbs as decomposable units calling upon a compositional interpretation of their significance. Calendar expressions are considered here as a conjunction of semantic operators (*since*, *by the end of*, *during*, *before*, etc) interacting with calendar base references.

3 From Texts to Structured Data

This section presents the global architecture (Fig. 1) of our proposal and describes the main workflow. The three major processes correspond to the population of the three different models that are manipulated: the linguistic model of calendar expressions, the calendar model (extension of iCalendar) and, in between, the pivot model (PivotObjectModel). The temporal knowledge acquisition system processes original data which consist of natural language texts. A first step is performed by TextFiltering and TextAnnotation modules which identify, extract and decompose the semantics of calendar expressions found in texts, thanks to lexicon lists and local grammars implemented in the form of Unitex[1] transducers. The output is post-treated to lift ambiguities and to instantiate the linguistic model.

A model transformation is applied to populate the PivotObjectModel with the instances of the linguistic model. A second model transformation is used to translate intensional expressions stored in the PivotObjectModel into their extensional equivalent counterpart (e.g.: *"on Mondays"* is transformed in *"on Monday, Jan 2"*, *"on Monday, Jan 9"*, etc). The output is depicted on a calendar widget that is used to correct possible misinterpretations, remove ambiguities or complete incomplete statements. A third model transformation can be used to translate PivotObjectModel instances into the

[1] Unitex: http://www-igm.univ-mlv.fr/~unitex

iCalendar standard (e.g.: for an export towards search engines). The PivotObjectModel can capture temporal information either from the output of the TextAnnotation process or from the CalendarEdition module. Data from any other source could be integrated thanks to a plain mapping of concepts between the sources and the PivotObjectModel.

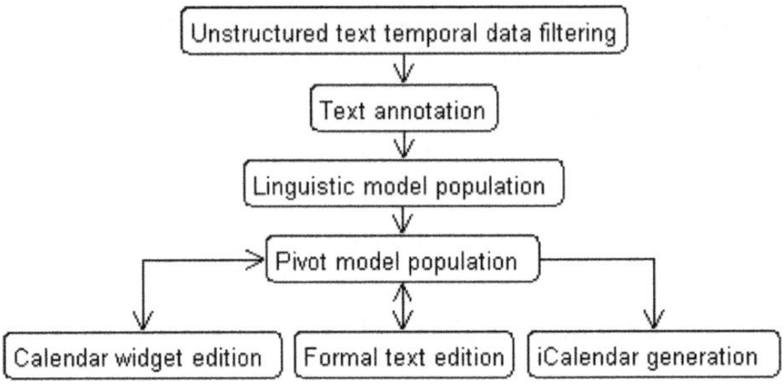

Fig. 1. General Workflow of the system

The PivotObjectModel extends the ISO19108 standard. Additional features are provided so that more semantics could be handled: e.g. intensional periodical occurrences, relative time positions between events (*"opening at lunchtime"*, lunchtime temporal properties being specified separately). The PivotObjectModel can readily bind temporal properties to these events. It provides an invariant structure that can easily be interfaced with other modules, either for populating the model or to retrieve temporal information.

Thanks to a formal grammar, all model instances can automatically be translated into a textual representation - a controlled language - and hence can without ambiguity be understood by a human operator as well as deterministically processed by a computer. In the wake of Natural Language Generation techniques, which produce natural language text from structured knowledge [15], it provides a controlled textual rendering of the model, so that user can easily understand/modify model instances. It enables an interaction between linguistic data and knowledge models, providing a manual edition of complex model instances.

4 Temporal Modeling

In this section we describe the pivot generic temporal model (PivotObjectModel) which centralizes the information from the source providers. We propose a general UML [16] object model for temporal events properties.

We selected the ISO19108 standard as a reference for modeling the basic concepts: Instant and Period. The main reasons for this choice are the following: (i) the object representation of the ISO19108 proves to be well fitted for being used in MDE as a pivot representation; (ii) the ISO191000 series treats of geographical information issues which are very commonly associated with temporal features.

4.1 Periodic Rule Model

For sake of brevity, we only discuss selected excerpts of our model[2] and exclude the part dedicated to exceptions. Let's first focus on the central concept in Fig. 2. The PeriodicRule class is the root element for defining periodicity issues about a PeriodicTemporalOccurrence. A PeriodicTemporalOccurrence is an aggregation of PeriodicRules. Each aggregated element indicates a simple periodic phenomenon (i.e.: only one Frequency). The composition of all elements in the set, results in the sum of the simple components. Consequently, the first property of a PeriodicRule is its Frequency. According to a common definition, a Frequency is a pair of values respectively indicating the number of occurrences (times attribute) that happen during a special time span (referenceDuration role).

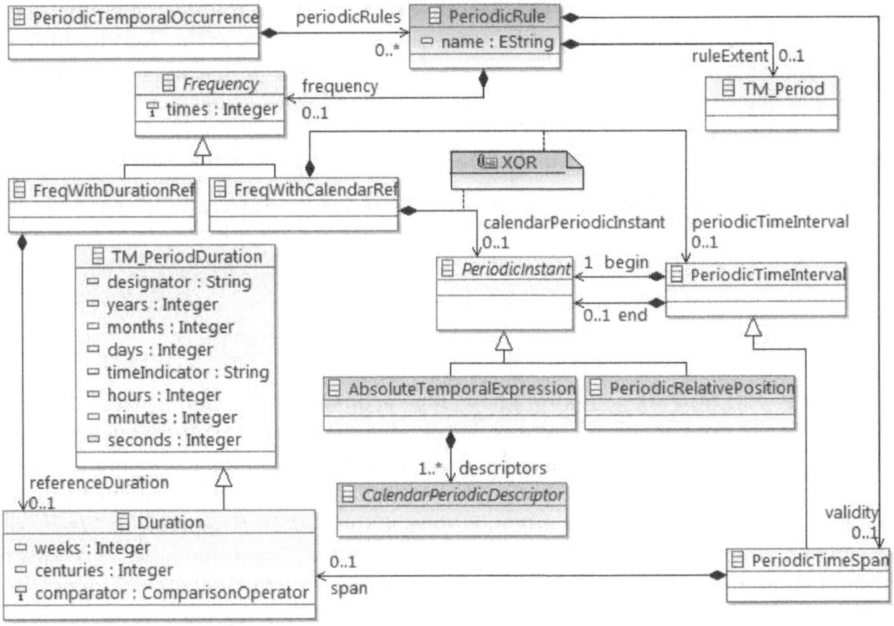

Fig. 2. Excerpt of the PeriodicTemporalOccurrence model

As shown in Fig. 2, referenceDuration ends in a Duration datatype. This might be too restrictive in practice, since only durations could then be referenced. Thus, we give access to the whole set of AbsoluteTemporalExpressions for specifying the beginning and the end of intervals *via* the role periodicTimeInterval. Intrinsic periodic CalendarPeriodicDescriptors can be specified (e.g.: "*each Monday*", "*each first Wednesday*"), providing means to specify the major calendar units. Instants may also be specified by adding a NumericRank to a calendar unit: e.g.: "*3rd Sunday, 28th week*".

The optional startTime attribute is specified for frequency, in order to anchor the first periodic phenomenon occurrence on a concrete calendar, i.e.: to define its phase

[2] All the classes prefixed by TM_ come from the ISO19108 standard.

once its frequency is known. As mentioned above, if no referenceDuration is given for a PeriodicRule, then a PeriodicTimeInterval must be specified with two properties, namely begin and end, which are AbsoluteTemporalExpression. Of course, constraints are to be checked, e.g.: begin precedes end for all occurrences, and both begin and end should have the same frequency), but begin and end occurrences may present a phase difference. This means that the length of PeriodicTimeInterval occurrences is not necessarily equal (e.g.: PeriodicTimeInterval occurring *"from the first Tuesday to the last Monday of each month"*). The class PeriodicRelativePosition is used to specify a PeriodicInstant in relation with another previously defined.

4.2 Rule Extent and Periodic Time Span

A periodic phenomenon is infinite. Time boundaries can however be provided, for instance to identify a starting point. The optional ruleExtent role specifies the period during which the PeriodicRule applies. The association end is a TM_Period with a beginning and an optional end. The semantics of ruleExtent is that all occurrences are valid inside the extent and invalid otherwise. A fixed time extent may prove insufficient to capture some situations which are not scarce among periodic events. As a matter of fact, the extent should itself often be periodic. This is the case in the following assertion: *"the event occurs each first week of the month from March to September"*. Therefore, a PeriodicTimeSpan is defined to specify the periodic time window: *"from March to September"*.

5 Capturing Temporal Knowledge of Access Periods

The generic workflow for temporal knowledge acquisition (Section 3) can be specialized in different domain specific cases. We studied a use case capturing access period information, i.e. the temporal properties that define the opening and closing hours of a given location. Such information is valuable for applications that intend to answer queries such as *"Which restaurants are open tonight after 10 p.m.?"* or *"Is there a supermarket opened on Sunday morning?"*. In accordance with the generic workflow, different strategies are implemented to ease acquisition: text filtering and annotation, calendar edition, formal text edition, to provide a controlled language view.

5.1 Access Period Information

Considering examples that define accessibility, it appears that the semantic decomposition of access periods is complex. They are composed of various temporal references: periodic references (*"opened every Monday"*), temporal intervals (*"from January 1st to March 11th"*), exceptions (*"except Tuesday"*), and specification of temporal units with different granularities (*"on Monday, from 8am to 8pm"*).

All these information are reflected in the linguistic model we propose (Fig. 3), which aims at being consistent with the way access periods are linguistically built up. An AccessPeriod is defined by one or several AbstractCalendarExpressions, which stand for CalendarExpressions or CalendarExpressionIntervals. Over a base or a set of base AbstractCalendarExpression, the definition of an AccessPeriod can aggregate exception or specification by using AbstractCalendarExpression. A CalendarExpressionInterval is linked to two CalendarExpressions, one of which is the start, the other being its end. A CalendarExpression (the core object in this model) is composed of the following main attributes: (i) the different time units that might enter in their composition, (ii) parts of day, parts of month and parts of year. A more detailed description of the linguistic model of calendar expressions is presented in [13].

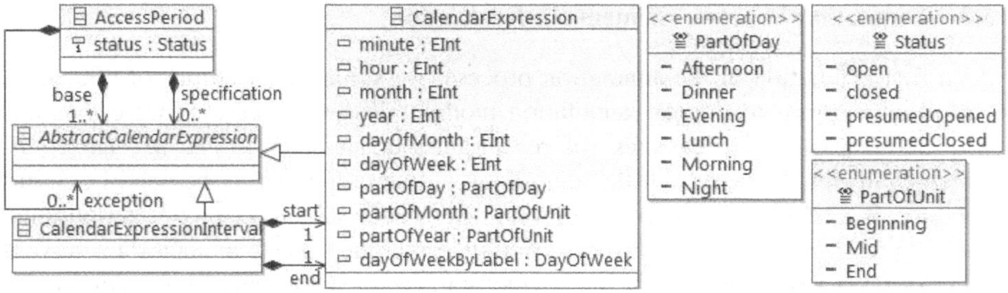

Fig. 3. Proposition for a linguistic modeling of access periods

5.2 Text Annotation

Natural language analysis is very convenient to enter periodic and complex temporal references defining periods of accessibility. Instead of filling complex forms, users can simply define access periods in natural language. Expressions denoting access periods are analyzed by a set of transducers (Finite State Machines) defined thanks to the NLP platform Unitex. The output breaks down the semantics of access period and describes the way they are linked to one another. The annotation tagset contains metadata for the temporal references and the relation between calendar expressions such as exception ("*Opened every day* *except on Wednesday*") or temporal granularity specification ("*on Sunday,* *from 9 a.m. to 12 p.m.*").

The annotation module is coupled with a normalization tool which completes and converts text annotation metadata into a structured format that corresponds to the linguistic model described in Subsection 5.1. After the annotation process, an automated post-treatment is necessary to lift ambiguities, in particular about the range of *exceptions* or *specifications*. For instance, in the expression "*Opened every day except on Tuesday, from 9 a.m. to 10 p.m.*", the specification (*from 9 a.m. to 10 p.m.*) should not be attached to the exception (*except on Tuesday*), but to the base expression (*every day*). This post-treatment also unfolds elliptic phrases (*closed on Tuesday and December 25*) and rebuilds their semantics in an explicit form (*closed on Tuesday and closed on December 25*). In its current state, the annotation process, nevertheless, shows limits. A simple rewriting process is sometimes required in order to filter external knowledge (such as school holiday, undefined bank holiday, or any lexicon that is external to the definition of temporal properties). For instance, for being fully interpreted by the annotation process, the *e.g. 2* listed in the introduction can be rewritten and simplified in the following way:

e.g. 2: *Opening times: Monday to Friday: Lunch (12 noon to 2pm) Dinner (6.30pm to 11pm). Saturday: Dinner (6.30pm to 11pm)*

e.g. 2 rewritten: *Opening times: Monday to Friday, from 12 noon to 2pm and from 6.30pm to 11pm. Saturday, from 6.30pm to 11pm.*

For now, the annotation process resources only cover the lexicon and structure of calendar expressions commonly used when defining access period. It could though progressively be extended to cover a larger lexicon.

5.3 Annotation Process: Elements of Evaluation

As a first evaluation of the annotation process, we submitted a corpus of 400 access period expressions to the text annotation module. These expressions were manually collected on various Web sites (of restaurants, theaters, etc). The *precision rate*, which evaluates the quality of the annotation output compared to the one of a human operator, is 82.25%. The scoring methodology was classic and straight: a well annotated expression receives a score of 1, any incorrect/incomplete annotation receives a score of 0. 71 expressions were not correctly interpreted and needed a simple rewriting process.

The interpretation process most commonly fails (1) when some external knowledge is required (such as the period covered by school holiday in the expression "*closed during school holidays*") and (2) when the system faces ambiguous definitions. For instance, the expression "*Opened Saturday and Sunday morning*" is ambiguous since it could mean that the location is open all Saturday or only Saturday morning. The system is deterministic. Then only one interpretation must be retained (in this case, only the first interpretation is given). These limits in the annotation process are not truly troublesome in the actual workflow, since the system is conceived to assist human operators who can modify the input, in case of unsatisfactory analysis.

5.4 Pivot Model Population, Temporal Reasoning and Edition

The translation of linguistic model instances into pivot model instances is achieved by model transformations written in Kermeta[3], which convert CalendarExpressions from the linguistic model into PeriodicRules conforming to the pivot model.

During this process, the module faces two main difficulties. (1) False contradictions management. For example, when dealing with the following expression "*Opening days: every day from 9am to 10pm. Closed on Tuesday*" the module raises a conflict: while a reader understands that "*Closed on Tuesday*" prevails over the former access period. The system wrongly detects contradictory information when it deals with Tuesdays, which are considered being opened and closed at the same time. (2) Symbolic or vague temporal unit management. The transformation from linguistic representation to concrete calendar representation can not be straightforward for symbolic or vague temporal units, such as: "*morning*", "*end of November*", etc. In such cases, the system relies on a set of mapping rules that can be parameterized (e.g. convert "*morning*" into a time interval e.g.: "*from 8am to 12 am*").

The calendar widget (Fig. 4) is the user interface for editing the annotation: it offers a convenient way for checking consistency of the text input's analysis.

[3] Kermeta: http://www.kermeta.org

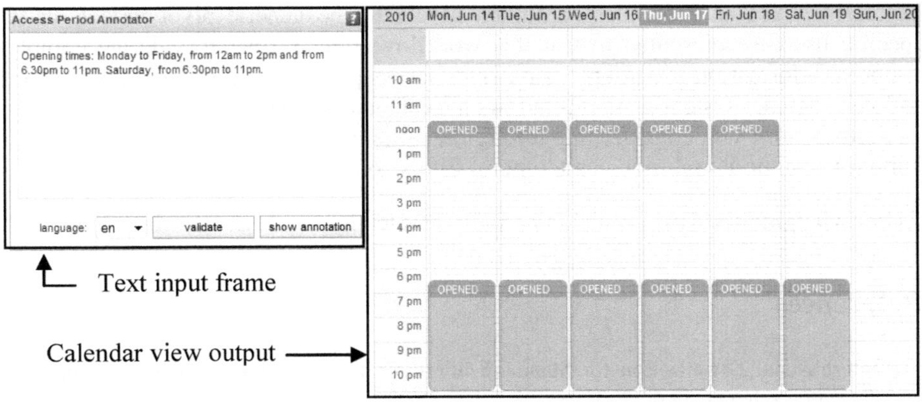

Fig. 4. Concrete calendar view of abstract access information[4] for e.g. 2

In connection with the PivotObjectModel, a textual grammar is specified and offers another convenient way to read the content of the data stored as instances of the pivot model. It allows an automated translation of any rule from the model into an equivalent counterpart expressed in a readable controlled language thus allowing the user to check the modeled data semantics. The translation is bi-directional and implemented with xText[5]. Fig. 5 shows an example of the grammar translator output with respect to the opening specification of a shop as: *"from Monday to Friday, 10 a.m. to 8 p.m. except Thursday"*. The generated text is using one periodic rule *"10 a.m. to 8 p.m."* and a time span which is also periodic *"from Monday to Friday"*.

// rule 1: 10 a.m. to 8 p.m. -	**rule: from each 10th hour to each 20th hour**
// from Monday to Friday	**using a time span as from each Monday to each Friday**
// except Thursday	**except each Thursday**

Fig. 5. Excerpt of text generated from pivot model instances with the grammar translator

6 Conclusion and Future Work

The generic workflow presented in this paper considers the temporal knowledge acquisition as a process which goes along from an unstructured text analysis to a structured and computable model of temporal data, which can then be presented through a controlled language representation. This controlled language can stand for a surrogate of the pivot model instances. In this workflow, the quality of the information analysis can be controlled by users who can interact with the calendar widget or with the controlled language representation, in order to create, correct or delete information. The model transformation component bridges both the linguistic model of temporal

[4] TKA (Temporal Knowledge Acquisition): http://client2.mondeca.com/AccessPeriodEditor/
[5] xText: http://www.eclipse.org/Xtext/

expressions and an iCalendar compliant model to the generic pivot model. In the specific use case presented to test this workflow, human operators define complex temporal information in a simple way, enter access period definition in a textual form and visualize the system's interpretation on a calendar widget.

Further work will consider integrating the system with a query engine, in order to build a Semantic Portal in which temporal filters could be used.

Acknowledgments. This project is partially granted by the ANR RMM2 project.

References

1. International Organization for Standardization: Text of 19108 Geographic information - Temporal schema, 55 p. (2002)
2. Hobbs, J.R., Pan, F.: An Ontology of Time for the Semantic Web. ACM TALIP. Special Issue on Temporal Information Processing 3(1), 66–85 (2004)
3. Dawson, F., Stenerson, D.: Internet Calendaring and Scheduling Core Object Specification (iCalendar) - RFC2445, RFC Editor (1998)
4. Carnap, R.: Meaning and Necessity. University of Chicago Press, Chicago (1947)
5. Schmidt, D.C.: Model-Driven Engineering. IEEE Computer Society Press, Los Alamitos (2006)
6. Bontcheva, K., Cunningham, H.: The Semantic Web: A New Opportunity and Challenge for Human Language Technology. In: 2nd ISWC Proceedings, Workshop on HLT for The Semantic Web and Web Services, Florida, October 20-23, pp. 89–96 (2003)
7. Pustejovsky, J., Castano, J., Ingria, R., Sauri, R., Gaizauskas, R., Setzer, A., Katz, G.: TimeML: Robust Specification of Event and Temporal Expressions in Text. In: IWCS Proceedings, Florida (2003)
8. Mani, I., Wilson, G.: Robust temporal processing of news. In: Proceedings of the 38th ACL, Hong Kong, pp. 69–76 (2000)
9. Setzer, A., Gaizauskas, R.: Annotating Events and Temporal Information in Newswire Texts. In: 2nd LREC Proceedings, Athens, pp. 64–66 (2000)
10. Schilder, F., Habel, C.: From Temporal Expressions to Temporal Information: Semantic Tagging of News Messages. In: ACL 2001 Proceedings, Workshop on Temporal and Spatial Information Processing, Toulouse, pp. 65–72 (2001)
11. Benveniste, E.: Problèmes de linguistique générale. In: Gallimard (ed.), Paris, vol. 2 (1974)
12. Bézivin, J.: On The Unification Power of Models. Software and System Modeling 4(2), 171–188 (2005)
13. Battistelli, D., Couto, J., Minel, J.-L., Schwer, S.: Representing and Visualizing calendar expressions in texts. In: STEP 2008, Venise (2008)
14. Teissèdre, C., Battistelli, D., Minel, J.-L.: Resources for Calendar Expressions Semantic Tagging and Temporal Navigation through Texts. In: 7th LREC, Valletta, May 19-21 (2010)
15. Reiter, E., Dale, R.: Building Natural Language Generation Systems. Journal of Natural Language Engineering, 3 Part 1 (1999)
16. OMG, Unified Modeling Language (UML): Superstructure. Version 2.2 (2009)

Using Machine Learning to Support Continuous Ontology Development

Maryam Ramezani[1], Hans Friedrich Witschel[1], Simone Braun[2], and Valentin Zacharias[2]

[1] SAP Research and
[2] FZI Forschungszentrum Informatik, Karlsruhe, Germany

Abstract. This paper presents novel algorithms to support the continuous development of ontologies; i.e. the development of ontologies during their use in social semantic bookmarking, semantic wiki or other social semantic applications. Our goal is to assist users in placing a newly added concept in a concept hierarchy. The proposed algorithm is evaluated using a data set from Wikipedia and provides good quality recommendation. These results point to novel possibilities to apply machine learning technologies to support social semantic applications.

1 Introduction

There are two broad schools of thought on how ontologies are created: the first views ontology development akin to software development as a - by and large - one off effort that happens separate from and before ontology usage. The second view is that ontologies are created and used at the same time, i.e. that they are continuously developed throughout their use. The second view is exemplified by the Ontology Maturing model [1,2] and by the ontologies that are developed in the course of the usage of a semantic wiki.

Machine learning, data mining and text mining methods to support ontology development have so far focused on the first schools of thought, namely on creating an initial ontology from large sets of text or data that is refined in a manual process before it is then used. In our work, however, we focus on using machine learning techniques to support continuous ontology development, in particular we focus on one important decision: given the current state of the ontology, the concepts already present and the sub/super concept relations between them - where should a given new concept be placed? Which concept should become the super concept(s) of the new concept?

We investigate this question on the basis of applications that use ontologies to aid in the structuring and retrieval of information resources (as opposed to for example the use of ontologies in an expert system). These applications associate concepts of the ontology with information resources, e.g. a concept "Computer Science Scholar" is associated to a text about Alan Turing. Such systems can use the background knowledge about the concept to include the Alan Turing text in responses to queries like "important British scholars". Important examples for such systems are:

– The **Floyd** case management system developed at SAP. In that system, cases and other objects (that are attached to cases, such as documents) can be tagged freely

P. Cimiano and H.S. Pinto (Eds.): EKAW 2010, LNAI 6317, pp. 381–390, 2010.

with terms chosen by the user. These terms can also be organized in a semantic network and this can be developed by the users. The Floyd system is usually deployed with a semantic network initially taken from existing company vocabulary.

- The **SOBOLEO** system [3] uses a taxonomy developed by the users for the collaborative organization of a repository of interesting web pages. There is also a number of similar social semantic bookmarking applications [4].
- The **(Semantic) Media Wiki** [5] system uses a hierarchy of categories to tag pages. We can view categories as akin to concepts and support the creation of new categories by proposing candidate super-categories.

All these system are "Web 2.0" style semantic applications; they enable users to change and develop the ontology during their use of the system. The work presented in this paper assists users in this task by utilizing machine learning algorithms. The algorithms suggest potential super-concepts for any new concept introduced to the system.

The rest of this paper is organized as follows. In section 2 we will present the previous research in this area and discuss how our work differs. In section 3 we describe the proposed algorithm for the recommendation of superconcepts. In section 4 we describe the methodology, the dataset and the results from the evaluation before section 5 concludes the paper.

2 Related Work

Many researchers have proposed the idea of creating ontologies from social tagging applications; from the terms users have assigned to information resources. [6] was one of the first who proposed social tagging systems as a semantic social network which could lead to the emergence of an ontology. An idea that is based on the emergent semantics proposed by [7] and the vision of a community of self-organizing, autonomous agents co-operating in dynamic, open environments, each organizing knowledge (e.g. document instances) and establishing connections according to a self-established ontology.

Van Damme et al. propose a 6-step methodology for deriving ontologies from folksonomies by integrating multiple techniques and resources [8]. These techniques comprise Levenshtein metric to identify similar tags, co-occurence and conditional probability to find broader-narrower relations and transitive reduction and visualization to involve the community. Future work shall include other existing resources like Google, WordNet, Wikipedia, ontologies for mapping. Likewise, [9] try to automatically enrich folksonomies using existing resources. They propose two strategies, one based on WordNet, the other using online ontologies, in order to map meaning and structure information to tags. Monachesi and Markus [10] developed an "ontology enrichment pipeline" to enrich domain ontologies with social tagging data. They evaluated different similarity measures to identify tags related to existing ontology concepts. These are symmetric (based on Jaccard) and asymmetric co-occurence and cosine similarity both of resource and user. They excluded tf and tfidf measures because they could not find any additional benefit in their test. Finally, they use DBpedia in combination with a disambigation algorithm based on Wikipedia in order to place the identified tags into the ontology. [11] suggests mapping tags to an ontology and presents the process of mapping in a simple example.

Other researchers have started solving the details of the problem using information retrieval techniques. [12] suggest creating a hierarchical taxonomy of tags by calculating the cosine similarity between tags, i.e. each new tag added to the system will be categorized as the child of the most similar tag. If the similarity value is less than a pre-defined threshold then the new tag will be added as a new category, which is a new child for the root. The problem with this algorithm is that there is no heuristic to find the parent-child relation. Any new similar tag will be considered as a child of the most similar tag previously added to the system even though it might be more general than the other tag. Markines et al. [13] present different aggregation methods in folksonomies and similarity measures for evaluating tag-tag and resource-resource similarity. Marinho et al. [14] use frequent itemset mining for learning ontologies from folksonomies. In this work, a folksonomy is enriched with a domain expert ontology and the output is a taxonomy which is used for resource recommendation.

The approach taken in this paper is different from the ones mentioned above in the sense that we suggest a recommendation approach to support end users in the collaborative maturing of ontologies [1,2], i.e. where anybody can add a new element to the ontology, and refine or modify existing ones in a work-integrated way. That means the ontology is continuously evolving and gradually built up from social tagging activities and not derived once at a specific time from the folksonomy. Our work provides a supporting tool for such ontology building by helping users with recommendation of semantic relationships, specifically super-subconcept relationships, between a new concept and the existing concepts.

3 Algorithm for Recommending Super-Concepts for New Concepts

We propose an algorithm for the recommendation of super-concepts for a new concept. This algorithm uses an existing concept hierarchy and assists the user in finding the right place for a new concept.

3.1 Degree of Sub-Super Relationship in a Concept Hierarchy

First we define a measure for the distance between a super concept and its sub concepts. We consider the shortest path distance between two concepts, starting from the sub concept and allowing only upward edges to be used to arrive at the super-concept. We call this"super-sub affinity" ("SSA"). To clarify how we find SSA, consider a concept hierarchy with a root A and two sub concepts B and C. Then SSA(A,B)=1, SSA(A,C)=1 and SSA(B,C)=0. If B has a sub-concept D, then SSA(A,D)=1/2. Note that SSA is not a symmetric relation, distinguishing it from common semantic similarity measures. In fact, the definition of SSA entails "if SSA(A,B)$\neq$0 then SSA(B,A)=0". We define SSA(A,A)=1. For more details about *SSA*, please refer to [18]. We store all SSA values in an $n \times m$ matrix where n is the number of concepts which have at least one sub-concept, m is the total number of concepts in the hierarchy, and the matrix diagonal is always 1. We will use this matrix in our recommendation algorithm for discovering super-concepts. The transpose of this matrix can be used for suggesting sub-concepts using the same algorithm. However, in this work, we focus only on recommending super-concepts.

3.2 Concept Similarity

In this section we define measures used to compare the similarity of the new concept to the existing concepts. We consider measures that use similarities in the concept names as well as measures that use contextual cues, i.e. secondary information available about the use of the concept.

For **string-based similarity** we use standard Jaccard similarity to find the degree of similarity among concepts with compound labels. Jaccard similarity is defined as: $J(A,B) = \frac{|A \cap B|}{|A \cup B|}$. where A and B are (multi-word) concepts. Using the Jaccard measure, the string-based similarity between each concept C_i and the new target concept C_t is defined as $sim_s(C_t, C_i) = J(C_t, C_i)$. For example the Jaccard similarity between two concepts "Computer" and "Computer Science" would be 1/2. Using this similarity measure, we find the set of k most similar concepts to the target concept C_t and we call this set N_s.

Context-based cues aim at using the context that the new concept has been used in to find similar concepts. Context has been defined by Dey [15] as any information that can be used to characterize the situation of an entity. In a social tagging system, for example, the context of a new tag entered into the system can be distinguished by the related resources, links between the resources, users who enter the tag, time, language and geographical information. In this work, we use the resources associated to a concept as a feature set to determine the context of the concept. We represent each concept C as a vector over the set of resources, where each weight, $w(r_i)$, in each dimension corresponds to the importance of a particular resource, r_i.

$$C = \langle w(r_1), w(r_2) ... w(r_{|R|}) \rangle \tag{1}$$

In calculating the vector weights, a variety of measures can be used. The weights may be binary, merely showing that one or more users have associated that concept to the resource, or it may be finer grained using the number of users that have associated that concept to the resource. With either weighting approach, a similarity measure between two vectors can be calculated by using several techniques such as the Jaccard similarity coefficient or Cosine similarity [16]. Cosine similarity is a popular measure defined as

$$Cosine(C1, C2) = \frac{C1.C2}{||C1|| \, ||C2||} \tag{2}$$

In this work, we use binary weighting for representing concepts as a vector of pages and Cosine similarity to find similar concepts. Thus, the similarity between each concept C_i and the new target concept C_t is defined as $sim_c(C_t, C_i) = Cosine(C_t, C_i)$. Using this similarity measure, we find the set of k most similar concepts to the target concept C_t and we call this set N_c.

We define a **hybrid similarity measure** by combining the string-based and contextual-based similarity measures. For that purpose, we use a linear combination of the similarity values found in each approach.

$$Sim_h(C_i, C_t) = \alpha Sim_s(C_i, C_t) + (1 - \alpha) Sim_c(C_i, C_t) \tag{3}$$

where $Sim_h(C_i, C_t)$ is the hybrid similarity value, and α is a combination parameter specifying the weight of string-based approach in the combined measure. If $\alpha = 1$, then

$Sim_h(C_i, C_t) = Sim_s(C_i, C_t)$, in other words the neighbors are calculated only based on string-similarity. On the other hand, if $\alpha = 0$, then only the contextual information is used for finding similar concepts. We choose the proper value of alpha by performing sensitivity analysis in our experimental section.

3.3 Prediction Computation

Based on the Super-Sub Affinity and the similarity measures defined above, we can now predict the degree of sub-super relationship (SSA) between the new concept and every other concept in the hierarchy. Our proposed algorithm is inspired by the popular weighted sum approach for item-based collaborative filtering [17].

Formally, we predict the SSA between the target concept and all other concepts C_i in the hierarchy as follows.

$$SSA_p(C_i, C_t) = \frac{\sum_{C_n \in N} SSA(C_i, C_n) * sim(C_t, C_n)}{\sum_{C_n \in N} sim(C_t, C_n)} \tag{4}$$

where $SSA_p(C_i, C_t)$ stands for the predicted SSA value for the pair (C_i, C_t), $SSA(C_i, C_n)$ stands for the actual SSA for (C_i, C_n), and $sim(C_t, C_n)$ is the similarity value between the target concept and neighbor concept which can be either string-based (Sim_s), contextual (Sim_c) or the hybrid (Sim_h) similarity. Thus N can be either N_s,N_c or N_h as described in section 3.2. Basically, SSA_p is predicted based on the location of the existing concepts that are similar to C_t; it becomes large when many of C_t's neighbors are close to the current candidate concept C_i in terms of SSA. Hence, the best candidates for becoming a super-concept of C_t are those C_i for which $SSA_p(C_i, C_t)$ is maximal. The weighted sum is scaled by the sum of the similarity terms to make sure the prediction is within the predefined range. In this work we have defined the direct sub-super affinity as 1. Thus, the nearer the prediction of $SSA(C_i, C_t)$ to 1, the more probable that C_i is super-concept of C_t.

3.4 Recommendation

Once the SSA values for all existing concepts and the new concept are calculated, the concept(s) with the highest SSA can be recommended as super-concept for the new concept. We can recommend a list of top n concepts with highest SSA prediction or we can use a threshold value and only recommend concepts with predicted SSA higher than the threshold. The threshold value (between 0 and 1) represents the "confidence" of the algorithm in recommendations. If there are no similar concepts found in step 1 or the predicted SSA values are lower than the threshold, the system does not make a recommendation which might mean that the new concept should be added as a new independent concept at the top of the hierarchy or that the system is not able to find the right place for the new concept.

4 Evaluation and Results

4.1 Data Set

To test our algorithms we need a Web 2.0 application where users can easily add new concepts and create semantic relations. We decided to use Wikipedia which is the most suitable web 2.0 application at hand. Hepp [19] theoretically proves Wikipedia as a reliable and large living ontology. We treat the categories of Wikipedia as concepts and the existing relationships between "Subcategories" as the seed concept hierarchy. Each category in Wikipedia has several associated pages, which we use as a context vector for the category as described in section 3.2. Thus, each category is represented as a binary vector over the set of pages. The weight of each page r_i for category C_j is 1 if page r_i is associated to category C_j and 0 otherwise.

For running our experiments, we focused on a small part of the English Wikipedia. We started from the category "Computer Science" as the root concept and extracted the sub-categories by traversing with breadth first search through the category hierarchy. Our final data set has over 80,000 categories. However, for our experiments we created three smaller data sets to compare how the size and properties of the seed concept hierarchy impact the results. Our smallest data set has 3016 categories with 47,523 associated pages. The medium data set has 9931 with 107,41 associated pages and the large data set has 24,024 categories with 209,076 pages. The average depth of the hierarchy is 3, 6 and 9 for those three data sets respectively.

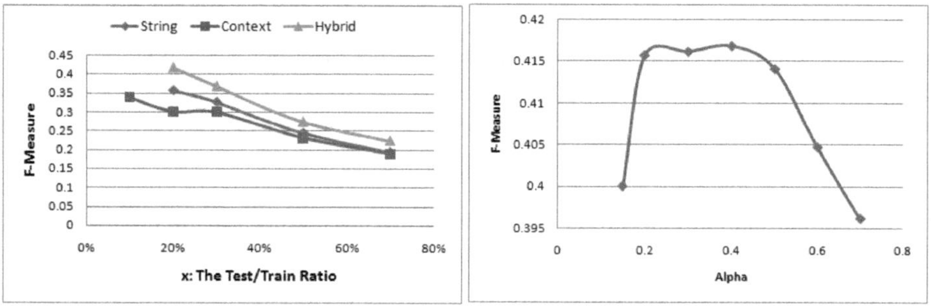

Fig. 1. Comparison of F-measure for different approaches by changing the test/train ratio x(on the left) and sensitivity of α in the hybrid algorithm(on the right)

4.2 Evaluation Methodology and Metrics

We divided the data set into a training set and a test set. Since we were interested to know how the density of the seed ontology affects the results, we introduced a variable that determines what percentage of data is used as training and test sets; we call this variable x. A value of $x = 20\%$ would indicate 80% of the data was used as training set and 20% of the data was used as test set. We remove all information of test cases from the data set to evaluate the performance of the algorithm. For each experiment, we calculate the SSA values before and after removing the test cases. If the test case has sub-concept and super-concept, after removing the test case, its sub-concepts will be directly connected to its super-concepts and the algorithm has to intelligently discover its original place in between the two concepts. For evaluation we adopt the common recall and precision measures from information retrieval. Recall measures the percentage of items in the holdout set that appear in the recommendation set and is defined as:

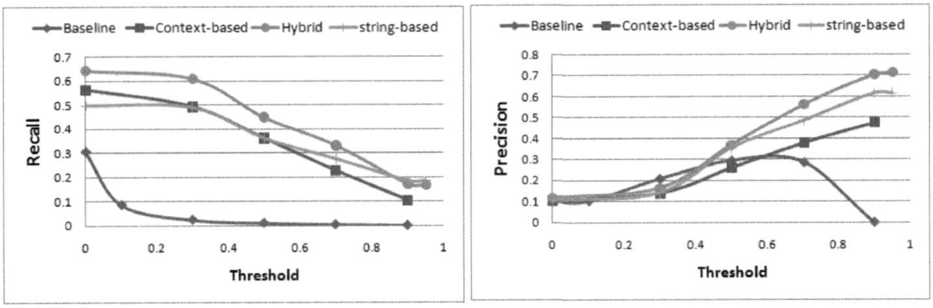

Fig. 2. Comparison of Precision and Recall of different algorithms for different threshold values

$recall = C_h \cap C_r|/|C_h|$ where C_h is the set of holdout concepts and C_r is the set of recommended concepts. Precision measures the percentage of items in the recommendation set that appear in the holdout set. Precision measures the exactness of the recommendation algorithm and is defined as: $precision = |C_h \cap C_r|/|C_r|$. In order to compare the performance of the algorithms, we also use F-measure defines as

$$F - Measure = \frac{2 \times Precision \times Recall}{Precision + Recall} \tag{5}$$

4.3 Experimental Results

In this section we present our experimental results of applying the proposed recommendation algorithm to the task of ontology maturing. In all experiments, we change the threshold value from 0 to 0.95 and record the values of precision and recall. As the threshold value increases, we expect precision to increase and recall to decrease since we recommend less items with higher confidence. In addition, to get a better view of performance of the algorithms, we use the notion of recall at N. The idea is to establish a window of size N at the top of the recommendation list and find recall for different numbers of recommendations. As the number of recommendation increases, we expect to get higher recall. In assessing the quality of recommendations, we first determined the sensitivity of some parameters. These parameters include the neighborhood size k, the value of the training/test ratio x, and the combination factor α. Our results show (not shown here) that there is a trade-off between better precision or better recall depending on the neighborhood size. We select $k = 3$ as our neighborhood size which gives better precision for high threshold values. To determine the sensitivity of the value of α in the hybrid algorithm, we conducted experiments with different values of alpha. The result of these experiments is shown in the right chart of figure 1 . From this chart we select the value of $\alpha = .4$ for the hybrid algorithm. To determine the effect of density of the seed concept hierarchy, we carried out an experiment where we varied the value of x from 20% to 70%. Our results are shown in the left chart of figure 1. As expected, the quality of recommendation decreases as we increase x. However, even with x=70%, our algorithm can still produce acceptable recommendations. For further experiments we keep x=20%.

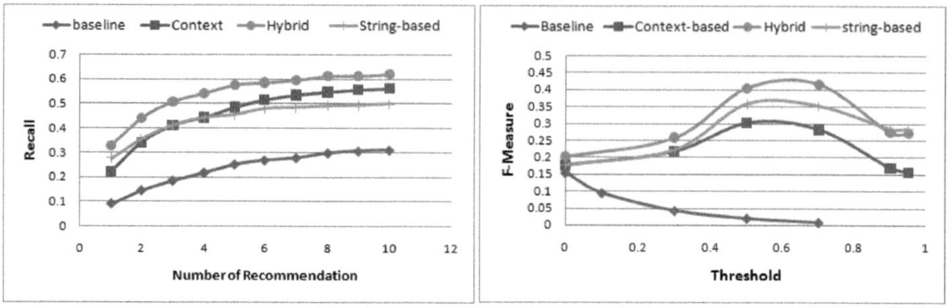

Fig. 3. Comparison of F-measure for different approaches by changing the threshold value(on the right) and Comparison of recall at N for different algorithms

Once we obtained the optimal values of the parameters, we compared the performance of the algorithm when using different similarity computation techniques. In addition,we compared our approach with a baseline algorithm suggested in [12]. The results of this comparison are shown in figure 2 and 3. The baseline algorithm uses the cosine similarity between concepts and recommends the concepts with highest cosine similarity. Basically, the baseline algorithm is similar to the first step of our algorithm where we find the k-nearest neighbors based on contextual cues. Figure 2 shows the precision and recall values as we change the threshold value and figure 3 shows the comparison using F-measure and Recall at N.

4.4 Discussion

Our results show that the hybrid similarity outperforms other approaches for both precision and recall for all thresholds and x values. We can observe from figure 2 that while contextual cues result in less precision than the string-based techniques, they produce slightly higher recall. That shows that string-based techniques can suggest more accurate recommendations but they do not have as much coverage as the context-based ones. Figure 3 compares the same algorithms using different measures. The right chart shows the F-measure for each algorithm as the threshold value changes and the left chart shows recall at N. Basically, we count the correct answers as we recommend N super-concepts. We can observe from these two charts that while hybrid similarity obviously outperforms other similarity measures, it is not trivial to determine if string-based measures are better than the context-based ones. The context-based cues outperform string-based ones when looking at the Recall at N while based on F-measure the string-based techniques outperform context-based ones.

In terms of continuous ontology development, picking a threshold of .7 from the right chart of figure 3 for the hybrid algorithm, this means that users who introduce a new concept into an existing ontology can count on almost 60% (see right of figure 2) of the recommendations received being correct and on a coverage of around 35% when looking through all recommendations and selecting the right ones.

4.5 Qualitative Evaluation

Although the precision and recall values from the experiments above are quite acceptable, we decided to investigate the actual results and find out in what cases the algorithm makes incorrect recommendations. We selected a random new concept "Botnets" and we observed the recommendation outputs. Table 1 shows the top 5 recommendations based on each technique. We can observe in this example that although not equal to the actual Wikipedia super-categories, the recommendations do make some sense.

Table 1. An example: Output of recommendation algorithm using different similarity cues. Recommendations are predicted super concepts of the new concept "Botnets"

Wikipedia	Contextual Cues	String-based Cues	Hybrid
Multi-agent systems	Artificial intelligence	Multi-agent systems	Multi-agent systems
Computer network security	Multi-agent systems	Computer network security	Artificial intelligence
	Computer architecture	Computer security organizations	Computer architecture
	Network architecture	Artificial intelligence	Computer network security
	Distributed computing	Computer architecture	Distributed computing

5 Conclusion and Future Work

We utilized recommender system technologies to support collaborative ontology maturing in a Web 2.0 application. We introduced a hybrid similarity measure by combining contextual and string-based cues to find the super concepts of a new concept. Our evaluation with the Wikipedia category hierarchy shows promising results. From the qualitative results we can see that our recommender in fact can produce better results than the calculated precision and recall indicate. Thus, the system can also be used directly in Wikipedia for improving the current category hierarchy.

In this work, we have used associated pages to a concept as contextual information. As future work, other contextual information such as links between pages, or user information can be considered as well. In addition, evaluation of the algorithms in an actual interactive social semantic bookmarking application can help us answer the question whether the generated recommendations are actually perceived as useful by the user.

Acknowledgments

This work was supported by the MATURE Project co-funded by the European Commission.

References

1. Braun, S., Kunzmann, C., Schmidt, A.: People Tagging & Ontology Maturing: Towards Collaborative Competence Management. In: From CSCW to Web2.0: European Developments in Collaborative Design. CSCW Series, pp. 133–154. Springer, London (2010)

2. Braun, S., Schmidt, A., Walter, A., Nagypal, G., Zacharias, V.: Ontology Maturing: a Collaborative Web 2.0 Approach to Ontology Engineering. In: Proc. of the WWW 2007 Workshop on CKC, CEUR-WS, vol. 273 (2007)
3. Zacharias, V., Braun, S.: SOBOLEO - Social Bookmarking and Lightweight Ontology Engineering. In: Proc. of the WWW 2007 Workshop on CKC, CEUR-WS, vol. 273 (2007)
4. Braun, S., Schora, C., Zacharias, V.: Semantics to the Bookmarks: A Review of Social Semantic Bookmarking Systems. In: Proc. of the 5th I-SEMANTICS, pp. 445–454 (2009)
5. Krótzsch, M., Vrandecic, D., Vólkel, M., Haller, H., Studer, R.: Semantic Wikipedia. Journal of Web Semantics 5, 251–261 (2007)
6. Mika, P.: Ontologies are us: A unified model of social networks and semantics. In: Gil, Y., Motta, E., Benjamins, V.R., Musen, M.A. (eds.) ISWC 2005. LNCS, vol. 3729, pp. 522–536. Springer, Heidelberg (2005)
7. Philippe, K.A., Ouksel, A.M.: Emergent Semantics Principles and Issues. In: Lee, Y., Li, J., Whang, K.-Y., Lee, D. (eds.) DASFAA 2004. LNCS, vol. 2973, pp. 25–38. Springer, Heidelberg (2004)
8. Damme, C.V., Coenen, T., Vandijck, E.: Deriving a Lightweight Corporate Ontology form a Folksonomy: a Methodology and its Possible Applications. Scalable Computing: Practice and Experience - Int. J. for Parallel and Distributed Computing 9(4), 293–301 (2008)
9. Angeletou, S., Sabou, M., Motta, E.: Improving Folksonomies Using Formal Knowledge: A Case Study on Search. In: Gómez-Pérez, A., Yu, Y., Ding, Y. (eds.) ASWC 2009. LNCS, vol. 5926, pp. 276–290. Springer, Heidelberg (2009)
10. Monachesi, P., Markus, T.: Using Social Media for Ontology Enrichment. In: Proc. of 7th ESWC, pp. 166–180. Springer, Heidelberg (2010)
11. Zhao, N., Fang, F., Fan, L.: An Ontology-Based Model for Tags Mapping and Management. In: Proc. of the Int. Conf. on CSSE, pp. 483–486. IEEE Computer Society, Los Alamitos (2008)
12. Heymann, P., Garcia-Molina, H.: Collaborative Creation of Communal Hierarchical Taxonomies in Social Tagging Systems. Technical Report 2006-10, Stanford University (2006)
13. Markines, B., Cattuto, C., Menczer, F., Benz, D., Hotho, A., Stumme, G.: Evaluating Similarity Measures for Emergent Semantics of Social Tagging. In: Proc. of the 18th Int. Conf. on WWW, pp. 641–650. ACM, New York (2009)
14. Balby Marinho, L., Buza, K., Schmidt-Thieme, L.: Folksonomy-Based Collabulary Learning. In: Sheth, A.P., Staab, S., Dean, M., Paolucci, M., Maynard, D., Finin, T., Thirunarayan, K. (eds.) ISWC 2008. LNCS, vol. 5318, pp. 261–276. Springer, Heidelberg (2008)
15. Dey, A.K.: Understanding and using context. Personal and Ubiquitous Computing 5(1), 4–7 (2001)
16. Van Rijsbergen, C.: Information Retrieval. Butterworth-Heinemann Newton, USA (1979)
17. Sarwar, B., Karypis, G., Konstan, J., Riedl, J.: Item-based collaborative filtering recommendation algorithms. In: Proc. of the 10th Int. Conf. on WWW, pp. 285–295. ACM, New York (2001)
18. Ramezani, M., Witschel, H.F.: An intelligent system for semi-automatic evolution of ontologies. In: Proceedings of 5th IEEE International Conference on Intelligent Systems IS 2010 (2010)
19. Siorpaes, K., Bachlechner, D.: Harvesting wiki consensus - using wikipedia entries as ontology elements. IEEE Internet Computing, 54–65 (2006)

Handling Markup Overlaps Using OWL

Angelo Di Iorio, Silvio Peroni, and Fabio Vitali

Department of Computer Science, University of Bologna
diiorio@cs.unibo.it, speroni@cs.unibo.it, fabio@cs.unibo.it

Abstract. A lot of applications handle XML documents where multiple overlapping hierarchies are necessary and make use of a number of workarounds to force overlaps into the single hierarchy of an XML format. Although these workarounds are transparent to the users, they are very difficult to handle by applications reading into these formats. This paper proposes an approach to document markup based on Semantic Web technologies. Our model allows the same expressiveness as XML and any other hierarchical meta-markup language, and, rather than requiring complex workarounds, allows the explicit expression of overlapping structures in such a way that search and manipulation of these structures does not require any specific tool or language. By simply using mainstream technologies such as OWL and SPARQL, our model – called EARMARK (Extremely Annotational RDF Markup) – can perform rather sophisticated tasks with no special tricks.

Keywords: EARMARK, OWL, change tracking, overlapping markup.

1 Introduction

In the past, overlapping markup has received ambivalent, almost schizoid considerations in the field of markup languages. On the one hand, overlaps were the hallmarks of bad HTML coders and naive HTML page editors, taking advantage of an unjustified benevolence in web browsers that would display basically any HTML regardless of proper nesting. On the other hand, overlaps have been a fringe, almost esoteric discipline of scholars in the humanities, competently used for arcane specifications of linguistic annotations and literary analysis.

But although the first type of usage was approached with scorn and the second with awe, they both fundamentally represent a situation that is more common than thought, and the scholars were only more aware, and not more justified, about the need to represent overlaps.

Overlaps are needed whenever multiple markup elements need to be applied over the same content, and these elements are independent of each other. In some (rather frequent) situations, this independence means that the content referred to by some elements is partially but not completely the same as the content referred to by other elements.

Yet of course SGML, and now XML, grammatically impose and require a strict hierarchy of containment generating a single mathematical tree of the document

P. Cimiano and H.S. Pinto (Eds.): EKAW 2010, LNAI 6317, pp. 391–400, 2010.

where no overlap is allowed. Thus, naively ignoring this requirement, carefully creating workarounds or inventing completely new markup languages, document authors have coped with this problem. But while new markup languages such as TexMecs [4] and LMNL [11] have but a small number of adepts and applications, workarounds such as segmentation, milestones or standoff markup [5] are frequently used and ubiquitous.

All workarounds manage to constrain secondary structural information so as not to break or obfuscate the main hierarchy that is expressed in the visible XML structure. But although this allows to manage multiple structures over the same content, this comes at a price: structures specified through workarounds are more difficult to find, identify and act upon than the structures in the main XML hierarchy.

In this paper we propose an alternative approach to overlapping that allows very simple tools to be used on all markup to generate sophisticated functionalities. Furthermore, rather than creating a completely new language requiring completely new tools and competencies, we propose to use Semantic Web technologies and tools to obtain much of the same results we would obtain with traditional XML tools.

Our proposal, EARMARK (Extremely Annotational RDF Markup), defines markup vocabularies by means of OWL ontologies [13], through which arbitrary markup over the same content can be expressed. Since each individual markup item is an independent assertion over some content or other assertions, overlaps stop being a problem, and similarly all other issues connected to physical embedding and containments, such as contiguity and document order.

Thus, while in previous works [6] [2] we concentrated on showing how XML documents could be converted in EARMARK and vice versa, and how to use workarounds when converting overlapping EARMARK structures into an XML document, in this paper we concentrate on identifying workarounds existing in real XML documents, and disentangle them into independent, direct EARMARK assertions on which sophisticated functionalities can then be generated.

The paper is structured as follows: in Section 2 we provide a brief overview of existing approaches to handle overlap using workarounds or brand new languages, and in Section 3 we provide a significative example of situations where overlaps exist today and sometimes in pretty mainstream situations. In Section 4 we introduce EARMARK, and in Section 5 we discuss an use case that should demonstrate the superiority of an EARMARK approach to a traditional XML one when overlaps come into question, and in Section 6 we draw some conclusions.

2 Existing Approaches to Overlapping

The need for multiple overlapping structures over documents using markup syntaxes such as XML and SGML is an age-old issue: much research has been carried out about techniques, languages and tools that allow users to create multiple hierarchies over the same content. A good review of them can be found in [1].

Some of such research proposes to use plain hierarchical markup (i.e., SGML and XML) and employ specially tailored elements or attributes to express the semantics of overlapping in an implicit way. For instance, the TEI Guidelines [9] present a number of different techniques that use SGML/XML constructs to force multiple hierarchies into a single one, including:

- *milestones* (the overlapping structures are expressed through empty elements to mark the boundaries of the "content"),
- *fragmentation* (the overlapping structures are split into individual non-overlapping elements that may even be linked through id-idref pairs) and
- *standoff markup* (the overlapping structures are placed elsewhere and indirectly refer to their would-be locations through pointers, locators and/or id/idref pairs).

Given the large number of techniques to deal with overlapping structures in XML, in [5] we presented a number of algorithms to convert XML documents with overlapping structures from and to the most common approaches.

Other research actually proposes to get rid of the theory of trees at the base of XML/SGML altogether, and use different underlying models and newly invented XML-like languages that allow the expression of overlaps through some kind of syntactical flourishing.

For instance, *GODDAG* [10] is a Direct Acyclic Graph whose nodes represent markup elements and text. Arcs are used to explicit represent containment and father-child relations. Since multiple arcs can be directed to the same node, overlapping structures can be straightforwardly represented in GODDAG. *Restricted GODDAGs*, a subset thereof, can be and has been linearized into TexMecs [4], a multi-hierarchical markup language that also allows full GODDAGs through appropriate non-embedding workarounds, such as standoff markup.

LMNL [11] is a general data model based on the idea of *layered text fragments and ranges*, where multiple types of overlap can be modelled using concepts drawn from the mathematical theory of intervals. Multiple serializations of LMNL exist, such as CLIX and LMNL-syntax.

The *variant graph* approach [8] is also based on graph theory. Developed to deal with textual variations – that generate multiple versions of the same document with multiple overlapping hierarchies – this theory proposes a new data model to represent literary documents and a graph linearisation (based on lists) that scales well even with a large number of versions. In the same conference, [7] presented another detailed survey about overlapping approaches, also discussing the MultiX^2 data model – that uses W3C standard languages such as XInclude to link and fetch text fragments within overlapping structures – and a prototype editor for the creation of multi-structured documents.

3 More Frequent than One May Think

So often overlapping structures have been considered as needed only in highly specific contexts (such as linguistics) and basically for scholars: solutions were complex since they were considered grounded in the intrinsic complexity of the topics themselves. Yet, overlapping structures can be found in many more fields than these, and even mainstream applications generate and use markup with overlapping structures. While the complexity of overlapping is hidden to the final user, application that consume such data may very well find it rather difficult to handle such information. In the following we discuss a significative context where overlapping already exist and fairly relevant information is encoded in multiple independent structures, leaving to special code the task of managing the complexity: word processors.

Word processors provide users with powerful tools for tracking changes, allowing each individual modification by individual authors to be identified, highlighted, and acted upon (e.g. by accepting or discarding them). The intuitiveness of the relevant interfaces actually hides the complexity of the data format and of the algorithms necessary to handle such information.

For instance, the standard ODT format used by Open Office – and similarly the DOCX format used by Microsoft Word – when saving change tracking information relies on two specific constructs for insertions and deletions that may overlap with the structural markup. While adding a few words within a paragraph does not imply the breaking of the fundamental structural hierarchy, any change that affects the structure itself (e.g. the split of one paragraph into two by the insertion of a return character, or vice versa the join of two paragraphs by the elimination of the intermediate return character) requires annotations to be associated to the end of a paragraph and the beginning of the next, in an unavoidably overlapping pattern. ODT uses milestones and standoff markup for insertions and deletions respectively, and also relies on standoff markup for annotations about the authorship and date of the change.

For instance, the insertion of a return character and a few characters in a paragraph creates a structure as follows:

```
<text:changed-region text:id="S1">
  <text:insertion>
    <office:change-info>
      <dc:creator>John Smith</dc:creator>
      <dc:date>2009-10-27T18:45:00</dc:date>
    </office:change-info>
  </text:insertion>
</text:changed-region>
<text:p>The beginning and
  <text:change-start text:change-id="S1"/></text:p>
<text:p>also<text:change-end text:change-id="S1"/>
  the end.</text:p>
```

The empty elements `<text:change-start/>` and `<text:change-end/>` are *milestones* marking respectively the beginning and the end of the range that constituted the insertion, while the element `<text:insertion>`, before the beginning of the document content, is *standoff markup* for the metadata about the change (author and date information). The deletion operation shows a similar behaviour.

4 EARMARK and Its Support for Overlapping Features

This section discusses a different approach to metamarkup, called EARMARK (Extremely Annotational RDF Markup) based on ontologies and Semantic Web technologies. The basic idea is to model EARMARK documents as collections of addressable text fragments, and to associate such text content with OWL [13] assertions that describe structural features as well as semantic properties of (parts of) that content. The overall approach is similar but more general, robust and extensible than [12]. As a result EARMARK allows not only documents with single hierarchies (as with XML) but also multiple overlapping hierarchies where the textual content within the markup items belongs to some hierarchies but not to others. Moreover EAMARK makes it possible to add semantic annotations to the content though assertions that may overlap with existing ones.

One of the advantages of using EARMARK is the capability to access and query documents by using well-known and widely supported tools for Semantic Web. In fact, EARMARK assertions are simply RDF assertions, while EARMARK documents are modelled through OWL ontologies. The consequence is that query languages (such as SPARQL) and actual existing tools (such as OWLAPI or Pellet) can be directly used to deal with even incredibly complicated overlapping structures.

The EARMARK model itself is defined through an OWL document (available at `http://www.essepuntato.it/2008/12/earmark`) specifying classes and relationships. The model introduces three separate base concepts: *docuverses*, *ranges* and *markup items*. Each of them is represented with different, disjoint OWL classes.

The textual content of an EARMARK document is conceptually separated from the annotations, and is referred to by means of assertions on the specific class *Docuverse*. This class refer to the collection of text fragments that can be interconnected to each other or transcluded into new documents.

The individuals of this class represent the object of discourse, i.e. all the text containers related to a particular EARMARK document. The following code snippets are written using the Manchester Syntax [3]; the prefixes *rdfs*, *owl* and *xsd* refer respectively to RDF Schema, OWL and XML Schema, while the empty prefix refers to the EARMARK own namespace.

```
Class: Docuverse
DataProperty: hasContent
  Characteristics: FunctionalProperty
  Domain: Docuverse
  Range: rdfs:Literal
```

Any individual of the *Docuverse* class can specify the actual content of the document using the property *hasContent*.

We then define the class *Range* for any text lying between two locations. A *range*, i.e, an individual of the class *Range*, is defined by a starting and an ending location (any literal) taking into account a particular docuverse through the properties *begins*, *ends* and *refersTo* respectively.

```
Class: Range
  HasKey: begins , ends , refersTo
ObjectProperty: refersTo
  Characteristics: FunctionalProperty
  Domain: Range
  Range: Docuverse
DatatypeProperty: begins
  Characteristics: FunctionalProperty
  Domain: Range
  Range: rdfs:Literal
DatatypeProperty: ends
  Characteristics: FunctionalProperty
  Domain: Range
  Range: rdfs:Literal
```

There is no restriction on locations used for the *begins* and *ends* properties: they define the way a range must be read. Note that, by using the *hasKey* OWL property, we assert that if there exist two ranges referring to the same docuverse and having the same begin and end locations, then they are the same range.

The class *MarkupItem* is the superclass defining artefacts to be interpreted as markup (such as elements and attributes).

```
Class: MarkupItem
DataProperty: hasGeneralIdentifier
  Characteristics: FunctionalProperty
  Domain: MarkupItem
  Range: xsd:string
DataProperty: hasNamespace
  Characteristics: FunctionalProperty
  Domain: MarkupItem
  Range: xsd:anyURI
```

A *markupitem* individual is a collection of individuals belonging to the classes *MarkupItem* and *Range*. It might have a name, specified in the functional property *hasGeneralIdentifier* (the term comes from the SGML term to refer to the name of elements), and a namespace, specified by using the functional property *hasNamespace*.

5 Using EARMARK

There are multiple applications for the EARMARK approach. The most interesting for this work is the capability of dealing with overlapping structures in an elegant and straightforward manner. Under EARMARK such structures do not need to be specified through complex workarounds as with XML, but they are explicit and can be easily rebuilt and accessed.

In fact, we do not expect all documents to be natively encoded with EARMARK. Thus, we developed an approach that takes as input an XML file and produces the corresponding EARMARK document in a finite amount of steps.

Details of such a process are out of the scope of this paper. Our goal here is to show that complex overlapping data structures can be disentangled into EARMARK assertions that can be processed and queried in a very simple way. Towards this goal, we now go into details of the scenario presented earlier: ODT change-tracking.

The ODT format uses complex data structures to store overlap generated by change-tracking facilities, as discussed in Section 3. These structures make it very difficult to search and manipulate the content by directly using XML languages and tools. Let us discuss a very simple example:

```
<text:changed-region text:id="S2">
  <text:deletion>
    <office:change-info>
      <dc:creator>Silvio Peroni</dc:creator>
      <dc:date>2009-10-27T18:45:00</dc:date>
    </office:change-info>
    <text:p>.</text:p>
  </text:deletion>
  <text:insertion>
    <office:change-info office:chg-author="Angelo Di Iorio"
      office:chg-date-time="2009-10-27T18:42:00"/>
  </text:insertion>
</text:changed-region>
<text:changed-region text:id="A2">
  <text:insertion>
    <office:change-info>
      <dc:creator>Angelo Di Iorio</dc:creator>
      <dc:date>2009-10-27T18:42:00</dc:date>
    </office:change-info>
  </text:insertion>
</text:changed-region>
<text:p>This is one paragraph<text:change-start text:change-
    id="S1"/>;
  actually, it was!<text:change-end text:change-id="S1"/>
  <text:change text:change-id="S2"/>
  <text:change-start text:change-id="A2"/></text:p>
<text:p><text:change-end text:change-id="A2"/>
  <text:change text:change-id="A3"/>
  <text:change-start text:change-id="A4"/>S
  <text:change-end text:change-id="A4"/>plit in two.</text:p>
```

The document was originally composed by a single paragraph: "*This is one paragraph that will be split in two.*". The user "Angelo Di Iorio" split the paragraph in two (change identified as A2), removed the text "*that will be*" (change A3), added a symbol "." at the end of the first paragraph (change A1, hidden by the following change S2, by Silvio Peroni) and capitalized the letter "*S*" at the beginning of the word "*split*" (change A4). Later, user "Silvio Peroni" substituted the final "." of the first paragraph with the text "*; actually, it was!*" (changes S1 and S2). Note that, for the sake of clarity, we did not show each element *text:changed-region* . It should not be difficult for the reader to picture them, following the discussion of Section 3.

Apart from difficulties in rebuilding the underlying overlapping structures from this complex (XML) syntax, applications have to face another issue: the fact that even simple queries become very complex. The complexity does not lie in the complexity of the information itself, but rather in the data structure over which the operation has to work.

For instance, assume that a reader is looking for "all text fragments inserted by Angelo Di Iorio". This very simple query ends up being surprisingly entangled when written in XPath:

```
for $id in //@text:id[../text:insertion//(dc:creator[. = '
    Angelo Di Iorio'] | @office:chg-author[. = 'Angelo Di
    Iorio'])] return //text:p//text()[(preceding-sibling::
    text:change-start[1][@text:change-id = $id] and following
    -sibling::text:change-end[1][@text:change-id = $id]) or
    ancestor::text:changed-region/@text:id = $id]
```

The EARMARK approach solves this issue is a very disciplined way. The point is that EARMARK stores overlapping data in a direct and elegant manner, that does not require tools to rebuild such information from twisted tree-based XML

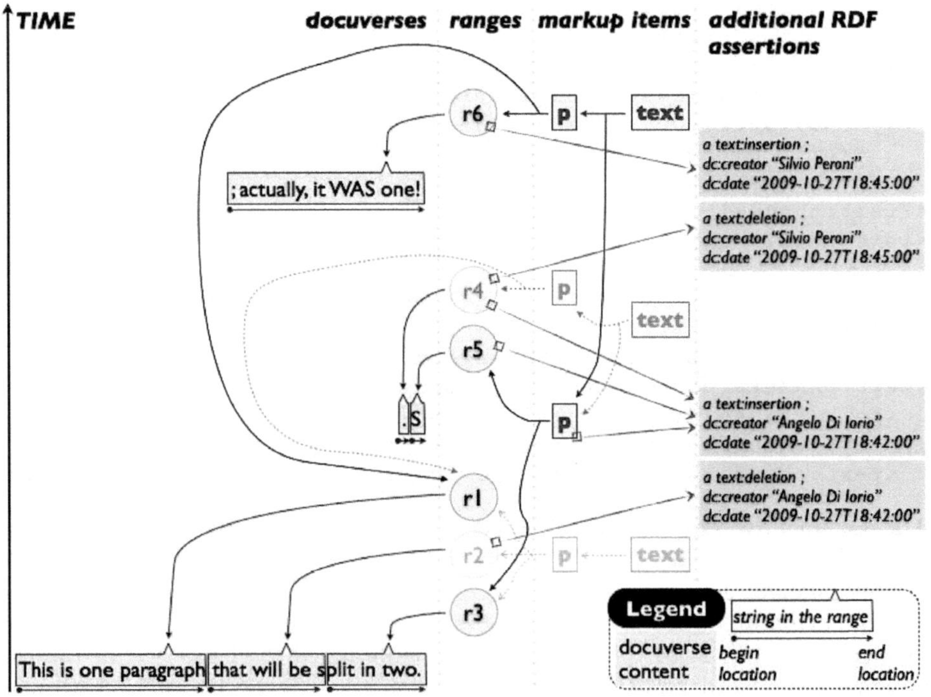

Fig. 1. Encoding the change-tracking use case with EARMARK data structures

structures. The information is already available and expressed through RDF and OWL statements.

Fig. 1 shows how the example could be modelled with EARMARK. All information about all three versions of the document are stored in a single EARMARK structure. In fact, there are three EARMARK elements, with general identifier set to "text", representing the three versions. Each of them is an ordered collection of other EARMARK elements, while the leaf items of each hierarchy are ranges. The arrows indicate a containment relationship, specified through the properties of the imported collection ontology, and model the tree structure of each version. Note that the EARMARK element with general identifier "text" of version 1 (looking the picture, the bottom one) contains only one paragraph – where paragraphs are all the elements with general identifier "p" – while the elements of versions 2 (central) and 3 (top), with the same general identifier "text", contain two paragraphs. In turn, those paragraphs contain fragments that compose the textual content of each version. The crucial aspect is that each text fragment is also annotated with (RDF) statements that indicates the type, the author and the date of each modification.

Fig. 1 is a graphic representation of the OWL ontology describing our example. Translating that content into an actual OWL files makes it possible to access and query it with Semantic Web tools. Powerful searches can be then performed without using niche tools or complex XPath expressions but simply through mainstream technologies such as SPARQL. Thus, the following SPARQL query:

```
SELECT ?r WHERE {
  ?r a text:insertion ; dc:creator "Angelo Di Iorio" }
```

represents the above-mentioned query ("*all text fragments inserted by Angelo Di Iorio*") running on the EARMARK document described so far.

6 Conclusions

The importance of XML lead researchers to design languages for overlapping markup that fit into the XML tree-based model. Multiple hierarchies are in fact forced into a single one that can be directly processed by languages such as XPath and XQuery. This paper discussed how using these languages for even simple needs is actually very difficult, even when the overlap is encoded applying the most common and robust strategies found in the literature.

The EARMARK approach is radically different and consists of specifying both markup structures and semantic annotations through an ontological approach. EARMARK associates OWL assertions to pieces of content and makes it possible to add RDF statements to the same content (or part of it). Multiple hierarchies can overlap without any limitation and without requiring the use of twisted syntactical workarounds. What makes our approach particularly interesting is that EARMARK documents are basically OWL ontologies. As a consequence, Semantic Web technologies – such as SPARQL – can be used *straightforwardly* to perform operations on their content.

Improving queries is not the only application of EARMARK. Validation is another interesting field we plan to investigate. The same ontological framework, in fact, can be used to prove properties concerning a document such as validity against a schema, compliance to co-constraint specifications or adherence to structural patterns.

References

1. De Rose, S.: Markup Overlap: A Review and a Horse. In: The Proceedings of the Extreme Markup Languages 2004 Conference, Montral, Canada (2004)
2. Di Iorio, A., Peroni, S., Vitali, F.: Towards markup support for full GODDAGs and beyond: the EARMARK approach. In: The Proceedings of Balisage: The Markup Conference 2009, Montreal, Canada (2009)
3. Horridge, M., Patel-Schneider, P.: OWL 2 Web Ontology Language: Manchester Syntax. W3C Working Group Note. World Wide Web Consortium (2009), http://www.w3.org/TR/owl2-manchester-syntax/
4. Huitfeldt, C., Sperberg-McQueen, C.M.: TexMECS: An experimental markup meta-language for complex documents. Working paper of the project Markup Languages for Complex Documents (MLCD). University of Bergen (2001)
5. Marinelli, P., Vitali, F., Zacchiroli, S.: Towards the unification of formats for overlapping markup. New Review of Hypermedia and Multimedia 14(1), 57–94 (2008)
6. Peroni, S., Vitali, F.: Annotations with EARMARK for arbitrary, overlapping and out-of order markup. In: The Proceedings of the Document Engineering 2009 Conference, Munich, Germany (2009)
7. Portier, P., Calabretto, S.: Methodology for the construction of multi-structured documents. In: The Proceedings of Balisage: The Markup Conference 2009, Montral, Canada (2009)
8. Schmidt, D., Colomb, R.: A data structure for representing multi-version texts online. International Journal of Human-Computer Studies 67(6), 497–514 (2009)
9. Sperberg-McQueen, C.M., Burnard, L.: TEI P5 Guidelines for Electronic Text Encoding and Interchange. The Association for Computers and the Humanities (2005)
10. Sperberg-McQueen, C.M., Huitfeldt, C.: GODDAG: A Data Structure for Overlapping Hierarchies. In: King, P., Munson, E.V. (eds.) PODDP 2000 and DDEP 2000. LNCS, vol. 2023, pp. 139–160. Springer, Heidelberg (2004)
11. Tennison, J., Piez, W.: The Layered Markup and Annotation Language. Paper Presented at the Late Breaking at Extreme Markup, Montreal, Canada (2002)
12. Tummarello, G., Morbidni, C., Pierazzo, E.: Toward textual encoding based on RDF. In: 9th ICCC Conference on Electronic Publishing, Leuven, Belgium (2005)
13. W3C OWL Working Group: OWL 2 Web Ontology Language Document Overview. W3C Recommendation. World Wide Web Consortium (2009), http://www.w3.org/TR/2009/REC-owl2-overview-20091027

Ontology Learning for Cost-Effective Large-Scale Semantic Annotation of Web Service Interfaces

Shahab Mokarizadeh[1], Peep Küngas[2], and Mihhail Matskin[1,3]

[1] Royal Institute of Technology (KTH), Stockholm, Sweden
[2] University of Tartu, Tartu, Estonia
[3] Norwegian University of Science and Technology (NTNU), Trondheim, Norway
shahabm@kth.se, peep.kungas@ut.ee, misha@kth.se

Abstract. In this paper we introduce a novel unsupervised ontology learning approach, which can be used to automatically derive a reference ontology from a corpus of web services for annotating semantically the Web services in the absence of a core ontology. Our approach relies on shallow parsing technique from natural language processing in order to identify grammatical patterns of web service message element/part names and exploit them in construction of the ontology. The generated ontology is further enriched by introducing relationships between similar concepts. The experimental results on a set of global Web services indicate that the proposed ontology learning approach generates an ontology, which can be used to automatically annotate around 52% of element part and field names in a large corpus of heterogeneous Web services.

Keywords: Ontology Learning, Web Services Annotation, NLP.

1 Introduction

The vision of web service technology to expose functionality of on-line services for system-to-system communication has resulted in deployment of considerable number of services on the Web. At the same time the Semantic Web initiative has provided methods, tools and knowledge structures for processing semantically enriched web services. Unfortunately, due to complexity of providing semantic information to web services, the visionary view of semantic web services has not been well accepted neither by industry nor governmental sector where semantic web services technologies could have the major impact. Hence vast majority of public web services lack semantic information and this, complemented with the increasing number of available web services, is the main obstacle in using semantic technologies either for exploiting or analyzing the existing web services. In the absence of core ontologies, annotation of existing web services is dependent on ontology development and ontology learning techniques. The latter refers to applying machine learning techniques for automatic discovery and creation of ontological knowledge [12]. In addition to outstanding ontology development obstacles [12] (being time-consuming and labor-intensive), ontology acquisition at the Web scale, such as we are aiming for, imposes extra burden primarily due to the large dataset size, heterogeneity of data and

P. Cimiano and H.S. Pinto (Eds.): EKAW 2010, LNAI 6317, pp. 401–410, 2010.

dynamicity of Web. Moreover, ontology acquisition solely from web service descriptions is a resource-demanding and error-prone task since majority of WSDL elements, which need annotations, lack textual documentation (around 95% of elements in our collection of ca 15 000 WSDL documents have no human-readable documentation attached). Furthermore, often the syntax of WSDL element names does not convey correct and complete picture of underlying semantics [1]. There have been efforts [14] [7] both in academia and industry to invent solutions for (semi) automatically annotating existing web services with standard semantic descriptions. The applicability of such solutions is hampered mainly by the annotation cost, as reported by Küngas and Dumas [2].

In this paper we first propose an unsupervised method for domain-independent ontology learning from web services corpus derived from a set of WSDL documents describing available Web services. The main purpose of the constructed ontology would be to facilitate semantic annotation of WSDL documents and XML schema for further analysis and usage of the Web services. The recall and precision of our approach is enhanced by utilization of natural language processing (NLP) techniques and linguistics resources (thesauri and acronym tables). The constructed ontology is then used to support automated annotation of data structure definitions in XML Schema and Web service interfaces in WSDL documents by using the heuristic-based automated annotation as proposed by Küngas and Dumas [2]. One of the specific applications of the constructed annotations is to increase the quality of Web services match-making. Matching of web services can then be used either during composition of new or analysis of existing web services.

The rest of this paper is organized as follows. In Section 2 we introduce our ontology development methodology and discuss requirements and design issues for the reference ontology. In Section 3 we present our ontology learning method, whereas the evaluation results are captured in Section 4. Finally, Section 5 reviews related work, while conclusions and discussion on future work are presented in Section 6.

2 Ontology Development Methodology

Our ontology development methodology is inspired from the ROD model proposed by Zhou [12] and is an incremental methodology consisting of multiple iterations. Accordingly, the methodology is based on a cycle of three consequence phases: design, learning and validation. While the ontology design phase involves identification of domain resources and analysis of requirements, the ontology learning phase embodies the core ontology learning and construction techniques. Ontology validation and evaluation of the generated ontology is the last phase of the cycle. After completion of a cycle and inspection of results, we will attempt to improve the results by integrating the resulting ontology with other ontologies and incorporating extra domain resources before executing another iteration.

In the ontology design phase, we identify the objectives and requirements for the target ontology, and determine applicability of relevant domain resources in our case. In addition, to comply with general characteristics of an ideal ontology [13] (e.g.

clarity, coherence, extendibility, etc), the target ontology needs to satisfy the following requirements with respect to objectives of web services analysis:

1. To maximize interoperability among web services (i.e. to increase number of matching web services);
2. To maximize the quantity of annotated web service elements;
3. To be evolvable and allow incremental ontology learning over time in order to accommodate frequent changes/updates in the web services domain.

We acknowledge that neither the above-mentioned list of requirements is complete nor all of its items can be achieved within a single iteration of ontology development. Therefore we have adopted an approach where we will refine the requirements after inspection of ontology validation, web services annotation and analysis results. Moreover, the ontology development methodology must accommodate the web scale ontology learning, which exposes additional requirements due to heterogeneity in documentation language, style and vocabulary, not to mention the requirements to computational complexity due to relatively large data set.

3 Ontology Learning Process

We follow a bottom-up approach for ontology learning by starting from processing the WSDL documents and gradually derive top-level ontological concepts and relations. As shown in Fig. 1, the ontology learning process consists of three steps where each step, in turn, is a pipeline of several tasks. The first step is mostly about extraction of relevant textual content and subsequent syntactic refinement, while the second step exploits the results of the first step to infer ontological concepts, relationships and instances. The last step deals with organization of the discovered concepts and relationships to improve the quality of discovered knowledge. In the following we explain in detail the activities involved in each step.

3.1 Information Elicitation

This step embodies our natural language processing scheme and uses components for syntactic refinement pattern extraction, term disambiguation and lexical similarity [6][1]. The step consists of following tasks:

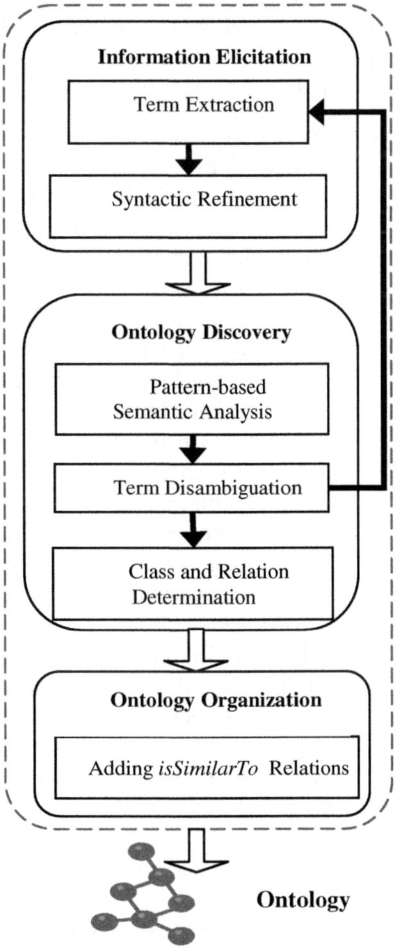

Fig. 1. Ontology Learning Steps

a) Term Extraction

Ontology learning from web service description can be performed at different levels of granularity, starting from the finest (XML schema leaf element names which are either of built-in XSD types or defined basic types) until more general levels with operations and services. Resulting ontologies can be used then to annotate the elements at the same level of granularity as the input elements. The focus of this work is based primarily on the finest granularity since once the finest elements of web services are semantically annotated, the resulting annotations can be propagated to coarse-grained elements [2]. Thus, first we will extract the list of fine-grained element names of the whole dataset (a corpus of WSDL documents). Next, out of the extracted list we choose a subset of most frequently presented element names, as proposed by Küngas and Dumas [2], for seeding ontology learning process. The extracted terms usually consist of multiple words (compound words or phrases).

b) Syntactic Refinement

The extracted terms may contain punctuations, shortened words, and abbreviations, misspelled and irrelevant words. Thus we need to normalize the terms to improve the quality of identified ontological concepts and relations in the generated ontology. Syntactic refinement task is constructed by using the following methods:

1. *Term Tokenization.* In context of schema leaf nodes, the extracted terms usually follow Camel case or Pascal case form, or separated by underlines and punctuations, which facilitate the tokenization process. We use these conventions for segmentation of terms into constituting tokens. The irrelevant words (such as single characters) and non-alphanumeric characters are also eliminated from the set of discovered tokens.
2. *Cleavage of Shortened Words and Abbreviations.* A term or the constituting words may refer to a domain terminology reflected as shortened word (e.g. pwd stands for password) or abbreviation (such as ASIN stands for Amazon Standard Identification Number). We utilize an auxiliary table for resolving such words into their corresponding complete syntactic forms.
3. *Known Compound Noun Determination.* The purpose of this method is to discover compound nouns (a sequential combination of two or more words) which convey a special meaning in general (e.g. first name) or in the underlying domain (e.g. login name). The compound nouns are treated as single units in the all subsequent word processing stages.
4. *Word Lemmatization.* Next, the words are transformed into their lemmas in order to look up them in the dictionary and later to provide unified naming conventions for labeling identified ontological concepts and relationships. Words which do not exist in dictionary are marked as stop words.
5. *Stop Word Removal.* Finally stop words are identified so that their sense will be excluded while we cluster terms based on their semantic similarity (see Section 3.3).

3.2 Ontology Discovery

This step concerns with exploited techniques, resources and tools for identifying the ontological concepts and relations from those set of refined terms resulted from previous step. The outcome of this step is our preliminary knowledge base (ontology + respective instances). The step consists of the following tasks.

a) Pattern-Based Semantic Analysis
We exploit the syntactic regularity patterns observed when composing a term out of multiple words. According to this observation vast majority of web service element names are noun phrases [1] while around 79% of the noun phrases in English language can be classified into one of two following patterns as reported by [3]:

- Pattern#1: $(Noun_1)+ \ldots +(Noun_n)$ e.g. *CustomerId*
- Pattern#2: $(Adjective_1)+ \ldots +(Noun_n)$ e.g. *SupportedImageType*

The patterns are highlighting the grammatical role of constituting words and their part of speech act. Both types of information (grammatical role and part of speech) can be extracted by employing grammatical dependency parser tools (e.g. MINIPAR tool [9]), which in addition discover dependency relationships of a given phrase. A dependency relationship is an asymmetric binary relation between a word, called *head,* and another word (or a set of words) named *modifier*, where *head* reveals the most emphasized word of the phrase (e.g. *CustomerId* would be resolved to pair {*head*: Identifier, *modifier*: Customer}). From dependency parser perspective, the above-mentioned patterns are identified as follows:

- **Pattern#1:** $(N|Word_n)$ $[(nn)(N|Word_1) + .. +(nn)\ (N|Word_{n-1})]$
- **Pattern#2:** $(N|Word_n)$ $[(mod)(A|Word_1)+ \ldots +(nn)\ (N|Word_{n-1})]$

In these patterns the first part, which is placed inside parentheses, refers to *head* of the phrase while the *modifier* segment is placed inside square brackets. Moreover, the words are annotated with their part of speech act (*N* for a noun and *A* for an adjective) and also grammatical roles (*mod* for an adjective relation, *nn* for a noun-noun relation). We harvest only terms complying with Pattern#1 or Pattern#2 as they provide the main ingredients for ontology learning.

b) Term Disambiguation
If all words in a term are determined as stop words, or when the *head* part is not a noun, then the term is considered as a vague term. These kinds of terms are disambiguated by replacing terms with respective operation names in WSDL from which input /output element names the particular term was extracted from. If the term appears in multiple operations, then we replace the single term with a concatenation of multiple operation names. We repeat the entire syntactic processing stages with new content but this time we simply discard ambiguous terms.

c) Class and Relation Determination
We rely on the following rules (Rule-1 and Rule-2) to exploit output of dependency parsing of each term to capture ontological classes and object property relationships. Construction of these rules is based on the following observations:

- According to Bourigault and Jacquemin [5] single-word terms denote broader concepts than multi-word terms. They appear more frequently in corpora and are therefore more appropriate for statistical clustering. In contrast to single-word terms that are too ambiguous and too generic, multi-word terms are more interesting for ontological motivation as they present finer concepts in domains. As single-word terms denote broader concepts than multi-word terms, and a compound noun inherits most of its semantic from its *head* [4], then we assume that the concept representing the *head* word subsumes the concept generalizing the entire term. Moreover, since *head* words cannot be decomposed further, we will regard them as concrete concepts in the ontology.

- The relation between *head* and *modifier* segment in case of *noun-noun (nn)* relationship resembles from grammatical point of view a kind of possessive authority for the *head* segment over an entire term. Based on this observation, has*Property* relationships among discovered concepts are asserted similarly to Guo et al [1].

Based on the aforementioned observations we introduce the following ontological concept identification rules:

Rule-1: *Terms, which are subject to Pattern#1 are initiating the assertion of following ontological concepts and relationships:*

- $Word_1$ hasProperty *Term,*
- *Term* subclassOf *Header.*

In Rule-1, *Term*, $Word_1$ and *Header* are all referring to concepts in an ontology. For example, term *SessionKeyIdentifier* complies with Rule-1, so the following axioms are added to the ontology: 1) *Session* isA *Class*, 2) *SessionKeyIdentifier* isA *Class*, 3) *Identifier* isA *Class*, 4) *Session* hasProperty *SessionKeyIdentifier, 5) SessionKeyIdentifier* subClassOf *Identifier.*

Rule-2: *Terms, which are subject to Pattern#2 are initiating the assertion of following ontological concepts and relationships*:

- *Term* subClassOf *Header*

In Rule-2, *Term* and *Header* are referring to concepts in an ontology. For example, term *SupportedType* complies with Rule-2, so the following axioms are added to the ontology: 1) *Type* isA *Class*, 2) *SupportedType* isA *Class, 3) SupportedType* subClassOf *Type.*

Using Rule-1 and Rule-2, we will generate an ontology automatically from the corpus of element names extracted from a set of web services descriptions in WSDL. In the last step, the initial set of (original) terms extracted from a collection of web service descriptions are assigned to their respective ontological representation as individuals.

3.3 Ontology Organization

In order to improve the quality and usability of generated ontology, the resulting ontology is investigated to determine extra relationship between concepts or to remove the redundant ones. In this work, we utilize lexical similarity between labels of ontology classes and augment the ontology with is*SimilarTo* relationship indicating that the classes on both side of this relationship convey a similar lexical semantic .We employ WordNet digital dictionary [10] and a WordNet lexical similarity library [8] to measure similarity between labels. We adopt an unsupervised agglomerative clustering approach to obtain clusters of similar classes. The clustering algorithm starts by putting every single data point (label of each concept) in one cluster to set up the initial clusters. Then, it measures pair-wise similarity distance of data points in one cluster against those belonging to other clusters and at each step merges two closest (most similar) clusters. The clustering process finishes whenever a single cluster remains or the similarity distance between two closest clusters does not meet a threshold. During our experiments, while manually evaluating the resulting ontologies, we observed that a threshold value of 85% is the minimum reasonable distance value. The similarity distance between two clusters is based on average dictionary-based affinity between entries of two clusters. The complexity of distance computation is of $O(n^2)$ due to need of cross-examination of each entry in one cluster against those in other clusters. From lexical analysis point of view, entries within a cluster are forming a synonym set. Thus, concepts in one cluster are pair-wise augmented with *isSimilarTo* relationship (e.g. Image *isSimilarTo* Picture).

4 Evaluation

The proposed ontology learning mechanism is implemented in Java by utilizing WordNet 3.0 as our reference dictionary, JWSL [8] library for measuring similarity between words, and MINIPAR dependency parser [9] for identifying the patterns. The generated ontology is represented in OWL format. During our experiments we used the set of ca 15000 WSDL documents from http://www.soatrader.com/web-services as a representative set of Web services. The evaluation data-set includes a sample subset of the services such that the frequency of input and output element names covers 20% (1858 unique terms) of names in the entire collected dataset. In order to validate correctness of the generated ontology, we manually constructed an ontology, using a methodology developed by Küngas and Dumas [2]. We refer to this handcrafted ontology as *golden ontology* in the rest of this paper.

As the generated ontology should also satisfy web service analysis requirements, we need to perform ontology evaluation from two perspectives. First, from ontology perspective we evaluate general ontological properties and validate the quality of a generated ontology against the golden ontology. Second, from web service annotation perspective we examine the quality and quantity of annotated web services using automatically generated ontology with respect to the golden ontology. We leave the latter evaluation case for the future work and focus on the former perspective in the rest of this paper. We perform evaluation of the automatically constructed ontology in two stages. While in the first stage, evaluation is performed over ontological classes, in the second stage ontological instances (WSDL/XSD leaf node elements) are used in evaluation. Fig. 2 presents the number of concepts and their instances in the automatically generated ontology and the golden ontology as well as the quantity of linguistically common concepts between the two ontologies and their instances.

4.1 Concept-Level Comparison

Out of 1853 unique terms in our evaluation data-set, our ontology learning system managed to process 1601 terms and assign them to their representative concepts (1813 concept) while the rest of the terms were ignored due to different reasons (i.e.

containing meaningless names, not complying with the determined patterns, etc). Clearly the number of concepts in generated ontology is larger with respect to the number of concepts in the golden ontology, since in our approach new concepts emerge due to following reasons. First, as a result of measuring linguistic and dictionary-based differences between underlying terms rather than considering actual semantics of terms (e.g. "legalDisclaimer" and "TermsAndConditions" where both convey same meaning while their ontological representation leads to several classes). Second, ontological concept discovery rules (Rule-1, Rule-2) break down a compound noun into several interrelated concepts. Hence, proportionally larger number of concepts is expected to be generated by our system compared to the number of instances.

For concept-level ontology comparison we exploited Falcon-AO [11], which aligns ontologies in two phases: first linguistic then structural (graph) matching. Authors of Falcon-AO have pointed out that their tool cannot use structural information for ontology alignment purpose if the underlying ontology is very large such as in our case. Hence, the ontology alignment result produced by Falkon-AO solely represents linguistics similarity between aligned ontologies. While the percentage of similar concepts over the two ontologies is only about 62% with respect to the concepts in the golden ontology, the number of instances captured by those common concepts is relatively high around 71% (1313 instances out of 1853). Since instance level evaluation can be performed over more than two third of the entire data set, a reasonable assessment can be expected despite of deficiencies of concept matching. Because the concepts in the golden ontology are not augmented with any other relations (i.e. object properties), we did not perform any comparison at this level.

4.2 Instance-Level Comparison

For instance-level comparison we compute precision (*P*) and recall (*R*) metrics to show the quality of our term classification approach only for those instances, which are assigned to the common concepts, which are presented by the last grey column in Fig. 2. Let's consider *E* as the set of instances belonging to those common concepts in a golden ontology, *C* (correct) as the number of instances in set *E*, which are classified correctly in the generated ontology, *I* (incorrect) as the number of instances in *E* which are misplaced (i.e. they are not assigned to the same concepts as instructed by the golden ontology) and *M* (missing) as the number of instances which appear in set *E* but they are not classified under the common concepts in generated ontology. Based on these definitions, we compute the precision and recall as following:

$$P = \frac{C}{C + I} \quad , \quad R = \frac{C}{C + M} \tag{1}$$

The size of *E* in our system is 1313, which equals $C+M+I$ where $C = 968$, $I = 60$ and $M = 278$. According to (1), we have precision of 85% and recall of 78%. High precision is achieved due to the syntactic quality of terms, following the syntactic patterns which we used during harvesting, and finally complying with respect to dictionary meanings in WordNet [10]. The quality of syntactic processing is also boosted by utilization of an auxiliary table to uncover known acronyms and compound nouns, which consequently improves both recall and precision.

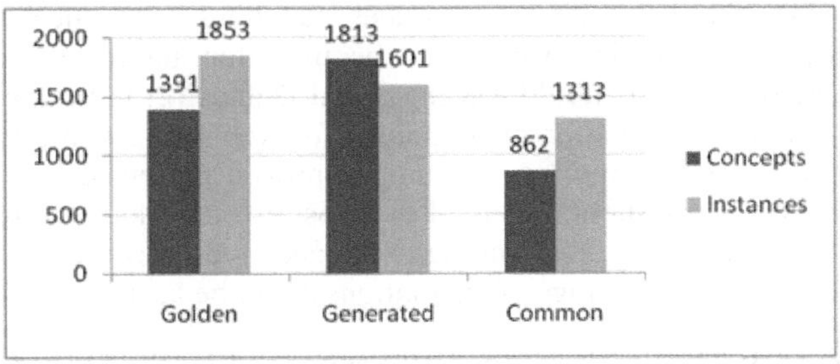

Fig. 2. Quantity of concepts & instances in generated ontology compared to golden ontology

5 Related Works

Proposed mechanisms for (semi-)automatic annotation and matching of web services are aiming for machine learning techniques and they diverge in availability of external resources, training data sets, quality and quantity of dataset and main purpose of annotation. Some machine-learning-based approaches such as [7] ,proposed by Heβ et al. need initially to train their system in order to generalize (semantic of training data) and predict semantic labels for (similar) unseen web services. As we target a large repository of absolutely not-annotated ad-hoc web services from different domains, applicability of such techniques is not clear. Similarly to our approach, Guo et al. [1] leveraged relation between words in phrases to establish ontological relationships between acquired concepts. While the authors tackle pair-wise service matching solution by aligning the generated ontology fragments, we intend to create an ontology to be utilized for analysis of web services. In addition, Guo et al. [1] take advantage of active domain experts and knowledge of web services domains in annotation. Neither of these two resources are practically available in our case due to size of the data set and lack of additional meta-knowledge about services. In a slightly similar work, Sabou et al. [6] described an automatic extracting method that learns domain ontologies from textual documentation attached to web services. Due to the fact that around 95% of web services in our data set come with no textual documentation, the applicability of their approach is not applicable in our case.

Several tools for semantic annotation of web services and transformation to semantic web service representations such as OWL-S by ASSAM [7], and WSDL-S/SA-WSDL [15] by Radiant [14] have been proposed. The aforementioned tools follow a semi-automatic approach for selecting the most appropriate domain ontology (for annotation purpose) and then mapping WSDL elements to respective ontological concepts. Due to explicit expert user intervention and reliance on pre-determined domain ontologies for annotation purpose, applicability of such solutions for large-scale annotation of web services is impractical despite of the fact that these solutions tend to provide high-quality annotations.

6 Conclusions and Future Work

In this paper we presented an ontology learning approach to be used for matching web services in large scale in the absence of a core ontology. The preliminary results show that the generated ontology captures correctly around 52% of entire data set, hence, providing a reasonable basis for web services matching in practical solutions. Our approach generates ontologies, which can be used for automated construction of annotation heuristics such as used by Küngas and Dumas [2] in their semi-automatic cost-effective semantic annotation methodology for web services interfaces. Thus one of the contributions of the ontology learning approach presented in this paper is to reduce the number of man-hours required in a cost-effective annotation scheme even further. As a future work we are planning to enhance the proposed ontology learning approach such that better coverage of annotations could be achieved automatically.

Acknowledgement. This work was partially supported by the Grant 621-2007-6565 from the Swedish Research Council.

References

1. Guo, H., Ivan, A., Akkiraju, R., Goodwin, R.: Learning Ontologies to Improve the Quality of Automatic Web Service Matching. In: IEEE Int. Conference on Web Services (ICWS 2007), pp. 118–125 (2007)
2. Küngas, P., Dumas, M.: Cost-Effective Semantic Annotation of XML Schemas and Web Service Interfaces. In: IEEE Int. Conference on Services Computing, pp. 372–379. IEEE Computer Society, Los Alamitos (2009)
3. European Collaborative Clamour Project: Linguistic Work Package Report (2000), `http://www.statistics.gov.uk/methods_quality/clamour/coordination/downloads/Clamourdec2000IRn2.doc`
4. Lieber, R.: Morphology and Lexical Semantics. Cambridge University Press, Cambridge (2004)
5. Bourigault, D., Jacquemin, C.: Term extraction + term clustering: an integrated platform for computer-aided terminology. In: 9th Conference on European Chapter of the Association for Computational Linguistics, pp. 15–22. ACL, Morristown (1999)
6. Sabou, M., Wroe, C., Goble, C., Mishne, G.: Learning domain ontologies for Web service descriptions: An experiment in bioinformatics. In: Proceedings of the 14th International Conference on World Wide Web, pp. 190–198. ACM, Japan (2005)
7. Heß, A., Johnston, E., Kushmerick, N.: ASSAM: A Tool for Semi-Automatically Annotating Semantic Web Services. In: McIlraith, S.A., Plexousakis, D., van Harmelen, F. (eds.) ISWC 2004. LNCS, vol. 3298, pp. 320–334. Springer, Heidelberg (2004)
8. Pirrò, G., Seco, N.: Design, Implementation and Evaluation of a New Similarity Metric Combining Feature and Intrinsic Information Content. In: Meersman, R., Tari, Z. (eds.) OTM 2008, Part II. LNCS, vol. 5332, pp. 1271–1288. Springer, Heidelberg (2008)
9. Lin, D.: Dependency-based Evaluation of MINIPAR. In: Workshop on the Evaluation of Parsing Systems, First Int. Conf. on Learning Resources and Evaluation, Spain (1998)
10. Miller, G.A.: WordNet: A Lexical Database for English. Communications of the ACM 38(11), 39–41 (1995)
11. Hu, W., Qu, Y.: Falcon-AO: A practical ontology matching system. Web Semantic 6(3), 237–239 (2008)
12. Zhou, L.: Ontology learning: State of the art and open issues. Information Technology and Management 8, 241–252 (2007)
13. Gruber, T.R.: Toward principles for the design of ontologies used for knowledge sharing. Journal of Human Computer Studies 43(5), 907–928 (1993)
14. Radiant: WSDL-S/SAWSDL Annotation Tool, `http://lsdis.cs.uga.edu/projects/meteors/downloads/index.php?page=1`
15. Kopecký, J., Vitvar, T., Bournez, C., Farrell, J.: SAWSDL: Semantic Annotations for WSDL and XML Schema. IEEE Internet Computing 11(6), 60–67 (2007)

Towards Hybrid Reasoning for Verifying and Validating Multilevel Models*

Nophadol Jekjantuk[1], Gerd Gröner[2], Jeff Z. Pan[1], and Edward Thomas[1]

[1] University of Aberdeen, United Kingdom
[2] University of Koblenz-Landau, Germany

Abstract. Ontologies and its reasoning services are expected to play an important role in many application domains, as well as in software engineering in general. In model-driven engineering (MDE), models, like UML models, represent and specify software systems. One problem with using ontologies within software engineering is that while model-driven engineering realizes a four-layer metamodeling architecture, the new version of OWL Web Ontology Language, called OWL 2, it supports only simple metamodeling. Moreover, the semantics of metamodeling in OWL 2 corresponds to the contextual semantics, which leads to non-intuitive results. Another issue is that the Open World Assumption (OWA) assumes a model is incomplete. Therefore, we could not validate some constrains in OWA. In this paper, we demonstrate multilevel (meta-) modelling using ontologies described in OWL FA, which has a well-defined fixed-layered architecture and semantics. As well as an approach to integrate Closed World Assumption(CWA) with OWA in order to use both assumptions for verifying and validating multilevel models.

1 Introduction

Ontologies and the Web Ontology Language (OWL) are well established for model descriptions and model management tasks. However, metamodelling is not supported by tractable OWL sub languages like OWL Lite, OWL DL. More complex languages like OWL Full provide metamodelling facilities, but OWL Full is not decidable.

Metamodeling, i.e. modelling across multiple modelling layers, dealing with Concepts and meta-concepts, is a key issue in model management and especially in model-driven software development (MDSD). Metamodels appear in application areas such as UML [19], Model Driven Architecture [4] and E-Commerce.

In model-driven software development, software developers would like to improve their software development processes by using reasoning mechanisms such as inconsistency checking of models. In order to do so they need to transform the software models that have a well-defined four-layered architecture into an OWL DL ontology, which does not support modelling, and reasoning over a layered architecture. In OWL DL, we can present classes and objects in two layers.

* This work has been partially supported by the European Project Marrying Ontologies and Software Technologies (MOST ICT 2008-216691).

P. Cimiano and H.S. Pinto (Eds.): EKAW 2010, LNAI 6317, pp. 411–420, 2010.

Therefore, developers need to sacrifice some meta-layers or compress it into two layers which lead to incomplete representation of the model. Thus, this could be the main reason why software developers ignore to use OWL ontologies and their mechanisms.

A common user complaint about OWL is that it does not provide a decidable sub-language which supports metamodeling. OWL 2 provides simple metamodeling which corresponds to the contextual semantics defined in [14]. However, this modelling technique is mainly based on punning. It has been shown in [17] that this can lead to non-intuitive results, since the interpretation function is different based on the context. There are various works which consider validation of UML models with OCL constraints like in [3,5,10,18,11]. However, none of these approaches account for a validation across multiple layers, i.e. validates models with respect to their metamodels. They validate models with model constraints and instances of the models, but they do not account for metamodels in their validation. However, for many applications, a two-layer validation without a metamodel is not adequate (cf. Section 2).

Another issue is that the description logics relies on open world assumption (OWA) which assumes incomplete information as default and allows for validating incomplete models. Therefore, we could not validate some constrains in OWA (cf. Section 4.3). The closed-world assumption (CWA) assumes that the elements in the model are known and unchanging. However, we would like to use beneficial from both assumptions to validate multilevel models.

There is work on closed world reasoning or local closed world reasoning (cf. [7]) for OWL knowledge bases like using epistemic operators as described in [8,6]. Hybrid knowledge representations are investigated in [12] to integrate both assumptions. However, none of those approach are consider on metamodeling.

In this paper, at first, we use OWL FA [17] to describe a multilevel models. Then, we use OWL FA reasoner [9] together with Local Closed World Assumptions (LCWA) engine to validate models covering multiple modelling levels. Thus, this will leverage the software development life cycle.

The paper is organized as follows. Section 2 outlines a metamodeling application which demonstrates dependencies between multiple levels. The need and requirement is described in Section 3. In the subsequent Sections, we demonstrated metamodeling based on description logics including the syntax and semantics of OWL FA, followed by the detailed description of how to represent multilevel models with metamodeling in ontologies as well as the need of closed world assumption are given in Section 4. In Section 5 we detailed the local closed world assumption, followed by an evaluation from experimental results in section 6 while a comparison with related works is contained in section 7.

2 A Motivating Example

This section gives an example to demonstrate the need for metamodeling enabled ontologies. Models are depicted in UML notations [1]. Metamodels are more than a syntactic language description of a modelling language; a metamodel is a description of the concepts of a modelling language specifying the structure and the kind of information that can be handled [15].

Example 1. Models and metamodels are commonly used in model-driven software engineering (MDSE). In order to improve software development processes, new technologies, which provide reasoning support like consistency checking of models and metamodels, are beneficial. In MDSE, each model layer can contain both class and object definitions (cf. [2]). However, this leads to undecidability problems in model validation w.r.t the complexity of the model. In ontology engineering, ontologies for metamodeling like OWL FA separate classes and objects into different layers in order to maintain the decidability of the language.

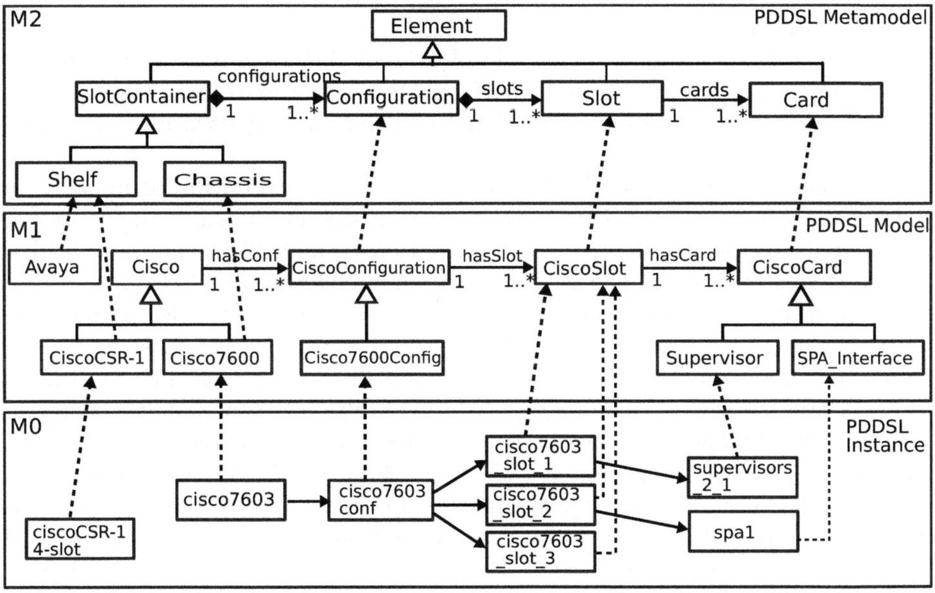

Fig. 1. Layered Architecture for a Physical Device Model

In Figure 1, a layered modelling architecture is demonstrated for physical device modelling (an application of configuration management). A physical device domain specific language (PDDSL) is a domain specific language (DSL) for physical devices which is used in business IT system modelling. The figure depicts three layers M_0, M_1 and M_2. M_3 is a Meta-metamodeling layer which is not included in the example. The arrows between the layers demonstrate instance relationships, the arrows within a layer are concept relations (like object properties and subclass hierarchies).

Cisco, CiscoConfiguarion, CiscoSlot and CiscoCard are instances of some classes from the M_2 layer. At the same time, these artifacts are concepts in the layer M_1 and each of these concepts can contain some instance from layer M_0. The rest of the relationships in a layer like concept subsumption and object properties are represented by the arrows.

There are additional modelling constraints imposed on different layers. In layer M_2, a model designer requires that each SlotContainer has a Configuration and each Configuration may contain some Slot, Each Slot may contain some Card. configurations, slots, and cards are expressed as ObjectProperty. Moreover, the modeller requires the disjointness of the two classes Chassis and Shelf. There are also three ObjectProperty assertions from the layer M_2 to layer M_1: configuration(Cisco, CiscoConfiguration), slots(CiscoConfiguration, CiscoSlot) and cards(CiscoSlot, CiscoCard).

In layer M_1 a model designer requires that each Cisco have at least one Configuration. Each CisoConfiguration may contain one or more CiscoSlot and each Slot may contain CiscoCard. hasConfig, hasSlot and hasCard are expressed as ObjectProperty.

Additionally, in a concrete model in M_1, the modeller requires the disjointness of the classes Supervisor and SPA_interface. Moreover, Cisco7600Config. can have only three CiscoSlot and Cisco7600_Slot_1 can contain only card from Supervisor class.

A crucial task in model-driven engineering is the validation of models and metamodels. A valid model refers to its metamodel and satisfies all the restrictions and constraints. However, the validation of multiple layers may lead to inconsistency even if the consistency is satisfied between all adjacent layers.

For instance in the previous described scenario, the model on M_1 and also the corresponding metamodel on layer M_2 are consistent. The inconsistency occurs when they are combined, i.e. consider the modelling restrictions like equivalence or disjointness for the whole model, covering multiple layers simultaneously instead of only two adjacent layers. If one would like to add Avaya is a Shelf and Avaya is equivalent to concept Cisco7600 in M_1. Here, Avaya and Cisco7600 are concepts in layer M_1. This equivalence condition does not cause any inconsistency of the modelling layer (M_1 and M_0 for instances). However, combined with the constraints on the metamodel layer M_2 which requires the disjointness of Shelf and Chassis, this leads to a contradiction and therefore to an inconsistent ontology. Without capturing multiple layers, this inconsistency is not detected since the adjacent layers M_1, M_0 and M_2, M_1 are consistent on its own.

Although, OWL FA allows us to capture a multilevel models and validate it with its reasoning mechanism. In some cases we cannot validate the multilevel models suitably because OWL FA in realizes the open world assumption (OWA). we will discuss through an example in section 4.3.

3 User Requirement

In this section, we describe the requirements for the PDDSL modelling architecture from Section 2 for physical devices from a PDDSL user (language user) point of view. The PDDSL user models physical devices and their configurations in layer M_1. In usual OWL (-DL) conceptual two-layer models, this could be the

TBox in order to account for modelling and reasoning in the modelling layer and instance layer.

For modelling of physical network devices in PDDSL, the user (PDDSL modeller) requires the following modelling support.

- Planning of Network: The modelling frameworks enable restrictions and suggestions of components that can be used in the current model configuration. These restrictions and suggestions are based on the corresponding metamodel in layer M_2.
- Consistency checking of devices and configurations: The consistency of the devices and configurations which are modelled in layer M_1 are checked and validated with respect to the corresponding metamodels. The metamodels are defined in the layer M_2.
- Data quality analysis: The user checks whether a configuration on M_0 is instance of a modelled configuration on M_1, or for a given configuration in M_0 the most specific configuration model in M_1 is searched.

The realization of these service requirements depends on the modelling possibilities and on the reasoning services that are available for the model. To realize a single requirement, a two-layered model is appropriate. However, if more of these requirements have to be realized simultaneously, two layers are not enough.

4 Metamodeling Based on Description Logics

In the following we present OWL FA and semantics together with how to use OWL FA to represent a multilevel models. Then we discuss why the Open World Assumption is not enough for validating the multilevel models.

4.1 OWL FA Syntax and Semantics

OWL FA [17] enables metamodeling. It is an extension of OWL DL, which refers to the description logic $\mathcal{SHOIN}(\mathcal{D})$. Ontologies in OWL FA are represented in a layered architecture. This architecture is mainly based on the architecture of RDFS(FA) [16].

OWL FA specifies a stratum number in class constructors and axioms to indicate the strata they belong to. Let $i \geq 0$ be an integer. OWL FA consists of an alphabet of distinct class names $\mathbf{V}_{\mathrm{C_i}}$ (for stratum i), datatype names $\mathbf{V}_{\mathrm{D}}$, abstract property names $\mathbf{V}_{\mathrm{APi}}$ (for stratum i), datatype property names $\mathbf{V}_{\mathrm{DP}}$ and individual (object) names ($\mathbf{I}$); together with a set of constructors (with subscriptions) to construct class and property descriptions (also called *OWL FA-classes* and *OWL FA-properties*, respectively).

Let $\mathsf{CN} \in \mathbf{V}_{\mathrm{C_i}}$ be an atomic class name in layer i ($i \geq 0$), R an OWL FA-property in layer i, $o \in \mathbf{I}$ an individual, $T \in \mathbf{V}_{\mathrm{DP}}$ a datatype property name, and C, D OWL FA-classes in layer i. Valid OWL FA-classes are defined by the abstract syntax:

$$\begin{aligned} C ::= {} & \top_{\mathrm{i}} \mid \bot \mid \mathsf{CN} \mid \neg_{\mathrm{i}} C \mid C \sqcap_{\mathrm{i}} D \mid C \sqcup_{\mathrm{i}} D \mid \{o\} \mid \exists_{\mathrm{i}} R.C \mid \\ & \mid \forall_{\mathrm{i}} R.C \mid \leqslant_{\mathrm{i}} nR \mid \geqslant_{\mathrm{i}} nR \mid \\ & (\text{if i} = 1)\ \exists_1 T.d \mid \forall_1 T.d \mid \leqslant_1 nT \mid \geqslant_1 nT \end{aligned}$$

The semantics of OWL FA is a model theoretic semantics, which is defined in terms of interpretations. In other words, The semantics of two layers which can be considered as TBox and ABox are same as in OWL DL. The idea of OWL FA is that the interpretation depends on the layer but is still an OWL DL interpretation. Given an OWL FA alphabet **V**, a set of built-in datatype names $\mathbf{B} \subseteq \mathbf{V}_{\mathrm{D}}$ and an integer $k \geq 1$, an *OWL FA interpretation* is a tuple of the form pair $\mathcal{J} = (\Delta^{\mathcal{J}}, \cdot^{\mathcal{J}})$, where $\Delta^{\mathcal{J}}$ is the domain (a non-empty set) and $\cdot^{\mathcal{J}}$ is the interpretation. In the rest of the paper, we assume that i is an integer such that $1 \leq i \leq k$. The interpretation function can be extend ObjectProperty assertionsed to give semantics to OWL FA-properties and OWL FA-classes. Let $RN \in \mathbf{V}_{\mathrm{APi}}$ be an abstract property name in layer i and R be an abstract property in layer i. Valid OWL FA abstract properties are defined by the abstract syntax: $R ::= RN \mid R^{-}$, where for some $x, y \in \Delta_{\mathrm{A}_{\mathrm{i}-1}}^{\mathcal{J}}$, $\langle x, y\rangle \in R^{\mathcal{J}}$ iff $\langle y, x\rangle \in R^{-\mathcal{J}}$. Valid OWL FA datatype properties are datatype property names. The interpretation function is explained in detail in [17].

4.2 Modelling Multilevel Models with OWL FA

In this section, we present the way of express multiple-layered model with OWL FA. Although the layer numbers can/should be encapsulated by tools, there are two rules of thumb to help users to get the number right. Firstly, the subscript numbers are only used to indicate a sub-ontology (e.g. $\mathcal{O}_2$), a constructor (e.g. $\exists_2$), or axiom symbols (e.g. $\sqsubseteq_2$, $:_2$) in a sub-ontology. Secondly, subscript numbers for constructors and axiom symbols indicate the sub-ontology that the class descriptions constructed by these constructors and axioms belong to.

The following example shows how to model a physical device ontology with OWL FA notation. According to PDDSL modelling architecture from Section 2, we can represent the class, property and instance relations in the M_2 layer. Example 2 shows how to describe class constructs, constraint by and class and property assertions using OWL FA notation.

Example 2. PDDSL Model on M_2 layer expressed in OWL FA:

$$\mathsf{SlotContainer} \sqsubseteq_2 \mathsf{Element} \tag{1}$$

$$\mathsf{Shelf} \sqsubseteq_2 \mathsf{SlotContainer} \tag{2}$$

$$\mathsf{Chassis} \sqsubseteq_2 \mathsf{SlotContainer} \tag{3}$$

$$\mathsf{Configuration} \sqsubseteq_2 \mathsf{Element} \tag{4}$$

$$\mathsf{Slot} \sqsubseteq_2 \mathsf{Element} \tag{5}$$

$$\mathsf{Card} \sqsubseteq_2 \mathsf{Element} \tag{6}$$

$$\mathsf{SlotContainer} \sqsubseteq_2 \exists_2 \mathsf{configurations.Configuration} \tag{7}$$

$$\mathsf{Configuration} \sqsubseteq_2 \exists_2 \mathsf{slots.Slot} \tag{8}$$

$$\mathsf{Slot} \sqsubseteq_2 \exists_2 \mathsf{cards.Card} \tag{9}$$

$$(\mathsf{Cisco},\ \mathsf{CiscoConfiguration}) :_2 \mathsf{configuration} \tag{10}$$

$$\mathsf{Cisco7600} :_2 \mathsf{Chassis} \tag{11}$$

Due to limitations of space, we could not show the complete OWL FA ontology in this paper. However, the class, property and instance relations in M_1 layer can be described in the same manner.

4.3 Closed and Open World Assumption in OWL FA

Knowledge representation in OWL and in OWL FA in general realizes the open world assumption (OWA). The open world assumption assumes incomplete information. More precisely, we can only use known statements to infer information. In the semantic web, this assumption is beneficial in order to build a knowledge base that can be further extended and enriched. In contrast, in the closed world assumption each statement that is unknown is assumed to be false, i.e. we assume our knowledge base is complete. In some applications, the closed world assumption is assumed like in database systems and in model-driven engineering. Hence, for certain validation tasks in multi-level models closed world assumption or closed world reasoning is required.

Let take follow assertions to demonstrate the difference of closed and open world assumption. We consider the assertions as an excerpt of the ontology from layer M_1 to M_0. These assertions are describe for some Cisco7600Config instances and the cards CiscoCard instances that are plugged into the slots. supervisors_2_1, supervisors_3_1, and supervisors_3_2 are instance of Supervisors. (cisco7603_slot_1, supervisors_2_1) $:_1$ hasCard, (cisco7603_slot_2, supervisors_3_1) $:_1$ hasCard, and (cisco7603_slot_3, supervisors_3_2) $:_1$ hasCard are Object propeties assertion.

A device modeller is interested whether a certain card of type SPA_Interface is used in any of the current configurations of type Cisco7600Config.. SPA_Interface is a subclass of CiscoCard in M_1 (cf. Fig. 1). Assumed there is no assertion in the ontology, that explicitly states that there is a configuration with a slot that is connected to a card of type SPA_Interface.

Using standard open world assumption we cannot answer this question since the absence of an assertion that assigns such a card of type SPA_Interface to a configuration does not imply that there is no such configuration. In contrast, using the closed world assumption, we can conclude from the ontology that there is no such configuration that uses a card of type SPA_Interface.

5 Local Closed World Assumption

The Local Closed World Assumption (LCWA) allows selective parts of an otherwise open world ontology to be locally closed. This means that the reasoner cannot assume the existence of any additional individuals or property relationships between classes or properties which are within the domain of the closed elements. For example, under the open world assumption, given the axiom $C \sqsubseteq \exists R.D$; the reasoner would assume the presence of a relationship R between every explicit instance of the class C and some instance of the class D, whether or not it was explicitly stated. If we locally close the class D, then the reasoner could only assume such a relationship with an explicit member of D. If the reasoner could not make this assumption, for example, if R was an inverse functional property, and all instances of D were already accounted for in the property R, this would render the ontology inconsistent.

To close a class in an ontology, we simply enumerate all known members of that class, and add a new axiom to the ontology stating that the class is equivalent to that set of individuals. This requires a language that can express nominals, such as OWL DL, or OWL2.

To close a property, we must add a new axiom for each instance of the property which can be inferred from the ontology. For each instance of a property $R(i_1, i_2)$, we add new axioms such that $\exists R.\{i_2\} \equiv \{i_1\}$ and $\exists R^-.\{i_1\} \equiv \{i_2\}$. Furthermore, we take the set of all inferrable instances of the property $(i_{d1}, i_{r1}), \ldots, (i_{d1}, i_{rn})$ and state that $\exists R \equiv \{i_{d1}, \ldots, i_{dn}\}$ and $\exists R^- \equiv \{i_{r1}, \ldots, i_{rn}\}$.

6 Experimental Result

In this section, we compare results between using OWL FA tool kit with Local Closed World Assumption (LCWA) and without it, to validate physical device ontology. Without using LCWA, we might not be able to validate multilevel models. Let us consider the following OWL FA ontology.

$$\mathsf{Shelf} \sqsubseteq_2 \neg\mathsf{Chassis} \tag{12}$$
$$\mathsf{Cisco7600} :_2 \mathsf{Chassis} \tag{13}$$
$$\mathsf{CiscoCRS1-4Slot} :_2 \mathsf{Shelf} \tag{14}$$
$$\mathsf{Cisco7603} :_1 \mathsf{Cisco7600} \tag{15}$$
$$\mathsf{CiscoCRS1-4Slot-1} :_1 \mathsf{CiscoCRS1-4Slot} \tag{16}$$
$$\mathsf{CiscoCRS1-4Slot-1} \approx_0 \mathsf{Cisco7603} \tag{17}$$

A $\mathsf{Cisco7603}$ is stop working and it need to be replace. One would like to know that it is possible to use $\mathsf{CiscoCRS1-4Slot-1}$ instead. Then, the modeller immediately make $\mathsf{CiscoCRS1-4Slot-1}$ become equivalent to $\mathsf{Cisco7603}$ and validate it with OWL FA Toolkit. The expected answer should be invalid but the OWL FA Toolkit returns valid according to Open World Assumption(OWA). In OWA, even $\mathsf{Cisco7600}$ has one individual in the knowledge base it does not means that $\mathsf{Cisco7603}$ is only one individual of $\mathsf{Cisco7600}$. $\mathsf{Cisco7600}$ can have infinite individual which is not define yet. The axioms $\mathsf{CiscoCRS1-4Slot-1} \approx_0 \mathsf{Cisco7603}$ does not make $\mathsf{Cisco7600}$ become equivalent to $\mathsf{CiscoCRS1-4Slot}$. Therefore, this multilevel models is still valid.

Now, we use new version of OWL FA tool kit with included local closed world assumption engine. Then, We close concept $\mathsf{Cisco7600}$ and $\mathsf{CiscoCRS1-4Slot}$. The result of validation will be inconsistent.

7 Related Work

OWL FA was introduced in [17] for metamodeling in OWL. Motik [14] addressed metamodeling in OWL with two different semantics. The contextual semantics (or π-semantics) uses punning, i.e. names are replaced by distinct names for concepts, individuals and roles. This is like the different representation of an object in the OWL DL ontologies $\mathcal{O}_i$ in OWL FA. OWL2 [13] provides simple metamodeling features which is based on the contextual approach. The other semantics is the HiLog semantics (or ν-semantics). The HiLog semantics is stronger than the π-semantics. The concepts and individual interpretations are not independent.

In [20] spanning objects are used in order to have different interpretations for objects that are instances and classes simultaneously. Compared to OWL FA one spanning object refers to one ontology $\mathcal{O}_i$.

Berardi et al. [3] apply DL Reasoning to UML class diagrams. The expressiveness of UML diagrams and constraints are restricted to the expressiveness of the DL $\mathcal{ALC}^-$. Basic conceptual modelling including model constraints is demonstrated for UML diagrams in OWL The consistency check of a UML class diagram is then reduced to concept satisfiability in $\mathcal{ALC}^-$. However, the verification is only performed on the conceptual level, without accounting for a metamodeling architecture.

8 Conclusion

In this paper, we have presented an approach to verify and validate multilevel models that describe in OWL FA by using hybrid-reasoning approach. At first, we described the requirements for verifying and validating of multilevel models through a practical example. Then, we detailed the need and requirements from software engineering. In the subsequent Section, we demonstrated Metamodeling based on description logics including the syntax and semantics of OWL FA, followed by the detailed description of how to represent multilevel models with metamodeling in ontologies and the need of closed world assumption. Later we detailed about local closed world assumption. The early experimental results show that OWL FA and its reasoner could benefit a software modeller in order to leverage the software development life cycle.

We have shown how to use the OWL FA Toolkit to verify and validate reasoning over multilevel models and we plan to incorporate these into the TrOWL[1] reasoning infrastructure. In the future, we would like to apply the fixed-layer architecture to OWL 2 DL that has more expressive power than OWL DL. Moreover, we plan to provide tools along with a reasoning mechanism for OWL 2 FA.

References

1. OMG Unified Modeling Language (OMG UML) Infrastructure. Version 2.2 (2009), `http://www.omg.org/spec/UML/2.2/Infrastructure`
2. Atkinson, C., Gutheil, M., Kennel, B.: A Flexible Infrastructure for Multilevel Language Engineering. IEEE Trans. Software Eng. 35(6), 742–755 (2009)
3. Berardi, D., Calvanese, D., De Giacomo, G.: Reasoning on UML class diagrams. Artificial Intelligence 168(1-2), 70–118 (2005)

[1] http://www.trowl.eu

4. Brown, A.: An introduction to Model Driven Architecture. IBM Technical Report (2004), http://www-128.ibm.com/developerworks/rational/library/3100.html
5. Cabot, J., Clariso, R., Riera, D.: Verification of UML/OCL Class Diagrams using Constraint Programming. In: Software Testing Verification and Validation Workshop, pp. 73–80 (2008)
6. Donini, F.M., Nardi, D., Rosati, R.: Description logics of minimal knowledge and negation as failure. ACM Transactions on Computational Logic (TOCL) 3(2), 225 (2002)
7. Etzioni, O., Golden, K., Weld, D.: Tractable Closed World Reasoning. In: Proc. of Knowledge Representation, KR (2004)
8. Grimm, S., Motik, B.: Closed World Reasoning in the Semantic Web through Epistemic Operators. In: CEUR Proceedings of the OWL Experiences and Directions Workshop, Galway, Ireland, Citeseer (2005)
9. Jekjantuk, N., Gröner, G., Pan, J.Z.: Reasoning in Metamodeling Enabled Ontologies. In: Proceeding of the International Workshop on OWL: Experience and Directions, OWL-ED 2009 (2009)
10. Kaneiwa, K., Satoh, K.: Consistency checking algorithms for restricted UML class diagrams. In: Dix, J., Hegner, S.J. (eds.) FoIKS 2006. LNCS, vol. 3861, pp. 219–239. Springer, Heidelberg (2006)
11. Malgouyres, H., Motet, G.: A UML Model Consistency Verification Approach based on Meta-Modeling Formalization. In: SAC 2006: Proceedings of the 2006 ACM Symposium on Applied Computing, pp. 1804–1809. ACM, New York (2006)
12. Motik, B., Horrocks, I., Rosati, R., Sattler, U.: Can OWL and Logic Programming live together happily ever after? In: Cruz, I., Decker, S., Allemang, D., Preist, C., Schwabe, D., Mika, P., Uschold, M., Aroyo, L.M. (eds.) ISWC 2006. LNCS, vol. 4273, pp. 501–514. Springer, Heidelberg (2006)
13. Motik, B., Patel-Schneider, P.F., Parsia, B.: Owl 2 web ontology language: Structural specification and functional-style syntax. W3C Recommendation (October 27, 2009)
14. Motik, B.: On the properties of metamodeling in owl. J. Log. Comput. 17(4), 617–637 (2007)
15. Ober, I., Prinz, A.: What do we need metamodels for?
16. Pan, J.Z., Horrocks, I.: RDFS(FA) and RDF MT: Two Semantics for RDFS. In: Fensel, D., Sycara, K., Mylopoulos, J. (eds.) ISWC 2003. LNCS, vol. 2870, pp. 30–46. Springer, Heidelberg (2003)
17. Pan, J.Z., Horrocks, I., Schreiber, G.: OWL FA: A Metamodeling Extension of OWL DL. In: Proceeding of the International Workshop on OWL: Experience and Directions, OWL-ED 2005 (2005)
18. Roe, D., Broda, K., Russo, A., Department of Computing: Mapping UML models incorporating OCL constraints into Object-Z. In: Imperial College of Science, Technology and Medicine, Department of Computing (2003)
19. UML. Unified Modeling Language, http://www.uml.org/
20. Welty, C.A., Ferrucci, D.A.: What's in an instance? Technical report, RPI Computer Science (1994)

Representing, Proving and Sharing Trustworthiness of Web Resources Using *Veracity*

Grégoire Burel, Amparo E. Cano, Matthew Rowe, and Alfonso Sosa

Oak Group, Department of Computer Science,
University of Sheffield,
Sheffield, United Kingdom
{g.burel,e.cano,m.rowe,a.sosa}@dcs.shef.ac.uk

Abstract. The World Wide Web has evolved into a distributed network of web applications facilitating the publication of information on a large scale. Judging whether such information can be trusted is a difficult task for humans, often leading to blind trust. In this paper we present a model and the corresponding *veracity* ontology which allows trust to be placed in web content by web agents. Our approach differs from current work by allowing the trustworthiness of web content to be securely distributed across arbitrary domains and asserted through the provision of machine-readable proofs (i.e. by citing another piece of information, or stating the credentials of the user/agent). We provide a detailed scenario as motivation for our work and demonstrate how the ontology can be used.

1 Introduction

The World Wide Web (WWW) facilitates the contribution of ideas spanning a large information network. The visibility of this information introduces the problem of *what* to trust and *whom* to trust. Currently it is up to web users to make a conscious decision whether to believe what they are reading or not. Trust needs to be derived using automatic means despite relying on error prone user generated content. For example, the *Wikipedia biography controversy*[1] highlighted the issue of information trustworthiness for human and software agents that might exist independently of the reliability of an information source [1]. As a consequence, it is necessary to not only trust information provenance but also information content in order to confirm the quality of a piece of data. This paper addresses trust in a piece of information published on the WWW through the use of Semantic Web (SW) technologies which we define as a *proposition*. A *proposition* can be any piece of web content which is identified by a URI - akin to a resource or statement via reification in SW terms. We present a lightweight decentralised trustworthiness model describing the need to assert proofs in a trust decision and an ontology named *Veracity*.

[1] The Wikipedia biography controversy, `http://en.wikipedia.org/wiki/Wikipedia_biography_controversy`.

P. Cimiano and H.S. Pinto (Eds.): EKAW 2010, LNAI 6317, pp. 421–430, 2010.

2 Trustworthiness Evaluation of Online Resources

The definition of trustworthiness is not absolute but highly contextual since it encapsulates social and personal concepts such as reputability, popularity, reliability and likelihood [2]. We define a proposition as trustworthy if the carried information is reliable, commonly accepted as true given pre-existing trusted knowledge and stable over time. Basing trustworthiness only on social or personal concepts may lead to mistakes, as there is no explicit rationale behind this type of trust endorsement. As a consequence, it is important to base trustworthiness on rational and socially independent variables.

2.1 Trustworthiness Evaluation Scenario

Consider Alice, a journalist, preparing an article about Einstein. In order to write her article, she needs to find as much reliable information as possible. During her search on Internet she may find different information about the famous scientist written by different known and unknown authors. Imagine that Alice finds the following proposition on some obscure website: "Einstein worked at the University of Berlin and was a physicist". For evaluating the trustworthiness of the proposition Alice can 1) Use her personal knowledge about Einstein; 2) Identify the author of the proposition as a "trusted authority" or as a reliable person given the current context; 3) Identify if the author has the knowledge required for asserting the information about Einstein; 4) Search for external trustworthy information that asserts a similar statement; 5) Ask a domain expert for estimating the trustworthiness of the proposition.

In the first case, Alice just needs to compare if her beliefs match the proposition. This case is unlikely since she does not actually know anything about the scientist yet. The second case implies that the editor of the information is reliable in general or in the terms of Alice. The third technique requires Alice to look for information about the author of the proposition that confirms that he knows directly or not about Einstein (e.g. the author may be a "physicist"). In the fourth case, she needs to look for external information or a reference that confirms the considered proposition. Finally, the last case requires Alice to find somebody that knows directly about the topic.

3 Related Work

Artz and Gil [3] distinguish between different methods that can be applied for deriving trust on the WWW and SW such as policy management, provenance analysis and content trust. We now review approaches in each of these areas.

Trust Policies: Information integrity and identification ensure that the parties involved in a trust situation cannot be altered separately. Generally, two approaches are taken for ensuring this integrity: the first involves the utilisation of a centralised server designed for managing a trust assertion [4,5,6]; the second involves distributed mechanisms for managing integrity such as digital signatures[2]. Compared to distributed systems, centralised systems are rather limited since a relation of trust must exist between a trust server and a relying party to work properly. These systems are also often unable to cope with proposition changes or require cache systems [7].

Information Provenance: Information provenance relies on the assumption that trust in a proposition can be estimated using the trust owned by an agent and network analysis. Hartig and Zhao [8] and Golbeck [9] explain how trustworthiness of data is based on assessing its provenance (author, timeliness, etc). Heath et al [6] identify factors influencing the trust between social entities given a particular proposition, Ziegler et al [5] and Carroll et al [10] present different trust metrics that can be used in social networks and similar work in [6] calculates trust ratings from a semantic social network. Several ontologies exist for expressing trust in a given proposition such as the Web Of Trust (WOT)[2] ontology - expressing author identity and trust for a given RDF resource - and the Trust Ontology[3] - for modelling the relation of trust between agents according to a given topic.

Content Trust: According to Gil and Artz [2], evaluating trustworthiness based on information provenance is limited due to the utilisation of indirect and non-contextual knowledge, instead the authors propose evaluating the trustworthiness of information based on its content and context rather than its author. Similarly the TRELLIS [7] application constructs relations between propositions, thereby providing trust in content without provenance information and the Proof Markup Language [11] (PML) ontology is designed to represent metadata about propositions - in the context of question answering. Both TRELLIS and PML do not provide proposition signatures and versioning thus confining its applicability to centralised data.

Current research focuses on the information provenance [4,5,6], content trust [7], policies and metrics [4,5] independently. Metrics can be applied independently of a model meaning that trust metrics may be applied using a similar model. Unfortunately, there is no existing model encompassing the representation of provenance, content trust and supporting the reliability of these statements independently of server side assumptions (centralised server/authority).

4 Requirements

Our scenario (section 2) outlines the need for a model that supports each of the techniques that Alice can apply for evaluating the trustworthiness of a proposition. Referring back to the scenario; in the first case Alice merely relies on her knowledge of the given proposition, which therefore does not necessitate trustworthiness. As a consequence this step is out of scope with modeling trustworthiness, thus to support the other cases the following needs must be fulfilled:

[2] Web Of Trust (WOT), `http://xmlns.com/wot/0.1/`

[3] The Trust Ontology, `http://trust.mindswap.org/ont/trust.owl`

Identify a proposition: To establish the veracity in a piece of information the proposition must be identifiable.

Describe the trustworthiness of a proposition: Once a trust decision is made, a formal description of that decision must be given.

Identify an agent: It is necessary to identify accurately the people or agents involved in the evaluation of the trust of a proposition. Particularly, the person asserting trust on the proposition must be identified. Moreover the identity of the agent must be protected so that it cannot be reused.

Provide agent credentials: Should an agent state their position on the veracity of a proposition, it is essential that the agent provides proof of their background knowledge when making such a statement about the proposition.

Provide supporting information: Should an agent find a piece of information external to a given proposition that supports or refutes the proposition's veracity, then the agent should be able to cite this piece of information.

Security of assertions: In order to provide a secure environment for the trustworthiness assertion, a mechanism should exist to verify that an agent really asserted a particular trustworthiness value on a particular proposition.

Reliable assertions: A modification in a proposition should invalidate all the previous trustworthiness assertions related to this piece of information.

No predefined trust assumptions: The veracity of a proposition should not require any a priori trust relations. Particularly, it should not assume the existence of a central authority for verifying the validity of a trust assertion.

5 Towards a Shared Model of Rational Trustworthiness

Previous ontologies are either incomplete or rely on a controlled network or do not define clearly the mechanism behind an assertion of trust over a proposition. In the context of our scenario, it is required to provide a distributed model that enable the assertion of explanatory trust.

5.1 Knowledge Factors in Trust

According to our definition, a proposition is trustworthy if it is admitted to be true given some *proven* background knowledge. Our definition relies on the use of rational and explicit contextual information for the assertion of trust over a proposition. However, current models [7,5,10,6,8] have no formal descritpion that ensures that a trustworthiness assertion has been performed according to our definition. Gil and Artz define *Entity Trust* and *Content Trust* models for asserting the trustworthiness of a proposition. However, despite adding a stronger context to their content trust model, Gil and Artz's definition incorporates fuzzy parameters that remain hard to evaluate automatically and impartially due to their social entailment. As a result, a strict model that relies on automatically processable and rational variables is requiered. Such type of representation needs to symbolise the factual knowledge that a *third-party* uses for making a trust decision. In this paper, we refer to *Social Trustworthiness* as the model of trust based on fuzzy factors while we use the term of *Rational Trustworthiness* for a trust assertion based on verified and valid information.

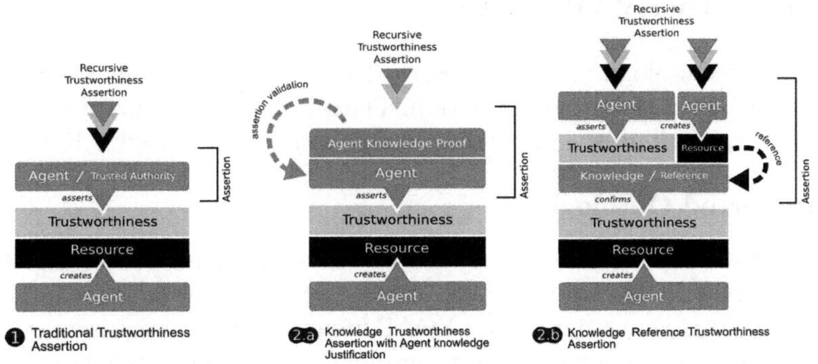

Fig. 1. Social Trustworthiness (1) and Rational Trustworthiness (2) — 2.a) Justifying Social Trustworthiness; 2.b) Knowledge Reference

5.2 Social Trustworthines vs. Rational Trustworthines

Even if trustworthiness is asserted through social means (Fig. 1.1), its reliability can be verified through rationality. The difference between social and rational trust is that the former relies exclusively on an unconditional trust in a person's judgment, while the latter uses supporting trust statements that can be used for evaluating the quality of a trust judgment of a person in a particular concept based on known facts. However, Social trust can still become rational by adding judgment justification statements that prove the personal knowledge of the user. This type of rational trust is summarised in Fig. 1.2. When asserting trustworthiness on a piece of information (resource), a user can justify his decision by proving that he has knowledge about the information he wants to prove as trustworthy or not (for example, by showing that his judgement about the proposition 'Einstein was a physicist' is valid because 'As Einstein, he is a physicist'). Rational trust can also be asserted by directly referring to supporting information rather than referring to a social assertion. In this context, the trustworthiness of a statement is not endorsed by a person given some knowledge but endorsed directly by another source of information or reference through a user assertion (Fig. 1.3). In this context, the trustworthiness relation becomes dereferenced to the cited knowledge.

5.3 Sharing Trustworthiness

Representing trustworthiness on the WWW demands some attention to the effect of the distribution of information in an open network. Without particular measures, it becomes evident that it is easy to either falsify the content of a proposition, its authorship or the agent behind a trust assertion. It is important to not depend on a closed or controlled network for maximising the spreading of trustworthiness information across the network. Because, the necessity of secure trustworthiness assertions is a technical issue our approach for dealing with these problems is discussed in the implementation described in the following section.

6 The Veracity Ontology

The Veracity Ontology[4] (VO) is designed for representing our trustworthiness model described in the previous section. The ontology is organised through three levels of trustworthiness: 1) Social; 2) Knowledge; 3) Knowledge Reference.

6.1 Imported Ontologies

The VO reuses the FOAF ontology for modeling the agents asserting the trustworthiness information on a resource while the WOT ontology is imported for managing `foaf:Agent`[5] signatures. FOAF fits perfectly the requirement of representing the social components of our ontology. The WOT ontology supports the insertion of a public key into a FOAF profile. This assertion enables the creation of a web of trust through the use of digital signatures. Digital signature ensures that: 1) The provenance of a web resource cannot be falsified easily; 2) A web resource cannot be modified without revoking the provenance of the information. This ontology is useful in a distributed environment where trustworthiness can be asserted anywhere. The WOT ontology ensures that these assertions cannot be falsified thus providing a solid base for valid assertions.

6.2 Core Components

The VO relies on the concepts of agent, proposition and trustworthiness. An agent models the agents asserting a trustworthiness value to a specific entity. It represents the social component of our ontology. A proposition is a model of a web resource (or a semantic statement) on which trustworthiness information can be inserted. Trustworthiness defines if an information is trustworthy or not.

foaf:Agent: An agent is modeled using the FOAF ontology (Fig. 2). We decided not to directly reuse the `foaf:Document` class since it does not map to an arbitrary `rdfs:Resource`. However, the resources of an entity are modeled using similar concepts in order to be aligned easily to DC Terms[6] and, depending on the context, to `foaf:Document` if necessary.

Proposition: A `Proposition` borrows concepts from FOAF and DC without referring directly to them. However, it is possible to align the properties of a `Proposition` to DC properties depending of the final application. The `Proposition` properties are inspired by several properties from the FOAF ontology, such as `foaf:sha1` for the `has_checksum` property and properties from the DC ontology such as `dc:creator` for `has_maker`. The checksum enables the identification of a specific version of a `Proposition` and the creator property asserts which `foaf:Agent` created the resource. The `topic` property is similar to `foaf:topic`; it can be used for deriving the creator's knowledge and the trustworthiness of an assertion (Fig. 2).

---

[4] The Veracity Ontology, `http://purl.org/net/veracity/ns#`.

[5] The classes and properties are written using the `Typewriter font` and prefixed with the corresponding ontology. If no prefix is provided, the Veracity ontology is used.

[6] DCMI Metadata Terms, http://dublincore.org/documents/dcmi-terms/

Trustworthiness: For modeling the trustworthiness of a `Proposition` we must assert a value which denotes an entity as trustworthy or not. Our model (Fig. 2) identifies two trust levels represented as a property of `TrustWorthiness`: A resource may be trusted or not. Therefore we define the `TrustWorthiness` class which has the `trusted` property. The range of this property depicts the instance of the class as being either trustworthy or not. `TrustWorthiness` is associated with a `Proposition` using the `has_trustworthiness` relation. Therefore the `Proposition` now has an associated trust value.

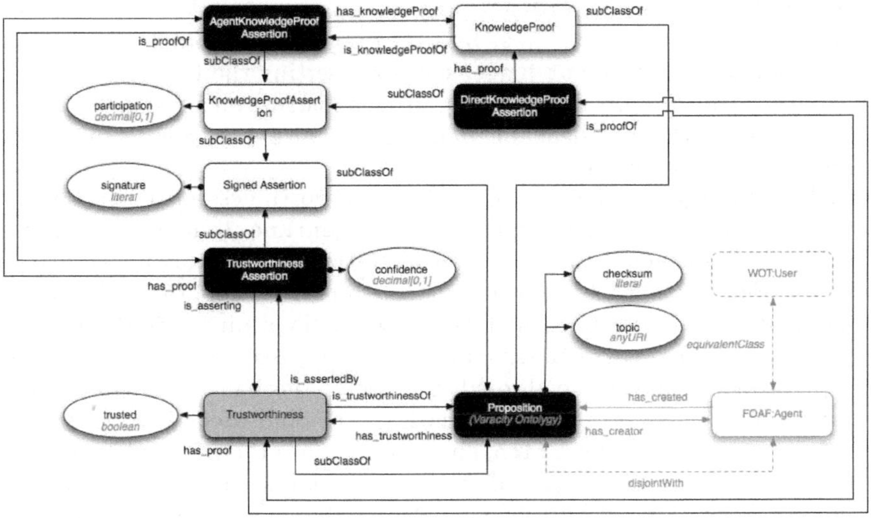

Fig. 2. The Veracity Ontology

6.3 Trustworthiness Assertion Components

A `TrustWorthiness` value cannot be really used before being endorsed by another entity that vouches for a particular `TrustWorthiness` value (trustworthiness assertion). The VO defines three different types of assertions that can be combined in a recursive fashion in order to model deep assertions and support the application of complex trust analysis metrics. In order to ensure that a resource is not changed after being endorsed, each type assertion is defined as a subclass of `SignedAssertion`. As a consequence, an assertion inherits the `checksum` property of a `Proposition`. A `TrustWorthiness` value also inherits from `Proposition` for the same reasons. As said previously, the model needs to prevent an agent from using the identity of another one for making fake assertions. A way to guarantee that an assertion is correct is to use Digital Signatures (DS). In the VO, DS are asserted using the WOT ontology. By merging the `wot:User` class from WOT with the `foaf:Agent` class from FOAF we can associate a public key with any `foaf:Agent` for matching the agent with a unique public key. As a consequence, each trust assertion can be associated with a unique DS that can be matched with a specific Agent.

TrustworthinessAssertion: This class manages a type of assertion that only relies on social information. This assertion implements the model described in the Fig. 1. As a consequence, for being used by a trust metric, the entity asserting a `TrustworthinessAssertion` must be identified as a trusted authority during a trustworthiness evaluation. Because the VO uses FOAF for modeling entities and any type of assertion is a subclass of `SignedAssertion`, a `TrustworthinessAssertion` is a relation between a `foaf:Agent` DS (using the `signature` property) and a `TrustWorthiness` (using `has_trustworthiness` and `is_assertedBy` properties). For allowing a more precise description of trustworthiness, the `confidence` property inserts a confidence level of the endorsement of `TrustWorthiness` by a `foaf:Agent`. The confidence models the accuracy of a `foaf:Agent` judgement for asserting the trustworthiness of a `Proposition`. For instance, by supporting a distrust on a resource (`trusted` set to *false*) with a confidence of *1.0* means that an `foaf:Agent` is sure that the information is not valid.

AgentKnowledgeProofAssertion: This trustworthiness assertion goes on the top of a `TrustworthinessAssertion`. An `AgentKnowledgeProofAssertion` assertion implements the first level of Rational Trustworthiness described in the Fig. 1.2.a. This assertion enables an entity to justify the personal knowledge used by a particular `foaf:Agent`. Typically, a `foaf:Agent` that performs a `TrustworthinessAssertion` may justify his decision by using a proof of his knowledge through the use of the `has_proof` property of a `TrustworthinessAssertion`. Similarly to the `confidence` property used in a `TrustworthinessAssertion`, an agent may use the `participation` property for defining how much of the personal knowledge participates in his decision. The linked information may have different formats. However, the relation between the user, the knowledge and the endorsed proposition should be semantically defined for enabling automatic trustworthiness validation.

DirectKnowledgeProofAssertion: This assertion refers to the Rational Trust described in the Fig. 1.2.b. A `DirectKnowledgeProofAssertion` enables an agent to cite a resource that tends to validate or invalidate a `Proposition`. Contrary to a `AgentKnowledgeProofAssertion`, this type of proof does not imply that the agent citing the resource has knowledge concerning the cited resource. The agent makes an explicit relation between two documents and presents how a cited document participates in a `Trustworthiness` relation. So, this relation enables the propagation of trust from a cited resource to a `Proposition`. An agent may also use the `confidence` property for specifying how strong is the relation between the two resources.

6.4 Fulfillment of the Requirements

The VO fulfils the previous model requirements. The proposed ontology enables the assertion of a trustworthiness value in a secure way thanks to the WOT ontology and the `trusted` property on usual web resources or semantic web resources. By reusing the FOAF and WOT ontologies, agents can be uniquely identified. The need for a contextual knowledge and knowledge references is satisfied respectively by an `AgentKnowledgeProofAssertion` and a

Table 1. Veracity Compared to the Existing Models

	Prop. Ident.	Desc. of Trust.	Agent Ident.	Agent Cred.	Info. Supp.	Secure Assert.	Reliable Assert.	No Prev. Trust
Trust Ont.	○	○	•	•	–	–	–	–
WOT/Konfidi	○	○	•	•	–	•	○	•
TRELLIS [7]	•	•	•	•	•	•	○	–
PML [11]	•	•	•	○	•	•	–	–
Veracity	•	•	•	•	•	•	•	•

Abbreviations: • = Yes. ○ = Limited/Implicit. – = No.

DirectKnowledgeProofAssertion. Because each assertion can be performed by anybody, the ontology satisfies the requirement of third-party assertions. Finally, the use of digital signatures enforces trusted assertions. The Table 1 summarises the differences between the VO and the existing ontologies.

7 Trustworthiness Evaluation Using *Veracity*

Considering the scenario from section 2, Alice might find that the University of Berlin trust assertion on the proposition "Einstein was a physicist" is enough to confirm the veracity of the proposition. The identification of the university as a "trusted authority" or an agent, can be asserted through the use of a TrustworthinessAssertion.

Alice can also find a similar trust assertion on another website. However, the author of the assertion, Bohr, is unknown to Alice. As expressed in the scenario, Bohr can prove that he is a physicist using a AgentKnowledgeProofAssertion in order to be trusted by Alice in the context of the proposition.

In the fourth case of the scenario, Alice needs to find external resources that provide a similar proposition. The VO can be used by a third-party agent for asserting a reference to external information. For instance, one could refer to the DBpedia page of Einstein since it states that "Einstein was a physicist". As a consequence, if DBpedia is considered by Alice as a "trusted authority", the initial proposition becomes trustworthy automatically. This assertion can be supported directly by using a DirectKnowledgeProofAssertion:

```
@prefix vo: <http://purl.org/veracity/ns#> .
<http://example.com/Albert_Einstein#physics> a vo:Proposition .
<http://example.com/Albert_Einstein#physics> vo:has_trustworthiness _:bnode1 .
_:bnode1 a vo:Trustworthiness .
_:bnode1 vo:trusted "true"^^xsd.boolean.
_:bnode1 vo:has_proof _:bnode2 .
_:bnode2 a vo:DirectKnowledgeProofAssertion .
_:bnode2 vo:has_proof <http://dbpedia.org/resource/Albert_Einstein> .
```

The last case is solved indirectly: Alice cannot seek expert advice but she has access to third-party assertions since each assertion can be done by any agent.

8 Conclusions

We have presented an approach for modeling the veracity of information on the web. Our model enables the verification of a proposition at the information level in a reliable and distributed fashion rather than relying only on its provenance. To prove the veracity of a piece of information it employs: 1) A Trustworthiness assertion, which links a statement to a trusted authority or agent; 2) An Agent Knowledge Proof Assertion, which proves that an agent is credited to label a statement as being trusted or not; and 3) A Direct Knowledge Proof Assertion, which proves that a statement is trusted by providing a reference to another statement.

Acknowledgements. The research leading to these results has received funding from the EU project WeKnowIt (ICT-215453).

References

1. Chesney, T.: An empirical examination of wikipedias credibility. First Monday 11(11) (2006)
2. Gil, Y., Artz, D.: Towards content trust of web resources. Web Semantics: Science, Services and Agents on the World Wide Web 5(4), 227–239 (2007)
3. Artz, D., Gil, Y.: A survey of trust in computer science and the semantic web. Web Semantics 5(2), 58–71 (2007)
4. Golbeck, J., Hendler, J.: Accuracy of metrics for inferring trust and reputation in semantic web-based social networks. In: Motta, E., Shadbolt, N.R., Stutt, A., Gibbins, N. (eds.) EKAW 2004. LNCS (LNAI), vol. 3257, pp. 116–131. Springer, Heidelberg (2004)
5. Ziegler, C., Lausen, G.: Spreading activation models for trust propagation. In: Proceedings of the 2004 IEEE International Conference on e-Technology, e-Commerce and e-Service (EEE 2004), pp. 83–97. IEEE Computer Society, Los Alamitos (2004)
6. Heath, T., Motta, E., Petre, M.: Computing word-of-mouth trust relationships in social networks from semantic web and web 2.0 data sources. In: Proceedings of the Workshop on Bridging the Gap between Semantic Web and Web (2007)
7. Gil, Y., Ratnakar, V.: Trusting information sources one citizen at a time. In: Horrocks, I., Hendler, J. (eds.) ISWC 2002. LNCS, vol. 2342, pp. 162–176. Springer, Heidelberg (2002)
8. Hartig, O., Zhao, J.: Using Web Data Provenance for Quality Assessment. In: SWPM (2009)
9. Golbeck, J., Hendler, J.: Inferring binary trust relationships in web-based social networks. ACM Trans. Internet Technol. 6(4), 497–529 (2006)
10. Carroll, J.J., Bizer, C., Hayes, P., Stickler, P.: Named graphs, provenance and trust. In: Proceedings of the 14th International Conference on World Wide Web, Chiba, Japan, pp. 613–622. ACM, New York (2005)
11. McGuinness, D.L., Ding, L., da Silva, P.P., Chang, C.: Pml 2: A modular explanation interlingua. In: Proceedings of AAAI, vol. 7 (2007)

Enhancing Content-Based Recommendation with the Task Model of Classification

Yiwen Wang[1], Shenghui Wang[2], Natalia Stash[1], Lora Aroyo[12], and Guus Schreiber[2]

[1] Eindhoven University of Technology, Computer Science
{y.wang,n.v.stash}@tue.nl
[2] VU University Amsterdam, Computer Science
{l.m.aroyo,schreiber}@cs.vu.nl, swang@few.vu.nl

Abstract. In this paper, we define reusable inference steps for content-based recommender systems based on semantically-enriched collections. We show an instantiation in the case of recommending artworks and concepts based on a museum domain ontology and a user profile consisting of rated artworks and rated concepts. The recommendation task is split into four inference steps: realization, classification by concepts, classification by instances, and retrieval. Our approach is evaluated on real user rating data. We compare the results with the standard content-based recommendation strategy in terms of accuracy and discuss the added values of providing serendipitous recommendations and supporting more complete explanations for recommended items.

1 Introduction

In recent years, the Semantic Web has put great effort on the reusability of knowledge. However, most work deals with reusable ontology and ontology patterns, there is hardly any work on reusable reasoning patterns [4]. Following the terminology defined by van Harmelen and ten Teije [4], we aim to identify reusable knowledge elements for content-based recommender systems based on semantically-enriched collections. As a first attempt, we show an instantiation in the domain of museums. We analyze our demonstrator[1] (called the "CHIP Art Recommender") and decompose the recommendation task into four inference steps: (i) realization (recommending concepts explicitly related to rated artworks via artwork features; (ii) classification by concepts (recommending concepts explicitly related to rated concepts via semantic relations); (iii) classification by instances (recommending concepts implicitly related to rated concepts using the method of instance-based ontology matching); and (iv) retrival (recommending artworks based on both rated and recommended concepts).

2 Task and Inference Steps

The CHIP Art Recommender stores the user profile in the form of both a set of rated artworks/instances and a set of rated concepts. Based on the user profile

[1] http://www.chip-project.org/demo/

P. Cimiano and H.S. Pinto (Eds.): EKAW 2010, LNAI 6317, pp. 431–440, 2010.

Table 1. The task of content-based recommendation

Input:	a user profile characterized as both a set of instance $I_{profile}$ and a set of concepts $C_{profile}$
Knowledge:	an ontology O = (T, I) consisting of a terminology T and an instance set I
Output:	a set of related concepts $(C^i \cup C^j \cup C^k)$ with C^i: Recommend($I_{profile}$, O) = {(i, ∈, c^i) | ∃i: i ∈ $I_{profile}$ ∧ i ∈ c^i} C^j: Recommend($C_{profile}$, T) = {(c^j ∼ c) | ∃c: c ∈ $C_{profile}$ ∧ c^j ∼ c} C^k: Recommend($C_{profile}$, O) = {(c^k ≃ c) | ∃c: c ∈ $C_{profile}$ ∧ c^k ≃ c ∧ i ∈ c ∧ i ∈ c^k} and a set of related instances I' with I': Recommend($C_{profile}$, C^i, C^j, C^k, O) = {(i', ∈, c')| c' ∈ ($C_{profile} \cup C^i \cup C^j \cup C^k$) ∧ i' ∈ c'}

and the museum domain ontology, the system recommends both related artworks and related concepts via explicit and implicit relations.

As described in Table 1, we use formal preliminaries to define the task of content-based recommendation: a terminology T is a set of concepts c organized in a hierarchy. Instance i is a member of such concepts c and this is described as *(i, ∈, c)* where ∈ refers to the membership relation. An ontology O consists of a terminology T and a set of instances I. Sometimes we write *(T, I)* instead of O if we want to refer separately to the terminology and the instance set of the ontology. In our case, instances refer to artworks and each artwork is described with a number of concepts. Based on the semantically-enriched Rijksmuseum collection [6], we specify three different kinds of relations: (i) artwork feature, (ii) semantic relation, and (iii) implicit relation.

(i)Artwork feature is an explicit relation between an artwork and a concept, denoted as $(i, \in, c)$. For example, the artwork "The Night Watch" is related to the concept "Rembrandt van Rijn" via the artwork feature "*creator*", the concept "Amsterdam" via the artwork feature "*creationSite*" and the concept "Militia" via the artwork feature "*subject*".
(ii)Semantic relation is also an explicit relation, but it links two concepts, denoted as $(c_i, \sim, c_j)$. In our case, based on the semantically-enriched museum collections, there are are not only domain-specific relations (e.g. *teacherOf, style*), but general relations (e.g. *broader/narrower*) as well [6].
(iii)Implicit relation connects two concepts that do not have a direct link between each other, denoted as $(c_i, \simeq, c_j)$. This relation is built based on common artworks these two concepts both describe, although there are no explicit/direct links between them.

To decompose the task of content-based recommendation, we identified four inference steps (see Fig. 1): (i) realization, (ii) classification by concepts, (iii) classification by instances, and (iv) retrieval.

Realization is the task of finding a concept c that describe the given instances i.
- Definition: Find a concept c^i such that $O \vdash i \in c^i$
- Signature: $i \times O \mapsto c^i$

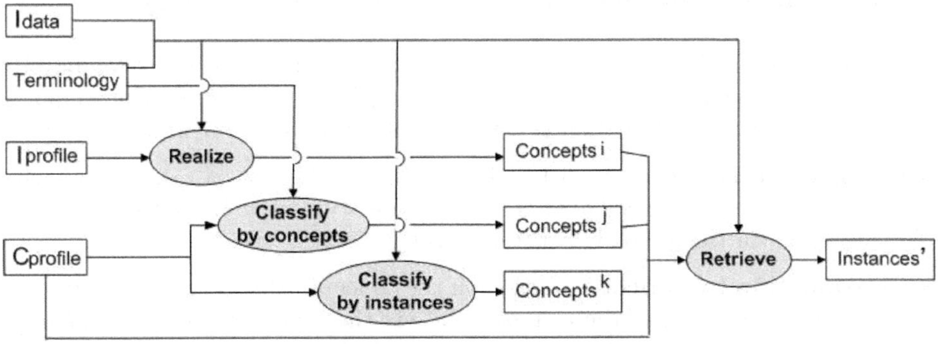

Fig. 1. Inference steps for the task of content-based recommendation

Classification by concepts is the task of finding a concept c^j which is directly linked to the given concept c through a semantic relation $\sim$ in the hierarchy of terminology T.

• Definition: Find a related concept c^j through various semantic relations $\sim$ (e.g. *broader, narrower, teacherOf, birthPlace*, etc.) in the terminology such that $T \vdash c \sim c^j$

• Signature: $c \times T \mapsto c^j$

Classification by instances is the task of finding a concept c^k which shares sufficient common instances with the given concept c using the instance-based ontology matching $\simeq$.

• Definition: Find a concept c^k through the instance-based ontology matching $\simeq$ such that $O \vdash c \simeq c^k \wedge \mathrm{i} \in \mathrm{c} \wedge \mathrm{i} \in c^k$

• Signature: $c \times O \mapsto c^k$

Retrieval is the inverse of realization: determining which instance *i'* belong to the related concept *c'*, where *c'* is a element of the unification of $C_{profile}$, C^i (Realization), c^j (Classification by concepts) and c^k (Classification by instances).

• Definition: Find an instance *i'* such that $i' \in c'$ where $c' \in (C_{profile} \cup C^i \cup C^j \cup C^k)$

• Signature: $c' \times O \mapsto i'$

Compared with the original definition of recommendation and its corresponding inference steps from van Harmelen and ten Teije [4], we extended the inference step of classification, which now consists of two components: classification by concepts and classification by instances. The main differences are: firstly, we applied much more different types of semantic relations [6] in the step of classification by concepts compared with the original classification which only uses the subsumption relation [4]; secondly, we proposed a new component "classification by instances", which explores the implicit relations between concepts using the method of instance-based ontology matching from Issac et al. [2].

3 Semantic-Enhanced Recommendation Strategy

Suppose the user likes the artwork "The Little Street", concepts "Rembrandt van Rijn" and "Venus", Fig. 2 shows how the CHIP system recommends related concepts and artworks based on the user profile by taking four inference steps.

• **Realization**: Based on the artwork "The Little Street", it recommends the concept "Johannes Vermeer" via the artwork feature *creator* and the concept "Townscape" via the artwork feature *subject.*

• **Classification by concepts**: Based on the concept "Rembrandt van Rijn", it recommends the concept "Pieter Lastman" via the semantic relation *studentOf* and the concept "Baroque" via the semantic relation *style.*

• **Classification by instances**: Based on the concept "Rembrandt van Rijn", it recommends the concept "Chiaroscuro" because they share sufficient (by setting the threshold) common artworks. Based on the concept "Venus", it recommends concepts "Francois van Bossuit" and "Aphrodite" also because of the sufficient common artworks they describe.

• **Retrieval**: Based on three sets of concepts: (i) rated concepts ("Rembrandt van Rijn" and "Venus"); (ii) explicitly related concepts via artwork features and semantic relations ("Johannes Vermeer", "Townscape", "Pieter Lastman" and "Baroque"); and (iii) implicitly related concepts ("Chiaroscuro", "Francois

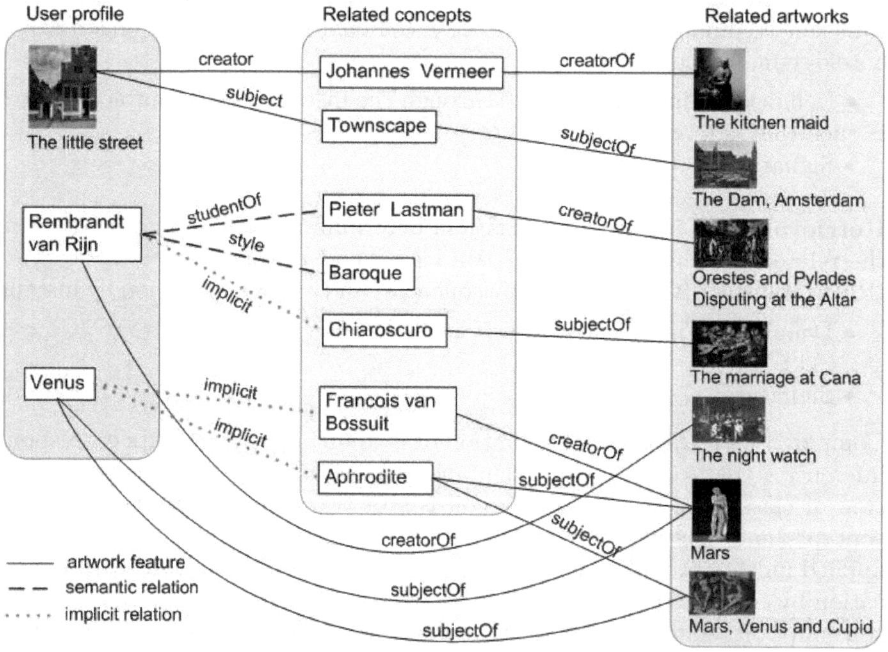

Fig. 2. Example of semantically-enhanced recommendations

van Bossuit" and "Aphrodite"), it recommends artworks "The Kitchen Maid", "The Dam, Amsterdam", "Orestes and Pylades Disputing at the Altar", "The Marriage at Cana", "The Night Watch", "Mars" and "Mars, Venus and Cupid" via artwork features *creatorOf* and *subjectOf*.

3.1 Computing the Explicit Value for the Steps of Realization and Classification by Concepts

In a previous user study [6], we explored the use of various explicit relations between artworks and concepts for recommendations. These relations include: (i) artwork features between an artwork and concepts (e.g. *creator*); and (ii) semantic relations between two concepts within one vocabulary (e.g. *broader*) and across two different vocabularies (e.g. *style*).

Using the existing user ratings collected from this study, we investigated the preliminary weights $W_{(r)}$ (see Table 2) for each explicit relation $R_{(i,j)}$, which is either an artwork feature between an artwork i and a concept j or a semantic relation between two concepts (i and j). For example, the relation between artwork "The Little Street" and concept "Johannes Vermeer" is *creator*, denoted as $R_{(TheLittleStreet,JohannesVermeer)}$ = *creator*. From Table 2, we know that the weight of this relation $W_{(creator)}$ is 0.67. In the formulas below we write $W_{(i,j)}$ instead of $R_{(i,j)}$ and $W_{(r)}$.

Considering that a rated item (either an artwork or a concept) could be linked to multiple items via various explicit relations, we need to normalize the weight(s) for each related item. As shown in Fig. 3, the rated item i_1 is linked to items j_1 and j_2. The relation between i_1 and j_1 is *creator* and the corresponding weight of *creator* is denoted as $W_{(i_1,j_1)}$. From Table. 2, we know that $W_{(i_1,j_1)}$ (creator) is 0.67, $W_{(i_1,j_2)}$ (subject) is 0.50, $W_{(i_2,j_1)}$ (teacherOf) is 0.43, and $W_{(i_2,j_3)}$ (style) is 0.63.

Table 2. Weights of explicit relations

Relation	creator	creation Site	subject	style	birth Place	death Place	teacher Of	aat Broader	tgn Broader	ic Broader
Weight	0.67	0.35	0.50	0.63	0.32	0.26	0.43	0.53	0.22	0.50
Inverse Relation	creator Of	creation SiteOf	subject Of	style Of	birth PlaceOf	death PlaceOf	student Of	aat Narrower	tgn Narrower	ic Narrower
Weight	0.68	0.31	0.54	0.61	0.28	0.21	0.44	0.55	0.16	0.52

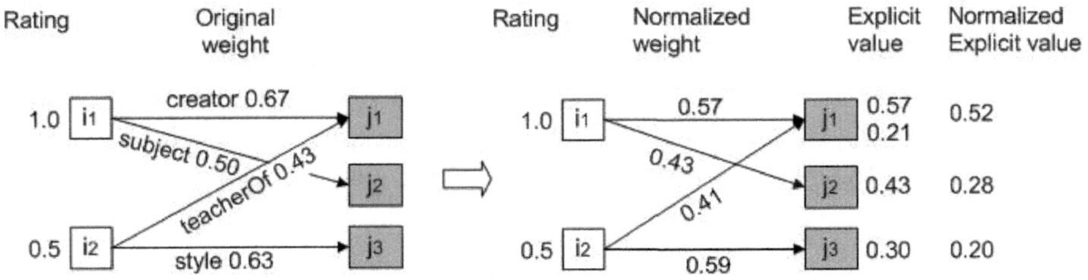

Fig. 3. Example of calculating the normalized explicit value

To normalize the weights, Formula 1 is applied. For example, based on i_1, the normalized weight of j_1: $NW_{(i_1,j_1)} = \frac{0.67}{0.67+0.50} = 0.57$ and the the normalized weight of j_2: $NW_{(i_1,j_2)} = \frac{0.50}{0.67+0.50} = 0.43$. In this way, we could calculate that based on i_2, normalized weight of j_1: $NW_{(i_2,j_1)} = \frac{0.43}{0.43+0.63} = 0.41$ and the normalized weight of j_3: $NW_{(i_2,j_3)} = \frac{0.63}{0.43+0.63} = 0.59$.

Formula 1: Normalized weight	Formula 2: Explicit value	Formula 3: Normalized explicit value
$NW_{(i,j)} = \frac{W_{(i,j)}}{\sum_{j=1}^{J} W_{(i,j)}}$	$Exp_{(i,j)} = NW_{(i,j)} \times R_{(i)}$	$NExp_{(j)} = \frac{\sum_{i=1}^{I} Exp_{(i,j)}}{\sum_{i=1}^{I}\sum_{j=1}^{J} Exp_{(i,j)}}$

Based on the normalized weights and user ratings, the next step is to compute the semantic value, see Formula 2. Based on i_1, the semantic values of j_1 and j_2 are: $Exp_{(i_1,j_1)} = 0.57 * 1.0 = 0.57$, and $Exp_{(i_1,j_2)} = 0.43 * 1.0 = 0.43$. Based on i_2, $Exp_{(i_2,j_1)} = 0.41 * 0.5 = 0.21$, and $Exp_{(i_2,j_3)} = 0.59 * 0.5 = 0.30$.

Finally, we also need to normalize these semantic values for each related item, see Formula 3. $NExp_{j_1} = \frac{0.57+0.21}{0.57+0.21+0.43+0.30} = 0.52$; $NExp_{j_2} = \frac{0.43}{0.57+0.21+0.43+0.30} = 0.28$; and $NExp_{j_3} = \frac{0.30}{0.57+0.21+0.43+0.30} = 0.20$.

3.2 Computing the Implicit Value for the Step of Classification by Instances

Sometimes there is no explicit relations between two concepts, however, they could be actually very similar or close to each other via some implicit relations. For example (see Fig. 2), "Rembrandt van Rijn" is famous for his technique using strong contrast of light and dark shading, which in Italian corresponds to "Chiaroscuro"; "Francois van Bossuit" often took "Venus" as a subject to paint; and "Venus" in Roman refers to "Aphrodite" in Greek. Compared with the "obvious recommendations" via explicit relations, these implicitly related concepts might be surprisingly new/unknown to users. The main challenge is to define how close these two concepts are in the collection.

To address this issue, Issaac et al. [2] propose a method of instance-based ontology matching. The basic idea is that the more significant the overlap of artworks of two concepts is, the closer these two concepts are, and the level of significance is calculated by the corrected Jaccard measure, see Formula 4. In the formula, the set of instances described by a concept c is called the extension of c and abbreviate by C^i. The $JCcorr(C_1^i, C_2^i)$ measures the fraction of the refinement (by choosing the factor of 0.8) of instances described by both concepts C_1 and C_2 relative to the set of instances described by either one of the concepts [2].

$$JCcorr(C_1, C_2) = \frac{\sqrt{|C_1^i \cap C_2^i| \times (|C_1^i \cap C_2^i| - 0.8)}}{|C_1^i \cup C_2^i|} \quad \text{(Formula 4: Corrected Jaccard measure)}$$

Adopting this method, we calculated the Corrected Jaccard values for all pairs of concepts in the collection. In general, the higher the Corrected Jaccard value is, the more common artworks these two concepts described. Below we give a brief look at the Corrected Jaccard values for some pairs of concepts:

0.96 (Sculptural studies – Terracotta models)
0.91 (unknown lacquerer – Lacquerware)
0.85 (Hermes – Mercury)
0.75 (Food and other objects – Still lifes with food)
0.63 (Militias – Militia paintings)
0.50 (Hinduism – Hindu deities)
0.40 (Still-life painting – Food and other objects)
0.30 (Drinking games – Sport and Games)
0.20 (Cupid – Love and Sex)
0.15 (Polychromy – Golden Legend)
0.10 (Rendering of texture – Woman)

There are in total 24249 pairs of concepts and the range of the Corrected Jaccard value is between 0 and 1. Looking at these values and checking the corresponding number of artworks the pair of concepts describe in common, we set 0.20 as a preliminary threshold, which might needs more refinement in the future. An example for the threshold 0.20 is "Cupid" and "Love and sex", which describe 8 artworks in common out of 40 artworks that are described by either one of these two concepts. In comparison, the Corrected Jaccard value between "Rendering of texture" and "Woman" is 0.10 and they describe 4 artworks in common out of 41 artworks.

After getting the Corrected Jaccard values for all concept pairs, we follow the same steps (Formula 1, 2 and 3) as the calculation of the explicit semantic value in Section 3.1. The only difference is that we use the Corrected Jaccard value to replace the original weight between two concepts and then normalize the Corrected Jaccard value in Formula 1. In the end, we will get a normalized implicit value $NImp_{(j)}$ for each implicitly related concept j.

3.3 Combining the Explicit and Implicit Values for the Step of Retrieval

Considering a related concept j could be linked to rated items via not only explicit relations but also implicit relations, we need to combine values from these two parts in order to get a final prediction $PreC_{(j)}$ for recommendation. Inspired by the work from Mobasher et. al [3], we set a parameter α to combine these two parts, see Formula 5. This combination parameter α measures the strength of the explicit and implicit components with respect to the current context. Taking two extreme examples: When α is 1, the system recommends items purely based on explicit relations and this will work well if the collection is well structured with rich semantic relations. When α is 0, it recommends items purely based on implicit relations which is suitable for recommender systems working on databases without semantic structures between concepts. Ideally, the parameter α could be manually set by the user, or dynamically adapted by the system, which enables the flexibility of the recommendation algorithm.

$$PreC_{(j)} = \alpha \times NExp_{(j)} + (1 - \alpha) \times NImp_{(j)}$$
(Formula 5: Prediction for related concepts)

After collecting related concepts via both explicit and implicit relations, the system retrieves related artworks based on these related concepts. Since there are only explicit relations, which are artwork features between concepts and artworks, we only need to compute the normalized semantic value for related artworks, which is explained in details in Formula 3.

4 Evaluation and Discussion

In the evaluation, we use the existing user ratings collected from the previous study [6]. There were 48 users that participated in this study. They used the CHIP Art Recommender to browse the Rijksmuseum collection, which contains 729 artworks and 4320 art concepts. Each user rated 53 items (artworks and concepts) on average. We evaluate the recommendation accuracy and discuss the added values of providing serendipitous recommendations and explanations for recommended items.

To measure the recommendation accuracy, we compute the standard Mean Absolute Error (MAE) by Leave-one-out cross validation [1]. MAE measures the average absolute deviation between ratings and predictions. Although there are a number of variables influencing the MAE (e.g. the parameter α, the weights for explicit relations and the threshold for the Corrected Jaccard value), in this evaluation, we only look at the impact of α on MAE in order to get a first insight and we leave the experimentation with other variables to future work.

In order to see whether the semantic-enhanced content-based recommendation (SE-CBR) strategy in general improves or hamper the accuracy, we also measure the MAE for the standard content-based recommendation (CBR) strategy, which was applied in the previous version of the system [5]. The standard CBR takes the inference steps of realization and retrieval, but no classification by concepts and instances, which means that based on user rated items, standard CBR only recommends items via artwork features.

Note that ratings in our system are based on a 5-star scale, which refers to -1, -0.5, 0, 0.5, 1. Thus the maximum possible value for MAE is 2 and the minimum value is 0. The lower MAE represent the higher recommendation accuracy. In Fig.4, we observe that: (i) Compared with CBR (MAE is 0.4855), SE-CBR reaches a much lower MAE, which is in the range of 0.3137 (α is 0) and 0.3181 (α is 1). It shows that although recommending more items, SE-CBR does not sacrifice the recommendation accuracy, surprisingly, it even improves the accuracy compared with CBR. (ii) The impact of α on MAE for SE-CBR is not significant, with a slight increase from 0.3137 (α is 0) to 0.3181 (α is 1). The reason could be that we set a very high threshold (0.20) for the Corrected Jaccard value when selecting implicitly related items. Among all 24249 pairs of concepts in the collection, only 4% (1175 pairs) has the Corrected Jaccard value above 0.20 and most of these pairs are either synonyms or very similar to each

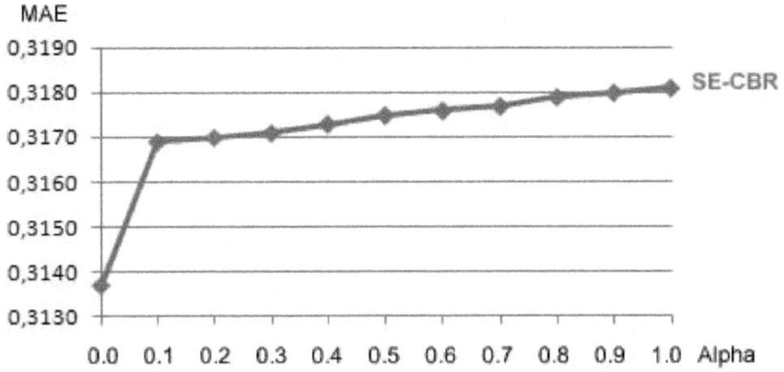

	Alpha	MAE
SE-CBR	0.0	0.3137
	0.1	0.3169
	0.2	0.3170
	0.3	0.3171
	0.4	0.3173
	0.5	0.3175
	0.6	0.3176
	0.7	0.3177
	0.8	0.3179
	0.9	0.3180
	1.0	0.3181
CBR		0.4855

Fig. 4. MAE for SE-CBR and CBR

other, e.g. "Unknown lacquerer"-"Lacquerware" and "Food and other objects"-"Still lifes with food". The high similarity ensures a high accuracy for implicit recommendations. When α is 0, it only recommends implicitly related concepts which are kind of synonyms in our case and thus it reaches the lowest MAE value of 0.3137. Considering the majority (75%: 18186 concept pairs) has the Corrected Jaccard values between 0.01 and 0.10, if we set a threshold in a lower range, it will bring a lot of noisy recommendations, which might significantly decrease the recommendation accuracy. Besides the threshold for the Corrected Jaccard value, there are a number of parameters (e.g. weights for explicit relations) that influence the accuracy. We plan to try a machine learning based approach instead of the manual turning in follow up work.

As Herlocker et al. [1] argued, accuracy alone is not sufficient for selecting a good recommendation algorithm. A serendipitous recommendation helps a user find a surprising and new/unknown item that he/she might not have otherwise discovered. Besides, explanations of why an item was recommended also helps users gain confidence in the system's recommendations. As illustrated in Fig. 2, if a user likes the famous Dutch painter "Rembrandt van Rijn", the standard CBR could only recommend the artwork "The Night Watch" via the artwork feature *creatorOf*. In comparison, the SE-CBR could recommend more items besides "The Night Watch": (i) by taking the step of classification by concepts, it recommends concepts "Baroque" (*style*) and "Pieter Lastman" (*studentOf*) based on the semantic relations between concepts; (ii) by taking the step of classification by instances, it recommends an implicitly related concept "Chiaroscuro" based on instance ontology matching; (iii) by taking the step of realization, it recommends artworks "The Marriage at Cana" and "Orestes and Pylades Disputing at the Altar" based on all related concepts. For each recommended item, the system provides the explanation of "Why recommend", which automatically derives relations between the user's rated items and recommended items from the domain ontology. In such a way, the user could receive not only more recommended items, but also more complete explanations, which could help them better understand the recommendations. A further user study is needed to evaluate the aspects of serendipity and explanations.

In this work, our intention was to identify reusable knowledge elements for content-based recommender systems based on semantically-enriched collections. We demonstrated our approach in the domain of museum art collections. In future work, we plan to test this approach for different applications and ontologies.

Acknowledgements

We greatly appreciate the contribution of Annette ten Teije from VU University Amsterdam for providing the inspiration to our work and the discussion of the results.

References

1. Herlocker, J.L., Konstan, J.A., Terveen, L.G., John, Riedl, T.: Evaluating collaborative filtering recommender systems. ACM Transactions on Information Systems 22, 5–53 (2004)
2. Isaac, A., van der Meij, L., Schlobach, S., Wang, S.: An empirical study of instance-based ontology matching. In: Aberer, K., Choi, K.-S., Noy, N., Allemang, D., Lee, K.-I., Nixon, L.J.B., Golbeck, J., Mika, P., Maynard, D., Mizoguchi, R., Schreiber, G., Cudré-Mauroux, P. (eds.) ASWC 2007 and ISWC 2007. LNCS, vol. 4825, pp. 253–266. Springer, Heidelberg (2007)
3. Mobasher, B., Jin, X., Zhou, Y.: Semantically enhanced collaborative filtering. In: Berendt, B., Hotho, A., Mladenič, D., van Someren, M., Spiliopoulou, M., Stumme, G. (eds.) EWMF 2003. LNCS (LNAI), vol. 3209, pp. 57–76. Springer, Heidelberg (2004)
4. van Harmelen, F., ten Teije, A., Wache, H.: Knowledge engineering rediscovered: towards reasoning patterns for the semantic web. In: 5th International Conference on Knowledge Capture (K-CAP 2009), pp. 81–88 (2009)
5. Wang, Y., Stash, N., Aroyo, L., Gorgels, P., Rutledge, L., Schreiber, G.: Recommendations based on semantically-enriched museum collections. Journal of Web Semantics 6(4), 43–58 (2008)
6. Wang, Y., Stash, N., Aroyo, L., Hollink, L., Schreiber, G.: Semantic relations for content-based recommendations. In: 5th International Conference on Knowledge Capture (K-CAP 2009), pp. 209–210 (2009)

Extending Open Rating Systems for Ontology Ranking and Reuse

Holger Lewen[1] and Mathieu d'Aquin[2]

[1] Institute AIFB, Karlsruhe Institute of Technology (KIT), Germany
holger.lewen@kit.edu
[2] Knowledge Media Institute (KMi), The Open University, United Kingdom
m.daquin@open.ac.uk

Abstract. Ontology reuse saves costs and improves interoperability between ontologies. Knowing which ontology to reuse is difficult without having a quality assessment. We employ user ratings to determine the user-perceived quality of ontologies. The combination of an Open Rating System (ORS), user ratings, and information on trust between users, allow us to compute a personalized ranking of ontologies. In this paper, we present our extension, the Topic-Specific Trust Open Rating System (TS-ORS). To overcome the limitations of the ORS, the TS-ORS features topic-specific trust and multi-faceted ratings. In a user study, we show that having user ratings and result ranking based on a TS-ORS significantly facilitates ontology assessment and selection for the end user.

1 Introduction

Ontology reuse reduces costs and development effort [1]. Ontology engineers save time when they reuse existing ontological content—entire ontologies or parts thereof. A typical problem users face today when they try to reuse existing ontological content is the selection of the most appropriate ontology for their task. This is because the assessment of ontologies is a time-consuming and nontrivial task. So far, no automatic evaluation technique exists that can judge the quality of an ontology the way a human can. The ability to rely on the experience of other users can lessen the assessment effort considerably. Because of this we gather user-based evaluations of ontological content in our Cupboard[1] ontology publishing system [2]. Based on these evaluations we provide user-perceived quality information on the content, and, together with information on inter-user trust, we compute a user-specific (personalized) ranking of ontological content.

Our TS-ORS provides a complete ranking framework for multi-faceted ratings based on fine-grained inter-user trust and meta-trust statements. In Cupboard, we expose the ontology ratings, and provide a personalized ontology ranking based on scores computed by the TS-ORS. The main contributions of this paper are: We extend the current state of the art ORS, introduced in Section 2, to overcome two major limitations: We introduce a fine-grained topic-specific

[1] `http://cupboard.open.ac.uk/`

P. Cimiano and H.S. Pinto (Eds.): EKAW 2010, LNAI 6317, pp. 441–450, 2010.

trust system including the ability to provide meta-trust, and allow multi-faceted ratings (see Section 3 for a description of our TS-ORS). We then show how the TS-ORS was adapted for ontology ranking in Cupboard (see Section 4). A user-study confirms our hypothesis that employing the TS-ORS in an ontology reuse scenario facilitates the selection and reuse of ontological content significantly compared to state of the art ontology search engines (see Section 4). Related work can be found in Section 5, followed by a conclusion in Section 6.

2 Open Rating Systems

An ORS is a system that allows users to write reviews and give ratings to arbitrary content. Other users can then trust or distrust the reviewers. Based on the trust information and the reviews collected, the system can generate a ranking for both reviews and reviewed content. The concept of ratings and meta-ratings (other users rating the ratings) has found wide adoption in the e-commerce world. A prominent example are the user reviews found on Amazon.[2]

One of the key components of the ORS model is the trust users express towards each other. The Web of Trust (WOT) these user-to-user trust statements form can be used for both *local* (user-specific) and *global* (user-agnostic) trust computation, as shown in Section 3. In order to demonstrate the differences between the original ORS model and our extension, we first present Guha's model [3], and then our extension in detail.

Model: Guha's ORS model consists of the following components:

1. A set of objects $O : \{o_1, o_2, o_3, \cdots\}$ that can be rated.
2. A set of agents $A : \{a_1, a_2, a_3, \cdots\}$ that participate in the ORS.
3. A set of possible values for ratings of objects $D : \{d_1, d_2, \cdots\}$.
4. A set of possible values for trust ratings of agents $T : \{t_1, t_2, \cdots\}$.
5. A partial function $R : A \times O \rightarrow D$ corresponding to agent ratings on objects.
6. A partial function $W : A \times A \rightarrow T$ corresponding to inter-agent trust.

Limitations of the ORS: First, there is no concept of a multi-faceted review, that means, it is only possible to provide an overall rating for an object, and not for the different aspects of an object (cf. the signature of the rating function R). In case certain aspects of an object are good, and others are bad, this derivation from the average is lost. In the context of ontology evaluation, for example, an ontology can be highly reusable, while only covering a limited part of the intended domain. In this case, reusability and domain coverage represent aspects that can be reviewed independently. Analyzing Cupboard data, we discovered that indeed many ontologies have a variance in the ratings on their different aspects. Taking one ontology space[3] we looked for cases where a reviewer provided reviews for every aspect of an ontology, allowing to compute an average rating this reviewer might have given in case only an overall rating would have been allowed. Based on 145 ratings, which would correspond to 29 overall ratings in the

[2] `http://www.amazon.com/`

[3] `http://cupboard.open.ac.uk:8081/cupboard/Experiment1`

ORS, we computed the mean variance between aspects as 0.85. This validated the extension of ORS with multi-faceted reviews.

Second, reviewers do not always write either good or bad reviews, but depending on the ontology and aspect they review, they can be trusted differently. Indeed, we observed many users that trust a review from a particular reviewer and distrust another review from that same reviewer. In the ORS model, the trust function W only stores global trust or distrust (covering all reviews of a user). To overcome this, we implement a more fine-grained trust management.

3 Topic-Specific Trust Open Rating Systems

Model: We introduce aspects of objects that can be rated, and extend the rating function R and the trust function W. In the TS-ORS model, we reuse O, A, D, T from Guha's ORS model (see Section 2) and introduce:

- A set of object aspects $X : \{x_1, x_2, x_3, \cdots\}$
- A partial function $R : A \times O \times X \to D$. R corresponds to the rating of an agent on one certain aspect of an object. Let $B_R \subseteq A \times O \times X$ denote the set of all triples for which R is defined, i.e., for which ratings exist.
- A partial function $W : A \times A \times O \times X \to T$, which corresponds to the trust of an agent in another agent for a specific aspect–object combination.

We assume all sets to be finite. In this paper we use the term *user* or *reviewer* to refer to agents from A. In our model, a reviewer has to justify each rating R with a textual review justifying the rating. We refer to the textual justification as the *review*, and to the actual D value as the *rating*. In this section, we separate the description of the model and algorithms from our concrete instantiation. The adaptation of the TS-ORS for ontology ranking alongside default values for parameters from the following algorithms can be found in Section 4.

Meta-trust Statements in the TS-ORS Model: Users express trust on the level of an aspect of an object (see definition of W). For the convenience of users, we defined and allow the use of meta-trust statements, which are trust statements covering more than one object–aspect combination. They can be seen as shortcuts to making many W statements (see Table 1).

Table 1. Allowed User-to-User Meta-trust Statements

Statement	Signature	Explanation
W	$A \times A \times O \times X \to T$	Trust to review a specific aspect of a specific object
W_X	$A \times A \times O \to T$	Trust to review all aspects of a specific object (for arbitrary aspects of X)
W_O	$A \times A \times X \to T$	Trust to review a specific aspect of all objects (for arbitrary objects of O)
W_{OX}	$A \times A \to T$	Trust to review all aspects of all objects (for arbitrary aspects of X and objects of O)

Algorithms: In the following we show how the trust information stored in W and the meta-trust statements can be used to provide a ranking of reviews for a given aspect–object combination, and also the computation of an overall rating for objects (taking R into account). The process starts with the materialization of meta-trust to normal trust statements. We then use the trust information to compute trust values for each user, which can be used to rank reviews. Based on the top ranked reviews, we can compute an overall rating of objects.

Meta-trust Propagation: Since the meta-trust statements are not part of the model, we have to materialize them to single W statements before the trust computation. The materialization is based on our intuition that more specific trust statements (those covering a smaller scope) are more authoritative: $W \succ W_X \succ W_O \succ W_{OX}$ ("$\succ$" meaning more authoritative). The materialization is performed based on the above order, i.e., starting with all statements in the form W, then processing all statements in the form W_X, then W_O, and finally W_{OX}. For each of the meta-trust statements, their scope is checked and then the value of the statement is propagated to the object–aspect level. Existing trust information is not overwritten in this process. For example, if a meta-trust statement has been made for an object (W_X), it is checked which aspects of this object are not covered by trust statements yet, and the value of the meta-trust statement is used for these aspects. We refer to the final outcome of the materialization as W'. Using meta-trust statements, it is possible for example to distrust other users globally, but to trust them for a certain object o_n (since the statement on the object is more authoritative than the global statement, the users will be distrusted for all objects except for o_n).

Computing Trust Values for Ranking: After the meta-trust has been materialized, all statements are in the form of W, and trust ranks can be computed. Note that in contrast to Guha's ORS, we compute individual trust relationships for every aspect of every object (every $o_n x_k$ combination for $o_n \in O, x_k \in X$).[4] For each $o_n x_k$ combination, we define two matrices storing trust and distrust. The trust matrix $\mathbf{T}$ has entries $t_{ij} \in \{0, 1\}$. If $t_{ij} = 1$, user u_i trusts u_j according to W', otherwise no information is available. Analogously, the distrust matrix $\mathbf{D}$ has entries $d_{ij} \in \{0, 1\}$ capturing the distrust. Given $\mathbf{T}$ and $\mathbf{D}$, we can compute the *GlobalTrustRank* (GTR) (a relabeled Page-Rank [4], see Equation 1), *GlobalDistrustRank* (GDR) (from [3], see Equation 2), and using Algorithm 1 (which is based on [5]) the local trust matrix $\mathbf{F}$ and the interpretation matrix $\mathbf{I}$.

$$GTR_{i+1}(u_u) = (1 - d) + d \cdot \left(\sum\nolimits_{v \in T_v} \frac{GTR_i(v)}{N_v} \right) \tag{1}$$

where u_u is the user whose GTR is computed, $v \in T_v$ is the user trusting u_u, N_v is the total number of users user v trusts, d is a damping factor between 0 and 1,[5] and i is the number of iterations the algorithm has run. Intuitively speaking,

[4] In the following, whenever we use the subscript $o_n x_k$ for matrices or ranks, it means that they contain the data relevant to this $o_n x_k$ combination.

[5] Based on [4], it is usually set to 0.85 for fast convergence of ranks.

GTR assigns trust to users based on how many other users trust them and how trusted the users trusting them are.

$$GDR(u_u) = \sum_{v \in B_v} \frac{GTR(v)}{N_v} \quad (2)$$

where u_u is the user whose *GDR* is computed, $v \in B_v$ is the user distrusting u_u, N_v is the total number of users user v distrusts. *GDR* is taking into account who distrusts a user and how high the *GTRs* of the distrusting users are.

We base our Local Trust Computation Algorithm (see Algorithm 1) on work from Guha et al [5], who investigated trust and distrust propagation in a WOT based on real world data. The algorithm uses the 4 different kinds of atomic trust propagation shown in Table 2. It employs a combination of these trust propagation techniques to propagate trust within the WOT. Distrust is only propagated 1 step (statements from distrusted users are discounted), since the semantics of propagation for distrust are not clear [5]. After the local trust matrix **F** is computed, it is interpreted. This is done by first checking which of the resulting entries f_{ij} were originally trusted or distrusted, and initializing the interpretation matrix **I** based on that information. Then, for each row in **F** the values are ordered, and unknown interpretations for entries f_{ij} are determined by comparison to the interpretation of neighboring entries.

Ranking Reviews at the Aspect Level of an Object: When a user requests the reviews for an object–aspect combination, the reviews for that combination have to be ranked by the TS-ORS to be provided in a user-specific order. If a user is logged in, we can base the user-specific ranking on the *local* trust information. This ranking is also influenced by a parameter $\alpha \in [0, 1]$ that the user can provide to combine global trust (*GTR*) and distrust (*GDR*) to a *GlobalCombinedRank* (*GCR*). The higher α is, the more emphasis is put on the *GTR*. In case a user is logged in, we use Algorithm 2, in the other case Algorithm 3. Algorithm 2 ranks reviews based on the information who is trusted and who is distrusted, and the local trust value from **F**. In case **F** cannot be interpreted, *GCR* values are used. Algorithm 3 can only rank based on the *GCR* values, since the user is unknown. Thus its ranking cannot be personalized.

Computing an Overall Rating of an Object: Each object has aspects $x_k \in X$ it can be reviewed on. The user can choose how to weigh each aspect for computing the overall rating of an object by specifying a weight $\mu_k \geq 0$ for each aspect $x_k \in X$. In case no rating exists for an aspect, we distribute its weight to the remaining aspects. The user can also decide on how many top-ranked ratings per aspect the computation is based. This is done with the parameter $N \geq 1$. $N = 3$ means, for example, that the top-3-ranked ratings are considered. Another parameter $\nu \in (0, 1]$ can be specified that determines how the top-N-ranked ratings are combined. The closer ν is to 0, the more emphasis is put on the top-ranked ratings, if $\nu = 1$ a linear combination is computed. We use Algorithm 4 to compute the overall rating. The ranking of reviews is determined by Algorithm 2 or 3, based on whether a user is logged in or not. With this

Input: Trust Matrix $\mathbf{T}$, Distrust Matrix $\mathbf{D}$
Output: Local Tust Matrix $\mathbf{F}$, Interpretation Matrix $\mathbf{I}$

$\mathbf{C} := \beta_1 \cdot \mathbf{T} + \beta_2 \cdot \mathbf{T}^\intercal\mathbf{T} + \beta_3 \cdot \mathbf{T}^\intercal + \beta_4 \cdot \mathbf{T}\mathbf{T}^\intercal$
$\mathbf{F} := \sum_{k=1}^{K} \gamma^k \cdot (\mathbf{C}^{(k)} \cdot (\mathbf{T} - \mathbf{D}))$
Initialize $\mathbf{I} := \mathbf{T} - \mathbf{D}$
foreach $j \in A$ **do**
  Compute a sequence $a(1), a(2), \ldots, a(|A|)$ such that:
  – for all $a \in A$ there is exactly one $i \in \{1, \ldots, |A|\}$ such that $a(i) = a$
  – for all $i \in \{1, \ldots, |A| - 1\}$ we find that $f_{ja(i)} \leqslant f_{ja(i+1)}$
  To simplify notation, we use $i_{ja(0)}$ and $i_{ja(|A|+1)}$ to denote 0. Small letters with subscripts denote entries in the matrices.
  repeat
    foreach $m \in A$ **do**
      if $i_{ja(m)} = 0$ **then**
        $i_{ja(m)} := 1$
        if $\Big((i_{ja(m-1)} + i_{ja(m+1)} \leq -1) \lor \big((i_{ja(m-1)} = -1 \land i_{ja(m+1)} = 1) \land ((f_{ja(m+1)} - f_{ja(m)}) > (f_{ja(m)} - f_{ja(m-1)}))\big) \lor \big((i_{ja(m-1)} = 1 \land i_{ja(m+1)} = -1) \land ((f_{ja(m+1)} - f_{ja(m)}) < (f_{ja(m)} - f_{ja(m-1)}))\big)\Big)$ **then**
          $i_{ja(m)} := -1$
        if $i_{ja(m-1)} = i_{ja(m+1)} = 0$ **then**
          $i_{ja(m)} := 0$
  until *no further changes occur in* $\boldsymbol{I}$;
  foreach m **do**
    if $f_{ja(m)} = t_{ja(m)} = d_{ja(m)} = 0$ **then**
      $i_{ja(m)} := 0$

Algorithm 1. Local Trust Computation

extension it is possible to compose an overall rating using ratings on different aspects and based on topic-specific trust statements.

In a simulation, which can be found in our Technical Report [6], we show how TS-ORS provides better ranking results than the ORS.

4 Adaptation of the TS-ORS to Ontology Ranking

The idea of employing user ratings for ontology evaluation has first been proposed by Noy et al. [7] in 2005. In the context of ontology evaluation, the set of objects O can contain complete ontologies, parts of an ontology (modules), or even URIs of classes. In Cupboard we instantiate the aspects X based on Gangemi's work on ontology evaluation [8], using: reusability, correctness, complexity, domain coverage and modeling. We allow users to review ontologies either they or other users uploaded. We currently assume that the ratings on ontology aspects cover all axioms of an ontology. If users wish to only rate parts of an ontology, they can do so by extracting these parts using state of the art modularization techniques, and then uploading them as a separate ontology to

Table 2. Atomic Trust Propagation based on [5]

Propagation	Operator	Description
Direct Propagation	$\mathbf{T}$	If A trusts B, someone trusted by B should also be trusted by A
Co-Citation	$\mathbf{T}^\intercal \cdot \mathbf{T}$	If A trusts B and C, someone trusting C should also trust B
Transpose Trust	$\mathbf{T}^\intercal$	If A trusts B, someone trusting B should also trust A
Trust Coupling	$\mathbf{T} \cdot \mathbf{T}^\intercal$	If A and B trust C, someone trusting A should also trust B

Cupboard. We are aware that providing highly customizable algorithms with many different aspects can confuse users, since knowing which parameter has which effect on the result is not trivial. It is important to note that many parameters have to be chosen once when instantiating the system, and thereafter are normally not changed. Moreover, providing reasonable default values allows users to interact with the system without providing their own values, while still enabling expert users to take full advantage of the flexibility of the system. In Cupboard, for T and D, we chose $T = \{\mathit{trust}, \mathit{distrust}\}$ and $D = \{1, \cdots, 5\}$, because many users are familiar with the 5 star rating schema and the possibility to assign trust and distrust (e.g., from Amazon.com). We assume the D values are equidistant. For the trust computation in Cupboard we use $\beta_1 = 0.4, \beta_2 = 0.4, \beta_3 = 0.1, \beta_4 = 0.1$, and $\gamma = 0.9$, based on an analysis of the evaluation results from [5]. We propagate trust 7 steps ($K = 7$ based on the idea of 6 degrees of separation [9]). For the user-specific part of the algorithms we use $\alpha = 0.7, N = 1, \nu = 0.8$ and $\mu_k = 1/|X|$ as default values, unless we have user-specified values.

In the following we show how exposing the user reviews and providing ontology ranking based on the TS-ORS can facilitate ontology reuse for the user.

Reuse User Study: The typical ontology reuse process consists of finding ontologies to reuse, then assessing and selecting them, and finally integrating them. Up to now, ontology search engines do not provide help for ontology selection to users searching for ontological content to reuse. Since rating systems

Input: $o_n \in O, x_k \in X, GTR_{o_n x_k}, GDR_{o_n x_k}, \mathbf{F}_{o_n x_k}, \mathbf{I}_{o_n x_k}, \alpha_i \in [0,1], a_i \in A$
Output: Sorted Reviews

foreach $(a_j, o_n, x_k) \in B_R$ **do**
    $GCR(a_j) := \alpha_i \cdot GTR_{o_n x_k}(a_j) - ((1 - \alpha_i) \cdot GDR_{o_n x_k}(a_j))$
    Assign to the review $(a_j, o_n, x_k) \in B_R$ a triple $(i_{ij}, f_{ij}, GCR(a_j))$
Based on these triples, reviews are sorted in descending lexicographic order (meaning columns are sorted descending, starting with i_{ij} and then considering f_{ij} to sort entries where the i_{ij} value is identical, and then considering $GCR(a_j)$ if both values for i_{ij} and f_{ij} are identical)

Algorithm 2. Review Ranking if the User Can be Identified

Input: $o_n \in O, x_k \in X, GTR_{o_n x_k}, GDR_{o_n x_k}, \alpha \in [0,1]$
Output: Sorted Reviews
foreach $(a_j, o_n, x_k) \in B_R$ **do**
  $GCR(a_j) := \alpha \cdot GTR_{o_n x_k}(a_j) - ((1-\alpha) \cdot GDR_{o_n x_k}, (a_j))$
  Assign to the review $(a_j, o_n, x_k) \in B_R$ a value $GCR(a_j)$
Based on these values, reviews are sorted starting with the highest value.

Algorithm 3. Review Ranking if the User Cannot be Identified

Input: $o_n \in O$, ranked sets of reviews
  $B_{o_n x_k} = \{(a_{j1}, o_n, x_k), \cdots, (a_{jm}, o_n, x_k)\} \subseteq B_R$ for each $x_k \in X$,
  $\nu \in (0,1]$, $N \geqslant 1$, μ_k for each $x_k \in X$
Output: Rating D_{o_n}
For a given $o_n x_k$ combination, we use the notation $(a_{ji}, o_n, x_k) \in B_{o_n x_k}$ to refer to the i-th ranked result.
foreach $x_k \in X$ **do**
  $N := \min(N, |B_{o_n x_k}|)$
  if $N = 0$ **then**
    $D_{o_n x_k} := 0$
    $\mu_k := 0$
  else
    $D_{o_n x_k} := \frac{1}{N} \sum_{i=1}^{N} \left((\nu^i / \sum_{s=1}^{N} \nu^s) \cdot R(a_{ji}, o_n, x_k) \right)$
foreach $k = 1, \cdots, |X|$ *with* $\mu_k \neq 0$ **do**
  $\mu_k := \mu_k / \sum_{l=1}^{|X|} \mu_l$
$D_{o_n} := \sum_{x_k \in X} \mu_k \cdot D_{o_n x_k}$

Algorithm 4. Computation of an Overall Rating

can be used to facilitate exactly this step in the reuse process, we ran a user study comparing the helpfulness of our TS-ORS compared to ontology search engines available on the Web and against Watson. For the experiment, we extended the Watson plug-in [12] for the NeOn Toolkit[6] to get the user evaluations from Cupboard and base the result ranking on the overall ratings as computed by Algorithm 4. We refer to this plug-in as the Cupboard plug-in. The experiment had 20 participants from 6 different institutions (17 PhD students, two postdocs and one professor). We assigned each participant to one of three groups. The task for each group was to extend a given ontology reusing existing ontological content. All groups had access to online ontology search engines. Group 1 had no additional plug-ins to facilitate the reuse process. Group 2 had the Watson plug-in at their disposal, and Group 3 could use the Cupboard plug-in. All participants filled out a questionnaire. The detailed experiment description and analysis of both the resulting ontologies and the questionnaire results can be found in [13]. We focus here on the key findings with regard to the three challenges of finding,

[6] `http://neon-toolkit.org/`

Table 3. Partial questionnaire results including two-sided p values for pairwise group comparison based on Fisher's exact test [10] with Yate's continuity correction [11]

Question: Did you have trouble finding ontology statements to reuse?						
	Group 1	Group 2	Group 3	p Gr. 1 vs Gr 2.	p Gr. 1 vs Gr. 3	p Gr. 2 vs Gr. 3
Yes	6	1	1	0.0047	0.0047	1
No	0	6	6			
Question: Did you have trouble selecting ontology statements to reuse?						
	Group 1	Group 2	Group 3	p Gr. 1 vs Gr 2.	p Gr. 1 vs Gr. 3	p Gr. 2 vs Gr. 3
Yes	5	5	0	1	0.0047	0.021
No	1	2	7			
Question: Did you have trouble integrating ontology statements to reuse?						
	Group 1	Group 2	Group 3	p Gr. 1 vs Gr 2.	p Gr. 1 vs Gr. 3	p Gr. 2 vs Gr. 3
Yes	5	1	0	0.0291	0.0047	1
No	1	6	7			

selecting and integrating reusable ontological content. Table 3 provides the three most important questions covering these three challenges. As is evident from the table, users using either the Watson or the Cupboard plug-in had no trouble finding or integrating ontological content, compared to users who only could use ontology search engines on the Internet (based on p values, the findings are highly significant for $p = 0.0047$ and significant for $p=0.0291$). Group 3, which had the results ranked based on user ratings, stated they had no problem selecting ontology statements compared to both the Watson group (whose result ranking was based on Lucene), or group 1 which was using a plethora of Semantic Web search engines on the Internet. Again, this result is statistically significant and shows that users have less problems selecting content when offered TS-ORS ranking and scores compared to the current state of the art.

5 Related Work

Our closest related work is Guha's work on Open Rating Systems [3], and trust propagation [5]. To overcome limitations of the related work, we have extended the model with ratings on aspects of objects, and provided a comprehensive framework for fine grained topic-specific trust and meta-trust expression. In contrast to the related work, we present a full algorithmic description and complete framework for the computation of personalized ratings based on ratings on objects and fine-grained user trust.

6 Conclusion

We have presented the TS-ORS which features multi-aspect object reviews and topic-specfic trust. The user study based on our implementation inside Cupboard has shown that users have significantly fewer problems selecting ontological content to reuse when provided user-based information on the quality of the ontologies, as delivered by our TS-ORS, compared to other state of the art ontology search engines.

Acknowledgements

Research reported in this paper was partially funded by the European Commission through the IST project ACTIVE (ICT-FP7-215040). We thank Markus Krötsch, Denny Vrandecic, Elena Simperl, Andreas Harth, Thanh Tran, Barry Norton, Sudhir Agarwal, and Natasha Noy for their valuable feedback.

References

1. Simperl, E.P.B., Popov, I.O., Bürger, T.: Ontocom revisited: Towards accurate cost predictions for ontology development projects. In: Aroyo, L., Traverso, P., Ciravegna, F., Cimiano, P., Heath, T., Hyvönen, E., Mizoguchi, R., Oren, E., Sabou, M., Simperl, E. (eds.) ESWC 2009. LNCS, vol. 5554, pp. 248–262. Springer, Heidelberg (2009)
2. d'Aquin, M., Lewen, H.: Cupboard – A Place to Expose your Ontologies to Applications and the Community. In: Aroyo, L., et al. (eds.) ESWC 2009. LNCS, vol. 5554, pp. 913–918. Springer, Heidelberg (2009)
3. Guha, R.: Open rating systems. In: 1st Workshop on Friend of a Friend, Social Networking and the Semantic Web (2004)
4. Page, L., Brin, S., Motwani, R., Winograd, T.: The pagerank citation ranking: Bringing order to the web. Technical report, Stanford University, CA, USA (1998)
5. Guha, R., Kumar, R., Raghavan, P., Tomkins, A.: Propagation of trust and distrust. In: Proc. of the Thirteenth International World Wide Web Conference, pp. 403–412. ACM Press, New York (May 2004)
6. Lewen, H.: Simulation-based Evaluation of the Topic-Specific Trust Open Rating System. Technical report, Universität Karlsruhe (TH) (June 2009), `http://www.aifb.uni-karlsruhe.de/WBS/hle/paper/TR2.pdf`
7. Noy, N., Guha, R., Musen, M.: User ratings of ontologies: Who will rate the raters. In: Proceedings of the AAAI 2005 Spring Symposium on Knowledge Collection from Volunteer Contributors (2005)
8. Gangemi, A., Catenacci, C., Ciaramita, M., Lehmann, J.: Modelling ontology evaluation and validation. In: Sure, Y., Domingue, J. (eds.) ESWC 2006. LNCS, vol. 4011, pp. 140–154. Springer, Heidelberg (2006)
9. Milgram, S.: The small world problem. Psychology Today 2(1), 60–67 (1967)
10. Fisher, R.: On the interpretation of χ 2 from contingency tables, and the calculation of P. Journal of the Royal Statistical Society 85(1), 87–94 (1922)
11. Yates, F.: Contingency tables involving small numbers and the χ 2 test. Supplement to the Journal of the Royal Statistical Society, 217–235 (1934)
12. d'Aquin, M., Motta, E., Dzbor, M., Gridinoc, L., Heath, T., Sabou, M.: Collaborative semantic authoring. IEEE IS 23(3), 80–83 (2008)
13. Lewen, H.: Facilitating Ontology Reuse with a Topic-Specific Trust Open Rating System. Technical report, Universität Karlsruhe (TH) (June 2009), `http://www.aifb.uni-karlsruhe.de/WBS/hle/paper/TR3.pdf`

HyperTwitter: Collaborative Knowledge Engineering via Twitter Messages

Martin Hepp

Universität der Bundeswehr München, E-Business & Web Science Research Group
Werner-Heisenberg-Weg 39, 85577 Neubiberg, Germany
mhepp@computer.org

Abstract. A recent trend in the evolution of the Web is the massive contribution of small chunks of content by regular users, typically in combination with mechanisms for fostering social interaction. Such is often referred to as microblogging, with Twitter, Identi.ca, and Google Buzz being the most widely known services. In this paper, we propose to use the underlying interaction pattern, and existing respective services, for the collaborative construction and maintenance of structured knowledge representations. We define (1) a syntax for embedding triple-like statements in Twitter messages, (2) develop a transformation into RDF, (3) suggest mechanisms for controlling the inclusion of such statements made by other users, (4) exploit the resulting graph for query expansion, and thereby provide a direct incentive for users to adopt our syntax; and (5) demonstrate the approach by means of a prototype implementation[1]. The resulting RDF graphs can be combined easily with other Semantic Web data.

Keywords: Microblogging, Twitter, Extreme Tagging, RDF, Folksonomies, Tagging, Knowledge Acquisition.

1 Overview

Microblogging services, in particular Twitter, Identi.ca, and Google Buzz have gained wide popularity. A 2009 Nielsen study [1], for example, reports an increase in Twitter user numbers from 475 k to over 7 Million between February 2008 and February 2009. In such services, contributions are limited to very short, plain text messages (140 characters in the case of Twitter), which typically forces users to take some cognitive effort for verbalizing thoughts or at least shortening existing pieces of content prior to publication. Mechanic copy-and-paste will usually fail due to the limited message length, or will at least require a very well-thought selection of the source fragment for the copy-and-paste operation. Thus, the majority of Twitter posts (called "tweets" or "status updates" in jargon) represent some human effort in processing information. Even the relaying of another user's message (called "retweeting") is based on human judgment and reflects a cognitive effort.

[1] For additional details, please see the HyperTwitter Technical Report [26].

P. Cimiano and H.S. Pinto (Eds.): EKAW 2010, LNAI 6317, pp. 451–461, 2010.

Twitter and most other microblogging services support users in filtering relevant content by a simple yet effective syntactical convention for *user identifiers* (@username) and *keywords* (#keyword, called "hashtag" in jargon). This allows spotting messages directed to a particular user or containing a particular keyword effectively. For instance, Twitter users can easily introduce multiple users to each other or point users who are monitoring a particular hashtag to a new Web resource:

```
@paulsmith : You should talk to @petermiller
#html5 developers: look at http://foo.com/
```

Based on simple string comparison techniques for such significant tokens, the service can link the millions of isolated short messages and build a densely meshed graph, representing social proximity and shared interests.

Unfortunately, Twitter hashtags and, to a lesser degree, Twitter user identifiers suffer from tag ambiguity (the same tag may stand for multiple meanings), tag heterogeneity (multiple tags are in use for the same meaning), and the lack of relationships between tags (e.g. super/subtag relations). The same problems are known from traditional social tagging systems; for an overview of those problems, see e.g. [7, pp. 74-76]. In Twitter, for example, it is very common that participants of an academic conference cannot immediately agree upon one authoritative hashtag for that event, which leads to disconnected messages about the same conference, because some posts contain the hashtag `#ekaw10` and others contain `#ekaw2010`.

The user community has only weak social instruments or techniques at hand for dealing with such synonymous tags. Very frequently, Twitter users spotting the use of synonymous tags will post messages like:

```
Please use #ekaw instead of #ekaw10 or #ekaw2010
```

Such messages will be visible for any user watching any of the three variants and hopefully foster convergence. Also, we can often see that organizers of events try to stimulate consensus ex ante by publishing a hashtag recommendation.

In this paper, we will describe how a minimal extension of the existing Twitter syntax will allow Twitter users to

1. consolidate multiple synonymous hashtags for their future queries,
2. express hierarchical or other types of relationships between multiple tags,
3. introduce tags for types of properties betweet arbitrary resources, and
4. use popular Web vocabularies like FOAF, SIOC, Dublin Core, GoodRelations, and others inside Twitter messages.

The guiding principle is to provide a mechanism that is (1) immediately useful for the user contributing the additional content but is at the same time (2) suitable for sharing contributions along social networks, so that many people can benefit from it.

From such augmented tweets, we can easily construct an RDF graph that can be used to improve the recall of search operations on Twitter and that can be exported and combined with any other RDF data on the Web of Linked Data. Since all augmented statements remain regular Twitter messages, they can be shared with others via *Twitter lists* (grouping posts by a selected set of people) or *retweeting*, i.e. confirming and relaying a message to all individuals reading your own posts. The main idea is to provide a direct incentive for users to contribute useful statements in the extended syntax, which can be shared and used for weaving a Web of Linked Data.

2 Collaborative Knowledge Engineering via Twitter Messages

In this section, we describe how a lightweight syntactical convention can support users of the Twitter microblogging service to (1) consolidate synonymous hashtags relevant to them and (2) author rich contributions for the Web of Linked Data.

2.1 Motivating Example

Very often, Twitter users cannot immediately agree upon a single authoritative hashtag for a topic, which makes it hard to spot all tweets related to that topic. Also, individuals and organizations often use multiple Twitter user IDs, which makes it hard to monitor all tweets from these accounts in one turn. Imagine the hashtags `#munich` and `#muenchen` were in use for the German city of Munich, and the users `@mfhepp` and `@hypertw` would relate to the same individual. While we could manually expand a query `"#munich @mfhepp"` to `"#munich OR #muenchen @mfhepp OR @hypertw"`, we cannot model and thus reuse and share the underlying equivalency relationship. Also, we cannot express more subtle relationships between tags, like the fact that one tag is more specific than another tag, nor model useful relationships between other resources.

2.2 HyperTwitter Syntax Proposal

With a lightweight syntactical convention based on the established Twitter syntax for tags ("#paris") and users ("@mfhepp"), we can empower Twitter users to embed machine-accessible statements into their tweets, which can then be used for query expansion or combined with other RDF data sources. Basically, we (1) suggest to use "=" or "sameas" for expressing equivalence between tags or between user IDs, (2) "subtag" for expressing that one tag is more specific than a second one, (3) allow introducing arbitrary new properties between elements by means of a preceding greater sign, and (4) support popular CURIEs [2] (e.g. `foaf:knows`).

Our proposed syntax for triple-like statements inside Twitter messages ("trippletweets") is as follows:

```
tripletweet := { subject predicate object [ . tripletweet]}
subject := { @userid | #hashtag | http_uri }
predicate := { = | sameas | subtag | a | >property |
prefix:suffix }
object := { @userid | #hashtag | http_uri | "value" |
prefix:suffix }
userid := [-_a-zA-Z0-9\.]+
hashtag := [-_a-zA-Z0-9\.]+
http_uri := http://[-_a-zA-Z0-9\./?&%#]+
```

```
property := [-_a-zA-Z0-9]+
prefix := { foaf: | tag: | gr: | sioc: | rdfs: | rdf: | skos:
| owl: | dc: | dcterms: | rev: }
suffix := [-_a-zA-Z0-9]+
value := "[^"]+"
```

The elements subject, predicate, and object, as well as multiple tripletweets must be separated by one or more valid whitespace characters in the given encoding. The combination of prefix:suffix is a subset of all CURIEs [2].

2.3 Usage

In the following, we illustrate the use of our proposed syntax.

Simple examples

```
#newyork sameas #nyc
```

The hashtag #newyork is equivalent to #nyc (formally: tag:equivalentTag).

```
#iswc09 subtag #iswc
#tennis subtag #sports
```

The hashtag #iswc09 is a specialization of #iswc and the hashtag #tennis is a specialization of #sports.

```
@mfhepp = @martinhepp
```

The user @mfhepp is the same individual as the user @martinhepp. Note that the formal semantics of "=" and "sameas" depends on the type of the subject and object of the statement. For pairs of tags, it is `tag:equivalentTag`, for individuals it is `owl:sameAs`, and for http_uris is also `owl:sameAs`. For other pairs of entities, the statement is unsupported.

Using predefined vocabularies

```
@mfhepp foaf:knows @kidehen
@mfhepp foaf:name "Martin Hepp"
@mfhepp foaf:birthday "07-11"
```

The user @mfhepp knows the user @kidehen. The name of user @mfhepp is "Martin Hepp. His birthday is July 11.

```
#iswc09 skos:broader #iswc
```

The tag #iswc09 is related to the tag #iswc via the `skos:broader` property. This is equivalent to "#iswc09 subtag #iswc".

```
@microsoft a gr:BusinessEntity
@microsoft rdf:type gr:BusinessEntity
```

The user @microsoft is an instance of the class BusinessEntity in the GoodRelations ontology.

Introducing new tags for types of relationships

```
#munich >translation #muenchen
@mfhepp >dob "1971-07-11"
@mfhepp >hasname "Martin Hepp"
```

The hashtag #munich is related to the hashtag #muenchen via a property labeled with "translation". The user @mfhepp has a property labeled "dob" (date of birth) with the value "1971-07-11".

Using http URIs

```
@mfhepp >attends http://www.iswc2010.org/
http://iswc2010.org/ >successor http://iswc2009.org/
```

The user @mfhepp is related via a relationship labeled "attend" to something for which the Web page is http://www.iswc2010.org/. Note that the Web of Linked Data requires distinct URIs for events and for Web pages about events, so we cannot use the HTTP URI directly as the object of the statement but have to mint a new URI and link back to the original URI via `foaf:topic`. Also note that abbreviated URIs (bit.ly etc.) should be expanded prior to that, but are not in the current prototype.

Multiple statements in a single tweet

```
@mfhepp foaf:knows @kidehen . @mfhepp foaf:name "Martin Hepp"
```

The user @mfhepp knows the user @kidehen and the real name of @mfhepp is "Martin Hepp". Note that the whitespace is significant in here.

2.4 Representation in RDF

In the following, we describe how rich statements matching our syntax can be represented in RDF. This allows both the flexible implementation of query expansion (e.g. whether you just want to expand hashtags and user IDs by *equivalent* ones, or expand a query from a single user to *everybody from his social network*), and other more generic usages of the data.

As a key design choice, we suggest one global namespace for all hashtags in Twitter. This increases access to tags but excludes tag disambiguation. Our motivation for that decision is that in Twitter, other than in typical tagging systems, tags are first and foremost used *as tokens to receive the attention of others*, i.e., they are designed to be global. Of course, multiple users or communities may produce "tag collisions" by that, but there is a strong incentive to use globally valid hashtags. In Twitter, hashtags have a stronger global reach than in other social tagging systems, because one does not invent tags for personal retrieval *but for being visible by others*.

Note that this does not mean than one could not control the subset of statements to be used for personal query expansion or other purposes, because HyperTwitter allows defining the single user or group of users whose messages should be parsed and included in the RDF representation. See subsection 2.5 for more details.

Our RDF transformation uses the three Web ontologies FOAF, SKOS, and the Tag Ontology for representing users, tags, and popular relationships.
Note that in the following, the prefixes definitions for the URIs of HyperTwitter users, tags, properties, and data elements are omitted for brevity. They can be found at http://semantictwitter.appspot.com/.

Users

```
users:<userid> a foaf:Agent;
```

Note: The preceding hash is **not** included in the URI.

Tags

```
tags:<hashtag> a tag:Tag;
                 tag:name "<hashtag>".
```

HTTP URIs

```
data:<http_uri> foaf:topic <http_uri>.
```

All non-standard characters of the string <http_uri> will be encoded before compiling the subject URI. For example, the URI http://purl.org/ will be represented as

```
data:http%3A%2F%2Fpurl.org%2F
```

It may be a good idea to first try to expand abbreviated URIs (e.g. http://bit.ly/…).

Property tags

```
props:<property> a rdf:Property .
```

New properties do not immediately have any formal semantics beyond being `rdf:Property`, but can be found via SPARQL queries. Then, heuristics can be applied based on the frequency of usage, the types of values attached, and the lexical analysis of the property name.

CURIEs for Properties

For the supported prefixes, i.e. foaf, tag, gr, sioc, rdfs, rdf, owl, skos, dc, dcterms, and rev, the standard expansion to full URIs as per [2] is being used.

Predefined properties "=" and "sameas"

```
tags:<hashtag1> tag:equivalentTag tags:<hashtag2>
users:<user1> owl:sameAs users:<user2>
data:<http_uri1> owl:sameAs data:<http_uri2>
```

The formal semantics of "=" / "sameas" depends on the type of the subject and object of the statement. For pairs of tags, it is `tag:equivalentTag`, for individuals it is `owl:sameAs`, and for http_uris it is also `owl:sameAs`. For pairs of other types, such statements are ignored in the transformation.

Predefined property "subtag"

```
tags:<hashtag1> skos:broader tags:<hashtag2>
```

We use the SKOS [3] properties for hierarchy relations. Note that this is supported for pairs of tags only.

Predefined property "a"

```
users:<user1> rdf:type prefix:suffix.
data:<http_ouri1> rdf:type prefix:suffix
```

The predefined property "a" is equivalent to `rdf:type` and can be meaningfully applied only to users and newly minted http URIs as the subject, and classes in the supported Web vocabularies, given as CURIEs, as the object.

2.5 Trust and Filtering

It is important to be able to control the origin of tweets to be included. For example, different users or group of users may disagree on whether particular hashtags are equivalent for them. We propose to use existing Twitter techniques for selecting subsets of tweets for a particular purpose: In the simplest form, a user will trust only his / her own tweets containing statements of equivalence or hierarchical relationships for query expansion. Alternatively, one can manage a specific list on Twitter that defines a set of users whose tweets should be considered for query expansion or other purposes. Such lists can be private or public.

Even if one decides to trust one's own statements only, it is possible to find and use other users' statements by simply retweeting them. So if a friend of yours makes the statement "`<hashtag1> = <hashtag2>`" and you find that useful, you can add it to your own query expansion and relay it to people following you in one turn by retweeting.

3 Implementation and Evaluation

A reference implementation of the HyperTwitter syntax is available at http://semantictwitter.appspot.com/. The overall goal was to provide a service that is immediately useful for each individual user, thus creating an incentive for adopting the proposed syntax. At the same time, the RDF content of all public Twitter messages is made accessible for further research and novel applications. For more details on the implementation and a preliminary evaluation, please check the HyperTwitter Technical Report [26].

4 Related Work

HyperTwitter is related to and partly inspired by the following branches of work.

Meta-models of Tagging and Extensions: While tagging was introduced as an informal technique for attaching descriptors to resources in a collaborative setting, mainly to support the performance of retrieval, the huge amount of respective tagging data soon triggered interest in research to exploit this data for deriving more formal knowledge representations; for an overview of related questions, see *Gruber* [4]. A first step was the development of ontologies for sharing tags and tagging data, with

Newman's **Tag Ontology** [5] being an early approach that has gained wide popularity. Other researchers proposed extended tag ontologies, mainly for facilitating access to the underlying social structures of tagging and for supporting the semantic enrichment of tags, e.g. by disambiguating homonymous tags. Two major efforts in this direction are **SCOT** [6] and **MOAT** [7]. For a comprehensive review of tag ontologies, see [8] and [9]. Our approach uses Newman's tag ontology for representing the tag entities found in HyperTwitter statements. This could be mapped easily to equivalent classes in additional tag ontologies.

The two most relevant works (and a direct inspiration) for creating the HyperTwitter prototype are **Extreme Tagging** [10] and **Tag4Tags** [11]. Both basically suggest to expand the domain of tagging activities from tagging a resource to tagging tags (in the case of Extreme Tagging), and other types of resources. Such can help to use tagging for consolidating personal or public tag usage and for authoring knowledge representations, since triples of tags can be understood as triples in the RDF model. HyperTwitter applies the idea of Tags4Tags and Extreme Tagging to the significant tokens in free-text microblogging, e.g. user IDs and hashtags.

Syntactical Conventions for Embedding Semantics into Microblogging: Almost all microblogging services rely on simple syntactical conventions for marking up content in messages, e.g. using the hash sign as a prefix for tags/keywords and the "at" sign for user IDs. In the past three years, several proposals have been made to define additional syntactic conventions for representing richer structures.

On the high end of granularity is **MicroTurtle (µttl)** [12] by *Inkster*, a specification for embedding small RDF graphs into microblogging messages using the Turtle syntax. MicroTurtle is very similar to our approach. The main differences are that (1) we use a simpler, linear syntax that is closer to tagging than to RDF and has convenient shortcuts for tag consolidation, which is likely a key motivation for users to use rich structures in messages; (2) we did develop and deploy a reference implementation, and (3) we introduced a simple yet effective message for managing the inclusion of messages to the semantic representation by "trust" lists or user IDs.

TwitterData [13] is a proposal by *Fast* and *Kopsa* for encoding property-value pairs in Twitter messages, e.g. "`San Francisco Airport $lat 37.612804 $long -122.381687`". Other than HyperTwitter, it focuses on property-value pairs instead of triples. Also, a mapping to Semantic Web standards has been announced but is not yet available. **MicroSyntax** [14] is a community effort to identify and document lightweight syntactical conventions for encoding information in Twitter messages and other short user contributions. The initiative also aims at supporting convergence among competing syntaxes and at creating reference implementations. **Picoformats** [15] is an initiative led by *Messina* to define syntactical conventions for communications and for executing simple commands via short text messages, originally intended for command-line interfaces, SMS, and other devices. It also refers to other conventions, e.g. MicroTurtle or TwitterData. **Twitter Nanoformats** [16] is another specification for embedding lightweight semantics into short messages. For example, it suggests the prefixes "L:" for locations, "event:" for events, and "time:" for temporal data. **Triple tags**, also called "machine tags" on Flickr and on other services, are a convention for representing property-value pairs with explicit namespacing in short messages [17]. A popular usage is geo data, e.g. "geo:long=50.123456".

Semantic Microblogging: Very recently, there have been several proposals of lifting Twitter content to the Semantic Web technology stack in order to make it accessible for SPARQL queries that combine Twitter data with other RDF data on the Web. For example, **SemanticTweet** by *Flinter* is a straightforward service that automatically constructs a FOAF graph from a Twitter user's social network [18].

More sophisticated contributions are on one hand the work by *Nowack* [19] and on the other hand the **SMOB** (Semantic-MicrOBlogging) framework [20]. Nowack's work lifts Twitter content to RDF and makes it accessible to SPARQL. While the usage of machine tags (see above) is being discussed, it does not support the authoring of explicit triple statements in tweets, limiting the accessible content to user IDs, SIOC relations, URIs, and property-value pairs. SMOB allows exposing Twitter content in RDF in a similar way but also supports aligning tags or modeling relationships using existing vocabularies. The focus in SMOB is on exposing the obvious meta-data using standard vocabularies. A main difference of our approach is that we additionally foster the introduction of new tags for relationships so that the convenience of free tagging can be used for predicates as well.

Other works: Approaches of maintaining and consolidating tags have been discussed by several authors, e.g. by *Golov, Weller*, and *Peters* [21]. Their **TagCare** system allows users to collate their tags from multiple tagging systems and to express semantic relations for future query expansion and other purposes.

Another stream of research aims at mining ontologies from tagging data, which can also be used for query expansion. A prominent example is the work by *Specia* and *Motta* [22]. They propose an automatic approach for deriving formal relations between tags from the combination of tagging data, existing Web ontologies, and other Web resources like Wikipedia. A major difference to our work is that the focus is on a fully automated extraction of formal representation, while we provide a syntax and application for the contribution of human judgment.

As far as Twitter query expansion is concerned, there are already first approaches, e.g. **TipTop** [23], a semantic Twitter-based search engine which seems to use mining and NLP techniques to extract relevant content for a given search from Twitter. However, it does not provide any RDF export of the data and can thus not be integrated with other Semantic Web resources or technology.

5 Discussion and Conclusion

At the time of writing, the amount of Twitter messages posted reaches 50 million tweets per day, which is an average of 600 tweets per second [24]. That means that users contribute an unprecedented amount of content, time, and intelligence, which may be very rewarding to tap for weaving a dense and current Web of Linked Data. Both for maintaining ontologies and facts in knowledge bases, the delayed inclusion of user feedback has kept on being a major bottleneck towards powerful intelligent knowledge-based systems; for a discussion, see e.g. [25]. Our approach reuses the ideas of Extreme Tagging [10] and Tags4Tags [11], i.e. using free tagging for modeling new types of relationships, for the challenge of knowledge authoring by means of microblogging.

Acknowledgments: HyperTwitter is inspired by the Tags4Tags approach as described by Leyla Jael García-Castro et al. [11].

References

1. NielsenWire: Twitter's Tweet Smell of Success, http://blog.nielsen.com/nielsenwire/online_mobile/twitters-tweet-smell-of-success/
2. CURIE Syntax 1.0. A syntax for expressing Compact URIs. W3C Candidate Recommendation, January 16 (2009), http://www.w3.org/TR/curie
3. SKOS Simple Knowledge Organisation System Reference. W3C Recommendation, August 18 (2009), http://www.w3.org/TR/skos-reference
4. Gruber, T.R.: Ontology of Folksonomy: A Mash-Up of Apples and Oranges. International Journal on Semantic Web and Information Systems (IJSWIS) 3, 1–11 (2007)
5. Tag Ontology: An Ontology for Tags, http://www.holygoat.co.uk/owl/redwood/0.1/tags/
6. SCOT: Let's Share Tags!, http://scot-project.org/
7. Passant, A., Laublet, P., Breslin, J.G., Decker, S.: A URI is Worth a Thousand Tags: From Tagging to Linked Data with MOAT. International Journal on Semantic Web and Information Systems (IJSWIS) 5, 72–94 (2009)
8. Kim, H.L., Passant, A., Breslin, J.G., Scerri, S., Decker, S.: Review and Alignment of Tag Ontologies for Semantically-Linked Data in Collaborative Tagging Spaces. In: 2008 IEEE International Conference on Semantic Computing (ICSC 2008), pp. 315–322. IEEE Computer Society, Washington (2008)
9. Kim, H.L., Scerri, S., Breslin, J.G., Decker, S., Kim, H.-G.: The State of the Art in Tag Ontologies: A Semantic Model for Tagging and Folksonomies. In: International Conference on Dublin Core and Metadata Applications, Berlin, Germany, pp. 128–137 (2008)
10. Tanasescu, V., Streibel, O.: Extreme Tagging: Emergent Semantics through the Tagging of Tags. In: First International Workshop on Emergent Semantics and Ontology Evolution (ESOE 2007), Busan, Korea, vol. 292, pp. 84–94 (2007), CEUR-WS.org
11. García-Castro, L., Hepp, M., García, A.: Tags4Tags: Using Tagging to Consolidate Tags. In: Bhowmick, S.S., Küng, J., Wagner, R. (eds.) DEXA 2009. LNCS, vol. 5690, pp. 619–628. Springer, Heidelberg (2009)
12. MicroTurtle (μttl), http://buzzword.org.uk/2009/microturtle/spec
13. Twitter Data. A Simple, Open Proposal for Embedding Data in Twitter Messages, http://twitterdata.org/
14. Microsyntax.org: Deep Structure of the Real-time Stream, http://www.microsyntax.org/about-microsyntax/
15. Picoformats, http://microformats.org/wiki/picoformats
16. Microblogging Nanoformats: Twitter (or Jaiku) Nanoformats Proposal, http://microformats.org/wiki/microblogging-nanoformats
17. Tag (metadata), section: Triple Tags, http://en.wikipedia.org/wiki/Triple_tag#Triple_tags
18. SemanticTweet. Twitter Meets the Semantic Web, http://semantictweet.com/
19. Turn Twitter Into Your Personal Assistant, http://www.devx.com/semantic/Article/40869
20. SMOB: Semantic-MicrOBlogging Framework, http://smob.me/

21. Golov, E., Weller, K., Peters, I.: TagCare: A Personal Portable Tag Repository. In: Proceedings of the Poster and Demonstration Session at ISWC 2008, Karlsruhe, vol. 401 (2008), CEUR-WS.org
22. Specia, L., Motta, E.: Integrating Folksonomies with the Semantic Web. In: Franconi, E., Kifer, M., May, W. (eds.) ESWC 2007. LNCS, vol. 4519, pp. 624–639. Springer, Heidelberg (2007)
23. TipTop Search Engine, `http://feeltiptop.com/`
24. Measuring Tweets. Twitter Blog Post (February 22, 2010), `http://blog.twitter.com/2010/02/measuring-tweets.html`
25. Hepp, M.: Possible Ontologies: How Reality Constrains the Development of Relevant Ontologies. IEEE Internet Computing 11, 90–96 (2007)
26. Hepp, M.: HyperTwitter: Collaborative Knowledge Engineering via Twitter Messages, Technical Report 2010-01, Universität der Bundeswehr München, PDF at `http://www.heppnetz.de/files/hypertwitter-TR.pdf`

TagSorting: A Tagging Environment for Collaboratively Building Ontologies

Leyla Jael García-Castro[1], Martin Hepp[1], and Alexander García[2]

[1] Universität der Bundeswehr München, Werner-Heisenberg-Weg 39, 85779 Neubiberg, Germany
leyla.garcia@ebusiness-unibw.org, mhepp@computer.org
[2] University of Bremen, Bibliothekstrasse 1, 28359 Bremen, Germany
cagarcia@uni-bremen.de

Abstract. Social Tagging Systems (STS) empower users to classify and organize resources and to improve the retrieval performance over the tagged resources. In this paper we argue that the potential of the social process of assigning, finding, and relating symbols in collaborative tagging scenarios is currently underexploited and can be increased by extending the meta-model and using this extension to support the emergence of structured knowledge, *e.g.* semantic knowledge representations. We propose a model that allows tagging as well as establishing relations between any pair of resources, not just objects and tags. Moreover, we propose to use this extension to enrich and facilitate the process of building semantic knowledge representations. We (1) provide a formal description for our approach, (2) introduce an architecture to facilitate semantic knowledge derivation, and (3) present a preliminary experiment.

Keywords: Social Web, Semantic Web, tagging, folksonomies, meta-model, emergent semantics, Web 3.0, collaborative ontology engineering.

1 Introduction

Social tagging systems (STS) have become increasingly popular and useful within the Web 2.0; simplicity and immediate benefits for end users are amongst the likely rationales behind this broad adoption [1]. STS allow agents, *i.e.* users, to freely associate terms, *i.e.* tags, to resources; these systems also facilitate the classification and organization of such resources. Tags gathered in this way are mainly used to improve retrieval performance over the tagged resources [2], and also to promote social interaction by enabling the construction of social networks based on the common interests that they represent [3].

Despite major advancements, ontology engineering still faces the challenge to properly involve broad audiences and to integrate and reuse existing knowledge [4-7]. Although STS have proven to provide significant benefits, deriving semantic knowledge representations, *e.g.* ontologies and taxonomies, from STS is still difficult [8-10]; typical problems are rooted in variations amongst tags as well as the heterogeneity of systems [3]. On one hand, tags can be ambiguous. For instance *sf*

P. Cimiano and H.S. Pinto (Eds.): EKAW 2010, LNAI 6317, pp. 462–472, 2010.

could mean both *San Francisco* and *Science Fiction*. Also, links amongst different but related tags (synonyms and spelling and morphological variants) are scant. Furthermore, tags introduce heterogeneity of aggregation, *i.e.* different levels of granularity or expertise, which leads to data precision conflicts [2, 11-13]. On the other hand, STS do not share a common representation for the tagging activity, making it difficult to share and reuse tagging data across them [14].

In this paper we propose a novel approach aiming to facilitate the emergence of richer semantic structures from the information gathered by means of STS. We have reused and extended previously proposed meta-models representing STS [1, 15-17] improving the use of both the social and the tagging process. Our model explicitly supports the representation of relations amongst taggable objects, *i.e.* resources, tags, and agents. For instance, it is possible to represent the relation *isCapitalOf* between the tags *Munich* and *Bavaria* as well as adding meaning to numerical tags, *e.g. IBM wasFoundedIn 1896*. The application of our model facilitates deriving baseline ontologies, *i.e.* a draft version containing few but seminal elements of an ontology from input contributed by broad user audiences.

This paper is organized as follows: In Sections 2 and 3 we present our main approach, in particular the model and architecture. In Section 4 we describe a preliminary experiment and evaluation. In Section 5 and 6 we summarize and discuss related work. In Section 7 we conclude our work and point to future extensions.

2 TagSorting: Ontologies from Social Tagging Systems

Our approach, named *TagSorting*, is based on Card Sorting, a knowledge acquisition technique that has been used to facilitate the ontology building process, mainly those tasks related to the concepts hierarchy. In our case, *tags* and *relations* act as cards that have to be organized. TagsSorting is built upon the *HyperTag* model [18] that allows establishing relations as tags on any duplet of tags. We aim at (1) obtaining a taxonomy and (2) also *ad hoc* and other useful relations by the application of the Card Sorting approach.

The *HyperTag* model is built upon existing meta-models representing STS data so they can easily interoperate. Those models share the structure (*subject*, *predicate*, *object*) to represent tagging, more specifically (*agent*, *tag*, *resource*): they also share relations such as *associatedTag*, *taggedBy* and *taggedResource* [1, 14-17, 19, 20], see left side of Fig. 1. *HyperTag* introduces a simple, yet likely very effective, extension to the common arrangement in existing meta-models. As illustrated on the right side of Fig. 1, our model introduces a wider understanding for *Resource* and *Tag*. As in the traditional STS structure, the *subject* remains an *agent* and the *predicate* remains a *tag* but the *object* has been extended in our model: We have widened the range of taggable objects from single resources to resources, with agents and tags being also considered resources, plus duplets of such resources. With the tagged duplets, we can represent a relation between a pair of taggable objects, *i.e.* (*subject*, *object*). The HyperTag model ultimately aims to facilitate the process of building ontologies using STS as the primary source; in order to achieve this goal, we propose a layered architecture supporting a participative ontology building process in an incremental and iterative way, see Fig. 22.

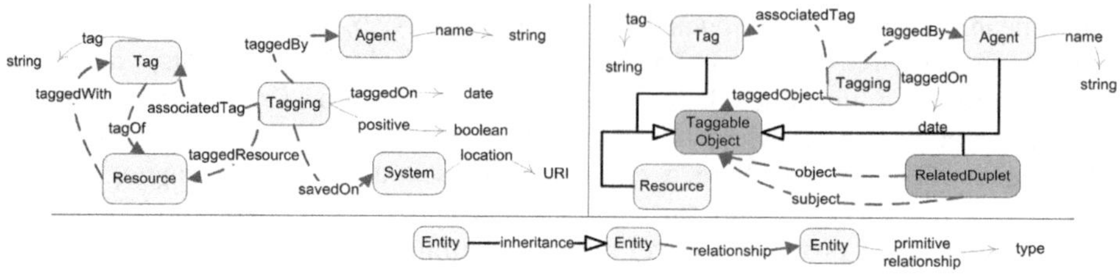

Fig. 1. Current meta-model and *HyperTag* meta-model for STS

In the **first stage**, the project manager, *i.e.* a person or a group, defines a project: (i) the domain of the target ontology, (ii) the goals of building this ontology, (iii) the team participating in the project, (iv) a repository of local and online ontologies that will be used for suggestions, mappings, and disambiguations, (v) the set of rules to describe tags as Concept, String, Integer, Double, Boolean, Date, or URI, and (vi) the set of rules to categorize tags and relations as entities defined in the ontologies in the repository. In the **second stage**, the project manager generates the tags that will be used as seed entities, mainly representing concepts and primitive types, *i.e.* numbers, dates, and strings. The seed generation uses regular STS providing APIs to access their data, *e.g.* Delicious (http://delicious.com/) and Connotea (http://www.connotea.org/), and takes advantage of methods and statistics in order to include those tags that are more representative: the project manager can filter by agents, tagging dates, related tags, most used tags, and minimum length of tags.

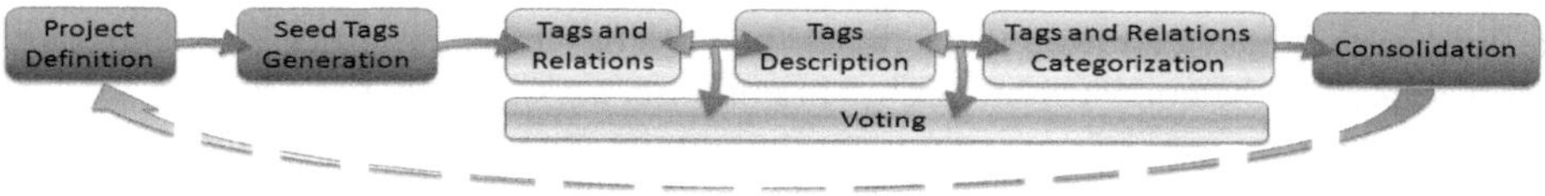

Fig. 2. TagSorting incremental and iterative process

The next three stages correspond to the ontology building process and are carried out by the team, they can be done in a sequential or parallel way, and thus every person can do it in its own way. In the **third stage,** the participants take seed tags and relate them by attaching a tag to a duplet; whenever they feel the need, they can also create new tags. Participants are provided with suggestions based on: (i) predefined relations commonly used in mapping approaches, (ii) predefined relations selected from one or more ontologies in the repository, (iii) online ontology mining by using approaches such as SCARLET [21], and (iv) auto-complete from the initially typed letters. In the **fourth stage** the participants describe tags as Concept, String, Integer, Double, Boolean, Date, and URI, following a scenario-specific meta-model, while in the **fifth stage** they attach categories to tags and relations, *i.e.* they tag the tags and relations with terms from a predefined vocabulary; these two stages are optional because they can be done automatically based on rules defined by the project management. The **sixth stage** is done in parallel and consists in voting for tags and relations; anytime a participant uses/adds a tag a new vote is counted, optionally, they can also attach short explanations. The **seventh stage** is done by the project manager and consists of a consolidation process. Initially a consolidation is automatically generated taking into account all participants' taggings and votes; then the project manager does a final review and the approved ontology version is released. This version can be part of the process for a new version or a new ontology by including it into the repository and categorization rules.

TagSorting annotates agents, tags, relations, and taggable objects by means of the *HyperTag* model, which makes it possible to publish tagging data as RDF and thus optionally as Linked Open Data. In this way, it is possible to use SPARQL queries to extract useful information, and similarly to LODr, the tagging data becomes part of the Semantic Web so semantic search engines, *e.g.* Watson (http://watson.kmi.open.ac.uk), and SPARQL endpoints, *e.g.* Virtuoso (http://virtuoso.openlinksw.com/) can make use of it.

3 Preliminary Experiment

We conducted an experiment to find out whether our approach is a feasible way to collect meaningful data within a tagging environment in order to derive models in a specific domain. We wanted to evaluate (i) whether people are able to think in graphs and triplets, (ii) whether participants understand the *TagSorting* process, and (iii) how they use the process to perform specific modeling tasks. The goal of the experiment was to manually model the Google Nexus One phone as a product and was explained to the participants by means of written instructions and supported by a practical example from a different domain. All participants were students from the Universität der Bundeswehr in Munich. They received cards for the seed tags, descriptors, categories, and some suggested relations taken from the GoodRelations ontology. Three participants were from the business management degree program, and five from business information systems, all of them with at least basic command of social Web platforms such as wikis and tagging systems. Some had basic knowledge in modeling UML class and Entity-Relation diagrams. Participants had two weeks to achieve the goal, and they were allowed to work individually or by pairs as well as to comment, share, and compare their models.

The seed tags where generated during the second week of February 2010 using data from Delicious and the search facility that it offers. The keywords where *nexus* and *one* and the relevant time-frame was from January 1st to 31st of 2010, the first month of Nexus One in market. We obtained a total of 2555 tags and took 25% of them (875 tags reported on the first 35 pages of results) and used as seed tags only those returning at least one hit on http://www.google.com. The 26 resulting seed tags were: android, buy, cellphone, design, flash, gadget, google, hardware, info, iphone, mobile, money, network, news, nexus, nexus_one, nexusone, one, opensource, phone, phones, product, smartphone, technology, web, and wishlist. From the eight initial participants we got five models since some of them decided to merge their models, thus we got two individual models and three collaborative models. One of the individual models was dismissed since the participant did not attend the intial instructions and decided to model the social process behind buying a phone instead modeling the Google Nexus One phone as a product based on his lack of task understanding.

In the four collected models, we identified a total of 94 concepts, 31 strings, 6 booleans, 6 floats, 8 integers, 2 dates, and 70 relations. The four models mainly showed: (i) physical characteristics (buttons and dimensions), additional features (camera) and applications; (ii) name variants, similar phones, and applications; (iii) hierarchy (smartphone, cellphone, phone), physical characteristics (dimensions), additional features (camera and GPS), and applications; and (iv) hierarchy information, and applications. All participants agreed that seed tags facilitated the modeling task; however two participants felt forced to use all seed tags, which we did not intend. All of the 26 seeds where used, 17 in at least two different models as well as 4 new tags. For those tags used in at least three models and described at least once as concepts, we analyzed the descriptors and classified them as correct, arguably correct, and wrong; as an example, we present the first five classifications in Table 1.

Table 1. Frequency and classification for more common tags

Tag	Frequency	Classification 1			Classification 2		
		Desc.	Freq.	Analysis	Desc.	Freq.	Analysis
google	100%	Concept	50%	Correct	String	50%	Wrong
iphone	100%	Concept	75%	Correct	String	25%	Wrong
smartphone	100%	Concept	50%	Correct	Boolean	25%	Arguably correct
android	75%	Concept	66.6%	Correct	Boolean	33.3%	Arguably correct
cellphone	75%	Concept	33.3%	Correct	Boolean	33.3%	Arguably correct

As far as the relations are concerned, similarities were harder to find, mainly because of lexical variations. From the four models we identified 70 relations corresponding to 54 different relations that could be narrowed down to 45 by means of specialized algorithms, *i.e.* lexical proximity and distance, see Table 22 for a summary of lexical variations on relations. We observed that consolidating descriptors before relating entities could facilitate consensus; also, we found that recommendation and social mechanisms could facilitate the consolidation of relation types, *i.e.* object or datatype, domains, and ranges, as well as relations reuse.

Table 2. Lexical variations on relations

Relation	Used in # models	Variations
hasAManufacturer	2	hasManufacturer
hasApp	3	has Applications, hasApps
hasHeight	2	hasHight
hasReleasedDate	2	isReleasedOn
hasVariant	3	hasAVariant, isVariantOf

The experiment showed that concepts are easier to identify and consolidate than relations. Descriptors, *i.e.* concept, boolean, date, integer, float, and string, were more used than categories likely since those require a deeper knowledge of the domain;

descriptors also facilitated distinguishing between object and datatype properties. From the collected models it is possible to semi-automatically derive an ontology: first we identified entities, *i.e.* hypertag:tag, and relations, *i.e.* hypertag:relatedDuplet; then we use descriptors, *i.e.* tags on tags, to define entities as classes or primitive types, which is also useful to decide whether a relation is an object or a datatype property. This first version of the domain model can be refined by the project manager and the final version can evolve by repeating the TagSorting process.

4 Related Work

Work related to our approach can be grouped into two main categories:

Representing Social Tagging Systems. STS have been represented by means of meta-models and ontologies. In both cases, approaches involve agents (A), tags (T), resources (R), and tagging (TA), which represent an agent assigning a tag to a resource; some of the models also add other dimensions such as time and systems on which the annotations took place.

Mika [15] proposed a basic meta-model that represents STS as a graph where A, T, and R are the vertices and TA are the arcs. Hotho *et al.* [1] adds a component ($\prec$) to allow sub/super-ordinate relations between tags. Tanasescu & Streibel [20] do not distinguish between R and T (RT); they allow tagging tags in order to add meanings, thus they consider a direction (D) that represents directional annotations of relations between entities (RT).

Newman [17] proposes a basic ontology where TA is a triplet; he also offers object properties between tags to represent similarity: *relatedTo* and *equivalentTo*. Knerr's ontology [22] aims to provide a single entry point to different STS: *Time* refers to the tagging date, *Domain* specifies the STS, *Visibility* can be private, public, or protected, and *Type* is related to the resource nature, *e.g.* video, image, and website. Gruber [16] shares the basic Newman's model and includes the system (S) on which annotation took place; also agents are allowed to vote [+/–] for tags in order to reduce spam. The Meaning-of-a-tag ontology (MOAT) extends Newman's ontology and provides a way for users to attach meanings (M) to their tags; a meaning relies on a resource and is part of the tagging (TA). Finally, the semantic cloud of tags ontology (SCOT) represents the structure and semantics of tagging data by means of a cloud of tags and facilitates importing and exporting amongst different systems (S).

Consolidating Knowledge in Social Tagging Systems. Consolidation of tagging data has been used to facilitate emergent semantics and semantic mapping; it has also been used to allow agents to maintain and transport their personal tagging vocabulary.

Folksontology [23], Tang *et al.* [9] and Folks2Onto [8] propose semi-automatic approaches in order to derive ontologies from STS. Folksontology [23], proposes an approach to derive ontologies from STS by means of (i) datasets obtained from STS in order to determine pair of related tags, enriching tags with hierarchical relations, and agents and tags clusters, and (ii) disambiguation and cleaning techniques based on online lexical resources usage as well as concepts and relations, e.g. homonyms and synonyms. Tang *et al.* [9] introduce a learning approach to derive ontologies capturing the hierarchical semantic structure from STS. The authors propose a probabilistic model for tags and tagged resources, which is jointly used with some divergence measures to quantitatively distinguish relations amongst tags. The hierarchical structured is derived from those relations; with this approach is possible to identify synonymy as well as hypernym relations. Folks2Onto [8] proposes a software-based approach to turn STS into ontologies by means of mappings. It supports Technorati (http://technorati.com) and Delicious as STS, and WordNet (http://wordnet.princeton.edu) and DublinCore (http://dublincore.org/) as ontologies. Folks2Onto first employs a retriever and a trainer in order to establish mappings, which will be used for the mapper to generate an RDF representation of the target ontology. Tanasescu & Streibel [20], Braum *et al.* [24], Golov, Weller & Peters [25], and Sharif [26] propose specific STS in order to facilitate ontology derivation. Tanasescu & Streibel [20] propose Extreme Tagging, which aims to extend STS in order to allow the collaborative construction of knowledge bases; this is achieved by means of allowing agents to tag resources as well as tags. In this way it is possible to obtain hierarchy relations as well as other kinds of semantic associations. Similarly to Extreme Tagging, the Mature Project [24] aims to use STS to allow emergent semantics and deriving ontologies; in this project, Braun *et al.* do not extend the basic STS meta-model but define an ontology building process supported by an STS-based application: The first phase is the emergence of ideas by means of tags introduced by agents; the second one is the consolidation of data and the emergence of a common vocabulary through the reuse and adaption of tags; in the third phase the tags are organized according to a hierarchy and ad hoc relations; the last phase deals with the axiomatization and is carried out by domain experts. It captures semantics by adding background knowledge. Same as the Mature Project, TagCare [25] also offers a STS but the purpose here is allowing agents to maintain and transport their personal tagging vocabulary across different platforms. It aims to help agents to apply the same tags uniformly in different platforms based on a so-called "personomy", *i.e.* a cross-platform personal tagging vocabulary. In TagCare, agents are allowed to consolidate their tagging data as well as to create their own vocabulary hierarchy, synonyms relations, and cross-references. Finally, Sharif's [26] approach aims to use the flexibility from STS and the structured model of knowledge from ontologies in order to complete the process of knowledge representation on the Web. He proposes to improve searching, navigation, and integration and retrieval in STS, and lowering entry barriers in ontology building, which is achieved by means of a model, *i.e.* an ontology representing STS, and two sub-models, one for the knowledge acquisition and organization and the other one for knowledge discovery.

5 Discussion

Several positive effects of STS have been reported in the literature, e.g. by [2, 23, 24]: (i) Tags facilitate the navigation over tagged resources without imposing predefined categories on users; (ii) the social process on STS allows discovering implicit relationships, and similar skills, tasks, or interests; and (iii) collaborative filtering and recommendations support the emergence of consensus and the consolidation of meta-data. Our approach takes advantage of all those mentioned strengths.

Our *HyperTag* conceptual model is built upon the work by Mika [15] and byNewman [17] and is compatible with the work by Gruber [16] and by Passant & Laublet [19]. It allows tagging tags as described by Tanasescu & Streibel [20], as well as defining hierarchical relationships as those available in Bibsonomy (http://www.bibsonomy.org/). It is also designed to remain compatible with (i) existing approaches to derive formal structures from tagging data such as FLOR [11] and SCARLET [21], (ii) normalization and disambiguation techniques such as [27-29], (iii) the addition of meaning to tags by using URIs [19], and (iv) techniques and tools for tag data consolidation amongst platforms [14].

The *TagSorting* approach is comparable to others also aiming to build ontologies based on social Web platforms such as the Maturing Project [24], STYLid [30], and MyOntoloy [31]. The *TagSorting* architecture aims to facilitate building conceptual models including mappings, whereas the other approaches focus only on taxonomies and hierarchies. Similarly to the other approaches, *TagSorting* allows the participation of regular users, domain experts, and ontology engineers; it is also suitable for building domain ontologies, which are considered dynamic and evolving. Consensus, convergence and strategies for identifying concepts also rely on social mechanisms. The consolidation of knowledge takes into account privileged users [24, 31], usage and popularity [30], as well as online knowledge mining. *TagSorting* facilitates the reuse of knowledge in STS as well as online ontologies by harvesting existing knowledge as proposed by [11, 21, 32] while the others reuse mainly their own knowledge representations [24, 30] or specific sources such as Wikipedia and eClassOWL [31].

6 Conclusions and Future Work

In this paper we (1) analyzed the advantages of using the *HyperTag* conceptual model to represent tagging and relations between an extended set of taggable objects, (2) presented and discussed our *TagSorting approach* to support ontology building within a STS environment in a collaborative way, and (3) compared it with similar approaches, illustrating the advantages and limitations, (4) reported on a preliminary experiment and associated results.

The *HyperTag* model and the *TagSorting* approach rely on STS characteristics, *e.g.* architecture of participation, collaborative environment, and support for the emergence of consensus and consolidation of meta-data. *HyperTag* allows agents to establish free relations between any pair of taggable objects, thus facilitating the reuse of semi-structure knowledge, *i.e.* tagging data, in the ontology building process. Our model exploits the potential and strengths of STS, keeping the simplicity and offering new possibilities to agents by means of the proposed extension of the taggable objects. This facilitates capturing and establishing morphological and semantic variations for tags [16], building hierarchical and *ad hoc* relations, building and maintaining semantic-social networks based on tagging, and improving the search & retrieval, and knowledge reuse by exploiting the tagging structure [33].

TagSorting facilitates the process of building ontologies based on information gathered on STS environments; however a further evaluation is required to improve and tune our approach and to overcome some difficulties related to the consolidation and lexical variations in both entities and relations by means of community consensus based on use, popularity, and voting mechanisms. Another feasible applications of the *HyperTag* model will also be evaluated, *e.g.* explicitly interlinking tagging communities by combining relations across agents, controlled vocabularies, taxonomies or ontologies, and inference rules; for instance, knowing that Lisa *is mother of* Maria, and Maria *is married to* Nathan, it would be possible to infer that Lisa *is mother in law of* Nathan. Using the *HyperTag* model and the *TagSorting* architecture in different scenarios, we expect to achieve: (i) consolidation and interlinking knowledge and communities amongst STS, (ii) deriving lightweight ontologies from STS, and (iii) establishing an STS environment to facilitate ontology building.

References

1. Hotho, A., Jäschke, R., Schmitz, C., Stumme, G.: Information Retrieval in Folksonomies: Search and Ranking. In: Sure, Y., Domingue, J. (eds.) ESWC 2006. LNCS, vol. 4011, pp. 411–426. Springer, Heidelberg (2006)
2. Specia, L., Motta, E.: Integrating Folksonomies with the Semantic Web. In: Franconi, E., Kifer, M., May, W. (eds.) ESWC 2007. LNCS, vol. 4519, pp. 624–639. Springer, Heidelberg (2007)
3. Kim, H.-L., Scerri, S., Breslin, J., Decker, S., Kim, H.-G.: The State of the Art in Tag Ontologies: A Semantic Model for Tagging and Folksonomies. In: International Conference on Dublin Core and Metadata Applications, Germany (2008)
4. Corcho, O., Fernández-López, M., Gómez-Pérez, A.: Methodologies, tools and languages for building ontologies: where is their meeting point? Data & Knowledge Engineering 46, 41–64 (2003)
5. Garcia, A., Gibson, F., O'Neill, K., Garcia-Castro, L., Corcho, O., Lord, P., Stevens, R.: The melting point, communities of practice developing ontologies. In: Chen, H., Wan, Y., Cheung, K. (eds.) Semantic e-Science, Annals of Information System. Springer, Heidelberg (2009)
6. Hepp, M.: Ontologies: State of the Art, Business Potential, and Grand Challenges. In: Springer (ed.) Ontology Management: Semantic Web, Semantic Web Services and Business Applications, pp. 3–22 (2007)
7. Gruber, T.: Grand Challenges for Ontology Design. ONTOLOG, vol. 2009 (2007), `http://ontolog.cim2003.net/cgi-bin/wiki.pl?ConferenceCall_2007_2003_2001` (retrieved March 15, 2009)
8. Almeida, A., Sotomayor, B., Abaitua, J., López-de-Ipiña, D.: Folk2Onto: Bridging the gap between social tags and ontologies. In: European Semantic Web Conference, Tenerife, Spain (2008)
9. Tang, J., Leung, H., Luo, Q., Chen, D., Gong, J.: Towards Ontology Learning from Folksonomies. In: International Joint Conference on Artificial Intelligence, Pasadena, CA, USA (2009)
10. van Damme, C., Hepp, M., Siorpaes, K.: FolksOntology: An Integrated Approach for Turning Folksonomies into Ontologies. In: European Semantic Web Conference - Workshop Bridging the Gap between Semantic Web and Web 2.0, Austria (2007)
11. Angeletou, S., Sabou, M., Motta, E.: Semantically Enriching Folksonomies with FLOR. In: European Semantic Web Conference - Workshop on Colletive Intelligence and the Semantic Web, Tenerife, Spain (2008)

12. Golder, S.A., Huberman, B.A.: Usage patterns of collaborative tagging systems. Journal of Information Science 32, 198–208 (2006)
13. Passant, A.: Using Ontologies to Strengthen Folksonomies and Enrich Information Retrieval in Weblogs: Theoretical background and corporate use-case. In: International Conference on Weblogs and Social Media, USA (2007)
14. Kim, H.-L., Breslin, J., Yang, S.-K., Kim, H.-G.: Social Semantic Cloud of Tag: Semantic Model for Social Tagging. In: Nguyen, N.T., Jo, G.-S., Howlett, R.J., Jain, L.C. (eds.) KES-AMSTA 2008. LNCS (LNAI), vol. 4953, pp. 83–92. Springer, Heidelberg (2008)
15. Mika, P.: Ontologies Are Us: A Unified Model of Social Networks and Semantics. In: Gil, Y., Motta, E., Benjamins, V.R., Musen, M.A. (eds.) ISWC 2005. LNCS, vol. 3729, pp. 522–536. Springer, Heidelberg (2005)
16. Gruber, T.: Ontology of Folksonomy: A Mash-up of Apples and Oranges. International Journal on Semantic Web & Information Systems 3 (2007)
17. Newman, R.: Tag Ontology Design, vol. 2009 (2004), `http://www.holygoat.co.uk/projects/tags/` (retrieved February 16, 2009)
18. García-Castro, L.J., Hepp, M., García, A.: Tags4Tags: Using Tagging to Consolidate Tags. In: Bhowmick, S.S., Küng, J., Wagner, R. (eds.) Database and Expert Systems Applications. LNCS, vol. 5690, pp. 619–628. Springer, Heidelberg (2009)
19. Passant, A., Laublet, P.: Meaning of A Tag: A Collaborative Approach to Bridge the Gap Between Tagging and Linked Data. In: International World Wide Web Conference - Linked Data on the Web Workshop, China (2008)
20. Tanasescu, V., Streibel, O.: Extreme Tagging: Emergent Semantics through the Tagging of Tags. In: International Workshop on Emergent Semantics and Ontology Evolution, Korea (2007)
21. Sabou, M., d'Aquin, M., Motta, E.: SCARLET: SemantiC relAtion discoveRy by harvesting onLinE onTologies. In: Bechhofer, S., Hauswirth, M., Hoffmann, J., Koubarakis, M. (eds.) ESWC 2008. LNCS, vol. 5021, pp. 854–858. Springer, Heidelberg (2008)
22. Knerr, T.: Tagging ontology- towards a common ontology for folksonomies, vol. 2009 (2006), `http://tagont.googlecode.com/files/TagOntPaper.pdf` (retrieved November 5, 2009)
23. van Damme, C., Hepp, M., Siorpaes, K.: FolksOntology: An Integrated Approach for Turning Folksonomies into Ontologies. In: European Semantic Web Conference - Workshop Bridging the Gap between Semantic Web and Web 2.0, Austria (2007)
24. Braun, S., Schmidt, A., Walter, A., Nagypal, G., Zacharias, V.: Ontology Maturing: a Collaborative Web 2.0 Approach to Ontology Engineering. In: International World Wide Web Conference - Workshop on Social and Collaborative Construction of Structured Knowledge (CKC), Canada (2007)
25. Golov, E., Weller, K., Peters, I.: TagCare: A Personal Portable Tag Repository. In: International Semantic Web Conference, Karlsruhe, Germany (2008)
26. Sharif, A.: Combining ontology and folksonomy: an integrated approach to knowledge representation. In: World Library and Information Congress (IFLA General Conference and Assembly), Milan, Italy (2009)
27. Gracia, J., Trillo, R., Espinoza, M., Mena, E.: Querying the Web: A Multiontology Disambiguation Method. In: International Conference on Web Engineering, USA (2006)
28. Sabou, M., d'Aquin, M., Motta, E.: Using the Semantic Web as Background Knowledge for Ontology Mapping. In: International Semantic Web Conference - Workshop on Ontology Matching, Grecia (2006)

29. Yeung, C.A., Gibbins, N., Shadbolt, N.: Understanding the Semantics of Ambiguous Tags in Folksonomies. In: International Workshop on Emergent Semantics and Ontology Evolution, Korea (2007)
30. Shakya, A., Takeda, H., Wuwongse, V.: StYLiD: Social Information Sharing with Free Creation of Structured Linked Data. In: World Wide Web Conference - Workshop on Social Web and Knowledge Management, China, pp. 33–40 (2008)
31. Siorpaes, K., Hepp, M.: myOntology: The Marriage of Ontology Engineering and Collective Intelligence. In: European Semantic Web Conference - Workshop Bridging the Gap between Semantic Web and Web 2.0, Austria (2007)
32. Garcia-Silva, A., Szomszor, M., Alani, H., Corcho, O.: Preliminary Results in Tag Disambiguation using DBpedia. In: International Conference on Knowledge Capture - Workshop on Collective Knowledge Capturing and Representation, Redondo Beach, CA, USA (2009)
33. Oren, E., Möller, K.H., Scerri, S., Handschuh, S., Sintek, M.: What are Semantic Annotations (2006)

QuiKey – An Efficient Semantic Command Line

Heiko Haller

Forschungszentrum Informatik (FZI), Germany
heiko.haller@fzi.de

Abstract. QuiKey is an interaction approach that offers interactive fine grained access to structured information sources in a light weight user interface. It is designed to be highly interaction efficient for searching, browsing and authoring semantic knowledge bases as well as incrementally constructing complex queries. Empirical evaluation using a comparative GOMS Analysis and a user study confirm interaction efficiency.

1 Introduction

Many knowledge management systems, especially those which rely on highly structured information and meta data being entered and maintained by users, fail because users do not make this additional effort. This may be one of the reasons why semantic technologies have, so far, not found widespread use in knowledge management systems, although semantic meta data would undoubtedly improve findability, interoperability and, in general, automated processing of information and knowledge items. QuiKey is a user interface concept that provides a light-weight, generic tool for searching, browsing and editing structured information in a fine-granular way. Additionally, and in the same interaction paradigm, QuiKey allows the construction of simple semantic queries as well as combining these simple queries to more complex ones in a step-by-step manner. QuiKey's main design goal is efficient interaction. It is targeted to cover the following use cases: targeted search of information (e.g. someone's phone number or someone's girlfriend's e-mail address), fast information entry (e.g. adding a new contact and linking her to an existing project), text search, formulating simple queries (e.g. all members of a certain project), set-based browsing [1] (explained in Section 2.2) and incrementally constructing complex queries (e.g. getting a list of members of projects financed by the EU that live in Portugal).

This paper describes the interaction design of QuiKey, and its current prototypical open source implementation together with a twofold evaluation study to substantiate its claims.

2 Design

The primary design goal of QuiKey was to make interaction as efficient as possible. Everything should be done with the least interaction effort necessary. While interaction efficiency is generally desirable, it is even more crucial for mobile

P. Cimiano and H.S. Pinto (Eds.): EKAW 2010, LNAI 6317, pp. 473–482, 2010.

devices where typing is usually cumbersome. The secondary design goal was, to have a minimalistic screen design that is also suitable for constrained screen space like in mobile devices.

The following principles have guided the interaction design of QuiKey:

- Everything can be done with the keyboard alone. While mouse interaction is always possible, it is never required. This avoids unnecessary costly switches between input media (also referred to as "homing" in user interaction literature [2]).
- There is only one mode for everything. Searching, browsing, authoring and querying is all done in the same consistent way of interaction.
- Short feedback cycles to reduce error-proneness. All parts of a complex interaction (items, relations, query operators and such) are implicitly or explicitly selected from lists of existing things, and the structure of the current operation is reflected visually. Like this, misspellings or syntax errors are greatly avoided and if they occur they are easy to notice.

Fig. 1. Text Search: A number of items is shown that match the search string "love me"

QuiKey is organized around the notion of *parts*. A part can be an existing item, a relation, a new text string or a command. Depending on the types and order of the parts entered, it is decided what action to take. The following are the main functionalities of QuiKey. As explained below, they are tightly interwoven.

2.1 Text Search

The simplest functionality that is also usable without any understanding of the structure of semantic knowledge models, is full text search. While search terms are entered, a list or ranked results is displayed based on a set of matching rules explained below. The best hit is preselected, so any item can be addressed by mere text entry without the need to use any special keys for syntax elements or selection. Of course, other items can also be selected via arrow keys or mouse. The following ordered list of ranking principles determines the ranking of text search results in QuiKey:

- a perfect match between search string and item text is best
- matching the beginning of an item is better than matching it anywhere else
- matching full words is better than matching a prefix only
- matching prefix is better than matching an arbitrary substring only
- matching the complete, coherent search string is better than matching single search words separately
- matching several search words in the right order is better than random order

This text search functionality is used throughout QuiKey wherever an item, relation type or such needs to be identified and it is one of the reasons that make QuiKey efficient. For example, to bring the item "Michael Jackson" to the top position out of 43270 named entities, it suffices to type "m jac".

2.2 Browsing

Starting with an item selected by text search, a user can navigate the knowledge base through its graph structure hop by hop by hitting the tab key.

When an item is jumped to, all corresponding statements (triples) about this item are displayed – sorted by relation types. When an item and a relation are selected (e.g. Madonna→has genre)[1], all statements matching this pattern are displayed as in Figure 2. From there, any statement can be selected to jump to the target object of the statement (in our example a particular album). Like this, a user can browse from entity to entity with the pattern *item→relation→item→relation→item...* (e.g. `Madonna`→`has album`→`Like a Virgin`→`has genre`→`Pop music...`).

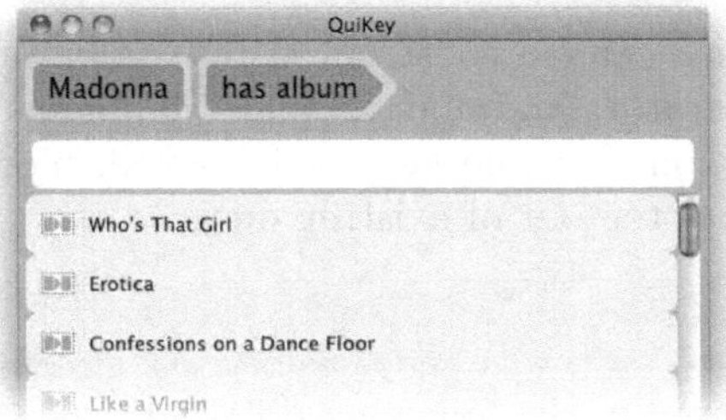

Fig. 2. Browsing: A list of all albums of madonna is shown after selecting the item "Madonna" and the relation type "has album"

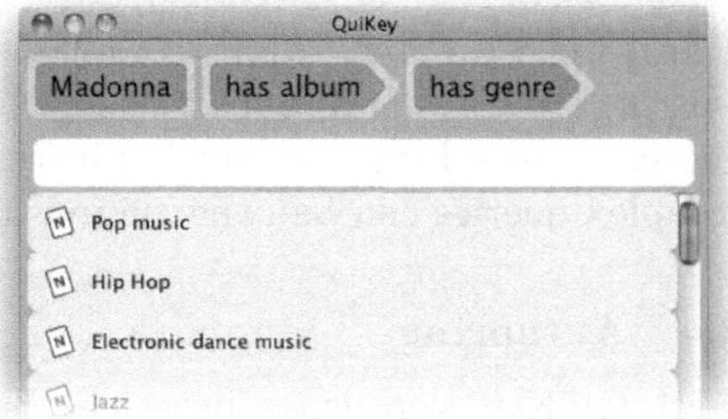

Fig. 3. Set-based browsing: A list of all genres of all albums of madonna is shown

Set Based Browsing. It is also possible to browse from sets of items to related sets by using the pattern *item→relation→relation...* For example, `Madonna`→`has album`→`has genre` would give a list of all genres of all albums of Madonna as in Figure 3.

[1] The arrow symbol →is used here to separate input parts, which is done with the tab key in QuiKey.

2.3 Queries

Constructing complex, possibly nested, queries over structured or semi-structured data with a text-based query language (like querying an RDF [3] graph with SPARQL [4] or formulating ASK Queries in Semantic MediaWiki [5]) is difficult: every slight syntax error or misspelling makes the whole query fail or (worse) return unintended results. And there is usually no feedback as to where the error lies because complex queries are formulated and evaluated as a whole only. QuiKey tackles these two common problems:

(1) Misspellings and syntax errors. are largely avoided because instead of requiring the user to write a whole query in some complicated syntax, in QuiKey, simple queries are constructed by browsing interactively, selecting from existing items and without the need of syntactical characters.
(2) To facilitate modular construction of complex queries. in a step-by-step manner, each query can be saved and referred to as a special query item:

Saving Queries. In QuiKey, like in facetted browsing, the border between browsing and query construction is blurred. In fact, the two above browsing examples already form semantic queries. Such simple queries can be persisted by inserting a name, under which the query should be saved, in the respective position of the pattern as a placeholder – prefixed by a question mark. For example: `Madonna→has album→?Madonna's albums` would save a new query item named "Madonna's albums" that represents all of madonna's albums. The placeholder does not need to be in the last position, e.g., the pattern `?Madonna's Genres→is genre of→is album of→Madonna` would save a query item representing all genres of all albums of Madonna.

Complex Queries. More complex queries can be constructed by combining existing saved queries with the logical operators `and` and `or` (e.g. Madonnas's genres→and→Jacko's genres). Since also complex queries can be saved, more complex queries can be constructed step by step out of existing ones.

2.4 Authoring

With QuiKey, knowledge bases can be altered in the following different ways:

Adding Items. To add a new text item to the knowledge base, it is enough to just type the text and press enter.

Adding Statements. To make statements about existing items, the statement can be entered in a subject→predicate→object pattern, separated by tab-keys. So, for example, `Michael Jackson→has album→This Is It` would add this statement to the knowledge model. Only that the user would not even have to type in the whole labels because parts that are already known can be chosen from the suggestions list while typing in auto-completion manner. So, for this example, it is actually enough to type in `m jac→h albu→This Is It`.

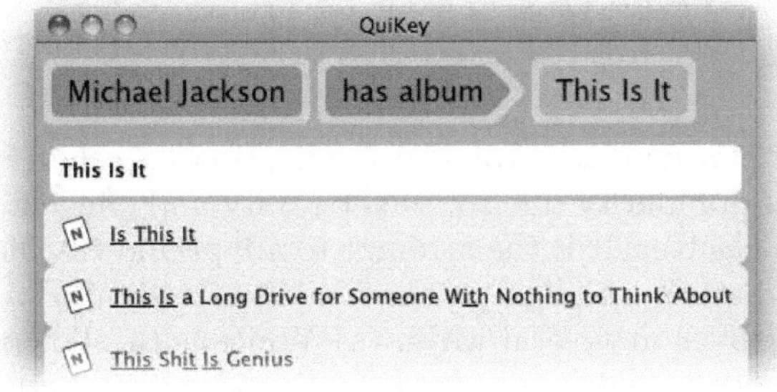

Fig. 4. Adding Several Objects: A new item "This Is It" is about to be created together with the statement that it is an album of Michael Jackson

Adding Items and Statements Together. If not all three parts in such a statement are known objects, the respective items or relation types are also added to the knowledge base. So, in the above example, if "This Is It" is not a known item, it would directly get created, together with the statement that it is an album of Michael Jackson. To avoid accidentally creating new items instead of reusing existing ones, the respective part is highlighted in yellow during interaction, i.e. before the action is executed. This can bee seen in Figure 4.

3 Implementation

QuiKey was initially developed as part of the semantic desktop project nepomuk[2]. For more information on semantic desktop systems in general, see [6] and [3]. While the QuiKey approach could be used with any kind of graph-based knowledge base, the current implementation uses a back-end and data model called CDS (Conceptual Data Structures) that has also been developed in the nepomuk project. The Java based CDS-API also features an in-memory inverted sub-string index, that serves QuiKey's text search functionality. The preliminary set of matching items is then ranked by quikey according to the matching rules described in Section 2.1. For performance reasons, the search depth of QuiKey's matching rules can be adjusted by the user. However, even with all rules enabled, text searches with up to 4 search words are executed well below one second on a knowledge base with 43270 items on a 2.4 GHz Intel core duo processor – with up to 3 search words, results are usually perceived as instantaneous. Since the expressiveness of neither CDS nor QuiKey's queries exceeds EL++[7], there could also be optimized implementations that scale to very large knowledge bases without slowing down user experience. For more information about CDS, see [8].

QuiKey's current open source implementation is based on Java/Swing. Today, QuiKey is deployed to complement iMapping, a visual knowledge workbench [9] that is also based on CDS and developed in nepomuk. For more information about iMapping and to get the latest version of both iMapping and QuiKey, see `http://imapping.info/`.

---

[2] `http://nepomuk.semanticdesktop.org`

[3] `http://semanticdesktop.org`

4 Related Work

4.1 Quicksilver

Quicksilver[4] by Nicholas Jitkoff is a kind of advanced application launcher for the Mac that has gained a lot of popularity due to its versatility and efficiency. QuiKey is mainly inspired by quicksilver. It is the attempt to adapt and transfer quicksilver's highly efficient interaction paradigm to the semantic desktop. However, QuiKey differs from Quicksilver in several ways: (a) While both allow to browse structured information models, Quicksilver is for finding and acting upon certain desktop objects. QuiKey is a generic authoring and query tool for graph-based knowledge bases. (b) Quicksilver matches the letters of the search string entered in the exact order only. It does not distinguish separate search words and will e.g. not match "Ontology Web Language" to "Web Ontology Language".

4.2 Parallax

Parallax by David Huynh [1] is probably the most convenient user interface to date to explore large amounts of structured data. Parallax is an experimental front end to Freebase[5], a website that offers a large amount of open structured data. A video that is also embedded in the parallax home page[6] nicely explains the benefits of semantic search in general and parallax in particular. It features the notion of set-based browsing, where navigation takes place from one set of things to another related set of things (e.g. from Michael Jackson's albums to their genres). It partly addresses the same use cases as QuiKey (querying large graph based knowledge bases through navigation), and features a visually much richer user interface (many navigation options per view, picture content, thumbnail previews, et c.).

5 Evaluation

The main claim of QuiKey's interaction design, to be highly interaction efficient, has been evaluated in two phases: First, in a comparative interaction analysis according to the KLM-GOMS method, where QuiKey has been measured against Semantic MediaWiki and parallax. Second, in a user study, where actual interaction times have been measured for QuiKey in order to validate the outcomes of the GOMS analysis. To that end, a set of tasks has been defined, by means of which the respective tools could be compared.

5.1 Tasks and Data

The goal that was chosen as a basis for the evaluation, was to construct a conjunctive query that yields the answer to the question *Which musical genres do*

[4] Original homepage: `http://blacktree.com/?quicksilver`
[5] `http://www.freebase.com/`
[6] `http://www.freebase.com/labs/parallax/`

Madonna and Michael Jackson have in common?. This goal fulfills the following requirements: (a) It can be decomposed into single steps that cover a wide range of QuiKey's functionalities (searching for items, browsing their properties, constructing simple and complex queries and adding new items). (b) It is comparable to other tools that offer similar functionality. (c) It is easy to understand because the musical domain is common knowledge. (d) A large amount of structured data is publicly available. In fact, an export from freebase of the music domain has been taken (artists, albums, genres etc.). It was filtered down to yield a data set of 26115 items that was highly interconnected to allow for complex semantic queries but small enough to run smoothly with the current CDS back end which was designed to handle personal knowledge management data fast and in memory rather than large imported data sets.

This goal can be broken down to the following sub-tasks:

1. Find out what albums Madonna has made. (text search, browse)
2. Find out what genres these albums have. (browse set)
3. Save this as a persistent query. (save query)
4. Do the same (1–3) for Michael Jackson.
5. Intersect these two saved queries. (construct complex query)

These sub-tasks have been used for comparison in the GOMS analysis and the user study.

5.2 GOMS Analysis

KLM-GOMS is a method developed by Card, Moran & Newell [2] to estimate the time it takes a user to complete simple interactive tasks using a keyboard and mouse[7]. This was done for each of the three tools. Once for the most efficient way the tool could theoretically be used for the task and once for the typically expected way (e.g. query code was formatted with white space, query names were more verbose ("Jacko genres" instead of "MJgen") and search words were spelt out instead of only to the point necessary.

The tools that were chosen for comparison are Semantic Mediawiki[8], [5] and parallax[9], [1]: Semantic MediaWiki with its ASK query language is probably the most widely used semantic knowledge modeling tool that also allows to construct complex and persistent queries. Parallax is probably the most convenient user interface to date to explore large amounts of structured data.

Results. The resulting estimates of interaction time needed are shown in Table 5.2. Unfortunately, in parallax it appears not to be possible to intersect existing queries or sets. Saving a current query also seems not to be possible. However a straight forward way how this would be done in parallax' interaction paradigm is apparent and so this way was guessed as an approximation. As can

[7] for an overview see `http://en.wikipedia.org/wiki/KLM-GOMS`

[8] `http://semantic-mediawiki.org/`

[9] `http://www.freebase.com/labs/parallax/`

Table 1. KLM-GOMS analysis for the sub tasks in comparison. Typically expected interaction and theoretically minimal paths of interaction are computed separately. Overall results for QuiKey are bolded for comparison with Table 2.

	SMW		**parallax**		**QuiKey**	
task	typical	minimal	typical	minimal	typical	minimal
one-time overhead per query	8.2	8.2	0	0	0	0
elementary query Madonna	13.2	13.0	10.8	10.8	7.5	6.1
elementary query M. Jackson	16.4	16.1	13.1	13.1	8.1	6.4
increment to chain query (x2)	18.3	17.2	7.2	6.6	3.5	2.9
increment to save (x2)	19.4	19.4	8.2	6.5	7.5	5.8
intersection query	21.0	21.0	n/a	n/a	10.7	7.6
overall time w/o intersection	113.2	110.4	54.8	50.3	**37.5**	**30.0**
overall time incl. intersection	134.2	131.4	n/a	n/a	**48.2**	**37.6**

be seen in Table 5.2, QuiKey is theoretically more interaction efficient than any of the two compared tools on any of the tasks. This means that, learnability, interaction styles and error-pronenes aside, it is theoretically possible to complete these tasks faster in QuiKey than in the other tools. What remains to be shown is that QuiKey can actually be *used* in this efficient way by real users:

5.3 User Study

In order to determine whether QuiKey can be used by real users as efficiently as it is designed to be, we let 16 testers perform the above defined set of tasks. All testers were familiar with semantic technologies in general. 3 of the testers were female, 13 male. The age of the testers ranged from 23 to 36. 14 of the 16 testers had never used QuiKey before and only one was already familiar with it.

Each tester went through the following process:

1. Short introduction to QuiKey: basic functionalities and interactions that are needed for the tasks were explained and demonstrated. Testers were asked to try out the interactions and explore the model and the tool until they feel confident in using it. (This took up to 8 minutes.)
2. A screen capture tool was started, that recorded screen content, audio, key strokes and the users via screen cam.
3. Testers were then asked to carry out the set of tasks. Instructions were given sequentially one by one, whenever the previous step was completed.

Later, keystrokes and interaction times were determined from the captured video with a precision of 18 frames per second.

Results. The mean number of keystrokes and interaction times are listed in Table 2 along with their confidence intervals[10]. The last column lists the minimal interaction times any user had needed to complete the task. Since these values come from different users they do not add up to the overall times. The overall

[10] http://en.wikipedia.org/wiki/Confidence_interval

Table 2. Mean times and key strokes needed for sub-tasks. (confidence intervals for p=.05%)

	keystrokes		measured time		
task	mean	±CI	mean	±CI	minimum
elementary query Madonna	10.8	±1.1	9.2	±1.2	4.8
elementary query M. Jackson	12.7	±1.9	8.9	±1.5	4.3
increment to chain query (x2)	7.6	±0.4	7.1	±0.8	3.2
increment to save (x2)	18.7	±2.6	8.7	±1.2	2.5
intersection query	20.1	±2.7	16.0	±3.1	8.1
cum. interaction time w/o intersection			**50.1**	±6.4	**31.8**
cum. interaction time incl. intersection			**66.1**	±9.1	**38.9**

minimum times instead reflect the time of the overall single fastest user. These minimum times are included in the table because they prove for each task how fast it *can* actually be done. Comparing the bolded values shows that the overall GOMS estimation of minimal interaction times were very close to the actual minimal times. This supports the GOMS estimations in general. Mean interaction times were somewhat longer than estimated for typical use. This may well be due to the fact that most of the testers were first time users. Also, during user testing it was noticed that search words were often spelt out completely instead of only to the extent needed (e.g. "Michael Jackson" instead of "m jac"). This is because users do not check results after every keystroke while typing known words. However in situations where keyboard interaction is more costly, like on mobile devices or touchscreens, for motion impaired users, or for long or unfamiliar words, the use of shorter search strings becomes more relevant.

6 Conclusion

Some of the claims, why the interaction approach of QuiKey is beneficial may be convincing by argument and some may be hard to prove in a lab study. But the the fundamental claim of interaction efficiency has been well confirmed through GOMS analysis and the user study.

Additional functionalities that are subject of future work include

- displaying short explanations about what a pattern means during interaction interacting, before it is executed, so the user knows what is going to happen and giving unobtrusive confirmations on actions completed,
- a way to interactively construct complex queries from scratch without the need to name and save intermediate queries,
- improving matching rules during use and automatically learning shortcuts for frequently used items,
- more expressive query operators including negation,
- history and undo
- using QuiKey as an additional front-end to Semantic MediaWiki
- developing a mobile version, where some of QuiKey's minimalist interactions have a bigger benefit, because typing is more costly.

Acknowledgements

This Work has partially been financed by the European Commission in the projects NEPOMUK (IST-FP6-027705) and MATURE (IST-FP7-216356). Special thanks go to Florian Simon for the implementation work of QuiKey.

References

1. Huynh, D., Karger, D.: Parallax and companion: Set-based browsing for the data web. Technical report, Metaweb, MIT (2009), `http://davidhuynh.net/media/papers/2009/www2009-parallax.pdf`
2. Card, S.K., Moran, T.P., Newell, A.: Psychology of Human-Computer Interaction. Lawrence Erlbaum, Mahwah (1983)
3. Manola, F., Miller, E.: Resource Description Framework (RDF) primer. W3C Recommendation (2004), `http://www.w3.org/TR/rdf-primer/`
4. Prud'Hommeaux, E., Seaborne, A.: Sparql. W3C Candidate Recommendation (June 2007)
5. Krötzsch, M., Vrandecic, D., Völkel, M., Haller, H., Studer, R.: Semantic wikipedia. Journal of Web Semantics 5, 251–261 (2007)
6. Sauermann, L., Kiesel, M., Schumacher, K., Bernardi, A.: Semantic Desktop. In: Blumauer, A., Pellegrini, T. (eds.) Social Semantic Web, pp. 337–362. Springer, X.media.Press, Heidelberg (2009)
7. Krötzsch, M., Rudolph, S., Hitzler, P.: Complexity boundaries for horn description logics. In: Proceedings of the 22nd AAAI Conference on Artficial Intelligence, Vancouver, British Columbia, Canada, pp. 452–457. AAAI Press, Menlo Park (2007)
8. Völkel, M., Haller, H.: Conceptual data structures for personal knowledge management. Online Information Review 33(2), 298–315 (2009)
9. Haller, H., Abecker, A.: Imapping – a zooming user interface approach for personal and semantic knowledge management. In: Toms, E., Bernstein, M., Millard, D. (eds.) Proceedings of the Hypertext Conference. ACM, New York (2010) (in Print)
10. Haase, P., Herzig, D.M., Musen, M., Tran, D.T.: Semantic wiki search. In: Aroyo, L., Traverso, P., Ciravegna, F., Cimiano, P., Heath, T., Hyvönen, E., Mizoguchi, R., Oren, E., Sabou, M., Simperl, E. (eds.) ESWC 2009. LNCS, vol. 5554, pp. 445–460. Springer, Heidelberg (2009)
11. Miller, G.A.: The magical number seven, plus or minus two: Some limits on our capacity for processing information. Psychological Review 63, 81–97 (1956)

Kali-ma: A Semantic Guide to Browsing and Accessing Functionalities in Plugin-Based Tools

Alessandro Adamou, Valentina Presutti, and Aldo Gangemi

Semantic Technology Lab, ISTC-CNR

Abstract. It is typical of plugin-based platforms such as the Eclipse RCP to be extensible by addition of functionalities. Such systems can undoubtedly benefit from having a vast developer community contributing to their enrichment. However, the proliferation of functionalities plugged in a system can be detrimental to its usability and bring confusion and clutter, as users who lack prior knowledge of the available features and how to access them can be unable to spot those that suit their needs.

We present Kali-ma, a tool that equips Eclipse-based ontology engineering platforms with a GUI that allows users to browse and access plugin functionalities. The Kali-ma interface is dynamically generated by matching installed plugins with ontologies that describe their capabilities in the Semantic Web. It can adapt to selected criteria for classifying tools, and its approach is portable across systems supporting other domains, such as software engineering and business process management.

1 Introduction

With ontologies becoming an established technology in the Semantic Web, several studies are being conducted on usability and quality aspects of user interaction with ontology tools, in an effort to address user-friendliness as a key requirement. From an analysis of existing ontology development tools such as the Protégé3[1], and their usage by seasoned ontology engineers, experts have reported a certain degree of intuitiveness, at the cost of complex support for visualization and operations that go beyond mere ontology editing [3,12].

One factor contributing to these usability-related drawbacks comes from the plugin-based nature of these ontology development tools, as are those that extend the Eclipse Rich Client Platform (RCP)[2]. While on one hand this approach is desirable for extensible software platforms, on the other hand it may lead to "creeping featurism", i.e. the uncontrolled proliferation of features in a software product. This may cause protracted or even aborted development schedules, and likely results in products that are overly complicated from the perspective of users with any level of expertise. Plugin-based platforms developed by large communities run remarkable risks of becoming feature creep. Third parties may provide their own additional functionalities, be they simple features e.g. support

[1] Protégé, `http://protege.stanford.edu/`

[2] Eclipse IDE and Rich Client Platform, `http://www.eclipse.org`

P. Cimiano and H.S. Pinto (Eds.): EKAW 2010, LNAI 6317, pp. 483–492, 2010.

for a certain file format, or full-fledged end-user tools running on top of the platform. They can do so at any time and remain agnostic as to how other parties are integrating their own functionalities on the user interface level. Thus, an instance of such a platform may appear to end-users as a mixture of different interpretations that each contributor gave of the user interface datamodel.

We provide here a threefold contribution: (i) a Semantic Web approach for re-organizing functionalities in plugin-based tools; (ii) a tool named *Kali-ma* that provides ontology platform users with a dashboard-like user interface for an overview of immediately accessible plugin-based functionalities; (iii) an evaluation of Kali-ma based on feedback from a sample of a community of practitioners.

With our Semantic Web approach (or Kali-ma approach), users can browse plugins as explicitly associated with *what can be done with them*, and select the one(s) they need based on this association. This method is independent on specific component containers, thus it can be applied to any plugin-based tool (cf. Section 3). It uses semantics in order to decouple the reasoning and interaction capabilities from the domain model, i.e. the representation of knowledge concerning the domain (product lifecycle management, software engineering, business modeling, ontology lifecycle management etc.) supported by a plugin-based tool.

As a proof-of-concept, we present *Kali-ma*[3], a tool that provides NeOn Toolkit (NTK)[4] users with a dashboard for managing their interaction with functionalities provided through plugins[5]. Kali-ma is itself a semantic tool, since it applies the semantic approach mentioned above. It uses an ontology network that describes the ontology design domain, namely *codolight* and its extensions, in order to classify plugins in terms of customizable design-related criteria, and make users benefit from such classification when browsing and accessing the plugins available in their running instance of the NTK. Plugin descriptions are published on the Web in the form of OWL ontologies[6], which are dynamically aggregated by Kali-ma at runtime. The approach can be applied to other platforms supporting ontology design such as Protégé3, Protégé4 and TopBraid[7]. Furthermore, it can be also ported across different domains by replacing its ontological component with adequate ontologies for the specific supported domain.

The next section introduces existing semantic approaches for organizing or interacting with data and software components. Section 3 introduces the cross-platform and cross-domain approach, while Section 4 describes how this is applied to the context of ontology engineering in the NeOn Toolkit. Before concluding and anticipating future work, Section 5 provides an insight on the preliminary user-based evaluation that led to the current version of the Kali-ma tool.

---

[3] In the rest of the paper, by *Kali-ma* we refer to the tool, while we explicitly indicate it when we refer to the *Kali-ma approach*.

[4] An extensible ontology lifecycle management platform, `http://www.neon-toolkit.org`

[5] The NeOn Toolkit was subsequent to [4] but it is implemented as a plugin-based tool, hence it suffers from what we want to address with the Kali-ma approach.

[6] For simplicity, we do not distinguish between ABox and TBox and just use the term "ontology" for addressing both the assertional and terminological components.

[7] TopBraid, commercially available at `http://www.topquadrant.com`

2 Related Work

The concept of “semantic user interface” has seen a multitude of different interpretations. The most prominent one is the development of GUIs for browsing the Semantic Web, annotating data in a local environment with machine-readable metadata, or filtering the annotated data for user manipulation. The Kali-ma approach is merely tangential to these aspects, as it concentrates on customizing the GUI based on semantic properties of the underlying domain model.

In the field of *Semantic Desktops*, the **Haystack** project [9] delivered an RDF-based personal information manager, which uses a declarative ontological approach to define layout constraints for interface objects. However, Pietriga et al. argue [8] that declarative approaches, being tightly bound to specific representation paradigms, are hardly portable across widget toolkits. In response, they proposed the **Fresnel** RDF vocabulary for application-independent data presentation, possibly the most mature proposal to date. Fresnel-based rendering engines are implemented in numerous recent RDF browsers today.

The **NEPOMUK** project delivered an open-source specification of a cross-platform, language-independent framework for Social Semantic Desktops [6]. In its presentation layer, user interfaces are provided on-the-fly for each service on the NEPOMUK desktop, which is seamlessly bridged with third-party applications by means of add-ons and plugins. Demonstrators for KDE and Eclipse RCP are reference implementations of parts of the NEPOMUK specification.

Aside from interaction, the field of software engineering has brought significant and diverse research work. The **Treaty** framework [1] provides an infrastructure for the runtime assembly of OSGi components in an Eclipse RCP environment. Its use of semantic technologies focuses on an extensible OWL vocabulary of Java types for identifying interfaces and unit tests for executing and validating component contracts. Kali-ma relies instead on higher semantic abstraction for classifying plugins, although work is being done for the construction of dynamic component pipelining, which grounds semantic plugin descriptions to the level of Java type checking. As for project lifecycle management, the work presented by Silva Parreiras et al. in [11] proposes the use of ontologies for model-driven software development. Another approach can be found in *Collaborative Protégé*3, a Protégé3-based tool supporting collaborative ontology design [10]. It uses an ontology that describes collaborative workflows for storing and querying metadata information during collaborative ontology design processes.

As for existing ontology engineering environments, we refer to the work done within the NeOn project [4], which carried out usability studies targeting ontology editors *Swoop*, *TopBraid*, *Protégé*3 and *Protégé*4. The resulting analysis has concluded that these tools lacked support for hastening repeated tasks and allowing users to customize the user interface by filtering unwanted or overly complex information. In other words, they proved to be *monotonic*, in that plugins only add new interface elements (tabs in Protégé, views, perspectives and menus in TopBraid etc.) that cannot be adequately filtered according to user needs. Kali-ma's effort to skim and simplify GUIs is based on these grounds.

3 A Cross-Platform Software Approach

The Kali-ma approach is based on representing a whole software component of the host platform as a network of ontologies. These instruct the host platform as to which of its own components should be taken into consideration when presenting functionalities to end-users, and how they relate to each other and to the activities that are performed in managing the lifecycle of a resource.

The size and complexity of this *ontological subsystem* are affected by three factors: *(i)* the desired granularity for representing the engineering domain that the software platform in question addresses; *(ii)* the amount of functionalities and plugins to be classified; *(iii)* the amount of criteria that engineers may wish to choose from when classifying available plugins, and the complexity of rules that encode these criteria. Following this intuition, we can group the required ontologies into three interconnected components.

The **engineering domain model** is an ontology that describes the notions that occur in the design and management of resources involved in the engineering processes supported by the platform. This component addresses the need for formalizing design tool descriptions in terms of input/output data (and the corresponding knowledge types handled), functionalities, interface objects and interaction patterns. Kali-ma makes a twofold usage of this model: first, plugins are formally described in terms of it; second, they are automatically classified based on rules and user preferences. It is at the discretion of knowledge engineers to establish which concepts in this domain model should be developed in depth and which existing domain or foundational ontologies, if any, should be reused. In the case of our Kali-ma tool for ontology design, we have opted for the *codolight* ontology network, which will be further described in the next sections.

Plugin descriptions are plugin-specific OWL modules, each describing what types of task a certain plugin can help accomplish, what types of knowledge representation it can handle, and so on. These modules depend on and reuse parts of the engineering domain model, namely (at a minimum) the classes and properties that define the knowledge processed in input and output by software components, and supported design functionalities. An OWL plugin description does not necessarily *assert* what categories a plugin should belong to when classified: if it does not, it should then instantiate all the required relations that would allow a DL reasoner to *infer* additional categories. These ontologies are located anywhere in the Semantic Web and aggregated at runtime. The means to aggregate them and maintain pointers to them are arbitrary, but in our proof-of-concept we use a description registry which is itself encoded in OWL.

Classification criteria and rules instruct software agents, such as OWL managers and DL reasoners, as to which categories should be considered for classifying tools, and what relationships exist between these categories and aspects of the engineering domain defined above. In general, these criteria and rules should support any given set of plugin descriptions compliant with the domain model. A criterion is identified by an OWL object property, and its relation to plugins is either directly asserted by reusing a property from the domain model, or inferred from complex rules that combine more such properties. In the latter case, new defined classes and properties must be part of the classification criteria and rules component. In our proof-of-concept, we will define three criteria for ontology design: one inherited directly from the domain model, one with a flat set of simple categories defined *ex-novo*, with no reasoning required, and one with a complex set of rules from which the appropriate categories are inferred.

The ontologies described above are then treated in a similar fashion as dynamically linked software libraries, but since they are not hardcoded into the software itself (unless developers choose otherwise), they do not require any static recompilation. In addition, being encoded in OWL, the stated facts make sense in the outside world and can be semantically interpreted by other human and software agents, with no need for *a priori* knowledge of what tools to classify.

The ontological nature of this architectural component eases task-based plugin discovery, while staying faithful to software architecture principles, with the advantage of being entirely *cross-platform*. As such, this component is open not only to update, but also to replacement with ontologies that serve completely different purposes, granted that they are aligned with the specifications of the ontological subsystem. For example, software engineers may want to use the Kali-ma GUI to manage and interact with their Eclipse IDE and its plugins to perform tasks like modeling UML diagrams, performing unit tests, or actually writing code. This can be achieved by replacing ontological subsystem components with the following: (i) a model that describes the software engineering aspects, a fine example being *Seontology* [2]; (ii) descriptions of known Eclipse plugins for software engineering, based on this model; (iii) a set of rules that provide a taxonomy of defined classes for software engineering aspects.

When preserving the context of ontology engineering and migrating to another development environment, our approach still makes sense if the ontological component is retained. In our proof-of-concept, the domain model is aligned with the Protégé workflow ontology [10] and other formal models for ontology design. Thus, if Kali-ma is ported to this platform and ontological descriptions of Protégé plugins exist, it is possible to offer the Kali-ma GUI to Protégé users.

4 The Kali-ma Tool

The proof-of-concept to our proposed approach (cf. Section 3) comes as a piece of software named *Kali-ma*. Its main feature is to provide the NeOn Toolkit with an interaction mode that allows end-users to manage ontology project lifecycles easier and under the guidance of their preferred model for ontology design capabilities. By default, we offer a choice of three such models, to be described in Section 4.1. Kali-ma can be directly installed through the NTK update feature[8].

The Kali-ma user interface is a floating layer, called *dashboard*, on top of the standard NeOn Toolkit window (see Figure 1). By means of the dashboard, users have an overview of all plugins available within their running instance of

[8] Online documentation available at `http://stlab.istc.cnr.it/stlab/KaliMa/v1.0`

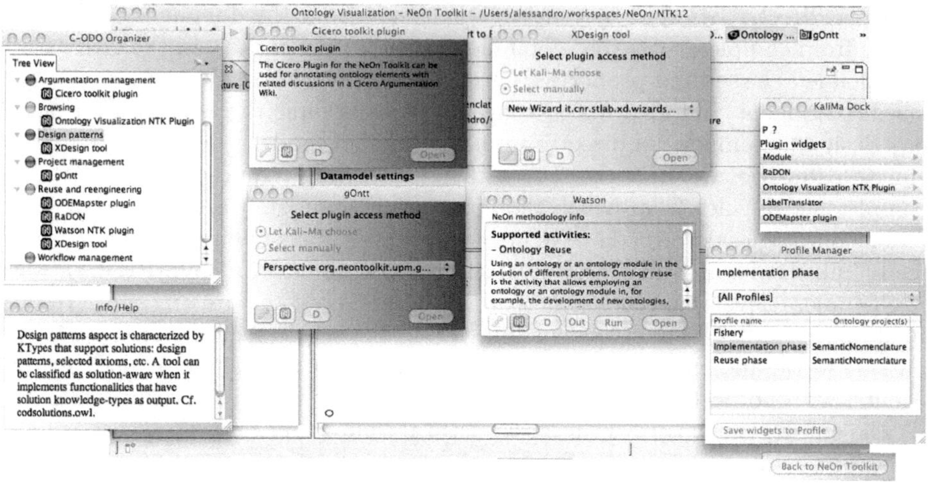

Fig. 1. The Kali-ma dashboard on top of the NeOn Toolkit window. Sorted by column, top to bottom then left to right: the *CODO organizer*; the *helper widget*; widgets representing the Cicero, gOntt, XDesign Tools, and Watson plugins; the *dock* with placeholders for five more plugin widgets; the *profile manager*; the NeOn Toolkit *switch*.

NTK, together with a description of them. The most relevant interaction aspect is the possibility to access such plugins without knowing or caring about the interaction path to launch a certain NTK plugin. Kali-ma takes the burden of hiding such interaction path and driving the user directly towards the interactive mode of the specific plugin, be it a single window, wizard or composite panel. This is achieved through widgets that represent installed plugins, an example being the four middle widgets depicted in Figure 1.

The dashboard also includes several utility widgets. The *CODO organizer* shows all available plugins classified by a selectable criterion, so that users can browse them and select the ones of interest. The *profile manager* allows the user to manage custom dashboard configurations, called profiles; such operations include saving a certain set of widgets and binding it to a certain project. The *helper* provides realtime information on the element (plugins, categories etc.) that the user is interacting with, i.e. as the user selects an element in the dashboard, the helper provides guidance on what it is and how to use it. The *dock* maintains placeholders for widgets that the user needs but does not wish to be visible at all times, thus allowing dashboard cleanup without having to edit the corresponding profiles. It is possible to switch between the dashboard view and the standard NTK interface view by one click at all times.

Kali-ma is a semantic tool, in that it is able to discover, categorize and access known NTK plugins by leveraging their OWL descriptions: plugin widgets are dynamically created at each new run of Kali-ma based on such OWL descriptions posted on the Web by plugin providers. In order to benefit from Kali-ma features, a plugin needs to have a description of itself on an online registry (whose location can be customized by the user), which itself is a minimalistic ontology.

4.1 Ontology Infrastructure and Reasoning

In this proof-of-concept, all parts of the the ontological subsystem proposed for the Kali-ma approach (cf. Section 3) are instantiated for the domain of networked ontology design and its application to the NeOn Toolkit software platform.

codolight[9] was our choice for the *engineering domain model* of ontology design. It is a lightweight networked ontology that addresses the need for formalizing ontology design tool descriptions in terms of input/output data (knowledge types), functionalities, interface objects and interaction patterns. Codolight is composed of nine modules: *kernel*, *data*, *projects*, *workflows*, *argumentation*, *solutions*, *tools*, *interaction*, and *interfaces*. An extensive description of these (rather intuitively labelled) modules can be found in [5]. For computational and social interoperability, *codolight* is aligned to several ontologies describing the Semantic Web: the Ontology Metadata Vocabulary [7], DOAP[10], the Software Ontology Model[11], Sweet Tools[12] and the Collaborative Protégé ontology [10].

To minimize the cost of annotating NeOn Toolkit plugins, we are providing a Web form for the semi-automatic generation of RDF code that describes plugins in *codolight*, hence called the *CODO-o-matic* service[13]. The Kali-ma tool is able to gather plugin descriptions via a description registry, which is a simple ontology containing mappings between individuals representing plugins and the physical URIs of the ontologies describing them. These URIs are declared as values for `rdfs:isDefinedBy` annotations on OWL individuals representing plugins.

We have identified three significant *classification criteria and rules* for ontology design, and made them selectable through the Kali-ma preferences:

1. *Design functionalities*, defined *ex-novo* by plugin providers as instances of the class `codo:DesignFunctionality`. This is the simplest criterion for plugin providers to support.
2. *NeOn activities*, part of the methodological guidelines defined by the NeOn Project for building networked ontologies. They are defined in an ontology that mirrors the glossary of activities in the NeOn Methodology [13]. Support for them is asserted explicitly by plugin providers and requires no inferencing. Experienced NTK users are more likely to be familiar with this criterion.
3. *Ontology design aspects*, six specialized design functionalities defined in the *designaspects* ontology as equivalent classes: a NTK plugin is classified as supporting one of these aspects by logical inferencing on the defined axioms.

Classification by the third criterion is the one that requires inferencing. Design aspects allow us to classify design tools into categories that are defined by the type of knowledge that is accepted in input, or produced in output. For example, the class of tools that allow to perform some reuse or reengineering of existing knowledge resources are defined as follows (in Manchester OWL Syntax):

---

[9] Codolight, `http://www.ontologydesignpatterns.org/cpont/codo/codolight.owl`
[10] Description Of A Project, `http://trac.usefulinc.com/doap`
[11] Software Ontology Model, `http://www.i.uzh.ch/ddis/evo/`
[12] Sweet Tools, `http://www.mkbergman.com/new-version-sweet-tools-sem-web/`
[13] CODO-o-matic, currently available at `http://150.146.88.63:8080/codomatic`

```
Class: ReuseReengineeringTool
EquivalentTo:
   (hasAspect value ReuseReengineering),
EquivalentTo:
   (codtools:implements some
      (specialization:specializes value ReuseReengineering)),
EquivalentTo:
   (codtools:hasInputType some ({coddata:DataStructureKType ,
      coddata:LinguisticKType , coddata:OntologyAxiomKType ,
      coddata:NetworkedOntologyKType , coddata:OntologyKType ,
      coddata:OntologyElementKType , [...] }))
    and
   (codtools:hasOutputType some (coddata:OntologyMappingKType,
      coddata:NetworkedOntologyKType , coddata:OntologyElementKType ,
      coddata:OntologyAxiomKType , coddata:OntologyKType , [...] }))
```

Per this formula, *something* is classified as a reuse or reengineering tool iff:

1. it is said to have that aspect as a value; or
2. it is said to implement a functionality that on its turn is said to be a specialization of the `ReuseReengineering` aspect; or
3. it has one or more values from a given list as input knowledge types, and one or more values from a given list as output knowledge types[14].

The third definition is of course the most important, since the first one is there to associate the aspect with the tool, and the second is there in case the aspect is conveyed by a functionality already associated with `ReuseReengineering`.

5 Evaluation

We have conducted a preliminary user evaluation, in order to understand the perception of the Kali-ma approach with respect to user needs emerged in [4] and tune implementation choices to improve usability. The users involved were 12 representatives of a community of practitioners, recruited for a three-day training course on ontology design with the NeOn Toolkit, and using Kali-ma during the second day. All users belonged to organizations approaching the use of Semantic Web technologies and facing the problem of designing ontologies. They can be classified as: software developers (2), software developers with some knowledge on Web ontologies (5), and information management officers (5). Participants filled a questionnaire[15] consisting of 47 items, mostly on a Likert scale[16], 12 of

[14] The rationale behind this rule is that the tool takes as input a certain knowledge resource, and includes in its output either the same knowledge resource (thus reusing it), or another type of knowledge resource (thus transforming, or *reengineering* it.)

[15] Available at `http://stlab.istc.cnr.it/documents/kalima/kalima_questionnaire.docx`

[16] The five-level scale ranged from 1 ("Strongly disagree") to 5 ("Strongly agree").

which aimed at evaluating usability and friendliness of Kali-ma interaction (e.g. "The Kali-ma interface includes elements I don't want to have around all the time."). Other items aimed at understanding user background (e.g. frequency of usage of ontology editors), familiarity and preferences for UI types, and collecting feedback for improvement. We proceeded to analyze the results as follows.

The 12 questions related to Kali-ma interaction had variable Likert polarity, in that agreement indicated positive judgement in some cases and negative judgement in others. We therefore normalized the scale polarity so that agreement always indicated positive feedback, in order to make responses comparable. The five Likert levels were then mapped to three groups: *negative*, *neutral*, and *positive*, in order to have a brief yet comprehensive indication of the results. We then computed the average number of "checks"[17] for each score and each question. These scores were compared to the expected values for a neutral distribution of scores, i.e. where the result indicates *no* positive or negative tendency. The actual distribution of the evaluation result deviated from the neutral distribution by 14,8% towards the positive score, which makes the result promising.

A deeper analysis of the scores and suggestions by the single groups established that most non-positive scores came mainly from software developers, while the group of information management officers (who represent our main target) gave mainly positive scores. Negative scores seem to depend partly on the familiarity of software engineers with the standard Eclipse-based interface, implying that they found the Kali-ma interaction method to be unusual in that context. This speculation was confirmed by informal discussions with testers after the evaluation session. Most suggestions were on how to improve interaction by adding: (i) realtime guidance, (ii) customization features and (iii) nicer graphic solutions. The current Kali-ma release includes solutions that address such aspects, namely: (i) the *helper* widget; (ii) customizable classification criteria; (iii) diverse icons and colors for distinguishing widgets based on their categories.

6 Conclusion

We have presented a semantic software approach for re-organizing and accessing functionalities in plugin-based tools. We have also developed and presented Kali-ma, an implementation of this approach for an ontology engineering platform.

Ongoing development is focused on further exploiting OWL plugin descriptions for pipelining functionalities by "design-by-contract" principles. Based on compatibility between output and input knowledge types handled by plugins, Kali-ma will allow their widgets to be concatenated into complex operations to be performed from within the widget UI itself. An implementation that relies on Java type-checking and the Eclipse RCP extension mechanism is already in place, and we are now working on lifting compatibility detection to high-level semantics. We also plan additional task-based user evaluation, where separate user groups are assigned tasks to perform with and without the aid of Kali-ma, in order to measure a possible improvement of the time needed to complete them.

[17] A check indicates that the user marked a Likert level that maps to a certain score.

Acknowledgements

The present work was carried out within the scope of the NeOn project for supporting the lifecycle of networked ontologies, `http://www.neon-project.org`

References

1. Dietrich, J., Jenson, G.: Components, contracts and vocabularies - making dynamic component assemblies more predictable. Journal of Object Technology 8(7), 131–148 (2009)
2. Dillon, T.S., Chang, E., Wongthongtham, P.: Ontology-based software engineering - software engineering 2.0. In: Australian Software Engineering Conference, pp. 13–23. IEEE Computer Society, Los Alamitos (2008)
3. Duarte, S.P., Pinto, H.S., Peralta, D.N., Mamede, N.J.: Using Protege-2000 in reuse processes. In: Proceedings of the OntoWeb-SIG3 Workshop at the 13th International Conference on Knowledge Engineering and Knowledge Management EKAW (2002)
4. Dzbor, M., Buil Aranda, C., Motta, E., Gómez-Pérez, J.M.: Analysis of user needs, behaviours and requirements on ontology engineering tools. Deliverable D4.1.2, NeOn project (2008)
5. Gangemi, A., Presutti, V.: The collaborative ontology design ontology (v2). Deliverable D2.1.2, NeOn project (2009)
6. Groza, T., Handschuh, S., Moeller, K., Grimnes, G., Sauermann, L., Minack, E., Mesnage, C., Jazayeri, M., Reif, G., Gudjonsdottir, R.: The NEPOMUK Project - on the way to the Social Semantic Desktop. In: Pellegrini, T., Schaffert, S. (eds.) Proceedings of I-Semantics 2007, JUCS, pp. 201–211 (2007)
7. Hartmann, J., Sure, Y., Haase, P., Palma, R., Suárez-Figueroa, M.C.: OMV – Ontology Metadata Vocabulary. In: Welty, C. (ed.) Ontology Patterns for the Semantic Web Workshop, Galway, Ireland (2005)
8. Pietriga, E., Bizer, C., Karger, D., Lee, R.: Fresnel: A Browser-Independent presentation vocabulary for RDF. In: Cruz, I., Decker, S., Allemang, D., Preist, C., Schwabe, D., Mika, P., Uschold, M., Aroyo, L.M. (eds.) ISWC 2006. LNCS, vol. 4273, pp. 158–171. Springer, Heidelberg (2006)
9. Quan, D., Huynh, D., Karger, D.: Haystack: A platform for authoring end user semantic web applications. In: Fensel, D., Sycara, K., Mylopoulos, J. (eds.) ISWC 2003. LNCS, vol. 2870, pp. 738–753. Springer, Heidelberg (2003)
10. Sebastian, A., Noy, N.F., Tudorache, T., Musen, M.A.: A generic ontology for collaborative ontology-development workflows. In: Gangemi, A., Euzenat, J. (eds.) EKAW 2008. LNCS (LNAI), vol. 5268, pp. 318–328. Springer, Heidelberg (2008)
11. Silva Parreiras, F., Staab, S., Pan, J.Z., Miksa, K., Kühn, H., Zivkovic, S., Tinella, S., Assmann, U., Henriksson, J.: Semantics for software modeling. In: Sheu, P., Yu, H., Ramamoorthy, C.V., Joshi, A.K., Zadeh, L.A. (eds.) Semantic Computing, p. 25. IEEE Press/Wiley (2008)
12. Storey, M., Lintern, R., Ernst, N., Perrin, D.: Visualization and Protege. In: Proceedings of 7th International Protege Conference (2004)
13. Suárez Figueroa, M., Gómez-Pérez, A. (eds.): NeOn Methodology: Scenarios for Building Networks of Ontologies (2008)

Constructing Understandable Explanations for Semantic Search Results

Björn Forcher[1], Thomas Roth-Berghofer[1,2], Michael Sintek[1], and Andreas Dengel[1,2]

[1] Knowledge Management Department, German Research Center for Artificial Intelligence (DFKI) GmbH Trippstadter Straße 122, 67663 Kaiserslautern, Germany
[2] Knowledge-Based Systems Group, Department of Computer Science, University of Kaiserslautern, P.O. Box 3049, 67653 Kaiserslautern
{first.lastname}@dfki.de

Abstract. MEDICO aims to develop an intelligent, robust, and scalable semantic search engine for medical images. The search engine of the MEDICO demonstrator RadSem is based on formal ontologies and designated for different kinds of users such as medical doctors or patients. An explanation facility integrated into RadSem justifies search results by showing a connection between query and result. The constructed explanations are depicted as semantic networks containing various medical concepts and labels. This paper addresses the tailoring of justifications to different kinds of users regarding such quality aspects as understandability or amount of information. A user experiment shows that under certain conditions the quality of justifications can be pre-estimated by considering the usage frequency of medical terms in natural language.[1]

Keywords: explanation, understandability, semantic search.

1 Introduction

The research project MEDICO aims (among other things) at developing an intelligent semantic search engine for medical documents and addresses different kinds of users, such as medical doctors, medical IT professionals or patients. The ultimate goal of the project [1] is to realize a cross-lingual and modality-independent search for medical documents, such as medical images or clinical findings Representational constructs of formal ontologies are used to annotate and retrieve medical documents. Currently, the MEDICO demonstrator RadSem [2] employs the Foundational Model of Anatomy (FMA) [3] and the International Classification of Diseases, Version 10 (ICD-10)[2].

[1] This research work was supported in part by the research program THESEUS in the MEDICO project, funded by the German Federal Ministry of Economics and Technology (01MQ07016). Responsibility for this publication lies with the authors.
[2] `http://www.who.int/classifications/apps/icd/icd10online`

P. Cimiano and H.S. Pinto (Eds.): EKAW 2010, LNAI 6317, pp. 493–502, 2010.

Since semantic search results are often hard to understand and not necessarily self-explanatory, explanations are helpful to support users. Medical IT professionals, for instance, may want to test the search engine. Here, explanations are interesting when the system presents unexpected results. It may turn out that the implementation or the used ontologies are incorrect. Hence, explanations can help to correct a system or improve it. By contrast, patients are not interested in the exact implementation of the search algorithm. Instead, they may want to learn something about the medical domain or to refine their search request.

For addressing these issues, we developed and integrated an explanation facility into RadSem that is used to justify search results by constructing a connection between search and annotation concepts. Justifications are depicted as semantic networks in an attempt to make search results more plausible for users. Finding a connection the facility also exploits the mentioned ontologies. Thus, the explanation contains several medical concepts and labels. As medical laypeople cannot associate any label with corresponding concepts a justification may not be understandable for all of them. By contrast, medical experts may prefer explanations that fit their professional language.

Understandable explanations are not necessarily useful explanations in case they are too general. The information content of the explanation must be able to satisfy the explanation need of the user whereas the explanation itself should not contain too much information [4].

In this paper, we describe our approach to construct tailored explanations regarding understandability for medical experts and laypeople. We propose a method which helps the explainer to assess the quality of alternative justifications in order to choose the best. A user experiment shows that under certain conditions the quality of justifications can be pre-estimated by considering the usage frequency of medical terms in natural language. The long-term goal of our work is to develop methods that help to derive general and specific user models that can be used in explanation components to construct suitable justifications.

The paper is structured as follows. The next section gives a short overview about relevant research on explanation generation. Section 3 describes briefly the semantic search engine RadSem and presents our work of constructing explanations. Section 4 contains our research about understandability of medical terms. Section 5 describes the user experiment and discusses our current approach that can be used for tailoring explanations to different user groups. We conclude the paper with a brief summary and outlook.

2 Related Work

Explanation facilities were important components of Expert Systems (ES) supporting the user's needs and decisions. Swartout and Moore formulated five desiderata for ES explanations that also apply for knowledge-based systems, among them *Fidelity* and *Understandability* [5]. Fidelity means that the explanation must be an accurate representation of what the ES really does. Hence, explanations have to build on the same knowledge the system uses for reasoning. Understandability comprises various factors such as *User-Sensitivity* and *Feedback*. User-Sensitivity addresses the user's goals and preferences but also his knowledge with respect to the system and the corresponding domain. Feedback is very important because users do not necessarily understand a given explanation. The system should offer certain kinds of dialogue so that users can inform themselves on parts they do not understand.

Wick and Thompson [6] developed the Reconstructive Explainer (REX), which implements the concept of *reconstructive explanations* for ES. REX transforms a trace, *i. e.*, a line of reasoning, into a plausible explanation story, *i. e.*, a line of explanation. The degree of coupling between the trace and the explanation is controlled by a filter that can be set to one of four states regulating the transparency of the filter. The more information of the trace is let through the filter, the more closely the line of explanation follows the line of reasoning. We took up the theme of (re-)constructing explanations in our current work.

3 Explanation Component of RadSem

MEDICO uses Semantic Web standards as representation formalism for domain knowledge and annotations. Medical ontologies such as the Foundational Model of Anatomy ontology (FMA) and terminologies such as the International Classification of Diseases, Version 10 (ICD-10) make up the MEDICO Ontology Hierarchy [7] covering various aspects of clinical data management and medical background knowledge. Biomedical ontologies and terminologies are useful for indexing medical data as studies show [8,9].

RadSem is a semantic annotation and retrieval prototype developed for MEDICO. It provides a simple search interface with an auto-completion mechanism that helps selecting appropriate ontological search terms. RadSem employs the structure of FMA and ICD-10 for searching the annotations of medical documents. For example, when searching for 'Hand' a radiograph may be returned annotated with the concept 'Distal Phalanx of Index finger'. In this case, RadSem leverages the part-of hierarchy of the FMA to find the image. Self-evidently, the subclass-of hierarchies are also used to find adjacent concepts and respective images. As FMA and ICD-10 are available in several languages annotating and searching are offered even across language boundaries.

For justifying retrieval results the explanation component reveals a connection between search and annotation concepts [10]. Since RadSem does not offer a trace the explanation component performs some kind of reconstructive explanation (Section 2). In this case, a search concept corresponds to the input and an annotation concept corresponds to output in the line of explanation, whereas the story in between is constructed by the explanation facility using the ontologies FMA and ICD-10 as knowledge base. Both ontologies are transformed into a semantic network, *i. e.*, a mathematical graph. Thus, constructing the line of explanation for semantic search in MEDICO can be reduced to a shortest path problem. We chose Dijkstra's Algorithm [11] to solve this problem assuming an equal distribution of edge path costs, *i. e.*, each property has the same cost.

Explanations (like any kind of knowledge) have two different aspects: form and content [12]. With respect to the *Understandability* desideratum we chose semantic networks as they are an understandable alternative to text [13] representing qualitative connections between concepts.

However, the component has two general problems. The first issue is with the generation itself. Dijkstra's Algorithm, by design, determines only one shortest path. Hence, potential alternative explanations are not found which may be better in a certain context with respect to different user groups. In addition, the path contains a certain number of concepts and thus, the amount of information is fixed. Potentially, the explanation path contains too much or too few information depending on path length. The second issue concerns the understandability of justifications. In particular the FMA provides several synonyms for labelling a concept. Currently, the explanation facility uses the *preferred label* to represent a certain concept in the explanation path. Most probably, not all users can associate the preferred label with a corresponding concept.

In the following section we present a theoretical framework to solve the second problem. For a given explanation path the framework is used for selecting appropriate labels regarding different user groups.

4 Understandability of Medical Terms

We developed a simple approach to improve understandability of semantic search results which is based on a past user experiment as presented in [10]. It emanates from the hypothesis that the degree of knowledge about medical terms correlates with the usage frequency in daily language [14]. The more often a (medical) term is used in natural language the more users 'know' that (medical) term, and, thus, the better understandable it is. In order to handle the usage frequency of terms in daily language a useful statistical measure are frequency classes. Let C be a text corpus and let $f(t)$ denote the frequency of a term $t \in C$. The frequency class $c(t)$ of a term $t \in C$ is $\lfloor log_2(f(t^*)/f(t)) \rfloor$, where t^* denotes the most frequently used term in C [15]. In many English corpora, t^* denotes the term 'the' which corresponds to frequency class 0. Thus, a more uncommonly used term has a higher frequency class. In the following, we refer to any frequency class $c(t) = i$ as c_i, whereas the maximum frequency class is denoted with c_{max}.

For evaluating the personal estimation of medical knowledge only German terms of FMA and ICD-10 consisting of one word were selected. For each frequency class $c_{th}, \ldots, c_{max}$ we selected a random set of terms of the same size. We considered only frequency classes at certain threshold c_{th} because all terms below are generally known. All selected terms were randomly subdivided into four tests each containing a varying number of frequency classes. Every test person had to estimate their knowledge about each term of exactly one test on a scale from 1 to 5 indicating their *Personal Knowledge Estimation* (PKE).

Two kinds of users participated in the experiment: medical experts and laypeople. Regarding laypeople, the experiment result confirms the hypothesis above. In contrast, the average PKE per term of medical experts is generally very high so that a trend could not be observed. However, the result of the experiment reveals an interesting problem concerning the flection of words in the German language. The term 'Zecken' (ticks) has a significantly lower frequency class as the base word 'Zecke' (tick) and thus, is more often used.

The main objective of the past experiment was not to verify a correlation between users' degree of knowledge and frequency classes. In fact, the intention was primarily to denote intervals of frequency classes as a means of prognosis whether user groups probably know a term or require supporting information. As medical experts are quite familiar with medical terms of the used ontologies we focus on medical laypeople in the following and consider experts again in discussion of Section 5. For that purpose, we defined a general function $p(c_i)$ that predicts the familiarity of terms belonging to the frequency class c_i. The function is based on 3 intervals of frequency classes representing a generalisation of the PKE scale. Handling the flection problem, we introduced the function $c_{min}(t)$ which determines first the stem of the term and then all inflected forms of the stem. The result of $c_{min}(t)$ is the minimum frequency class of all inflected forms. If $n, m \in N_0$ and if $n < m$, the function $p(c_i)$ is defined as follows:

$$p(c_\epsilon) = \begin{cases} \text{well known,} & \text{iff } c_0 \leq c_\epsilon < c_n \\ \text{in need of support,} & \text{iff } c_n \leq c_\epsilon < c_m \\ \text{completely unknown,} & \text{iff } c_m \leq c_\epsilon \leq c_{max} \end{cases}$$

With respect to the experiment results, the parameters for medical laypeople are $n = 15$ and $m = 21$. In this case, the term 'Hand' (hand) is a *well known* term, in contrast to the term 'Pemphigus' (pemphigus) which is probably a *completely unknown* term for most people.

In the experiment setting we only considered one-word terms. However, labels of the FMA comprise normally more than one word, such as 'Distale Phalange des Zeigefingers' (Distal phalanx of index finger). A simple assumption is that an average value of all words can be used to determine the familiarity of the whole concept label. But in this case, we face certain problems. First, stop words namely 'des' (of), have a very low frequency class which probably distort the average value. Second, medical terms consisting of several words may contain known and unknown words. In these cases it is not clear if all words influence the level of familiarity in the same way, for instance, 'Phalange' (phalanx) and 'Zeigefinger' (index finger). In a preliminary experiment we found out that only one word in a compound can influence the understandability significantly. Considering only the maximum frequency class in this context is not useful although it has a very strong impact. However, the problem is less serious the lower the distance between the highest and lowest frequency class is. Third, if a label contains multi-word expressions single words are not suitable to predict the level of familiarity. Consider the label 'The Lord of the Rings'. Probably all people know the single words but not all the corresponding concept. This is especially a problem in the English Language, but less problematic in the German Language.

For the described problems we implemented a function that predicts the level of familiarity of a label l consisting of several words or multi-word expressions. The function $p_{rms}(l, c_\phi, \sigma_c)$ is used by our explanation component to select the most understandable label if a prediction is possible. The function has two threshold parameters. c_ϕ is used to filter stop words. σ_c ensures that the maximum distance between frequency classes is not too big. The steps are as follows: (1) Detect all independent words and multi-word expressions of label l. The result is a set of terms $W_t = [w_{t1}, \ldots, w_{to}]$. (2) Remove all words $w_q \in W_t$ if $w_q < c_\phi$. The remaining set is $W_s = [w_{s1}, \ldots, w_{sp}]$. (3) Calculate the root mean square mean $\overline{x} = \frac{1}{p}(c_{min}(t_{s1}) + \ldots + c_{min}(t_{sp}))$. (4) Determine the standard deviation $\sigma = \sqrt{\frac{1}{p}\sum_{j=1}^{p}(c_{min}(t_{sj}) - \overline{x})^2}$. (5) If $\sigma > \sigma_c$ return result *unpredictable* else return $p(\overline{x})$.

We used the root mean square $rms_c(l, c_\phi)$ here to calculate the central tendency of a set of frequency classes in order to put emphasis on high frequency classes. Other average values such as median, geometric or harmonic mean may also be of interest. However, the function $max_c(l)$ is used in the following section to determine the maximum frequency class of all terms contained in l. In this case, a stop word threshold is not necessary.

5 User Experiment and Discussions

In the previous sections we described how we improved the quality of explanations by selecting understandable labels for ontological concepts. As mentioned before, besides understandability the amount of information also effects the quality of an explanation. As German is the mother tongue of the test persons and the FMA does not provide German labels for all concepts, we just consider the ICD-10 for the experiment. Corresponding experiments with the FMA are part of our future work.

The user experiment presented here has two goals. The first goal addresses the amount of information or the number of concepts in an explanation. Here, the question is, whether users favour the complete path between search and annotation concept or a shorter variant. This is not only a user-specific problem. For instance, in mobile applications the information presentation is limited so it must be shortened somehow. In the following we refer to concepts between search and annotation concept as bridging concepts. The second goal of the experiment aims to select an appropriate bridging concept. Our hypothesis is that we can adapt the approaches in Section 4 to determine which concept is the best bridging concept. As mentioned before, a concept label should not contain too common or too specific information. We think that a concept label should be a known label close to the *in need of support* limit regarding medical laypeople.

The experiment setting represents real explanation scenarios in RadSem regarding documents that are annotated with disease concepts of ICD-10. Hence, the test cases must fulfil two fundamental characteristics. First, the search concept must be at least *in need of support* because we assume that most RadSem users search only for familiar information. Second, the potential, retrieved document is annotated with at least one concept which is *in need of support.* Here, we focus on justifications for single annotation concepts and not for integrated justifications of all annotations. If users know the annotation concept there is not necessarily an *explanation need*. Finally, the search must be *explainable*. Thus, the explanation path must contain at least one intermediate concept.

In the experiment we considered paths with a length of four which is also the maximum path length regarding ICD-10. Although an explanation path can be much longer with respect to FMA, the proposed length covers most explanation cases of RadSem. The reason here is that RadSem uses a depth limit for its search algorithm to prevent a possible precision loss [16]. Hence, explanation paths much longer than four occur rarely. An exemplary test case is presented in Figure 1. The first concept corresponds to the search concept (magnifier symbol) and the last to the annotated concept (bitmap symbol). In the following we refer to the first concept as A, to the second as B, etc, and to the corresponding labels as l_A, l_B, etc.

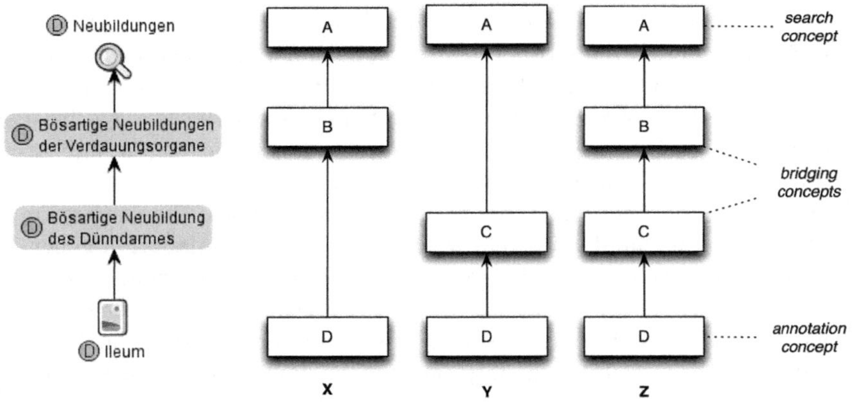

Fig. 1. Explanation Test Case (on the left). The explanation paths run from the search concept to the annotation (and, thus, found) concept via one or two bridging concepts.

For the experiment, we generated 50 distinct and random explanation paths including labels. We considered only labels with length 5 to 85 characters. The lower limit is intended to avoid abbreviations, the upper limit to avoid annoying labels which would probably falsify the test. We implemented the following conditions to generate possible explanation paths:

1. $max_C(l_D) \leq c_{max}$
2. $max_C(l_B) < c_{max}$ or $max_C(l_C) < c_{max}$
3. $max_c(l_A) + \delta_1 < max_c(l_D)$
4. $max_c(l_A) < +max_c(l_B) + \delta_2 < max_c(l_D)$ or $max_c(l_A) < +max_c(l_C) + \delta_2 < max_c(l_D)$
5. $\delta_1 < \delta_2$

All five conditions must be fulfilled for path generation. The first two conditions ensure that only labels are used where a frequency class is available in order to obviate the compound problematic. In the current setting we chose $\delta_1 = 2.5$ and $\delta_2 = 4.5$.

In the experiment, two variants of each selected explanation path Z are generated (Figure 1): variant X and Y. They are derived by either removing concept C or B, and by connecting B to D or connecting A to C respectively. Thus, a variant set contains X and Y and the full path Z. We constructed three test variants containing 50 explanation cases. Each test variant contains exactly 1 element of each variant set. Hence, a test variant contains a random number of path variants X, Y and Z.

In order to determine whether the explanation path is presented in a real explanation request the test persons have to state whether they know the first and the last concept. On a scale ranging from *good*, *rather good*, *middle*, *rather bad* to *bad*, we derived whether the test person would have requested the corresponding explanation. Only if a test person chooses *middle* or better for the first and *middle* or worse for the last concept, the case is used for the evaluation.

For obtaining the experiment goals the test persons have to rate the explanation. Here, we use the same scale as presented above. The rating indicates which path variants are preferred most. If test persons prefer exactly one bridging concept, the path variants X and Y together must be compared to Z. Finally, we compare the ratings of the path variants X and Y to the average frequency class of the bridging concept label. We assume a too low or a too high average frequency class to influence the explanation rating.

Finally, users can comment on the explanation cases. The intention was twofold: On the one hand, to reveal weak points in the explanation generation, and on the other hand to explain possible outliers in the experiment results.

In total, 30 test persons participated in the experiment. Each test variant was done as often as any other one and thus, the evaluation is based on 1500 rated explanation paths. We focused only on medical laypeople as medical experts should know most terms of ICD-10 (cf. Section 4). For that reason, we ensured that all tests persons did not have a profound medical qualification or knowledge.

To verify our hypotheses we evaluated the experiment as follows. For each path variant in each test variant we built the arithmetic mean of all corresponding ratings. We considered only those ratings in the calculation where test persons had an explanation need. For each variant set we chose the best rated variant and counted its frequency obtaining the following result: $X = 62\%$, $Y = 26\%$, $Z = 12\%$. Comparing X and Y to Z the test persons seem to prefer exactly one bridging concept.

Now the question is which path variant is probably the best one with respect to medical laypeople. In other words, the explainer needs a method to compare the quality of both variants X and Y. In case l_B is *known* and l_C is *unknown* path variant X is most likely the best one. However, consider a case in which both labels l_B and l_C are *in need of support*. It is suspected that the broader concept according to the ontology hierarchies is the better bridging concept. But a broader concept does not necessarily entail a lower average frequency class of its label, so that l_C may be better understandable than l_B. Hence, several cases must be considered to select the best path variant for medical laypeople. For this purpose, we use the frequency class border c_n between *known* and *in need of support* labels as additional decision criterion. The following listing describes all cases where $p_{rms}(l_B, c_\phi, \sigma_c) = p_{rms}(l_C, c_\phi, \sigma_c)$. In all other cases we choose the more understandable label and if there is no prediction possible due to σ_c we choose path variant Z.

1. If $quad_c(l_B, \sigma_c) \leq quad_c(l_C, \sigma_c) < c_{border}$ use l_C.
2. If $quad_c(l_C, \sigma_c) < quad_c(l_B, \sigma_c) < c_{border}$ use l_B.
3. If $c_{border} \leq quad_c(l_B, \sigma_c) \leq quad_c(l_C, \sigma_c)$ use l_B.
4. If $c_{border} \leq quad_c(l_C, \sigma_c) < quad_c(l_B, \sigma_c)$ use l_C.

The application of this method has the following result. In case $c_n = 15$ and $\sigma_c = 4.5$ there are 31 cases in which the level of familiarity can be pre-estimated. Here, the success of the proposed method is 77% in contrast to a random prospect of success of 50%.

So far, we considered only medical laypeople. Regarding medical experts, the shortening seems less complicated. As mentioned before, medical experts are familiar with almost all terms in the FMA and ICD-10. Hence, we propose to choose label l_C because it is the narrower concept in the ontology which probably more useful for medical experts. As said before this has not been evaluated yet.

In our experiment we describe a very specific setting as we considered only a maximum path length of 4. However, the experiment showed that a bridging concept is a useful mean to reduce the complexity of an explanation. In addition, it was not intended to determine the best possible explanation. Even a human teacher in school who knows his students cannot do that. Only a dialogue with explanatory character can help to solve the whole explanation need of users [17], and a bridging concept provides a suitable start for such an explanation dialogue.

6 Summary and Outlook

In this paper we presented the explanation facility of the MEDICO Demonstrator RadSem. It uses a kind of reconstructive explanations to justify semantic search results of RadSem. The justifications are constructed with two ontologies (FMA, ICD-10) and the shortest path algorithm of Dijkstra.

In order to improve the quality of constructed explanations we described a simple approach that enables the explanation component to shorten explanations for different kinds of users regarding understandability. The shortening method is based on the hypothesis that understandability can be pre-estimated by considering the usage frequency of medical terms in natural language. The method provides first hints for constructing suitable and understandable explanations which may also be used to derive more expressive user models.

The presented justification may not be the best for all targeted user groups. For this reason, users should be able to ask for a different justification using alternative paths, which need not necessarily be shortest paths. Furthermore, we plan to integrate further interaction and exploration functionality for realising more sophisticated dialogues between user and explanation component.

References

1. Möller, M., Sintek, M.: A scalable architecture for cross-modal semantic annotation and retrieval. In: Dengel, A.R., Berns, K., Breuel, T.M., Bomarius, F., Roth-Berghofer, T.R. (eds.) KI 2008. LNCS (LNAI), vol. 5243, pp. 391–392. Springer, Heidelberg (2008)
2. Möller, M., Regel, S., Sintek, M.: RadSem: Semantic annotation and retrieval for medical images. In: Aroyo, L., Traverso, P., Ciravegna, F., Cimiano, P., Heath, T., Hyvönen, E., Mizoguchi, R., Oren, E., Sabou, M., Simperl, E. (eds.) ESWC 2009. LNCS, vol. 5554, pp. 21–35. Springer, Heidelberg (2009)
3. Rosse, C., Mejino, J.L.V.: The Foundational Model of Anatomy Ontology. In: Anatomy Ontologies for Bioinformatics: Principles and Practice, vol. 6, pp. 59–117. Springer, Heidelberg (2007)
4. Richards, D.: Knowledge-based system explanation: The ripple-down rules alternative. In: Knowledge and Information Systems, vol. 5, pp. 2–25 (2003)
5. Swartout, W.R., Moore, J.D.: Explanation in second generation expert systems. Second Generation Expert Systems, 543–585 (1993)
6. Wick, M.R., Thompson, W.B.: Reconstructive expert system explanation. Artif. Intell. 54(1-2), 33–70 (1992)
7. Möller, M., Sintek, M.: A generic framework for semantic medical image retrieval. In: Proc. of the Knowledge Acquisition from Multimedia Content (KAMC) Workshop, 2nd International Conference on Semantics And Digital Media Technologies, SAMT (2007)
8. Marwede, D., Schulz, T., Kahn, T.: Indexing Thoracic CT Reports Using a Preliminary Version of a Standardized Radiological Lexicon (RadLex). Journal of Digital Imaging 21(4), 363–370 (2007)
9. Marwede, D., Fielding, J.M.: Entities and relations in medical imaging: An analysis of computed tomography reporting. In: Applied Ontology, vol. 2, pp. 67–79. IOS Press, Amsterdam (2007)
10. Forcher, B., Schumacher, K., Sintek, M., Roth-Berghofer, T.: Evaluating the intelligibility of medical ontological terms. In: Proceedings of the 5th Workshop on Knowledge Engineering and Software Engineering, KESE 2009 (2009)
11. Dijkstra, E.W.: A note on two problems in connexion with graphs. Numerische Mathematik 1, 269–271 (1959)
12. Kemp, E.A.: Communicating with a knowledge-based system. In: Brezillon, P. (ed.) Improving the Use of Knowledge-Based Systems with Explanation (1992)
13. Wright, P., Reid, F.: Written information: Some alternatives to prose for expressing the outcomes of complex contingencies. Journal of Applied Psychology 57(2), 160–166 (1973)
14. Hayes, D.P.: The growing inaccessibility of science. Nature 356, 739–740 (1992)
15. zu Eissen, S.M., Stein, B.: Intrinsic plagiarism detection. In: ECIR, pp. 565–569 (2006)
16. Hollink, L., Schreiber, G., Wielinga, B.: Patterns of semantic relations to improve image content search. Web Semantics: Science, Services and Agents on the World Wide Web 5(3), 195–203 (2007)
17. Du, G., Richter, M.M., Ruhe, G.: An explanation oriented dialogue approach and its application to wicked planning problems. Computers and Artificial Intelligence 25(2-3) (2006)

Ontology Engineering with Rough Concepts and Instances

C. Maria Keet

KRDB Research Centre, Free University of Bozen-Bolzano, Italy
keet@inf.unibz.it

Abstract. A scenario in ontology development and its use is hypothesis testing, such as finding new subconcepts based on the data linked to the ontology. During such experimentation, knowledge tends to be vague and the associated data is often incomplete, which OWL ontologies normally do not consider explicitly. To fill this gap, we use OWL 2 and their application infrastructures together with rough sets. Although OWL 2 QL is insufficient to represent most of rough set's semantics, the mapping layer of its Ontology-Based Data Access framework that links concepts in the ontology to queries over the data source suffice to ascertain if a concept is rough, which subsequently can be modelled more precisely in an OWL 2 DL ontology. We summarise the trade-offs and validate it with the HGT ontology and its 17GB genomics database and with sepsis, which demonstrates it is an encouraging step toward comprehensive and usable rough ontologies.

1 Introduction

It has been noted that scientist want to use ontologies together with data, such as hypothesizing that some subclass or relation exists and subsequently to validate this either in the laboratory or against the instances already represented in the knowledge base [1]. For such a putative new concept, one would want to be able to find those instances with the right combination of object and data properties, i.e., taking a 'guessed' collection of attributes that is subsequently experimentally validated against the data (e.g., [2]). Such guessing includes dealing with incomplete or otherwise *vague* data and information. Ideally, for all relevant individuals belonging to the putative concept, each value of the chosen properties is distinct, but this may not be the case due to the limited data or insufficiency of the selected properties so that some individuals are indistinguishable from each other and therewith instantiating a *rough concept* that represents the intensional aspects of the rough set. Despite the vagueness, it still can be useful in the ontology engineering process to include such a rough concept in the ontology

Hence, a *rough ontology* can be useful. To support such usage of ontologies, one needs a language with which one can represent, at least, rough concepts as the intensional representation of the corresponding rough set and a way to persistently relate the instance data to the rough concepts. Various extensions of Description Logics (DL) and OWL languages have been proposed for rough ontologies [3,4,5,6,7,8], which diverge in commitment as to which aspects of rough sets are included in the ontology language and they concern theory instead of demonstrating successful use of the rough ontology in ontology engineering. As it turns out, there is no perfect DL language, reasoner, and

P. Cimiano and H.S. Pinto (Eds.): EKAW 2010, LNAI 6317, pp. 503–513, 2010.

ontology development tool that does it all with respect to the semantics of rough sets, nor will there be if one adheres to the hard requirement of staying within the decidable fragment of first order logic, let alone within the tractable zone. However, some results can be obtained already: in addition to representing most of rough sets' semantics with the recently standardised OWL 2 DL, the linking to data and, moreover, ascertaining if a concept is really a rough concept can be achieved within the framework of Ontology-Based Data Access (OBDA) [9] by exploiting the mapping layer. To demonstrate it is not merely theoretically possible to have rough concepts and vague instances in one's ontologies, but that it is indeed practically possible, we take the use cases about horizontal gene transfer (HGT) with a hypothesized (rough) concept Promiscuous Bacterium, and demonstrate how this can be modelled more precisely in an OWL 2 DL ontology (but not used with the data) and deployed in an OBDA system using a simpler ontology (roughly in OWL 2 QL) so that the instances from the 17GB large HGT-DB database can be retrieved using a structured process of automation and manual intervention.

The remainder of the paper is structured as follows. We summarise the theoretical assessment on the feasibility of rough ontologies in Section 2. Experimental results with rough concepts and with vague instances will be presented in Section 3 and we close with conclusions in section 4.

2 Rough Concepts and Rough Ontology Languages

To be able to have a correspondence of a rough set with a rough concept in a rough ontology and to represent its essential characteristics, we first outline the basics of rough sets following the standard "Pawlak rough set model" [10] and then summarize requirements and trade-offs to include such roughness features in DL-based OWL ontologies.

2.1 Rough Sets

The Pawlak rough set model is depicted informally in Fig. 1 and formally, it is as follows. $I = (U, A)$ is called an *information system*, where U is a non-empty finite set of objects and A a finite non-empty set of attributes and such that for every $a \in A$, we have the function $a : U \mapsto V_a$ where v_a is the set of values that attribute a can have. For any subset of attributes $P \subseteq A$, one can define the equivalence relation $\text{IND}(P)$ as $\text{IND}(P) = \{(x, y) \in U \times U \mid \forall a \in P, a(x) = a(y)\}$ so that $\text{IND}(P)$ generates a partition of U, which is denoted with $U/\text{IND}(P)$. If $(x, y) \in \text{IND}(P)$, then x and y are *p-indistinguishable* with respect to the attributes in P. From the objects in universe U, we want to represent set X such that $X \subseteq U$ using the attribute set P where $P \subseteq A$. X may not be represented in a crisp way—the set may include and/or exclude objects which are indistinguishable on the basis of the attributes in P—but it can be approximated by using lower approximation, $\underline{P}X = \{x \mid [x]_P \subseteq X\}$, and upper approximation, $\overline{P}X = \{x \mid [x]_P \cap X \neq \emptyset\}$, where $[x]_P$ denotes the equivalence classes of the p-indistinguishability relation. The *lower approximation* is the set of objects that are *positively* classified as being members of set X, i.e., it is the union of all equivalence classes in $[x]_P$. The *upper approximation* is the set of objects that are *possibly* in X; its complement, $U - \overline{P}X$, is the *negative region* with sets of objects that are definitely not in X (i.e., $\neg X$). Then, "with every rough set we associate two *crisp* sets, called *lower* and *upper approximation*" [10], which is commonly denoted as a tuple $X = \langle \underline{X}, \overline{X} \rangle$. The difference between the lower and upper approximation, $B_P X = \overline{P}X - \underline{P}X$, is the *boundary region* of which its objects neither can be classified as to be member of X nor that they are not in X; if $B_P X = \emptyset$ then X is, in fact, a crisp set with respect to P and when $B_P X \neq \emptyset$ then X is rough w.r.t. P. The *accuracy of approximation*, $\alpha_P X$, provides a measure of how well the rough set approximates the target set with respect to P, e.g., $\alpha_P X = \frac{|\underline{P}X|}{|\overline{P}X|}$. Clearly, if $\alpha_P X = 1$, then the boundary region $B_P X$ is empty and thus X is crisp. Useful for reasoning is that $\underline{P}X \subseteq X \subseteq \overline{P}X$.

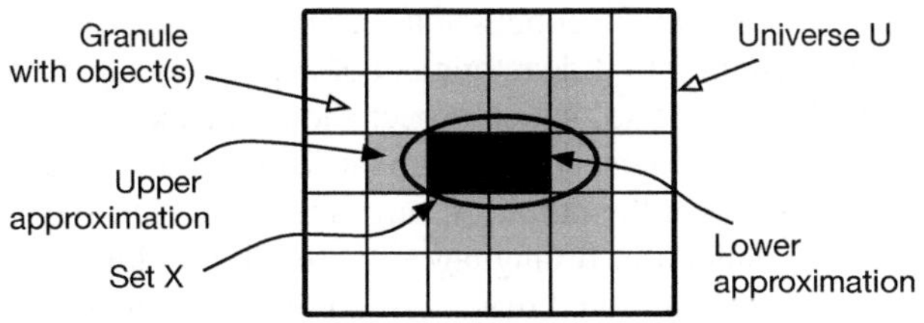

Fig. 1. A rough set and associated notions (Source: based on [10])

2.2 Prospects for Rough OWL Ontologies

Due to space limitations, only the outcome of the analysis will be summarised here; a more comprehensive assessment and argumentation is described in [11].

OWL ontologies use a richer language [12] than the simple $I = (U, A)$ of rough sets, in particular concerning how to represent 'attributes' of a concept $C \in \mathcal{C}$ (with object properties $R \in \mathcal{R}$ or data properties $D \in \mathcal{D}$) and object properties' properties. Another difference is that we need a model-theoretic semantics for lower and upper approximation, $\underline{C}$ and $\overline{C}$, and rough concept, "$\wr C$", and impose that the attributes used to compute $\underline{C}$ and $\overline{C}$ are represented in the ontology.

The semantics of the approximations is straightforward, with E denoting the reflexive, symmetric and transitive indistinguishability (i.e., equivalence) relation: $\underline{C} = \{x \mid \forall y : (x, y) \in E \rightarrow y \in C\}$ and $\overline{C} = \{x \mid \exists y : (x, y) \in E \wedge y \in C\}$. Regarding rough sets' tuple notation, $X = \langle \underline{X}, \overline{X} \rangle$, there can be an analougous one for concepts, $\wr C = \langle \underline{C}, \overline{C} \rangle$, but this cannot be represented as such in the ontology. A solution to this is to 'flatten out' the tuple by relating $\underline{C}$ and $\overline{C}$ to $\wr C$ with newly introduced object properties, say, $lapr$ and $uapr$ (i.e., quantifying over *sets*, not objects that are member of the respective sets). This enables one to make explicit the knowledge about how the three concepts relate to each other: $\wr C$ is identified by the combination of its $\underline{C}$ and $\overline{C}$, which is analogous to a weak entity type in EER, i.e., for each $\wr C$, there is exactly one $\underline{C}$ and one $\overline{C}$, and vv. Last, for rough set's A, the set of 'attributes' in OWL amounts to $\mathcal{R} \cup \mathcal{D}$, and each $p_i \in P$ to compute the rough concepts must have $\wr C$ as its domain.

Overall, we now have a more precise notion of $\wr C$ cf. the tuple notation in [6], use both $\mathcal{R}$ and $\mathcal{D}$ for the 'attributes' of the concepts (cf. $\mathcal{R}$ only in [5,8]), include the properties of the indistinguishability relation (cf. their omission in [7] or a similarity relation [3]), and adhere to proper declaration of $\underline{C}$, $\overline{C}$, and $\wr C$ in that they all have the same collection of properties from $\mathcal{R} \cup \mathcal{D}$ (cf. different sets of attributes in [8]).

Nevertheless, there are still three aspects to sort out for practical rough ontologies: the necessity to represent the indistinguishability relation E, the identity of a rough concept by its lower and upper approximation by means of identification constraints involving OWL object properties, and linking the ontology to (large amounts of) instances to ascertain if a putative rough concept is indeed rough or not. Currently, there is no single DL or OWL language that can handle all three features, or even two of the three. Narrowing the gap between 'offer and demand' by inventing a new language is impractical: real identification of $\wr C$ requires second order logic, or, as approximation, identification constraints for each rough concept, which is likely to increase the computational complexity even further. Therefore, we shall push the envelope of extant languages and tools and make concessions regarding semantics and performance in order to gain better insight into if development of a new language and corresponding tools are worth the effort and if so, which aspect should be tackled first, and to assess the amount of uptake by ontologists to experiment with rough concepts. For *practical* reasons, then, we narrow down the ontology languages to the DL-based OWL species, because they are W3C standardised languages, there are ontology development tools for them, they have several automated reasoners, and they are the DL of choice among the (bio-)ontologists. E's reflexivity, symmetry and transitivity, can be represented with OWL 2 DL [12]. Currently, $\wr C$ can only be added as a "`RoughC`" with its relations to the approximations so that it serves as human communication, i.e., there is no computational significance other than deducing $\underline{C} \sqsubseteq C \sqsubseteq \overline{C}$ based on the declared knowledge in the TBox. Then, given it is the interplay with the actual instances that is crucial for roughness, we need also a system that can handle large amounts of data, which currently locks one into *DL-Lite*/OWL 2 QL in the OBDA framework with QuOnto [9] that can represent even less of rough set's semantics (and of the subject domain) than OWL 2 DL. This issue can be counterbalanced partially by exploiting the mapping layer, although this is not ideal because it is not as transparent and maintainable as representing the subject domain semantics in the ontology, but we can assess our rough concepts and instances.

3 Experimentation with a Rough Ontology and Vague Instances

Given the aforementioned trade-offs, we will demonstrate how one can have either an ontology with rough concepts represented fairly comprehensively regarding their semantics (Experiment 2 and 3) or have it with more limited semantics but linked to the data and be able to perform the actual hypothesis testing against the data (Experiment 1). To be fair to the latest technologies for expressive OWL species, we also experiment with a more expressive ontology with little data by revisiting the sepsis experiment of [8] in Experiment 3.

3.1 Materials and Methods

Methodology. Different strategies for both experimentation and use of rough ontologies in operational ontology-driven information systems are possible. Because the link to data is crucial for rough ontologies, we commence with the OBDA approach and subsequently move to a more expressive language. The methodological steps for the first two experiments are as follows:

1. Develop a basic ontology in OWL 2 QL or *DL-Lite*$_{\mathcal{A}}$ stored as an OWL file;
2. Obtain the relational database in Oracle, DB2, MySQL, or PostgreSQL;
3. Set up the OBDA system;
4. Declare the mappings between the classes and properties in the OWL ontology and SQL queries over the database in the OBDA system;
5. Find all rough concepts with respect to the data through posing ontology-mediated queries (in SPARQL or EQL-Lite), evaluating the result set, and adding the concepts to the ontology;
6. Migrate this ontology to an expressive OWL species, such as OWL 2 DL: (i) declare the semantics from the `WHERE` clause in the SQL query of the mapping layer as object and data properties in the ontology; (ii) add upper and lower approximations of each rough concept; (iii) add the indistinguishability object property with its properties (reflexive, symmetric, transitive); (iv) add the axioms relating the approximations to the rough concepts and vv.;
7. When the rough reasoning services are implemented, run the reasoner with the enhanced ontology to check satisfiability and consistency.

For step 6 in experiment 2, the following considerations are adhered to. Recollecting the relevant part of OWL 2's direct semantics [12]: take a vocabulary V with, among others, V_C denoting the set of classes, and its corresponding class interpretation function $\cdot^C$ that assigns to each class $C \in V_C$ a subset $(C)^C \subseteq \Delta^I$, and V_{OP} the set of object properties where $\cdot^{OP}$ is the object property interpretation function that assigns to each object property $OP \in V_{OP}$ a subset $(OP)^{OP} \subseteq \Delta^I \times \Delta^I$. We add rough concept, upper, and lower approximation such that $\wr\mathtt{C}, \overline{\mathtt{C}}, \underline{\mathtt{C}} \in V_C$, add the indistinguishability relation `Ind` over $\Delta^I \times \Delta^I$ such that `Ind` $\in V_{OP}$ and the ontology contains the assertions: `ReflexiveObjectProperty(a:Ind)`, `SymmetricObjectProperty(a:Ind)`, and `TransitiveObjectProperty(a:Ind)`, and assign the semantics to the classes:

$$(\overline{\mathtt{C}})^I = \{x \in \Delta^I \mid \exists y \in \Delta^I, (x,y) \in \mathtt{Ind} \wedge y \in \mathtt{C}^I\} \quad (1)$$

$$(\underline{\mathtt{C}})^I = \{x \in \Delta^I \mid \forall y \in \Delta^I, (x,y) \in \mathtt{Ind} \rightarrow y \in \mathtt{C}^I\} \quad (2)$$

$$(\wr\mathtt{C})^I = (\langle \underline{\mathtt{C}}, \overline{\mathtt{C}} \rangle)^I = \langle (\underline{\mathtt{C}})^I, (\overline{\mathtt{C}})^I \rangle \quad (3)$$

which amounts to the assertions for any $\overline{\mathtt{C}}$ and $\underline{\mathtt{C}}$ in OWL 2 DL functional syntax,
`EquivalentClasses(`$\overline{\mathtt{C}}$ `ObjectSomeValuesFrom(a:Ind a:C))` and
`EquivalentClasses(`$\underline{\mathtt{C}}$ `ObjectAllValuesFrom(a:Ind a:C))`
Recollect that (3) is approximated in an ontology by adding the two properties, `uapr`, `lapr` $\in V_{OP}$ that each have $\wr$C as domain, and cardinality exactly 1: `ObjectProperty-Domain(a:upar a:`$\wr$`C)`, `ObjectPropertyDomain(a:lapr a:`$\wr$`C)`, `ObjectExact-Cardinality(1 a:uapr a:`$\overline{\mathtt{C}}$`)`, and `ObjectExactCardinality(1 a:lapr a:`$\underline{\mathtt{C}}$`)`. This is added to the ontology for each rough concept and its approximations.

Materials. Linking data from one or more data sources to an ontology is carried out with the OBDA system based on the theory and tools described in [9]. In short, the *semantic layer* was realised with Protégé 3.3.1 and the OBDA plugin for Protégé, with which one develops and inspects the OWL ontology and declares the mappings between the classes and properties in the ontology and SQL queries over the data source (persistently stored in an `.obda` file). The *application layer* is the OBDA plugin for Protégé as well, which allows the user to pose the SPARQL user-queries over the ontology and inspect the query answer. The automated reasoner that takes care of unfolding and rewriting the SPARQL user-query into the SQL query over the data sources is QUONTO. The *data layer* consists of a single Oracle 10g database based on the HGT-DB database [14] that stores data about horizontal gene transfer and was kindly made available for testing purposes by its developers.

The ontology language for this particular implementation of the OBDA system is the OWL-ized DL language *DL-Lite*$_\mathcal{A}$ [9]. From an ontologist perspective, the *DL-Lite*$_\mathcal{A}$ ontology for OBDA, and in particular the HGT 'application ontology', has typical characteristics of a logic-based simple conceptual data model, which has 31 classes, 32 object properties, 61 data properties, and 108 subclass axioms that deal with organisms and their properties (such as name, amount of genes, and chromosomes) and genes with their properties (such as its function, location, and its statistics).

For the OWL2 DL representation of the HGT ontology and rough concepts, Protégé 4.0 was used with Fact++. The domain knowledge for Experiment 3 is taken from [8] and also required OWL 2 DL. Protégé 4.0 with Pellet 2.0 and FaCT++, and Racer Pro Preview 2.0 were used and the experiments were carried out on a Macbook Pro with Mac OS X v 10.5.8 with 2.93 GHz Intel core 2 Duo and 4 GB memory.

The supplementary files—ontologies, mappings, queries, and data—are available online through `http://obda.inf.unibz.it/obdahgtdb/obdahgtdb.html`.

3.2 Results

The setting for the first and second experiment about HGT is as follows. A geneticist has an idea about what a "promiscuous bacterium" is because some bacteria transfer and receive much more genes from other bacteria than others do. It is not fully understood who they are and why this is the case, hence the first step is to analyse the data using properties that indicate a certain promiscuity so as to find bacteria with comparatively many anomalous (foreign) DNA in their chromosome.

Experiment 1 (Promiscuous bacteria in OBDA). We specify a first attempt for representing the notion of PromiscuousBacterium in the ontology as a subtype of Organism, so that it must have more than 5 so-called FlexibleHGTgeneClusters (a set of overlapping, adjacent or nearby genes on the chromosome that are horizontally transferred) and the Percentage of genes on the chromosome that are predicted to be horizontally acquired as > 10. Given the limitations of the language and to not have the intended meaning of PromiscuousBacterium (as in (9), below) partially in the ontology and partially in the mapping layer, we chose to put all properties in the OBDA mapping layer; that is, we have PromiscuousBacterium $\sqsubseteq$ Organism in the OWL ontology, and then made a mapping between PromiscuousBacterium in the ontology and an SQL query over the relational database (see Fig. 2): the head of the mapping with the class in the ontology and those attributes in the database with which we identify a promiscuous bacterium, is shown with the line `PromiscuousBacterium(getPromBact($abbrev,$ccount, $percentage))` under mapping `M:0` and the mapping body, i.e., SQL query over the

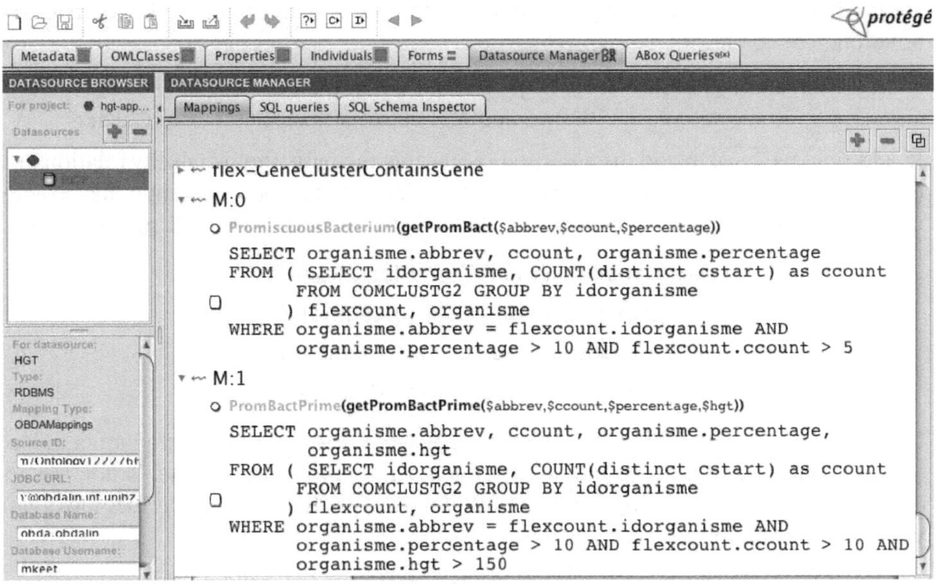

Fig. 2. Mappings for PromiscuousBacterium and its subclass PromBactPrime in the OBDA plugin

database, below it. Querying the database through the ontology with a SPARQL query using the OBDA Plugin for Protégé and answered using QuOnto, 98 objects are retrieved where *Dehalococcoides CBDB1* (dehaloc) and *Thermotoga maritima* (tmar) are truly indistinguishable bacteria, i.e. they have the same values for all the selected and constrained attributes. A few others are very close to being so, such as *Pelodictyon luteolum DSM273* (plut) and *Synechocystis PCC6803* (synecho3) who have both 6 clusters and 10.1% and 10.2%, respectively, which, practically, still lie within the error-margin of genomics data and its statistics; see online material for the full result set. Thus, by virtue of dehaloc and tmar, PromiscuousBacterium is a rough concept.

To improve the accuracy and examine if we can turn a subconcept of PromiscuousBacterium into a crisp one, a *new* data property about the number of predicted genes that are horizontally transferred—NrPredHGTgenes with integer values, set to >150—is added and the second attribute set at >10 gene clusters, which thus *revises* the assumption of what a promiscuous bacterium really is, i.e., we have a "PromBactPrime" in the ontology such that PromBactPrime $\sqsubseteq$ PromiscuousBacterium. The head and body of the mapping are depicted under M:1 in Fig. 2. The query answer has only 89 objects and this change eliminated the indistinguishability of dehaloc and tmar, hence PromBactPrime is a *crisp* concept with respect to the data stored in the database. ◇

Experiment 2 (Promiscuous bacteria in OWL 2 DL). In contrast to the OBDA setting in Experiment 1, it is possible to represent the subject domain semantics of promiscuous bacteria in the OWL 2 DL ontology itself instead of in the mapping layer. The PromiscuousBacterium is a subclass of Organism in the HGT ontology with an additional object- and a data property, so that it must have more than 5 flexible hgt-gene clusters (FlexibleHGTgeneCluster) and the percentage of genes on the chromosome that are predicted to be horizontally acquired, Percentage, greater than 10. In compact DL notation, we then have:

$$\text{PromiscuousBacterium} \equiv \text{Organism} \sqcap \exists\, \text{Percentage.real}_{>10} \sqcap \geq 6\ \text{hasHGTCluster.FlexibleHGTGeneCluster} \tag{4}$$

In addition, we have to add the assertions regarding the indistinguishability relation `Ind` (see Section 3.1 for relational properties) and that Promiscuous Bacterium has exactly one lower and one upper approximation, PromBactLapr and PromBactUapr, as follows:

$$\text{PromiscuousBacterium} \sqsubseteq\ = 1\ \text{lapr.PromBactLapr} \tag{5}$$

$$\text{PromiscuousBacterium} \sqsubseteq\ = 1\ \text{uapr.PromBactUapr} \tag{6}$$

$$\text{PromBactLapr} \equiv \forall\, \text{Ind.PromBact} \tag{7}$$

$$\text{PromBactUapr} \equiv \exists\, \text{Ind.PromBact} \tag{8}$$

Given that we already know from Experiment 1 that PromiscuousBacterium is indeed a rough concept and that the proposed refinement, i.e., PromBactPrime, is not, the additional crisp concept requires only the full definition without relating it to a lower and upper approximation:

$$\text{PromBactPrime} \equiv \text{PromiscuousBacterium} \sqcap \exists\, \text{Percentage.real}_{>10} \sqcap \geq 11\ \text{hasHGTCluster.FlexibleHGTGeneCluster} \sqcap \exists\, \text{NrPredHGTgenes.integer}_{>150} \tag{9}$$

Querying or instance classification with this OWL 2 DL version and the HGT data, however, is currently not feasible. ◇

Experiment 3 (Revisiting septic patients). Patients may be septic or are certainly septic, according to the so-called *Bone criteria* and Bone criteria together with three out of another five criteria, respectively. For instance, the Bone criteria (from [8]) can be encoded in OWL as being an `EquivalentClass` to `BoneSeptic`, as follows:

```
(hasDiagnosis some Infection and
hasSymptom some (Hypoperfusion or Hypotension or OrganDysfunction)
and (((temperature some int[> 38] or temperature some int[<36])
  and (respiratoryRate some int[>20] or paco2count some int[<32]))
  or ((temperature some int[>38] or temperature some int[<36]) and
      heartRate some int[>90])
  or ((temperature some int[>38] or temperature some int[<36]) and
   (leukocyteCount some int[<4000] or leukocyteCount some int[>12000]))
  or ((respiratoryRate some int[>20] or paco2count some int[<32]) and
      heartRate some int[>90])
  or ((respiratoryRate some int[>20] or paco2count some int[<32]) and
   (leukocyteCount some int[<4000] or leukocyteCount some int[>12000]))
  or (heartRate some int[>90] and (leukocyteCount some int[<4000] or
   leukocyteCount some int[>12000]))))
```

The respective encodings in Protégé 4.0 and RacerPro 2.0 preview are available online as supplementary material, as well as data of 17 'patients' such that there are indistinguishable patients and the boundary region is not empty. Protégé 4.0 with Pellet 2.0 did not work at all. Protégé 4.0 with FaCT++ works well with a few dummy concepts and a few instances, but the esoteric definitions for septic appeared to be more challenging: it crashed with an encoding including `Ind` and, with or without `Ind`, upon saving and reopening the `.owl` file, it had reordered the braces in the definition in such a way as to change its meaning so that it does not classify all 17 individuals correctly.

These observations are probably due to the fact that the software used is still in the early stages. RacerPro 2.0 Preview never crashed during exerimentation and did return the correct classifications within about 2 hours (the slow response time is likely due to the heavy use of data properties with the concrete domains; Volker Haarslev, personal communication). While the latter is an encouraging result because it works with the real definitions and a small data set, the automated reasoning clearly does not scale to [8]'s thousands of patients. ♢

3.3 Discussion

While a rough ontology such as the amended HGT ontology in OWL 2 DL did provide a more comprehensive and transparent way of representing the declarative knowledge of putative and actual rough concepts, it was only with the less expressive OWL 2 QL-based OBDA-enabled system that it could be experimentally validated against the data and that it was *certain* that there was no need to add approximations for PromBactPrime in the ontology. Taken together, the ontologies, OBDA, and ontology development tools with their respective reasoners provide a means to represent the steps of successive de-vaguening during experimentation, they make the selected properties explicit, and, if desired, one can keep both ≀PromiscuousBacterium and PromBactPrime in the ontologies without generating inconsistencies. The two-step process with OBDA and OWL 2 DL might seem cumbersome, but is an advance with respect to traceability compared to separately querying the database with undocumented one-off queries and adding the obtained knowledge to the OWL 2 DL ontology.

The feasibility to extend languages or tools to reflect the representation of the roughness semantics and the experimentation in ontology engineering using a reasoner, is theoretically, and thus also practically, limited. As last resort, one can add a RoughC $\sqsubseteq \top$ and let all rough concepts in the subject domain be subsumed by RoughC so that the modeller informally can keep track of the rough concepts in the ontology. For OWL 2 DL, one can also define an extension as outlined in Section 3.1, which is similar to that of [6]'s $\mathcal{RDL}_{AC}$. However, there is little to gain in automated reasoning due to scalability issues as illustrated in the experiments. The added value of such extensions may be questioned and the following two avenues will yield more usefulness from a knowledge engineering perspective.

The first direction where improvements may be achieved, is to partition the data source and import only data into the ABox of one or a few objects at a time, carry out the instance classification, export the results, merge the results after each classification step, and then assess the results; however, one-off scripting is not ideal. Alternatively, a sophisticated modularization of both the ontology and the data(base) so as to execute the reasoning only on small sections of the ontology and database (in the direction of, e.g., [15]) might be an option in the near future. The second option concerns usability: although rough ontologies work as proof-of-concept, the procedure to carry it out is not user-friendly. One may be able to turn into a feature the interaction between the more precise representation in OWL 2 DL and the linking to data with OWL 2 QL (or a similar tractable language) by upgrading it to a named scientific workflow. This guides the developer to carry out in a structured, traceable, and repeatable manner the tasks to experiment with ontologies, the associated data, and the rough concepts.

4 Conclusions

Extending OWL ontologies with the core notions of rough sets revealed both theoretical and practical challenges. Given rough sets' semantics, there is no, nor will there be, a DL-based OWL species that can represent all these aspects precisely, although expressive languages, such as OWL 2 DL, come close and some tools, such as RacerPro, can handle complex rough concept descriptions with a small amount of data. However, it is the interaction with large amounts of data that makes any extension with roughness interesting and necessary to find rough concepts, which is possible with the Ontology-Based Data Access framework. Validation of the theoretical assessment was carried out through experimentation with rough concepts and vague instances using the HGT case study and sepsis. Current and future work pertains to looking further into modularization to achieve a platform for hypothesis-driven usage of rough ontologies that will reap the greatest benefits to meet the users' requirements.

Acknowledgements. I thank Umberto Straccia, Ferdinando Bobillo, and Mariano Rodríguez-Muro for feedback during the experimentation.

References

1. Keet, C.M., et al.: A survey of requirements for automated reasoning services for bio-ontologies in OWL. In: Proc. of OWLED 2007, CEUR-WS, vol. 258 (2007)
2. Marshall, M.S., et al.: Using semantic web tools to integrate experimental measurement data on our own terms. In: Meersman, R., Tari, Z., Herrero, P. (eds.) OTM 2006 Workshops. LNCS, vol. 4277, pp. 679–688. Springer, Heidelberg (2006)
3. Bobillo, F., Straccia, U.: Supporting fuzzy rough sets in fuzzy description logics. In: Sossai, C., Chemello, G. (eds.) ECSQARU 2009. LNCS, vol. 5590, pp. 676–687. Springer, Heidelberg (2009)
4. Fanizzi, N., et al.: Representing uncertain concepts in rough description logics via contextual indiscernibility relations. In: Proc. of URSW 2008, CEUR-WS, vol. 423 (2008)
5. Ishizu, S., et al.: Rough ontology: extension of ontologies by rough sets. In: Smith, M.J., Salvendy, G. (eds.) HCII 2007. LNCS, vol. 4557, pp. 456–462. Springer, Heidelberg (2007)
6. Jiang, Y., Wang, J., Tang, S., Xiao, B.: Reasoning with rough description logics: An approximate concepts approach. Inform. Sciences 179, 600–612 (2009)
7. Liau, C.J.: On rough terminological logics. In: Proceedings of the 4th International Workshop on Rough Sets, Fuzzy Sets and Machine Discovery (RSFD 1996), pp. 47–54 (1996)
8. Schlobach, S., Klein, M., Peelen, L.: Description logics with approximate definitions—precise modeling of vague concepts. In: Proc. of IJCAI 2007, pp. 557–562. AAAI Press, Menlo Park (2007)
9. Calvanese, D., et al.: Ontologies and databases: The DL-Lite approach. In: Tessaris, S., Franconi, E., Eiter, T., Gutierrez, C., Handschuh, S., Rousset, M.-C., Schmidt, R.A. (eds.) Reasoning Web 2009. LNCS, vol. 5689, pp. 255–356. Springer, Heidelberg (2009)
10. Pawlak, Z., Skowron, A.: Rudiments of rough sets. Inform. Sciences 177(1), 3–27 (2007)
11. Keet, C.M.: On the feasibility of description logic knowledge bases with rough concepts and vague instances. In: Proc. of DL 2010, CEUR-WS, Waterloo, Canada, pp. 314–324 (2010)

12. Motik, B., Patel-Schneider, P.F., Cuenca-Grau, B.: OWL 2 web ontology language: Direct semantics. W3c recommendation, W3C (October 27, 2009)
13. Motik, B., et al.: OWL 2 Web Ontology Language Profiles. W3c recommendation, W3C (October 27, 2009), http://www.w3.org/TR/owl2-profiles/
14. Garcia-Vallvé, S., et al.: HGT-DB: a database of putative horizontally transferred genes in prokaryotic complete genomes. Nucleic Acids Research 31(1), 187–189 (2003)
15. Lutz, C., Toman, D., Wolter, F.: Conjunctive query answering in the description logic EL using a relational database system. In: Proc. of IJCAI 2009. AAAI Press, Menlo Park (2009)

Building Large Lexicalized Ontologies from Text: A Use Case in Automatic Indexing of Biotechnology Patents

Claire Nédellec, Wiktoria Golik, Sophie Aubin, and Robert Bossy

MIG, INRA, Jouy en Josas
firstname.lastname@jouy.inra.fr

Abstract. This paper presents a tool, TyDI, and methods experimented in the building of a termino-ontology, i.e. a lexicalized ontology aimed at fine-grained indexation for semantic search applications. TyDI provides facilities for knowledge engineers and domain experts to efficiently collaborate to validate, organize and conceptualize corpus extracted terms. A use case on biotechnology patent search demonstrates TyDI's potential.

Keywords: Knowledge engineering, knowledge acquisition from texts, life sciences.

1 Introduction

The recent development of semantic search engines in specific domains reveals a new need for ontologies that support automatic dense and fine-grained indexing in specific domains. The main limit of the approach is the low availability of adequate indexing resources – linguistic and semantic in specific domains. The work described in this paper takes place in the context of developing semantic search engines in the agronomy domain, for which we use the generic WebAlvis information retrieval system [1]. In this context, we consider the ontology structure as a hierarchy of concepts and the indexing of the text as the annotation of local and independent text phrases by concept labels. The lexical variability and the ambiguity of the terms that denote concepts are processed in the lexical level that bridges the formal conceptual level to the text [2]. The state of the art in section 2 reveals a strong need for termino-ontology acquisition assistants. Section 3 presents TyDI's main functionalities and the methods it allows for the cooperative design of ontologies from texts. Finally, a use case in the biotechnology patents domain shows how TyDI supports the collaboration between a domain expert and a knowledge engineer through a user-friendly interface.

2 Context

2.1 Requirements

Domain-specific semantic information retrieval systems require a termino-ontology. A termino-ontology is defined as an ontology comprising a hierarchy of concepts and the most complete set of terminological and lexical manifestations of each concept.

P. Cimiano and H.S. Pinto (Eds.): EKAW 2010, LNAI 6317, pp. 514–523, 2010.

The lack of resources is particularly manifest for building scientific and technical information systems. Available terminologies and thesauri generally do not provide formal *is_a* links and most ontologies in the agronomy domain (*e.g.* Gene Ontology [3], the Open Biological and Biomedical Ontologies [4]) are hardly usable for fine-grained indexing because of the domain inadequacy or the lack of lexicalization. Corpus-based extraction of terms is recognized as a rich source of knowledge for termino-ontology design, preserving the explicit links between the text, the lexical and the conceptual level [5]. Term extractors propose term candidates from the text that fulfill linguistic patterns or word co-occurrence criteria. Their application ensures a large coverage of the domain, resulting in lists that can reach several thousands of term candidates. Despite the recent advances in term extraction and ontology learning, such lists still need manual curation and structuring in order to be usable in semantic IR. The efficiency of this work relies on a tool that must allow the selection and the structuring of terms and concepts in a user-friendly way. Ergonomics is particularly crucial for direct use by the expert, so that s/he would focus on domain knowledge acquisition rather than on specific linguistic and formal modeling issues.

2.2 State of the Art

Ontology acquisition from texts has been widely studied in the last decade, resulting in a number of tools that assist the ontology engineer in the various steps of ontology design from term selection to semantic modeling.

Ontology learning frameworks provide integrated pipelines for automatically computing concepts, relations between concepts and inference rules from text analysis, either linguistic or statistical. Several tools have been proposed, among which Text2Onto [6], Asium [7], OntoLearn [8] and OntoLT [9].These automatic approaches make useful suggestions that have to be validated and integrated into the knowledge model. Although some of them like as Asium and Text2Onto provide a user validation interface, they do not address the modeling issue with the flexibility of ontology editors.

Closer to our requirements, term validation interfaces and ontology editors assist the manual design of domain specific terminologies and ontologies respectively. The validation of sets of term candidates is often tackled as the simple task of selecting and rejecting words and phrases extracted from a corpus, supported by spreadsheet-like software. It shortly reveals its limits and inappropriateness, especially for term context analysis in the source corpus and cooperative design. The web application TermExtractor [10] stands as an exception as the validation can be compiled from a vote by different users. Unfortunately the validation interface cannot be used as standalone without the associated term extraction tool. At the end of the spectrum, ontology editors like Protégé [11], OboEdit [12] - in the biomedical community-KAON [13] assist ontology creation, edition, browsing, reuse and merging in languages based on formal semantics such as OWL. If they offer user-friendly interfaces for managing concepts and roles, they remain difficult to adopt quickly for simple hierarchy modeling by a domain expert. Finally none of these tools provides facilities for defining concept lexicalization from term candidates extracted from corpus.

The most complete tool with respect to our needs is undoubtedly Terminae [5] that provides an explicit link between the lexical and terminological levels and the conceptual level. It provides a high level of traceability, necessary for the maintenance of the resource. Its limit towards our requirements is the formal distinction between the lexical and conceptual knowledge as materialized by distinct actions and windows in the interface. While this feature makes sense when the ontology design is achieved by knowledge engineers, it turns to act as a hindrance for the domain expert, who has a topic-centered approach of knowledge modeling and needs to transparently handle knowledge from different types at the same time.

3 Cooperative Ontology Building from Text

This section details TyDI elementary functions and describes how these functions are combined in methodological steps taking into consideration the cooperative relationship between domain experts and a knowledge engineer.

3.1 TyDI

User cooperation and ontology design traceability relies on a client-server architecture based on the *NetBeans* technology and a PosgreSQL RDBMS for storage. This architecture ensures robustness and flexibility. The input of the TyDI system is a set of term candidates; it supports the YaTeA [14] term extractor format and CSV files. TyDI interface also offers advanced and intuitive navigation and control over the termino-ontology. A TyDI documentation and screenshot are available from [15].

Term candidates are displayed with their linguistic information. The user can specify the columns to be displayed and their order. The content of the term grid is computed by filters specified by the user. The context of each term in the source corpus and its properties can be viewed in specific frames. Distinct frames are dedicated to local structuring and to global modeling. Additional functionalities worth mentioning are the external search facilities (*e.g.* Google, Wikipedia); display of the sub-terms of a given term; exploitation of the term morpho-syntactic variations as computed by the FastR tool [16]; grouped actions via multi-row selection; OWL, OBO and tsv (tab separated values) export.

Term filters include numeric criteria (word count and number of occurrences), used for selecting either short, generally generic terms or long, more specific and generally less frequent terms. The user can select terms with shallow criteria (surface form patterns) or linguistic criteria (surface form, lemma, head, expansion and syntactic category). For instance, one can define filters that displays all terms sharing the same head or all sub-terms syntactically embedded in a given term. These criteria can be combined with Boolean operators. For example, the filter "head term = *tree*" combined sub-terms filter yields the list: *tree*, *mature tree*, *mature avocado*, *mature avocado tree*, *medium-sized mature avocado tree* among which the expert will easily invalidate incomplete term candidates (*mature avocado*) and too specific term candidates (*medium-sized mature avocado tree*).

The filter and sorting functionalities are also useful to build the terminology structure. TyDI facilitates the examination of close terms along various axes. For instance *Head* and *Expansion* columns highlight semantic relations reflected by the term composition: distributional semantic relations (e.g. *insect resistance / bacteria resistance*, *stationary phase / stationary stage*), multidimensional traits (*e.g. plant resistance = resistance of the plant* vs. *insect resistance = resistance to the insects*) and hyperonymy (*e.g. mature tree / mature avocado tree*). These functionalities also help defining synonymy equivalence classes through unconventional term usages, abbreviations, acronyms and rhetoric figures such as metonymy (*e.g. gene activation* vs. *expression activation*) or ellipsis (*e.g. terminator sequence* vs. *terminator*). TyDI allows to qualify specific types of synonymy, *i.e.* acronymy, typographic variation, quasi-synonymy and translation.

A specific frame is used for local modeling of the lexical representation of ontology concepts with terms. Defining a new concept consists in creating a concept label from the term grid or in selecting the label from an existing term synonym class. A dedicated frame provides facilities for structuring the concept hierarchy, for navigating through the ontology and for performing major revisions.

TyDI supports collaborative work by allowing concurrent validations of each term. It maintains in a distinct property the validation status according to each user. The validation status includes a label and a comment where the user can record justifications and questions. The validation status of other users may be visible or hidden depending on the specific application needs; TyDI thus supports open, blind or double-blind validation schemes. Validation statuses also offer filter and sorting criteria, so one can retrieve terms for which a consensus or a controversy exists.

3.2 Strategies for Building Ontologies from Text

TyDI is independent from methodological strategies of information processing and knowledge modeling: bottom-up, top-down or topic-centered as distinguished in [17]. In fact they are not exclusive and complement each other in the same project as shown in the use case (section 4).

The bottom-up strategy consists in gathering large sets from the whole set of terms extracted from a corpus. Terms are validated in a systematic way by sorting them by shallow properties like the surface form, the number of occurrences or the word count. The most frequent terms, if specific enough, are analyzed in order to scope the main themes. This strategy proves useful for a first approach of the data and for reckoning the data contents.

The top-down strategy aims at structuring the ontology by relating existing sub-trees. It starts from ontology overview, and then moves on toward details, by breaking down the model into layers, filling the ontology from high level concepts to more specific concepts. With this approach, modelers have a global insight of the model, allowing them to locate gaps in the model. This strategy is a preliminary step to team work where each participant has specific expertise and is responsible for a particular area of the model.

The topic-centered strategy is more focused: the aim is not to cover a large part of the data, but to focus on local model parts. It starts from a specific term and performs a search in order to assemble a maximum of similar terms within new related classes.

The filtering used here is more sophisticated than in the bottom-up strategy, since composition terms analysis and morpho-syntactic variation are extensively used. This strategy is preferred by domain experts who concentrate on a precise issue, usually delaying the strict observation of modeling principles.

The two former strategies prove both useful for modeling at the leaf level (bottom-up approach) and at more abstract levels (top-down approach), while the latter (topic-centered) is convenient for locally populating ontology labels and synonym classes.

3.3 A Cooperative Process

TyDI is intended for both domain experts and knowledge engineers who collaborate relying on complementary skills. Thus TyDI is designed for concurrent cooperative work. Our main hypothesis is that the domain expert shall play an active role in knowledge modeling through a direct use of the tool. We believe that a strong involvement of the domain expert is both efficient and gratifying. We also assume this involvement is feasible with the help of appropriate methodologies of cooperation between the expert and a knowledge engineer, and the use of an appropriate tool as an interface between them. We discuss here the respective contribution of the expert and the engineer and how TyDI can act as the medium tool. These general principles will be illustrated in the use case in section 4.

In this context, the design of a termino-ontology requires that both the expert and the knowledge engineer acquire some knowledge of the objective and constraints of the other party. The knowledge engineer (KE) enforces the target application and processing tools constraints. S/he also trains the expert to use TyDI functionalities at different acquisition phases. By learning how to use the tool, the expert is allowed to grasp the practical consequences of these constraints, as well as some of the underlying principles of terminology and formal modeling. S/he validates domain terms using his/her background knowledge and context facilities of TyDI while the KE relies on linguistic clues, composition related functionalities and document context to check the well-formedness of validated terms.

During the construction of synonym equivalence classes, the expert proposes preferred terms and synonyms, while the KE discusses the preference according to the term frequency and linguistic constraints such as length. S/he also checks that synonymy and hyperonymy relations are strict enough and do not denote weak relatedness with respect to the application requirements. S/he may suggest additional synonyms by analyzing similar terms and term context in the corpus.

The specific cases of ellipses, metonymies and metaphoric usage are debated in order to distinguish hyperonyms, synonyms and non-related variants. The debate is ideally collegial and requires references and inspiration from external resources of the application domain. During this interaction the KE acquires the domain basic notions empowering him to be more autonomous so the expert can concentrate on more complex issues. Finally the KE role is also to help expert in choosing the best strategy for ontology design (see section 3.2). For instance, when the expert goes too deep in specific topics and looses the view of the global direction, the KE may suggest alternative strategies such as top-down structuring of the existing knowledge chunks.

4 Use Case: Ontology Building from Biotechnology Patents

We present here a practical experiment of collaborative ontology design supported by TyDI. The target application is the semantic search of patents in the biomass exploitation domain for the VegA project [18]. The patent belongs to the ECLA patent class A01H: *New plants or processes for obtaining them; plant reproduction by tissue culture techniques,* referred to as *New Plant* domain in the following. That work was set up to meet the actual needs of intellectual property engineers and biology experts in technology watch and evaluation of freedom to operate. The IR application is now operational and publicly available [19]. The patent collection consists of the 21,039 OEB patent documents in English as available from esp@cenet web service. The *title*, *abstract* and *claims* sections were used for the term extraction and then indexed by the termino-ontology. YaTeA software extracted 65,529 terms imported into TyDI. A plant biology expert and a knowledge engineer collaborated to the *New Plant* termino-ontology building. They interacted remotely by using TyDI interface to visualize the results of their actions in real time, and by email and phone for planning. The design consisted of four phases: (1) shallow term filtering, (2) topic-based exploration of the terms, (3) term validation, classification and local modeling, and (4) global modeling and concept formalization. According to section 3.2, the two first phases belong to the *bottom-up* strategy, the third part is representative of the *topic-centered* strategy and the fourth one is an example of the *top-down* strategy.

4.1 Shallow, Non Semantic List Filtering

Given that the term candidates were automatically extracted, the list contained incorrect and irrelevant terms. The first stage consisted in cleaning the terms list by shallow filtering and was mostly performed by the KE. She attempted both to delete most incorrect forms and to group inflexions and derivations into synonyms classes. Since the list contained many morphological variants (e.g. *public controversies*, *public controversy*, *Public controversy*) that were missed by the lemmatization step, the engineer wrote explicit rules to merge them automatically, the merged terms were still visible on the TyDI interface for traceability purposes. After merging, the number of terms decreased by about 11% (7,403 terms). The most frequent incorrect forms, were identified by sorting the terms of the surface form column by alphabetical order that highlights badly segmented terms starting with special characters (*%,[,“*). Other numerous irrelevant terms were identified thanks to the surface form filter: rhetorical terms and terms relative to the genre of documents (*in addition, claim, main objectives)*, terms containing irrelevant adjectives or demonstratives (*previous study, this disease*), over-general and ambiguous terms (*intensity*, *product*, *concentration*).

A lot of hapax, often resulting from incorrect segmentation or POS tagging were found out by sorting terms by their occurrence frequency and tagged as invalid.

4.2 Topic-Based Terms Exploration

The goal here was to identify important domain themes. To filter the terms, the expert and KE used shallow clues such as frequency and length of terms. Frequency sort highlights representative terms of recurrent themes in the corpus (ex. *DNA sequence:* 542 occ., *transgenic plant:* 664 occ.). They also sorted terms by number of words, giving priority to short (monolexical) terms to identify general items (*e.g. polymer, breeding, phenotype, disease*) or, on the contrary, giving priority to longer multilexical terms to identify domain specific items (*e.g. herbicide resistant acetohydroxyacid synthase*). In parallel, the interaction with the KE became more fluent as the expert familiarized with TyDI, learnt its main functionalities as well as the terminology and formal ontology fields. Concurrently, the KE discovered the main biological notions.

4.3 Terms Validation, Terms Classification and Local Modeling

In this phase, the expert selected a seed term as representative of one relevant theme (*e.g. maize cell*), then he browses through terms by following different types of semantic roles in order to cover thoroughly the theme of the elected theme. The user combined different filtering criteria at the surface level (*e.g.* regular expression match) or at the linguistic level (same head, same expansion). This kind of unbounded navigation allowed the expert to discover alternative semantic axes (*maize cell* vs. *maize culture*), or semantically close elided terms (*maize plant cell*).

Since, a lot of terms turned out to be semantically close, the expert benefited from the filter display to gather them within classes. To check the meaning of an ambiguous term, he displayed its context and queried search engines from TyDI interface. We observed that when checking for valid terms candidates, the expert is naturally impelled to group and structure the terms within semantic classes and subclasses, and thus to conceptualize them into a local model in a continuous schema. Even though this blurs the formal frontier between the lexical and the conceptual levels, for efficiency reasons the distinction should not be enforced at the operational level in the user interface. The expert handled both: terms linked by synonymy relationship (*virus resistance, viral resistance* and *resistance to virus*) choosing a class representative (*virus resistance*) and classes linked by *is_a* relationship (*geminivirus resistance, potyvirus resistance is_a virus resistance).*

Thanks to the multi-window view, the expert was able to quickly populate existing synonyms and hyperonyms classes and to create new ones by looking for other terms displayed within the grid. Moreover the expert distinguished different synonymy sub-cases corresponding to linguistic variation types: typographic variants (*indole butyric acid* and *indolebutyric acid*) and acronyms (*IBA*). Other synonyms resulted from previous machine processing (*e.g.* OCR error: *Brassica oleracea*, *Brassica oieracea*).

4.4 Global Modeling and Concepts Formalization

At this stage, the respective roles of expert and knowledge engineer became well-defined: conceptualization and modeling of term classes belonged mostly to the domain expert, whereas the KE made sure generality relations were strict and consistent with formal knowledge modeling rules, and also helped the expert resolve consistency problems. The term classes produced during the previous stage were used as a basis for ontology design. Each class representative was reevaluated as denoting an ontology concept, while outclass terms were systematically considered as potential candidates for denoting new concepts. Supported by the engineer, the expert massively gathered synonyms that were spread across the terminology (e.g. *Brassica iuncea* and *Brassica iuncea plant* with their synonyms). As already observed in previous modeling experiences, the restriction to only *is-a* relations sometimes led the expert to gather related concepts in informal concept bags instead of formalizing them into different hierarchies, *e.g. resistance to infection, to disease, to pathogen.* The formalization of such bags depends on the application requirement. In fact, in the A01H domain the distinction between the three types of resistance is considered as irrelevant for semantic document searching. Alternatively, he gathered concepts related to different issues because of the similarity of their labels, *e.g. solar energy* and *metabolizable energy* denote respectively the source of the energy and the capability of the plant to metabolize it. The KE systematically reviewed the topics investigated by the expert in order to overcome these problems.

During that stage, the expert proceeded by creating several general concepts, then by populating the ontology with more specific concepts and enriching more in depth issues in which the expert is particularly versed. In order to correct the bias of the single expert view and the potential lack of representativeness of the training corpus, an expert of the biomass domain handed to the domain expert an additional list of topics representative of the documents. He also relied on relevant external information resources, *i.e. Mesh* and *Agrovoc* for structuring the highest levels of the ontology, choosing relevant concept labels.

4.5 Ontology Building Results

The design of the *New Plant* termino-ontology took 6 weeks, which is very short compared to our comparable previous semantic search application developments with Yatea using a spreadsheet and Protégé instead of TyDI. 21,960 (37%) terms were validated and 10,603 (18%) terms were deleted. 5,967 (10%) terms belong to 2680 synonym classes which are linked to the same number of hierarchical concepts.

The development of an instance of WebAlvis allowed us to evaluate the quality of a sample of the termino-ontology through an IR application. The evaluation results are available from [15]. This evaluation showed the high quality of the resource with regard to formal and lexical criteria, thus validating our methodology.

5 Conclusion

The improvement of semantic information retrieval systems, especially in highly specific domains, depends on the quality of the knowledge representing resources developed. Specific domain knowledge acquisition from corpus is a work in progress and requires appropriate methodologies and enhanced tools.

We specified that fine-grained document analysis applications (Information Retrieval, Information Extraction) require formal ontologies with rich lexicalization. This kind of resource is hardly available and its acquisition is very time-consuming.

We proposed a methodology for building lexicalized ontologies where the domain experts are strongly involved, to the point they also contribute to the modeling of the resource. We demonstrated that this involvement can be efficient with the help of an appropriate methodology and a specialized tool to help knowledge engineers and domain experts to work collaboratively. We presented the TyDI software through the use case of a patent retrieval application for the biotechnology domain. We are currently improving TyDI based on feedback collected during this experiment. Immediate future developments will focus on handling polysemy and integrating available ontologies and terminologies. Long terms improvements include ontology learning features (distributional semantics, Hearst-like patterns) and better collaboration support (history management, locks, conflict resolution functions).

We are involved in several projects in different domains that will provide more use cases, giving the opportunity to improve both TyDI and our methodology.

Acknowledgement. The authors acknowledge of TyDI development by Frédéric Papazian. They also thank Bernard Teyssendier, the domain expert for his contribution to the *New Plant* ontology. This work is funded by Quaero program.

References

1. Bossy, R., Kotoujansky, A., et al.: Close Integration of ML and NLP Tools in BioAlvis for Semantic Search in Bacteriology. In: Burger, A., et al. (eds.) Proceedings of the Workshop on Semantic Web Applications and Tools for Life Sciences, UK (2008)
2. Nédellec, C., Nazarenko, A., Bossy, R., et al.: Information Extraction. In: Staab, S., Studer, R. (eds.) Ontology Handbook. Springer, Heidelberg (2009)
3. Ashburner, M., Ball, C.A., et al.: Gene ontology: tool for the unification of biology. The Gene Ontology Consortium. Nature Genetics 25, 25–29 (2000)
4. Smith, B., Ashburner, M., Rosse, et al.: The OBO Foundry: coordinated evolution of ontologies to support biomedical data integration. Nature Biotechnology 25, 1251–1255 (2007)
5. Aussenac-Gilles, N., Després, S., Szulman, S.: The TERMINAE Method and Platform for Ontology Engineering from Texts. In: Buitelaar, P., Cimiano, P. (eds.) Bridging the Gap between Text and Knowledge - Selected Contributions to Ontology Learning and Population from Text, pp. 199–223. IOS Press, Amsterdam (2008)
6. Cimiano, P., Völker, J.: Text2Onto - A Framework for Ontology Learning and Data-driven Change Discovery. In: Proceedings of the 10th International Conference on Applications of Natural Language to Information Systems (NLDB), Spain (2005)
7. Faure, D., Nédellec, C.: A corpus-based conceptual clustering method for verb frames and ontology acquisition. In: LREC Workshop on Adapting Lexical and Corpus Resources to Sublanguages and Applications, Spain (1998)
8. Navigli, R., Velardi, P.: Learning Domain Ontologies from Document Warehouses and Dedicated Web Sites. In: Computational Linguistics, vol. 30, pp. 151–179 (2004)
9. Biemann, C.: Ontology Learning from Text: A Survey of Methods. LDV Forum 20, 75–93 (2005)
10. Sclano, F., Velardi, P.: TermExtractor: a Web Application to Learn the Shared Terminology of Emergent Web Communities. In: Proc. of I-ESA, Portugal (2007)
11. Noy, N.F., Sintek, M., et al.: Creating Semantic Web Contents with Protégé-2000. In: IEEE Intelligent Systems, vol. 16, pp. 60–71 (2001)
12. Day-Richter, J., Harris, M.A., et al.: OBO-Edit - an ontology editor for biologists. Bioinformatics 23, 2198–2200 (2007)

13. Volz, R., Oberle, D., et al.: KAON SERVER - A Semantic Web Management System. In: Proc. of the WWW-2003 Alternate Track on Practice and Experience, Hungary (2003)
14. Aubin, S., Hamon, T.: Improving Term Extraction with Terminological Resources. In: Salakoski, T., Ginter, F., Pyysalo, S., Pahikkala, T. (eds.) FinTAL 2006. LNCS (LNAI), vol. 4139, pp. 380–387. Springer, Heidelberg (2006)
15. TyDI web page, http://bibliome.jouy.inra.fr/Ekaw.en.html
16. Jacquemin, C.: A Symbolic and Surgical Acquisition of terms Through Variation. In: Wermter, S., Scheler, G., Riloff, E. (eds.) IJCAI-WS 1995. LNCS, vol. 1040, pp. 425–438. Springer, Heidelberg (1996)
17. Uschold, M., Gruninger, M.: Ontologies: Principles, Methods and Applications. Knowledge Engineering Review 11(2), 93–136 (1996)
18. VegA, http://www.inra.fr/arpvega/
19. AlvisNLP for A01H, http://bibliome.jouy.inra.fr/A01H/index.php

ReBEC: A Method for Capturing Experience during Software Development Projects

Gerardo Matturro[1] and Andrés Silva[2]

[1] Universidad ORT Uruguay, Cuareim 1451, 11200 Montevideo, Uruguay
matturro@uni.ort.edu.uy
[2] Universidad Politécnica de Madrid, 28660 Boadilla del Monte, Madrid, Spain
asilva@fi.upm.es

Abstract. In software organizations, usual ways to capture the experience project team members acquire are based on methods such as project postmortem analysis, post-project revisions and others alike. Their main drawback is that the experience capture is done (if ever) after project completion, which leads to the risk of losing it if, as usually occurs, team members are finally not available. This paper introduces ReBEC (Reflection-Based Experience Capture), an approach that enables organizations to integrate the experience capture activities into daily software project tasks. We also present the case study of the implementation of this approach in a software organization. The study results show that ReBEC allows an earlier capture of knowledge and experience compared to existing approaches, and identify sources of knowledge as well as lessons learned and proposals of best practices.

Keywords: Knowledge management, software engineering, experience capture.

1 Introduction

The knowledge and experience that team members acquire as they carry out a software project conforms a valuable asset for organizations that aim to improve their software practices and processes for future projects [1]. For this to happen, software organizations should assure that the knowledge gained in a project is not lost, and it must be first captured and then, stored and managed for reutilization [2] [3]. Common approaches for capturing that knowledge and experiences are based on techniques such as semi-structured interviews [4], [5] or by applying methods such as project postmortem analysis [6], post-project revisions [7] and legacy sessions [8], among others. The main drawback of these approaches is that the capturing process usually takes place at a later time then of the occurrence of the experience itself and it is required that the people who own the experience be available to participate in this capturing process, which in general is not possible.

In this paper we present an approach to capture software project experience that differs from the above mentioned methods mainly in two aspects: the way the experience is captured, and the moment in the project life cycle this capture takes place.

This remainder of this article is organized as follows. In section 2 we present a general overview of the existing approaches for capturing software project experiences

P. Cimiano and H.S. Pinto (Eds.): EKAW 2010, LNAI 6317, pp. 524–533, 2010.

along with their main weaknesses. In section 3 the concept to reflective practice is introduced as a key element in the design of our approach. Section 4 is devoted to present a general overview of ReBEC, with a description of the phases it is structured, and to introduce the "reflective guides", the proposed knowledge management tool used to capture experience. In section 5 we present the case study we conducted in a software organization to study the application of our approach. In section 6 we discuss the conclusion of the study. Finally, in section 7 we present the conclusions of the article and describe the future works and research lines.

2 Related Works and Criticisms

Several methods have been proposed for capturing of knowledge and experiences that project team members acquire as they carry out a software project.

The project post-mortem analysis [6] comprises three phases: preparation, data collection, and analysis. In the preparation phase all the documentation generated during the project is reviewed in order to determine the goals for the postmortem analysis. The data collection phase is the moment in which the relevant project experience is gathered and, once the important topics have been identified, they are prioritized before proceeding with the analysis phase. During this last phase, a feedback session is conducted in order to analyze the data collected and to find the causes for positive and negative experiences.

The legacy sessions [8] refers to the working sessions where project team members identify innovations and improvements that they have performed in their projects and that are potentially valuable for future users. A legacy session consists of four parts. The first part consists of a brainstorming session to identify potential legacies (apprenticeships that have the potential of being re-used by the members of the project team or by other members of the organization). In the second part, the participants synthesize the results of the former phase categorizing them as "processes", "products" or "people", and an element is chosen for subsequent discussion. The third phase is the detailed discussions of the chosen element for, in the fourth phase, create a summary of the revision done.

The post-project reviews [7] are a way to provide a formal mechanism to transfer experience from a project team to an organizational memory once the project has finished and while these experiences are still fresh in the minds of the participants. The captured experience is stored in a repository of learned lessons whose purpose is to facilitate the organization, maintenance and spread of the captured knowledge.

All the above described methods are characterized by the fact that the capture of experience is done later in time with regard to the actual occurrence of the experience, generally after finishing the project or by the time it has reached a relevant milestone.

The main problem with these approaches is that they arrive very late in the life of a project, if they are ever done, because when a project is finished, team members are almost immediately reassigned to a new one, taking with them their individual knowledge, and there is no time for such reviews [9], [10], [11], [12], [13].

Thus, to separate in time the experience and its subsequent capture involves some risks. Experience might be lost if team members are no longer available because they have been assigned another project or they have abandoned the organization.

Based on these considerations, a new approach is needed as long as: 1) it previously establishes the specific types of knowledge and experiences that are interesting to capture and 2) the capture of the knowledge and experience happens while the project is under execution.

Another topic that is central to our approach is the concept of "reflection". Raelin defines *reflection* as the practice of periodically stepping back to ponder the meaning to self about what has recently transpired. Reflection illuminates what has been experienced by self, providing a basis for future action [14]. Reflection is considered to be an essential part of a learning process and reflective practice is the method by which reflection is made a conscious and structured activity. Reflection should be built into every activity, project or work piece in order to maximize learning from everyday activity [15]. Schön introduced the reflective practitioner perspective in which professional rethink and examine their work during and after accomplishing the creative process [16].

According to Hazzan and Tomayko, an analysis of the software engineering field, and the kind of work that software engineers usually perform, supports applying the reflective practitioner perspective to software engineering [17].

One traditional tool used in reflection activities is the reflective journal. A reflective journal records a learning item that took place as a result of reflecting on experiences and situations [15].

3 Proposed Approach for Experience Capture

Based on the considerations detailed in the previous section, we have defined a different viewpoint for capturing the knowledge and the experience that is acquired during software projects execution. This new viewpoint is characterized by a) incorporating the perspective of the reflective practice and the use of reflective diaries in the activities of software projects, b) take into account the problems pointed out in section 2 related to the traditional forms of post-mortem analysis and similar methods and c) integrating the experience capture process with the activities of software projects and software processes improvement efforts.

3.1 General Overview

Our approach is structured in four phases, as shown in Figure 1. From the set of the software practices and processes in use in the organization, in the Capture Objectives Definition phase a set of knowledge and experience capture objectives are establish for those software practices and processes that the organizations wants to improve. Based on these objectives, in the next phase the reflective guides are created. These guides contain a series of questions or sentences whose purpose is to guide and facilitate the analysis and reflection over the realization of the project tasks by the members of the project team.

Once these guides have been elaborated, the next step consists of assigning those guides to the members of the project teams who, during the execution period of their project tasks, use the guides to register their reflections and impressions, the difficulties found, unexpected events and similar considerations in relation to the way they those tasks are actually performed.

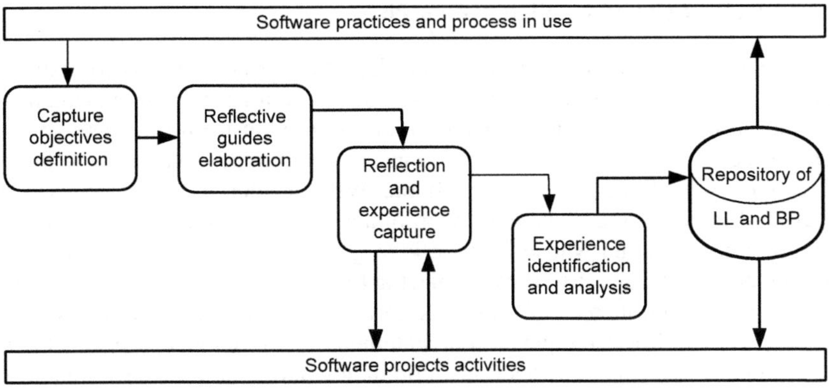

Fig. 1. Graphical representation of the proposed approach

Once the project tasks are finished and the questions or sentences have been answered, the guides are collected for analysis and for identifying new knowledge and experiences captured in the answers. This last activity provides, for the next phase, the inputs of new knowledge and personal experience in order to carry out the process of identifying and taking out the lessons learned during the execution of the project activities and the identification of the proposal of best practices that, later, will be incorporated to a Repository of Learned Lessons and Best Practices.

These new captured experiences and knowledge will impact the manner in which project activities will be carried out in the future. They will become a basis for incorporating improvements to current practices and processes in use. This sequence of activities can be repeated in an iterative way to incrementally manage the creation of knowledge and the organizational learning based on experience, integrating the knowledge and experience management activities with software projects and software process improvement initiatives.

3.2 The Experience Capture Objectives Definition Phase

The purpose of this phase is to define the objectives of knowledge and experience capture for the target practices, techniques or software processes. To define these objectives we propose to use the well-known Bloom's taxonomy of educational objectives [18]. The way to express the capture objectives is to formulate questions and sentences that, taking into account the cognitive processes associated with the different levels of Bloom´s taxonomy, point to those aspects of the practices or processes from which we will try to capture experience. Asking questions is nothing new. The difference here is that these questions are asked "before" the team members perform their project activities and not "after" those activities has been performed. In this way, respondents know in advance the questions he/she will have to answer later, and find them in a better position to reflect on and to give a more detailed answer.

To elaborate these reflective questions or sentences, it is necessary to take into account: a) the concepts related to the practices, techniques or software processes in relation to which the experience is going to be captured and b) certain keywords usually associated with each level of Bloom´s taxonomy, that express corresponding cognitive operations. Lists of key words can be found in [18].

3.3 The Reflective Guides Elaboration Phase

One the experience capture objectives are defined, the next step is to elaborate the reflective guides. As we define them, these guides are a knowledge management tool whose purpose is to guide the reflection done by project team members about those project aspects from which it is desired to gather experiences, according to the experience capture objectives previously defined. We consider the reflective guide as a special kind of reflective diary that incorporates questions and statements elaborated in the previous step, and whose purpose is to guide the analysis and the reflection of team members with regard to those project activities that were assigned to them, and to focus their attention on those aspects of their activities from which we want to gather experience. For each question or statement, team members will be able to provide an answer with those reflections, comments and problems encountered during the execution of his/her project tasks.

3.4 The Reflection and Experience Capture Phase

Once the reflective guides have been elaborated, they are handed in to the members of the project team who are responsible to carry out the project activities respective of which the objectives to capture experience were formulated. This delivery is done in a brief meeting in which team members are given an explanation about the purpose and content of the guides, and how they are supposed to use them as part of their project activities. During this phase then, team members should use the guides as an aid to analyze and to reflect on the execution of their project activities, and to record their reflections and experiences as a way to answer the reflective questions or statements.

3.5 The Experience Identification and Analysis Phase

Once the project activities related to the reflective guides have finished and the team members have answered the questions, the guides are collected back for their analysis. This analysis consists in extracting from the answers those passages that might be considered "lessons learned" during the realization of project activities, and those passages that have the potential of becoming proposals for "best practices". The learned lessons and the proposals of best practices obtained will be incorporated into a repository to make them accessible to the rest of the organization (see Fig. 1).

3.6 The Repository of Lessons Learned and Best Practices

This repository, in our proposal, has a tree-like structure, based on the software engineering knowledge areas provided by the Guide to the Software Engineering Body of Knowledge [19]. Each leaf of the tree points to the actual lessons learned and/or best practices related to their corresponding knowledge area. Any team member in a new project will be able to access the repository and find the lessons learned and best practices relevant for the projects activities he or she is carrying out.

To ensure these knowledge assets are used in new software projects, when the reflective guides are assigned to team members they will include references to the lessons learned and best practices in the repository related to the project activities they are going to perform. In Figure 1, this is represented by the arrow that goes from the Repository to the "software project activities".

Going through several iterations over the same project activities, those lessons learned and best practices can be continuously refined and, when they became stable, the knowledge and experiences they represent can be formally integrated into the organizational software process specification. In Figure 1, this is represented by the arrow that goes from the Repository to "Software practices and process in use".

4 Empirical Study

To illustrate our approach and the use of reflective guides, we present here the study conducted from April to July of 2009 at the Software Factory (ORTsf), an academic unit within the Software Engineering department of the Universidad ORT Uruguay.

4.1 Research Questions and Projects Selected for the Study

The two research questions for the study were stated as follows: 1) How to capture the knowledge and experience that team members acquire during software projects, in a way that such capture is done earlier than with existing approaches; 2) What kind of knowledge and experience can be captured by using the reflective guides.

The strategy chosen was a case study [20]. The conditions of the context are particularly important to be considered because we aim to study the proposed approach as embedded into the daily working activities of the members of a real software project team working in real software development.

Three independent software development projects were considered in this study, as shown in Table 1. The project teams were integrated by 3 to 5 students of the last course of Systems Engineering career at the University. In each team, typical roles in software projects, like project manager, requirements engineer, architect, developer and tester, were distributed among its members. A working condition for the teams was to work together on-site (in the facilities of the University) for at least 10 hours weekly, in order to promote team cohesion and also to have a similar working ambience to that of a software organization. The remaining 20 expected weekly hours in the project, the students had the freedom to work at the University or in any other alternative place at their choice. Each project had a "real" customer, namely, an organization, independent of the University, to which the products was targeted. This characteristic of the chosen projects makes the work of the project groups similar to that in software development organizations: several projects being developed simultaneously, not uniform development practices through the different projects, and different deadlines, handing in dates and commitments with the respective customers.

Table 1. Projects selected for the empirial study

Name	Description	Persons
COODESOR	Management system for a dentistry medical organization	4
GESA	Management system for the Uruguayan accreditation organism	3
SCPI	Investment projects follow up and control system	5

4.2 Reflective Guides Content and Elaboration

The first step in defining the contents of the reflective guides, is to define which practices and processes they will focus on. In ORTsf there is historical data regarding the software practices that are usually assessed as "inefficient" when performed by project teams. Based on this data, we use ReBEC to capture experiences aimed to improve the processes of defining metrics for project management.

We used this software engineering activity as a base for the definition of the aims of capturing the experience and for elaborating the reflective guides for the case study. The questions and statements included in the guides were elaborated by the first author in cooperation with a member of the ORTsf staff who, based on working experiences with other former project teams, has good knowledge about the specific aspects of the chosen practices that are important to take into account.

4.3 Data Collection and Analysis

The reflective guides were elaborated and given to the project managers of the competing teams, who used them during their project activities and returned them back with all questions answered. What follows are extracts of those answers for some of the reflective questions. The full guides with the complete answers can be obtained from the first author.

Question 3 and extracts of answers are presented in Table 2.

Table 2. Answers to question 3 (Level 4, Analysis, of Bloom's taxonomy)

Q. 3: According to your experience, how could you overcome the difficulties for identifying metrics useful for your project?
COODESOR: ... *today the difficulty we have is identifying some metric that is missing from our point of view ... to overcome this I will be reading the literature on the issue and I also want to meet with the Manager role tutor to learn how we are situated related to metrics.*
GESA: ... *we used documentation from previous projects, meetings with role tutors for project management tasks and meetings with the group tutor.*
SCPI: *With the help of the project's tutor, of the reviewer and the SQA role tutor ... the information available in the Software Factory web site was very useful ...*

Question 5 and extract of answers are presented in Table 3.

Table 3. Answers to question 5 (Level 6, Evaluation, of Bloom's taxonomy)

Q. 5: Report, in a few lines, the lessons learned during the metrics planning process.
COODESOR: ... *what I can say is that, given that I work in a maintenance project, I have observed the differences between a maintenance project and a development project ...*
GESA: ... *the metrics used in other projects cannot always be reused, each project must be evaluated by itself and individual metrics defined for that project. What we hear in class or read in books may not always be applicable to the project we are carrying out.*
SCPI: ... *we realized that just the "theoretical" framework is not enough, because metrics need to be adapted to the project's reality.*

Finally, question 7 and extract of answers are presented in Table 4.

Table 4. Answers to question 7 (Level 5, Synthesis, of Bloom's taxonomy)

Q. 7: Of those metrics-related management activities you carried out, which ones you consider your performance was adequate and which should be improved?
COODESOR: *...having a talk with the team to make them understand the significance of time records...define the metrics to be used at the very beginning of the project, something that I did not do because of lack of experience and, establishing them after X time after the project had begun it is harder to collect the information needed for metrics to represent reality ... the metrics to use have been well selected ... avoiding collecting metrics that do not contribute too much and that consume more time from the project.*
GESA: *I consider that the activity records of the group members were correctly carried out. I would improve the iteration estimation task ...*
SCPI: ... *we still cannot say what we did right or wrong ... later on, when we use the collected data, we may actually know the errors we made in planning.*

To answer the research questions asked in sub-section 5.1, we proceeded to perform a qualitative analysis of the answers given by the people taking part. This analysis comes from abstracting away those elements that are considered to be important or pertinent to answer the research questions [21]. In our case, these elements were chosen from those answers that present chunks of experience acquired during project activities. To refer to these sections of the answers, in the following we will use the convention (Project Name, Question number from which the answer was extracted).

With regard to the first research question, the analysis of the answers indicates that they refer to accurate aspects derived from the experience of having executed the project activities, elaborated during the period in which the definition of the project management metrics activities were performed. One of the criticisms formulated to the existing approaches for capturing experience is that the process of capturing usually happens once the project is finished. With the reflective guides, this capturing process occurred while projects unfold, because team members were asked to use the reflective guides and to elaborate the answers as part of their project tasks.

With regard to the second research question, the analysis of the answers allows us to identify sources of knowledge, learned lessons and proposals of best practices.

Regarding the identification of the source of knowledge, the answers allow us to identify sources of explicit as well as of tacit knowledge. Expressions such as "...meetings with role tutors... and with the group tutor..." (GESA,3), "...with the help of the project tutor, the reviewer and the SQA role tutor..." (SCPI,3) enable identification of tacit knowledge sources. Similarly, expressions such as "...we used documentation from previous projects..." (GESA,3), "...the information available in ORTsf web site was very useful..." (SCPI,3) indicate sources of explicit knowledge.

The knowledge and experience captured in the guides enable us the identification of lessons learned, derived also from carrying out the project tasks. Expressions such as "...something I did not do because of lack of experience and that were more difficult to collect a long time after the project had begun..." (COODESOR,7), "...metrics need to be adapted to the project's reality..." (SCPI,5) show learned lessons during the project activities.

With regard to the identification of proposals of best practices, expressions such as "...having a team meeting to make them realize the significance of keeping time records..." (COODESOR,7), "...establishing the metrics to be used at the very beginning of the project..." (COODESOR,7) may be considered recommendations to follow that, adequately developed, will allow the formulation of best practices.

5 Conclusions and Further Work

In this article we presented ReBEC, a new approach for capturing experiences in software projects, by using a knowledge management tool we named "reflective guides". Different from the pre-existing approaches discussed in section 2, the proposed method is based on a previous establishment of the specific types of knowledge and experiences that are interesting for capture, and on the capture of this knowledge and experience as projects unfold, instead of waiting to capture them once the project is over. In this way, problems and inconveniences that arise from postponing the capture of experience after the project ends, as discussed in section 2, are solved.

We also presented an empirical study for an implementation of the proposed approach in a software organization, with the purpose of showing that the reflective guides constitute an adequate tool for the capture of knowledge and experience that members acquire during the realization of a software project. The reflective guides were used by the project managers of the selected projects as an aid to facilitate the reflection on their respective project activities, and as guidelines to capture the knowledge and experience they acquired while doing their project activities. The qualitative analysis of the answers allowed us to gather, at least, three kinds of knowledge artifacts: sources of knowledge in the organization, lessons learned during the execution of project activities, and proposals of best practices.

Based on these positive results, in ORTsf we are planning to extend the use of the reflective guides to capture experiences from other software engineering activities.

One aspect that requires additional work is the possibility of enrichment of the answers to the reflective questions, in order to allow team members to add more details or enhanced descriptions of their experience. At first sight, this can be done by introducing the role of a facilitator to help team members in improving their abilities to reflect and to write better answers.

Another question that also deserves further research relates to the time consumed by team members in answering the reflective guides and the other activities of ReBEC, such as reflective guides preparation and the analysis of the answers given, and how it compares with the times required to carry out the other methods presented in section 2. We consider that it is necessary not only to have quantitative data about this timing. Qualitative data is also needed in order to take into consideration the quality and richness of the results obtained with ReBEC, compared to others methods.

References

1. Briand, L.: On the many ways software engineering can benefit from knowledge engineering. In: Proc. 14th International Conference on Software Engineering and Knowledge Engineering, pp. 3–6 (2003)
2. Rus, I., Lindvall, M.: Knowledge Management in Software Engineering. IEEE Software 19(3), 26–38 (2002)

3. Antunes, B., Seco, N., Gomes, P.: Knowledge management using semantic web technologies: An application in software development. In: Proc. 4th International Conference on Knowledge Capture, pp. 187–188 (2007)
4. Komi-Sirvio, S., Mantyniemi, A., Seppanen, V.: Toward a practical solution for capturing knowledge for software projects. IEEE Software 19(3), 60–62 (2002)
5. Scott, L., Jeffrey, R.: An anatomy of an experience repository. In: Proc. of the 2003 International Symposium on Empirical Software Engineering, pp. 162–173 (2003)
6. Birk, A., Dingsoyr, T., Stalhane, T.: Postmortem: never leave a project without it. IEEE Software 19(3), 43–45 (2002)
7. Harrison, W.: A software engineering lessons learned repository. In: Proc. 27th Annual NASA Goddard/IEEE Software Engineering Workshop (2003)
8. Cooper, L., Majchrzak, A., Faraj, S.: Learning from project experiences using a legacy-based approach. In: Proc. 38th Hawaii International Conference on System Sciences (2005)
9. Basili, V., Lindvall, M., Costa, P.: Implementing the Experience Factory as a set of experience bases. In: Proc. 13th International Conference on Software Engineering and Knowledge Engineering, pp. 102–109 (2001)
10. Desouza, K., Dingsøyr, T., Awazu, Y.: Experiences with conducting project postmortems. In: Proc. 38th Hawaii International Conference on System Sciences (2005)
11. Cooper, L.: Converting project team experience to organizational learning. In: Proc. 40th Hawaii International Conference on System Sciences (2007)
12. Bjørnson, F.: Knowledge management in software process improvement, Doctoral Thesis, Norwegian University of Science and Technology (2007)
13. Zedtwitz, M.: Organizational learning through post-project reviews in R&D. R&D Management 32(3), 255–268 (2002)
14. Raelin, J.: Work-based learning. Prentice Hall, Upper Saddle (2002)
15. Clifford, J., Thorpe, S.: Workplace learning and development. Kogan Page, London (2007)
16. Schön, D.: Educating the reflective practitioner. Jossey-Bass, San Francisco (1987)
17. Hazzan, O., Tomayko, J.: Reflection and abstraction in learning software engineering's human aspects. IEEE Computer 38(6), 39–45 (2005)
18. Bloom, B., Engelhart, M., Furst, E., Hill, W., Krathwohl, D.: Taxonomy of educational objectives. In: Handbook I: Cognitive domain. David McKay, New York (1956)
19. Abran, A., Moore, J.: Guide to the software engineering body of knowledge. IEEE Computer Society, Los Alamitos (2004)
20. Yin, R.: Case study research. Design and methods. Sage, Thousand Oaks (2003)
21. Blaxter, L., Hughes, L., Tight, M.: How to research. Open University, Philadelphia (1996)

Reasoning by Analogy in the Generation of Domain Acceptable Ontology Refinements

Laura Moss[1,2,3], Derek Sleeman[1,2], and Malcolm Sim[2]

[1] Department of Computing Science, University of Aberdeen, Aberdeen, AB24 3FX
[2] University Section of Anaesthesia, Pain, & Critical Care Medicine, Glasgow Royal Infirmary, Glasgow, G4 0SF
[3] Department of Clinical Physics, University of Glasgow, Glasgow, G12 8QQ
lauramoss@nhs.net

Abstract. Refinements generated for a knowledge base often involve the learning of new knowledge to be added to or replace existing parts of a knowledge base. However, the justifiability of the refinement in the context of the domain (domain acceptability) is often overlooked. The work reported in this paper describes an approach to the generation of domain acceptable refinements for incomplete and incorrect ontology individuals through reasoning by analogy using existing domain knowledge. To illustrate this approach, individuals for refinement are identified during the application of a knowledge-based system, EIRA; when EIRA fails in its task, areas of its domain ontology are identified as requiring refinement. Refinements are subsequently generated by identifying and reasoning with similar individuals from the domain ontology. To evaluate this approach EIRA has been applied to the Intensive Care Unit (ICU) domain. An evaluation (by a domain expert) of the refinements generated by EIRA has indicated that this approach successfully produces domain acceptable refinements.

Keywords: Ontology Refinement, Analogical Reasoning, Medicine.

1 Introduction and Related Work

Bundy [3] suggests that ontologies (like any defined knowledge base) evolve over time; a model can only capture a finite description of the world, decisions made in the modelling of the domain can be *"overturned by experimental evidence or changes in specification"*. Previous approaches to (semi-automatic) ontology construction (also considered as ontology learning [16]) generally rely on a large text corpus to automatically extract concepts and relationships, for example, Text2Onto [5]. The validation and verification of ontologies is also a widely covered research topic (for a summary see [14]). The competency of an ontology is often evaluated using several distinct approaches: the first by testing the ontology against a list of competency questions which it should be able to answer, and the second by checking aspects of structural consistency using tools such as ODEClean [8]. For an ontology, incompleteness and incorrectness can exist at

P. Cimiano and H.S. Pinto (Eds.): EKAW 2010, LNAI 6317, pp. 534–543, 2010.

both the structural level (TBox) and the instance (individual) level (ABox). The field of ontology evolution can provide some support for ontology refinement (e.g. [12]) and attempts have recently been made at automating the process [15]. However, the majority of previous work (ontology learning, validation, and evolution) has focused on the refinement (or creation) of the taxonomic structure of an ontology, and removing inconsistencies in ontologies (e.g. [9],[10]); the validity of values associated with individuals in an ontology has been largely neglected.

The approach presented in this paper generates refinements for *individuals* in an ontology (rather than the TBox) and differs from previous time consuming and knowledge intensive approaches by using *existing* domain knowledge contained in analogous individuals. Gentner [7] describes reasoning by analogy as *"a kind of reasoning that applies between specific exemplars or cases, in which what is known about one exemplar is used to infer new information about another exemplar"*. The use of reasoning by analogy in ontology engineering is mainly confined to reuse processes such as mapping, and merging of ontologies, and has largely not been explored in ontology refinement; one notable exception is the LEARNER system [4] which generates refinements for incomplete ontologies. The approach described in this work extends previous work by generating refinements (automatically) for *both* incomplete and incorrect ontology individuals.

The rest of this paper is organised as follows; section 2 discusses the approach implemented in EIRA to generate ontology refinements and its application to the Intensive Care Unit (ICU) domain; section 3 details an evaluation of the refinements generated; section 4 discusses conclusions and future work.

2 Reasoning by Analogy to Generate Refinements

2.1 EIRA

EIRA, an existing knowledge-based system has previously been applied in the ICU domain to produce explanations for anomalous patient responses to treatment[1]. Figure 1 provides an overview of EIRA (the following numbers in brackets correspond to numbers in the figure). EIRA's explanation generation process starts when an ICU clinician enters an anomaly into EIRA (1). EIRA can also detect (if possible) additional anomalies at the same time as the clinician detected anomaly (2). The explanations produced by EIRA are generated by the application of strategies with (medical) domain knowledge represented in several ontologies (3)(4). A number of explanations for the anomaly are then presented to the ICU clinician (5). To identify the strategies (algorithms) implemented in EIRA, interviews were held with ICU clinicians during which they were asked to provide explanations for a number of pre-identified anomalous patient responses to treatment. These interviews and explanations were subsequently analysed and high level strategies used by the clinicians were extracted and implemented in EIRA.

[1] For further details see [11].

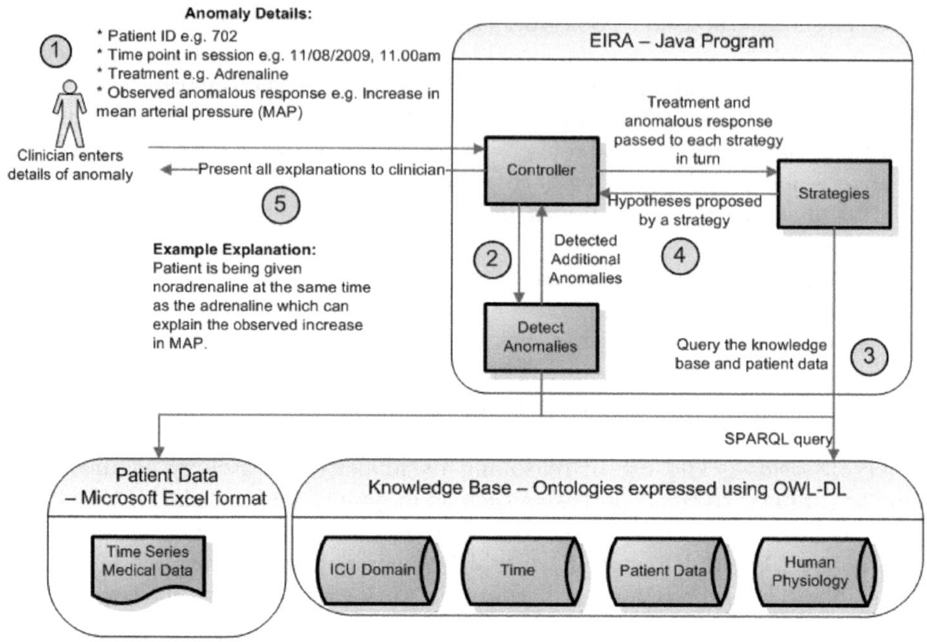

Fig. 1. Overview of EIRA

2.2 Generating Ontology Refinements

EIRA has been recently extended to reason by analogy to generate ontology refinements. For each explanation produced by EIRA, the clinician using the tool can respond by dismissing it, fully agreeing with it, or specifying that the explanation requires further (clinical) investigation. If the clinician dismisses the explanation, EIRA analyses the reasoning processes that generated the explanation[2]. An incorrect explanation indicates that either the strategies used by EIRA to produce the explanation were inappropriate or parts of EIRA's knowledge base are incorrect. The work described focuses on the refinement of EIRA's knowledge base; approaches to refine incorrect or insufficient rules (as strategies can be considered to be rules) have previously been explored in the theory revision literature (e.g.[6]). Of course, the knowledge base in EIRA may not only contain incorrect knowledge, it may also be incomplete, which prevents explanations from being generated. Incomplete knowledge may be identified when a query of the knowledge base fails to return any results. To refine the knowledge base (for both incorrect and incomplete individuals) it is proposed that knowledge about concepts and individuals which are *similar* to the erroneous concept(s) is used to suggest refinements. The following definition of similarity

[2] It is assumed that the ICU clinician provides a gold standard to commence the *generation* of a refinement, however, a consensus between multiple clinicians will be required before the refinement is actually *implemented* in the knowledge base.

has been applied: two individuals can be considered similar if they are both instances of the same class (or immediate super-class).

The process of generating a refinement starts when either EIRA has detected missing information in the knowledge base or a clinician has stated that an explanation is incorrect. In both cases the SPARQL [2] queries used by EIRA are examined to identify the areas of the knowledge base potentially requiring refinement[3]. For each SPARQL query, the following high-level steps are followed:

1. Determine the type (class) of the individual containing a missing or incorrect property value(s) (the subject of the SPARQL triple).
2. Examine other individuals of the same (or similar) type.
3. Identify from these, individuals which have at least one value for the property (the predicate) used in the SPARQL triple.
4. Suggest refinements to the knowledge base which involve the property values of the other individuals.

To allow the domain expert/s to consider the impact of a proposed refinement to the ontology, EIRA identifies (using the Explanation Ontology, described later) previously correct explanations generated from the parts of the domain ontology for which a refinement has now been generated. A domain expert is asked to consider the impact of the refinement which may result in the following responses: 1) decline the current refinement as the associated change to a previous explanation is not acceptable, 2) accept the refinement because it does not change previous explanations, and 3) re-analyse a (previously correct) explanation as it is now considered to be incorrect in light of the proposed refinement.

Generating Refinements for Incomplete Individuals. To identify incomplete parts of EIRA's knowledge base, the results from SPARQL queries used in EIRA are examined; when a SPARQL query fails to return any results, the parts of the ontology queried require further investigation.

A SPARQL query can fail to return any results when either the information in the ontology does not match the components of the query, or information is missing from the knowledge base. When a SPARQL query fails, it is examined further by dividing the query into (triple) patterns, investigating each pattern in turn. The following types of triple patterns are used in EIRA's algorithms (the examples are taken from the ICU domain)[4]:

- **A** - RDF-Term, RDF-Term, Variable, e.g.
  <http://www.owl-ontologies.com/unnamed.owl#Hypoadrenal Crisis>
  <http://www.owl-ontologies.com/unnamed.owl#additionalSymptoms>
  ?additionalSymptom.

[3] SPARQL is a W3C recommended query language for RDF (Resource Description Framework [1].), and is used to query ontologies.

[4] It is acknowledged that other types of triple patterns (e.g. Variable, Variable, Variable) could theoretically occur in a SPARQL query, however, they are not currently used in the implementation of EIRA.

– **B** - Variable, RDF-Term, RDF-Term, e.g.
?symptom
<http://www.owl-ontologies.com/unnamed.owl#clinicalFeatures>
<http://www.owl-ontologies.com/unnamed.owl#DecreaseHeartRate>.

– **C** - Variable, RDF-Term, Variable, e.g.
?condition,
<http://www.owl-ontologies.com/unnamed.owl#additionalSymptoms>
?symptom.

Triple pattern of type A is the simplest to investigate. In the example given, if the triple pattern did not return any results, it can be determined that 'Hypoadrenal Crisis' has no associated additional symptoms in the ontology. In this example, additional symptoms for 'Hypoadrenal Crisis', can be suggested by using individuals which are similar to 'Hypoadrenal Crisis'. To enable this the class (or super-class) of the subject in the triple (T) being examined is determined and other individuals of this class are identified. For each individual identified, if an object (property value) is associated via the same predicate (property) as in T, then the object is suggested as a refinement for the original triple. The algorithm only examines the class and super-class of the individual as moving further up the class hierarchy reduces the likelihood that suggestions acceptable to a domain expert will be found. Following the above example, the ontology is queried to determine the type (class) of 'Hypoadrenal Crisis', which in this case is 'Adrenal Disorder'. Other individuals with type 'Adrenal Disorder' are then retrieved from the ontology (e.g. 'Phaeocromocytoma'), if none are found then the super-class of the type ('Adrenal Disorder') is examined (e.g. 'Metabolic Disorder'). When another, similar, individual is identified it is examined to determine if the 'additionalSymptoms' property relates it to another individual. For example, it can be determined that 'Phaeocromocytoma' is associated with 'HighHeartRate' and 'Anxiety' via the 'additionalSymptoms' property. A refinement for the 'Hypoadrenal Crisis' class may then be suggested in which 'HighHeartRate' and 'Anxiety' are associated with 'Hypoadrenal Crisis' via the 'additionalSymptoms' property.

For triple pattern types B and C, if no results are returned by the query these triple patterns are not investigated further unless the triple patterns exist as part of a sequence of triple patterns. For example, if triple pattern B in the example given does not return any results, then it can be inferred that no individuals exist in the ontology with a value for the 'clinicalFeatures' property of 'DecreaseHeartRate' and hence it is not an appropriate scenario for refinement. Similarly, if triples of pattern type C fail, then it is not possible to make a suggestion as no other individuals exist in the ontology to compare against. The only situation where it may be possible to make suggestions for values using type B or C triples is when they occur as part of a sequence of triple patterns within the same query (i.e. the SPARQL query examines several parts of the knowledge base), in these scenarios information can be used from the other triple patterns in the query. For example, the following SPARQL query contains two triple patterns (the first of type B and the second of type A):

SPARQL query: SELECT ?symptom WHERE ?symptom
<http://www.owl-ontologies.com/unnamed.owl#clinicalFeatures>
<http://www.owl-ontologies.com/unnamed.owl#IncreaseHeartRate>.
<http://www.owl-ontologies.com/unnamed.owl#Phaeocromocytoma>
<http://www.owl-ontologies.com/unnamed.owl#additionalSymptoms> ?symptom

The first triple pattern (TP1) would not be examined as its subject is an unknown concept (i.e. a variable, '?symptom'). The algorithm would then proceed to examine the second triple pattern (TP2); if it does return results and further, if the variables in both triple patterns have the same variable name (i.e. '?symptom'), then TP2 can be used to enable a further examination of TP1. This is achieved by substituting '?symptom' in TP1 with each value for '?symptom' from the results of TP2. For example, once it has been determined that 'Phaeocromocytoma' has the 'additionalSymptom', 'HighHeartRate', it is possible to examine TP1 by replacing '?symptom' with 'HighHeartRate'.

Generating Refinements for Incorrect Individuals. For each explanation generated by EIRA, which the domain expert classifies as incorrect, the associated SPARQL queries are identified from an Explanation Ontology. The Explanation Ontology models (domain-independently) the explanations generated by EIRA. Figure 2 provides a visualisation of the Explanation Ontology.

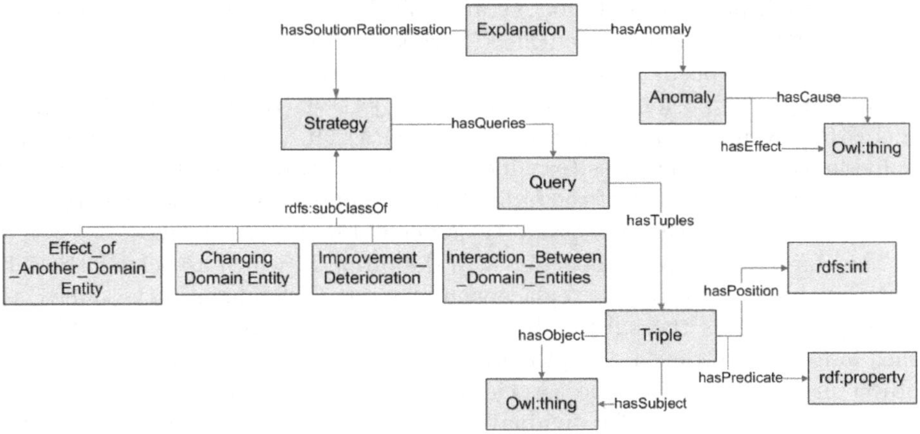

Fig. 2. Explanation Ontology Schema

The identified SPARQL queries are then segmented into triple patterns and examined further (as discussed in the previous section). The following types of refinements can be suggested by EIRA: replace the property value, remove the property value associated with an individual, and change the property associating the individual and property value. EIRA systematically determines if refinements can be generated for each type of refinement. For example, if the ontology (incorrectly) contains the 'expectedEffect' property relating the individual, 'Verapamil', with the property value, 'IncreaseHR' (i.e. verapamil is expected to increase a patient's heart rate), then the following refinements may be suggested by EIRA:

1. **Replace property value**, e.g. replace 'IncreaseHR' with another value, for example, 'DecreaseHR'.
2. **Remove the property value associated with an individual**, e.g. remove the property value, 'IncreaseHR', associated with 'Verapamil' via the 'expectedEffect' property.
3. **Change the property associating the individual (subject) and property value (object)**, e.g. relate 'Verapamil' and 'IncreaseHR' via another property, for example, the 'conditionalDrugEffect' property

The first type of refinement involves the examination of similar individuals to suggest a replacement value (object) which the property (predicate) should relate the (triple's) subject to. To enable this, EIRA determines if the class (or super-class) of the subject in the triple (T) contains other individuals. For each individual (I) identified, the value (V) related to I by the same property as T is noted. If V is associated with at least 25%[5] of the individuals examined then V is recommended as a refinement for T. Following the above example, if 'Verapamil' (the subject) and 'Propranolol' are individuals of the same super-class and it is observed that the property 'expectedEffect' relates 'Propranolol' to 'DecreaseHR', then the refinement suggested is to set 'DecreaseHR' as the value of the 'expectedEffect' property for 'Verapamil'; that is, expectedEffect(Verapamil, IncreaseHR) becomes, expectedEffect(Verapamil, DecreaseHR).

The second type of refinement removes the erroneous property value, and so the subject is no longer related to the object via the property. To achieve this EIRA examines each triple (T) in the SPARQL query and retrieves other individuals of the same class (or super class if no instances exist) as the subject in T. If greater than 50% of the individuals do not have the same property as T then it is suggested that the property associated with T is removed.

The third type of refinement replaces the property which associates the subject and object. To suggest a replacement property, individuals of the same class (or super-class) as the subject in the triple (T) are examined by EIRA. For each individual retrieved, the property which associates the individual with the object in T are noted (if the association occurs). If an identified property occurs in more than 50% of individuals examined then the property is suggested as a refinement for T. Following the previous example, if 'Verapamil' (the subject) and 'Propranolol' are individuals of the same super-class and it is observed that 'Propranolol' is related to the 'IncreaseHR' individual via the 'conditionalDrugEffect' property, then the algorithm suggests that the 'expectedEffect' property relating 'Verapamil' and 'IncreaseHR' is effectively replaced with the 'conditionalDrugEffect' property. In this case, the refinement of the knowledge base would involve: expectedEffect(Verapamil, IncreaseHR) being replaced by conditionalDrugEffect(Verapamil, IncreaseHR).

[5] The threshold levels applied in the three types of refinements have been agreed with an ICU clinician as sensible levels for this domain.

3 Evaluation

To evaluate whether the use of reasoning by analogy in EIRA (to suggest refinements to incomplete and incorrect ontology individuals) produced acceptable results, refinements generated by EIRA were presented to an ICU clinician for evaluation. To generate the refinements, test cases were created, each consisting of a medical treatment and anomalous response (as identified by an ICU clinician [11]), this information was entered into EIRA and on each occasion EIRA failed to produce an explanation, or produced an incorrect explanation, the subsequent ontology refinements generated by EIRA were noted.

3.1 Evaluating Refinements Generated for Incomplete Individuals

The test cases did not query all parts of the knowledge base (as the queries are based on the anomalies entered) and hence refinements were not generated for all the properties in the domain ontology. To produce a complete set of refinements, examples of missing property values (not previously identified by the test cases) were manually identified from the knowledge base and details entered into EIRA.

EIRA produced (manually and automatically as described above) 46 refinements which were presented to the clinician. The clinician was asked to state whether each refinement was clinically acceptable. For 7 out of the 46 possible refinements a mistake had been made and refinements had been generated for properties which should contain property values unique to the individual (e.g the name of a drug) and these were removed[6]. A further 2 refinements were not commented on by the clinician as he felt he lacked the required clinical knowledge.

For the remaining 37 refinements which the clinician did comment on, a total of 23 refinements (62.2%) were accepted by the ICU clinician and 14 refinements (37.8%) were classified as not acceptable; for these 14 refinements, the clinician stated that the property values suggested were not acceptable. In addition, for 7 cases, the clinician did not agree that the two compared individuals were similar (the majority of these cases had generated refinements judged as unacceptable). For these later cases it is suggested that the taxonomy (TBox) of the ICU domain ontology requires further refinement.

3.2 Evaluating Refinements Generated for Incorrect Individuals

Incorrect explanations generated by EIRA (as identified previously by an ICU clinician in [11]) were selected from the Explanation Ontology and refinements subsequently generated. A total of 72 explanations (instances) were contained in the Explanation Ontology. 11 of these explanations had previously been evaluated by an ICU clinician as incorrect (the remaining 61 were evaluated as correct

[6] These refinements are not considered as incorrect in the evaluation as the clinician agreed that it is completely meaningless to generate refinements for these properties. EIRA has subsequently been updated.

or required further clinical investigation). For 7 of the 11 incorrect explanations, the ICU clinician had previously suggested why the explanation was incorrect (i.e. suggested a refinement to the knowledge base) in interviews described in [11].

The evaluation of the refinements generated for an incorrect knowledge base consisted of two stages: the first identifies if the refinements made by the ICU clinician (for 7 of the incorrect explanations) could be reproduced by EIRA, and the second determines if refinements generated by EIRA for the remaining 4 'unexplained' incorrect explanations were acceptable to a domain expert. In the first stage of the evaluation, EIRA reproduced 4 out of the 7 refinements suggested by the ICU clinician; the refinements EIRA produced for the remaining 3 explanations (which did not match the previous clinician's refinements) were subsequently evaluated by an ICU clinician. In the second stage of the evaluation, refinements were generated by EIRA for the remaining 4 (out of 11) incorrect explanations for which the ICU clinician *did not* previously suggest any refinements. A total of 19 refinements were generated by EIRA and viewed by an ICU clinician. For two (out of the 19 refinements) generated by EIRA, the clinician again felt he lacked the required clinical knowledge to evaluate the refinements. Out of the remaining 17 refinements, the clinician agreed that 10 out of the 17 (58.8%) refinements were acceptable. If the refinements from both sets of evaluation are considered, the overall acceptance of the refinements generated by EIRA for an incorrect knowledge base is 61.9%.

4 Conclusions and Future Work

The results indicate that (ABox) ontology refinements, acceptable to a domain expert for both an incomplete and incorrect ontology, can be generated by reasoning by analogy. Further, this approach has the following advantages: *existing domain knowledge* contained in ontology individuals is used, thereby avoiding the requirement for additional domain datasets (which are often unavailable) and/or time consuming to acquire; this work indicates that *domain acceptable* refinements can be generated when the TBox of an ontology is organised from the same perspective as the properties for which the property values are being transferred; and finally the use of SPARQL queries and domain expert feedback allows for relatively easy *identification* of ABox elements requiring refinement.

Plans for future work include: the implementation of more complex definitions of similarity in EIRA as the ICU clinician disagreed at several points that the identified individuals were similar, Ricklefs et al [13] provide a comparison of such ontology similarity metrics; an extended evaluation, firstly by asking further ICU clinicians to evaluate EIRA's refinements, both individually and as a group to form a consensus evaluation, and secondly, an evaluation to determine whether the refinements accepted by the domain expert improve the number of satisfactory explanations generated by EIRA; finally, an exploration of the use of reasoning by analogy in EIRA to generate *new* domain knowledge.

Acknowledgments. Kathryn Henderson and Jennifer McCallum (CareVue Project) & the staff and patients of the ICU Unit, Glasgow Royal Infirmary. This work was an extension of the routine audit process in Glasgow Royal Infirmary's ICU; requirements for further Ethical Committee Approval have been waved. This work was supported under the EPSRC's grant number GR/N15764.

References

1. RDF, `http://www.w3.org/RDF/` (accessed October 2009)
2. SPARQL, `http://www.w3.org/TR/rdf-sparql-query/` (accessed October 2009)
3. Bundy, A.: Why Ontology Evolution Is Essential in Modelling Scientific Discovery. In: Proceedings of the 2008 AAAI Fall Symposium on Automated Scientific Discovery (2008)
4. Chklovski, T.L.: A System for Acquiring Commonsense Knowledge by Analogy. In: Proceedings of 2nd International Conference on Knowledge Capture (2003)
5. Cimiano, P., Völker, J.: Text2Onto. In: Natural Language Processing and Information Systems, pp. 227–238 (2005)
6. Craw, S., Sleeman, D.: Automating the Refinement of Knowledge-Based Systems. In: Proceedings of the Ninth European Conference on Artificial Intelligence (1990)
7. Gentner, D.: Analogical Reasoning, Psychology of. In: Encyclopedia of Cognitive Science. Nature Publishing Group (2002)
8. Guarino, N., Welty, C.A.: An overview of OntoClean. In: Handbook on Ontologies in Information Systems, pp. 151–172 (2004)
9. Horridge, M., Parsia, B., Sattler, U.: Laconic and Precise Justifications in OWL. In: Sheth, A.P., Staab, S., Dean, M., Paolucci, M., Maynard, D., Finin, T., Thirunarayan, K. (eds.) ISWC 2008. LNCS, vol. 5318, pp. 323–338. Springer, Heidelberg (2008)
10. Lam, J., Pan, J., Sleeman, D., Vasconcelos, W.: A Fine-Grained Approach to Resolving Unsatisfiable Ontologies. In: Proceedings of the 2006 IEEE/WIC/ACM International Conference on Web Intelligence, WI-2006 (2006)
11. Moss, L., Sleeman, D., Sim, M., Booth, M., Daniel, M., Donaldson, L., Gilhooly, C., Hughes, M., Kinsella, J.: Ontology-Driven Hypothesis Generation to Explain Anomalous Patient Responses to Treatment. Knowledge-Based Systems 23, 309–315 (2010)
12. Noy, N., Chugh, W., Liu, M., Musen, M.: A Framework for Ontology Evolution in Collaborative Environments. In: Cruz, I., Decker, S., Allemang, D., Preist, C., Schwabe, D., Mika, P., Uschold, M., Aroyo, L.M. (eds.) ISWC 2006. LNCS, vol. 4273, pp. 544–558. Springer, Heidelberg (2006)
13. Ricklefs, M., Blomqvist, E.: Ontology-Based Relevance Assessment: An Evaluation of Different Semantic Similarity Measures. In: Meersman, R., Tari, Z. (eds.) OTM 2008, Part II. LNCS, vol. 5332, pp. 1235–1252. Springer, Heidelberg (2008)
14. Sure, Y., Gómez-pérez, A., Daelemans, W., Reinberger, M.L., Guarino, N., Noy, N.F.: Why Evaluate Ontology Technologies? Because They Work! IEEE Intelligent Systems 19, 74–81 (2004)
15. Zablith, F., Sabou, M., d'Aquin, M., Motta, E.: Using Background Knowledge for Ontology Evolution. In: Proceedings of International Workshop on Ontology Dynamics (IWOD) at ISWC (2008)
16. Zhou, L.: Ontology Learning: State of the Art and Open Issues. Information Technology and Management 8, 241–252 (2007)

Evaluations of User-Driven Ontology Summarization

Ning Li and Enrico Motta

Knowledge Media Institute
The Open University
Milton Keynes, United Kingdom
{n.li,e.motta}@open.ac.uk

Abstract. Ontology Summarization has been found useful to facilitate ontology engineering tasks in a number of different ways. Recently, it has been recognised as a means to facilitate ontology understanding and then support tasks like ontology reuse in ontology construction. Among the works in literature, not only distinctive methods are used to summarize ontology, also different measures are deployed to evaluate the summarization results. Without a set of common evaluation measures in place, it is not possible to compare the performance and therefore judge the effectiveness of those summarization methods. In this paper, we investigate the applicability of the evaluation measures from ontology evaluation and summary evaluation domain for ontology summary evaluation. Based on those measures, we evaluate the performances of the existing user-driven ontology summarization approaches.

Keywords: Ontology Summarization, Evaluation, Semantic Web.

1 Introduction

Ontology Summarization, in recent years, has been recognised as an important tool, driven by users, to facilitate ontology understanding and help users quickly make sense of an ontology in order to support tasks like ontology reuse [1][2][3]. It has provided the basis for a number of user-centric technologies, such as the novel interactive frameworks for ontology visualization and navigation KC-Viz[1] and the online ontologies sharing and reusing system Cupboard[2]. Though there are a number of works in literature for ontology summarization, their evaluations are rather isolated from one another and there lacks a comparative view among the ontology summarization approaches. In fact, there lacks a systematic overview of what evaluation measures are there available and applicable for ontology summary evaluation.

As stated in [4], a key factor that makes a particular discipline or approach scientific is the ability to evaluate and compare the ideas within the area. For ontology summarization, evaluation measures can be very different depending on what drives or motivates the ontology summarization. For example, for task-driven ontology summarization, the evaluation can be task-specific and objective in that the criterion

[1] http://neon-toolkit.org/wiki/KC-Viz
[2] http://kmi-web06.open.ac.uk:8081/cupboard/

P. Cimiano and H.S. Pinto (Eds.): EKAW 2010, LNAI 6317, pp. 544–553, 2010.

can be based on whether the ontology summary satisfies the requirements of the specific task as the original ontology does while gaining the expected benefits such as reduced ontology size. Whereas for user-driven ontology summarization, the ultimate goal is to serve the user with the help of ontology engineering tools, and therefore the evaluation can be subjective as well as objective. In this paper, we focus on the evaluation of user-driven ontology summarization, which has not been systematically addressed in literature. The main contributions of this paper consist in the following two aspects, one is to provide a systematic view of the evaluation measures for ontology summary with focus on user-driven ontology summarization, and the other is to evaluate two user-driven ontology summarization systems in a comparative way using evaluation measures investigated here.

This paper is organized as follows. In section 2, we provide an introduction to ontology summarization and a review of the ontology summarization works in literature in a categorical view. Following this, we focus on the introduction of user-driven ontology summarization works. Section 3 presents an investigation of evaluation measures and their applicability in ontology summary evaluation. In Section 4, we give our evaluation results in a comparative way of the two user-driven ontology summarization approaches. Section 5 concludes the paper with discussions.

2. Ontology Summarization

2.1 Ontology Summarization Overview

Motivated by the definition of text summarization in natural language processing, the authors in [2] provided a definition for ontology summarization as "the process of distilling knowledge from ontology to produce an abridged version for a particular user (or users) and task (or tasks)". According to this definition, the information content of a summary depends on either user's needs or/and task's requirements. This is one way of classifying the ontology summarization works in literature. In following, we provide a categorical view of the ontology summarization approaches.

Driving force. Ontology summarization is mostly driven by certain needs of users or tasks that are observable to ontology engineers. Task-driven ontology summarization works include winnowing ontology from very large size to the size only necessary to meet the needs of querying tasks [5], downsizing Abox to improve the scalability of ontology reasoning tasks [6]. User-driven ontology summarization focuses on the needs of users to understand and make sense of ontology quickly in large-scale ontology spaces, such as the work in [1][2][3] which will be the focus of this paper and will be given more details in Section 2.2.

Working unit of summarization. Driven by different motivations, ontology summarization can operate at different levels and on different constitutional components of ontology. For example, in [6], the summarization object is ABox with aims to improve the scalability of reasoning tasks for ontologies containing large ABoxes. The work in [2][3] operates on RDF sentence in order to have summaries which contain both terms (concepts and properties) and relations among the terms. Whereas in [1], summaries contain only concepts with the belief that they are more effective in just helping user to know what this ontology is about than further details like how the ontology is structured which may have an adverse impact of confusing inexperienced users, and also with the observation that further navigation of more details of the whole ontology from key concepts is feasible and practical.

Extractive or abstractive. For text in natural language, summarization can be extractive in that summaries are produced by selecting a subset of the elements in the original document, or abstractive by rephrasing the information content of the original document [7]. Although summaries produced by humans are typically not extractive, most of the scientific researches on summarization, notably text summarization, are on extractive summarization because abstractive summarization is much harder to implement due to problems of semantic representation, inference and natural language generation. Though some problems in text summarization like semantic representation, inference are no longer difficult to solve in ontology summarization, most of the ontology summarization works in literature are also extractive because, unlike text which is natural language that can be expressed in many different ways, ontology is a formalized representation of knowledge having a much simpler but stricter syntax and semantics. Also, Ontology is already a carefully selected, by domain experts, bunch of concepts as well as their relations, properties and facts.

2.2 User-Driven Ontology Summarization

Contrary to task-driven ontology summarization, the ultimate goal for user-driven ontology summarization is to satisfy user's needs, which can be a very subjective matter. Therefore, it is not so easy to define a clear boundary of whether one summary is getting the job done or done better than another unless some clearly specified and commonly agreed criteria are laid. Therefore in following sections, we focus on the introduction of user-driven ontology summarization techniques, which will lead to the systematic investigation of ontology summary evaluation measures.

We have referred to three pieces of works, and the only three to the best of our knowledge, for user-driven ontology summarization aiming to facilitate ontology understanding. The work in [1] extracts key concepts as the best representatives of ontology and hence as ontology summary. In [1], a number of criteria were jointly considered, and correspondingly a number of algorithms were developed and linearly combined, to identify key concepts of an ontology. The criteria include: *name simplicity* which favors concepts that are labeled with simple names while penalizing compounds; *basic level* which measures how "central" a concept is in the taxonomy of the ontology; *density* highlights concepts which are richly characterized with properties and taxonomic relationships; *coverage* aims to ensure that no important part of the ontology is neglected; and *popularity* indentifies concepts that are commonly used. The summarization results, i.e. key concepts, were evaluated against human assessors' summaries, referred to as "ground truth". A good agreement has been found between algorithm-generated summaries with "ground truth".

There are other two works in [2] and [3] which also look into ontology summarization to facilitate user quickly make sense of what an ontology is about, but do not have the intention to support further exploitation of the ontology once user gets interested. Different from the work in [1], in [2] and [3], the authors take RDF sentence as the basic unit for summarization and extract the most salient/important sentences as summarization results. By constructing an RDF sentence graph with RDF sentences as vertices and links among them as edges, the authors calculate, for each vertex, a "centrality" value that determines the relative importance of a vertex within the graph. This work is largely motivated by the work of a graph-based text summarization [7]. Therefore, when it comes to evaluation, a lot of lessons have been learnt from the evaluation of text summarisation, which will be introduced with more details in Section 3.2.

3 Ontology Summary Evaluation

With those works around to do ontology summarization aiming to facilitate ontology understanding, it is more important than intriguing to compare their performances using similar, if not the same, evaluation measures in order to assist users in deciding the suitability of each approach to their own purpose. When approaching ontology summary evaluation, experiences have been gained from the two topics ontology summarization tries to cover or combine, apparently one is ontology evaluation, and the other is summary evaluation.

3.1 Ontology Evaluation

Ontology evaluation has been continuously researched since the beginning of ontology-supported engineering and the semantic web. However, there has not been a published work on ontology summary evaluation. There are similarities and dissimilarities between these two topics and therefore some, if not all, of the ontology evaluation approaches may be applicable for ontology summary evaluation. The ontology evaluation has been surveyed in work [4] and [8] and concisely summarized in [9]. Basically, the evaluation can be done automatically or manually and the evaluation can be carried out at different evaluation levels, which refer to the aspects of the ontology that are evaluated. A majority of the work in literature focus on the following three levels. 1) **Application-driven ontology evaluation**, in which the quality of an ontology is directly proportional to the performance of an application that uses it, 2) **Gold Standard based ontology evaluation**, where the quality of the ontology is expressed by its similarity to a manually built Gold Standard ontology, 3) **Corpus coverage ontology evaluation**, in which the quality of the ontology is represented by its appropriateness to cover the topic of a corpus.

Since ontology summarization aims to capture the most important parts of ontology while maintaining the focus of the conceptualized knowledge domain, theoretically, the above three types of evaluation schemes could be applied to ontology summary evaluation in a similar way as to ontology evaluation. However, as pointed out in [9], it has been recognized that they all have various levels of barriers to overcome when fulfilling ontology evaluation tasks. When it comes to ontology summary evaluation, these barriers actually become less prominent attributed fundamentally to the fact that the comparison now is not between two ontologies which most probably contain many different lexicons as well as concepts structured in many different ways, but between the original ontology and a subset of it. For example, in **Application-driven ontology evaluation**, problems lie in (a) the difficulty of assessing the quality of the supported task (e.g. search) and (b) creating a "clean " experimental environment where no other factors but the ontology influences the performance of the application [9]. When this type of evaluation is applied to ontology summary evaluation, these problems are no longer problems if the ontology summarization process is guided by the application, such as in [5] where the summarization is guided by the queries received from any dependent applications. When the guiding applications are then used to evaluate the resulted summary to check, for example, whether it can answer all the queries as the original ontology does, whether it can reduce the query-answering time etc. It tends to be straightforward and much easier than evaluating the original ontology. In **Gold Standard based ontology evaluation**, one of the difficulties encountered is that comparing two ontologies is rather difficult. According to [10], one of the few works on measuring the similarity between ontologies, ontologies can be compared at two different levels: lexical and conceptual. Lexical comparison assesses the similarity between the lexicons (set of labels denoting concepts) of the two ontologies. At the conceptual level the taxonomic structures and the relations in the ontologies are compared. These problems become easier in ontology summary evaluation, as seen in [1][2], because the comparison now is between candidate summaries with "gold standard" summary of the same ontology, also known as human assessors' "ground truth". Not only the size of ontology summary is a lot smaller than original ontology, also they are all confined to conceptual knowledge of the same domain. The same applies to the **Corpus coverage ontology evaluation**, though it has not been practiced in literatures for ontology summary evaluation. In the case of ontology summary evaluation, the topic coverage check is between candidate summaries and the original ontology and among candidate summaries without concerning how well the original ontology covers the topic in general and therefore much easier to implement. The applicability of ontology evaluation schemes for ontology summary evaluation and their practices in related work are listed in Table 1.

Table 1. Ontology evaluation schemes for ontology summary evaluation

Ontology evaluation Schemes	Applicable for ontology summary evaluation	Practiced in
Application-driven	Yes	[5]
Gold Standard based	Yes	[1][2]
Corpus coverage	Yes	N/A

3.2 Summary Evaluation

Just as experiences can be and has been gained from text summarization to do ontology summarization, lessons can be learned from the evaluation of text summarization to do the evaluation of ontology summarization. This happens in the work of [2] where graph-based text summarization techniques were applied in ontology summarization. The authors evaluated the summary quality as well as the effectiveness of ontology summarization techniques using measures similar to the evaluation of text summarization. According to [11], many evaluation measures proposed for text summarization can be classified into three categories: **Recall-based**, **Sentence-rank-based** and **Content-based**. In general, one measure will produce one score for each summary produced by one technique. If summaries produced by one technique consistently produces higher scores by all measures than those produced by other techniques and thus has a higher average score, it is reasonable to believe that the summarization technique that produces the summaries with higher scores is a better technique.

Recall-based measures rely on human assessors to extract "ground truth" summaries first and then compare machine-generated summaries with them by counting the number of sentences they have in common. Therefore, the more sentences a summary has *recalled* from the "ground truth", the higher the evaluation score will be. Though intuitive and simple, recall-based evaluation measures fall short in a number of aspects. Firstly, they introduce a bias because human assessors are used and, in extracting sentences of a document, the agreement among assessors is typically quite low [12]. Secondly, a small change in the summary output (by replacing one sentence with another equally good one which happens not to match majority "ground truths") could change the evaluation score dramatically. This measure is practised in [1] between machine-generated summaries with "ground truth". **Sentence-rank-based** evaluation measures also rely on human assessors to produce "ground truth". However, instead of producing summaries that simply contain the most representative sentences of a document, each assessor is asked to rank the sentences of a document in the order of their importance in the summary. All machine-generated summaries also contain the rankings of the sentences. Kendall's *tau* statistic [13] can then be used to quantify a summary's agreement with a particular "ground truth". This *tau* measure is used in [2] to compare the performances of different "centrality"-based summarization methods among themselves and with "ground truth". **Content-based** measures, as the name indicates, calculate the similarity of the summary content to the full document content. The content similarity can be simply realized by finding the "term frequency" vectors of summaries and those of documents, and then calculating inner product value of two vectors which will result in a score indicating how similar the two vectors are [11]. In practise, "ground truth" can also be used as an alternative to the full document, though not a necessity as in the two measures mentioned above. That is to say, if "ground truth" is available, the similarity comparison can be carried out against the "ground truth" instead of the full document. This is what was practised in [2], where "vocabulary overlap" is used instead of "term frequency" to measure the similarity between machine-generated summaries with "ground truth". In this context, recall-based measures can be loosely regarded as a special case of content-based measures. The applicability of ontology evaluation schemes for ontology summarization evaluation and their practices in related work are listed in Table 2.

Table 2. Summary evaluation scheme for ontology summary evaluation

Summary evaluation schemes	**Applicable for ontology summary evaluation**	**Practiced in**
Recall-based	Yes	[1]
Sentence rank based	Yes	[2]
Content-based	Yes	[1][2]

4 User-Driven Ontology Summary Evaluation: A Comparative Discussion

So far, the few works as explained in Section 2.2, which are user-driven and have focus on ontology summarization to facilitate ontology understanding remain unrelated and have not been evaluated on a common ground. Therefore, it is hard for readers to infer how well each system performs in a comparative way. As described in Section 3 that, among the only few, the works in [1] and [2] deploy measures compliant with those from both ontology evaluation and summary evaluation to evaluate their summarization results. In specific, they both deploy **Gold Standard based** and **Content-based** evaluation measures. To be specific, they both rely on human assessors' "ground truth" contents, with which the summarization results are compared by content. Given this commonality, in this section, we will present the evaluation of the two works in a comparative way by setting up a common ground for comparison. Not only will it serve as a test case for our claims that ontology summarization, like any other scientific work, can and should be evaluated by similar, or the same, measures, also it provides an indicative view of how state-of-the-art user-driven ontology summarization approaches perform and hence allows users to decide the suitability of each approach to their own purpose. The evaluation in [3] is excluded here because it could not rely on human assessors' "ground truth" information and hence lack the common ground with the other two approaches.

In the work of [2], the basic unit of summarization is RDF sentence, which is, in a nutshell, an integrated information unit that can be a single RDF statement without any blank node or a set of RDF statements connected by blank nodes. Using RDF sentence as basic distilling unit instead of terms (namely concepts), the authors claimed that it would provide extra knowledge of how the terms are related in the ontology and therefore provide a more comprehensive understanding of the ontology. However, in their work, not all, but only "generic" RDF sentences are considered in ontology summary while excluding "special" sentences. The "generic" there referred to RDF sentences which are mapped from axioms of atomic class and property whereas the "special" referred to sentences containing axioms specifying equivalence between class restrictions for example. However, in the work of [1], the basic working unit for summarization is concepts only. This is due to the fact that this work was mainly driven by a foreseen use case scenario, that is to facilitate the graph-based visualisation and navigation for large-scale ontologies. For ontology visualisation tools, concepts are the most fundamental component and play the most important role which interlinked with each other with the links among them being either properties or axioms of classes, such as *isA* relations. When ignoring the links between atomic classes and ignoring the atomic properties in the results of [2], we obtain a set of result which contains concepts only as the results in [1]. The results in these two works can therefore be evaluated comparatively by jointly applying **Gold Standard based** and **Content-based** measures.

In our evaluation, we use two test onotlogies *biosphere*[3], *financial*[4] which have been used in [1] as test ontologies because they have much larger vocabularies than

[3] http://sweet.jpl.nasa.gov/ontology/bioshpere.owl
[4] http://www.larflast.bas.bg/ontology

those used in [2], and contain no properties that are subject to extraction by the summarization approaches in [2] hence enhancing the comparability of these two works. Using approaches in [2] with their online services[5], we obtain the most salient RDF sentences, from which we extract the first 20 concepts as key concepts in their order of appearance in the summarised RDF sentences by ignoring the links among them. We then calculate the number of key concepts that agree with "ground truth", i.e. "gold standard", that is the majority, over 50%, opinion of the human assessors to reduce the versatile subjectivity of individual assessors. Eight assessors with good experience in ontology engineering were asked to extract 20 concepts they considered the most representatives for each ontology. The statistics of the test ontologies, the number of key concepts agreed by more than 50% of human assessors and the number of key concepts extracted by those two summarization approaches are listed in Table 3. Table 4 and Table 5 list the 20 key concepts extracted by the two summarization approaches respectively with key concepts that agree with respective "ground truth" highlighted using italic font. The "ground truth" of *biosphere* ontology include *Animal, Bird, Fungi, Insect, Mammal, MarineAnimal, Microbiota, Plant, Reptile, Vegetation*, and that of *financial* ontology include *Bank, Bond, Broker, Capital, Contract, Dealer, Financial_Market, Order, Stock.*

Table 3. Statistics of ontology and ontology summarization results

Ontology	No. of concepts	No. of concepts in "ground truth"	No. of key concepts extracted by approach in [1]	No. of key concepts extracted by approach in [2]
biosphere	87	10	8	6
financial	188	9	6	6

Table 4. Key concepts extracted by summarization approach in [1]

Ontology	Key Concepts
biosphere	*Animal, Bacteria, Bird*, Crown, Fish, *Fungi*, FungyTaxonomy, Human, Litter, LivingThing, *Mammal, MarineAnimal*, Marine- Plant, *Microbiota*, MicrobiotaTaxonomy, Mold, Mushroom, *Plant, Vegetation*, Yeast
financial	Agent, *Bond, Capital*, Card, Cost, *Dealer*, Financial_Asset, Financial_Instrument, *Financial_Market*, Money, *Order*, Organization, Payment, Price, Quality, Security, *Stock*, Supplier, Transaction, Value

We can see from the results that, with respect to the total number of concepts in the test ontologies which are 87 and 188 respectively, there is a quite high correlation between the results from these two approaches. This means that though they work on different units of ontology and different methodologies are used to do ontology summarization, the results in terms of concepts are close. This is due to the fact that calculating the "centrality" of RDF sentences in [2] having similar effects with calculating *basic level, density* and *coverage* in [1] because they all work on the topology and taxonomy aspects of ontology. By comparing them in details, we can tell the influence of each approach on the final results. The results from [1] approach contain more

[5] http://iws.seu.edu.cn/services/falcon-f/ontosum/

Table 5. Key concepts extracted by summarization approaches in [2]

Ontology	Key Concepts
biosphere	*Plant*, LivingThing, *Vegetation*, *Microbiota*, *Animal*, MicrobiotaTaxonomy, *Fungi*, FungiTaxonomy, MarinePlant, *Mammal*, Fish, Canopy, Macroalgae, Macroalgae, Anemone, Mushroom, Protist, BlueGreenAlgae, Foraminifer, VegetationCover
financial	Financial_instrument, financial_asset, security, *bond*, asset, agent, financial_agent, *organization*, *capital*, finicial_ mean, debt_instrument, *market*, financial_market, municipal_bond, market_agent, *stock*, *contract*, supplier, corporate_bond, government_bond

simple names, i.e. non-compound names, and more popular names than those from [2] approach. This is not surprising because the latter approach works only on ontology structures whereas the earlier one works not only on ontology structures, but also on *name simplicity* and *lexical popularity*.

5 Discussions and Conclusions

This paper provides an overview of state-of-the-art ontology summarization approaches in a categorical view first, and then focuses on the introduction of user-driven ontology summarization approaches. With aims to evaluate user-driven ontology summarization approaches on a common ground, in this paper, we systematically investigate evaluation measures from both ontology evaluation and summary evaluation domains and inspect their applicability for ontology summary evaluation. After spotting the commonality between the evaluation measures used by the existing ontology summarization approaches. We provide our evaluation results on two of the user-driven ontology summarization approaches by looking at them together in a comparative way. This evaluation confirms the comparability of those ever-isolated approaches given a common ground and a same set of evaluation measures, and also provides an indicative view of how well each approach performs in comparison with each other.

User-driven ontology summarization has provided the basis for a number of user-centric technologies, such as KC-Viz and Cupboard, and also for experiments in *Cautious Knowledge Sharing* [14], where ontology providers only advertise ontologies through automatically generated summaries, rather than in their entirety. It has also been used to index ontologies repositories using key concepts only, as opposed to indexing ontologies using the totality of their concepts [14]. The results showed a slight degradation in performance but apparently with a significant decrease in the index size. This will simplify the deployment of semantic repositories in scenarios such as those envisaged by the SmartProducts project[6], where we aim to deploy semantic technologies in domestic devices with very limited RAM and computational power. Therefore, evaluations of ontology summary are of paramount importance to the development of effective summarization approaches to ensure their performances in different scenarios.

[6] http://www.smartproducts-project.eu/

References

1. Peroni, S., Motta, E., d'Aquin, M.: Identifying Key Concepts in an Ontology Through the Integration of Cognitive Principles with Statistical and Topological Measures. In: 3rd Asian Semantic Web Conference, Bangkok, Thailand (2008)
2. Zhang, X., Cheng, G., Qu, Y.: Ontology Summarization Based on RDF Sentence Graph. In: 16th Inter. World Wide Web Conference Banff, Alberta, Canada, May 8-12 (2007)
3. Zhang, X., Cheng, G., Ge, W., Qu, Y.: Summarizing Vocabularies in the Global Semantic Web. Journal of Computer Science and Technology 24(1), 165–174 (2009)
4. Brank, J., Grobelnik, M., Mladenic., D.: A Survey of Ontology Evaluation Techniques. In: Conference on Data Mining and Data Warehouses (SiKDD), Ljubljana, Slovenia (2005)
5. Alani, H., Harris, S., O'Neil, B.: Winnowing Ontologies Based on Application Use. In: Sure, Y., Domingue, J. (eds.) ESWC 2006. LNCS, vol. 4011, pp. 185–199. Springer, Heidelberg (2006)
6. Fokoue, A., Kershenbaum, A., Ma, L., Schonberg, E., Srinivas, K.: The Summary Abox: Cutting Ontologies Down to Size. In: Cruz, I., Decker, S., Allemang, D., Preist, C., Schwabe, D., Mika, P., Uschold, M., Aroyo, L.M. (eds.) ISWC 2006. LNCS, vol. 4273, pp. 343–356. Springer, Heidelberg (2006)
7. Erkan, G., Radev, D.R.: LexRank: Graph-based Lexical Centrality as Salience in Text Summarization. Journal of Artificial Intelligence Research 22, 457–479 (2004)
8. Hartmann, J., Sure, Y., Giboin, A., Maynard, D., Suarez-Figueroa, M.C., Cuel, R.: Methods for Ontology Evaluation. Knowledge Web Deliverable D1.2.3 (2005)
9. Sabou, M., Lopez, V., Motta, E., Uren, V.: Ontology Selection: Ontology Evaluation on the Real Semantic Web. In: Workshop: Evaluation of Ontologies for the Web (EON) at 15th International World Wide Web Conference, Edinburgh (2006)
10. Maedche, A., Staab, S.: Measuring Similarity between Ontologies. In: Gómez-Pérez, A., Benjamins, V.R. (eds.) EKAW 2002. LNCS (LNAI), vol. 2473, p. 251. Springer, Heidelberg (2002)
11. Donaway, R.L., Drummey, K.W., Mather, L.A.: A Comparison of Rankings Produced by Summarization Evaluation Measures. In: ANLP/NAACL Workshop on Automatic Summarization, pp. 69–78 (2000)
12. Jing, H., McKeown, K., Barzilay, R., Elhadad, M.: Summarization Evaluation Methods: Experiments and Analysis. In: American Association for Artificial Intelligence Spring Symposium Series, pp. 60–68 (1998)
13. Sheskin, D.J.: Handbook of Parametric and Nonparametric Statistical Procedures. CRC Press, Boca Raton (1997)
14. Lopez, V., Guidi, D., Motta, E., Peroni, S., d'Aquin, M., Gridinoc, L.: Evaluation of Semantic Web Applications. OpenKnowledge Project Deliverable, D8.5 (2008)

A Visualization Service for the Semantic Web

Sean M. Falconer[1], Chris Callendar[2], and Margaret-Anne Storey[2]

[1] Stanford Center for Biomedical Informatics Research, Stanford University, USA
[2] University of Victoria, Canada
sfalc@stanford.edu, {ccallend,mstorey}@uvic.ca

Abstract. The Web presents an opportunity to openly collaborate and share visualizations of semantic web data. Many desktop tools for visually exploring ontologies exist; however, few researchers have investigated how visualizations could be used in an online environment to enhance the semantic web. In this paper, we present our experience with developing a visualization service for the semantic web. We discuss the advantages and challenges with moving to a web-based platform, as well as the features of the service through several case studies. We reflect on this experience and provide recommendations for future work and data integrations.

1 Introduction

Over the past decade, many ontology visualization tools have been developed to help users understand, create, and manipulate ontologies [8]. Visualization of ontologies is often considered to be a benefit as we can rely on powerful human cognitive and perceptual abilities not possible with pure textual representations.

Tools and repositories for semantic web resources and ontologies have been migrating from desktop environments to the interactive Web. Yet online visual tools for interacting, understanding, and browsing these information repositories and ontologies is sorely lacking. For example, Swoogle[1], contains over 10,000 ontologies in its index. However, the tools available for browsing, exploring and interacting with these ontologies are still primarily relegated to the desktop.

Much of the research focus for ontology visualization has been on how to better support navigation of the ontology graph within desktop tools. Little research has looked at how visualization could potentially play a larger role in supporting collaboration and adoption of semantic web technology. The web browser has become the universal interface, allowing researchers and application developers to reach a far larger audience than previously thought possible [3]. The Internet makes it easy to share results and collaborate over vast distances. There is no need to download special tools, and with the advent of Web 2.0, the Web has grown into an interactive environment.

In this paper, we present a web-based visualization service, called FlexViz. We discuss advantages and challenges with developing web-based visualizations, features of our service, and several example case studies.

---

[1] http://swoogle.umbc.edu

P. Cimiano and H.S. Pinto (Eds.): EKAW 2010, LNAI 6317, pp. 554–564, 2010.

2 Web-Based Visualization

The Web is gradually becoming a platform for visualization. Internet-based visualizations like tag clouds are now a standard navigational component of many websites. The NameVoyager [10], which lets users interactively explore historical name data, drew 500,000 visits within two weeks of its launch. Many Eyes, a project from IBM, has combined visualization with social computing[2]. Users of the site can upload new data sets and apply different visualizations to the data to facilitate analysis. The visualizations and data are shared, allowing other users to apply new views, discuss particular visualizations, and rate views.

Despite this trend, few researchers (see [7] for exception) have explored the utility of web-based visualizations of semantic web data. The Web, as a platform for exploring and interacting with structured information, is very attractive. Below we explore some of these potential advantages.

Reach a larger audience: One of the greatest features of the Web is instant usability. Downloads of special software are unnecessary, the browser has become the universal interface. The accessibility of online applications greatly enhance their adoption potential. Part of the success and popularity of the NameVoyager application was due to its public nature. Anyone can use the application, which has instant ramifications for all aspects of the site. The Web opens an application up to the "accidental user".

Social data analysis: Web-based visualization changes the focus of visualization from task-oriented problem solving to social data analysis [10]. Users can engage deeply with online visualizations and web applications, opening the topic area to in-depth social analysis [6]. Again, "accidental users", bring different perspectives and different backgrounds, which may change how the application is used. For example, the various mash-ups that have been created with Google Maps [5].

Reduce task complexity: Integration with existing web applications potentially reduces task complexity. As in the previously mentioned Swoogle browsing example, with a web-based visualization, the steps requiring a user to download and load the ontology into an editor are removed.

Tracking user behavior: Tracking in desktop environments can be difficult, as the information must be collected on the client and then forwarded to a server. However, the deployment of visualizations on the Web, particularly as hosted services, make collecting this information seamless and straightforward. An application can collect rich statistical information about their users' behaviors. This data can later be used to help improve the tool and service as well as test the adoption of new features.

Even with these advantages, few web-based ontology visualizations currently exist. Moreover, the existing visualizations, like AmiGO[3], lack interactivity and

[2] `http://manyeyes.alphaworks.ibm.com`

[3] `http://amigo.geneontology.org`

are not tightly integrated with the surrounding application. Benjamins *et al.* state that one of the six essential challenges for the semantic web is visualization support [1]. Addressing this challenge is difficult. There are several technical hurdles that must be overcome. Below we discuss several of these technical issues.

Performance: Ontologies can be very large and complex. For example, SNOMED CT, an extremely comprehensive medical terminology, contains approximately 300,000 terms and over 1 million relationships[4]. Many existing visualization tools rely on the ontology being completely stored in memory, which is not feasible for large ontologies like SNOMED CT. Web-based technologies for creating visualizations often have limited rendering performance and severe memory constraints.

Screen real estate: Even relatively small ontologies, can be difficult to visualize. Often, ontologies are visualized as a node-link diagram, which is susceptible to labeling issues and a cluttered display [8]. Managing these issues in a desktop environment is a design challenge, but on the Web, there are further constraints. Web browsers often use between 100 to 200 pixels for tabs, menus, and navigation controls. This severely limits the available canvas for a visualization.

Integration: Seamless integration with existing web applications is key to the successful adoption of a web-based visualization. This can be potentially difficult. With newer, less widely adopted technologies, users of the tool may be forced to download plugins as with Microsoft's Silverlight technology. Also, multiple technologies may need to be integrated to allow the existing web infrastructure to communicate with the visual elements.

Development environment: The choice of a development environment for supporting the visualization is difficult. A variety of potential technologies exist; SVG, Java applets, Flash, Silverlight, Firefox canvas object, etc. Each technology has advantages and disadvantages and depending on the nature of the application, the choice in technology may change.

Although there are advantages to supporting more web-based visualizations of semantic web services, there are also many challenges that must be faced. In the next section, we discuss the development and design philoposhy of FlexViz.

3 Developing FlexViz

Following a similar design philosophy as adopted by many Web 2.0 services, we wished to make FlexViz easily extensible, thus allowing the Web community to apply new data sources as they see fit. The first version of FlexViz was released in January 2008. Since then, there have been three major releases[5].

3.1 Features

The feature requirements for FlexViz were based on our years of experience developing tools for ontologies and structured data sources. Below, we provide an overview of some of the FlexViz functionality.

[4] `http://www.nlm.nih.gov/snomed`

[5] FlexViz source code: `https://sourceforge.net/projects/flexviz/`

Layouts: FlexViz supports many different graph layouts. These include vertical/horizontal tree layouts, circle layouts, spring layouts, and grid-based layouts. Layouts provide a way to automatically position nodes for legibility. New layouts can be easily integrated and applied.

Filtering: FlexViz allows a developer to specify different types of nodes and arcs. The complexity of the represented graph can be reduced by applying filters to specific node and arc types. Additionally, specific nodes can be filtered via a right-click menu. The menu allows the user to hide a particular node or the children of that node. User-driven filter helps address some of the performance concerns with web-based visualizations.

Navigation: To help support scalability, besides simple filtering, FlexViz supports step-wise node expansion. The initial view for a graph is restricted to the local neighborhood of the in-focus node. That is, only the focal node along with its immediate neighbors based on un-filtered arc types is displayed. Nodes that can be expanded further are shown with a plus icon. For simple graphs, double-clicking these nodes expands the node to display its local neighborhood based on the in-memory graph representation. However, for larger data repositories, the double-click event potentially invokes a web service call to retrieve the local neighborhood for the selected node. This call takes place asynchronously, retrieving the relevant information and eventually updating the graph. The data is cached for fast retrieval on repeated calls.

Interaction: Nodes can be dragged and re-positioned as the user desires. The graph also supports panning and zooming. The contents of the graph can be re-positioned by toggling either the "fit to screen" or "expand graph" options. The "fit to screen" button will re-position all nodes and arcs to be displayed within the viewable canvas area of the graph. Depending on the size of the graph, overlapping can occur. The user can either manually move nodes or use the "expand graph" option to make items visible. These options help to address the canvas real estate issue.

Search: The label associated with a node can be searched for within the in-memory representation of the graph. Term completion for this search is also available. The matching node is highlighted and the graph view pans to display the node. The search interface can also be extended for specific applications to support asynchronous searching (see Section 4.1 for discussion).

Exporting: FlexViz views can also be exported, either as XML or as a static graphic. For specific applications, this feature can be extended to facilitate data-specific extraction (see Section 4.1 for discussion).

The above features are some of the basic features support provided by FlexViz. The functionality can be easily extended depending on the requirements of the given domain and task. In the next section, we explore three example extensions and integrations of the FlexViz toolkit, demonstrating the flexibility available.

4 Visualizing Semantic Web Data

The FLEXVIZ toolkit provides a generic library to create web-based graph representations. However, the usefulness of the toolkit derives from the applications that extend it. In this section, we discuss three such extensions: BioPortal integration, FOAF support, and Bio-Mixer. The extended application stack for FLEXVIZ is shown in Fig. 1.

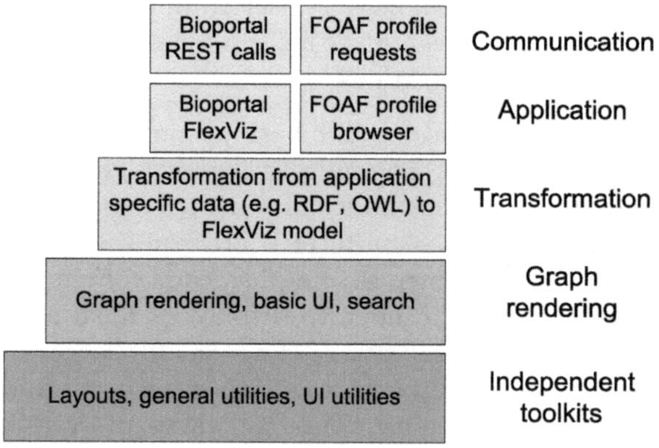

Fig. 1. FLEXVIZ application stack. The top layer consists of application specific communication services, like REST calls to BioPortal. The second layer consists of specific application instances of FLEXVIZ. The third tier is the transformation layer, where application specific data like RDF or OWL is transformed into the FLEXVIZ model. The fourth and fifth tiers are the generic FLEXVIZ toolkit libraries.

4.1 BioPortal

BioPortal has been developed as part of the National Center of Biomedical Ontology (NCBO. BioPortal provides a repository of biomedical related ontologies and resources. Ontology exploration is supported via searching or selection of a particular ontology. Ontology concepts can be explored through a class browser, similar to the class browser found in Protégé. Users of BioPortal may explore the existing ontologies to understand and learn a new ontology; it is also a critical step for ontology evaluation, sharing, mapping, and resource management.

The ontology view is essentially an indented list of the ontology classes, which forces the ontology's representation into a tree structure rather than a graph. As a result, the tree only displays inheritance relationships and not property relations. Furthermore, classes in an ontology potentially have multiple parents, which in a tree cannot be adequately represented. The class must be duplicated for each parent, which has been shown to be confusing to users [4].

To help address these deficiencies, we worked with the BioPortal development team to provide FLEXVIZ as an ontology browsing service. The BioPortal specific extension of FLEXVIZ is stored on our own servers, and seamlessly integrated

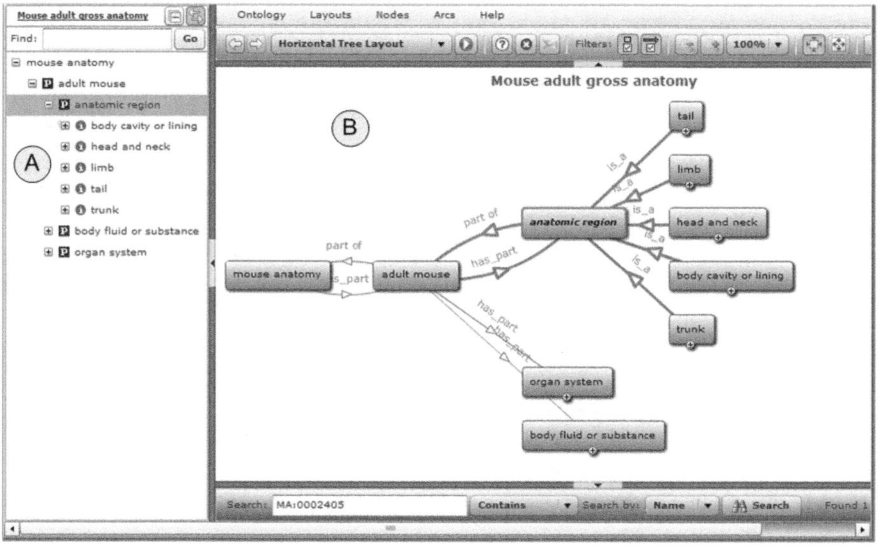

Fig. 2. Visualizing the Mouse Adult Gross Anatomy within BioPortal. (A) shows the class tree browser, while (B) shows the FLEXVIZ graph rendering. The term *anatomic region* is the current focal term, and this is synchronized between the two views.

into BioPortal (see Fig. 2)[6]. All communication with BioPortal occurs through the REST services provided by BioPortal for accessing ontology-related data. All expansion, search, and focus operations result in a service call to BioPortal.

Several ontology specific extensions were incorporated into the BioPortal FLEXVIZ application. We included an extension to the concept node context menu called "Link to concept". Similar to the "Link" feature in Google Maps or YouTube, this feature allows a user to share a particular visualization with another person via a specific URL or through auto-generated HTML that supports an embedded view. Both approaches allow users to share, link, or embed specific visualizations into their web pages and blogs. We incorporated this feature to facilitate collaboration and provide a light-weight mechanism to deploy instances of FLEXVIZ wherever users deem appropriate.

Natively, a FLEXVIZ view can be extracted as an image, which is useful for scientists using BioPortal when they wish to embed a particular ontology snapshot into a research paper or document. However, we are also working on supporting OWL and RDF extraction. This feature would support users with the task of extracting a portion of an ontology.

Figure 2 shows an example of the FLEXVIZ integration in BioPortal. The figure shows a visualization from part of the Mouse Adult Gross Anatomy, where *anatomic region* is the focal term. The tree representation displayed in Fig. 2(A) is an extension of the base user interface implementation of FLEXVIZ. This

[6] Source code: `https://bmir-gforge.stanford.edu/gf/project/flexviz/`

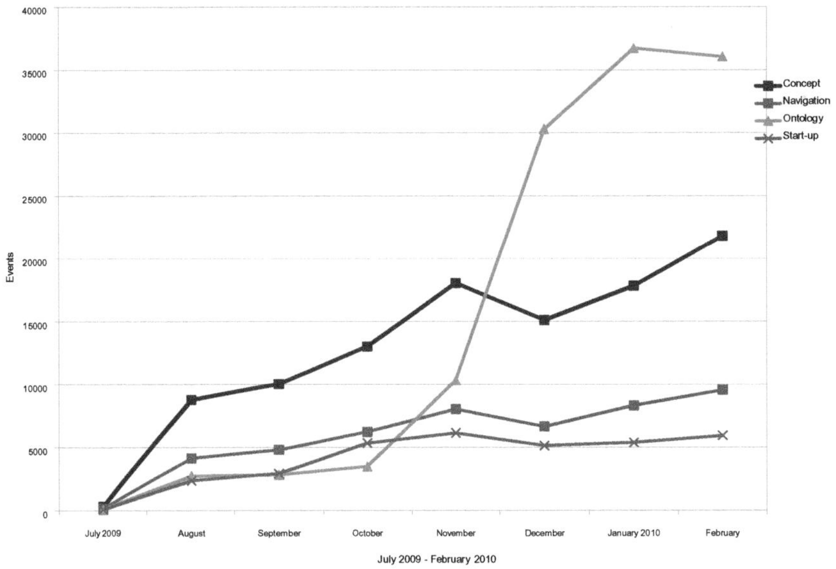

Fig. 3. Concept, navigation, ontology, and start-up events over an eight month period

extension helps to support synchronization between the tree and graph view as well as allow us to gather statistics about user browsing behavior.

Since July of 2009, we have been logging the usage of FLEXVIZ. Figure 3, shows the number of concept, navigation, ontology, and start-up events that have been executed with FLEXVIZ over an eight month period. Concept events are captured when a user request requires information about a particular concept, while navigation events are interaction events that do not require specific data to be loaded, for example, when a graph layout is applied. Ontology events are captured when a new ontology is selected and loaded and finally, start-up events occur when the visualization is first loaded.

4.2 FOAF

The Friend of a Friend (FOAF) project is attempting to create a web of machine-processable descriptions of people, the relationships between them, and the things they do [2]. With the growing number of social networking sites like Facebook, Twitter, Twine, and MySpace, Internet users must re-create their public profiles and the links to their friends over and over within each service. FOAF provides a standard, structured means to deal with this problem.

A FOAF profile consists of a RDF file describing a particular individual and the description of their friends. A user can make their profile available online, and potentially the profile could be shared between existing social networking services. Collections of profiles and the interconnections between people and their friends form a graph structure. Provided the friends listed in the `foaf:knows`

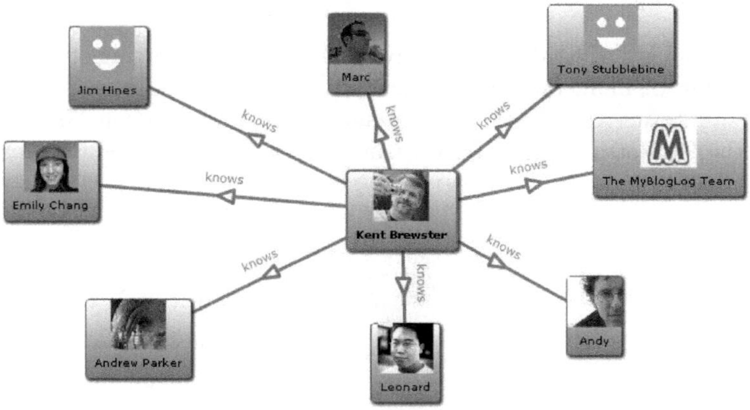

Fig. 4. Screenshot of the FOAF BROWSER canvas

property also have pointers to their own FOAF profiles, the graph structure can be walked by requesting the given RDF FOAF file through HTTP. In this example of FLEXVIZ, we extend the toolkit to make use of this explicit profile graph structure. The extended version, called the FOAF BROWSER, helps users browse existing FOAF profiles and the interconnections between them.

We integrated with FOAF to help demonstrate the flexibility of our service, as FOAF is one of the most well known examples of the semantic web. Similar to the BioPortal integration, we created extensions to FLEXVIZ at the *Communication*, *Application*, and *Transformation* layers (see Fig. 1). The communication extension uses HTTP to download the RDF files associated with a given FOAF profile, while the application extension consists of user interface extensions specific to FOAF, and finally the FOAF data is parsed and transformed into the FLEXVIZ model in the transformation extension.

Figure 4 shows an example of the FOAF BROWSER rendering a single FOAF profile. The FOAF BROWSER uses the `foaf:depiction` property to render a graphical representation of the given person. If this information is not available, a default graphic is used. The nodes (people) in the graph are labeled using the `foaf:name` property, and all profile property information is available when a user moves their mouse over a given node. Provided a known person has a `foaf:seeAlso` property specified, double-clicking the node results in a new HTTP request to download the corresponding FOAF profile. As a result, the graph is expanded to display the new information.

We re-used the "Link to" idea from the BioPortal integration, thus facilitating users with integrating a visual representation of their FOAF profile into their own web pages. We also extended the filters available for pruning a graph to support specific FOAF properties. Finally, we extended the interaction features of the FLEXVIZ graph to support a zoom effect when a node is brushed by the mouse pointer. Moving the mouse over a node results in that node growing in size in order to make the FOAF user's picture easier to see.

4.3 Bio-Mixer

Bio-Mixer[7] is a web-based mashup environment for supporting the exploration and re-mixing of biomedical ontologies. Ontology terms and mappings can be explored in interactive views such as timelines, lists and graphs. The graph view extends the BioPortal specific implementation of FLEXVIZ (see Fig. 5)[8].

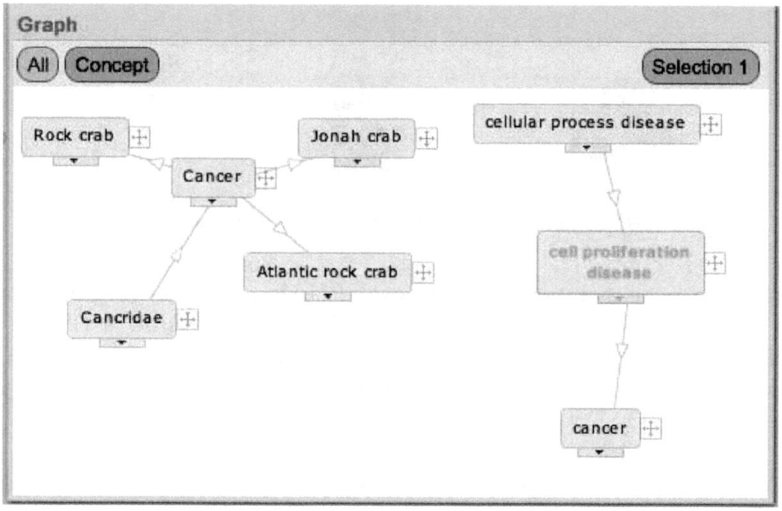

Fig. 5. Screenshot of the graph widget from Bio-Mixer. Two concept neighborhoods are displayed from two different ontologies.

Although Bio-Mixer uses the Bioportal FLEXVIZ implementation, this use case is significantly different. Bio-Mixer demonstrates how customizable the look-and-feel and application behaviors are for FLEXVIZ. For example, Bio-Mixer integrates multiples types of visualizations and supports synchronized interaction between them. To support this, Bio-Mixer uses the public methods in FLEXVIZ for attaching listeners to various graph events. Bio-Mixer also uses completely different styling to seamlessly integrate FLEXVIZ.

5 Discussion

The three case studies presented in the previous section illustrate the flexibility of the FLEXVIZ service for semantic web applications. The design and generality of the toolkit took several iterations and many new ideas are still being explored. Below, in reference to the FLEXVIZ service, we discuss the advantages of web-based visualizations that we previously introduced.

[7] `http://bio-mixer.appspot.com/`

[8] Source code: `http://code.google.com/p/bio-mixer/`

Reach a larger audience: Integration with BioPortal is allowing biomedical ontologies and FlexViz to reach a much larger audience. As more ontology repositories become available online, visualizations like FlexViz will need to be available to help users browse and understand the contents of the available ontologies. As was shown in Section 4.1, there has been a growing adoption of the FlexViz tool over a reasonably short period of time.

Social data analysis: This requires wide-spread adoption, which we are still evaluating. However, early usage is promising. The "Link to" feature will help facilitate this process for users as both users of FOAF and BioPortal can easily share their visualizations.

Reduce task complexity: To evaluate this, extensive user testing and iterative design is required. In our initial design, we tried to leverage other tools built for the Web that tend to use standard user interface controls that users may be familiar with. We developed FlexViz to reduce the complexity with certain types of tasks, like comparing and evaluating ontologies on the Web, and understanding FOAF profile relationships.

Tracking user behavior: We log data from the BioPortal FlexViz integration to help us understand how users are using the visualization. This will help guide us as we make further improvements to the tool.

With respect to the challenges of web-based visualizations mentioned earlier, we have attempted to address *performance* by supporting incremental navigation and search-based navigation. This helps to reduce the amount of data that must be asynchronously requested from our application-specific end-points. User tracking will also help us more easily tailor what is displayed based on previous user navigation patterns. Technology *integration* is getting easier as technologies for the Web improve. Choosing Flex as our development technology has helped to reduce integration overhead. For example, the BioPortal application integrates with FlexViz via an `iframe` with a URL pointer to our server. We have developed the BioPortal extension to have a similar look and feel as the native BioPortal so that users will not realize they are interacting with a different tool. However, FlexViz can be re-styled on demand for any particular application, as shown by the BioMixer integration. Like integration, *development environments* for web-based technologies are improving. The Google Web Toolkit along with various AJAX toolkits are making it easier for developers to create interactive web applications.

6 Conclusion

There are many advantages to developing more interactive visualization tools for the semantic web. Existing work consists primarily of static images or text representations. In our research, it took several iterations and experimentation with various technologies to create a generic toolkit that can readily be extended to a variety of semantic web resources. In the future we plan to continually enhance the performance and functionality of FlexViz. We also plan to perform more comprehensive evaluation of the FLEXVIZ tool and use the feedback to help improve our design. We propose that online visualizations can greatly enhance user tasks on the semantic web as well as help to promote semantic web technologies. The Web offers researchers the opportunity to provide tools that help users explore new information spaces, collaborate, and take part in social data analysis [10].

Acknowledgments

This work was supported by the National Center for Biomedical Ontology, under road map initiative grant U54 HG004028 from the National Institutes of Health.

References

1. Benjamins, R., Contreras, J., Corcho, O., Gomez-Perez, A.: Six Challenges for the Semantic Web. In: KR 2002 Workshop on Formal Ontology, Knowledge Representation and Intelligent Systems for the Web (2002)
2. Brickley, D., Miller, L.: FOAF Vocabulary Specification (2005), http://xmlns.com/foaf/0.1
3. Brodlie, K.: Visualization over the World Wide Web. In: Scientific Visualization Conference, pp. 23–29. IEEE Computer Society, Los Alamitos (1997)
4. Falconer, S.M., Storey, M.-A., Yamauchi, T.: CogZ: Evaluating Cognitive Support for Semi-Automatic Terminology Mapping (2009) (Under review)
5. Floyd, I.R., Jones, M.C., Rathi, D., Twidale, M.B.: Web Mash-ups and Patchwork Prototyping: User-driven technological innovation with Web 2.0 and Open Source Software. In: Proceedings of the 40th Annual Hawaii International Conference on System Sciences, pp. 86–96. IEEE Computer Society, Los Alamitos (2007)
6. Frost, J.H., Massagli, M.P.: Social Uses of Personal Health Information Within PatientsLikeMe, an Online Patient Community: What Can Happen When Patients Have Access to One Anothers Data. Journal of Medical Internet Research 10(3) (2008)
7. Hirsch, C., Hosking, J., Grundy, J.: Interactive Visualization Tools for Exploring the Semantic Graph of Large Knowledge Spaces. In: Workshop on Visual Interfaces to the Social and Semantic Web (2009)
8. Katifori, A., Halatsis, C., Lepouras, G., Vassilakis, C., Giannopoulou, E.: Ontology visualization methods—a survey. ACM Computing Surveys 39(4), 10–43 (2007)
9. Mackinlay, J., Shneiderman, B.: Information visualization, Using Vision to Think. Academic Press, London (1999)
10. Wattenberg, M.: Baby Names, Visualization, and Social Data Analysis. In: INFOVIS 2005: Proceedings of the 2005 IEEE Symposium on Information Visualization, Washington, DC, USA, vol. 1. IEEE Computer Society, Los Alamitos (2005)

How Much Semantic Data on Small Devices?*

Mathieu d'Aquin, Andriy Nikolov, and Enrico Motta

Knowledge Media Institute, The Open University, Milton Keynes, UK
{m.daquin,a.nikolov,e.motta}@open.ac.uk

Abstract. Semantic tools such as triple stores, reasoners and query engines tend to be designed for large-scale applications. However, with the rise of sensor networks, smart-phones and smart-appliances, new scenarios appear where small devices with restricted resources have to handle limited amounts of data. It is therefore important to assess how existing semantic tools behave on such small devices, and how much data they can reasonably handle. There exist benchmarks for comparing triple stores and query engines, but these benchmarks are targeting large-scale applications and would not be applicable in the considered scenarios. In this paper, we describe a set of small to medium scale benchmarks explicitly targeting applications on small devices. We describe the result of applying these benchmarks on three different tools (Jena, Sesame and Mulgara) on the smallest existing netbook (the Asus EEE PC 700), showing how they can be used to test and compare semantic tools in resource-limited environments.

1 Introduction

With the rise of sensor networks, smart-phones and smart-appliances, new scenarios appear where a number of small devices with restricted resources each have to handle limited amounts of data. In particular, the SmartProducts project [1] is dedicated to the development of "smart products" (namely, cars, airplanes and kitchen appliances) which embed "proactive knowledge" to help customers, designers, and workers in communicating and collaborating with them. Concretely, Smart Products rely on a platform using small computing devices (such as gumstix[1]) which process, exploit, and expose knowledge related to the product they are attached to through the use of semantic technologies.

While building such a platform, an obvious issue concerns the performance of semantic technologies on the considered hardware. Indeed, existing tools are usually designed for large scale applications and data, deployed on high performance servers, and possibly taking benefit from distributed computing approaches. A few initiatives have emerged that aim at providing tools dedicated to small devices[2], but these are not yet mature enough to be employed in the considered

* Part of this research has been funded under the EC 7th Framework Programme in the context of the SmartProducts project (231204).

[1] `http://www.gumstix.com/`

[2] See e.g., MobileRDF (`http://www.hedenus.de/rdf/`) and microJena (`http://poseidon.elet.polimi.it/ca/?page_id=59`)

P. Cimiano and H.S. Pinto (Eds.): EKAW 2010, LNAI 6317, pp. 565–575, 2010.

scenarios. On the other hand, it is unclear whether popular systems such as Jena[3] or Sesame[4] could actually be used, how they would perform, and how they would compare on resource-limited hardware. Of course, it can always be argued that semantic processing can be applied remotely, on a server, so that the small device only has to act as an interface to semantic data, without having to handle it directly. In such cases however, mechanisms have to be put in place to ensure the availability of this data in all the different environments in which the device might be used, while maintaining appropriate levels of security and privacy. For this reason, one of the main rational underlying this work is to gain the ability to answer the question, "How much semantic data can we store and process on small devices?", so that we can also evaluate, in a given application, how much of the data *have to* be processes externally.

Several benchmarks have been devised to assess and compare the performance of semantic tools (see e.g., [2,3]). However, here again, the current focus on large-scale applications makes these benchmarks inadequate to answer the above question. They indeed assume the availability of sufficient resources to run the considered tools on the large amounts of test data they contain. In addition, as they work at large scale, these benchmarks tend to focus only on two criteria to evaluate performance: the size of the data and the response time. When working at a smaller scale, other characteristics than size (e.g., the distribution of entities in classes, properties and individuals) can have a significant impact on the tools' performance. More importantly, to test the ability of a particular tool to run on a small device, other performance criteria need to be considered, which are often assumed to be available in sufficient quantities in large-scale benchmarks (namely, memory and disk space).

For these reasons, we created a set of "smaller-scale" benchmarks for tools implementing semantic technologies. In practice, each of these benchmarks corresponds to a set of ontologies (i.e., semantic documents) varying in size and with common characteristics (in terms of complexity and distribution of entities). We also use a set of eight generic queries of varying complexities to be executed on each of the ontologies in each of the benchmarks. Therefore, running each benchmark individually allows us to analyze the behavior of the considered tools in specific situations (according to particular data characteristics) and comparing the results of different benchmarks helps in understanding the impact of parameters other than the size of the ontology on various performance measures.

We experimented with running the created benchmarks on three popular tools—Jena, Sesame and Mulgara—with different configurations, on a very limited netbook (the Asus EEE PC 700, also called 2G Surf). This netbook has specifications in similar ranges to the kind of devices that are envisaged in the SmartProducts project. Hence, measuring response time, memory consumption and disk space while running our benchmarks on this device allows us to evaluate the ability and limitations of each of the tested tools if employed in concrete, small-scale scenarios.

---

[3] `http://jena.sourceforge.net/`

[4] `http://openrdf.org`

2 Benchmarks for Small to Medium Scale Semantic Applications

In this section, we propose a new set of benchmarks for small to medium scale applications. Each benchmark is made of two components: 1- a set of ontologies (semantic documents) of varying sizes; and 2- a set of queries of varying complexities (common to all the benchmarks).

2.1 Ontology Sets

The sets of ontologies to be used for testing semantic tools have been built following two main requirements. First and most obviously, they had to cover ontology sizes from very small (just a few triples) to medium-scale ones (hundreds of thousands of triples). As expected, and shown in the next section, medium-scale ontologies represent the limit of what the best performing tools can handle on small devices. Second, these sets of ontologies should take into account the fact that, especially at small-scale, size is not the only parameter that might affect the performance of semantic tools. It is therefore important that, within each set, the ontologies vary in size, but stay relatively homogeneous with respect to these other characteristics. In this way, each set can be used to test the behavior of semantic tools on a particular type of ontologies (e.g., simple ontologies containing a large number of individuals), while comparing the results obtained with different ontology sets allows us to assess the impact of certain ontology characteristics on the performance of the considered tools. In addition, we also consider that relying on real-life ontologies (i.e., ontologies not automatically generated or composed for the purpose of the benchmark) would lead to more exploitable results.

In order to fulfill these requirements, we took advantage of the Watson Semantic Web search engine[5] to retrieve sets of real life ontologies[6] of small to medium sizes. We first devised a script to build sets of ontologies from Watson grouping together ontologies having similar characteristics, therefore building homogenous sets with respect to these characteristics. The parameters employed for building these groups are the ratio $\frac{Number\ of\ Properties}{Number\ of\ Classes}$, the ratio $\frac{Number\ of\ Individuals}{Number\ of\ Classes}$ and the complexity of the ontological description, as expressed by the underlying description logic (e.g., $\mathcal{ALH}$). The 2 first parameters were allowed a derivation of more or less 50% from the average in the group (ontologies rarely have exactly the same values for these characteristics). As a result of this automatic process, we obtained 99 different sets of ontologies. We then manually selected amongst these sets the ones to be used for our benchmarks, considering only the sets containing appropriate ranges of sizes (see summary of the selected benchmark ontology sets in Table 1).

[5] `http://watson.kmi.open.ac.uk`

[6] Here we use to word ontology to refer to any semantic document containing RDF descriptions, including documents containing individuals.

Table 1. Summary of the 10 benchmark ontology sets. The name of each set is given according to its number in the original automatic process. Size is in number of triples.

Name	Ontos	Size range	Ratio prop./class	Ratio ind./class	DL Expressivity
12	9	9-2742	0.65-1.0	1.0-2.0	$\mathcal{ALO}$
37	7	27-3688	0.21-0.48	0.07-0.14	$\mathcal{ALH}$
39	79	2-8502	no class	no class	-
43	56	17-3696	0.66-2.0	4.5-20.5	-
53	21	3208-658808	no property	no individual	$\mathcal{EL}$
54	11	1514-153298	no property	no individual	$\mathcal{ELR}+$
56	20	8-3657	no class	no class	-
58	35	7-4959	1.41-4.0	no individual	$\mathcal{AL}$
66	17	1-2759	no property	no class	-
93	11	43-5132	1.0-2.0	13.0-22.09	-

2.2 Queries

Since our benchmarks are derived from various, automatically selected ontologies, we needed a set of queries generic enough to give results on most of these datasets. We therefore devised eight queries of varying complexities, which are based on the vocabularies of the RDFS, OWL, and DAML+OIL languages:

1. *Select all labels.* This is a basic query which returns all *rdfs:label* datatype values.
2. *Select all comments.* This query returns all *rdfs:comment* values. Usually these values are longer than *rdfs:label*, but more scarce.
3. *Select all labels and comments.* This query checks the ability of the tool to deal with OPTIONAL clauses.
4. *Select all RDFS classes.* This is a basic query which returns RDF resources of type *rdfs:Class*. Its results can be different depending on whether reasoning is applied and whether the tool is aware of the *subClassOf* relation between RDFS and OWL classes.
5. *Select all classes.* This query explicitly searches also for OWL and DAML classes in addition to RDFS classes. The query constructs a union of several clauses.
6. *Select all instances of all classes.* This query contains the clauses of the previous query augmented with joint patterns. The set of results for this query varies depending on whether reasoning is applied: reasoning produces more answers to the query because each instance belonging to a subclass is inferred to belong to a superclass as well.
7. *Select all properties applied to instances of all classes.* This query adds an additional joint pattern to the previous one.
8. *Select all properties by their domain.* This query centers on properties and is also supposed to return different sets of results depending on the reasoning mechanism enabled.

The SPARQL queries corresponding to the descriptions above are also available at `http://watson.kmi.open.ac.uk/small-scale-benchmarks`.

3 Applying the Benchmarks

In our experiments, we focused on two goals: 1- Testing the behaviour of popular semantic data storage tools on a resource-constrained device; and 2- comparing the performance ranking of the same tools when processing small and to medium scale datasets.

As a hardware platform to conduct the experiments we selected the Asus EEE PC 2G Surf netbook (the oldest version of Asus EEE netbooks) with 900 MHz CPU, 512 MB RAM and Puppy Linux[7] installed. This provides a good reference platform as it has similar specifications to common embedded computing devices[8], as well as to top-of-the-range smart-phones[9] while being reasonably convenient to use.

We have selected three of the popular semantic data store tools, which provide Java API interface: Jena, Sesame 2, and Mulgara[10]. We did not test some other storage tools specifically designed for handling large scale datasets such as Virtuoso or 4store because of their high initial resource requirements (e.g., Virtuoso installation requires 62MB of disk space). Because Jena and Sesame provide ontological reasoning capabilities, we tested these tools in two modes: without reasoning and with RDFS reasoning to estimate the additional resource usage caused by inferencing. The following test system configurations were used:

- Jena TDB v0.8.2.
- Jena TDB v0.8.2 with the Jena native RDFS reasoner.
- Sesame v2.2.4 with the RDF Native SAIL repository.
- Sesame v2.2.4 with the RDFS Native SAIL repository (i.e., with reasoning).
- Mulgara v2.1.6 (Lite).

Each test consisted of the following steps:

1. Creating an empty data store.
2. Loading an ontology into the data store.
3. Running queries 1-8.
4. Measuring the disk space taken by the data store.
5. Cleaning the data store (physically deleting the corresponding files).

For each step we measured the time cost and the size of the Java heap space used by the virtual machine. Because of the resource limitations of the chosen netbook, we have restricted the maximum heap size to 400 MB.

3.1 Results

Table 2 gives a summary of all the results obtained after running the 5 different tool configurations described above on our 10 benchmark ontology sets. We can

[7] http://www.puppylinux.com/

[8] For example, the SmartProduct project employs Overo Air gumstix with 600 MHz CPU and 256 MB RAM.

[9] For example, the Apple iPhone 3GS has a 600Mhz CPU and 256 MB of RAM, and the Sony Ericsson XPeria X10 has 1GHz CPU and 1GB of memory.

[10] http://www.mulgara.org/

Table 2. Average measures for the different tools using the different benchmark sets

Benchmark	12	37	39	43	53	54	56	58	66	93
Jena No Reasoning										
# of ontologies treated	9	7	78	56	19	11	20	35	17	11
% of overall size processed	100%	100%	80%	100%	43%	100%	100%	100%	100%	100%
Avg. load time/triple (ms)	54	26	48	12	1	2	37	32	271	13
Avg. memory/triple (KB)	267	86	265	80	1	1	180	199	1023	32
Avg. disk space/triple (KB)	9	2	14	3	0.17	0.19	4	5	27	0.93
Avg. time query/Ktriple (ms)	2460	969	1722	604	232	149	1448	1155	8067	442
Avg. # of query results	22	114	0.87	13	3318	2874	7	12	0.97	80
Avg. time/K query result (ms)	6089	4564	601	1297	335272	147	6456	1480	1998	2913
Jena RDFS Reasoning										
# of ontologies treated	9	6	78	56	2	1	20	34	17	11
% of overall size processed	100%	39%	80%	100%	0%	0%	100%	44%	100%	100%
Avg. load time/triple (ms)	65	32	50	12	2	6	38	33	254	13
Avg. memory/triple (KB)	284	106	282	85	2	5	191	216	1035	34
Avg. disk space/triple (KB)	7	2	14	3	0.17	0.19	4	5	27	0.93
Avg. time query/Ktriple (ms)	13317	10363	10717	4110	15078	28307	10732	37353	44078	2710
Avg. # of query results	75	113	240	357	551	297	99	130	87	216
Avg. time/K query result (ms)	17403	64531	5606	3144	955122	1381216	13461	79262	23116	6481
Sesame No Reasoning										
# of ontologies treated	9	7	78	56	21	11	14	7	17	11
% of overall size processed	100%	100%	80%	100%	100%	100%	9%	1%	100%	100%
Avg. load time/triple (ms)	12	6	7	3	1	1	9	17	38	3
Avg. memory/triple (KB)	32	12	29	10	0.16	0.23	28	62	115	5
Avg. disk space/triple (KB)	0.51	0.24	0.53	0.21	0.1	0.12	0.47	1	1	0.15
Avg. time query/Ktriple (ms)	2334	987	1235	336	43	60	1738	3955	9816	408
Avg. # of query results	22	114	0.87	53	8329	2874	2	1	1	80
Avg. time/K query result (ms)	3899	2905	710	1877	117	272	1984	4587	750	1844
Sesame RDFS Reasoning										
# of ontologies treated	9	7	78	56	21	11	14	7	17	11
% of overall size processed	100%	100%	80%	100%	100%	100%	9%	1%	100%	100%
Avg. load time/triple (ms)	16	10	8	4	3	4	11	25	50	5
Avg. memory/triple (KB)	55	17	50	17	0.23	0.34	46	107	160	8
Avg. disk space/triple (KB)	1	0.45	0.96	0.4	0.14	0.18	0.96	2	3	0.25
Avg. time query/Ktriple (ms)	2942	1156	1578	401	122	152	2100	5670	14277	511
Avg. # of query results	58	153	29	102	10617	3882	22	16	53	154
Avg. time/K query result (ms)	3389	3172	1272	610	99367	31836	1405	2685	1585	1322
Mulgara										
# of ontologies treated	9	7	78	56	19	11	20	35	17	11
% of overall size processed	100%	100%	80%	100%	43%	100%	100%	100%	100%	100%
Avg. load time/triple (ms)	141	54	132	49	2	2	105	110	595	27
Avg. memory/triple (KB)	139	49	141	41	0.43	0.62	96	101	522	17
Avg. disk space/triple (KB)	3778	1650	6090	2175	32	43	5757	7261	43412	1451
Avg. time query/Ktriple (ms)	9909	5875	5340	2651	1291	1399	4896	4719	27589	2704
Avg. # of query results	22	114	0.87	53	3318	2874	7	12	0.97	80
Avg. time/K query result (ms)	14916	9056	2942	16256	885	1390	3780	6655	4713	5466

distinguish 2 sets of measures in this table: measures related to the performance of the tools (e.g., loading time) and measures related to their robustness (i.e., their ability to process large numbers of heterogeneous, real-life ontologies). Indeed, concerning robustness, each benchmark was run automatically for each tool, processing the ontologies in the corresponding set in an order of size. When a tool crashed on a particular ontology, unless an obvious error could be corrected, the test on the corresponding benchmark was interrupted. As can be seen from Table 2, the different tools tend to break on different benchmarks (with benchmark 39 being commonly problematic to all of them). In addition, while the application of RDFS inferences does not seem to affect the ability of Sesame to process ontologies (it consistently breaks on the same ontologies, and no other), Jena tends to be a lot less robust when reasoning is applied, especially on medium size ontologies, most likely due to the increase in its need for resources. All together, Mulgara and Jena without reasoning appear to be the most robust tools with 8 out of 10 benchmarks being covered at 100% (here, percentage is expressed with respect to the sum of all the triples in all the ontologies of the benchmark). The fact that they can process exactly the same number of ontologies can be explained by the fact that Mulgara uses Jena as a parser.

Regarding performance measures, we give more details below on the behavior of each tool configuration concerning loading time, memory consumption, disk space and query response time. However, generally, it appears quite clearly that Sesame (without reasoning) tends to outperform the other tools at small-scale. As we will see, this is less true at medium-scale, and other benchmarks have shown that, at large-scale, the difference between Sesame and Jena tends to be inverted [3]. This can be explained by the fact that Jena and Mulgara generally allocate larger amounts of resources straight from the start, while an "empty Sesame" is very lightweight. In other terms, it seems that the "fixed cost" associated with processing ontologies with Sesame is significantly lower than the one of Jena and Mulgara, whereas the "variable cost" appears to be higher. While this turns out to be a disadvantage at large-scale, it certainly makes Sesame a stronger candidate in the scenarios we consider here, i.e., small-scale, resource-limited applications.

Loading time refers to the time (expressed in milliseconds) taken by each tool to parse the file containing the ontology, create the internal data structures necessary to process this ontology, and store the information contained in the ontology in these internal structures. Naturally, this measure depends a lot on

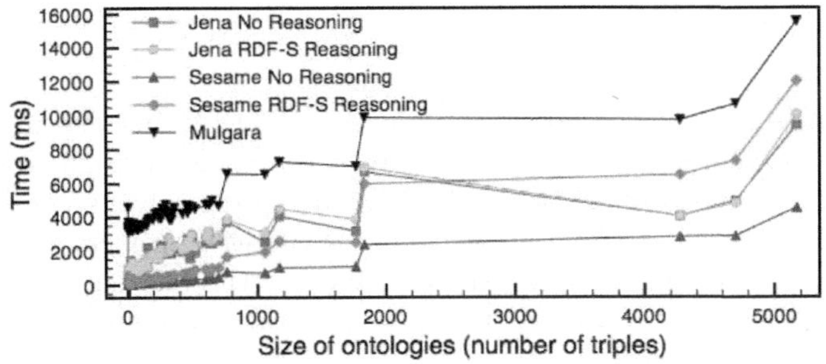

Fig. 1. Loading time with respect to size of the ontologies in benchmark 39

the storage device employed, but the way each tool represents the ontologies internally also has a significant impact. Indeed, as can be seen from Table 2, loading ontologies takes significantly less time for Sesame than for any other of the tested tool. Mulgara, on the other hand, creates many indexes for the data, which clearly impacts negatively on this measure. It can be noticed that applying RDFS reasoning with Sesame influences loading time, with supposedly some inferences being drawn already when initializing the ontology model, while it is not the case for Jena. Figure 1 shows a typical evolution of loading time with respect to the size of the ontology (using benchmark 39). Here we can see that Sesame was able to load more than 5000 triples in less than 5 seconds without reasoning, compared to around 12 seconds with reasoning. Mulgara took almost 16 seconds. It is interesting to see also how Jena loads ontologies apparently independently from the use of RDFS reasoning.

Having compared the results obtained for different benchmarks, we can observe that the tools behave consistently with respect to loading time independently from variables other than size. Sesame with reasoning, however, performs better than Mulgara for small ontologies only, and ends up taking longer for ontologies above a few thousand triples. Also, loading time appears to be slightly higher for ontologies with the same number of triples but more expressive description logics. This could be explained by a higher density of description for classes in these cases.

Memory consumption is described in Table 2 by providing the average memory space required (in kilo-bytes) per triple in each ontology. As for loading time, this is measured right after having loaded the ontology from the file, evaluating the amount of memory required to make the model accessible. Here, Sesame appears again to be the best performing tool at small scale, both when applying reasoning and not. While using reasoning in Sesame add an increment to memory consumption, for Jena reasoning does not have a significant impact on the memory consumption at loading time. Regarding memory consumption, Mulgara seems to be generally less demanding than Jena (both with reasoning and without). While differences appear on average between benchmarks of different sizes, within benchmarks, no correlation is visible between the size of the ontologies and the memory consumption (due to the use of persistent storage on disk), except for Jena which shows a slight, linear increase of memory consumption with size.

Disk space is also measured at loading time, calculating the overall size at the location on the local disk where each of the tools keep their stores. Here again, Sesame stands out as being the least demanding when reasoning is not applied, but also, to a smaller extent when reasoning is applied. Since Jena does not store the results of inferences, there are very little differences in terms of required disk space when applying RDFS reasoning and when not. While Jena and Sesame perform comparably, Mulgara can be seen as being extremely demanding in terms of disk space. Indeed, contrary to Sesame, which almost does not require any disk space at all when running without any ontology loaded, Mulgara

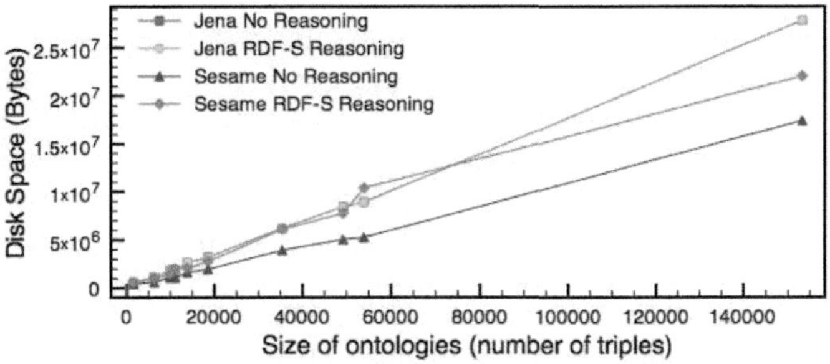

Fig. 2. Disk space consumption at loading time with respect to size of the ontologies in benchmark 54

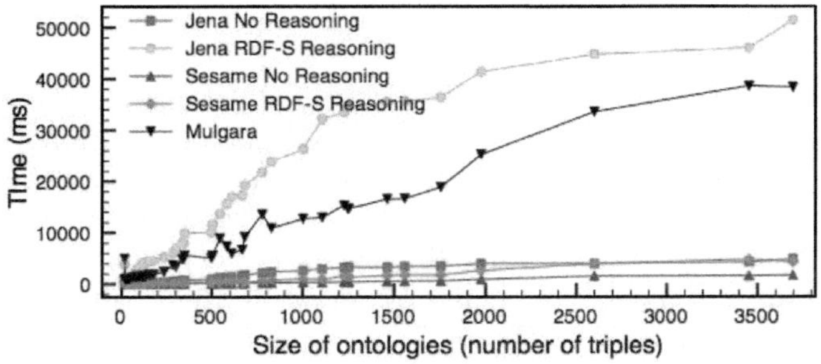

Fig. 3. Query response time (sum on all the 8 queries) with respect to size of the ontologies in benchmark 43

allocates a lot of space for storage structures such as indexes at starting time (in our experiments, around 150MB), which makes it a very weak candidate in scenarios where small-scale ontologies are processed on devices with limited storage space. As shown in the graph Figure 2 looking at benchmark 54, disk space seems to increase linearly with the size of the ontology for Jena and Sesame. Mulgara is absent from the graph (as it was orders of magnitude higher than the others), but here as well, disk space consumption increases linearly, with a slightly lower factor than Sesame and Jena. In the example Figure 2, for more that 15 000 triples, Sesame takes between 15 MB and 20 MB of disk space depending on whether reasoning is applied, and Jena takes almost 30 MB.

Query time is measured when executing the 8 queries defined in Section 2.2. While analyzing the results for each individual query could help identifying some fine-grained behavior, we focus here on the global performance of the tools and consider the overall time to execute the 8 queries. Looking at the average results presented in Table 2, Sesame and Jena appear to be performing well, in similar ranges, when reasoning is not applied. However, as already noticed before, these two tools apply different strategies concerning inferencing. Indeed, Sesame applies and stores results of inferences when loading the ontology (making loading time higher), while Jena applies reasoning at query time. This difference appears very clearly in the results concerning query times. In accordance with its "pre-inferencing" strategy, Sesame provides results with inferences in times very close to the ones without inferencing. For Jena, however, applying reasoning leads to a very significant increase in query time. This difference in behavior is visible in the graph Figure 3, showing the sum of the times required to execute our 8 queries in relation to the size of the ontologies in benchmark 43. As can be seen, even if it does not include any reasoning facility, Mulgara performs relatively badly compared to Jena and Sesame. Indeed, while Jena without reasoning, as well as Sesame both with and without reasoning are able to execute queries in near real-time even on such a small device as our netbook, Mulgara and Jena with reasoning would need up to 38 and 50 seconds respectively to provide results for an ontology of less than 4 000 triples.

Another interesting observation concerns the differences in the results of the queries. Indeed, looking at Table 2, the three tool configurations which do not apply reasoning obtain reasonably consistent results on our set of queries (on the benchmarks where they all managed to process the same number of ontologies), meaning that they interpret SPARQL queries in very similar ways. However, while analyzing the number of results obtained by the two tools applying reasoning, significant differences appear. The explanation to this phenomenon is that, in addition to having different strategies on when to apply reasoning, these tools implement RDFS inferences differently, with Jena generally obtaining more results (i.e., entailing more new statements). Additional investigations would be required to find out whether this is the result of different interpretations of the semantics of RDFS, of incomplete results from Sesame, or of incorrect results from Jena.

4 Conclusion

In this paper, we have established a set of small to medium scale benchmarks to test the performance of semantic tools on small devices with limited resources. Using these benchmarks and through extensive tests we have shown that tools such as Sesame, and to a smaller extent Jena, were able to cope reasonably well with small-scale ontologies on a very resource limited netbook. These results provided new insights into the behaviour of semantic data management tools in comparison with large-scale benchmarking tests of the same tools. Of course, the benchmarks we developed can be used to test any other semantic tool on any other platform, providing the availability of the necessary underlying infrastructure on such a platform. While the results obtained are encouraging, they also validate our intuition that existing semantic technologies are developed with large-scale applications in mind and that more work is needed to develop semantic software infrastructures dedicated to small-scale applications running with limited hardware resources.

References

1. Sabou, M., Kantorovitch, J., Nikolov, A., Tokmakoff, A., Zhou, X., Motta, E.: Position paper on realizing smart products: Challenges for semantic web technologies. In: Workshop: Semantic Sensor Networks (SSN 2009), ISWC (2009)
2. Guo, Y., Pan, Z., Heflin, J.: LUBM: A benchmark for OWL knowledge base systems. Journal of Web Semantics 3(2-3), 158–182 (2005)
3. Bizer, C., Schultz, A.: The Berlin SPARQL benchmark. International Journal on Semantic Web and Information Systems 5(2), 1–24 (2009)

A Semantic Approach for Learning Objects Repositories with Knowledge Reuse

Isabel Azevedo[1], Rui Seiça[2], Adela Ortiz[1], Eurico Carrapatoso[2], and Carlos Vaz de Carvalho[1]

[1] Instituto Superior de Engenharia do Porto, GILT, R. de São Tomé, 4200 Porto, Portugal
{iazevedo,adela,cvc}@dei.isep.ipp.pt
[2] Faculdade de Engenharia da Universidade do Porto, R. Roberto Frias, Porto, Portugal
ruiseica@gmail.com, emc@fe.up.pt

Abstract. In this paper we discuss how the inclusion of semantic functionalities in a Learning Objects Repository allows a better characterization of the learning materials enclosed and improves their retrieval through the adoption of some query expansion strategies. Thus, we started to regard the use of ontologies to automatically suggest additional concepts when users are filling some metadata fields and add new terms to the ones initially provided when users specify the keywords with interest in a query. Dealing with different domain areas and having considered impractical the development of many different ontologies, we adopted some strategies for reusing ontologies in order to have the knowledge necessary in our institutional repository. In this paper we make a review of the area of knowledge reuse and discuss our approach.

Keywords: Semantic Web, ontology selection, ontology reuse.

1 Introduction

Formal ontologies have been seen as a way to state content specific understandings for many knowledge-sharing tasks, in the form of conceptualizations of the world of interest.

In a study from 2007 [1], the participants were asked about what motivated them to use ontologies. The answers showed that the two main reasons were the need to share a common understanding of the structure of information among people or software agents (69.9 percent), and the requirement to enable the reuse of domain knowledge (56.3 percent).

However, the creation of ontologies leads to some costs, not only time, and it is often not considered a simple process, even if many methodologies have emerged. The creation of ontologies cannot be done automatically and requires, to a considerable degree, human input. Furthermore, unlike what happened in Software Engineering, ontology creation and other Semantic Web methodologies are not fully matured. Actually, the same study already referred before found that 60 percent of the users do not apply any methodology for developing ontologies.

P. Cimiano and H.S. Pinto (Eds.): EKAW 2010, LNAI 6317, pp. 576–585, 2010.

Ontology reuse has been seen as a viable alternative to having ontologies with reduced expenses. But, reusing ontologies is not a simple process. It starts by finding the possible candidates, and then it is necessary to rank them, and select one or more in accordance to those characteristics that were considered important. It could be argued that it is simpler to develop one from scratch but it is not always possible to find an expert and a knowledge engineer that can dedicate the required time to that. Furthermore, it brings new costs in finding, selecting and revision tasks, in which significant automation is not possible, except, to some extent, for the discovery of ontologies.

Nonetheless, due to the incapability of developing ontologies from scratch for a large number of different domains to use in an institutional repository, the reuse of ontologies has emerged as a feasible solution.

The rest of the paper is organized as follow. In section 2 we briefly discuss the foundations of knowledge reuse in general and ontology reuse in particular. In the third section we present the TREE (Teaching Resources for Engineering Education) repository, explain the reasons for considering the reuse of ontologies and the adopted strategies for finding and selecting the appropriate ontologies. Finally, the last section discusses the empirical evaluation carried out, states some conclusions and the planned work for the next months.

2 Knowledge Reuse

Knowledge processes frequently entail the creation or reuse of knowledge, and the methods appropriate for one, may not be convenient for the other [2].

According to Alavi et al., knowledge reuse is the process by which an entity is capable of finding and applying shared knowledge [3]. The reuse of knowledge components probably started to be considered as an important subject when the Knowledge Sharing Effort, sponsored by some American organizations aiming to support the sharing of knowledge among systems, suggested the connection of reusable units to build knowledge-based systems in 1991 [4].

Markus identified three main players in the process of reusing knowledge [5]:

- *Knowledge producer*—the knowledge creator, who registers explicit knowledge or transforms tacit knowledge into explicit,
- *Knowledge intermediary*— the agent that adapts knowledge for reuse, with many roles, including sharing it,
- *Knowledge consumer*—the person or system that recovers the suitable knowledge piece and makes use of it.

The same questions that emerged from knowledge reuse, appeared, to some extent, in the attempts to reuse ontologies. Indeed, reusability is (or should be) an underlying property of ontologies. They are often seen as a way to allow "knowledge sharing and reuse" [4], as the concepts represented in an ontology become explicit, reliable and convenient to share and, then, to reuse.

As ontologies have been more and more used in many domains, several ontologies have been made available on the Web, with different scope and quality. One of the motivations to make ontologies available is that an increase in their use and revision can boost their quality. Also, the applications that use them become (more) interoperable and are provided with a deeper, machine-processable understanding of the underlying domain.

Therefore, ontology reuse started to be considered, following the trend started in knowledge, in general, and even before that, the tendency in the software engineering field.

Pinto recognizes two purposes for reusing ontologies [6]:

- *Ontology merging* - By merging different ontologies, another one is built with the combined concerned parts;
- *Ontology integration* - Different ontologies are used to build a new one, but with modifications and extensions.

The more the knowledge is available, the greater the likelihood of being reused. Thus, there are some tools that make easier finding ontologies suitable for some purpose. They do play a role in ontology reuse situations, acting as knowledge intermediaries. These tools are:

- *Ontology registry* – It is an application used to register ontologies, maintaining some description fields, statistics about their contents, and a link to each registered ontology. A registry does not provide a central storage for ontologies, but a searchable list of them.
- *Ontology repository* – It maintains a local copy of ontologies, and their different versions, if they exist. This kind of tools usually only provide browse functionalities.
- *Ontology search engine* – It does not require an active action from ontology developers. This kind of tools automatically searches for and indexes the ontologies they discover. Some examples are Swoogle [7], Watson [8], Sindice [9] and Falcons (http://iws.seu.edu.cn/services/falcons/objectsearch/index.jsp). They vary in the metadata provided for each ontology, but there is not any standard for ontology metadata and exchange.

These kinds of tools facilitate the findability of suitable ontologies, but they differ in the way they describe ontologies and in the provided metadata, usually without any information about domain of interest, creation date or authorship, for instance.

Currently, there are more than 10.000 online ontologies (http://swoogle.umbc.edu/), which do not mean that finding the suitable ontologies have become much easier. The problem has become to select the best ontology from many available. Related to this topic is the ranking of ontologies. Search engines usually rank the found ontologies using one or more of the following approaches:

- *Popularity* – Ontologies are ranked in accordance with the number of times they are referred to in other ontologies. That method is followed by Swoogle (http://swoogle.umbc.edu), with some drawbacks, although consistent with the idea that the most used in other ontologies should had been considered suitable by many people;
- *Ontological structure* – By applying metrics that estimate how elaborate is the knowledge structure of an ontology structure, the "goodness" of an ontology can be estimated. Some of the approaches use the relation between the number of classes and properties [10], the centrality of a class in the whole hierarchy

(Centrality measure [11]) or estimates how richness is a concept defined (Density measure [11]);

- *Concept coverage* –It is related to how well a concept is covered in an ontology. The matches between the query term and the labels in an ontology are regarded, and weighted in accordance to how perfect in the matching, usually just carried out at lexical level.

3 TREE Repository

As part of the project CASPOE (PTDC/EIA/65387/2006 – Semantic and Pragmatic Characterisation of Learning Objects), a three-year project funded by the Portuguese Foundation for Science and Technology, we have been developing a prototype for an institutional learning object repository, named TREE (Teaching Resources for Engineering Education), which uses ontologies and extracted keywords to represent the semantics of learning resources [4, 5], digital objects that could be used to achieve an educational purpose. It has been populated with some materials from courses taught at ISEP, a higher education institution.

Although TREE is a repository for resources that might be used in engineering courses, it is a heterogeneous document repository as it covers different knowledge areas, such as Law, Linguistics, Environmental Sciences and Mathematical and Computer Sciences. At this moment it is on an Intranet only accessible by students, teachers and staff people.

We use Fedora (Flexible Extensible Digital Object Repository Architecture - http://www.fedora-commons.org/) repository system with some add-ons.

An important factor for the adoption of Fedora was the possibilities offered for the construction of new metadata profiles different from the base version provided. We have adopted metadata standards associated with the practice of teaching and learning, such as IEEE Learning Object Metadata [12], which consider not just metadata fields related to authorship, identification and brief descriptions of content.

Fez (http://fez.library.uq.edu.au/wiki/Main_Page) is used as a Web interface to Fedora; it is an open-source software for creating and maintaining a highly flexible web interface to the Fedora software.

The documents included in the repository are divided into communities related to different scientific areas. Each community has one or more collections assigned to diverse knowledge sub-areas, related to different courses in our institution.

Users can find resources browsing through the communities and collections hierarchical structure, searching through the tags assigned to resources or metadata fields. Under the latter hypothesis, users can search documents through the specification of keywords.

Ontologies are used for the purpose of having the core concepts of a domain well-related in order to improve the performance of information retrieval in the TREE repository. The information in the ontologies should answer what concepts are related to another given one. Thus, the reasons for the adoption of ontologies in the TREE repository are twofold:

- Allow a detailed description of the resources;
- Improve the results by applying a query expansion method.

When a document is submitted to the TREE repository, some metadata fields are automatically or semi-automatically filled. One of those is the keyword metadata (a subelement of the General element in the IEEE LOM standard), which can have multiple values.

The ontologies are used to find additional concepts related to those extracted. Then, the user can accept the desired ones. It is worthwhile to note that this process was found necessary when realized that users are really very concise when filling forms, with detrimental results in subsequent searches.

We developed a module to expand the query terms provided by the TREE users. Each time a query is submitted, every term in it is expanded to related ones. The expansion uses ontologies, considering subsumption or supersumption relations (up to two levels), equivalence and other relations, and instance data, but allowing the users to agree or not with the use of the additional terms.

3.1 Ontology Reuse in the TREE Repository

Figure 1 generically delineates the architecture of the semi-automated module for ontology reuse. It takes two inputs: a list of domain concepts and the online ontologies found through semantic search engines using the given concepts.

Among many tools that facilitate the discovery of ontologies we selected Swoogle for its easy integration in the repository and the summary supplied with the results. Swoogle applies the algorithm OntoRank, which is quite analogous to PageRank, which is used by Google search engine.

At our institution each course has a description in English, which is mandatory, with some predefined fields to be supplied; one of them is related to the course contents. It is simple to extract the relevant concepts for each course considering that specific field. Nevertheless, those responsible for courses can specify others and disregard or correct some of the extracted ones. That enumeration of the important terms corresponds to one of the recommended steps to follow when developing an ontology.

For each desired concept, we apply a singularisation algorithm, and '`Distributed Databases`' is changed into '`Distributed Database`', for instance. That approach augments the number of perfect correspondences later. Then, using those concepts we compose a query that is submitted to Swoogle REST based service, which returns a RDF/XML document containing a short summary for each of them, which is used to predict relevancy.

Having C_1, C_2, … C_N as the singularized concepts for a course, we harmonize them, namely replacing white spaces with dashes. Then we first try queries with all the concepts, after disregarding those not covered by any online ontology. Thus, we might have a query with N terms, and then the system tries N-1 terms, and so on. Having all concepts covered (by at least a predefined number of ontologies) or having tried each concept alone, the process is finished. Often ontologies with only one single concept are not related to the domain of interest. Also, a query using only one search string might result in excessive results to be analysed. For instance, a query with 'table' as search string provides 935 results.

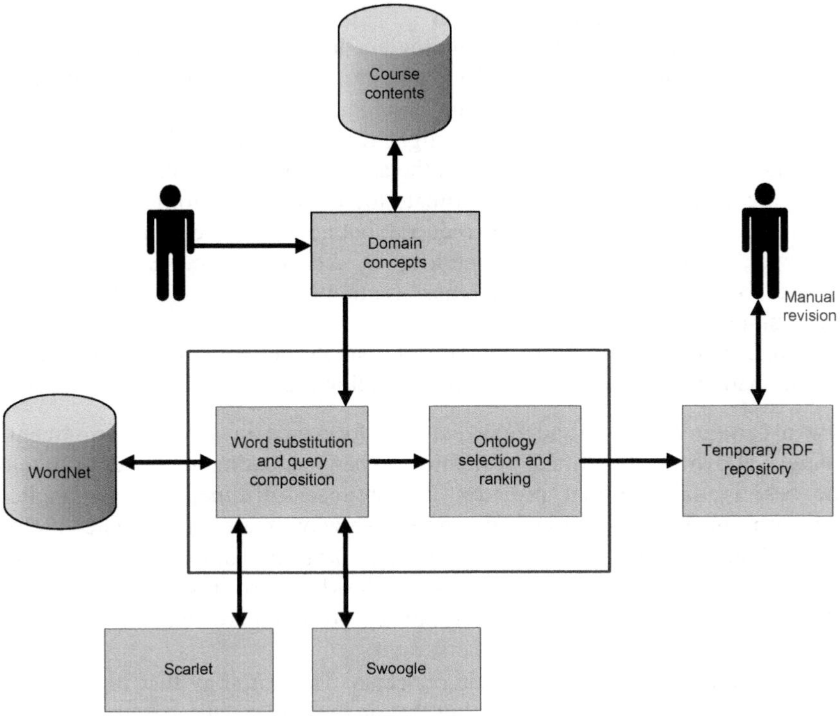

Fig. 1. Architecture of the semi-automated ontology reuse module

For the ontology retrieval we consider labels of instances, classes and properties in ontologies lexically matching the query terms. As some other relevant concepts could remain unnoticed, some related projects try a more conceptual matching [13] [14] and expand the initial concepts using WordNet [15], an electronic lexical database created by the Cognitive Science Laboratory of Princeton University. However, we found that approach more useful when applied in a later step, discussed in section 3.2.2.

There are three possibilities when trying to find adequate ontologies:

- One or more ontologies are found with all the desired concepts;
- The system returns different ontologies with most of the concepts, but the set of ontologies covers all of terms;
- It is impossible to find an ontology with one or more of the concepts. When this happens, we try to find relevant synonyms in the field under analysis and we repeat the process again.

Before carrying out the process of ontology selection, the ontologies whose URIs correspond to dead links are disregarded and the others are checked to verify if they are syntactically correct, and then they are ranked.

Once the found ontologies are fully analysed, the chosen ones are stored and manipulated using Jena (http://jena.sourceforge.net) and Sesame (http://sourceforge.net/projects/sesame/) frameworks.

3.1.1 Ontology Ranking and Selection

With the growing demand for reuse ontologies, there has been a need for criteria and standards to find out their quality. Once a system is reusing ontologies, their quality might affect the quality of the resulting ontologies, and the desirable functioning of the system. Deficiencies in modeling might remain unknown for a long time until unpredictable or poor query results catch the attention of someone.

Applying evaluation methods to estimate the quality of ontologies and rate them, the likelihood of that problem can be reduced, but not entirely eliminated.

However, evaluating a single ontology is different from evaluating a set of ontologies to decide on the one(s) to reuse, as an intensive evaluation of all candidates is not feasible.

Although more specific for evaluation of a single ontology at a time, some of the more automatic approaches for ontology evaluation are:

- Use a certain ontology and realize its performance in a real environment with interest, allowing a functional evaluation. When evaluating a number of ontologies, the best is the one that provides the optimal fulfillment for an application. However, this technique is not often a feasible way to test and evaluate ontologies.
- Use a Gold Standard ontology. The most similar to this one is considered the most suitable one and should be adopted. Some drawbacks of this approach are the lack of availability of the optimum ontology to compare with others, and the comparison itself, namely how to perform it.
- Realize the coverage of the domain concepts. The ontology that includes most of the concepts is the one to be used, but that analysis is usually based on matching at lexical level, as stated before.

We evaluate and rank the discovered ontologies considering three different aspects, each one leading to a different number. These considered characteristics are: their concepts coverage (considering the distance between the provided terms and those in the ontology), popularity (ontoRank value provided by Swoogle) and knowledge richness (the number of classes and properties, considered all triples).

During the concepts coverage analysis, some extraneous matching can occur between the terms provided and those in the ontology when carried out at lexical level, but applying a similarity metric that possibility can be avoided to certain extend, but not completely.

After computing the Levenshtein metric to estimate the distance between strings, only the terms that match some class, property or instance label greater than a defined threshold, are regarded.

For any given ontology, we calculate the ratio between the sum of similarities of occurrences and the number of occurrences for each domain concept.

Once a list of possible appropriate ontologies is ranked, an ontology engineer analyses it and manually selects the most suitable ones, occasionally with the assistance of an expert from that area, namely when two or more ontologies have very similar ranking values. In that case, competency questions might be considered to decide on the most appropriate ontology. They have also proved valuable to detect missing parts of knowledge. For example, considering the database domain, an ontology extract might have to address the following competency questions:

- Which are the Normal Forms?
- Which are the subsets of SQL statements?

A final ontology is obtained from the merging from one or more ontologies, and then assigned to a collection in the TREE repository.

3.1.2 Additional Strategies Adopted to Find Online Ontologies

When no ontology is found covering a certain concept provided, and yet relying on the information provided by the search engine Swoogle, we verify if the ontologies already found for others have some variations of them. For instance, finding ontologies with the term '`relational_model`' for the Database field is unsuccessful. But analyzing the ontologies already found, we can discover a similar one: '`relational_data_model`', as explained before.

It is worth to note that many semantic search engines do not satisfactorily consider wildcards, although accepting them. Thus, our first attempt to submit queries using wildcards like 'relational*model', for example, was unsuccessful.

In addition, we try word substitution through WordNet, after some ontologies have possibly been found. WordNet is structured semantically, containing nouns, verbs, adjectives and adverbs. Words that are synonymous are grouped together in synsets - synonym sets. Polysemous words in WordNet are included in more than one synset and each synset leads a different sense. For instance, the concept '`data modelling`', which appears in a database course description, is not contained in any online ontology. Considering sister terms, hypernyms (words from ancestor synsets) and hyponyms (words from descendant synsets), there many possible substitutions for '`modelling`' from different synsets, such as '`modeling`', '`molding`', '`moulding`', '`model`', '`pattern`', and so on. When we have already found some ontologies for the other concepts supplied, we check if one of them applies the terms provided by WordNet, as a class, a property or instance, and in this case we consider that new concept as a substitute for the one initially specified.

When no ontology was already found using the terms provided by WordNet, we exploit Scarlet java API (http://scarlet.open.ac.uk/) to verify if there are some relations between the probable substitutes supplied by WordNet and the other terms provided, choosing then the one with most relations found or found in the same ontologies. Scarlet (SemantiC relAtion discoveRy by harvesting onLinE onTologies) is "a technique for discovering relations between two concepts by harvesting the Semantic Web" [14], whose usage was first envisaged for ontology matching. We regard all type of relations, more than one ontology and inheritance depth equals to 5.

When all other attempts have proved unsuccessful to find ontologies related to a concept, we ask for a set of documents containing that concept, which is used for ontology extraction, with some parts subsequently incorporated into the ontology already obtained earlier, after some revision. However, this last approach is significantly more time-spending than the others.

4 Conclusions

In this paper we presented a case study about ontology reuse. Based on the literature review and this particular case study, we have identified some issues that should be attended in order for the reuse of ontologies to increasingly become a reality.

Even though the TREE repository was designed for engineering resources, the adopted approaches can be used for other areas as well.

The basic version of the repository was evaluated using resources from four different courses, whose responsible people complemented the concepts gathered from the course description.

The initial results were very encouraging. The empirical evaluation revealed the practical usefulness of the discussed approaches and the users were generally satisfied with the efficiency of the information retrieval. However those responsible for courses were not so pleased with the time spent in all the activities, but a full automation of the whole process of discovering, selecting and revising ontologies is impossible. Also, some performance issues were highlighted but, as most of the process is carried offline, that point is not a main concern for the upcoming months.

Some detected errors have been corrected and we plan to further evaluate the whole system via quantitative measurements in the next months.

Finally, our approach to reuse ontology has some similarities with the one described in [13], but we have achieved more automation in some steps, namely we do not ask for user feedback before using WordNet for finding suitable substitutions for domain concepts, relying on information available on the Semantic Web.

Acknowledgments. The work described in this paper has being developed under the project CASPOE - Characterization Semantics and Pragmatics of Educational Objects (PTDC/EIA/65387/2006), with funding from the Portuguese Foundation for Science and Technology.

References

1. Cardoso, J.: The Semantic Web Vision: Where Are We? IEEE Intelligent Systems, 84–88 (2007)
2. Davenport, T.H., Jarvenpaa, S.L., Beers, M.C.: Improving knowledge work processes. Sloan Management Review 37, 53–65 (1996)
3. Alavi, M., Leidner, D.E.: Review: Knowledge Management and Knowledge Management Systems: Conceptual Foundations and Research Issues. MIS Quarterly 25, 107–136 (2001)
4. Nechs, R., Fikes, R., Finin, T., Gruber, T., Patil, R., Senator, T., Swartout, W.: Enabling Technology for Knowledge Sharing. AI Magazine 12, 36–56 (1991)
5. Markus, M.L.: Toward a theory of knowledge reuse: Types of knowledge reuse situations and factors in reuse success. Journal of Management Information Systems 18, 57–93 (2001)
6. Pinto, H.S., Gomez-Perez, A., Martins, J.P.: Some Issues on Ontology Integration. In: Proc. of IJCAI 1999's Workshop on Ontologies and Problem Solving Methods: Lessons Learned and Future Trends, Stockholm, Sweden (1999)

7. Ding, L., Finin, T., Joshi, A., Pan, R., Cost, R.S., Peng, Y., Reddivari, P., Doshi, V., Sachs, J.: Swoogle: A Search and Metadata Engine for the Semantic Web. In: Proceedings of the Thirteenth ACM Conference on Information and Knowledge Management (2004)
8. d'Aquin, M., Sabou, M., Dzbor, M., Baldassarre, C., Gridinoc, L., Angeletou, S., Motta, E.: Watson: A Gateway for the Semantic Web. In: European Semantic Web Conference (ESWC 2007), Innsbruck, Austria (2007)
9. Oren, E., Delbru, R., Catasta, M., Cyganiak, R., Stenzhorn, H., Tummarello, G.: Sindice.com: A document-oriented lookup index for open linked data. International Journal of Metadata, Semantics and Ontologies 3 (2008)
10. Buitelaar, P., Eigner, T., Declerck, T.: OntoSelect: A Dynamic Ontology Library with Support for Ontology Selection. In: The International Semantic Web Conference (Demo Session), Hiroshima, Japan (2004)
11. Alani, H., Brewster, C.: Metrics for Ranking Ontologies. In: Fourth International Evaluation of Ontologies for the Web Workshop held as part of the 15th International World Wide Web Conference, Edinburgh, United Kingdom (2006)
12. IEEE: IEEE Standard 1484.12.1-2002, Learning Object Metadata, LOM (2002)
13. Cantador, I., Fernández, M., Castells, P.: Improving Ontology Recommendation and Reuse in WebCORE by Collaborative Assessments. In: Proceedings of the 1st International Workshop on Social and Collaborative Construction of Structured Knowledge (CKC 2007), at the 16th International World Wide Web Conference (WWW 2007), Banff, Canada, vol. 273 (2007)
14. Brewster, C., Alani, H., Dasmahapatra, S., Wilks, Y.: Data-driven Ontology Evaluation. In: Proceedings of the 4th International Conference on Language Resources and Evaluation, Lisbon, Portugal (2004)
15. Miller, G.A.: WordNet: A Lexical Database for English. New Horizons in Commercial and Industrial Artificial Intelligence. Communications of the ACM 38, 39–41 (1995)

Author Index

GPSR Compliance

The European Union's (EU) General Product Safety Regulation (GPSR) is a set of rules that requires consumer products to be safe and our obligations to ensure this.

If you have any concerns about our products, you can contact us on ProductSafety@springernature.com

In case Publisher is established outside the EU, the EU authorized representative is:

Springer Nature Customer Service Center GmbH
Europaplatz 3
69115 Heidelberg, Germany

Batch number: 10704693

Printed by Printforce, the Netherlands